Lawrenceville Press

A Guide to Microsoft® Office 2010

Jan Marrelli

ISBN 978-0-82195-780-6 (Softcover)

© 2011 by Paradigm Publishing, Inc.
875 Montreal Way
St. Paul, MN 55102
E-mail: educate@emcp.com
Web site: www.emcp.com

19 18 17 16 15 14 13 12 11 10   1 2 3 4 5 6 7 8 9 10

We have strived to make this the most comprehensive and easy to understand Microsoft Office 2010 text available. *A Guide to Microsoft Office 2010* focuses on teaching students business application software, including word processing, spreadsheet, database, desktop publishing, presentation graphics, and business-oriented utilization of the Internet through a project-based, hands-on approach. It also introduces computer terminology, hardware, software, operating systems, and information systems as they relate to the business environment.

This text is designed to be used in beginning through advanced business application courses and provides approximately 80 to 120 hours of study.

The text starts with a Microsoft Office Basics chapter, which explains the Office interface, file management, searching the Web, Outlook and e-mail, and Office help. Additional chapters explain Word, Excel, Access, PowerPoint, Publisher, and OneNote and include the many new features of Office 2010. The integration of data between the Office applications is covered throughout the text.

For the best classroom experience for both student and instructor, our comprehensive text includes hands-on practices, critical-thinking review questions, and projects of varying difficulty levels. The projects are designed to teach global awareness and financial, economic, and business literacy. Many projects extend the chapter by teaching additional concepts and techniques.

Students must have access to the Microsoft Office 2010 software to complete the practices and exercises in this text.

The text is available in both softcover and e-book editions.

Design and Features

Each chapter contains the following elements:

- *Key Concepts* — identifying the learning outcomes of the chapter.

- *Hands-on Practices* — requiring the student to test newly learned skills using the computer after concepts are presented and discussed.

- *Sidebars, Tips, and Alternatives* — presenting additional topics, tips, and alternative methods in the margin.

- *Chapter Summaries* — reviewing the concepts covered in the chapter.

- *Vocabulary Sections* — presenting a list of new term and definitions and a list of commands and buttons covered in the chapter.

- *Review Questions* — providing immediate reinforcement of new concepts.

- *Projects* — applying the knowledge in the chapter to a variety of business-related projects.

- *Appendix* — digital image concepts are presented to support application use.

- *Online Resources* — materials that complement and extend this text are free for download. Supplements cover operating systems, personal finances, IT careers, computer technology, the Web, and keyboarding skills. The supplements and all the files students need to complete the practices and exercises are found at www.lpdatafiles.com.

- *Data Files* — Data files are downloaded at www.lpdatafiles.com. In the Practices and Projects, file names in all capitals indicate a data file.

Projects

Many of the projects in this text revolve around six fictitious companies:

- *Freelance Writer* — Composition and editorial projects.

- *Travel... With a Purpose* — Travel agency that provides educational tours.

- *Study Time Tutoring* — Tutoring business.

- *Align Computers* — Computer sales and service.

- *Entrepreneur* — Students pick a business for their projects.

- *Yolanda's Catering* — Restaurant catering business.

Some of the projects extend the concepts covered in the text by introducing new topics or additional features of the application.

Instructor Ancillaries

The Teacher Resource CD contains:

- *Lesson Plans* Lessons in PDF format keyed to the chapters in the text. Each lesson includes assignments, teaching notes, worksheets, and additional topics.

- *PowerPoint Presentations* Topics keyed to the text are in PowerPoint files for presentation.

- *Vocabulary* Word files of the vocabulary presented in the text.

- *Rubrics* Rubrics keyed to exercises in the text for assessment.

- *Worksheets* Problems that supplement the exercises in the text provide additional reinforcement of concepts.

- *Review Question Answers* Answers for the review questions presented in the text.

- *Data Files* The files students need to complete the practices and projects in the text, the worksheets in the Teacher Resource Materials, and the case questions in the EXAM*VIEW*® question banks.

- **EXAM***VIEW*® **Software** Question banks keyed to the text and the popular EXAM*VIEW*® software are included to create multiple tests, quizzes, and additional assessment materials.

- *Answer files* Answers to the practices, review questions, projects, worksheets, and EXAM*VIEW*® case questions.

Distance Learning Course Cartridges:

Distance Learning Course Cartridges are available for use on various platforms. Using these files, instructors can provide a syllabus, assignments, quizzes, study aids, and other course materials online; hold e-discussions and group conferences; send and receive e-mail and assignments from students and manage grades electronically.

About the Author

Jan Marrelli has authored numerous Lawrenceville Press computer applications and programming texts along with their accompanying teacher resource materials. She has taught computer applications and programming courses at both the College and high school level as well as participating in curriculum development and assessment projects for the Ontario Ministry of Education.

Using This Text

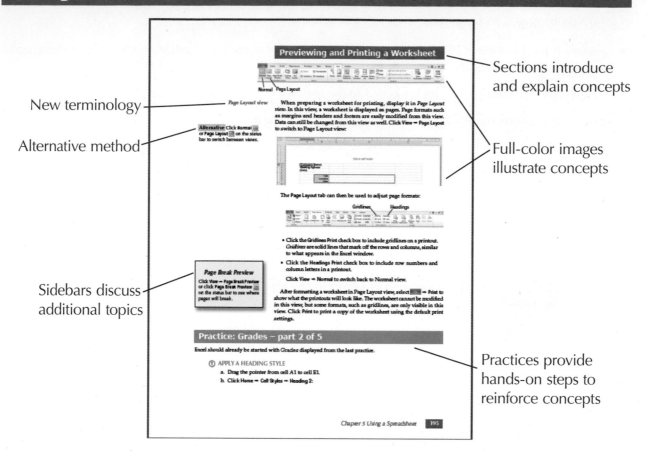

New terminology

Alternative method

Sidebars discuss additional topics

Sections introduce and explain concepts

Full-color images illustrate concepts

Practices provide hands-on steps to reinforce concepts

This text begins with a chapter that covers the basics of using Microsoft Office 2010. It is recommended that you begin with Chapter 1 and then the application chapters can be completed in any order. For example, you can complete the Excel chapters 5 through 8 before completing the Word chapters 2 through 4.

Within each chapter, you will find:

Alternatives – Other ways to perform actions.

TIPs – Additional information that complements the text.

Sidebars – Additional topics that complement the text.

Text in the margin – Indicates new terminology and subtopics.

Practices – Concepts are presented, discussed, and then followed by a "hands-on" practice that allows you to try out newly learned skills using the computer. The practices also serve as excellent reference guides for review. Some practices stand alone, while others build on work completed in previous practices. Therefore, it is recommended that the practices are completed in the order in which they are presented.

The end of each chapter contains:

Chapter Summaries – Concepts covered in the chapter are reviewed.

Review Questions – Critical thinking questions that will let you review and deepen your understanding of the concepts covered in the chapter.

Vocabulary Sections – A list of new terms and definitions and a list of the commands and buttons covered in the chapter.

Projects – Projects vary in difficulty. Some require collaboration with peers, and others introduce new topics or additional features of the application. The ✿ icon in an project title indicates that files used were created or modified in an earlier exercise.

Additional support:

Appendix – Concepts relating to digital images are presented at the end of the text.

Online Resources – Materials that complement and extend this text can be downloaded for free from www.lpdatafiles.com. Supplements cover operating systems, personal finances, IT careers, computer technology, the Web, and keyboarding skills, and additional topics.

Data files – Files needed to complete the practices and exercises in the text can be downloaded from www.lpdatafiles.com.

Index – Looking for a concept? Check the index at the end of the text.

Screen Resolution

Screen captures in this text were created using 1280 x 1024 resolution; screens with a higher resolution may appear slightly different. For example, using the screen resolution of 800 x 600, a Ribbon appears as:

Whereas, with a screen resolution of 1680 x 1024, the Ribbon appears as:

Note, for example, that the lower screen resolution displays just an image on the Date & Time 🔣 button instead of an image with text 🔣 Date & Time . Different screen resolutions may also result in an extra 'click' being required to execute a command. For example, adding a cover page using 800 x 600 resolution requires the user to click Pages → Cover Page in the Home tab. Whereas, with 1680 x 1024 resolution, the user just needs to click Cover Page in the Home tab. To address the differences in screen resolution, Ribbon instructions are specified using visuals of the button and the group the button is located in is specified.

Table of Contents

Chapter 1
Microsoft Office Basics

Chapter 2
Using a Word Processor

Chapter 3
Formatting Documents

Chapter 7
Creating Charts

Chapter 8
Advanced Spreadsheet Techniques

Chapter 9
Working with a Database

Chapter 10
Relational Database Techniques

Chapter 11
Analyzing Data in a Database

Chapter 12
Creating Presentations

Chapter 13
Advanced PowerPoint Features

Chapter 14
Desktop Publishing

Chapter 15
Using OneNote

Appendix
Digital Images

Index

A Guide to Microsoft Office 2010

What is Microsoft Office?

Microsoft Office 2010 is a Windows application that consists of several applications, each designed to perform specific tasks:

Outlook 2010 is an e-mail client with tools for organizing and searching e-mail.

Word 2010 is a word processor application used to produce professional-looking documents such as letters, résumés, and reports.

Excel 2010 is a spreadsheet application used to organize, analyze, and chart data.

Access 2010 is a database application used to generate forms, queries, and reports from the data it stores.

PowerPoint 2010 is a presentation application used to organize and format slides.

Publisher 2010 is a desktop publishing application used to create publications such as newsletters and business reports.

OneNote 2010 is a notetaking and information management application.

Microsoft Office is designed to create a productive and efficient work environment. Each application has a similar look and feel making it possible to transfer skills learned in one application to another. Data can be easily duplicated between the applications, reducing the time required to produce a document. For example, spreadsheet data can be easily added to a word processor document without having to retype the information.

Operating System

All computers run software called an *operating system* (OS). The OS allows the computer to run other software and perform basic tasks, such as communicate with the user and keep track of files and folders. Types of operating systems include Windows, Linux, and Mac OS. For more information about a specific OS, visit www.lpdatafiles.com.

The Microsoft Office Interface

window

Running an Office application displays an area on the screen called a *window* where the user interacts with the software. The window is the application *interface*, which includes a File tab, Quick Access Toolbar, and the Ribbon. Other common features include:

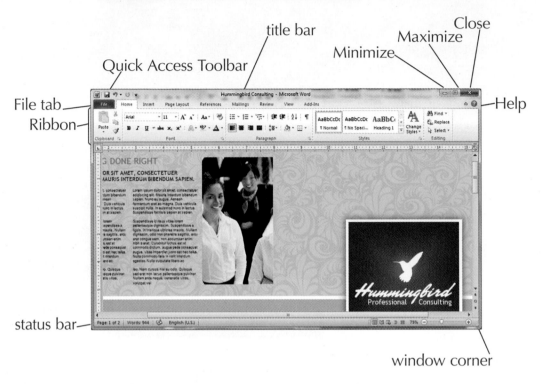

* The file name of the open document is displayed in the **title bar**.

* Click the **File tab** to display Backstage view which includes file management options such as opening and saving.

keyboard shortcut

* Click a button on the **Quick Access Toolbar** to execute a command or press the button's *keyboard shortcut*. As a reminder of a keyboard shortcut, a ScreenTip is displayed when pointing to a button:

TIP Keyboard shortcuts can increase productivity because hands remain on the keyboard when executing a command.

* Click a tab on the **Ribbon** to access groups of commands.

* Click **Minimize** to hide a window.

TIP A minimized window has an application icon on the Windows taskbar which can be clicked to display the window again.

* Click **Maximize** to expand the window to fill the screen.

* Click **Restore Down** to restore the window to its smaller size. Restore Down replaces Maximize when a window has been maximized.

* View information about the document in the **status bar**.

* Drag the **window corner** to size the window.

* Drag the **scroll bars** to view unseen parts of the document.

* Click **Close** to close the window.

* Click **Help** to display a window with Microsoft Office help.

TIP The numeric keypad, located on the right of most keyboards, can make entering numeric data more efficient. It also allows easy access to the mathematical operators +, −, *, and /. Num Lock must be on before numbers can be entered. Press the Num Lock key to toggle between on and off.

TIP The shape of the mouse pointer will change depending on the situation.

TIP Clicking a specific location in a document moves the insertion point to that position.

Using Input Devices

Input devices are used to communicate with an application. Common input devices include the keyboard, mouse, CD/DVD drive, USB drive, and disk drive. The *keyboard* is used to enter text and numeric data:

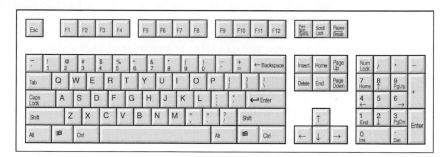

Press a key to enter that character at the insertion point. The *insertion point* is the blinking vertical line that indicates where the next character will be typed. Press and hold the **Shift key** while pressing a character key to enter uppercase letters or the character shown above a number or symbol on a key. The **Enter key** is used to end a paragraph or terminate a line of text.

Other keys and key combinations are used to move the insertion point or modify existing text:

- Press an **arrow key** to move the insertion point within existing text without erasing or entering text. **Ctrl+arrow** key moves the insertion point from word to word in a document.

- Press the **Home key** or **End key** to move the insertion point to the beginning or end of a line of text, respectively. **Ctrl+Home** and moves the insertion point to the beginning of the document, **Ctrl+End** to the end.

- Press the **Delete key** to erase the character to the right of the insertion point. Characters to the right move over to fill the gap.

- Press the **Backspace key** to erase the character to the left of the insertion point. Characters to the right move over to fill the gap.

- Press the **Esc (Escape) key** to cancel the current operation. The specific effect of the Esc key depends on the current operation.

- Press the **Page Up** or **Page Down key** to move, or *scroll*, a document in a window.

The *mouse* is used to select commands and respond to application prompts. When using a mouse, a *mouse pointer* is displayed on the screen. To *point* to an object, slide the mouse until the pointer is positioned on the object and then select the object by pressing the left mouse button. The mouse can be used to perform other actions. *Double-click* means to press the left mouse button twice in rapid succession. *Right-click* means to press and release the right mouse button quickly. These actions have different effects depending on the object the mouse is pointing to. A mouse may contain a *wheel*, which can be rotated to scroll through a document.

Most handheld computers use a *stylus pen* to perform the same functions as a mouse. Laptop computers are typically equipped with a *touchpad* or *pointing stick* instead of a separate mouse.

① **START THE WORD 2010 APPLICATION**

    a. Ask your instructor for the appropriate steps to start Microsoft Office Word 2010.

    b. Locate the features of the window, such as the File tab ▮File▮, Ribbon, Quick Access Toolbar, and the insertion point.

② **USE THE MOUSE TO MANIPULATE THE WINDOW**

    a. Slide the mouse. Note how the mouse pointer moves on the screen.

    b. If the window is maximized, use the mouse to click Restore Down ▮ to decrease the size of the window, otherwise click Maximize ▮.

    c. Click Minimize ▮ to hide the Word window.

    d. On the taskbar, click ▮W▮ to again display the Word window. Maximize the window if it is not already.

③ **TYPE TEXT**

    a. Type the following without pressing the Enter key: The Office 2010 applications are considered business productivity tools because they help users get organized, efficiently manage data, and easily create documents and publications.

    b. Press the Home key. The insertion point moves to the start of the line.

    c. Press the End key. The insertion point moves to the end of the line.

    d. Press the Enter key to end the paragraph. Type your first and last name.

    e. Press the appropriate key combinations to move the insertion point to the start of the document.

    f. Move the insertion point to the left of the "O" in "Office."

    g. Press the Delete key the appropriate number of times to delete the words "Office 2010" and the space that follows 2010.

TIP The Ribbon may appear slightly different depending on your screen resolution. Screen resolution is adjusted in the Control panel.

The → Symbol

In this text, the → symbol indicates that a command should be executed. For example, "Select ▮File▮ → Open" means to click the File tab and then select the Open command. A second → symbol indicates that a button option should be selected. For example, "Click Home → Paste → Paste Special" means to click ▮ (the part of the button with an arrow) and then select Paste Special.

Using the Ribbon

The *Ribbon* is an interface element that groups related commands into tabs. Each tab displays buttons, boxes, and other options for executing commands. For example, the Home tab on the Word Ribbon displays a set of commands for editing text:

tabs

Dialog Box Launcher   buttons

Some buttons display text to indicate their purpose. If a button displays only a graphic, point to the button to display a ScreenTip with its name. To execute a command, click a button. For commands such as Font, a box is provided for entering the font name or selecting one from a list. Buttons with an arrow have additional options to choose from. For example, click Home → Font Color ▲ to apply the default color or click ▾ in Home → Font Color ▲▾ to select a different color. Commands can also be accessed by

Chapter 1 Microsoft Office Basics

access key

TIP Press Alt once to display access keys for the Quick Access Toolbar and Ribbon.

pressing the Alt key and an *access key*. For example, press Alt+H+FC to change the font color.

The Ribbon changes depending on the activity. For example, inserting a graphic adds a Picture Tools Format tab to the Ribbon:

contextual tab

The Format tab is an example of a *contextual tab*. It remains on the Ribbon for as long as those commands may be needed. In this example, the contextual tab remains for as long as the graphic is selected.

If more space is needed for viewing a document, click Minimize the Ribbon ^. The minimized Ribbon displays only tabs:

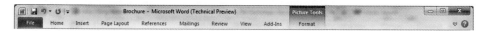

To restore the Ribbon, click Expand the Ribbon ⌄.

Within a tab, buttons are grouped. For example, the Home tab contains the Clipboard, Font, Paragraph, Styles, and Editing groups. Tab groups often

dialog box launcher

include a *Dialog Box Launcher*. Click the Dialog Box Launcher ⊡ to display a dialog box of options related to that group. For example, clicking the Font Dialog Box Launcher displays:

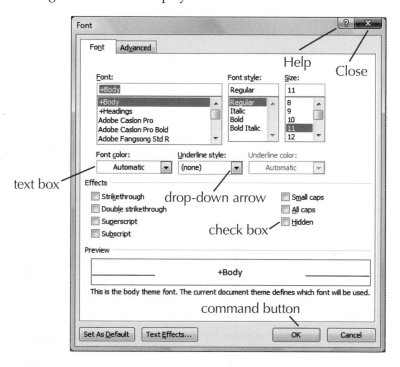

TIP Press the Tab key to move from option to option in a dialog box to increase productivity. Once an option is selected, press an arrow key or the spacebar to change the value for a selected option.

TIP An ellipsis (…) after a command name in a menu or a name on a command button indicates that a dialog box will appear.

- Click the **drop-down arrow** to display a list of options.

- Click **check boxes** to select or clear options.

- Type information in a **text box**.

- Select a **command button** to initiate an action.

- Click **Help** ⊡ to display a window with information about using the dialog box.

- Click **Close** 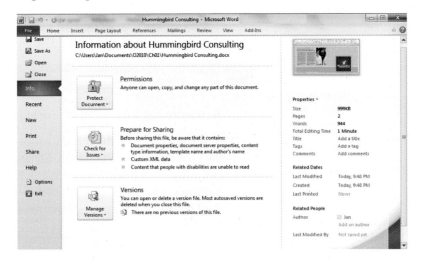 to remove a dialog box without applying any options. Select Close, Cancel, or press the Esc key to perform the same function.

The *default button* is the button displayed with a thicker border when the dialog box is first displayed. The default button can be selected by pressing the Enter key. In the Font dialog box, OK is the default button.

Backstage View

Click the File tab ▮▮ to display *Backstage view,* which displays file management options:

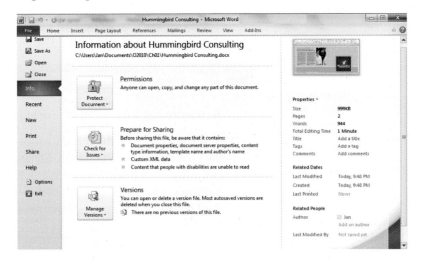

The Info tab displays information about the document including the file size, word count, and when the document was last modified and printed. To return to the document, click any of the tabs across the top of Backstage view or press the Esc key.

Saving Files

Once a document has been created in an application, it should be saved as a file. A *file* is a collection of related data stored on a lasting medium, such as a hard disk. A saved file can be loaded into memory for further editing at a later time. The modified document must then be saved again to *overwrite* the original file with the changed file. A good work habit is to save a document often as it is being modified to prevent accidental loss from a power interruption or network problem.

A file must be given a name to identify it. A *file name* is a unique name for a file stored on disk. When a new document is created, the title bar displays a general description, such as Document1 or Book1, until the document is saved. Select ▮▮ → Save or click Save ▯ (Ctrl+S) on the Quick Access Toolbar to save a document. The Save As dialog box is displayed the first time a file is saved:

Default Settings

A default setting is the setting that is automatically selected unless it is changed by the user.

TIP Click Properties to edit the document properties.

Storage Media

Files can be stored for later retrieval on various types of storage media, such as magnetic (hard disk), optical (CD, DVD) or semiconductor (USB Flash drive).

Address bar

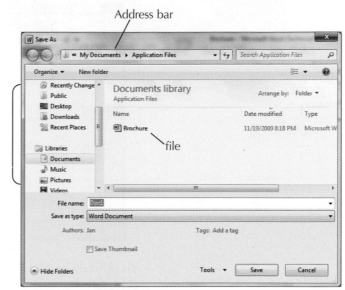

Navigation pane

file

Files are organized into *folders* 📁. In the dialog box above, the Application Files folder contains one file named Brochure in the File list. The Save As dialog box has features for navigating to the appropriate folder for storing the file:

- The **Address bar** displays the location where the file will be saved. To navigate to a different location, click an arrow in any part of the Address bar and then click a drive or folder location:

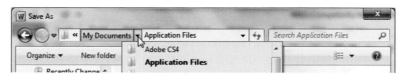

TIP Click `New folder` in the Save As dialog box and then type a descriptive name to create a new folder in the current location.

- The **Navigation pane** displays folders and locations. Click a folder or location in the Navigation pane to display those contents.

- The File name box should be changed to a name that is valid and descriptive of the file's contents. A valid file name can contain letters, numbers, spaces, and the underscore character (_), but cannot contain colons (:), asterisks (*), question marks (?), and some other special characters. Examples of valid, descriptive file names are Biology Paper, GADGETS LOGO, and Memo 2011 02 09.

TIP The Address bar displays a breadcrumb style path to the last folder name listed.

extension

Applications automatically add an extension to the file name when saved. An *extension* indicates the file type and is used by the application to recognize files. Word 2010 automatically adds the .docx extension to file names.

Printing a Document

To print a document, select ▬▬ File ▬▬ → Print, which displays Print options in Backstage view:

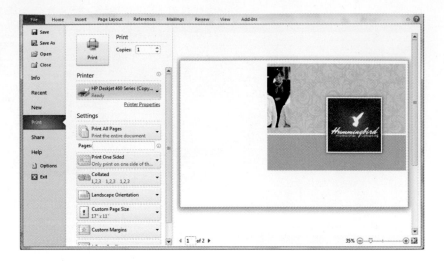

TIP Always save before printing.

TIP To print pages 1 through 10 and page 15, type 1-10, 15 in the Pages box.

To print more than one copy of the document, type or select a number in the Copies box and then select Print. To print specific pages, type the appropriate page number or range of pages in the Pages box and then select Print. Additional print options are discussed later in the text.

Practice: Working with a Document – part 2 of 3

Word should be already started with text typed into a new document.

① **SAVE THE DOCUMENT**

   a. On the Quick Access Toolbar, click Save ☐. The Save As dialog box is displayed.

   b. Use the Address bar and the File list below it to navigate to the appropriate location for the file to be saved. You may have to ask your instructor for instructions on navigating to the appropriate folder.

   c. The file name in the File name box needs to be replaced with a descriptive file name. In the File name box, type: Application Practice

   d. Select Save. The file is saved in the selected location with the name Application Practice and the file name is displayed in the title bar of the document window.

② **PRINT THE DOCUMENT**

   a. Select ▰ File → Print. Print options are displayed. The options available will vary depending on the printer or printers connected to your workstation or network.

   b. Set the Copies to 1, if it is not already.

   c. Select Print. The document is printed.

Closing a Document

When finished working on a document, it should be saved and then closed. *Closing a document* means that it is removed from the application window and the file is no longer in the computer's memory. Select ▰ File → Close to close a document. A warning dialog box is displayed if the document has been modified since it was last saved.

Quitting an Application

Quitting an application means that the application window is removed from the desktop and the program is no longer in the computer's memory. To quit an Office application, select the exit command. For example, to exit Word, select  File → Exit. Close ▬✗▬ in the upper-right corner of the application window can also be used to quit the application.

Opening a File

Opening a file transfers a copy of the file contents to the computer's memory and then displays it in an application window. To open a file, select File → Open, which displays the Open dialog box:

Use the Address bar and File list to navigate to the appropriate file. Click the file name and then select Open to display the file.

To organize the File list alphabetically or chronologically, click a column heading such as Name or Date modified. To filter the File list, point to a heading and then click ▼ to display options:

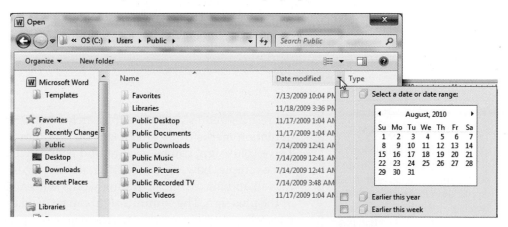

Word should already be started with Application Practice displayed from the last practice.

① **CLOSE APPLICATION PRACTICE**

Select ▣ File → Close. The document is removed from the Word window.

② **OPEN A DOCUMENT**

a. Select ▣ File → Open. The Open dialog box is displayed.

b. Navigate to the location of Application Practice. You may have to ask your instructor for instructions on navigating to the appropriate folder.

c. In the File list, click Application Practice and select **Open**. The Application Practice document is again displayed in a window.

③ **QUIT WORD**

Select ▣ File → Exit. The Word window is closed.

Searching the Web

TIP Other Web browsers include Firefox, Chrome, Opera, and Safari.

search engine

TIP For more information about the Web and Internet Explorer, visit www.lpdatafiles.com.

When researching information for a document, one widely used resource is the World Wide Web. The Web is used to search and access information on the Internet and requires a Web browser application, such as Microsoft Internet Explorer to view the Web site pages.

A *search engine* is used to locate information on the Web. Search engines search a database of Web pages for specified words or phrases and then list the hyperlinks to the pages containing the text. Search engine Web sites include:

Google (www.google.com)   **Yahoo!** (www.yahoo.com)

Ask (www.ask.com)   **Bing** (www.bing.com)

To locate information in a search engine, *search criteria* must be specified. Most search engines include categories to help specify search criteria. For example, in Google select Images to search just for images:

Search Engines

A search engine usually works by sending out an agent, such as a spider. A spider is an application that gathers a list of available Web page documents and stores this list in a database that users can search.

There are several ways to specify search criteria. Surrounding phrases with quotation marks finds Web pages that contain the entire phrase exactly. The + (plus sign) can be used to find pages that contain specified words. For example, hawaii +museum matches pages that contain the words Hawaii and museum. Separating words with a space has the same effect as the plus sign. The – (minus sign) can be used to exclude unwanted Web pages. For example, hawaii –museum matches pages that contain the word Hawaii but not the word museum.

The +, –, and space can be combined to produce more precise search criteria. For example: university + connecticut –yale.

The logical operators AND, OR, and NOT are sometimes used to specify search criteria. The operator AND has the same effect as the + and space. The operator OR is used to find Web pages that contain one word or another or both. For example, florida OR hotel returns links to pages containing Florida, hotel, and Florida and hotel. The operator NOT has the same effect as – (minus sign).

Boolean expression

When operators are used in search criteria, a Boolean expression is formed. A *Boolean expression* evaluates to either true or false. For example, the criteria hawaii +museum evaluates to true when a Web page contains Hawaii and that same Web page contains museum. When an expression evaluates to true, a link to the Web page is displayed.

Practice: Searching the Web

You will need a Web browser and Internet access to complete this practice.

① **GO TO THE GOOGLE SEARCH ENGINE**

    a. Start Internet Explorer.

    b. In the Address box, replace the existing URL with www.google.com:

    c. Press Enter. The Google home page is displayed.

② **TYPE SEARCH CRITERIA**

    a. In the search box, type: seven wonders of the world

    b. Click Google Search to start the search. After a few moments a list of Web site hyperlinks are displayed. How many pages match the criteria?

    c. Scroll down to display the results of the search, then click one of the hyperlinks that interests you. A new page is opened.

③ **SELECT OTHER WEB PAGES LOCATED IN THE SEARCH**

    a. On the toolbar, click Back ⬅. The Web site hyperlinks are again displayed. Click a different hyperlink.

    b. Continue this process to access additional pages.

④ **DEFINE CRITERIA USING LOGICAL OPERATORS**

    a. Refine the search criteria to: seven wonders of the world +new and see how many Web page matches there are.

    b. Refine the search criteria to: seven wonders of the world +new –ancient and see how many Web page matches there are.

    c. Click a few of the hyperlinks to determine if the Web pages include the information that is being searched for.

⑤ **GO TO THE BING SEARCH ENGINE**

    a. In the Address box, replace the existing URL with www.bing.com, the URL for Bing's home page, and then press Enter. The Bing home page is displayed.

b. In the **Search** box, type stonehenge and then click the Search button. After a few moments a list of Web site hyperlinks are displayed. Note the number of Web page matches there are.

c. Use the Google search engine (www.google.com) to find Web pages matching stonehenge. How many pages match the criteria? How does the Bing search compare to the Google search?

⑥ **CLOSE THE BROWSER**

Click **Close** [x] to close the browser window.

Citing Web Sources

TIP Citing sources is also discussed in Chapter 4.

If information from a Web site is to be referenced or quoted in a report, essay, or other document, a citation must be used to give credit to the original author and allow the reader to locate the cited information. A widely accepted form for citation is published by the Modern Language Association (MLA) in its publication *MLA Handbook for Writers of Research Papers, Sixth Edition.*

In general, a citation for material located at a Web site should look similar to:

TIP MLA no longer requires the use of URLs in MLA citations because Web sites are not static and typically documents can be located by searching the title in a search engine. If an instructor still requires the use of URLs, they are placed in angle brackets after the date of access.

> Author's Last Name, First Name. "Article Title." *Site Title.* Publisher Name, Last-updated date. Web. Access date. <URL>.

If no publisher name is available, n.p. should be used and if no publication date is listed, n.d. is used.

A citation of a page on a Web site:

> Marrelli, J. "How to use Internet Explorer". *Lawrenceville Press - Download Data Files.* Lawrenceville Press, 23 Dec. 2010. Web. 15 May 2011.

A citation of an article in an online magazine should include a volume number or issue number:

> Schiffman, Paula. "Making Vinegar at Home." *Vinegar Monthly Vol. 1*, Lawrenceville Press. May 2010. Web. 30 Oct. 2011.

A citation of a posting to a blog or discussion group:

> Cruz, Anthony. "Are Orchestras Going Downhill?" *Oboe Discussion Group.* Oboe DGP, 10 June 2010. Web. 23 Nov. 2011.

Avoiding Plagiarism

All sources of information that are used to support research must be cited. This includes e-mail messages, graphics, sounds, video clips, and news-groups postings.

Multitasking

Multitasking is an operating system feature that allows more than one application to run at a time. When using multitasking effectively, tasks are completed more efficiently. For example, a report that requires a chart and some research could be completed by having Word, Excel, and a Web browser running at the same time and then switching between them to organize the information into the Word document.

thumbnail

The Windows taskbar displays icons for each open application. Point to an application icon to display a *thumbnail*, or miniature version, of each open document:

TIP Press Alt+Tab to switch between open documents.

Click a document thumbnail to maximize the window.

Practice: Sample Citation

You will need a Web browser and Internet access to complete this practice.

① **START WORD**

    a. Start Word. A new, blank document should be displayed.

    b. Type An example citation: and press Enter.

② **START THE BROWSER**

    a. Start Internet Explorer. Note that there are two icons on the taskbar. One icon for the Word document and one for the browser.

    b. In the Address box of the browser, type www.lpdatafiles.com/surfing and then press Enter. The Surfing Web site is displayed.

    c. Review the information on the Web page. Locate the author's name, the title, and the last updated information.

③ **CREATE A CITATION**

    a. On the taskbar, click the icon for the Word document. The Word window is again displayed. Note that the insertion point is in the same position as it was left.

    b. Use the icons on the taskbar to switch between Word and the browser to determine information needed for the citation. In Word, type a citation for the Web site without pressing the Enter key. To italicize the site title, select the text and then click Home → Italic *I* :

        Wu, Ana. "Surfing the Web." *Surfing*. n.p., 12 May 2009. Web. 5 Jun 2011.

    c. Save the document naming it Sample Citation and then print a copy.

④ **QUIT THE APPLICATIONS**

   a. Close Sample Citation and then quit Word. The Word window is closed and the browser window is again displayed.

   b. Close the browser window.

Mailing List Server

A *mailing list server*, such as LISTSERV, manages Internet mailing lists. Special interest groups often use a mailing list for discussion purposes. When a subscriber posts, or e-mails, a message to the mailing list, every subscriber receives a copy. Mailing lists sometimes have a moderator who filters the messages before posting.

Top Level Domain

The domain name includes the top level domain after the dot. The top level domain indicates the domain type. For example, com indicates a commercial business and edu indicates educational institution.

What is E-Mail?

Once complete, a document can be e-mailed to the recipient. *E-mail* means electronic mail and is the sending and receiving of messages and files over a communications network such as a LAN (Local Area Network) or the Internet. E-mailing a document has many advantages, which include allowing a far-away recipient to receive a document very quickly. With Microsoft Office, documents can be e-mailed directly from within the application used to create the document or sent as an attachment.

An e-mail address is required in order to send and receive e-mail messages. E-mail addresses are provided when you sign up with an ISP (Internet Service Provider) or a Webmail service. A typical e-mail address is similar to:

user name   domain name

An *e-mail client* is software that is used to read messages, create and send messages, list and organize messages, and manage e-mail addresses in an address book. Outlook, Eudora, Yahoo! Mail, and Gmail are some popular e-mail clients. Yahoo! Mail and Gmail run in a Web browser and are called *Web-based e-mail clients* or *Webmail accounts*.

When an e-mail client sends or receives a message, it connects to an *e-mail server*, which is a computer running special software and connected to the Internet. The e-mail client typically connects to an *SMTP server* (Simple Mail Transfer Protocol) for outgoing mail. For incoming mail, a connection to a *POP3* (Post Office Protocol3) or *IMAP* (Internet Mail Access Protocol) server is made.

Unfortunately, when using e-mail there is the risk of receiving malicious code, such as viruses, Trojan horses, and worms. An e-mail client usually includes an e-mail filtering system, but antivirus software that runs in addition to the e-mail client is a necessity.

E-Mail Etiquette and Ethics

When communicating through e-mail, professionalism and courtesy are expected. E-mail etiquette for composing messages includes:

- Be concise.
- Use manners. Include "please" and "thank you" and properly address people you do not know as Mr., Ms., Mrs., Dr., and so on.
- Use proper spelling, grammar, and capitalization. Do not use all capital letters to type a message. All capitals are the equivalent of SCREAMING.

In general, re-read a message before it is sent. Always fill in the To box last to avoid sending a message before it is complete.

Using e-mail also requires following a code of ethics:

- Send messages through your account only. Do not try to deceive recipients by falsely representing yourself.
- Keep the subject in the message header short and truly representative of the message. Recipients may judge the authenticity of the message based on the subject and decide to delete the message. Antivirus software and e-mail filtering systems may send your message to the Spam or Junk E-mail folder if the subject is inappropriate.
- Use appropriate subject matter and language.
- Be considerate of other people's beliefs and opinions.
- Respond to e-mail messages in a timely manner.
- Do not attempt to access e-mail from someone else's account without permission.
- Do not give out someone else's e-mail address without first obtaining permission.

E-mail messages are not private. An e-mail message goes through several mail servers before it reaches the recipient, making it possible for others to intercept it. E-mail messages are also easily forwarded. When sending e-mail at work or school, it is important to remember that employers and school administrators have the right to read any e-mail messages sent over the corporate or school network, as well as the right to track online activity.

Spoofing

Spoofing is the unethical and illegal practice of providing a Subject that lures an individual into opening an e-mail about an entirely different topic. The CAN-SPAM Act of 2003 provides penalties for commercial e-mailers who send deceptive messages.

Encryption

One way to protect the privacy of an e-mail message is to encrypt the message, which converts the message to scrambled or cipher text. The recipient of the message needs a key to unscramble the message.

Using Outlook

The *Microsoft Outlook* e-mail client is a personal information manager with tools for managing e-mail messages. The Mail window appears similar to:

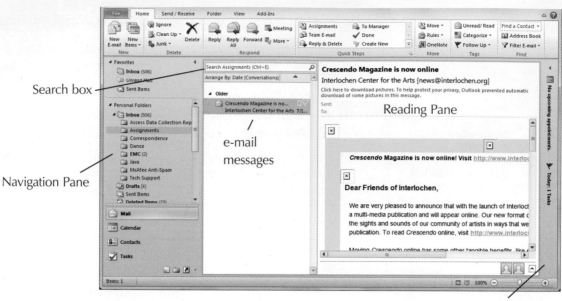

Search box

Navigation Pane

Reading Pane

e-mail messages

To-Do Bar

Mail Formats

The format of outgoing e-mail messages can be set to HTML, plain text, or rich text.

HTML is the default and recommended format because it is used by most e-mail clients. Plain text format is understood by most e-mail clients, but it does not support formatting, such as bold. Rich text format supports numerous formatting options, but is only understood by certain e-mail clients.

Select the Format Text tab to change the mail format.

TIP Outlook checks spelling as a message is typed. Right-click a wavy red line under a word to see spelling options.

TIP A copy (Cc) of an e-mail is often sent to group leaders, supervisors, or others who may need to be kept informed of a situation, but not actually interact with the e-mail recipients in the To box.

The *Mail window* contains several panes:

* The **Navigation Pane** lists folders where e-mail messages are stored.

* The next pane displays the e-mail messages stored in the selected folder, in this case the Inbox. This pane also contains the **Search box** for searching messages.

* The **Reading Pane** displays the selected message. The selected message is displayed with a *message header*, which contains the subject of the message, the recipients, and the sender.

* The **To-Do Bar** lists appointments and tasks.

To create a new e-mail message, select Home ➔ New E-mail :

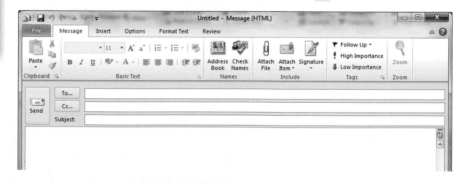

* In the Subject box, type a title that describes the message.

* In the large blank space, compose the message.

* In the To box, type the e-mail address of the recipient . If an e-mail message is to be sent to more than one individual, separate e-mail addresses with a semi-colon (;).

* In the Cc box, type the e-mail addresses of any recipients that are to receive a "carbon copy" of the e-mail.

* Click Send to send the message.

To retrieve messages from the e-mail server, click Send/Receive → Send/ Receive All Folders. New messages are placed in the Inbox folder and message headers are displayed in the second pane.

To reply to a selected message, click Home → Reply. A new message window containing the selected message is displayed. A new message, or reply, can be typed above the original message. Click Send to send the reply. By including the original message, the recipient will have a reference when reading the reply.

To print a message, click File → Print → Print. A message is move to the Deleted Items folder when Home → Delete is clicked.

Practice: E-Mail Messages – part 1 of 3

You will need Internet access and an e-mail address to complete this practice.

① **START OUTLOOK AND DISPLAY THE MAIL WINDOW**

Ask your instructor for the appropriate steps to start Outlook.

② **CREATE AN E-MAIL MESSAGE**

a. Select Home → New E-mail. In the displayed window, type a subject and message, replacing Classmate with a friend's name and Name with your name:

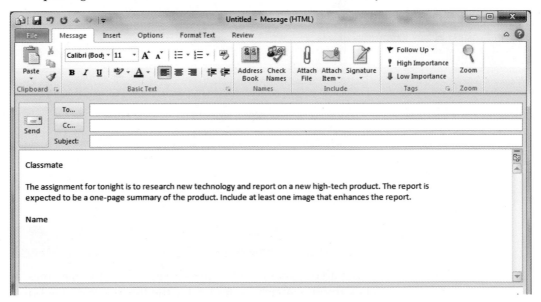

b. Exchange e-mail addresses with a classmate. Type your classmate's e-mail address in the To box. If your instructor is to receive a copy of the e-mail, then type your instructor's e-mail address in the Cc box.

c. Click Send. The e-mail message is sent.

③ **RECEIVE AND PRINT AN E-MAIL MESSAGE**

a. Click Send/Receive → Send/Receive All Folders. Messages are retrieved from the e-mail server and placed in the Inbox.

b. In the Inbox pane, select the message from your classmate. The message is displayed in the Reading Pane.

c. Click File → Print → Print.

④ **REPLY TO AN E-MAIL MESSAGE**

a. Click Home → Reply. A window is displayed with the original message and the sender's e-mail address in the To box. Note that the prefix "RE:" has been added to the beginning of the subject line in the Subject box.

b. Type the following message, replacing Name with your name: Thank you for sending the assignment. I think I will research microchip technology.   --Name

c. Click Send.

The Address Book

The *Address Book* stores contact names and e-mail addresses. Click Home → Address Book to view entries in the Address Book:

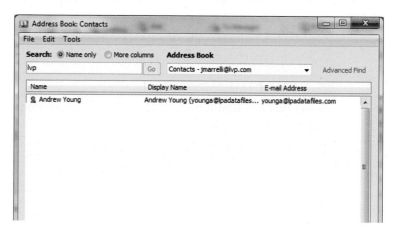

To add a new contact, select File → New Entry.

As an e-mail address is typed in the To or Cc box of a message window, a list of Address Book names appears. Use the arrow keys to select the appropriate address. An e-mail address can also be selected from the Address book by clicking To... or Cc... .

E-Mail Attachments

E-mail provides a way to quickly send a file. In a new message window, click Insert → Attach File to display the Insert File dialog box. Select a file and then select Insert. The name of the attached file is displayed in the Attachment box in the e-mail header.

The recipient can choose to save an attachment in an appropriate location or open it directly from the e-mail. To save a selected attachment, select Attachments → Save As. A dialog box is displayed. Navigate to the location for the file and then select Save. Attachments can also be saved by right-clicking the attachment and selecting Save As from the displayed menu.

native format

To open an attachment, the recipient will need to have the appropriate application. For example, if a Word file is attached, then the recipient must have Word to open the file. A Word file in its native format is recognized by the .docx extension in the file name. *Native format* is the format that an application normally uses for saving a file.

TIP In Word, options for attaching a PDF copy of the open document to an e-mail message are found in File → Share.

Sending files in their native format is necessary if the user is to edit the file, but inconvenient if the user simply needs to view the file. One solution is to attach a file that has been saved in text format. Files in text format typically have the extension .txt or .rtf. Text files can be opened by any word processor. The disadvantage of the text format is that some of the document formatting may be lost or changed. A more commonly used solution is to export a file to PDF format before attaching it to an e-mail.

PDF The *PDF* file format is widely used because all document formatting is preserved. To view a PDF, recipients use Adobe Reader, a free application from Adobe Systems that most users already have.

Practice: E-Mail Messages – part 2 of 3

You will need Internet access to complete this practice. Outlook should already be started from the last practice.

① **ADD AN ENTRY TO THE ADDRESS BOOK**

    a. Click Home → Address Book. The Address Book is displayed. Note the addresses currently listed.

        1. On the Address Book menu bar, select File → New Entry. Another dialog box is displayed:

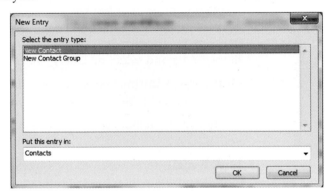

        2. In the Select the entry type box, select New Contact and then select OK. A Contact window is displayed.

        3. Complete the Full Name box and E-mail box entries using the name and e-mail address of a classmate. Note that Outlook automatically creates an entry for the File as box.

        4. Click Contact → Save & Close. The Contact window is removed and the contact appears in the Address Book.

        5. Click Close ❌ to remove the Address Book.

② **CREATE AN E-MAIL MESSAGE AND ADD AN ATTACHMENT**

    a. Click Home → New E-mail. A Message window is displayed.

    b. In the message window, click To. The Select Names dialog box is displayed.

        1. In the Name list, select the name of your classmate.

        2. At the bottom of the dialog box, click To.

        3. Click OK. The dialog box is removed and your classmate's e-mail address appears in the To box of the message window.

    c. In the Subject box, type: My Assignment

d. In the Message body, type the following, replacing Name with you name: Here is a copy of my assignment. Can you proofread it for me? Thank you. --Name

e. In the Message window, click Insert → Attach File. A dialog box is displayed.

    1. Navigate to ASSIGNMENT, which is a data file for this text.

    2. Select Insert. The file is attached to the message.

    3. The file size of the attachment is displayed to the right of the file name. What is the file size of ASSIGNMENT?

f. In the message window, click Send.

Organizing E-mail Messages

Related e-mail messages should be organized into folders. Outlook automatically creates some folders and rules that direct specific e-mail messages to the appropriate folders. These folders are displayed in the Navigation pane:

* **Inbox** stores received messages.

* **Sent Items** stores messages that have been sent.

* **Deleted Items** stores messages that have been deleted until they are permanently deleted or retrieved. Messages stored in the Deleted Items folder are permanently deleted by right-clicking the Deleted Items folder and selecting Empty Folder.

* **Drafts** stores unfinished messages that have been automatically saved by Outlook because they have been open for a time.

* **Outbox** stores messages that have been sent but not transmitted yet.

* **Junk E-mail** stores received messages that have a subject line or e-mail address which has been flagged by antivirus software or another e-mail filtering system.

The Inbox arranges e-mail messages by date. This arrangement can be changed to display e-mail messages alphabetically by sender, by recipient, or by subject. Changing the arrangement may help locate a message. However, related e-mail messages in the Inbox should be organized into folders with descriptive names to make it easy to locate messages. To create a new folder, right-click the folder name and then select New Folder. E-mail messages can then be dragged to the appropriate folder in the Navigation pane.

The Search box is used to search messages. For example, to search for e-mail containing the text research project, type those keywords into the Search box.

research project	×

As the keywords are typed, the current e-mail folder is searched and matching messages displayed with the keywords highlighted. To quit searching, click Close Search ×. Search criteria can be refined by selecting options in the Search tab that is displayed when the insertion point is placed in the Search box:

Rules

Rules help manage e-mail messages by automatically performing an action based on a condition. For example, move all messages from Susan Thompson to the Sales folder. To create a rule, select Home → Rules → Create Rule.

Conversation View

Conversation view groups e-mail messages by subject, even when the messages are in different folders.

Click Arrange By and select Date (Conversations) to arrange messages in Conversation view.

For example, to search for e-mail messages with the Subject Assignment in all Outlook mail folders, click Search → Subject, and type Assignment in the Search box and then click Search → Search All Subfolders.

E-mail Security

spam

E-mail is an effective way to communicate. Unfortunately, along with personal and business messages, most people also receive a lot of "junk e-mail," also called *spam*. Outlook has a Junk E-mail Filter, which catches obvious junk mail and automatically places it the Junk E-mail folder. This folder should be checked periodically to ensure a legitimate message has not accidentally been filtered to this folder. If a legitimate message is located in this folder, right-click the message and select Not Junk → Never Block Sender.

It is also possible to block messages from specific senders. Right-click a message from the sender to be blocked and select Junk → Block Sender. To view and edit the Blocked Senders list, select Home → Junk → Junk E-mail Options, which displays the Junk E-mail Options dialog box. Select the Blocked Senders tab to display those options:

TIP The Safe Senders tab in the Junk E-mail Options dialog box is used to ensure that e-mail from specified addresses will not be treated as junk e-mail.

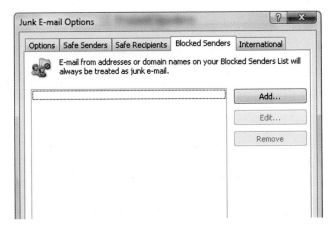

To remove a name from the Blocked Senders list, select the name and then select Remove. Blocked senders can also be added in this dialog box by selecting Add and typing the sender's e-mail address.

Cybercrime includes the delivery of malicious code in an e-mail message. Malicious code, such as viruses, Trojan horses, and worms may be delivered in an e-mail attachment or through spam. A message carrying malicious code can have a familiar e-mail address because address books are often the target. Messages from unfamiliar individuals or companies require extra precautions. Just opening an infected e-mail could execute malicious code.

viruses

Viruses have varying effects, such as displaying annoying messages, causing programs to run incorrectly, and erasing the contents of the hard drive. A *Trojan horse* appears like a useful computer program, but actually

Trojan horse

worm　causes damage to data and can download stronger threats. A *worm* is a malicious program that can replicate itself, use up a system's memory, and bring a system down.

phishing, pharming　A growing security threat is *phishing* and *pharming* (pronounced "fishing" and "farming") e-mails. Both involve online fraud and are forms of *identity theft*　cybercrime. This crime, also referred to as *identity theft*, seeks to obtain confidential information in order to rob an unsuspecting individual of his or her identity. Personal information, such as identification numbers or credit card numbers, should never be included in an e-mail message. E-mail messages that prompt you to visit a Web site to verify personal information should be deleted without visiting any Web site links or replying to the e-mail.

Outlook provides some protection from e-mail viruses and other malicious code by automatically blocking attachment files that contain code that can run without warning, such as .bat, .exe, .vbs, and .j files. However, precautions still need to be taken to minimize the possibility of malicious code damaging important data:

- Invest in antivirus software. Antivirus software will detect many types of viruses by scanning incoming e-mail messages before they are opened. If a virus is detected, the software will display a warning and try to remove the virus.

- Update the antivirus software frequently. New viruses are continually being created and new virus definitions must be downloaded on a regular basis in order for the antivirus software to be effective.

- Always save an attachment file and then virus-check the file before opening it. This precaution should be taken for all messages from known and unknown sources, since many viruses target address books and fool users into thinking the e-mail is from someone familiar.

- Protect your personal information and review bank and credit card statements regularly.

Practice: E-mail Messages – part 3 of 3

Outlook should already be started from the last practice.

① CHANGE ARRANGEMENT OF INBOX MESSAGES

    a. Display the Mail window if it is not already showing.

    b. At the top of the Inbox pane, click Arranged By. A menu is displayed:

c. In the menu, select From. Scroll to view all of the messages. Note that the e-mail messages are arranged in alphabetic order by the sender's name.

d. Arrange the messages by Subject.

e. Arrange the messages by Date (Conversations).

② **CREATE A NEW FOLDER**

    a. Right-click the Inbox folder. A menu is displayed.

        1. Select New Folder. A dialog box is displayed.

        2. In the Name box, type Assignments.

        3. In the Select where to place the folder list, select Personal Folders:

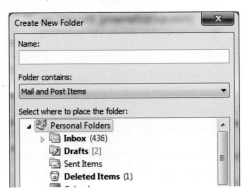

        4. Select OK. The new folder is created and displayed in the Navigation Pane.

③ **SEARCH FOR A MESSAGE AND MOVE A MESSAGE TO A FOLDER**

    a. In the Search box, type Assignment:

Messages with the text Assignment are displayed and the search text highlighted.

    b. Drag the Assignment message from the last practice to the Assignment folder. The message is moved.

    c. In the Navigation Pane, click Inbox to exit the search.

④ **QUIT OUTLOOK**

Using Microsoft Office Help

The Microsoft Office Help window is displayed by clicking Help ⑦ or by pressing the F1 key. Each Office application has its own specific Help window. For example, the Word Help window looks similar to:

TIP On the Help window toolbar, click **Change Font Size** to increase or reduce the size of the text in the Help window.

The Help window functions much like a Web browser. There is a toolbar with navigation buttons that go Back ⊙ or Forward ⊙ through visited topics. Other navigation buttons are Stop ⊗, Refresh ⊙, and Home ⌂. Print 🖨 is used to print the current contents of the Help window.

The Word Help home window includes a Word 2010 Help and How-to section with links to major topics:

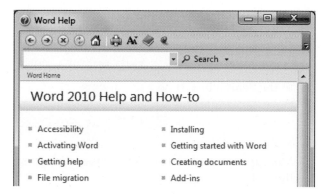

Click one of these links to display subcategories and a list of topics. Help also supports keyword search for finding help topics. Below the toolbar is the search box where search criteria is typed:

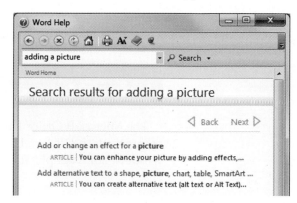

If there is a connection to the Internet, Help will browse topics at the Microsoft Office Online Web site. The Connection Status menu in the lower-right of the Help window indicates the source of the help content. Click the Connection Status menu to display commands for changing the help source.

① **DISPLAY THE WORD HELP WINDOW**

   a. Start Word.

   b. In the upper-right of the Word window, click Help ⑳. The Word Help window is displayed.

   c. In the lower-right corner of the window, click the Connection Status menu to display commands:

   d. If the connection status is currently online, then click Show content only from this computer.

   e. In the Browse Word Help topics, click <u>SmartArt graphics</u>. A list of topics is displayed.

   f. Change the connection status to Show content from Office.com.

   g. In the search box, type SmartArt graphics and press Enter. The list of topics is longer.

   h. Click Back ⬅.

② **BROWSE FOR HELP**

   a. Click <u>Collaboration</u>. Note the topics displayed.

   b. In the Topics list, click one of the subtopics. Related information is displayed.

   c. Scroll through the information.

③ **DO A KEYWORD SEARCH FOR HELP**

   a. In the search box, type .docx and then click Search. A list of topics is displayed.

   b. Click <u>Save a file</u>. Scroll through the information.

④ **USE THE NAVIGATION BUTTONS AND THEN CLOSE THE HELP WINDOW**

   a. On the toolbar, click Home ⌂. The home window is again displayed.

   b. Click Back ⬅. What is displayed?

   c. Click Forward ➡.

   d. Click Close ✖ in the upper-right corner of the window. The Word Help window is closed.

   e. Exit Word.

Microsoft Office 2010 is a Windows application that includes Outlook, Word, Excel, Access, PowerPoint, Publisher, and OneNote. Windows applications have an interface called a window, which include an File tab Quick Access Toolbar, and a Ribbon. The File tab displays Backstage view, which is used to save, print, close, quit, and open documents.

Input devices are used to communicate with a Windows application. A keyboard is used to enter text and numeric data. Other input devices include the mouse, stylus pen, and touchpad.

Folders are used to organize files, which are automatically given an extension when saved. A document is printed using the Print command. Closing a document means that it is removed from the application window and the file is no longer in the computer's memory. Quitting an application removes an application from the desktop and the program is no longer in the computer's memory. Opening a file transfers a copy of the file contents to the computer's memory and then displays it in a window.

A search engine is used to locate information on the Web. Search criteria is used to specify which pages are to be located. Operators including +, –, space, AND, OR, and NOT can be used in specifying criteria. When operators are used, a Boolean expression is formed.

There are guidelines for citing electronic material on the Internet. The primary purpose of a citation is to give credit to the original author and allow the reader to locate the cited information.

Multitasking is an operating system feature that allows more than one application to run at a time. The taskbar displays buttons that represent each open file or application.

E-mail is the sending and receiving of messages over a communications network such as a LAN or the Internet. To send and receive messages, an e-mail address and an e-mail client is required. The risks of using e-mail include receiving malicious code in an e-mail message. When communicating through e-mail, professionalism and courtesy are expected. This includes following e-mail rules of etiquette and a code of ethics.

Microsoft Outlook is an e-mail client. It includes an Address Book for storing contact names and e-mail addresses. Outlook has a Junk E-mail Filter, which catches obvious junk mail, or spam, and automatically places it in the Junk E-mail folder. It is also possible to block messages from specific senders.

The Microsoft Office Help window functions like a browser with buttons for going backwards and forwards through visited topics. Help browses the Microsoft Office Online Web site as well as content installed on the computer when Office was installed.

Access The Office database application.

Access key A key that is indicated by the underlined character in a command.

Address book Outlook tool that stores contact names and e-mail addresses.

Alt key Used with an access key to display a menu.

Boolean expression An expression that evaluates to either true or false.

Check box An element in a dialog box that allows the user to select or clear an option.

Click Pressing the left mouse button and releasing it quickly.

Closing a document Removing a document from the application window and the file from the computer's memory.

Command button An element in a dialog box that initiates an action when clicked.

Contextual tab A tab added to the Ribbon for certain activities.

Default button The button displayed with a thicker border when a dialog box is first displayed.

Double-click Pressing the left mouse button twice in rapid succession.

Drop-down arrow A text box feature that can be clicked to display a list of items to choose from.

E-mail Electronic mail. The sending and receiving of electronic messages and computer files over a communications network such as a LAN or the Internet.

E-mail client Software used to read, create, and send e-mail messages, list and organize e-mail messages, and manage addresses in an address book.

E-mail server A computer running special software and connected to the Internet.

Excel The Office spreadsheet application.

Extension Indicates the file type and is used by the application to recognize files.

File A collection of related data stored on a lasting medium, such as a hard disk.

File name A unique name for a file.

Folder Used to organize commonly related files.

Identity theft A crime that seeks to obtain confidential information in order to rob an unsuspecting individual of his or her identity.

IMAP server An e-mail server used for incoming mail.

Input device A device used to communicate with a Windows application.

Insertion point A blinking vertical line in a document that indicates where the next character typed will be placed.

Interface The area on the screen where the user interacts with a software application.

Keyboard Used to enter text and numeric data.

Keyboard shortcut A sequence of keys that executes a command.

Mail window The Outlook window containing e-mail tools.

Message header The portion of an e-mail message containing the subject, recipients, and sender of the message.

Microsoft Office 2010 A Windows application that consists of several applications, each designed to perform specific tasks.

Mouse An input device that is used to select commands and respond to application prompts.

Mouse pointer An image on the screen, usually in the shape of an arrow, that indicates the position of the mouse.

Multitasking An operating system feature that allows more than one application to run at a time.

Native format The format that an application normally uses for saving a file.

Navigation Pane The Mail window pane that lists folders where e-mail messages are stored.

OneNote The notetaking and information management application.

Opening a file Transferring a copy of the file contents to the computer's memory, which displays it in a window.

Outlook The Office e-mail client.

Overwrite The process of replacing an existing file with one that contains changes.

PDF File format which preserves all document formatting.

Pharming An e-mail security threat involving online fraud and identity theft.

Phishing An e-mail security threat involving online fraud and identity theft.

Point Sliding the mouse until the pointer is positioned on an object.

Pointing stick A pointing device that is sometimes found on a notebook computer.

POP3 server An e-mail server used for incoming mail.

PowerPoint The Office presentation application.

Publisher The Office desktop publishing application.

Quick Access Toolbar A group of buttons for executing commands.

Quitting an application Removing an application window from the desktop and the program from the computer's memory.

Reading Pane The Mail window pane that displays the contents of the selected message.

Ribbon Related commands that are divided into tabs.

Right-click Pressing and releasing the right mouse button quickly.

Scroll To bring unseen parts of a document into view.

Scroll bar Dragged to bring unseen parts of the document into view.

Search criteria The words or phrases used in a search.

Search engine Used to locate information on the Web.

SMPT server An e-mail server used for outgoing mail.

Spam Junk e-mail.

Status bar Displays information about a document.

Stylus pen A device on a handheld computer that performs the same functions as a mouse.

Taskbar A Windows operating system feature that displays buttons for each open file or application.

Text box An element in a dialog box that allows the user to enter information.

Thumbnail A miniature version of a document.

Title bar A horizontal bar that displays the name and type of document.

To-Do Bar The Mail window pane that lists appointments and tasks.

Touchpad A pointing device that is sometimes found on a notebook computer.

Trojan horse Malicious code that appears like a useful program.

Virus Malicious code attached to a program that may come as an e-mail attachment.

Web-based e-mail client E-mail client that runs in a browser.

Webmail account A Web-based e-mail client. *See* Web-based e-mail client.

Wheel A mouse component that can be rotated to scroll through a document.

Window The interface of a Windows application.

Window corner Dragged to size the window. Located in the bottom-right corner of the window.

Windows application Programs or software written by professional programmers to perform specific tasks and run under the Windows operating system.

Word The Office word processor application.

Worm Malicious code that can replicate itself, use up a system's memory, and bring down a system.

Address Book Displays the Address Book. Found on the Home tab.

Attach File Displays the Insert File dialog box. Found on the Insert tab in a new message window.

Back Displays a previous help topic. Found on the Help window toolbar.

Block Sender Blocks messages from specific senders. Found in the menu displayed by right-clicking a message and selecting Junk.

Cc... Displays the Address Book where a contact can be selected.

Close Removes a window or dialog box from the screen. Found in the upper-right corner of a window or dialog box.

Connection Status menu Contains commands for changing the source of help content. Found in the lower-right corner of the Help window.

Delete Moves an e-mail to the Deleted Items folder. Found on the Home tab.

Dialog Box Launcher Displays a dialog box. Found in a tab group on the Ribbon.

Exit Quits an application. Found in Backstage view.

File tab Displays Backstage view.

Forward Displays the next help topic. Found on the Help window toolbar.

Help Displays information about the dialog box elements. Found in a dialog box.

Help Displays the Microsoft Office Help window. Found in the upper-right corner of an Office application window.

Home Displays the Help home window. Found on the Help window toolbar.

Junk E-mail Options Displays options for junk e-mail. Found in Home → Junk.

Mail Message Displays a window for composing a mail message. New on the toolbar can be used instead of the command.

Mark as Not Junk Moves a message from the Junk E-mail folder to the Inbox folder. Found in the menu displayed by right-clicking an e-mail message in the Junk E-mail folder.

Maximize Expands a window to fill the screen. Found in the upper-right corner of a window.

Minimize Hides a window. Found in the upper-right corner of a window.

Never Block Sender Removes a sender from the Blocked Senders list. Found in the menu displayed by right-clicking a message and selecting Junk.

New E-mail Creates an new e-mail message. Found on the Home tab.

New Entry Displays the New Entry dialog box. Found in the File menu in the Address Book dialog box.

New Folder Creates a new folder in the Navigation Pane. Found in the menu displayed by right-clicking a folder in the Outlook Navigation pane.

Open Opens an existing document. Found in Backstage view.

Print Prints a document or e-mail. Found in Backstage view.

Print Prints a help topic. Found on the Help window toolbar.

Refresh Reloads a help topic. Found on the Help window toolbar.

Reply Used to create an e-mail message response to the selected message.

Restore Down Restores a window to its previous size. Found in the upper-right corner of a window.

Save Saves a document. Found in Backstage view. Save on the Quick Access Toolbar can be used instead of the command.

Save Attachments Saves an attachment. Found on the Attachments tab.

Send/Receive Sends and receives e-mail messages. Found on the Send/Receive tab.

Stop Stops a help topic from loading. Found on the Help window toolbar.

To... Displays the Address Book where a contact can be selected.

1. a) What does the File tab display?
   b) What does the Quick Access Toolbar contain?

2. Which key is used to move the insertion point to the beginning of a line of text?

3. How can the access key be determined?

4. a) What is a keyboard shortcut?
   b) Explain how keyboard shortcuts can increase productivity.

5. a) What is a contextual tab?
   b) How is the Ribbon minimized?

6. List three types of information displayed in the Info tab in Backstage view.

7. a) Why is it important to give files and folders descriptive names?
   b) Explain how you could use folders to organize your files.
   c) What does the extension at the end of a file name indicate?

8. a) List three search engine Web sites.
   b) What is search criteria?

9. a) List three logical operators.
   b) What is the name of the expression that is formed by using logical operators?

10. On August 2, 2011 you accessed a posting on the Clewiston Kite Surfing discussion group at http://www.lpdatafiles.com/kitesurf/color.txt. The posting was made by Tara Perez on the topic of kite colors on June 3, 2010. Write a citation that quotes Tara's posting.

11. List three examples of e-mail clients.

12. Why is it important to follow a code of ethics when using e-mail?

13. Why is the PDF format commonly used for e-mail attachments?

14. a) Explain how you could organize your e-mail messages into folders.
    b) Explain how to find all of the e-mails that contain the word "password."

15. a) What is spam?
    b) How can messages from specific senders be blocked?

16. List three ways to minimize the possibility of malicious code damaging data.

17. What are two ways to find information when using the Help window?

True/False

18. a) Access is a spreadsheet application.
    b) Publisher is an application used for desktop publishing.
    c) The title bar displays the file name and type of document.
    d) A window is hidden when Maximize 🔲 is clicked.
    e) Press the Home key to move the insertion point to the end of a line of text.
    f) Press the Alt key to cancel the current operation.
    g) Press the Esc key to exit Backstage view.
    h) An arrow on a button indicates that additional commands are available.
    i) The Format tab is displayed on the Ribbon when Word is started.
    j) The default button in a dialog box is selected by pressing the Enter key.
    k) Answer to History ? is an example of a valid, descriptive file name.
    l) Any changes made to a document after saving are automatically stored in the file on disk.
    m) The file extension .docx indicates the file was created in Excel 2010.
    n) It is possible to print only the second page of a document.
    o) A Boolean expression evaluates to either true or false.
    p) MLA is an accepted form for citations.
    q) A word processor application and a spreadsheet application can be running at the same time.
    r) Only one Word document can be opened at a time.
    s) Outlook is an e-mail client.
    t) E-mail messages are private.
    u) Phishing is a type of online fraud.
    v) A virus is a type of computer game.

Project 1

You are applying for a freelance writing contract. You need to provide details of your working environment.

a) In a new Word document, type Computer Environment and press Enter twice.

b) Type Microsoft Office Applications and press Enter. Type the names of the Microsoft Office applications available from your computer workstation, pressing Enter after each application name.

c) Type Input Devices and press Enter. Data is entered into a Windows application using an input device. Type the input devices connected to your computer, pressing Enter after each device.

d) Type Storage Media and press Enter. Files can be stored for later retrieval on various types of storage media, such as a disk, CD/DVD, Zip disk, or memory key. Type the types of storage media you are able to save your files on, pressing Enter after each type of storage media.

e) Type Output Devices and press Enter. Output devices display or store processed data. Monitors and printers are examples of display output devices. The CD/DVD burner and memory keys are examples of output devices used for storing data. Type the output devices connected to your computer, pressing Enter after each device.

f) Type Printer(s) and press Enter. Common classifications of printers include laser and dot matrix. A laser printer uses a laser and toner to generate characters and graphics on paper. An ink jet printer uses an ink cartridge to place very small dots of ink onto paper to create characters and graphics. Classify the type of printer(s) accessible to your computer.

g) Press Enter and then type your first and last names and the date.

h) Save the document naming it Computer Environment and print a copy.

Project 2

One of your first freelance writing assignments is to create an article on the importance of creating strong passwords and keeping your computer password a secret:

a) In a new Word document, type the title Computer Passwords and press Enter.

b) Type the following without pressing the Enter key: It is important to keep your password a secret so that other individuals cannot gain unauthorized access to your computer. Do not share your password with anyone and if you receive an e-mail requesting your password, even if it looks like it is from a legitimate source, do not provide the requested information.

c) Press Enter.

d) Type the following without pressing the Enter key: Strong passwords are more secure and are necessary for protecting your personal information. Passwords should appear to be a random string of characters. Words that are in a dictionary, a sequence of characters, or repeated characters are poor choices for passwords. A strong password will be lengthy with at least 8 to 14 characters. A combination of letters (both uppercase and lowercase), characters (numbers and letters), and symbols ($, %, #, and so on) make it more difficult for someone to try to retrieve your password. One technique for creating a strong password is to use a phrase, including the spaces, if possible.

e) In a new sentence, list two examples of what would be considered secure passwords and two examples of passwords that would be easy to guess.

f) Press Enter and then type your first and last names and the current date.

g) Save the document naming it Passwords.

h) Close the document.

Project 3

As a freelance writer, you decide you need a Web site to sell your services to consumers online. Learn more about e-commerce by completing the following exercise.

a) Open E-COMMERCE, which is a Word data file for this text. Read the document.

b) Press the Page Down key.

c) Press the Page Up key.

d) Position the insertion point at the start of the last paragraph, which starts "Wireless technology…"

e) Press the End key.

f) Press the Home key.

g) Position the insertion point after the period in the last sentence in the last paragraph.

h) Press Enter.

i) Type your first and last name.

j) Save the modified E-COMMERCE and print a copy.

k) Minimize the window.

l) Maximize the E-COMMERCE window and then close the document.

Project 4

You need to examine and evaluate Web site content as part of your job as a freelance writer.

a) In Internet Explorer, enter the URL: www.cnn.com

b) Read the content on the home page.

c) On what date was the Web page last updated?

d) Is the information incorrect or incomplete in order to give a particular or slanted view of a topic. Explain your answer.

e) Is the information truthful and trustworthy? Explain your answer.

f) In Internet Explorer, enter the URL: www.earthday.net

g) Repeat steps (b) through (e) for the Earth Day Network Web site.

Project 5

Another freelance writing assignment is on the topic of Carpal Tunnel Syndrome.

a) Conduct a search on the Internet using at least two search engines to find three Web pages that have information about Carpal Tunnel Syndrome.

b) Write a one-paragraph description of the injury.

c) In a second paragraph, write about possible treatments for the injury.

d) *Ergonomics* is the science that studies safe work environments. Many health-related issues, such as carpal tunnel syndrome are related to prolonged computer use. Research ergonomics and write a few paragraphs that outline preventative measures that can be taken to avoid health-related issues, such as carpal tunnel syndrome.

e) On a separate sheet titled References, cite each source.

f) Save the document as: Carpal Tunnel and print a copy

Project 6

Update your Outlook Address Book and organize your Inbox by completing the following steps.

a) Collect e-mail addresses from six people you would be likely to send e-mail messages to and are not in your Address Book.

b) Create six new entries in the Address Book.

c) Send an e-mail to a one of the individual's in your address book.

d) Organize your e-mail messages by creating two new folders, naming the folders appropriately, and then moving messages to the new folders.

Project 7

You have one more freelance writing assignment.

a) Conduct a search on the Internet to find information about a virus associated with an e-mail attachments.

b) Write a one-paragraph description of the virus. Include details, such as the damage caused by the virus and steps necessary to remove the virus.

c) On a separate sheet titled References, cite each source.

d) Save the document as: Email Attachments and print a copy

Chapter 2
Using a Word Processor

What is a Word Processor?

A *word processor* is a computer application used to create, modify, print, and e-mail documents. Professional-looking documents such as letters, résumés, and reports can be created using a word processor. The Microsoft Word 2010 word processor application window looks similar to:

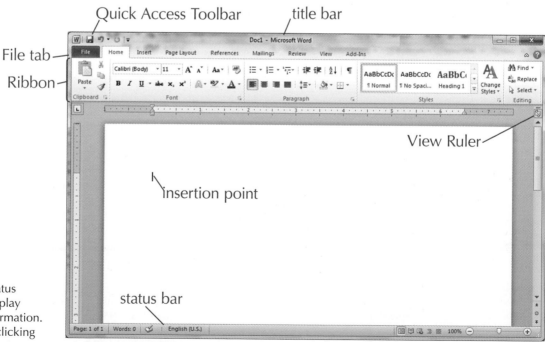

TIP Click a status bar item to display additional information. For example, clicking Words: displays additional word count statistics.

TIP A Word document is saved with a .docx extension. Word documents containing macros have a .docm extension.

The Word window displays information about a document and includes tools for working with documents:

- The file name of the current document is displayed in the **title bar**. The name Document1 is used temporarily until the document is saved with a descriptive name.
- Click the **File tab** [File] to display commands for opening, saving, and printing a document.
- Select commands and perform actions using the **Ribbon** and the **Quick Access Toolbar**.
- Click View Ruler [icon] at the top of the vertical scroll bar to display the rulers. The **rulers** show the paper size. Markers on the rulers are used to format text.
- The **insertion point** is the blinking vertical line that indicates where the next character typed will be placed. The insertion point blinks to draw attention to its location.
- View information about the current document in the **status bar**.

TIP Right-click the status bar to add additional information to the status bar, such as the Line number.

Creating Document Text

In a word processor document, typed text is placed at the insertion point. Any existing text automatically moves to the right to make room for the new text. Within a paragraph, allow the word wrap process to wrap text from line to line. The *word wrap* process automatically determines if the words to the right will fit on the end of the current line or if some must go on the next line. Press Enter to end a paragraph.

TIP If a new document is not displayed, select [File] → New → Blank Document → Create.

When Enter is pressed, blank space is automatically included after each paragraph. This is appropriate for certain documents such as a memo:

¶

¶

MEMO·TO: → Hannah·Rowswell¶

FROM:→ → Grace·Briglio¶

DATE:→ → 03/23/2011¶

SUBJECT: → Company·Policy·#3119¶

¶

Other documents, such as letters, should not have extra space after a paragraph:

June·8,·2011¶
¶
¶
Ms.·Kellie·Ramos¶
Puppy·Day·Care¶
34·Grover·Avenue¶
Jackson,·MN·61287¶
¶
Dear·Ms.·Ramos:¶
¶

One Space After a Period

How many spaces are typed after a period or other punctuation mark? Only one space is needed because the distance between each character is adjusted proportionally, making text easy to read.

Click Home → No Spacing before typing text if there should not be extra space after each paragraph in the document:

No Spacing

TIP If the AutoCorrect feature makes an unwanted correction, point to the correction. A blue bar is displayed. Move the pointer over the blue bar and click AutoCorrect Options ⅋ ⌄ to display options for reversing the correction.

As text is typed, the *AutoCorrect* feature in Word automatically corrects commonly misspelled words and incorrect capitalization. The total word count of the document is displayed in the status bar and updated as words are typed:

Editing Text

Undo Redo   Show/Hide

To *edit*, or modify, the contents a document, first position the insertion point where text is to be typed or deleted. Position the insertion point by pressing an arrow key, or move the pointer into the document until it changes to the *I-beam* (I) and click where the insertion point should appear.

Overtype Mode

Overtype mode means that as text is typed it replaces existing text, instead of the default insert mode. To use overtype mode, select ▭ → Options. In the **Advanced** options, select Use overtype mode.

---

formatting marks

To reverse the last action performed, on the Quick Access Toolbar click Undo ↺. Click Redo ↻ to repeat the last action performed. Click ⌄ in Undo ↺⌄ to display a list of the last actions performed and additional options.

Spaces, tabs (discussed later in the text), and paragraphs are not normally displayed as characters in a document, but they can be displayed as symbols. These symbols are called *formatting marks* and do not appear on paper when a document is printed:

tab mark   space mark

→ It·is·a·good·idea·to·show·formatting·marks,·so·that··you·can·find·mistakes·like·
two·spaces·between·words.¶

paragraph mark (Enter)

It is much easier to edit a document when formatting marks are visible. To display formatting marks, click Home → Show/Hide ¶ . Click Show/Hide ¶ again to hide the formatting marks.

Spelling and Grammar Checking

Word includes a *spelling checker* that automatically checks words by comparing them to a dictionary file. If a word is spelled incorrectly or is not in the dictionary file, a red wavy line appears below it. To correct the word, right-click it and then click the correct spelling from the menu:

Because the dictionary file does not contain every word in the English language, a red wavy line may appear below a correctly spelled word, such as a proper name. When this happens, the wavy line can be ignored because it does not appear on paper when the document is printed. To remove the red wavy line from all occurrences of that word in the document, right-click the word and select Ignore All from the menu.

Proofreading

Spelling and grammar checkers can increase the accuracy of a document. However, proofreading a document is still a very important step in the editing process. For example, a word may be spelled correctly but used inappropriately. Have a person other than the author proofread a document to increase the chances of finding spelling, grammar, and punctuation errors.

Word also has a *grammar checker* that displays a green wavy line below a phrase or sentence when a possible grammatical error is detected. Right-click the green wavy line to display suggested corrections:

A green wavy line may appear below an acceptable sentence. When this happens, the wavy line can be ignored, or it can be removed from the document by selecting Ignore Once from the menu.

A blue wavy line indicates that a word may be inappropriate in the context of the sentence. For example:

Practice: Request

The document created in this practice is a letter in the block style as defined in *The Gregg Reference Manual Tenth Edition* by William Sabin (© 2008 McGraw-Hill Companies, Inc.).

① **START WORD**

② **TYPE THE LETTER HEADING**

A *block style letter* is a letter style that is often used in business. The block style should also be used by individuals writing to a company or professional organization. A block style letter contains a heading, opening, body, and closing with all lines of text beginning at the left side of the page.

a. If the rulers are not visible above and to the left of the document, click View Ruler 🔲 above the vertical scroll bar.

b. Click Home → Show/Hide ¶ to display formatting marks, if they are not already showing. A ¶ marker is displayed to the right of the insertion point.

c. Click Home → No Spacing 🔲.

d. A letter heading includes a return address and date. Press Enter four times to move the insertion point down approximately 1 inch (2.54 cm).

e. Type the following address, press Enter twice, type the date, and then press Enter four times:

> ¶
> ¶
> ¶
> ¶
> 45·Maple·Avenue¶
> Centerville,·WY·11287¶
> ¶
> March·12,·2011¶
> ¶
> ¶
> ¶
> ¶

③ **SAVE THE LETTER**

On the Quick Access Toolbar, click Save 🔲. The Save As dialog box is displayed.

1. Navigate to the appropriate location for the file to be saved.

2. In the File name box, replace the existing text with Request and then select Save.

④ **TYPE THE LETTER OPENING**

The letter opening includes an inside address and salutation. Type the following:

March·12,·2011¶
¶
¶
¶
Ms.·Hannah·Laurant¶
Centerville·Neighborhood·Coordinator¶
City·Hall¶
12·Main·Street¶
Centerville,·WY·11287¶
¶
Dear·Ms.·Laurant:¶
¶
¶

⑤ **TYPE THE LETTER BODY AND CLOSING**

The letter body conveys the message of the letter, and the closing includes a complimentary closing and a signature line. Type the following letter body and closing. Ignore any red wavy lines that appear:

Dear·Ms.·Laurant:¶
¶
I·represent·the·Arbor·Neighborhood·Association,·which·includes·families·from·1ˢᵗ·Street·through·8ᵗʰ·Street,·east·of·Oak·Avenue·and·west·of·Poplar·Avenue.·We·would·like·to·participate·in·the·"Neighborhood·Cleanup"·campaign.·I·am·writing·to·request·that·a·representative·from·your·organization·speak·at·our·next·association·meeting.·Our·next·meeting·is·scheduled·for·Saturday,·April·16,·2011·at·the·pavilion·at·Poplar·Park.¶
¶
We·have·already·started·the·campaign·by·obtaining·a·brochure·and·free·trash·bags·from·your·office.·Our·association·is·relying·on·a·representative·to·offer·suggestions·for·a·cleanup·schedule·and·an·incentives·program·for·the·neighborhood·children.¶
¶
Thank·you·for·your·time.·I·look·forward·to·hearing·from·you·soon.¶
¶
Sincerely,¶
¶
¶
¶
Blaine·Feldman¶

⑥ **REMOVE THE RED WAVY LINE FROM CORRECTLY SPELLED WORDS**

a. Right-click either occurrence of "Laurant." A menu is displayed.

b. Select Ignore All. The red wavy line disappears from both occurrences of "Laurant."

⑦ **EDIT THE LETTER**

a. In the body of the letter the meeting time needs to be specified. Place the insertion point just before "Saturday" and then type 2:00 p.m. followed by a space.

b. In a new paragraph below Blaine Feldman's name, type your name.

⑧ **SAVE THE MODIFIED REQUEST, PRINT A COPY, AND CLOSE THE DOCUMENT**

Selecting Text

Editing is faster when text to delete or change is selected first. Select text by dragging the pointer over any amount of text, from a single character to several pages. *Selected text* is shown highlighted on the screen:

On a clear night, thousands of stars are visible in the sky, some brighter than others. The brightness of a star depends on its size, temperature, and distance from the Earth. A star's magnitude is the measure of its brightness. ¶

The second sentence is selected

Type to replace selected text with new text. Press the Backspace key or Delete key to remove the selected text. Click anywhere in the document or press an arrow key to remove the selection without deleting the text.

In addition to dragging the pointer, there are other ways to select text. Depending on the situation, one method may be more efficient than the other, increasing productivity:

- **Double-click a word** to extend the selection from the first character to the space after the word. **Triple-click** a paragraph to select the entire paragraph.

- **Hold down the Shift key and click a character** to extend the selection from the insertion point to the clicked character.

- **Hold down the Shift key and press an arrow key** to extend the selection from the insertion point to the character in the direction of the arrow key. **Hold down both the Ctrl and Shift keys and press an arrow key** to extend the selection from the insertion point to the word in the direction of the arrow key.

- **Hold down the Ctrl key and click anywhere in a sentence** to select the sentence.

- **Move the pointer to the left of the text (near the left edge of the page) until the pointer changes to ⤢ and click** to select the line of text to the right. **Double-click** to select the entire paragraph, and **triple-click** to select the entire document. **Drag up or down** to select multiple lines of text.

- Click Home → Select → Select All to select all of the text in the document:

Select

Cut, Copy, and Paste

Cut   Copy

Paste

Editing a document often requires moving and duplicating text. *Moving text* means that selected text is "cut" from one place in a document and then "pasted" into another place. *Duplicating text* means that selected text is "copied" from one place in a document and the copy "pasted" into another place. There are four steps to move or duplicate text:

1. Select the text to be moved or copied.

2. Click either Home ➞ ✂ Cut or Home ➞ 📋 Copy.

3. Place the insertion point in the document where the text is to be inserted.

4. Click Home ➞ Paste. Click Paste Options 📋(Ctrl)▾ to adjust the formatting:

Alternative To improve productivity, use Ctrl key shortcuts for **Cut** (Ctrl+X), **Copy** (Ctrl+C), and **Paste** (Ctrl+V).

TIP Resting the mouse pointer on a **Paste Options** icon displays a live preview of how the text will appear if that option is selected.

Keep Source Formatting

Keep Text Only

Clipboard

Cut or copied text is placed on the *Clipboard*, which is a designated area in memory. Paste places the most recent contents of the Clipboard at the insertion point. Text on the Clipboard remains there until different text is cut or copied or the computer is turned off.

Office Clipboard

The *Office Clipboard* stores the last 24 cut or copied items. Click the Clipboard group Dialog Box Launcher 🔲 to display the Clipboard task pane:

TIP To adjust the size of the Clipboard task pane click ▾, select **Size** and then drag to size the task pane.

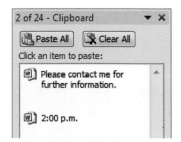

The Clipboard task pane

Click an item in the Clipboard task pane to paste it at the insertion point. To delete an item, point to the item and then click the arrow to display the Delete command. To close the Clipboard task pane, click **Close** ✖.

Text can be moved and duplicated between two or more documents. For example, cut text from one document can be pasted into a different document. Similarly, copied text can be pasted into a different document. After cutting or copying from one document, display the second document, position the insertion point, and then paste. The Office Clipboard can also be used to paste items into another Word document.

Practice: ORIENTATION – part 1 of 4

Word should already be started.

① **OPEN ORIENTATION**

    a. Open the ORIENTATION document, which is a Word data file for this text. The Gadgets, Inc. employee orientation document is displayed.

    b. Display formatting marks if they are not already showing.

② **MOVE A PARAGRAPH**

    a. Triple-click the second paragraph of text after the "Introduction" heading. The paragraph is selected:

> Gadgets, Inc.¶
> Employee·Orientation¶
>
> Introduction¶
>
> Training·new·employees·is·a·priority·at·Gadgets·so·that·our·customers·are·served·in·the·best·way· possible.·As·a·Gadgets·employee,·you·are·expected·to·implement·the·skills·and·information·that·you· learn·at·the·orientation.·A·company·is·only·as·strong·as·its·weakest·link.·Help·keep·us·strong!¶
>
> Welcome!·Gadgets,·Inc.·is·pleased·to·have·you·as·a·member·of·our·team.·Gadgets·employees·are· devoted·professionals·with·strong·work·ethics·and·positive·attitudes.·Your·orientation·leaders·will· provide·you·with·the·training·you·need.¶
>
> ¶

    b. Click Home → ✄ Cut . The paragraph is removed from the document.

    c. Place the insertion point at the beginning of the word "Training…."

    d. Click Home → Paste. The paragraph is moved to a different location.

    e. Save the modified ORIENTATION.

③ **PASTE TEXT FROM ANOTHER DOCUMENT**

    a. Open the HANDBOOK document, which is a Word data file for this text.

    b. Scroll to view the "Meeting" information.

    c. Place the insertion point just to the left of the second etiquette rule that reads "Use a handshake…."

    d. Press and hold the Shift key and then click at the end of the text that reads "…on the right shoulder." The selection includes:

> are·in·order,·say·something·similar·to·"Mr.·or·Ms.
>
> Use·a·handshake·for·greeting.¶
>
> Wear·a·name·tag·high·on·the·right·shoulder.¶
>
> Personally·accompany·clients·while·they·are·on·tl

    e. Click Home → 🗐 Copy . The text is copied to the Clipboard.

f. Close HANDBOOK. The ORIENTATION document is again displayed.

g. On the Home tab, click the Clipboard group Dialog Box Launcher 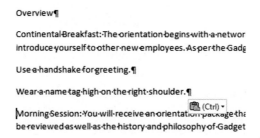. The Clipboard task pane is displayed with the copied etiquette rules.

h. Scroll the ORIENTATION document to display the paragraphs in the "Overview" section.

i. Place the insertion point at the beginning of the second paragraph, which reads "Morning Session…."

j. In the Clipboard task pane, click the "Use a handshake…" item. The text is copied into the ORIENTATION document:

Overview¶

Continental·Breakfast:·The·orientation·begins·with·a·networ
introduce·yourself·to·other·new·employees.·As·per·the·Gadg

Use·a·handshake·for·greeting.¶

Wear·a·name·tag·high·on·the·right·shoulder.¶

Morning·Session:·You·will·receive·an·orientation·package·tha
be·reviewed·as·well·as·the·history·and·philosophy·of·Gadget

k. In the Clipboard task pane, click Close ✕. The task pane is removed.

l. In a new paragraph at the end of the document, type your name.

m. Scroll to the beginning of the document. In the first paragraph, between the word "Welcome" and the exclamation point, type a comma followed by a space and your name.

n. Save the modified ORIENTATION and print only page 1.

Finding and Replacing Text

Find   Replace

A document can be easily searched for a specified character, word, or phrase. Click Home ➡ Find to display the Navigation pane where search text is entered. Matches are displayed in the Navigation pane. Click a match to navigate to that location in the document:

search for the word 'business'

It is also possible to search for objects in a document, such as graphics by clicking the Find Options and additional search commands arrow in the Navigation pane and selecting an option in the Find list:

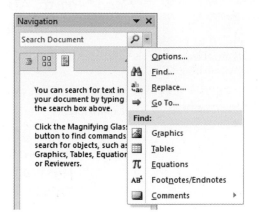

TIP The Find and Replace dialog box can also be displayed by clicking the Page: indicator on the status bar.

TIP If search options such as Match case are not displayed, select More in the Find and Replace dialog box.

To replace text with other text, click Home → Replace. Search text as well as replace text are entered in the Find and Replace dialog box.

To make a text search more specific, use options such as Match case and Find whole words only in the Find and Replace dialog box. Match case selects text with the same capitalization as the search text. For example, a search for Cat will not find CAT or cat. Find whole words only selects text that entirely matches the search text. For example, a search for fin will not find finer, stuffing, or muffin.

Formatting marks and other special characters are entered as search text by selecting them from the Special list at the bottom of the Find and Replace dialog box. For example, it may be helpful to find all occurrences of the word Tip at the beginning of a paragraph. Since all (except the first) paragraphs in a document have a paragraph mark before them, select Paragraph Mark from Special and then type Tip.

Formatting Characters

TIP When using the Home tab to format text, the live visual preview feature displays the selected text in the font or size that the pointer is resting on.

The way text appears on a page is called its *format*. Font, size, and style define a character's format. A *font* Calibri (Body) ▾ or *typeface* refers to the shape of characters. The default font in Word is Calibri. There are also fonts, such as Wingdings, that contain pictures called *dingbats*. Note how each font shapes characters differently:

Calibri: ABCDEF abcdef 1234567890

Cambria: ABCDEF abcdef 1234567890

Segoe Print: ABCDEF abcdef 1234567890

Courier: ABCDEF abcdef 1234567890

Wingdings: ✄✁✎✐✐☞ ♋♌♍♎♏♐ 📁📄📄📄📄📷📠☎📠📁

Font size 11 ▾ is measured in *points*, and there are 72 points to an inch. For example:

This is an example of 8 point Calibri.

This is an example of 10 point Calibri.

This is an example of 12 point Calibri.

This is an example of 14 point Calibri.

The way in which a character is emphasized is called its *font style*. Regular text, sometimes called normal text, is the default style. Other styles include:

Bold text B is printed darker so that words and phrases stand out on a page. It is often used for titles and headings.

Italic text I is slanted and is mostly used for emphasis.

Underline text U has a line under it and is mostly used for emphasis. Underline style should be used with caution so that it is not confused with a hyperlink.

Text effects A▾, such as shadow and bevel, can be applied to selected text.

Font color A is used to emphasize text. Color should be applied with readability in mind. Bright colors and many colors in a single document are not usually recommended.

Another text style is *superscript* x^2, which reduces the size of the text and raises it to the top of the current line. *Subscript* x_2 is a text style that reduces the size of the text and lowers it to the bottom of the current line:

In her 5th Avenue boutique, Dina Johannsen sold her designer perfume called "Dina's H_2O."

To remove all formatting, click Clear Formatting ✏.

Text can also be formatted using the Mini toolbar. Selecting text displays the Mini toolbar:

Consumer to consu Calibri (E ▾ 11 ▾ A˄ A˅ 彈 彈 ce w
intermediary, such a B *I* U ≡ ab˅ ▾ A ▾ ✑

Wireless technology has created a new way to conduct e for mobile commerce. Mobile commerce allows consum

Move the pointer over the Mini toolbar to fully display it. More than one button can be used to apply multiple formats, such as bold and italic.

The Font dialog box can also be used to change the formatting of selected text and is displayed by clicking the Font group Dialog Box Launcher ▣.

Previewing and Printing a Document

Previewing a document shows what printouts will look like. To preview an open document, select ▮File▮ → Print. Print settings are displayed in Backstage view:

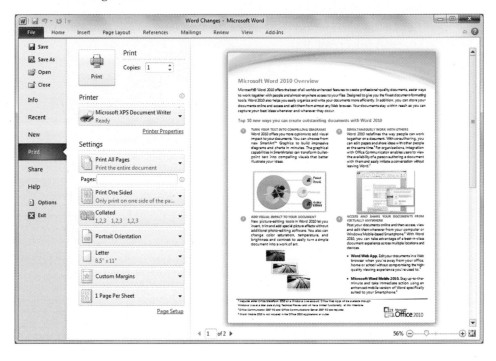

The document appears as it will be printed in the right side of the window. The zoom bar can be used to change the magnification of the document. Click 🔲 to view the entire page in the window. Click Next Page ▸ and Previous Page ◂ to scroll through the document. The vertical scroll bar can also be used to scroll a document.

Select Print to print the document or press Esc to return to the document window.

Hard Copy

A document printed on paper is often called a "hard copy."

Practice: ORIENTATION – part 2 of 4

Word should already be started with ORIENTATION displayed from the last practice.

① **FIND TEXT**

   a. Click Home → Find. The Navigation pane is displayed.

   b. In the Search box, type: training and then press Enter. Four occurrences of training are highlighted in the document.

   c. In the Navigation pane, click Next Search Result ▾ . The second occurrence of "training" is selected.

d. Click Next Search Result ▼ . The third occurrence is selected.

e. Click Next Search Result ▼ to find the fourth occurrence. Did you notice that "training" with a lowercase t as well as "Training" with an uppercase T were found?

② MODIFY SEARCH CRITERIA

a. In the Navigation pane, click the Find Options and additional search commands arrow and select Options:

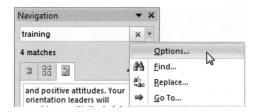

b. In the displayed dialog box, select the Match case check box:

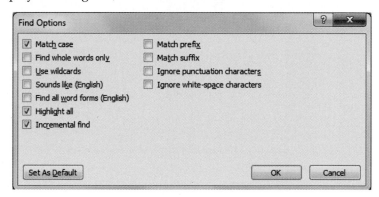

c. Select OK and then type training in the search box. Navigate to the two matches. Did any found words begin with an uppercase T?

d. Click ☒ to close the Navigation pane.

③ FIND A SPECIAL CHARACTER

a. Click Home → Replace. The Find and Replace dialog box is displayed. Click the Find tab and then click More if search options are not displayed.

b. Select Special → Paragraph Mark. The Find what box now contains: ^p

c. In the Find what box, after the ^p add: gadgets

d. Check that the Find what criteria is: ^pgadgets

e. Clear the Match case option.

f. Select Find Next. The word "gadgets" preceded by a paragraph marker is selected.

g. Select Find Next. A message dialog box is displayed. Select Yes and then select OK to remove the dialog boxes. Notice that the first occurrence of "gadgets" at the top of the document was not selected, because it is not preceded by a paragraph mark.

④ REPLACE TEXT

a. In the Find and Replace dialog box, click the Replace tab.

b. In the Find what box, replace the existing text with: devoted

c. In the Replace with box, type: dedicated

d. Select Find Next. If a dialog box is displayed, click Yes. The first occurrence is located and selected.

e. Select Replace. The selected text is replaced with "dedicated" and the rest of the text is scanned for another occurrence.

f. Select Replace. Another occurrence is found and replaced and a message dialog box is displayed. Select OK to remove the message dialog box.

g. Select Close. The dialog box is removed.

⑤ FORMAT THE TITLE

a. At the top of the document, select both lines of the entire title "Gadgets, Inc. Employee Orientation." The Mini toolbar is displayed.

b. On the Mini toolbar, change the font to Cambria, the size to 16, the font style to Bold, and the font color to the Purple at the far right of the Standard Colors:

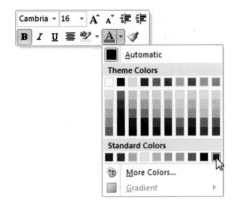

⑥ FORMAT TEXT

a. In the next line, select the "Introduction" title.

b. Click Home → Italic *I* . The selected text is italic.

c. Click Home → Bold **B** . The selected text is now both bold and italic.

d. Click anywhere in the document to remove the selection.

⑦ FORMAT THE REMAINING TITLES AS BOLD AND ITALIC

a. Scroll down page 1 and select the "Overview" title.

b. On the Mini toolbar, click Bold **B** and Italic *I* . The selected text is bold and italic.

c. Use either of the methods in Steps 6 and 7 to format the "What You Need to Know" and "See You Soon" titles as bold and italic.

⑧ UNDERLINE A PHRASE IN THE INTRODUCTION

a. Scroll to the top of page 1.

b. Select the words "pleased to have you" in the second sentence of the paragraph that begins "Welcome! ...."

c. Click Home → Underline **U** . The selected text is underlined.

d. Click anywhere to remove the selection.

⑨ REMOVE FORMATTING

a. Place the insertion point just to the right of the "d" in "pleased to have you" in the underlined text.

b. Hold down the Shift key and then press the right-arrow key until "to have you" is selected.

c. Click Home → Underline **U** . The selected text is no longer underlined.

d. Click Home → Italic *I* . The selected text is formatted as italic.

e. Click Home → Clear Formatting 💱. The selected text is no longer italic.

f. Click anywhere to remove the selection. Only the word "pleased" is underlined.

Check — Your document should look similar to:

Gadgets, Inc.¶
Employee·Orientation¶

Introduction¶

Welcome, Name! Gadgets, Inc. is <u>pleased</u> to have you as a member of our team. Gadgets employees are dedicated professionals with strong work ethics and positive attitudes. Your orientation leaders will provide you with the training you need. ¶

Training new employees is a priority at Gadgets so that our customers are served in the best way possible. As a Gadgets employee, you are expected to implement the skills and information that you learn at the orientation. A company is only as strong as its weakest link. Help keep us strong! ¶

⑩ PREVIEW AND PRINT THE DOCUMENT

a. Save the modified document.

b. Select [File] → Print. The ORIENTATION document is displayed in the preview area.

c. Use the Zoom bar to change the magnification to 120%.

d. Click Fit in Page 🔲. The entire page is displayed in the window.

e. Click ▶ . Page 2 of the document is displayed.

f. Click Print. The document is printed.

Paragraph Alignment

Align Text Left   Center   Justify
Align Text Right

The *alignment* of text in a paragraph refers to its position relative to the sides of the page:

- *Left aligned* is the default and means that the left edge of a paragraph is straight and the right edge of the paragraph is jagged. This format is most often used in letters and research papers.

- *Centered* means that the left and right edges of the paragraph are equally distant from the left and right sides of the page. Headings and titles are often centered.

- *Right aligned* means that the right edge of the paragraph is straight and the left edge is jagged.

- *Justified* alignment creates straight edges at both sides of a paragraph and is often used in newspapers and books.

Format Painter

Copy a paragraph's formatting, by placing the insertion point in the paragraph and clicking Home → ✓ Format Painter . The pointer changes to ⬚I. Click another paragraph to apply the formatting. If formats need to be pasted repeatedly, double-click Home → ✓ Format Painter . Click again to turn it off.

Alternative Use the Mini toolbar to center align a paragraph.

On the Home tab, click Align Text Left ≣, Center ≣, Align Text Right ≣, and Justify ≣ to format the paragraph that contains the insertion point. To format multiple paragraphs together, first select the paragraphs and then click an alignment button.

The Paragraph dialog box can also be used to change the formatting of selected text and is displayed by clicking the Paragraph group Dialog Box Launcher ⬚. Click the Indents and Spacing tab to display options for changing alignment.

Inserting Symbols

Symbol

Alternative Type (c) and the AutoCorrect feature changes it to ©.

There are symbols that do not appear on the keyboard, such as the copyright (©) and degree (°) symbols. To insert such symbols into a document, click Insert → Symbol and select a symbol. If the symbol is not shown, select More Symbols to display the Symbol dialog box. Click a symbol and then select Insert to place the symbol at the insertion point. Other symbols are displayed in the dialog box by selecting a font in the Font list.

Hyperlinks in a Document

Hyperlink

TIP If your hyperlink isn't automatic, click ▣ → Options. In the Proofing options, select AutoCorrect Options. Select the AutoFormat As You Type tab and select the Internet and network paths with hyperlinks check box.

When a Web site address (URL) is typed, Word automatically formats it as a hyperlink. For example, www.lpdatafiles.com. The user can then press the Ctrl key, which changes the pointer to ☝, and click the link to display the Web page in a browser window.

Word applies similar formatting to an e-mail address. For example: christina@lpdatafiles.com . A reader can press the Ctrl key and then click the link to display a new e-mail message window.

The Insert Hyperlink dialog box contains options for inserting a hyperlink into a document. To use this dialog box, click Insert → Hyperlink. Select a type of link from the Link to list and then type a label in the Text to display box. For Web page links, type a URL in the Address box. For an e-mail address link, type an address in the E-mail address box. The label is placed at the insertion point, but the URL will be followed when the reader clicks the label.

To remove the hyperlink from text, right-click the link and then select Remove Hyperlink from the menu.

TIP Refer to Chapter 1 for more information on e-mail, the Internet, and URLs.

Using a Thesaurus

Thesaurus

synonyms

antonyms

A *thesaurus* is a collection of *synonyms*, which are words that have similar meanings. For example, "chilly" is a synonym for "cool." A thesaurus also provides related words, phrases, and *antonyms*, which are words with opposite meaning. For example, "hot" is an antonym for "cool."

TIP Select a phrase instead of a word to view similar phrases in the thesaurus.

Place the insertion point in a word and then click Review → Thesaurus to display the Research task pane with results from searching the thesaurus file. To replace the selected word with one from the Research task pane, click the arrow to the right of the word and select Insert from the displayed menu. Thesaurus results can also be displayed by right-clicking a word, and then selecting Synonyms from the menu.

Alternative Press Shift+F7 to display the Research task pane.

Word uses a file for the thesaurus which does not contain every possible word in the English language. If the selected word cannot be found, suggested spellings are displayed in the Research task pane.

Practice: ORIENTATION – part 3 of 4

Word should already be started with ORIENTATION displayed from the last practice.

① **CENTER THE FIRST TWO LINES IN ORIENTATION**

   a. At the top of page 1, place the insertion point anywhere in the "Gadgets, Inc." title.

   b. Click Home → Center ≡ . The text is centered.

   c. In the next line of the document, right-click the text "Employee Orientation." A menu and the Mini toolbar is displayed

   d. On the Mini toolbar, click Center ≡ . The text is centered.

② **JUSTIFY THE PARAGRAPHS IN THE INTRODUCTION**

   a. Place the insertion point anywhere in the paragraph that begins "Welcome...."

   b. Hold down the Shift key and click in the last paragraph of the introduction, which begins "Training new employees...." Each paragraph in the Introduction now contains some selected text:

   Introduction¶

   Welcome, Name! Gadgets, Inc. is pleased to have you as a member of our team. Gadgets employees are dedicated professionals with strong work ethics and positive attitudes. Your orientation leaders will provide you with the training you need. ¶

   Training new employees is a priority at Gadgets so that our customers are served in the best way possible. As a Gadgets employee, you are expected to implement the skills and information that you learn at the orientation. A company is only as strong as its weakest link. Help keep us strong!¶

   c. Click Home → Justify ≡ . The paragraphs are justified.

   d. Click anywhere to remove the selection.

③ USE A THESAURUS

    a. In the second paragraph of the document, place the insertion point in the word "way" in the text "…best way possible."

    b. Click Review ➜ Thesaurus. The Research task pane is displayed with thesaurus results for "way."

    c. In the task pane, point to "manner," click the arrow, and then select Insert:

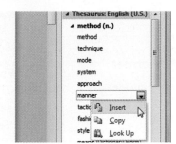

Gadgets, Inc.
Employee Orientation

dgets, Inc. is <u>pleased</u> to have you as a member of our team. Gadgets employees are
als with strong work ethics and positive attitudes. Your orientation leaders will
training you need.

yees is a priority at Gadgets so that our customers are served in the best <mark>way</mark>
ts employee, you are expected to implement the skills and information that you

    d. In the Research task pane, click Close ✕. The task pane is removed.

④ FIND A SYNONYM FOR THE WORD GLAD

    a. In the last paragraph of the document, right-click the word "glad."

    b. In the displayed menu, select Synonyms ➜ pleased.

⑤ INSERT A SYMBOL

    a. At the end of the document, press Enter to create a new paragraph below your name.

    b. Click Insert ➜ Symbol ➜ ©. The copyright symbol is placed at the insertion point.

    c. Type a space and then type: 2011 Gadgets, Inc.

⑥ ADD AN E-MAIL CONTACT AND A WEB SITE ADDRESS

    a. Place the insertion point just before the period in the last sentence that ends "human resources at extension #3872."

    b. Type a space and then type: or e-mail gadgets@lpdatafiles.com

    c. Place the insertion point after the period following the e-mail address and type a space. The e-mail address becomes a hyperlink.

    d. Type the sentence: You may also download this document from our Web site at www.lpdatafiles.com/gadgets.

    e. Type a space after the period:

> Gadgets, Inc. is pleased to have you on board. If you have any questions, please call human resources at extension #3872 or e-mail <u>gadgets@lpdatafiles.com</u>. You may also download this document from our Web site at <u>www.lpdatafiles.com/gadgets</u>. ¶

    f. Save the modified ORIENTATION.

⑦ TEST THE HYPERLINK

    This step requires a browser and Internet access. If either of these are not available, then skip this step.

    a. Press and hold the Ctrl key and then click <u>www.lpdatafiles.com/gadgets</u>. A browser window is opened and the Web site displayed.

    b. Close the browser window.

⑧ PRINT THE MODIFIED ORIENTATION

E-Mailing a Document

TIP Refer to Chapter 1 for more on e-mail and attachments.

E-mail is a fast and efficient message delivery system in which Word documents can be attached to a message. Select [File] → Share → Send Using E-mail → Send as Attachment to display an e-mail message window with the address boxes and the document as an attachment. Type the e-mail address of the recipient in the To box. The file name of the document automatically appears as the Subject. Type text in the message box if additional information should appear in the e-mail message and then click Send to send the message.

XPS Format

XPS format is an electronic file format that preserves formatting, similar to PDF format. To view XPS files, an XPS reader is required.

Word Send Using E-mail options also allow attachments to be sent in PDF or XPS format. Both of these formats ensure that the documents will look the same on most computers by preserving fonts, formatting, and images across platforms.

Selecting [File] → Share → Send Using E-mail → Send as Internet Fax sends the current document as a fax. In order to use this option, you must be registered with an Internet fax provider.

To keep computers safe from malicious code such as viruses, always save an attachment to the hard disk before opening it. Most antivirus programs are set up to automatically check a Word document for viruses when it is opened.

Practice: ORIENTATION – part 4 of 4

This practice requires Outlook and Internet access. Word should already be started with ORIENTATION displayed from the last practice.

(1) **E-MAIL THE DOCUMENT**

    a. Select [File] → Share → Send Using E-mail → Send as Attachment. An e-mail window is created with the ORIENTATION document as an attachment.

    b. Type the following message, replacing Name with your name:

        Attached is my completed ORIENTATION document.

        Name

    c. In the To box, type the e-mail address of your instructor.

    d. Click Send. The e-mail is sent to your instructor.

(2) **CLOSE ORIENTATION**

Reviewing a Document

New Comment   Track Changes

document collaboration

peer editing

Document collaboration means working with others to create, review, and revise a document to achieve the best end result. One form of collaboration is *peer editing*. It is always a good idea to have a peer edit a document because it is often difficult to catch mistakes, especially in a lengthy document that has been worked on for an extended time. Peer editing often involves "suggested" changes instead of changes that have to be made, such as spelling errors.

The peer editing process can involve providing a printout for a peer to write edits on, but this can be inefficient and inconvenient. Another way to gather input from a reviewer is to provide the document as a file that tracks changes. This method allows the reviewer to type edits and add comments directly into the document itself. Changes will be recorded as they are made so that the author can later decide which changes to keep and which to discard.

To start tracking changes in a document, click Review → Track Changes. The Track Changes button remains selected when changes are being tracked. When changes are made, edits appear similar to:

TIP The Accept and Reject buttons each have an option for accepting or rejecting all changes in the document.

To view the changes made by the reviewer, click Review → ⬆ Previous or Review → ⬇ Next in the Changes group. Click Review → Accept or Review → Reject in the Changes group to keep or remove the changes.

Comments can help explain edits. To add a comment, click Review → New Comment. Comments and tracked changes are collectively called *markup*. To display the reviewer's comments, click Review → Previous or Review → Next in the Comments group. Click Review → Delete to remove a comment.

Tracked changes and comments will print by default. To print the document without tracked changes, select ▪File▪ → Print, click the Print All Pages arrow and select Print Markup.

Before distributing a document to customers, employees, or other end users, be sure there are no comments or tracked changes stored in the document that may be accidentally seen. Comments must be deleted

TIP Right-click the status bar and select Track Changes to add a track changes indicator to the status bar.

and tracked changes must be accepted or rejected in order to be removed completely from the document or change Final: Show Markup in the Display for Review list to Final. The original document can be displayed by selecting Original in the Display for Review list. Changes to the document can also be viewed in the Reviewing Pane by selecting Review → Reviewing Pane → Reviewing Pane Horizontal.

Documents that are being reviewed and edited can be exchanged via e-mail. The author e-mails the document to a reviewer, who makes changes and adds comments. The document is then e-mailed back.

Version control is an important aspect of reviewing documents. When saving an attachment, the file name can be changed to indicate a new version. Common changes are adding a number to the file name or a descriptive phrase, such as "2011 10 14 Edits." By renaming the document, the original is kept on the hard disk without any tracked changes. This can be helpful if the document becomes corrupt or a file is needed that does not have tracked changes.

The types of changes a reviewer can make can be restricted before e-mailing the document. Click Review → Restrict Editing to display the task pane of options for restricting changes. A password is added to enforce the restrictions.

Reading a Document on Screen

Full Screen Reading   Zoom

Print Layout view is the default view in Word 2010. To better read a document in Print Layout view, the document can be magnified or reduced by clicking View → Zoom and selecting an option in the Zoom dialog box. To quickly zoom in and out of a document, drag the Zoom slider or click ⊕ or ⊖ in the bottom-right corner of the window:

TIP Page views can also be changed on the status bar:

As an alternative, click View → Full Screen Reading. *Full Screen Reading view* displays the document in a full screen to maximize the viewing space. Select [File] → Options → Open e-mail attachments in Full Screen Reading view to always have Word attachments open in Full Screen Reading view.

Practice: Benefit

This practice requires an e-mail client and Internet access. You are also required to work with a classmate and exchange documents through e-mail. Word should already be started.

① **CREATE NEW A DOCUMENT**

   a. Select **File** ➔ **New**.

   b. Select **Blank document** and then select **Create**. A new, blank document is displayed.

   c. Type the following text:

   > I am looking forward to my Gadgets, Inc. orientation. I believe I will benefit most from

   d. Complete the document by reading the ORIENTATION printout from the last practice and then writing about one event at the orientation that would be beneficial to you if you were the new employee.

   e. Click **View** ➔ **Full Screen Reading**. The document is displayed in Full Screen Reading view.

   f. Click **Close**. The document is again displayed in Print Layout view.

   g. In the bottom-right corner of the window, drag the Zoom slider back and forth. The view is zoomed in and out.

   h. Click **View** ➔ **Zoom**. A dialog box is displayed.

      1. Select **100%**.

      2. Select **OK**. The document is again displayed at 100% in Print Layout view.

   i. Save the document naming it Benefit Name where Name is your name.

② **RESTRICT EDITING AND E-MAIL THE DOCUMENT FOR REVIEW**

   a. Click **Review** ➔ **Restrict Editing**. The task pane is displayed.

   b. In the task pane, select the **Allow only this type of editing in the document** check box and in the list below it select **Tracked changes**.

   c. Click **Yes, Start Enforcing Protection**. A dialog box is displayed.

      1. In the **Enter a new password (optional)** box, type: 58we6kw

      2. In the **Reenter password to confirm** box, type 58we6kw and select **OK**. The document is protected from unintentional editing and ready to send to reviewers.

   d. Select **File** ➔ **Share** ➔ **Send Using E-mail** ➔ **Send as Attachment**. An e-mail window is created with the Benefit document as an attachment.

   e. Type the following message, replacing Name with your name: Please review this document and then send it back to me. Thanks! --Name

   f. In the **To** box, type the e-mail address of a classmate.

   g. Click **Send**. The e-mail is sent to your classmate for review.

③ **REVIEW A DOCUMENT**

   a. Check your e-mail.

   b. Open the e-mail from your classmate. Note that the e-mail message asks you to review the attached document.

   c. Save the attachment to the appropriate location.

   d. Open the file.

   e. Read through the document and make at least two changes.

f. Place the insertion point at the very beginning of the document.

g. Click **Review** → **New Comment**. The insertion point is moved to the comment.

h. Type: Don't forget to add a heading, opening, and closing to this letter!

i. Select [File] → **Share** → **Send Using E-mail** → **Send as Attachment**. An e-mail message is displayed with the Benefit document as an attachment.

j. Type the following message, replacing Name with your name:

   Here are my edits. --Name

k. In the **To** box, type the e-mail address of a classmate.

l. Click **Send**. The e-mail is sent to your classmate for review.

m. Close Benefit.

④ **REVIEW CHANGES**

a. Check your e-mail.

b. Open the e-mail reply from your classmate. The e-mail message includes the reviewed document as an attachment.

c. Save the attachment to the appropriate location naming it Benefit Name Revised where Name is your name.

d. Open the file.

e. Select **Review** → **Restrict Editing**. The task pane is displayed.

f. In the task pane, click **Stop Protection**. A dialog box is displayed.

   1. Type the password: 58we6kw

   2. Select **OK**.

g. Place the insertion point at the very beginning of the document.

h. Click **Review** → **Next** from the **Comments** group. The comment is selected.

i. Click **Review** → **Delete** from the **Comments** group. The comment is deleted.

j. Click **Review** → ⟳ Next from the **Changes** group. A tracked change is selected.

k. Evaluate the edit and then click either **Review** → **Accept** or **Review** → **Reject**.

l. Continue accepting or reject tracked changes until a message is displayed and then select **Yes**.

m. Save the modified document.

⑤ **CLOSE BENEFIT REVISED**

⑥ **QUIT WORD**

Chapter Summary

This chapter discussed Word, the Microsoft Office word processor application used to create, modify, print, and e-mail documents.

Typed text is placed at the insertion point, and the arrow keys move the insertion point within text. Word automatically determines if words will fit on the end of the current line or go on the next line in a process called word wrap. The word count of the document is displayed in the status bar and updated as words are typed.

Word automatically adds blank space after each paragraph. Use the **Home** tab to format paragraphs with no space after them.

Edits can be reversed or repeated using buttons on the Quick Access Toolbar. Formatting marks such as spaces and tabs, which do not appear on paper when printed, can be displayed to make editing easier. The Home tab is used to show and hide formatting marks.

Word includes a spelling checker and grammar checker. A red wavy line appears below a misspelled word, and a green wavy line below a grammatical error. A blue wavy line indicates a contextual error. Right-click a wavy line to display a menu of suggestions.

Text is selected by dragging the pointer, clicking, or using the keyboard. The Home tab is also used to select all the text in a document at once. Selected text can be moved or copied within a document or between two or more documents using the Home tab. The Office Clipboard stores the last 24 cut or copied items. Double-click an item in the Clipboard task pane to paste it at the insertion point.

A document can be searched for certain text, and text can be replaced with specified text using the Home tab. A search can be narrowed using options. Special characters can be entered as search text using the Special list.

The way text appears on a page is called its format, which can be changed using the Home tab or the Mini toolbar. A font or typeface refers to the shape of characters, and the size of text is measured in points. The way a character is emphasized is called font style, such as bold or superscript. Text color can also be changed. The alignment of text in a paragraph refers to its position relative to the sides of the page.

Symbols can be inserted in a document using the Insert tab. A document can include hyperlinks to a Web page or an e-mail address. Hyperlinks can be typed into a document or inserted using the Insert tab.

A thesaurus is a collection of synonyms, which are words that have similar meanings. The thesaurus in Word is displayed using the Review tab and also provides some antonyms, which are words with opposite meaning.

Document collaboration can be achieved by e-mailing documents that have been edited with changes tracked and comments added. The Review tab is used for collaboration. A document can be printed with or without tracked changes and comments showing. The types of changes a reviewer can make can be restricted. A document can be e-mailed as an attachment to a message. The View tab is used to change the way a document is displayed.

Vocabulary

Alignment The position of text relative to the sides of the page.

Antonym A word that has the opposite meaning of another word.

AutoCorrect A feature in Word that automatically corrects commonly misspelled words and incorrect capitalization.

Centered A format where the left and right edges of the paragraph are equally distant from the left and right sides of the page.

Clipboard A designated area in memory where cut and copied text is placed.

Dingbat A picture created by a special font such as Wingdings.

Document collaboration Working with others to create, review, and revise a document.

Duplicate text To make a copy of text and then place that copy at a different location in the document or into a completely different document.

Edit To modify the contents of a document.

Font The shape of a set of characters.

Font style The way a character is emphasized.

Format The way text appears on a page.

Formatting marks Special symbols, representing spaces, tabs, and paragraphs, that do not appear on paper when a document is printed.

Full Screen Reading view A Word view that makes reading a document on screen easier because text is larger.

Grammar checker A feature that automatically checks a document for grammatical errors.

I-beam The shape of the pointer when it is moved into a document.

Insertion point A blinking vertical line that indicates where the next character typed will be placed.

Italic A text style that makes text slanted.

Justified A format where both sides of the paragraph are straight.

Left aligned A format where the left edge of the paragraph is straight and the right edge is jagged.

Markup Comments and tracked changes.

Move text Delete text and then place that text at a different location.

Office Clipboard Stores the last 24 cut or copied items.

Peer editing A form of collaboration where a peer edits a document.

Point The unit used to measure the size of text. There are 72 points to an inch.

Previewing a document Shows what the printouts will look like.

Print Layout view The default document view.

Quick Access Toolbar A bar at the top of the window with buttons that are clicked to perform actions.

Regular The default font style.

Ribbon A bar near the top of the window with tabs of buttons that are clicked to perform actions.

Right aligned A format where the right edge of the paragraph is straight and the left edge is jagged.

Rulers Located at the top and left side of the document window, they are used for measuring and also contain markers for formatting text.

Selected text Text that is shown highlighted on the screen.

Spelling checker A feature that automatically compares words to those in a dictionary file to determine if they are spelled correctly.

Status bar A bar at the bottom of the screen that displays information about the current document.

Subscript Text that is reduced in size and lowered to the bottom of the current line.

Superscript Text that is reduced in size and raised to the top of the current line.

Synonym A word that has a similar meaning to another word.

Thesaurus A collection of synonyms.

Title bar A bar at the top of the Word window that displays the file name of the current document.

Typeface Commonly referred to as font. *See* font.

Underline A text style that puts a line under text.

Word processor A computer application used to create, modify, print, and e-mail documents.

Word wrap The process used to determine if the next word will fit on the end of the current line or if it must go on the next line.

Word Commands

Accept Makes a tracked change permanent. Found on the Review tab.

Align Text Left ≣ Left aligns the text in the selected paragraph. Found on the Home tab.

Align Text Right ≣ Right aligns the text in the selected paragraph. Found on the Home tab.

Bold **B** Formats selected text as bold. Found on the Home tab and on the Mini toolbar.

Center ≣ Center aligns the text in the selected paragraph. Found on the Home tab and on the Mini toolbar.

Close ✕ Closes a displayed task pane. Found in the upper-right corner of the task pane.

Copy ▤ Copy Places a copy of the selected text on the Clipboard, leaving the selected text at its original location. Found on the Home tab.

Cut ✂ Cut Moves the selected text to the Clipboard. Found on the Home tab.

Delete Deletes an item from the Clipboard. Found in the menu displayed by clicking the arrow of an item on the Office Clipboard.

Delete Deletes a comment. Found on the Review tab.

Find Displays a Navigation pane used to search a document for search text. Found on the Home tab.

Font Calibri (Body) ▾ Changes the font of selected text. Found on the Home tab and on the Mini toolbar.

Font Color A Changes the color of selected text. Found on the Home tab and on the Mini toolbar.

Font Size 11 ▾ Changes the size of selected text. Found on the Home tab and on the Mini toolbar.

Full Screen Reading A view in which text is larger and word wrap is changed so that fewer words appear on a line. Found on the View tab.

Grow Font A˙ Increases the size of selected text. Found on the Home tab and on the Mini toolbar.

Hyperlink Displays a dialog box used to insert a hyperlink into a document. Found on the Insert tab.

Ignore All Removes the red wavy line from all occurrences of that word in the document. Found in the menu displayed by right-clicking a red wavy line.

Ignore Once Removes the green wavy line from a sentence that contains a possible grammatical error. Found in the menu displayed by right-clicking a green wavy line.

Italic *I* Formats selected text as italic. Found on the Home tab and on the Mini toolbar.

Justify ≣ Justify aligns the text in the selected paragraph. Found on the Home tab.

Next ⇥ Next Selects the next tracked change. Found on the Review tab.

New Comment Adds a comment to a document. Found on the Review tab.

Next Selects the next comment. Found on the Review tab.

No Spacing AaBbCcDc ¶ No Spaci… Formats the text in a document to not have blank space after each paragraph. Found on the Home tab.

Paste Places the contents of the Clipboard at the insertion point. Found on the Home tab.

Previous ⇤ Previous Selects the previous tracked change. Found on the Review tab.

Previous Selects the previous comment. Found on the Review tab.

Print Prints a document. Found in File → Print.

Redo ↻ Repeats the last action performed. Found on the Quick Access Toolbar.

Reject Ignores a tracked change or removes a comment. Found on the Review tab.

Remove Hyperlink Removes the blue underline from a hyperlink. Found in the menu displayed by right-clicking the link.

Replace Displays a dialog box used to search a document for search text and change it to specified text. Found on the Home tab.

Restrict Editing Displays a task pane of options for allowing only comments to be added an tracked changes to be made to a document. Found on the Review tab.

Select All Selects all the text in a document. Found in Home → Select.

Send Sends the content of a document as an e-mail message. Found on an e-mail message.

Send as Attachment Sends the document as an e-mail attachment. Found in File → Share → Send Using E-mail.

Send as Internet Fax Sends the document as an Internet fax. Found in File → Share → Send Using E-mail.

Shrink Font A˙ Reduces the size of selected text. Found on the Home tab and on the Mini toolbar.

Show/Hide ¶ Displays formatting marks. Found on the Home tab.

Symbol Used to insert symbols into a document. Found on the Insert tab.

Synonyms   Displays a list of synonyms and an antonym for a word. Found in the menu displayed by right-clicking a word.

Text Effects A ˅   Applies a visual effect to selected text. Found on the Home tab.

Thesaurus Displays the Research task pane with synonyms. Found on the Review tab.

Track Changes   Records additions, deletions, and other changes in a document as they are made. Found on the Review tab.

Underline U   Formats selected text as underlined. Found on the Home tab and on the Mini toolbar.

Undo ↰   Reverses the last action performed. Found on the Quick Access Toolbar.

View Ruler ▨   Displays or hides the rulers. Found above the vertical scroll bar.

Zoom   Displays a dialog box used to magnify or reduce the document on screen. Found on the View tab.

1. a) How can the insertion point be moved down 3 lines and then 10 places to the right?
   b) How can the mouse be used to move the insertion point?

2. What is word wrap?

3. How can the word count of the document be determined?

4. a) How can the last action performed be reversed?
   b) Can the last action performed be repeated? If so, how?

5. How are formatting marks useful when editing a document?

6. a) What does a red wavy line indicate?
   b) What does a blue wavy line under a sentence indicate?

7. a) What happens if text is selected and then the Backspace key is pressed?
   b) List two methods for selecting an entire paragraph of text.

8. a) In a search for the word hat, how can you avoid finding the word that?
   b) What is the search text for finding the word The at the beginning of a paragraph?

9. Why would it be better to select Replace rather than selecting Replace All?

10. Fonts can be divided into three categories: *Serif fonts* have small strokes at the ends of characters that help the reader's eye recognize each letter. Serif fonts are more conventional and are used in large amounts of text. *Sans serif fonts* lack the decorative flourishes of serif fonts. Sans serif fonts are often used in headings to contrast with the body text:

Serif

No Serif (Sans Serif)

Decorative fonts have letters that are specially shaped and are neither serif nor sans serif. Some decorative fonts have a picture, rather than a letter, that corresponds to characters.

a) Refer to the "Formatting Characters" section in this chapter and then list the font name and category for each of the fonts presented in the fonts example in that section.
b) List an appropriate use for each type of font.

11. a) What is character size measured in?
    b) Would text in the body of a letter be better as size 10 or size 18? Why?

12. List two instances of when the subscript or superscript format should be used.

13. How can a hyperlink in a Word document be displayed in a Web browser?

14. How does peer editing help create a better document?

15. Why would a comment be added when reviewing a document? Give an example.

16. Can tracked changes be printed? If so, how?

17. What is Full Screen Reading view?

True/False

18. a) The Enter key is pressed at the end of each line of text in a paragraph.
    b) Press Ctrl+right arrow to move the insertion point to the beginning of the next word.
    c) Double-clicking a word selects that word and the line of text that it appears in.
    d) The Office Clipboard stores the last 50 copied or cut items.
    e) Shrink Font ᴬˇ and Grow Font Aˇ are used to change the font size of selected text.
    f) The Mini toolbar can be used to center align a paragraph.
    g) There is no way to include a © symbol in a Word document.
    h) Peer editing is a form of collaboration.

Project 1

As the manager of *Yolanda's Catering*, you have been asked to write a letter to Mrs. Kristine LeBon thanking her for her recent business.

a) In a new document create the following letter using the block style. Be sure to indicate **No Spacing** after the paragraphs, and press Enter four times before typing the return name and address.

¶
¶
¶
¶
123·Whippo·Lane¶
Butler,·PA·16001-7896¶
¶
January·9,·2011¶
¶
¶
¶
Mrs.·Kristine·LeBon¶
17·North·Main·St.¶
Reedsburg,·GA·04459-2233¶
¶
Dear·Mrs.·LeBon:¶
¶
I·am·writing·to·thank·you·for·your·recent·business.·We·are·always·appreciative·of·repeat·business·and·you·have·used·our·services·many·times.¶
¶
As·you·are·aware,·at·Yolanda's·we·pride·ourselves·on·serving·quality·food·using·impressive·presentation·techniques.·To·ensure·we·continue·to·meet·the·high·expectations·of·our·customers,·we·are·asking·you·to·complete·the·attached·short·survey·and·return·it·to·us·in·the·enclosed·envelop.¶
¶
We·look·forward·to·serving·you·again·in·the·near·future.¶
¶
Sincerely,¶
¶
¶
¶
Chris·Warheit¶
Manager¶

b) Check the document on screen and correct any errors and misspellings. Remove the red wavy line from correctly spelled words.

c) Save the letter naming it Thank You.

d) Make the following changes:

- Delete the word high in the second paragraph.
- Use the thesaurus to change the word appreciative in the first paragraph to an appropriate synonym.
- Add the following sentence to the start of the third paragraph in the body of the letter: Thank you again for your business.
- Change We look in the third paragraph to Yolanda's looks.

- Change Chris Warheit at the end of the letter to your name.

e) Check the document on screen and correct any errors and misspellings.

f) Save the modified Thank You and then print a copy.

Project 2

The sports editor a local newspaper likes the soccer article that you submitted. However, space limitations require that the article be between 150 and 160 words. Open SOCCER, which is a Word data file for this text, and complete the following steps:

a) Carefully read the article and determine which sentences and words are extraneous and which are necessary to maintain the focus of the article.

b) In a new document, copy and paste text from the SOCCER article to create a condensed story without losing the focus of the original article.

c) Check the word count on the status bar. Continue to edit the article to meet the space requirements of 150 to 160 words.

d) Save the document naming it Short Soccer Name replacing Name with your name.

e) E-mail the Short Soccer Name document for review to your instructor.

f) Preview the document and print a copy.

Project 3

Align Computers wants to create a document advising customers that a regular maintenance routine will help keep their computer in good condition. A maintenance routine should include cleaning the computer, maintaining the hard disk, and regularly updating virus protection and operating system software. COMPUTER MAINTENANCE contains some tips about keeping a computer in good condition. Open COMPUTER MAINTENANCE, which is a Word data file for this text, and complete the following steps:

a) Type your name below the "Computer Maintenance" title.

b) Format the title "Computer Maintenance" as Candara 14 point, bold, and centered.

c) Format the following headings as Candara 12 point, bold, and left aligned:

   "Cleaning"
   "Disk Maintenance"
   "Updating Software"

d) Input devices are devices from which the computer can accept data. Two input devices are discussed in the "Cleaning" section. Format the first occurrence of each input device name as italic.

e) Output devices are devices that display or store processed data. One output device is discussed in the "Cleaning" section. Bold the full name of the output device.

f) In the "Disk Maintenance" section, format the text "built-in" as bold and italic.

g) The "Updating Software" section explains what must be downloaded regularly to protect against new viruses. Format the name of the download as bold and italic.

h) Save the modified COMPUTER MAINTENANCE and print a copy.

Project 4

The local newspaper has hired you as an entertainment critic. A review should be written based on facts and without bias and should include:

- Title of the review and the critic's name
- Name and date of movie, concert, play, art exhibit, or event
- Date of review
- Intended audience (young children, children, teen, young adult, adult)
- Rating, if applicable (G, PG, PG-13, and so on)
- Type of movie, music, play, art, or event
- Name of producer or gallery and name of director, if applicable
- Name of actors, band members, artist, headliner, or main attraction
- Summary of the movie or play, without giving away surprises or the ending
- Comparison to similar movies, concerts, plays, art exhibits, or events
- Your overall rating

a) In a new document create a review of at least 350 words about a recent movie, concert, play, art exhibit, or similar event that you attended. Be sure to include the appropriate information as listed above.

b) Create a center aligned, bold title in a larger font size that has the name of the event that was reviewed.

c) Format any titles in the review as italic, such as the title of a movie or a song title.

d) Format the body of the review with justified alignment.

e) Add a paragraph at the end of the review with the number of words in the article.

f) Check the document on screen and correct any errors and misspellings.

g) Save the document naming it Entertainment Review and print a copy.

Project 5

Dr. Ellie Peterson and Dr. Jeremy Prow, owners of *Travel...With a Purpose* are studying coral reefs off the coast of Florida. They have created a funding proposal for their coral research.

a) Open PROPOSAL, which is a Word data file for this text, and make the following changes:

- Change the heading so it reads A PROPOSAL FOR CORAL RESEARCH at the top of the page.
- Change the word effect to affect in the "Summary" paragraph.
- Change the word accomplish to complete in the "Summary" paragraph.
- Delete the text state of the art in the "Purpose and Description" paragraph.

b) Check the document on screen and correct any errors and misspellings.

c) Center align and bold the headings "A PROPOSAL FOR CORAL RESEARCH" and "GROWTH STUDIES OF CORAL ON SOUTH FLORIDA REEFS."

d) Format the headings "Summary," "Purpose and Description," "Coral," and "Computerized Guide" as italic.

e) Center align and bold the "BUDGET" heading and format it in a larger font size.

f) Find the word greater in the proposal and then use the thesaurus to replace it with a synonym.

g) Replace all occurrences of aging with growth.

h) Save the modified PROPOSAL and print only page 1.

Project 6

Study Time Tutoring would like to create a handout that will help students take tests. The TAKING TESTS document gives directions on how to take a test, but the steps are listed out of order. Open TAKING TESTS, which is a Word data file for this text, and complete the following steps:

a) Use Cut and Paste to put the directions in a logical order.

b) Find a synonym for test and replace all occurrences of test with the synonym.

c) Below the directions, press Enter and then type your name.

d) Save the modified TAKING TESTS, preview the document, and then print a copy.

Project 7

Travel...With a Purpose is preparing a document on five sculptors that lived during the late 19th and early 20th centuries:

Sculptor	Country
Constantin Brancusi	Romania
Ronald Moody	Jamaica
Ivan Mestrovic	Croatia
Jacques Lipchitz	Lithuania
Pablo Gargallo	Spain

These sculptors were born in different countries and their art was influenced by events, movements, and cultures of those years common to the artists.

a) Open SCULPTORS, which is a Word data file for this text. It contains information about the five artists listed above. Cut and paste the paragraphs so that the sculptor information is in alphabetical order by country.

b) Save the modified SCULPTORS and print a copy.

c) Cut and paste the paragraphs so that the sculptor information is in chronological order by artist's birth date. Make sure your name remains at the end of the document.

d) Save the modified SCULPTORS and print a copy.

e) Use a library or the Internet to find the name of a work (a sculpture) by each artist, the materials used, and the year it was completed. Below each artist's biography, add the information about the artist's work and include a hyperlink to a Web site that contains additional information about the artist. Add a blank paragraph between artists.

f) Save the modified SCULPTORS and print a copy.

Project 8

As a freelance writer, you have been asked to take articles and combine then into one for environmental magazine:

a) In Word, open and review the WATER, CONSERVATION, and XERISCAPE documents, which are Word data files for this text.

b) In a new document create an article based solely on the information in the three documents printed in step (a). *Hint: Use copy and paste!* Include a title, introductory paragraph, supporting paragraph(s), and a closing paragraph.

c) Bold the document's title and format it as 14 point.

d) In a new paragraph at the end of the document, type By Reporter Name replacing Name with your name.

e) Format the body of the article with justified alignment.

f) Check the document on screen and correct any errors and misspellings.

g) Save the document naming it Water Conservation, preview the document, and then print a copy.

Project 9

You have decided to open a business. In your entrepreneurial adventure, you could design jewelry, build skateboards, design clothing, open a restaurant, or anything else you wish. You will need a flyer to promote the grand opening of your business. A *flyer* is a one-page document that is sent in the mail, hand delivered, or left out for pick up. The intended audience is prospective customers residing in the area of the business location. A flyer should have large elements to catch the reader's attention so that the reader immediately knows the general topic. The rest of the flyer should contain as much information as possible, including business name, address, phone number, e-mail address, Web site address, and fax number. These elements can be smaller because the flyer already has the reader's attention. A flyer should also include coupons or other promotions to draw the prospective customer into the store.

a) In a new document create a flyer that will be sent to prospective customers announcing your grand opening.

b) Assume the flyer will be printed in color and format the text appropriately. Decide which text should be used to get the reader's attention and make that text much larger. Experiment with different fonts for the larger text, and choose one that is easy to read and complements your business. Experiment with different ways of emphasizing the text.

c) Format appropriate paragraph alignments throughout the flyer.

d) Check the document on screen and correct any errors and misspellings.

e) Save the document naming it Grand Opening and then print a copy.

f) A rubric is used to assess the quality of a document. In a new document type the following text, typing two spaces between the "1 2 3 4 5" numbers and replacing Name with your name:

Flyer·Rubric·by·Name¶

This·rubric·can·be·used·to·assess·the·quality·of·the·Grand·Opening·exercise·in·Chapter·2.·¶

Instructions:··Circle·the·appropriate·number·using·the·following·scale:·¶

·1-Poor··2-Fair··3-Average··4-Good··5-Excellent¶

The·flyer·promotes·the·grand·opening·of·the·store.··1··2··3··4··5¶

The·flyer·is·appropriate·for·the·intended·audience.··1··2··3··4··5¶

The·fonts·used·in·the·flyer·enhance·the·message.··1··2··3··4··5¶

The·flyer·gets·the·reader's·attention.··1··2··3··4··5¶

g) Save the document naming it Flyer Rubric and print a copy.

h) Exchange printed flyers and rubrics with a classmate. Peer-edit your classmate's flyer using their rubric, and then exchange rubrics back. Based on the assessment by your peer, should any changes be made to the flyer?

Project 10

Word includes Equation Tools for writing equations with mathematical symbols. Commonly used equations are included, and any equation can be created.

a) Create a new document for **Study Time Tutoring**.

b) Type the following text, replacing Name with your name: Sample Equations by Name

c) Press Enter to create a new paragraph, then click Insert → Equation → Area of Circle. A formula that calculates the surface area of a circle with a radius r is inserted.

d) Press Enter to create a new paragraph, then click Insert → Equation → Pythagorean Theorem. A formula that calculates the relationship between the sides of a right triangle with legs a and b and hypotenuse c is inserted.

e) Press Enter to create a new paragraph, then click Insert → Equation → Insert New Equation. The Design tab is displayed. Note the Symbols and Structures groups. Create a sample equation.

f) Save the document naming it Equations and then print a copy.

g) Create a new document.

h) Type the following title, replacing Name with your name: NAME'S MATH QUIZ

i) Below the title, use the equation features to create a math quiz with at least 5 questions. Use your mathematics textbook as a resource.

j) Save the document naming it Math Quiz and then print a copy.

Chapter 3
Formatting Documents

Practice Data Files
TRAINING, GADGETS MAP

Project Data Files

INVENTORY, LEARNING JOURNAL,
WELCOME, TRAVEL, TELECOMMUTING, U.S.
PRESIDENTS, PROPOSAL

Formatting a Document

The formatting applied to a document can affect how the reader interprets the document, how easily the document is read, and the overall impression of the document. For example, if the text is very small and covers the entire page from edge to edge, it will be very difficult to read the text. If the text is too large and there is quite a bit of space between each line of text, the document could appear childish. Proper formatting is crucial in creating a professional-looking document.

Margins

Margins

Common Paper Sizes

To change the paper size, click
Page Layout → Size.

Letter	8.5" x 11"
Legal	8.5" x 14"
A3	297mm x 420mm
A4	210mm x 297mm
Tabloid	11" x 17"

Margins are the white space around the text on a page. Margin size affects the amount of text that a page can contain. Smaller margins leave more room for text. Wider margins mean less text. For example, widening the left and right margins decreases the number of characters that fit on a line. Narrowing the same margins increases the amount of text in a line. Similarly, larger top and bottom margins decrease the number of lines of text a page can contain and smaller top and bottom margins increase the amount of text on a page. The following examples contain the same text, but have different margins:

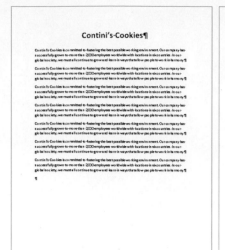

TIP To change units of measurement, click 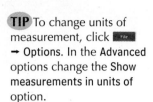 → Options. In the Advanced options change the Show measurements in units of option.

Alternative Click the Page Setup group Dialog Box Launcher ▣ to display the Page Setup dialog box.

The default or **Normal** margins in Word are 1 inch for the left, right, top, and bottom. Click **Page Layout** → **Margins** to display options for changing the margins. To format a document with margins that are not listed, click **Page Layout** → **Margins** → **Custom Margins**. The Page Setup dialog box with the **Margins** tab selected is displayed, and individual margins can be set.

Indenting Paragraphs

Indent Left and Indent Right

TIP Sections are discussed in Chapter 4.

Margin settings apply to an entire document and cannot be different from paragraph to paragraph (unless the document is divided into sections.) *Indents* decrease the width of lines of text in a paragraph. Indents are often used to set off paragraphs such as a quotation.

TIP To change only the left indent by 0.5", click **Home** → **Increase Indent** ᤏ or **Home** → **Decrease Indent** ᤎ.

The default indents are 0 inches, meaning that lines of text extend from the left margin to the right margin. Specify left and right indents to give a paragraph shorter line lengths:

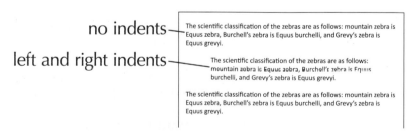

Alternative Click the Paragraph group Dialog Box Launcher ▣ and then use the Indents and Spacing tab to set indents.

To format a paragraph with indents, use **Page Layout** → **Indent Left** and **Page Layout** → **Indent Right**. The amount of indent is measured in inches. Setting indents affects only the paragraph that contains the insertion point, or multiple paragraphs selected together.

TIP Click View Ruler  above the vertical scroll bar to display the rulers.

Indents can also be set by dragging markers on the ruler:

When an indent marker is dragged, a dotted line appears that helps line up text.

Practice: TRAINING – part 1 of 6

① **OPEN TRAINING**

    a. Start Word.

    b. Open TRAINING, which is a Word data file for this text.

② **CHANGE THE MARGINS**

    a. Click Page Layout → Margins. Options for changing the margins are displayed.

    b. Click Wide. The left and right margins are now 2 inches. Scroll through the document and see the effect.

    c. Click Page Layout → Margins → Narrow. All the margins are now 0.5 inches. Scroll through the document and see the effect.

    d. Click Page Layout → Margins → Custom Margins. The Page Setup dialog box is displayed.

    e. Change the margin options as shown:

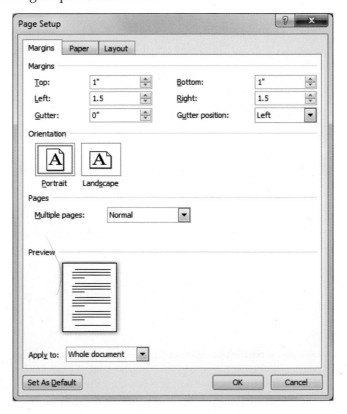

    f. Select OK. Scroll through the document and see the effect.

    g. Save the modified TRAINING.

③ INDENT A PARAGRAPH

    a. In the "Session Descriptions" section, which starts on page 1 and ends on page 2, place the insertion point in the paragraph that begins "Learn the difference…."

    b. On the Page Layout tab, change the Indent Left and Indent Right options to 0.5. The left and right sides of the paragraph are indented 0.5 inches.

④ INDENT OTHER PARAGRAPHS

    a. In the "Sessions Descriptions" section, place the insertion point in the paragraph that begins "Learn specific techniques…."

    b. On the ruler, drag the Left Indent marker to the 0.5" mark:

Organizational Skills
Learn specific techniques for organizing your professional image.

The left side of the paragraph is indented.

    c. On the ruler, drag the Right Indent marker to the 5" mark:

Organizational Skills
Learn specific techniques for organizing your work area to reflect a professional image.

The right side of the paragraph is indented.

    d. In the "Session Descriptions" section, place the insertion point in the paragraph that begins "Develop awareness…."

    e. Format the paragraph with 0.5" left and right indents.

⑤ SAVE THE MODIFIED TRAINING

Space Before and After a Paragraph

Spacing Before and After

Space between paragraphs makes the text easier to read and helps distinguish where paragraphs begin and end. The default formatting for a paragraph is no space before (above) the paragraph and 10 points of space after (below) the paragraph. Paragraphs of body text, such as in the body of a letter, are typically formatted in this manner. Headings are typically formatted with space before and some space after, which helps set the heading closer to the text that it is associated with:

paragraph with space after ———

paragraph with space before and after ———

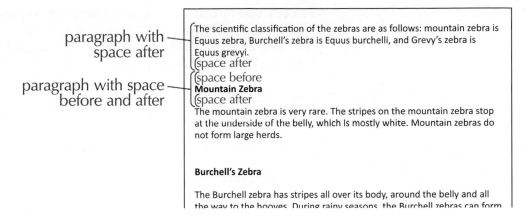

The scientific classification of the zebras are as follows: mountain zebra is Equus zebra, Burchell's zebra is Equus burchelli, and Grevy's zebra is Equus grevyi.

(space after

(space before
Mountain Zebra
(space after

The mountain zebra is very rare. The stripes on the mountain zebra stop at the underside of the belly, which Is mostly white. Mountain zebras do not form large herds.

Burchell's Zebra

The Burchell zebra has stripes all over its body, around the belly and all the way to the hooves. During rainy seasons, the Burchell zebras can form

Alternative Click the Paragraph group Dialog Box Launcher ⬚ and then use the Indents and Spacing tab to set space before or space after.

To change the space before or after a paragraph, use Page Layout ➔ Before and Page Layout ➔ After. The amount of space is measured in points. Setting space before or after affects only the paragraph that contains the insertion point, or multiple paragraphs selected together.

Line Spacing

Line and Paragraph Spacing

double spaced

The space between lines of text in a paragraph can be changed. The default formatting for a paragraph is 1.15 lines of space. Text that is *double spaced* adds more space between lines of text for notes or comments and can make a document easier to read:

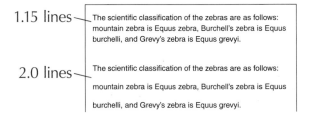

1.15 lines ———
The scientific classification of the zebras are as follows: mountain zebra is Equus zebra, Burchell's zebra is Equus burchelli, and Grevy's zebra is Equus grevyi.

2.0 lines ———
The scientific classification of the zebras are as follows: mountain zebra is Equus zebra, Burchell's zebra is Equus burchelli, and Grevy's zebra is Equus grevyi.

Click Home ➔ Line and Paragraph Spacing ‡≡▾ to display options for changing the amount of space between lines of text in a paragraph:

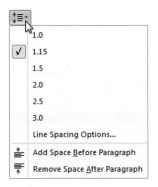

Select 2.0 to format a paragraph with double spacing. For additional spacing options, click Line Spacing Options to display the Paragraph dialog box. Setting line spacing affects only the paragraph that contains the insertion point, or multiple paragraphs selected together.

Practice: TRAINING – part 2 of 6

Word should already be started with TRAINING displayed from the last practice.

① CHANGE SPACE AFTER A PARAGRAPH

    a. At top of page 1, place the insertion point in the heading "Life-Long Learning Program."

    b. On the Page Layout tab, set After to 24 pt. More space is added below the "Life-Long Learning Program" heading.

② CHANGE SPACE BEFORE PARAGRAPHS

    a. In the "Session Descriptions" section, place the insertion point in the paragraph that begins "Learn the difference…."

    b. On the Page Layout tab, set Before to 6 pt. More space is added above the paragraph.

    c. In the "Session Descriptions" section, place the insertion point in the paragraph that begins "Learn specific techniques…."

    d. On the Page Layout tab, set Before to 6 pt.

    e. In the "Session Descriptions" section, place the insertion point in the paragraph that begins "Develop awareness…" and format the paragraph with 6 pts of space before.

③ CHANGE PARAGRAPH LINE SPACING

    a. Near the top of the document, place the insertion point in the paragraph of text that begins "Gadgets, Inc. is committed…."

    b. Click Home → Line and Paragraph Spacing ⬍≡▾ → 2.0. The paragraph of text is double spaced:

Gadgets, Inc.
Life-Long Learning Program

Gadgets, Inc. is committed to fostering the best possible working environment. Our

company has successfully grown to more than 2,000 employees worldwide with

locations in six countries. In our global society, we must all continue to grow and learn in

ways that allow people to work in harmony.

④ SAVE THE MODIFIED TRAINING

Tabs and Tab Stops

Tabs are used to position text within a line. Press the Tab key to insert a tab and move any text to the right of the insertion point over to the position of the next tab stop. Delete a tab by placing the insertion point to the left of the tab and pressing the Delete key. Any text is automatically moved to the left to fill the space previously created by the tab.

A *tab stop* specifies a location within the line of text. In Word, tab stops are displayed on the ruler above the document. A set of default tab stops are located at every half inch, but they do not appear on the ruler.

Tabs can be used to align text into columns of data. New tab stops are created at the appropriate intervals to align the data in columns:

Name	Age	Kennel	Feeding Time	Weight (kg)
Peach	12	19B	4 pm	8.5
Meatball	2	6C	6 pm	9.25
Mango	1	12A	6:30 pm	5.75
Booper	6	5A	2 pm	12.5

A tab stop can be set at any position on the ruler within the margins. When a tab stop is set, Word automatically removes the default tab stops to the left. For example, a tab stop set at 1.4 inches automatically removes the default tab stops at 0.5 and 1.0 inches. The default stop at 1.5 inches is not affected.

Text is aligned to a tab stop according to the type of tab stop:

- **Left Tab** ⬛ aligns the beginning of the text at the stop.
- **Right Tab** ⬛ aligns the end of the text at the stop.
- **Center Tab** ⬛ centers the text equidistant over the stop.
- **Decimal Tab** ⬛ aligns the decimal point (a period) at the stop.

Each type of tab stop is used in the text shown below. Note the markers on the ruler:

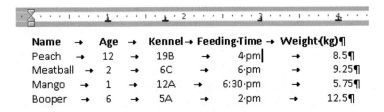

Tab stops are applied to the paragraph that contains the insertion point or to multiple paragraphs selected together. When the insertion point is moved through the text, the ruler changes to show the tab stops for the current paragraph.

Set a tab stop by first clicking the tab selector on the ruler until the type of tab stop to be created is displayed:

tab selector—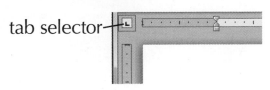

TIP A *Bar Tab* can also be set. A Bar Tab doesn't position text, it inserts a vertical bar at the tab position.

Click the white area of the ruler above the document to place a tab stop. The tab stop can be dragged to a new location if needed. For example, click the tab selector until Right Tab ⊐ is displayed and then click the ruler to create a right tab stop at that location.

To remove a tab stop, drag its marker downward, off the ruler. Any text that was aligned at a deleted stop is then aligned to the next tab stop.

The Tabs dialog box is useful for changing, editing, and deleting tab stops. Double-click a tab stop on the ruler to display the Tabs dialog box. In the dialog box, type the Tab stop position, select the appropriate Alignment, and then select Set to create a tab stop at that position. Repeat this procedure to create as many tab stops as needed. To remove a tab stop, select it from the Tab stop position list and then select Clear. Select Clear All to remove all the tab stops.

Selecting a Vertical Block of Text

Data formatted into columns often have different formatting applied to individual columns of data. To select a vertical block of text, hold down the Alt key and drag:

Name	→	Age	→	Kennel→	Feeding·Time	→	Weight{kg)¶
Peach	→	12	→	19B	→ 4·pm	→	8.5¶
Meatball	→	2	→	6C	→ 6·pm	→	9.25¶
Mango	→	1	→	12A	→ 6:30·pm	→	5.75¶
Booper	→	6	→	5A	→ 2·pm	→	12.5¶

Formatting can then be applied to the selected text. For example, click Home → Bold **B** to format selected data as bold:

Name	→	Age	→	Kennel→	Feeding·Time	→	Weight{kg)¶
Peach	→	12	→	**19B**	→ 4·pm	→	8.5¶
Meatball	→	2	→	**6C**	→ 6·pm	→	9.25¶
Mango	→	1	→	**12A**	→ 6:30·pm	→	5.75¶
Booper	→	6	→	**5A**	→ 2·pm	→	12.5¶

Practice: TRAINING – part 3 of 6

Word should already be started with TRAINING displayed from the last practice.

① **SELECT TEXT FOR FORMATTING**

    a. Display formatting marks if they are not already showing.

    b. Scroll to the "Schedule" section. The paragraphs in this section have a single tab between each column: one tab after "Session," "Day," and "Time." The information is difficult to read because tab stops have not been set.

    c. Select all the paragraphs in the "Schedule" section:

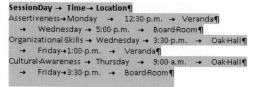

② SET TAB STOPS

a. At the far left of the ruler, click the tab selector until Left Tab ⊾ is displayed, if it is not already showing.

b. Click the ruler near the 2" mark. A left tab stop is created and the "Day" column is aligned at the stop.

c. On the ruler, drag the left tab stop marker to 1.75". The column of text is moved closer to the session names.

d. Click the tab selector until Right Tab ⊿ is displayed.

e. Click the ruler at 3.75". A right tab stop is created and the "Time" column is aligned at the stop.

f. Double-click any tab stop on the ruler. The Tabs dialog box is displayed.

   1. In the Tab stop position box, type: 4.75

   2. In the Alignment options, click Center.

   3. Select Set and then OK. A center tab stop is created and the "Location" column is aligned at the stop.

Check — Your document should look similar to:

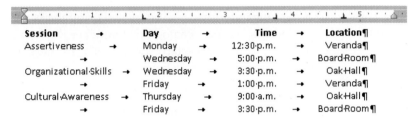

③ FORMAT A VERTICAL BLOCK OF TEXT

a. Press and hold the Alt key and drag from the beginning of the "Assertiveness" title to the end of the data in the first column:

b. Click Home → Italic *I* . The column of text is formatted as italic:

Session	→	Day	→	Time	→	Location¶
Assertiveness	→	Monday	→	12:30·p.m.	→	Veranda¶
	→	Wednesday	→	5:00·p.m.	→	Board·Room¶
Organizational·Skills	→	Wednesday	→	3:30·p.m.	→	Oak·Hall¶
	→	Friday	→	1:00·p.m.	→	Veranda¶
Cultural·Awareness	→	Thursday	→	9:00·a.m.	→	Oak·Hall¶
	→	Friday	→	3:30·p.m.	→	Board·Room¶

④ SAVE THE MODIFIED TRAINING

Hanging and First Line Indents

A paragraph can be formatted so that the first line is indented differently from the rest of the paragraph. When the first line of a paragraph is farther to the left than the rest of the paragraph, it is formatted with a *hanging indent*. A hanging indent is often used for lists, outlines, or for a bibliography entry:

TIP Creating a bibliography is discussed in Chapter 4.

Levy, Kristin. *The Complete Guide to Selling Inner-Spring Mattresses.* Chicago: Buffet Press, 2010.

To create a hanging indent, drag the Hanging Indent marker on the ruler:

A hanging indent can also be created using the Paragraph dialog box. Click the **Paragraph** group Dialog Box Launcher 🗗, then in the dialog box click the **Indents and Spacing** tab. Select **Hanging** in the **Special** list and specify the indent amount in the **By** box.

Another paragraph format is the *first line indent*, which indents the first line of the paragraph farther to the right than the rest of the paragraph. A first line indent is often used for text in a published book or paper. For example, this paragraph is formatted with a first line indent.

To create a first line indent, drag the First Line Indent marker on the ruler:

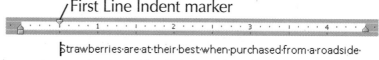

A first line indent can also be created using options in the **Indents and Spacing** tab in the Paragraph dialog box. Select **First line** in the **Special** list and specify the indent amount in the **By** box.

Setting hanging or first line indents affects only the paragraph that contains the insertion point, or multiple paragraphs selected together.

Creating Bulleted and Numbered Lists

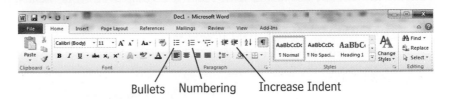

Bullets   Numbering   Increase Indent

TIP When formatting lists, complete paragraphs do not need to be selected as long as text from every paragraph is included in the selection.

In a *bulleted list*, each item is a separate paragraph formatted with a hanging indent, a bullet (•), and a tab. To create a bulleted list, first select the paragraphs in the list and then click Home → Bullets ☷ ▾ :

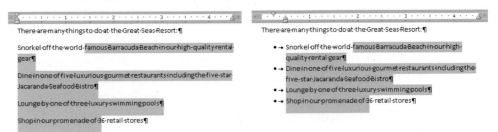

Bulleted lists are used when each item is equally important. *Numbered lists* show a priority of importance and are used, for example, for the steps in a recipe. To create a numbered list, first select the paragraphs and then click Home → Numbering ☷ ▾ :

Chicken·Rice·Soup¶

1.→ Pour·some·chicken·broth·into·a·large·saucepan·with·a·small· amount·of·chopped·celery·and·carrots·and·bring·it·to·a·rolling· boil.¶
2.→ Add·some·rice·and·cook·about·15·minutes·until·the·rice,·carrots,· and·celery·are·done.¶
3.→ Reduce·the·heat,·add·some·chopped·chicken,·and·simmer·for·3· minutes.¶
4.→ Serve·immediately·with·crackers·or·toast.¶

TIP Word automatically formats a paragraph as a list item if an asterisk or "1." is typed at the beginning of a paragraph.

Click Home → Increase Indent ☷ to increase the indent of bulleted or numbered items. To remove the bullets or numbering list formats, select the formatted paragraphs and then click Home → Bullets ☷ ▾ or Home → Numbering ☷ ▾ again.

A multi-level list can be created by selecting text, clicking the Multilevel list button and selecting a multilevel list style:

Bullet and Numbering Library

Click the arrow in the Bullets ☷ ▾ or Numbering ☷ ▾ buttons to select other bullet characters or different numbering formats.

Word should already be started with TRAINING displayed from the last practice.

① FORMAT A HANGING INDENT

a. Scroll to the "Instructors" section on page 2 and then select the two paragraphs about the instructors:

Instructors¶

Pat·Merlin·Well-known·for·innovative·teaching·techniques,·Pat·is·a·leader·in·assertiveness·training.·Pat·is·also·recognized·in·the·field·of·organizational·methods·for·the·business·world.¶

Francis·Neal·Francis·has·worked·with·hundreds·of·companies·world-wide·to·help·resolve·cultural·conflicts·and·teach·the·importance·of·cultural·diversity·within·an·organization.¶

b. On the ruler, drag the Hanging Indent marker to the 1" mark.

c. The paragraphs have hanging indents, but are still not formatted properly. Place the insertion point just after "Merlin" in the first instructor paragraph.

d. Delete the space and then press the Tab key.

e. Replace the space after the second instructor's last name with a tab.

Check – Your document should look similar to:

Pat·Merlin → |Well-known·for·innovative·teaching·techniques,·Pat·is·a·leader·in·assertiveness·training.·Pat·is·also·recognized·in·the·field·of·organizational·methods·for·the·business·world.¶

Francis·Neal → Francis·has·worked·with·hundreds·of·companies·world-wide·to·help·resolve·cultural·conflicts·and·teach·the·importance·of·cultural·diversity·within·an·organization.¶

② FORMAT A NUMBERED LIST

a. Scroll to the "Program Objectives" section on page 1.

b. Select the three paragraphs about program objectives:

Program·Objectives¶

Provide·a·professional·learning·environment·with·skilled,·knowledgeable·instructors.¶

Foster·an·interactive·teacher-student·relationship·to·maximize·learning.¶

Instill·a·level·of·confidence·in·each·and·every·learner·so·that·new·skills·will·be·implemented·with·ease.¶

c. Click Home → Numbering ≣ ▾. The paragraphs are formatted with numbers and a hanging indent. Click anywhere in the document to remove the selection:

Program·Objectives¶

1. → Provide·a·professional·learning·environment·with·skilled,·knowledgeable·instructors.¶
2. → Foster·an·interactive·teacher-student·relationship·to·maximize·learning.¶
3. → Instill·a·level·of·confidence·in·each·and·every·learner·so·that·new·skills·will·be·implemented·with·ease.¶

③ **FORMAT A BULLETED LIST**

   a. Scroll to the "Registration" section.

   b. Select the four paragraphs about registration.

   c. Click Home → Bullets ☷ ▾. The items in the list are formatted with bullets and a hanging indent:

Registration

- The Gadgets, Inc. Life-Long Learning Program is free to all employees.
- Each session is one hour in length.
- Sessions between 11:30 a.m. and 1:30 p.m. are brown-bag sessions. Please bring your own lunch. Beverages will be provided.
- Please RSVP to: gadgetsLLL@lpdatafiles.com

④ **SAVE THE MODIFIED TRAINING**

Headers and Footers

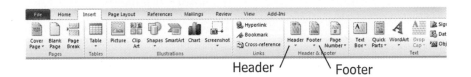

Header   Footer

A *header* is an area at the top of a page and a *footer* is an area at the bottom of the page. A header or footer is typically used to include the page number, file name, author's name, and the date on each page. To create a header or footer, click Insert → Header or Insert → Footer. A gallery of built-in designs is displayed. Click a built-in design and the document text dims, the header or footer is added, and the Design tab is displayed on the Ribbon:

TIP Header and Footer are found on both the Insert tab and the Design tab.

Alternative To add a blank header or footer, click Insert → Header → Edit Header or Insert → Footer → Edit Footer.

Type text to replace the placeholder and then format the text as needed. Use the Design tab to further customize the header or footer:

- Change the distance from the header or footer to the edge of the page using Header from Top ▣▾ or Footer from Bottom ▣▾.

- The header or footer is printed on each page of the document. To specify a different header and footer for the first page, select the Different First Page check box. The header and footer tabs on page 1 change:

Click Design → Go to Header or Design → Go to Footer to move the insertion point between the header and footer. Click Design → Close Header and Footer or double-click the body of the document to close the header and footer.

Double-click in the header or footer area to make it active again and allow for editing.

Adding Times, Dates, and Page Numbers

Page Number   Date & Time

TIP Many of the header and footer built-in designs contain page number and date placeholders.

Page numbers are helpful in documents that have more than one page. To add the page number at the insertion point in an existing header or footer, click Design → Page Number → Current Position.

If a header or footer has not yet been created, click:

- Insert → Page Number → Top of Page to create a header with a page number. Any existing header is replaced.

- Insert → Page Number → Bottom of Page to create a footer with a page number. Any existing footer is replaced.

- Insert → Page Number → Page Margins to add a page number in the left or right margins. To edit a page number in the margins, make the header active.

The page number can then be formatted as needed. When the document is printed, the appropriate page number will print on each page. To change the numbering style, click Page Number → Format Page Numbers. To delete a page number, click Page Number → Remove Page Numbers or select the page number and press the Delete key.

TIP Page Number and Date & Time are found on both the Insert tab and the Design tab.

It is easier to keep track of document revisions when printouts include the date and time they were printed. To add the date or time, select 🖾 Date & Time from the Insert or Design tab and then select a format from the displayed dialog box. Select the Update automatically check box in the dialog box to have the date and time automatically updated when a document is printed or opened. To delete the date or time, select it and press the Delete key.

To update the date and time in the document, place the insertion point within the date or time and then press F9 or click Update:

TIP To change the format of a date or time, right-click the date or time and then select Edit Field from the menu.

Adding and Editing Graphics

Graphics can be used to make a document more interesting and informative. Graphics in digital format come from various sources, including scanned artwork, digital camera pictures, screen captures, and illustration software. Click Insert → Picture to display the Insert Picture dialog box with a list of graphic files. A graphic inserted into a document is placed at the insertion point. Formats can then be applied to the paragraph and will affect the position of the graphic. For example, to center a graphic, place the insertion point in the paragraph that contains the graphic and click Home → Center ≡.

When a graphic is inserted, the Format tab is added to the Ribbon and is used to change the look of a selected graphic:

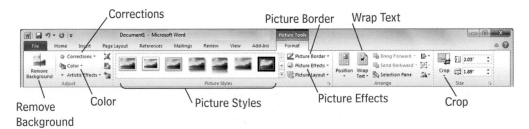

- Corrections displays options for sharpening and softening the image and for changing the brightness and contrast:

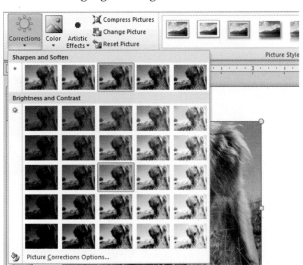

- Color options can be used to recolor the graphic:

• Artistic Effects displays a list of artistic effects:

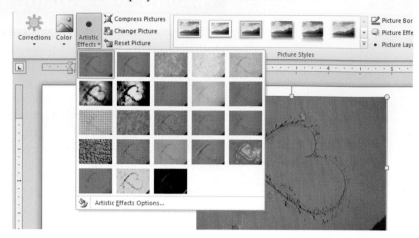

• 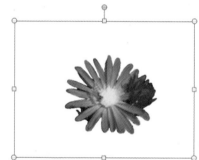 Compress Pictures compresses the picture to reduce the file size.

• Change Picture displays a dialog box used to select a different picture. The formatting and size of the current picture is preserved.

• Reset Picture discards all of the formatting changes.

• Picture Styles apply several picture formats in one click.

• Picture Border ▾ adds a border.

• Picture Effects ▾ adds effects such as bevels and shadows.

• Picture Layout ▾ converts the graphic to a SmartArt graphic.

• Background Removal removes unwanted parts of the graphic:

• Position lines up a selected graphic in a specific position on a page.

• Wrap Text displays options for changing the way text wraps around the graphic. For example, Wrap Text → Behind Text places the graphic behind the text:

- Crop trims away areas of the graphic that are not needed.
- Height and Width are used to size a graphic. Alternatively, point to a corner handle, which changes the pointer to ⤢ and then drag to size the graphic:

TIP Dragging a center handle causes distortion. Drag a corner handle to size a graphic without distorting it.

Drag the green handle to rotate the graphic.

Clip art are files of general-purpose graphics created by an artist using illustration software. Click Insert → Clip Art to display a task pane for finding clip art. Type a word or phrase in the Search for box and select Go to find all clip art that have the keywords in their description. To narrow a search, use the Search in list, which contains clip art collection names, and the Results should be list, which contains file formats. For example, type flower in the Search for box and then select Go to display clip art similar to:

Clips

Clip art is a type of clip. A clip is a single media file, which can be a picture, a sound, an animation, or a movie. The Clip Art task pane is used to search for clips.

To place a clip art graphic into the document, click the arrow to the right of the graphic and select Insert from the menu. To remove the task pane, click Close ✕ in the upper-right corner.

Cut, Copy, and Paste on the Home tab can be used to create copies or move a selected graphic. Press the Delete key to delete the selected graphic. Click anywhere in the document other than on the graphic to remove the handles.

Screenshots

To insert a screenshot into a document, select Insert → Screenshot to display a list of open windows:

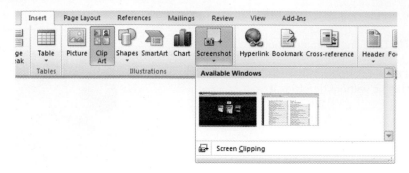

Clicking a window places a screenshot of the window in the Word document. To capture just a portion of the window, click Screen Clipping and then drag to select the screen clipping area.

OpenType Ligatures

TIP OpenType format is compatible with both Macintosh and Windows computers.

OpenType is a scalable font format that was developed by Microsoft and Adobe. Two or more letters combined into one character make a *ligature*. Open Type ligatures are used to create interesting font effects. For example:

Ligatures are not enabled by default. To enable this feature, right-click selected text and select Font. In the Font dialog box, select the Advanced tab and then select Standard Only in the Ligatures box:

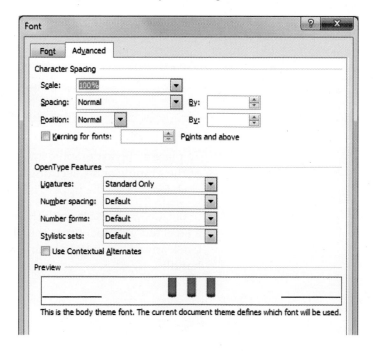

Word should already be started with TRAINING displayed from the last practice.

① **CREATE A HEADER WITH THE PAGE NUMBER**

   a. Click Insert ➜ Page Number ➜ Top of Page. A gallery is displayed.

   b. Scroll the gallery and click the **Bold Numbers 2** built-in design. The header is created with a centered page number "Page 1 of 3" and the **Design** tab is displayed on the Ribbon.

   c. Type your name followed by a space:

② **ADD THE DATE IN THE FOOTER**

   a. Click Design ➜ Go To Footer. The insertion point is moved to the footer.

   b. Click Design ➜ Date & Time. A dialog box is displayed.

      1. Select a format similar to **10/31/2011 5:22:48 PM**.

      2. Select the Update automatically check box.

      3. Select OK. A date and time that will automatically update are added.

   c. Click in the footer, and then drag to select the date and time.

   d. Click Home ➜ Bold **B** . The date and time are formatted as bold.

   e. Click Design ➜ Close Header and Footer. The header and footer are dimmed.

③ **INSERT A GRAPHIC AND FORMAT IT**

   a. Scroll to page 2 to the "Session Locations" section and place the insertion point at the beginning of the paragraph that begins "The walls of…."

   b. Click Insert ➜ Picture. A dialog box is displayed.

      1. Navigate to GADGETS MAP, which is a data file for this text.

      2. Select Insert. The picture is displayed at the insertion point.

   c. Click Format ➜ Color ➜ Dark Blue, Text color 2 Dark.

④ **POSITION THE GRAPHIC**

   a. Click Format ➜ Wrap Text ➜ Square. The text wraps around the graphic.

   b. Drag the map so that the top of the map is even with the first line of text in the "Session Locations" section and the right side of the map is about even with the right margin:

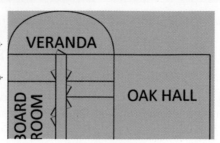

Session·Locations¶

Gadgets,·Inc.·is·committed·to· providing·a·professional·and· comfortable·environment·for·all· employees.·The·Veranda·room·is· a·bright,·airy·room·with·floor-to- ceiling·windows·that·look·out- onto·the·Bartholomew·Anderson· Memorial·Japanese·Gardens.·· Furniture·with·wicker·trim·and·a· variety·of·interior·plants·make· the·Veranda·room·a· comfortable,·inspiring·area·in·

Ⓢ SAVE THE DOCUMENT

Pagination

Page Break

Manual and Automatic Page Breaks

An inserted page break is called a "manual" or "hard" page break. Where Word ends one page and begins another is sometimes called an "automatic" page break.

Pagination is how a document is divided into pages. Word automatically determines how much text will fit on a page based on the amount of text and the document formatting. As a document is edited, Word automatically updates the pagination. To change pagination, insert a *page break*. Inserting a page break moves the text after the insertion point to the next page. To insert a break, press Ctrl+Enter or click Insert → Page Break.

To delete a page break, place the insertion point to the left of the page break and press the Delete key. The document repaginates and text from the next page moves up to fill the current page.

Creating Footnotes and Endnotes

Insert Endnote

Insert Footnote

Research papers and reports often include *footnotes* to cite sources. To add a footnote, place the insertion point in the text where the footnote number should appear and click References → Insert Footnote. A number is placed in the text and the insertion point is moved to a new footnote at the end of the document:

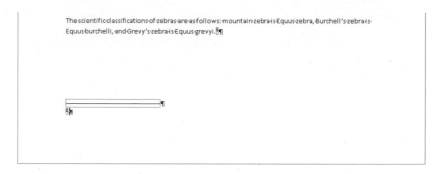

A separator line indicates the footnotes

TIP The standard format for footnotes is a 0.5 inch first line indent and a blank line above each footnote.

In a new footnote, the insertion point is placed to the right of the footnote number at the bottom of the page so that the footnote information can be typed and formatting applied.

By default, Word numbers footnotes with Arabic numerals such as 1 and 2. To change the number format, click the Footnotes group Dialog Box Launcher 🖺 to display the Footnote and Endnote dialog box. Options in this dialog box affect the number format, the starting number, and the location of the footnotes.

TIP Double-click the footnote number in the text to move the insertion point to the footnote at the bottom of the page.

Word sequentially numbers footnotes, and automatically renumbers footnotes when one is moved, inserted, copied, or deleted. To delete a footnote, delete the footnote number in the text, which automatically removes the reference from the bottom of the page.

endnotes

Endnotes appear on the last page of a document and are a common method of references for a research paper. To create an endnote, place the insertion point in the text where the endnote number should appear and click References ➡ Insert Endnote. A number is placed in the text and the insertion point is moved to the end of the document. By default, Word numbers endnotes with lowercase Roman numerals such as i and ii. Change the number format in the Footnote and Endnote dialog box.

TIP Creating a bibliography is discussed in Chapter 4.

Practice: TRAINING – part 6 of 6

The footnotes in this practice have the standard format as defined in *The Gregg Reference Manual Tenth Edition* by William Sabin (© 2008 McGraw-Hill Companies, Inc.). Word should already be started with TRAINING displayed from the last practice.

① **CREATE A FOOTNOTE**

a. In the first paragraph of the document, place the insertion point after the period after the last word, which reads "…harmony."

b. Click References ➡ Insert Footnote. Word inserts a 1 and the insertion point is moved to the bottom of the page where the footnote text can be typed. Note the separator line between the body of the document and the footnote.

② **ENTER THE FOOTNOTE TEXT**

a. Type the following text, allowing Word to wrap the text:

Chris Kemperstein, Working in Harmony: The Gadgets Philosophy (Atlanta: Caliper Press, 2010), p. 110.

b. Move the insertion point to the left of the footnote number and then press Enter.

③ FORMAT THE FOOTNOTE TEXT

   a. Select the book title, "Working in Harmony: The Gadgets Philosophy."

   b. Click Home → Italic I . The book title is now italic.

   c. Click anywhere in the footnote text. The book title is no longer selected and the insertion point is placed in the footnote.

   d. With the insertion point in the footnote text, drag the first line indent marker on the ruler to 0.5". The footnote now has a first line indent of 0.5 inches:

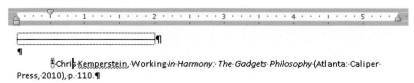

④ CHANGE THE PAGINATION

   a. Place the insertion point just to the left of the "S" in "Session Descriptions."

   b. Click Insert → Page Break. A page break is inserted, and text after the break is moved to the next page.

   c. Scroll to the "Instructors" heading on page 2 and place the insertion point just to the left of the "I" in "Instructors."

   d. Press Ctrl+Enter. A page break is inserted, and text after the break is moved to the next page.

   e. Scroll up and place the insertion point to the left of the page break:

   f. Press the Delete key. The page break is deleted.

   g. Press the Delete key again to delete the extra paragraph.

⑤ SAVE THE MODIFIED TRAINING, PRINT A COPY, AND CLOSE THE DOCUMENT

Templates

A *template* is a master document that includes the basic elements for particular types of documents. Templates are used again and again whenever a document of that type is needed. For example, office memos usually contain the same layout (To:, From:, Subject:, company logo, and so on), with only the topic changing for each new memo. Instead of typing the text, setting tab stops, and applying the formatting every time, a more efficient approach would be to create a template that contains the unchanging elements and then use this template each time a new memo is needed.

To create a template, type and format text in a new document. Select File → Save As to display a dialog box. Type a file name in the File name box, and select Word Template in the Save as type list. In the left pane of the dialog box, click Templates under the Microsoft Word heading and then select Save.

TIP A Word template is saved with a .dotx extension. Word templates containing macros have a .dotm extension.

To create a new document from a template, select ▮ File ▮ → New, then click My Templates to display a dialog box of templates.

When a template is used, Word creates a new, blank, untitled document that contains the same formatting and text as the template. This prevents accidentally saving over and changing the original template.

A variety of pre-created templates are accessible through Word. Select ▮ File ▮ → New to display available templates:

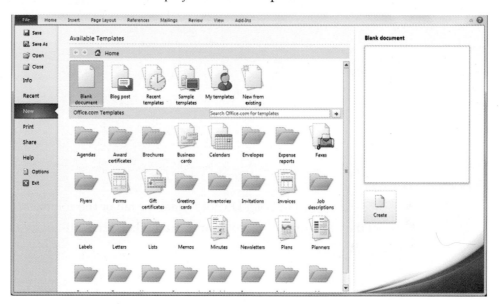

Click options in the Available Templates list to view and select *local templates*, which are stored on the computer. If the computer has an Internet connection, click options in the Office.com Templates list to view and download templates from Microsoft.

Practice: Generic Memo

The document created in this practice is a memo as defined in *The Gregg Reference Manual Tenth Edition* by William Sabin (© 2008 McGraw-Hill Companies, Inc.).

① CREATE A NEW BLANK WORD DOCUMENT

② TYPE TEXT AND FORMAT THE DOCUMENT

    a. Press the Enter key twice to move the insertion point down about 1 inch (2.54 cm) from the top margin.

    b. Type the following text, pressing the Tab key after each colon. Include two blank lines after the "SUBJECT" line:

```
                    ¶

                    ¶

                    MEMO·TO:  →   ¶

                    FROM:→¶

                    DATE:→¶

                    SUBJECT:  →   ¶

                    ¶

                    ¶
```

   c. Format each word as bold. Do not format the tab or the colon as bold.

   d. Select the paragraphs that contain text, and then set a left-aligned tab stop at 1".

   e. Click anywhere to remove the selection.

③ **SAVE THE TEMPLATE**

On the Quick Access Toolbar, click Save 💾. The Save As dialog box is displayed.

   1. In the **File name** box, type: Generic Memo

   2. In the **Save as type** list, select **Word Template**.

   3. In the left pane, click **Templates**.

   4. Select **Save**. The document is saved as a template.

④ **CLOSE THE TEMPLATE**

⑤ **CREATE A NEW DOCUMENT USING THE TEMPLATE**

   a. Select **File** ➔ **New**. The New Document dialog box is displayed.

   b. In the **Templates** list, click **My templates**. The New dialog box is displayed.

   c. Click the Generic Memo template and then select **OK**. A new document with the Generic Memo template text is displayed.

⑥ **CREATE A MEMO USING THE TEMPLATE**

   a. Type the following information into the memo headings, replacing Name with your name:

```
        MEMO·TO:  →   All·Employees¶

        FROM:     →   Name,·Assistant·Manager¶

        DATE:     →   March·16,·2010 ¶

        SUBJECT:  →   Vacation·Days¶
```

   b. Place the insertion point in the last blank paragraph of the document.

c. Complete the memo by typing the following text for the body of the memo:

¶

Effective·May·1,·each·employee·will·be·allotted·two·vacation·days·per·month.¶

⑦ SAVE, PRINT, AND THEN CLOSE THE DOCUMENT
    a. On the Quick Access Toolbar, click Save 🖫 . The Save As dialog box is displayed.
        1. Navigate to the appropriate location for the file to be saved.
        2. In the File name box, replace the existing text with Vacation Days Memo and then select Save.
    b. Print a copy of the memo and then close the document.

Creating an HTML File

HTML is the file format for documents viewed using a browser, such as documents on the Web. A document in HTML format is more versatile because Word is not needed to view it, just a browser, such as Internet Explorer. HTML documents can be viewed in Word, and are best viewed in Web Layout view.

TIP The MHTML (MIME HTML) format means that all the information for the document, including pictures, is saved within one single file.

To save a document as an HTML file, select ▮File▮ → Save As and then select a Web page type in the Save as type list. Click the Change Title button to give the Web page a descriptive *title*, which is text displayed in the title bar of the browser window. Click the Tags box to add a tag to the document. Tags are keywords, separated by semi-colons, used to organize and search for documents.

Saving a document as a Web Page creates an .htm file and a folder with the same name to store any supporting files associated with the document, such as graphics. Saving a document as a Single File Web Page creates an .mht file that contains all supporting information.

TIP In Internet Explorer version 8, press the Alt key to display the File menu.

To view the file in a Web browser, open a browser, such as Internet Explorer and select File → Open.

An HTML document opened in Word is displayed in Web Layout view.

Creating a PDF Document

PDF (Portable Document Format) is a file format that preserves document formatting. To save a Word document in PDF format, select ▮File▮ → Save As and then select PDF in the Save as type list. Adobe Reader is used to view a PDF document.

This practice requires browser software. Internet access is not required.

① CREATE A NEW WORD DOCUMENT

a. In a new document, type the following text, replacing Name with your name:

Contini's·Cookies·Annual·Picnic¶

All·employees·and·their·families·are·invited·to·attend.·Join·together·at·Foliage·Park·on·Saturday·from·11:30·a.m.·until·3:00·p.m.·for·food,·fun,·and·games.¶

Picnic·menu:¶

Hot·dogs,·hamburgers,·and·veggie·burgers¶

Potato·salad·and·garden·salad¶

Baked·beans,·coleslaw,·and·cookies¶

Lemonade,·iced·tea,·and·water¶

Games·include·horse·shoes,·softball,·and·a·three-legged·race!¶

Call·Name·at·555-1234· if·you·have·any·questions.·¶

b. Bold the title "Contini's Cookies Annual Picnic" and make it 24 points in size.

c. Format the four paragraphs of "Picnic menu" items as a bulleted list.

② INSERT CLIP ART

a. Add three blank paragraphs after the "…have any questions." paragraph.

b. With the insertion point in the last blank paragraph, click Insert → Clip Art. The Clip Art task pane is displayed.

    1. In the Search for box, type picnic and then click Go. Clip art is displayed.

    2. Point to an appropriate clip art graphic and then click the arrow that appears beside the graphic.

    3. In the menu, select Insert. The clip art is placed at the insertion point.

c. If the graphic is too large, drag a corner handle to size the graphic smaller. The entire document should fit onto one page.

d. Experiment with the Wrap Text options and apply a picture style.

③ SAVE THE DOCUMENT AND PRINT A COPY

a. Save the document naming it: Contini Picnic

b. Print a copy.

④ SAVE THE DOCUMENT AS AN HTML FILE

a. Select ▣ File → Save As. A dialog box is displayed.

    1. In the Save as type list, select Single File Web Page.

    2. Click Change Title. A dialog box is displayed.

3. Type a title as shown:

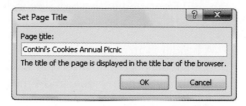

4. Select OK.

5. Select Save. The dialog box is removed and the document is displayed in Web Layout view.

⑤ OPEN THE HTML DOCUMENT IN A BROWSER

a. Start Internet Explorer.

b. Select File ➔ Open. A dialog box is displayed. If the File menu is not visible, such as in Internet Explorer version 8, press the Alt key to display the menu bar.

c. Navigate to the file and select Open.

d. Select OK. The Web page document is displayed.

e. Expand the window, if necessary, to view the entire document. Note the title in the title bar.

f. Close the browser window.

⑥ CLOSE CONTINI PICNIC AND QUIT WORD

Chapter Summary

This chapter discussed formatting documents to improve appearance and readability. Proper formatting is crucial in creating a professional-looking document.

Margins are the white region around text on a page. They affect the amount of text a page can contain. Margins are set using the Page Layout tab. Left and right indents affect the width of lines of text in a paragraph. Indents are set using the Page Layout tab or by dragging markers on the ruler.

By default, text is formatted with space after a paragraph. Space before and after paragraphs can be changed using the Page Layout tab. The line spacing of text in a paragraph is changed using the Home tab or the Paragraph dialog box.

Tabs are used to position text within a line. A tab stop specifies a location within a line of text and is displayed on the ruler above a document. The tab selector is used to set a tab stop. Tabs are also used to align multiple paragraphs of text into columns.

A vertical block of text is selected by holding down the Alt key and dragging. Once selected, formatting can be applied to the entire column.

Hanging indents and first line indents affect the width of the first line of text in a paragraph. These indents are set by dragging markers on the ruler or using options in the Paragraph dialog box.

Bulleted and numbered lists are paragraphs with a number or bullet, a tab, and formatted with a hanging indent. The Home tab is used to format lists.

A header is an area at the top of a page and the footer is an area at the bottom of the page. The Insert tab is used to display the header and footer. Page numbers and the date and time are added using the Insert tab.

Graphics from a file or clip art are added to a document using the Insert tab. The Format tab is used to change the look of a selected graphic. Pagination is how a document is divided into pages. Page breaks are added using the Insert tab or by pressing Ctrl+Enter.

Footnotes and endnotes used in research papers are created on the References tab. Remove a footnote or endnote by deleting its number from the text.

A template contains the basic elements for a particular type of document. A template is created by saving a document to the Templates folder as a Word Template type. To create a new document based on a template, click My templates in the New Document dialog box.

HTML documents are used for Web sites and for distributing documents to individuals that have browser software but do not have Microsoft Word. Use the Single File Web Page type to convert a document to a Web page.

Vocabulary

Bulleted list List created with each item as a separate paragraph formatted with a hanging indent, a character such as a bullet (•), and a tab.

Clip art A general-purpose graphic created by an artist using illustration software.

Double spaced Paragraph format that adds more space between each line of text.

Endnote Used to document a source. Found on the last page of a document.

First line indent First line of a paragraph that is farther to the right than the rest of the paragraph.

Footer Text that is printed at the bottom of each page.

Footnote Used to document a source. Usually located at the bottom of the page that contains the footnoted material.

Hanging indent First line of a paragraph that is farther to the left than the rest of the paragraph.

Header Text that is printed at the top of each page.

HTML The file format for documents viewed using a browser.

Indent Paragraph format that decreases the width of lines of text in a specific paragraph.

Ligatures Two or more letters combined into one character.

Margins The white region around the text on a page.

Numbered list List created with each item as a separate paragraph formatted with a hanging indent, a number, and a tab. Each number indicates an item's priority in the list.

OpenType A scalable font format.

Page break Changes where one page ends and another begins.

Pagination How a document is divided into pages.

Tab Used to position text within a line.

Tab stop Specifies a location within a line of text.

Template A master document that includes the basic elements for a particular type of document.

Title Text displayed in the title bar of a Web browser.

Word Commands

After Changes the amount of space after a paragraph. Found on the Page Layout tab.

Before Changes the amount of space before a paragraph. Found on the Page Layout tab.

Bottom of Page Creates a footer with a page number. Found in Insert → Page Number.

Bullets Formats a paragraph with a hanging indent and inserts a bullet and a tab to create a bulleted item in a list. Found on the Home tab.

Clip Art Displays the Clip Art task pane, which is used to insert clip art at the insertion point. Found on the Insert tab.

Close Header and Footer Closes the header and footer. Found on the Design tab.

Color Changes the colors in a selected graphic. Found on the Format tab.

Corrections Brightness, Contrast, Sharpen and Soften options. Found on the Format tab.

Crop Trims away areas of the graphic that are not needed in a selected graphic. Found on the Format tab.

Current Position Adds a page number at the insertion point. Found in Insert → Page Number.

Date & Time Date & Time Displays a dialog box used to insert the current date or time at the insertion point. Found on the Insert tab.

Footer Displays a gallery of footers. Found on the Insert tab.

Footer from Top Changes the distance from the footer to the edge of the page. Found on the Design tab.

Format Page Numbers Displays a dialog box used to change the page numbering style. Found in Insert → Page Number.

Go to Footer Moves the insertion point to the footer. Found on the Design tab.

Go to Header Moves the insertion point to the header. Found on the Design tab.

Header Displays a gallery of headers. Found on the Insert tab.

Header from Top Changes the distance from the header to the edge of the page. Found on the Design tab.

Height and Width Used to size a graphic. Found on the Format tab.

Increase Indent Increases the indent of bulleted or numbered items. Found on the Home tab.

Indent Left Indents the left side of a paragraph. Found on the Page Layout tab.

Indent Right Indents the right side of a paragraph. Found on the Page Layout tab.

Insert Endnote Places a number in the text and moves the insertion point to the end of the document. Found on the References tab.

Insert Footnote Places a number in the text and moves the insertion point to the bottom of the page. Found on the References tab.

Line & Paragraph Spacing Used to change the amount of space between lines of text in a paragraph. Found on the Home tab.

Margins Displays options used to format the margins of a document. Found on the Page Layout tab.

Numbering Formats a paragraph with a hanging indent and inserts a number and a tab to create a numbered item in a list. Found on the Home tab.

Page Break Inserts a page break at the insertion point. Found on the Insert tab.

Page Margins Creates a page number in the left or right margins. Found in Insert → Page Number.

Page Number Displays a gallery of built-in designs used to add a page number in the document. Found on the Insert tab.

Picture Displays a dialog box used to insert a graphic at the insertion point. Found on the Insert tab.

Picture Border Adds a border to a selected graphic. Found on the Format tab.

Picture Effects Adds effects such as bevels and shadows to a selected graphic. Found on the Format tab.

Picture Layout Converts a graphic to a SmartArt graphic. Found on the Format tab.

Position Displays options for lining up a selected graphic on the page. Found on the Format tab.

Remove Background Removes unwanted portions of an image. Found on the Format tab.

Reset Picture Removes the formatting from a selected graphic. Found on the Format tab.

Screenshot Inserts a screen shot of another open window. Found on the Insert tab.

Top of Page Creates a header with a page number. Found in Insert → Page Number.

Wrap Text Displays options for wrapping text around an object. Found on the Format tab.

1. Describe how formatting can affect the usability of a document.

2. How can the margins of a document be changed so the left margin is 2" and the right margin 3"?

3. What is the difference between formatting a paragraph with a 1" left indent using Page Layout → Indent Left ≣ and by dragging markers on the ruler?

4. a) Why are paragraphs of text formatted with space after each paragraph?
   b) How is the space before a paragraph changed?

5. a) Give an example of a document that is typically double spaced.
   b) How is the formatting of a paragraph changed to double spaced?

6. a) How can you tell where tab stops have been set?
   b) What default tab stops will automatically be removed when a tab stop is set at 3"?
   c) List the steps required to set a center tab stop at 2.25".

7. What type of data would be best aligned using a decimal tab stop?

8. What type of indent formats the first line of a paragraph farther to the left than the rest of the paragraph?

9. a) List the steps required to format a paragraph with a hanging indent of 0.25".
   b) Give an example of when a hanging indent is useful.

10. List the steps required to format six paragraphs as a bulleted list of six items.

11. When would a numbered list be used instead of a bulleted list?

12. a) What is a header?
    b) List three kinds of information that is often included in a header or footer.
    c) What option is selected to have the header not print on the first page?

13. a) What option is used to position a graphic relative to the text?
    b) List three sources of graphics.

14. Other than changing margins, what else can affect a document's pagination?

15. a) List two ways to insert a page break.
    b) How is a page break deleted?

16. a) What are footnotes used for?
    b) Compare and contrast uses and formatting of footnotes and endnotes.

17. a) What is a template?
    b) Give an example of when using a template could be helpful. Explain why.

18. Describe the usefulness of being able to save a Word document as an HTML file and as a PDF file.

True/False

19. a) Margin settings can change from paragraph to paragraph.
    b) Indents are often used to set off paragraphs such as a quotation.
    c) A paragraph in a new document is double spaced by default.
    d) Default tab stops are located at every inch on the ruler.
    e) A right tab stop aligns the end of the text at the stop.
    f) A hanging indent is part of the standard footnote format.
    g) The steps in a recipe should be formatted as a bulleted list, and the ingredients are best formatted as a numbered list.
    h) It is possible to have a different header and footer printed on the first page than on the rest of the pages.
    i) The keywords clip art are appropriate when searching for clip art of musical instruments.
    j) Cut, Copy, and Paste can be used to create copies of or move a selected graphic.
    k) Once inserted, page breaks cannot be deleted from a document.
    l) Footnotes appear at the bottom of the page by default.
    m) A Web page title is text displayed in the title bar of the Web browser.

Project 1

A portfolio is a collection of work that clearly illustrates effort, progress, and achievement of knowledge and skills. A portfolio can take the form a three-ring binder or similar container, or it can be stored in digital format. Samples of work included in portfolios are often called *artifacts*. A complete portfolio will also include written reflections about each artifact. Create a portfolio using artifacts created from the Projects in this text. The portfolio should contain:

- an inventory of the works produced
- artifacts
- a learning journal, which documents the skills acquired as a result of working through this text and reflects on each artifact

a) Open INVENTORY, which is a Word data file for this text. Replace Name with your name in the footer. Print a copy and place the hard copy at the front of the portfolio. Each time an artifact is added to the portfolio, it should be documented on the inventory sheet.

b) As assignments are completed, select artifacts for the portfolio. The artifacts selected for the portfolio should be "polished copies." This may require making edits to work that has already been assessed. Select artifacts that illustrate a range of skills and knowledge learned.

c) Each time an artifact is selected, open LEARNING JOURNAL, which is a Word data file for this text, and make an entry in the learning journal to document and reflect on the skills acquired as a result of completing the artifact. In the footer, replace Name with your name. When the portfolio is complete, place a copy of LEARNING JOURNAL after the artifacts.

d) Once a portfolio has enough content to use, it should be assembled and updated frequently.

Project 2

The WELCOME document contains a letter for new customers. Open WELCOME, which is Word data file for this text, and complete the following steps:

a) Format the title "Travel...With a Purpose" as 18 point, bold, and in a different font, with 24 points of space after the paragraph.

b) Insert TRAVEL, which is a graphic data file for this text. Size the picture appropriately. Format the graphic with Square text wrapping and position it to the right of the paragraph that begins "Travel...With a Purpose"

c) Change the top and left margins of the document to 2".

d) Create a footer with your name and right align the footer text.

e) Format the paragraphs of text about the hours at the bottom of the letter with the following tab stops:

- at 1.25" create a left tab stop (for the hours on Monday – Friday)
- at 2.75" create a left tab stop (for the hours on Saturday)
- at 4.25" create a left tab stop (for the hours on Sunday)

f) Format the column titles as italic, and the first column as bold.

g) Save the modified WELCOME and print a copy.

Project 3

You are creating an article about the advantages of telecommuting. Open TELECOMMUTING, which is a Word data file for this text, and complete the following steps:

a) Center align the following headings and format them as 14 point, bold, Tahoma, with 10 points of space before each paragraph:

"Computers in the Home Office"

"The Process of Telecommuting"

"Advantages of Telecommuting"

"Telecommuting in Coral County"

b) Underline the first sentence of the second paragraph that begins "Telecommuting is possible because...."

c) Change the margins to Narrow.

d) Insert a page break before the heading "Telecommuting in Coral County."

e) Create a header with your name centered.

f) Create a footer with the page number centered.

g) Format the paragraphs of text about the number of people and percentage of population with the following tab stops:

- at 2" create a right tab stop (for the number of people)
- at 3.5" create a right tab stop (for the percentage of population)

h) The column titles should be centered above the text in the columns. Format only the column titles "Number of People" and "Percentage of Population" to have the following tab stops:

- at 1.75" create a center tab stop (for "Number of People")
- at 3.5" create a center tab stop (for "Percentage of Population")

i) Bold the column titles.

j) Format the line that contains the totals as italic.

k) Create 0.5" left and right indents for the last paragraph on page 1, the one that begins "…if 10% to 20%…."

l) Place a footnote after the period ending the quote indented in step (k). Create the following footnote for the quote, formatting it in the standard format as practiced earlier in this chapter:

¶

Effy Oz, *Ethics for the Information Age* (Wm. C. Brown Communications, Inc., 2009).¶

m) Insert an appropriate clip art in a new paragraph above the heading "Computers in the Home Office." Center align the graphic. Size the graphic smaller if necessary so that the document prints on two pages.

n) Save the modified TELECOMMUTING and print a copy.

Project 4

As a freelance writer, you are writing on a story on how vitamins can be found in many different sources.

a) In a new document, type the following text, separating the columns with single tabs (do not precede the first column with a tab). Your text will not be arranged as shown here until tab stops have been set:

Vitamin	Purpose	Common Food Sources
A	skeletal growth, skin	green leafy or yellow vegetables
B1	metabolism of carbohydrates	whole grains, liver
B12	production of proteins	liver, kidney, lean meat
C	resistance to infection	citrus fruits, tomatoes
E	antioxidant	peanut or corn oils

b) Save the document naming it Vitamins.

c) Format all the paragraphs to have no space before or after.

d) Format all the paragraphs with the following tab stops:

- at 1.25" create a left tab stop (for the usage in body)
- at 3.5" create a left tab stop (for the common food sources)

e) Format the "Common Food Sources" column of data, except for the title, as italic.

f) At the top of the document, create a title with the text Learn About Vitamins. Format the title as bold, center aligned, with 24 points of space after.

g) Bold the column titles.

h) Subscript the "1" in "B1" and subscript the "12" in "B12."

i) Insert an appropriate clip art graphic above the title at the top of the document. Size the graphic smaller if necessary.

j) Create a footer with your name and right align the footer text.

k) Check the document on screen and correct any errors and misspellings.

l) Save the modified Vitamins and print a copy.

Project 5

To help a student study at *Study Time Tutoring*, you are preparing a list of United States presidents. Open U.S. PRESIDENTS, which is Word data file for this text, and complete the following steps:

a) Format the entire document with left tab stops at 0.75" and 4" and a right tab stop at 3.5". The text should be arranged in columns similar to:

Number	President	Years in Office	Party
1.	George Washington	1789-1797	(none)
2.	John Adams	1797-1801	Federalist
3.	Thomas Jefferson	1801-1809	Democratic-Republican
4.	James Madison	1809-1817	Democratic-Republican
5.	James Monroe	1817-1825	Democratic-Republican
6	John Quincy Adams	1825-1829	Democratic-Republican

b) Save the modified U.S. PRESIDENTS.

c) Bold the column titles.

d) Double space all the paragraphs.

e) Create a header with your name and center the header text.

f) Create a footer with the page number centered.

g) Save the modified U.S. PRESIDENTS and print a copy.

h) Save the document as an HTML file and then print a copy from a browser.

Project 6

At *Travel... With a Purpose*, you are preparing for a tour to the Hawaiian islands and want to provide the participants with information about volcano eruptions:

a) In a new document, type the following text, separating the columns with single tabs (do <u>not</u> precede the first column with a tab). Your text will not be arranged as shown here until tab stops have been set:

Island	Area (km2)	Tallest Peak	Peak Height (m)
Hawaii	6,501	Mauna Kea	4,139
Maui	1,174	Haleakala	3,007
Oahu	979	Kaala	1,208
Kauai	890	Kawaikini	1,573
Molokai	420	Kamakou	1,491
Lanai	225	Lanaihale	1,011
Niihau	118	Paniau	384
Kahoolawe	72	Lua Makika	443

b) Save the document naming it Hawaiian Islands.

c) Format all the paragraphs to have no space before or after.

d) Format all the paragraphs with the following tab stops:

- at 1.5" create a right tab stop (for the area)
- at 2.5" create a center tab stop (for the tallest peak)
- at 4.25" create a right tab stop (for the peak height)

e) In the paragraph with the column titles, change the right tab stop at 1.5" to a center tab stop at 1.25" and change the right tab stop at 4.25" to a center tab stop at 4".

f) Bold the column titles.

g) Format the entire "Tallest Peak" column of data, not the title, as italic.

h) Format all the text as 11 point Candara.

i) Create a header with the text The Hawaiian Islands in 24 point, bold text, center aligned, with 24 points of space after.

j) Superscript the "2" in the column title "Area (km2)."

k) Create a footer with your name and center the footer text.

l) Check the document on screen and correct any errors and misspellings.

m) Save the modified Hawaiian Islands and print a copy.

Project 7

At *Study Time Tutoring*, you are creating a review sheet for science:

a) In a new document, type the following text, separating the columns with single tabs (do <u>not</u> precede the first column with a tab). Your text will not be arranged as shown here until tab stops have been set:

Measurement	Units	Symbol	Formula
Area	square meter	m2	m2
Heat	joule	J	N x m
Power	watt	W	J/s
Force	newton	N	kg x m/s2
Pressure	pascal	Pa	N/m2
Velocity	meter per second	m/s	m/s

b) Save the document naming it Science Review.

c) Format all the paragraphs to have no space before or after.

d) Format all the paragraphs with the following tab stops:

- at 1.5" create a left tab stop (for the units)
- at 3.5" create a center tab stop (for the symbol)
- at 5" create a right tab stop (for the formula)

e) Superscript all four occurrences of "2."

f) Format the Formula data as Cambria font.

g) At the end of the document, insert three blank paragraphs. Type the following text, separating the columns with single tabs (do <u>not</u> precede the first column with a tab). Your text will not be arranged as shown here until tab stops have been set:

Formula	Name
C2H2	acetylene
H2O	water
K2SO4	potassium sulfate
NH3	ammonia
CH4	methane
C6H6	benzene

h) Format the new paragraphs to have no space before or after.

i) Format the new paragraphs to have only one tab stop, a left tab stop at 1".

j) In the new paragraphs, subscript all occurrences of numbers.

k) Format the Formula data as Cambria font.

l) At the top of the document, create a title with the text Science Review Sheet. Format the title as bold, center aligned, with 24 points of space after.

m) Bold all of the column titles in the document.

n) Create a header with your name and left align the header text.

o) Save the modified Science Review and print a copy.

Project 8

The Entertainment Review project created in Chapter 2, Project 4 needs additional formatting before the article can be submitted. Open Entertainment Review and complete the following steps:

a) Format the body of the review as double spaced.

b) Create a header with the text CRITIC'S CHOICE and center the text. Format the text as bold and 14 points.

c) Create a footer with your name and right align the footer text.

d) Save the modified Entertainment Review and print a copy.

e) Save the document as an HTML file and then print a copy from a browser.

Project 9

The Coral Research proposal modified in Chapter 2, Project 5 needs to be formatted. Open PROPOSAL and complete the following steps:

a) Change the top and bottom margins to 1.25" and the left and right margins to 1.5".

b) Insert a page break before the heading "Computerized Guide."

c) Format the paragraphs below the "BUDGET" heading with the following tab stops:

- at 0.75" create a left tab stop
- at 4.5" create a decimal tab stop

d) Format the three numbered paragraphs of stages on page 2 as a numbered list.

e) Insert a page break before the heading "Notes" at the bottom of page 2.

f) Create a header with your name and center the header text and a footer with the page number centered.

g) Save the modified PROPOSAL and print a copy.

Project 10

Align Computers wants to distribute an employee bulletin about electronic communication etiquette. For example:

Telephone Calls
Always state your name and the purpose of the call.

Cellular Phone
Refrain from talking on the phone while driving.

Speakerphone
Be sure there is no background noise.

Voicemail
Speak slowly and clearly.

E-mail
Use meaningful subject lines.

a) In a new document, type the title Electronic Communication Etiquette, press Enter, and then type the devices and rules listed in this Project.

b) Center align the title and format it as 20 point, bold, Consolas, with 24 points of space after. Bold the device names.

c) Generate three additional etiquette rules that apply to each device. Add the additional etiquette rules in separate paragraphs below the appropriate device name.

d) Format the etiquette rules under each title as a bulleted list.

e) Create a header with your name and right align the header text. Add a footer with the date and center the footer text.

f) Save the document naming it Etiquette and print a copy.

Project 11

In Chapter 2, Project 9 you decided to open a business. You will now use Word to create a logo for your new business venture. Create at least two designs to choose from. For example, Word was used to create the logo below:

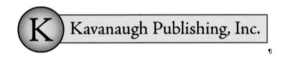

a) Use options on the **Format** tab to modify the logos. Experiment with various looks to come up with two very different logos.

b) Save the document naming it Logo Proposals and print a copy.

Project 12

A résumé summarizes accomplishments, education, and work experience. A traditional résumé is a printed document that is typically one page in length and lists a person's educational background, previous job experiences, skills obtained through education and work experience, and accomplishments, such as memberships, awards, and activities.

Create a résumé for yourself. You may want to use a template to help you create the résumé. Your résumé should contain the following:

• Four sections of information with the following titles: Education, Experience, Skills, and Accomplishments. The information in each section should be indented paragraphs.

• At least one bulleted or numbered list.

• A header with your name, address, and phone number.

• A footer with the text References available upon request.

Format the résumé appropriately, using emphasized text, two different fonts, two or three different sizes, and tabs and tab stops. Check the document on screen for errors and misspellings and make any corrections. Save the document naming it Basic Resume and print a copy.

Project 13

Multiple labels that contain the same text can easily be created in Word. This feature is useful for creating return address labels for use on envelopes. When printing a labels document, special adhesive paper with multiple labels on each page is used in the printer. The Avery® brand of adhesive labels is widely used, and the dimensions of many of its labels have been included in Word.

a) Create a new document and then click Mailings → Labels. A dialog box is displayed.

b) In the Labels tab of the dialog box, select Options. A dialog box is displayed.

   1. Select Page printers.
   2. In the Label vendors list, select Avery US Letter.
   3. In the Product number list, select 5267 and then select OK. The dialog box is removed.

c) In the Address box, type your first and last name and then press Enter. The insertion point is moved to the next line.

d) Type your street address, press Enter, then type your city, state, and zip (or province and postal code).

e) Select Full page of the same label and then select the New Document button. The dialog box is removed and a new document with labels is displayed.

f) Select Home → Select → Select All. All of the text in the document is selected. Change the font size to 8. The label text is now completely displayed in each label.

g) Save the document naming it Return Address Labels and print a copy.

Project 14

A résumé summarizes accomplishments, education, and work experience. Many companies scan résumés using an optical character reader (OCR) into a computerized database. They can then search the database of resumes for keywords that describe the qualifications required for a position. This is an efficient way to sort through hundreds of résumés. When submitting a résumé, it is a good idea to check with the company's Human Resources department to see if the company scans résumés, since the content and format of a scannable résumé differs greatly from that of a traditional résumé.

Scannable résumés consist of keyword summaries that contain job-related acronyms and terminology and are written using nouns instead of action verbs.

A scannable résumé has to be formatted so that it can be read properly by the OCR. Formatting used on traditional résumés, such as shading and lines, should be avoided because it can be misinterpreted. A scannable résumé should contain as little punctuation as possible. If punctuation is used with a word that may be a keyword, a space should be placed before the punctuation mark. A search for the word management might not recognize management, with a comma or management. with a period.

Guidelines for creating a scannable résumé are:

- Use white or other light-colored paper.
- Send the original copy, not photocopies.
- Do not use graphics, shading, bold, italic or underline formatting. Use all capital letters for headings.
- Avoid vertical lines, and if horizontal lines are used to separate parts of the resume, include space between the line and text.
- Use standard fonts such as Calibri, Arial, or Times New Roman.

- Do not fold or staple the resume.
- Put your name at the top of each page.
- Use left alignment.
- Use separate lines for address information.
- Do not use a hollow bullet (▫) because it could be interpreted as the letter "o." Use a regular bullet • or preferably * or -.

In a new document, create a scannable résumé using the No Spacing style by completing the following steps:

a) In a scannable résumé, all capital letters are used for the name in the heading, which is center aligned. Type the following text and format the paragraphs as centered:

THOMAS YOUNG
43 Main Street
Miami FL 33056
305-555-7879
youngt@Lpdatafiles.com

b) Résumé side headings vary depending on the résumé content. Example side headings include: Objective, Education, Experience, Computer Skills, Volunteer Experience, Hobbies, Leadership Skills, Organizational Skills, Awards, Accomplishments, and References. In a scannable résumé, side headings are typed in all capitals with one blank line above and below each side heading. Any formatting such as bold should not be applied to side headings. Type OBJECTIVE and press Enter twice.

c) Type the following objective:

A technical writing position where my writing and computer skills are used to produce clear and accurate technical training manuals.

d) The experience and skills sections below are written using keyword nouns instead of action verbs which are typically found on a traditional resume. Press Enter twice and then type the rest of the résumé. You may need to point to the blue bar below the dash and then click the AutoCorrect Options button and select Undo Automatic Bullets if the bullets automatically indent:

TECHNICAL WRITING EXPERIENCE

- Preparation of technical training manuals for cell phone users
- Preparation of technical training manuals for several brands of DVD players
- Preparation of sales brochures
- Production of customer viewable copy

COMPUTER SKILLS

- Mastery of Adobe Acrobat, Adobe InDesign, Microsoft Word
- Creation and maintenance of company Web sites
- Programming experience in Java, Pearl, and C++

ADMINISTRATIVE SKILLS

- Manage project teams
- Control of project expense budgets
- Deliver technical training
- Team player
- Excellent communication skills

EDUCATION

- BA in Visual Communication Design Ohio State University 2009

e) Save the document naming it Scannable Resume and print a copy.

f) A résumé is often the only impression an employer has of the application. Therefore, it is important to ensure that a résumé is error-free before it is submitted. Proofread the hard copy carefully and if necessary, edit and print a new copy of the résumé.

g) In a new document, create your own scannable résumé following the format outlined in this Project.

Project 15

A *blog* is a short term for a weblog, which is a piece of writing similar to a journal entry. The blog is then posted to a Web site that uses blogging software. *Blog* and *blogging* are also used to indicate writing and posting the blogs. A blog account is required to post a blog, and can be found at Web sites such as www.blogger.com.

Writing a blog is an easy way of expressing personal thoughts, as well as personal opinions, complaints, and experiences. News can be conveyed in a blog. Some blogs are meant to be seen by anyone with Internet access, and other blogs are set up for only a private circle of account holders to view. Companies and academic groups use blogs to expand discussions, manage teams, and keep information flowing.

Word documents can be published as blog posts, and blog posts can be created from scratch in Word. To post an open Word document, select **File** → Share → Publish as Blog Post. A blog post document is created from the open document. To create a new, empty blog post, select **File** → New →Blog post.

A blog post consists of a title and entry below it:

Titles of blogs are not necessarily descriptive, although the title usually indicates what kind of information is in the blog. A title that is a popular phrase or a creatively written statement usually indicate that the blog is a personal thought. A title that is more business-like indicates serious content.

a) Select New blog post in the New Document dialog box and then select Create. A new blog post is created. If the Register a Blog Account dialog box is displayed, select Register Later.

b) Click the text Enter Post Title Here and type: I'm on Project 15

c) Place the insertion point in the blank paragraph below the title and line. Type at least two paragraphs of your thoughts and experiences with this chapter, text, or Project.

d) Save the document by selecting **File** → Save, naming it Wednesday Blog.

e) Select **File** → Print to print a copy.

Chapter 3 Formatting Documents

Chapter 4
Advanced Formatting Features

Key Concepts

Formatting with styles and themes
Dividing a document into sections
Formatting columns
Using tables
Create a table of contents
Inserting SmartArt graphics
Hyphenating a document
Creating brochures and newsletters
Adding citations and a bibliography
Using text boxes

Practice Data Files

VOLCANOES, TUTORING, SPACE
TRANSMISSIONS

Project Data Files

ELEMENTS, SATURN

Styles

Quick Styles   Change Styles

body text, headings

TIP Styles makes it easy to have a consistent look throughout a document.

Quick Styles

Documents contain elements such as headings and body text. The main paragraphs in a document are *body text. Headings* are titles that are often bold and in a larger and different font than body text. These elements are set apart by their fonts, sizes, colors, and paragraph formats. Rather than apply each of these formats separately, a style can be used. A *style* is a named set of formats. With one click, multiple formats can be applied to selected text. Word includes styles, also called *Quick Styles*, to format body text ("Normal" style), different levels of headings, and other elements such as quotes:

STYLE	FORMATTING
Normal	11 pt Calibri, 10 pts space after
Heading 1	14 pt Cambria, bold, 24 pts space before, dark blue
Heading 2	13 pt, Cambria, bold, 10 pts space before, blue
Quote	11 pt, Calibri, italic, 10 pts space after

TIP Some features of Word use styles to differentiate between text. For example, a table of contents is automatically generated based on heading styles.

Normal style is automatically applied to paragraphs in a new document. To apply a different style, click in a paragraph or select multiple paragraphs and then click a Quick Style on the Home tab. To display the Quick Styles gallery, click More ⊽:

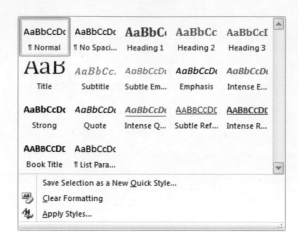

Translate

Select Review → Translate → Choose Translation Language to choose a translation language, such as Spanish or French. Then, you can use the Mini Translator in Word. Pointing to a word displays a quick translation.

Click **Clear Formatting** or click **Home → Clear Formatting**  to change the formatting of the paragraph to Normal style.

Styles are kept together in sets. The Quick Styles gallery shown above is the Default style set. Changing a Quick Style set changes all the styles used for body text, headings, and other elements. To change the style set, click **Home → Change Styles → Style Set** and select a set from the list. For example, selecting **Fancy** changes the style set to:

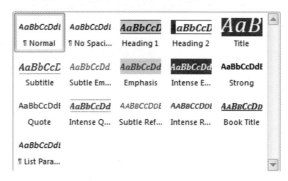

A style set can be modified further by selecting a **Colors** or **Fonts** option in the **Change Styles** menu:

Foundry Color   *Impact Font*

TIP Select text and then rest the pointer on a style to preview what the style will look like.

A new style can be created when the built-in styles are not appropriate. Right-click a formatted paragraph and select **Styles → Save Selection as a New Quick Style**. New styles are saved with the document, and remain available even when style sets are changed. To modify an existing style, right-click the Quick Style in the gallery and select **Modify**. A dialog box is displayed where changes can be made to the style's formatting.

To remove a style from the Quick Styles gallery, right-click the style and select **Remove from Quick Styles Gallery**.

① START WORD AND OPEN VOLCANOES

   a. Open VOLCANOES, which is a Word data file for this text, and display formatting marks if they are not already displayed.

   b. At the bottom of page 1, replace Name with your first name and last name.

② APPLY STYLES

   a. At the top of page 2, place the insertion point in the "Introduction" heading.

   b. Click Home → Heading 1. The Heading 1 style is now applied to the "Introduction" heading:

> **Introduction**¶
> A·volcano·is·a·location·on·the·surface·of·the·Earth··where·magma·has·erupted·out·of·the·interior·of·the·planet.·Magma·is·molten·rock,·which·has·melted·from·the·extreme·heat·(2200°C·to·5000°C)·and·

   c. Below the "Introduction" paragraph on page 2, place the insertion point in the "Volcano Facts" heading.

   d. Click Home → Heading 1.

   e. Scroll to the end of the document and apply the Heading 1 style to the "Conclusion" heading.

③ APPLY STYLES TO THE OTHER HEADINGS

   a. Scroll to the middle of page 2 and place the insertion point in the "Stages of Volcanic Activity" heading.

   b. Click Home → Heading 2.

   c. Scroll through the rest of the document and apply the Heading 2 style to the "Types of Volcanoes" and "Types of Lava Rocks" headings.

   d. Scroll to the top of page 1 and place the insertion point in the "Volcanoes" title.

   e. Click Home → More ▾. A gallery of Quick Styles is displayed.

   f. Click Title.

   g. At the bottom of page 1, apply the No Spacing style to the three paragraphs that begin with "By…" and end with "…2011 ."

④ APPLY AND MODIFY A STYLE

   a. Scroll to the middle of page 2 and place the insertion point in the "Eruption Stage" heading.

   b. Click Home → Heading 3 style.

   c. Scroll through the rest of the document and apply the Heading 3 style to the "Cooling and Inactive Stage," "Cinder Cones," "Shield Volcanoes," "Composite Volcanoes," "Basalt," "Obsidian," and "Andesite" headings.

   d. On the Home tab, right-click the Heading 3 style and select Modify from the menu. A dialog box is displayed.

   e. Click Italic *I* and then select OK. All of the text formatted with the Heading 3 style is now italic.

⑤ SAVE THE MODIFIED VOLCANOES

Table

cell A table consists of rows and columns of cells, which can contain text and graphics. The intersection of a row and column is called a *cell*. Cells can have borders, which make the information easier to read:

Element	Symbol	Atomic Number	Atomic Mass
Calcium	Ca	20	40.1
Gold	Au	79	197.0

row The table above has four columns and three rows. *Rows* are horizontal and
column *columns* are vertical. For example the first row contains titles, and the last column contains the "Atomic Mass" title and the mass amounts.

To create an empty table, click Insert → Table and move the pointer over the grid to select the number of cells for the table:

TIP To create a table from text that is separated by tabs, select the text and then click Insert → Table → Convert Text to Table.

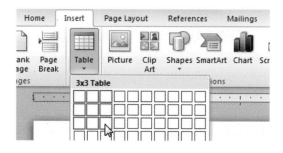

Click the grid to create the table and then type text into the individual cells. Press the Tab key to move from cell to cell.

When a table is created, Word automatically adjusts the column widths to be equal so that the table fills the space between the left and right
boundaries margins. The column and row borders are called *boundaries* and are used to change the width of a column or the height of a row:

Alternative Click Layout → Distribute Rows or Distribute Columns to distribute the width or height of columns or rows equally.

- Point to the right boundary, the pointer changes to ╫, and then drag the boundary to change the column's width.

- Point to the bottom boundary of a row, the pointer changes to ╪, and then drag to change the row's height.

- Double-click a boundary to change the height or width just enough to display the data entirely.

TIP The Design and Layout tabs are available when a table, row, or column is selected, or when the insertion point is in a cell.

After creating a table, a row or column may need to be added. Place the insertion point in a cell and click Layout → Insert Above to add a row above the selected row. Likewise, click Layout → Insert Below to add a row below, or Insert Left or Insert Right to add a column to the left or right of the insertion point. Delete a row, column, or entire table using Layout → Delete.

Formatting a Table

Alternative Point to the left edge of a cell, the pointer changes to ⬈, and then click to select the cell's contents.

Alternative Point to the left of a row, the pointer changes to ◿, and then click to select the row. Point to the top of a column, the pointer changes to ⬇, and then click to select the column.

Cells are selected prior to applying formatting. Position the insertion point and then click Layout → Select to display a menu of selection options:

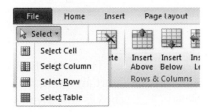

Formats such as fonts and font styles on the Home tab can then be applied to the contents of selected cells. Additional formatting options on the Layout tab:

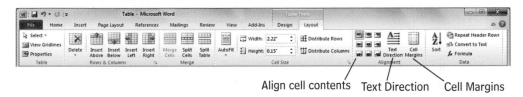

Align cell contents   Text Direction   Cell Margins

- Change the alignment of cell contents from left, center, or right, and from top, center, and bottom of the cell using the align cell contents buttons.
- Click Layout → Text Direction to rotate the text in the cell.
- Click Layout → Cell Margins to display a dialog box with options for changing the distance from the cell contents to the edges of the cell.

The Design tab contains formatting options:

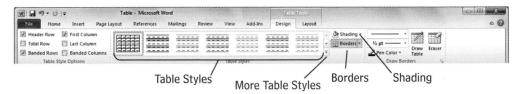

Table Styles   More Table Styles   Borders   Shading

Click a Table Style to apply it to the table. To change the cell borders, click Design → Borders and to change the shading, click Design → Shading. Borders and shading formats are applied to the selected row, column, or table.

As an alternative to creating and formatting a table, select Insert → Table → Quick Tables and select a Built-In table style:

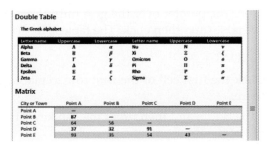

Sort   Formula

TIP To sort a single column, select the column before clicking Layout → Sort and then select the Sort column only check box.

TIP Ascending order is also called alphabetical order when the data is text and chronological order when the data is times or dates.

The contents of the rows in a table can be sorted based on a column. To sort an entire table, select the table and then click Layout → Sort. A dialog box is displayed with options that affect which column to base the sort on and how to sort the data. Ascending (low to high) or Descending (high to low) changes the order based on the text, number, or date.

Calculations can be performed in columns or rows that contain numbers. For example, the total calories in this table are calculated in the bottom-right cell:

Burger Components	Calories
Hamburger Patty	150
Bun	190
Ketchup	50
Total Calories:	390

To perform a calculation in the cell that contains the insertion point, click Layout → Formula. A dialog box is displayed with =SUM(ABOVE) in the Formula box, which indicates the numbers in the column above will be added and the total will be displayed. =SUM(LEFT) indicates the numbers in the same row and to the left of the cell will be added. Select a different function, such as AVERAGE, in the Paste function list. Select OK to perform the calculation. Format the numbers by selecting a format in the Number format list.

Once any data has changed in cells, right-click the cell that contains the calculation and select Update Field to recalculate the amount.

Practice: VOLCANOES – part 2 of 4

Word should already be started with VOLCANOES open from the last practice.

① **INSERT A TABLE**

    a. In the middle of page 2, place the insertion point in the blank paragraph after the sentence that ends "…the last eruption:" Display formatting marks if necessary.

    b. Click Insert → Table. A grid is displayed.

    c. Move the pointer over the grid until three columns and four rows are selected (a 3x4 table) and then click. The table is inserted into the document.

② **ENTER DATA**

    a. Click the first cell of the first row to place the insertion point, if it is not already there.

    b. Type Name and then press the Tab key. The insertion point is now in the second cell of the first row.

    c. Type Country and then press the Tab key.

d. Type Last Eruption and then press the Tab key. The insertion point is now in the first cell of the second row.

e. Enter the remaining data so that your table looks similar to:

Name¤	Country¤	Last·Eruption¤	¤
Mt.·Etna¤	Italy¤	2005¤	¤
White·Island¤	New·Zealand¤	2001¤	¤
Mt.·Hekla¤	Iceland¤	2000¤	¤

③ FORMAT THE DATA

a. Point to the top of the third column until the pointer changes to ↓ and then click. The third column is selected.

b. Click Layout → Align Top Right ▤. The data is right aligned.

c. Point to the left of the first row until the pointer changes to ⇗ and then click. The first row is selected.

d. Use the Home tab to format the row as 14 point and bold. The row height increases with the larger font size.

e. Click anywhere to remove the selection.

④ FORMAT THE TABLE

a. Point to the boundary between the "Name" column and the "Country" column until the pointer changes to ↔.

b. Drag the boundary to the left until the "Name" column is just slightly wider than the data. Word automatically changes the column width of the "Country" column so that the table still fills the space between the left and right margin.

c. Repeat parts (a) and (b) for the "Country" and "Last Eruption" columns. The table no longer fills the space between the left and right margin:

▪ *Eruption·Stage*¶
A·volcanic·eruption·occurs·when·lava,·gasses,·and·other·subterranean·matter·come·out·of·the·ground.·
The·exact·location·of·where·they·come·out·of·is·called·a·vent.·A·volcano·usually·has·more·than·one·vent.·
The·following·table·lists·three·volcanoes·and·the·date·of·the·last·eruption:¶

Name¤	**Country¤**	**Last·Eruption¤**¤
Mt.·Etna¤	Italy¤	2005¤¤
White·Island¤	New·Zealand¤	2001¤¤
Mt.·Hekla¤	Iceland¤	2000¤¤

¶

⑤ ADD A COLUMN AND FORMAT IT

a. Place the insertion point in any cell in the "Last Eruption" column.

b. Click Layout → Insert Left. A new column is inserted to the left.

c. Enter data into the new column:

Name¤	**Country¤**	**Height·(m)¤**	**Last·Eruption¤**¤
Mt.·Etna¤	Italy¤	3350¤	2005¤¤
White·Island¤	New·Zealand¤	321¤	2001¤¤
Mt.·Hekla¤	Iceland¤	1491¤	2000¤¤

d. Double-click the boundary between the last two columns. The "Height (m)" column is narrowed.

⑥ FORMAT A TABLE WITH BORDERS AND SHADING

a. Point to the left of the first row until the pointer changes to 𝒜 and then click. The first row is selected.

b. Click Design → Borders → Top Border. The top border formatting for this row is deselected, and the row no longer has a top border.

c. With the top row still selected, click Design → Shading and click the green color in the top row of Theme Colors. The first row is shaded green.

⑦ ADD A ROW AND CALCULATE DATA

a. Place the insertion point in any cell in the last row.

b. Click Layout → Insert Below. A new row is added to the bottom of the table.

c. In the last cell in the "Country" column, type: Average:

d. Format the text Average: as bold.

e. Place the insertion point in the text Average: and click Layout → Align Top Right ⊞. The text is right aligned.

f. Place the insertion point in the last cell in the "Height (m)" column.

g. Click Layout → Formula. A dialog box is displayed and the Formula box contains =SUM(ABOVE).

    1. Press the Backspace key until SUM(ABOVE) is deleted, but do not delete the equals sign =.

    2. In the Paste function list select AVERAGE. The formula is placed in the Formula box.

    3. In the formula, between the parentheses type ABOVE so that the formula calculates the average using the numbers in the column above it. Your dialog box should look similar to:

    4. Select OK. The calculation is performed and the cell displays the average height of the volcanoes, 1720.67.

Check — Your table should look similar to:

Name¤	Country¤	Height (m)¤	Last Eruption¤¤
Mt.·Etna¤	Italy¤	3350¤	2005¤¤
White·Island¤	New·Zealand¤	321¤	2001¤¤
Mt.·Hekla¤	Iceland¤	1491¤	2000¤¤
¤	**Average:¤**	1720.67¤	¤¤

⑧ FORMAT A TABLE WITH A STYLE

a. Scroll to the top of page 3, to the table that contains information about volcano types.

b. Place the insertion point in any cell in the table.

c. On the Design tab, click the Light Shading ▦ style.

(9) **SORT DATA IN A TABLE**

  a. Move the pointer over the table and click ⊞ in the upper-left corner of the table. The entire table is selected.

  b. Click Layout ➜ Sort. A dialog box is displayed.

  c. In the Sort by list, select Country.

  d. In the Type list, select Text if it is not already selected.

  e. Select Descending and then OK. The table is sorted by row based on the data in the country column, in descending order.

Check — your table should look similar to:

Name¤	Country¤	Volcano-Type¤	¤
Kilauea¤	United·States¤	Shield¤	¤
Mt. Egmont¤	New·Zealand¤	Composite¤	¤
Izalco¤	El·Salvador¤	Cinder·Cone¤	¤

(10) **SAVE THE MODIFIED VOLCANOES**

Creating a Table of Contents

Update Table

Table of Contents

A *table of contents*, or *TOC*, is a list of headings and corresponding page numbers in a document. A table of contents can be created automatically based on heading styles. To create a table of contents at the insertion point, click References ➜ Table of Contents and select a style from the displayed gallery of built-in styles.

Each entry in a table of contents is a hyperlink to the corresponding heading. Click a table of contents entry and then press the Ctrl key to change the pointer to 🖑:

TIP Select References ➜ Table of Contents ➜ Insert Table of Contents to display a dialog box of additional options for creating a table of contents.

TIP Select Insert ➜ Cover Page to display a gallery of predesigned cover pages that can be used in a document or report.

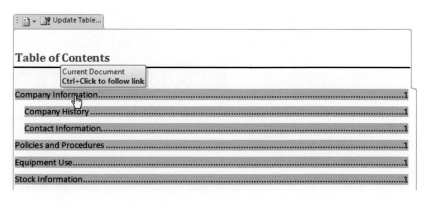

Click a TOC entry to scroll the document and place the insertion point in the corresponding heading.

Word does not automatically update a table of contents when changes are made to a document. Click a table of contents to make it active and then click Update Table in the upper-left corner:

Table of Contents

Alternative Press the F9 key to display the dialog box for updating a selected table of contents.

The Update Table of Contents dialog box is displayed. Select Update entire table to update any headings and corresponding page numbers.

To remove a table of contents, click References → Table of Contents → Remove Table of Contents.

Creating Sections in a Document

Breaks

Long documents often need to have different formatting applied to sections of the document. For example, pages two and three of a document may need to be formatted with two columns, while page one needs only one column.

section break

A *section break* is used to divide a document into sections. Click Page Layout → Breaks, which displays a list of breaks. Select Next Page to end a section and start a new section on the next page, or select Continuous to end a section and start a new section on the same page.

Right-click the status bar at the bottom of the document window and select Section to add an indicator to the status bar that indicates the section that contains the insertion point. When formatting marks are displayed, section breaks are identified by a double line and the type of break.

TIP Select Page Layout → Watermark to display a gallery of watermarks that can be used to insert ghosted text, such as Draft or Confidential, behind the content on the page.

Page formats, such as margins, are applied to only the current section by default. To apply a page format to the Whole document, use the Apply to list in the Page Setup dialog box.

To delete a section break, place the insertion point to the left of the break and press the Delete key.

Section Headers and Footers

Page Number   Link to Previous

A document divided into sections can have different headers and footers in each section. For example, in a report, the page numbers in the footer should start on the first page of the body of the report, not the title page.

By default, each section header and footer contains the same text as the previous section, as noted with the Same as Previous tab:

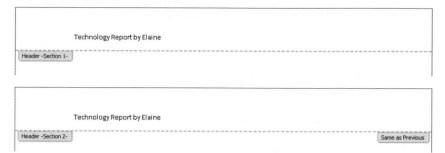

Technology Report by Elaine

Header -Section 1-

Technology Report by Elaine

Header -Section 2-   Same as Previous

Page X of X

Options for including the total number of pages are available if the section has more than one page.

Number Formats

Format	Type
1, 2, 3, ...	Arabic
- 1 -, - 2 -, - 3 -,...	Arabic
a, b, c, ...	letters
A, B, C, ...	letters
i, ii, iii, ...	Roman
I, II, III,...	Roman

To create a different header or footer in a section, place the insertion point in the header and then click Design → Link to Previous so that it is no longer selected. The text in the header area can then be changed and will appear on all pages in that section.

Different page numbering may be required for different parts of a document. *Front matter* is information that comes before the body of a report, such as the title page and table of contents, which are often numbered with small Roman numerals (i, ii, iii, and so on). The *body* of a report contains the information being presented and is usually numbered with Arabic numerals (1, 2, 3, and so on) starting at 1. To format different page numbers, click Design → Page Number → Format Page Numbers to display a dialog box. Select a format in the Number format list. Page numbering can be started at a different number by selecting Start at and then typing the new number.

Hyphenating a Document

Hyphenation

Hyphenating a document is a process that divides words, if necessary, at the end of lines with a hyphen (-) so that part of a word wraps to the next line. Hyphenation can smooth out very ragged right edges in left-aligned text and can lessen the space between words in justified text. To automatically hyphenate a document, click Page Layout → Hyphenation → Automatic. Select Manual to display each word as it is selected for hyphenation.

TIP In the Insert Hyperlink dialog box, change text in the Text to display box to affect what the hyperlink looks like in the document.

Practice: VOLCANOES – part 3 of 4

Word should already be started with VOLCANOES open from the last practice.

① **INSERT A TABLE OF CONTENTS**

a. Scroll to the top of page 2 and place the insertion point in the blank paragraph above the "Introduction" heading.

b. Click References → Table of Contents. A gallery of styles is displayed.

c. Click Automatic Table 2. A table of contents is created at the insertion point.

② USE A HYPERLINK IN THE TABLE OF CONTENTS

   a. Click an entry in the table of contents to make the table active.

   b. Click "Obsidian" in the table of contents.

   c. Hold down the Ctrl key until the pointer changes to 👆 and then click the Obsidian entry. The document is scrolled to the Obsidian heading, and the insertion point is placed in the heading.

③ INSERT A SECTION BREAK

   a. Scroll to page 2, below the table of contents, and place the insertion point to the left of the "I" at the beginning of the "Introduction" heading.

   b. Click Page Layout → Breaks → Next Page. A section break is inserted between pages 2 and 3 and the main text of the report is moved to page 3.

   c. If the status bar does not display "Section: 2," right-click the status bar and select Section and then click anywhere in the document. "Section: 2" is displayed because the insertion point is in section 2.

④ ADD A HEADER AND FOOTER

   a. At the top of page 2, click the table of contents. The table of contents is selected, an Update Table tab is displayed, and the status bar displays "Section: 1."

   b. Click Insert → Page Number → Bottom of Page → Plain Number 2. A footer is created with a centered page number.

   c. Click Design → Go To Header. The insertion point is moved to the header.

   d. Type your first and last names.

⑤ FORMAT THE PAGE NUMBERS IN EACH SECTION

   a. Click Design → Different First Page. The header and footer are removed from the title page of the document.

   b. Click Design → Go To Footer. The insertion point is moved to the footer of section 1.

   c. Click Design → Page Number → Format Page Numbers. A dialog box is displayed.

      1. In the Number format list, select i, ii, iii, ….

      2. Select OK. The dialog box is removed. Scroll to the bottom of the table of contents page. The page number in the footer is "ii" because it is the second page in the document.

   d. Click Design → Close Header and Footer. The header and footer are dimmed.

⑥ FORMAT THE PAGE NUMBER IN THE FOOTER OF SECTION 2

   a. Scroll through the document to view the dimmed footer text. Note that the page numbers in the footer in section 2 need to be formatted to start numbering at 1.

   b. On any page in section 2, double-click the footer.

   c. Click Design → Link to Previous 🖼 to deselect it. The footer in section 2 can now be formatted differently than the footer in section 1.

   d. Click Design → Page Number → Format Page Numbers. A dialog box is displayed.

1. Select the options as shown:

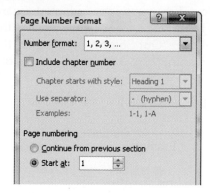

2. Select OK. The page number is formatted as Arabic numerals starting with number 1.

e. Click Design → Close Header and Footer. The header and footer are dimmed.

⑦ HYPHENATE THE DOCUMENT AND UPDATE THE TABLE OF CONTENTS

a   Click Page Layout → Hyphenation → Automatic. Word hyphenates the document. Scroll through the document and look for hyphenated words.

b. Scroll to the table of contents.

c. Click the table of contents to select it.

d. In the upper-left corner of the table of contents, click Update Table. A dialog box is displayed.

e. Select Update entire table and then OK. The table of contents now shows the correct page numbers.

⑧ SAVE THE MODIFIED VOLCANOES

Using Outline View

Outline View

To display a document in Outline view, click View → Outline. *Outline view* displays the organization of a document.

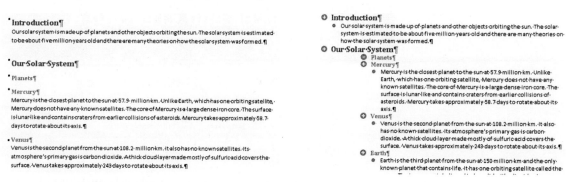

Print Layout view   *Outline view*

In Outline view, styles are used to determine heading levels and body text. Paragraphs are indented according to their levels, for example the Heading 1 style is at a higher level than Heading 2. In the example shown above, "Our Solar System" is in the Heading 1 style and "Planets" is Heading 2 style. Paragraphs with the Normal style are the lowest level.

A document can be edited by topic in Outline view using options on the Outlining tab:

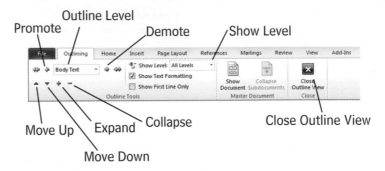

- Click **Promote** ⇐ or **Demote** ⇒ to apply the next higher or lower level style, respectively.

- Click **Demote to Body Text** ⇒⇒ to apply the Normal style, or **Promote to Heading 1** ⇐⇐ to apply the Heading 1 style.

- Click **Move Up** ▲ or **Move Down** ▼ to move the paragraph before or after the preceding paragraph, respectively.

- Click **Expand** ✛ or **Collapse** ➖ to display or hide the text under the heading containing the insertion point, respectively.

- Use **Show Levels** All Levels ▾ to display different heading levels. Body text is only displayed when **Show All Levels** is selected.

Icons next to text in the document in Outline view indicate levels:

- ● Body text
- ⊕ Headings followed by a paragraph with a lower level
- ⊖ Headings followed by a paragraph with the same level

Entire topics can be selected by clicking ⊕ next to a heading, which selects that heading and the text under it. Click Outlining → Move Up ▲ or Outlining → Move Down ▼ or drag ⊕ to move a selected topic. Click Outlining → Close Outline View to display the document in Print Layout view.

Citing Sources and Creating a Bibliography

A *bibliography* is a list of the sources cited and consulted in preparation of a document. A bibliography is usually on a separate page at the end of

citations

a document and is sometimes titled "Works Cited." Within a document, *citations* are used to refer to bibliography entries:

on was Salyut 1 and it was launched c
aunched. (Brooks, 1994) The first spa
the International Space Station was s
in use and still expanding with contir

This citation refers to the Brooks bibliography entry

Word maintains a Master List of sources for all documents. To add a new source or manage existing sources, click References → Manage Sources. A dialog box is displayed:

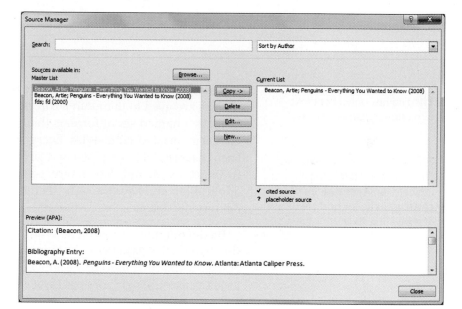

TIP When adding information for a source, select **Show All Bibliography Fields** check box for additional fields.

TIP MLA stands for Modern Language Association and APA stands for American Psychological Association.

Select New to add information for a source. Sources can be copied to or deleted from the Current List, which affect the open document. Sources are added automatically to the Current List when a source is cited in the document. Deleting a source from the current list does not remove it from the Master List.

To create a citation, place the insertion point where the citation should appear in the document and click References → Insert Citation. All sources in the Current List are displayed. Click a source to create the citation. To add page numbers, click the citation and then select Edit Citation:

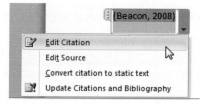

TIP Select **Edit Source** to edit the source for a citation.

A dialog box is displayed with options for adding page numbers and other modifications.

To create a bibliography, click References → Bibliography and click a format for the bibliography. A bibliography is created at the insertion point using all sources in the Current List. The bibliography is automatically updated when any changes are made to the sources in the Current List.

Word formats citations and bibliographies based on the selected bibliography style. To choose a bibliography style, use the Style list on the References tab. The list includes the commonly used MLA and APA styles.

Themes

Colors

Fonts

Themes

Effects

TIP Themes only affect text formatted in named styles

TIP At the top of the Font list, "(Body)" and "(Headings)" indicate the fonts used in the chosen theme for body text and heading styles.

Just as styles are used to maintain consistent formatting in a document, themes are used to maintain a consistent look in multiple documents. A *theme* is a named set of formats that change the colors, fonts, and other effects associated with styles. Every style is affected as well as elements such as tables, bibliographies, and tables of contents. Themes are accessible in Word, Excel, and PowerPoint, so that documents created in all three applications can have the same theme and look like part of a professional document package.

By default, the Office theme is applied to a new document. To change the theme, click Page Layout → Themes and click a theme in the gallery. To change formatting used in the applied theme, click Page Layout → Colors ▾, Page Layout → A Fonts ▾, or Page Layout → Effects ▾.

Practice: VOLCANOES – part 4 of 4

Word should already be started with VOLCANOES open from the last practice.

① **DISPLAY VOLCANOES IN OUTLINE VIEW**

   a. Scroll to the beginning of the body text and place the insertion point in the "Introduction" heading.

   b. Select View → Outline. The document is displayed in Outline view.

② **DISPLAY DIFFERENT LEVELS OF HEADINGS**

   a. Click Outlining → Show Level → Level 1. Only the headings with the Heading 1 style are displayed.

   b. Click Outlining → Show Level → Level 2. Heading levels 1 and 2 are displayed.

   c. Click Outlining → Show Level → Level 3. All three heading levels are displayed.

③ **MOVE THE "TYPES OF LAVA ROCKS" TOPIC**

   a. Click ⊕ next to the "Types of Lava Rocks" heading. The entire topic, including lower level headings, is selected.

   b. Click Outlining → Move Up ▲ . The selected topic is moved before the "Composite Volcanoes" heading.

c. Click Outlining → Move Up ▲ three more times. The selected topic is moved before the "Types of Volcanoes" topic and its headings:

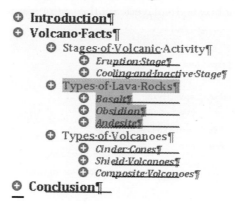

d. Click Outlining → Show Level → All Levels. Note that the text under each heading also moved.

e. Click Outlining → Show Level → Level 3.

f. Click Outlining → Close Outline View. The document is again displayed in Print Layout view.

④ INSERT A CITATION USING A PLACEHOLDER

a. Scroll to the middle of page 4 to the "Cinder Cones" heading and place the insertion point after the period at the end of the sentence "Cinder cone volcanoes are formed from explosive eruptions."

b. Click References → Insert Citation → Add New Placeholder. A dialog box is displayed.

c. Type Jensen and select OK. A placeholder is created for the citation:

e·eruptions.·(Jensen)·Because·the
cool·before·they·hit·the·ground.·∕

⑤ ADD AND MANAGE SOURCES

a. Click References → Manage Sources. A dialog box is displayed. Note the "Jensen" source from the placeholder just created, which appears in the Current List with a question mark next to it.

b. In the Current List, click "Jensen" and then select Edit. A dialog box is displayed. Set the options as shown:

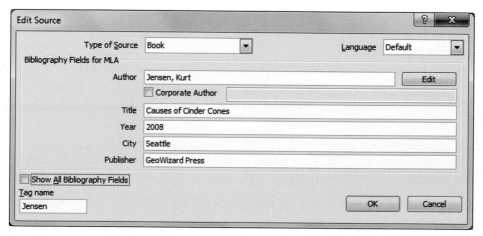

c. Select OK and then select Copy. The source is added to the Master List and Current List.

d. Select New. A dialog box is displayed. Set the options as shown:

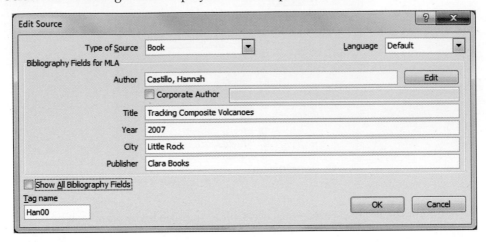

e. Select OK. The source is added to the Master List and Current List.

f. Select New. A dialog box is displayed. Set the options as shown:

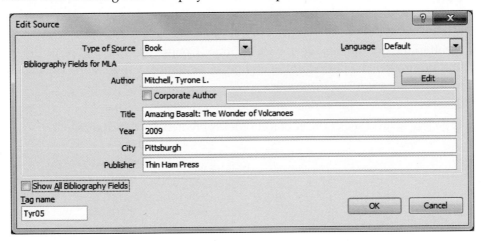

g. Select OK. The source is added to the Master List and Current List.

h. Click Close. The Source Manager dialog box is closed and the document is displayed with the Jensen citation active.

⑥ **EDIT A CITATION AND CHANGE THE STYLE**

a. On page 2 in the Cinder Cones section, click [Jensen] ▾ and select Edit Citation. A dialog box is displayed.

b. In the Pages box type 34 and select OK. The page number is added.

c. Click References → Style → APA if it is not already selected. The styles set by the American Psychological Association for use in research papers are followed to format the citation.

d. Click References → Style → MLA. The styles set by the Modern Language Association for use in research papers are followed to format the citation. Note the differences in the citation in the document.

⑦ **INSERT CITATIONS USING EXISTING SOURCES**

a. Scroll down to the "Composite Volcanoes" heading and place the insertion point after the period at the end of the paragraph which ends "…several kilometers."

   b. Click References → Insert Citation and then select the "Castillo, Hannah" source from the list. The citation is entered.

   c. Click [Castillo] and select Edit Citation. A dialog box is displayed.

   d. In the Pages box type 120-125 and select OK. Page numbers are added.

   e. Scroll up to the "Basalt" heading and place the insertion point after the period at the end of the paragraph which ends "…silica, or aluminum."

   f. Insert a citation for "Mitchell, Tyrone L."

   g. Edit the citation to reference page 62.

⑧ **INSERT A BIBLIOGRAPHY**

   a. Scroll to the end of the document and place the insertion point in the blank paragraph below the "Conclusion" heading.

   b. Click Page Layout → Breaks → Next Page in the list. A section break is inserted.

   c. Click References → Bibliography → Bibliography. A bibliography is created at the insertion point. Scroll up if necessary to view the bibliography.

⑨ **CHANGE THE THEME**

   a. Click Page Layout → Themes → Apex. The theme is changed from the Office theme to the Apex theme. Scroll through the document and note how the styles and elements have changed, which affects the look and the pagination of the document.

   b. Click Page Layout → Themes → Equity. The theme is changed again.

   c. Click Page Layout → Colors → Urban. The color scheme of the theme is changed but the fonts remain the same.

⑩ **UPDATE THE TOC AND FORMAT PAGE NUMBERS**

   a. Scroll to the second page of the document and click the table of contents to select it.

   b. In the upper-left corner of the table of contents, click Update Table. A dialog box is displayed.

   c. Select Update entire table and then OK. The table of contents is updated. The page number for the bibliography restarted at number 1.

   d. Scroll to the footer on the bibliography page and double-click the footer.

   e. Click Design → Page Number → Format Page Numbers. A dialog box is displayed.

      1. Select the Continue from previous section option and then select OK. The number in the footer changes to 3.

   f. Click Design → Close Header and Footer. The header and footer are dimmed.

   g. Scroll to the table of contents and update it again. The bibliography page number is now correct.

⑪ **SAVE, PRINT, AND CLOSE THE MODIFIED VOLCANOES**

Creating SmartArt Graphics

SmartArt graphics are diagrams that show relationships between elements and are used to illustrate information. *Elements* may be people, tasks, goals, statistics, or similar information. In a SmartArt graphic, elements are represented by shapes. To create a SmartArt graphic at the insertion point, click Insert → SmartArt which displays a dialog box:

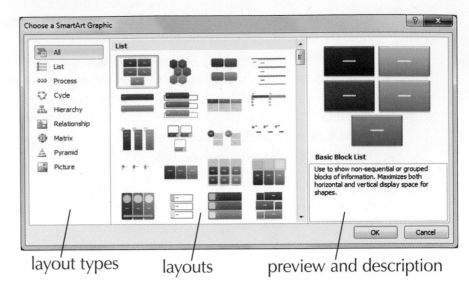

layout types   layouts   preview and description

TIP To display the Text pane, click Design → Text Pane or click on the selected SmartArt graphic.

TIP A flowchart can be created using a **Vertical Bending Process** layout, and then changing the shapes as needed for flowchart items.

TIP To make a Venn diagram, which shows overlapping relationships, use a **Relationship** layout.

Select a layout type to limit the displayed layouts to that type. Click a layout to view a preview and description. Select OK to place a SmartArt graphic at the insertion point. The Text pane is displayed. Type text in the Text pane or directly into the [Text] placeholders in the graphic. Use arrow keys in the Text pane to move between items, or create a new item by pressing the Enter key.

When creating a SmartArt graphic, consider the information that will be included and what message should be conveyed by the graphic:

- List layouts show non-sequential information.
- Process layouts illustrate steps in a timeline or a process.
- Cycle layouts illustrate steps in an ongoing process.
- Hierarchy layouts are used for decision trees or organization charts.
- Relationship layouts illustrate connections between elements or to a central element.
- Matrix layouts show separate parts relating to a each other or a to a whole.
- Pyramid layouts shows relationships in proportion to each other.

Formatting a SmartArt Graphic

Add Bullet   Promote   Demote

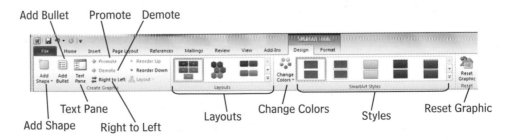

Text Pane   Layouts   Change Colors   Styles   Reset Graphic
Add Shape   Right to Left

A SmartArt graphic can be formatted and edited in many ways. The font, size, and font style of selected text is formatted using the Mini toolbar or options on the Home tab. To add additional shapes or items to a SmartArt graphic, click Design → Add Bullet ⊞ or Design → Add Shape. Click Design → Right to Left ⇄ to change the arrangement of shapes to a mirror image.

To move a selected shape up or down a level, click Design → Promote or Design → Demote ⇒.

To change the size of a shape, select the shape to display handles. Point to a corner handle, which changes the pointer to ⟋, and then drag to size the shape. Hold down the Shift key while dragging to proportionately size the shape. To change a shape, right-click the selected shape and select Change Shape in the displayed menu. To change the size of the entire SmartArt graphic, drag a resize handle in a corner of the graphic:

The look of a SmartArt graphic can be changed by applying styles, changing colors of the shapes, and changing the layout. To apply a style, click a SmartArt style on the Design tab. To change the colors of the shapes, click Design → Change Colors and then click a color combination in the displayed gallery. Themes affect the color combinations and styles applied to SmartArt graphics. Changing the theme changes the available color combinations and styles and the effects of the shapes.

Shapes and text can be formatted using options on the Format tab:

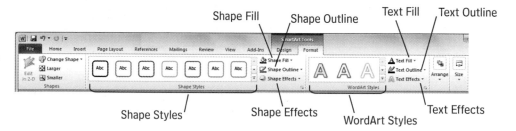

TIP Shapes can be sized using Format → Smaller and Format → Larger or changed using Format → Change Shape.

- Click Shape Fill, Shape Outline, Text Fill, or Text Outline to change the fill and outline of shapes and text. Shape Styles and WordArt Styles apply several formats at once.

- Click Shape Effects or Text Effects to change the look of shapes and text:

Layouts of the same layout type can be selected on the Design tab. To change the layout to a different layout type, click More Layouts and then select More Layouts to display the Choose a SmartArt Graphic dialog box.

Click Design → Reset Graphic to reverse the edits made to a SmartArt graphic.

Formatting a Document in Columns

Columns   Breaks

Columns are commonly used in newspapers, magazines, and other long publications to make lines of text easier to read. Columns are also used to format documents such as brochures. Click Page Layout → Columns and then select an option to format the document into columns. Click Page Layout → Columns → More Columns to display a dialog box with additional options:

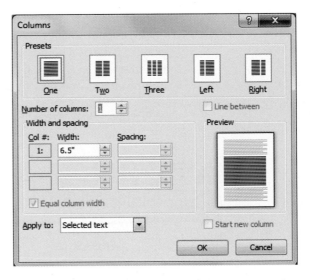

- Change the number of columns in the Presets options or type a number in the Number of columns box.
- To add a line between columns select the Line between check box.
- Change column widths in the Width and Spacing options.

column break   To control the flow of text between columns, place a *column break* where a column of text should end. Text after a column break is moved to the next column. To insert a column break at the insertion point, select Page Layout → Breaks [icon] → Column.

Creating a Brochure

Brochures are often used as advertising or as informative publications. A *brochure* is typically a single sheet of paper, printed on both sides, and folded two or three times to create a smaller publication that can be handed out, mailed, or placed in a strategic location where interested people can pick one up.

two-fold brochure   One common brochure layout is a *two-fold brochure*, which has six panels of information:

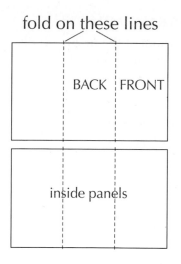

fold on these lines

BACK | FRONT

inside panels

TIP *Landscape orientation* means the paper is printed across the widest part, and *Portrait orientation* is when the paper is printed across the narrowest part.

Templates can be used to create brochures that already have graphics and formatting. To create a brochure from scratch, a two-page document is set up in landscape orientation with all margins 0.5" and three equal columns 1" apart. Click Page Layout ➞ Orientation ➞ Landscape to change the orientation of the page. Column breaks are used to start a new column, and a next page section break is used at the bottom of the "FRONT" panel (above) to start the second page.

purpose

audience

Text and graphics are added to the document and formatted with the purpose and the audience of the brochure in mind. The *purpose* of the brochure is the goal, for example to inform people about preparing taxes properly or to encourage people to hire you for your services. The *audience* of the brochure are the people that will read it.

The text and graphics in a brochure are restricted to narrow columns, and the design should consider the column width:

- Use left alignment for paragraphs of text. Headings are usually left aligned or centered.

- A font size of 8 to 12 point is best for paragraphs of text.

- Graphics should be appropriate for the purpose and audience.

When the brochure is finished, print a copy, fold it, and review it thoroughly before printing copies to distribute. If a printer does not have the capability to print both sides of the paper, print one side then put the paper back in the printer and print the other side. The Word document can also be brought to a printing company for professional printing on a variety of paper, and most companies have folding and mailing services.

Practice: TUTORING

① OPEN TUTORING AND APPLY PAGE FORMATTING

a. Open TUTORING, which is a Word data file for this text, and display formatting marks if they are not already displayed.

b. Click Page Layout ➞ Orientation ➞ Landscape. The document is formatted in landscape orientation.

c. Click Page Layout ➞ Margins ➞ Narrow. The margins are all 0.5".

② **INSERT A PYRAMID DIAGRAM**

a. At the bottom of the first page, place the insertion point in the blank paragraph below the words "Get to the TOP!"

b. Click Insert → SmartArt. A dialog box is displayed.

　　1. In the layout types, click Pyramid.

　　2. Click the Basic Pyramid ▲.

　　3. Select OK. A SmartArt graphic is created.

c. Click in the top [Text] placeholder and type: "A" students

d. Click in the middle [Text] placeholder and type: "B" students

e. In the bottom placeholder type: "C" students

f. Click anywhere in the SmartArt graphic except on text or a shape. The SmartArt graphic is selected, and none of the shapes or text objects are selected.

g. Drag a corner handle until the SmartArt graphic is half as tall and less than half as wide.

h. Click outside the SmartArt graphic. The graphic is no longer selected:

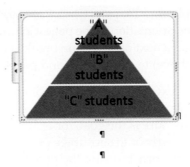

and their school work better. Whether you just need a little help to get through a diffic
ugh tutoring you gain knowledge and insight to different ways to attack problems and

③ **FORMAT THE DOCUMENT WITH COLUMNS**

a. Scroll to the top of page 1 and place the insertion point in the first paragraph.

b. Click Page Layout → Columns → Two. The document is formatted in two columns.

c. Click Page Layout → Columns → More Columns. A dialog box is displayed.

d. Change the Presets to Three and the Spacing to 1". When the spacing is changed, the Width may automatically adjust:

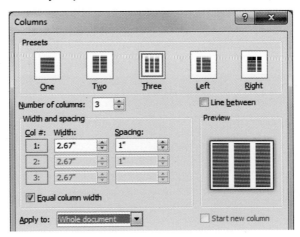

e. Select OK. The document is now set up for a brochure.

④ **FORMAT TEXT**

a. At the top of page 1, place the insertion point in the text "Your Report Card could look like:" and click Home ➡ Heading 1. The Heading 1 style is applied.

b. Place the insertion point to the left of "Your" in "Your Report Card could look like:" and press Enter three times. The text is moved down.

c. Place the insertion point in the blank paragraph below the report card table.

d. Select Page Layout ➡ Breaks ➡ Column. A column break is inserted and the text below the break is moved to the next column, which is the middle column:

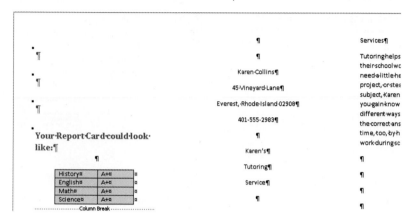

e. Place the insertion point at the top of the middle column and press Enter until the name and address are moved down near the middle of the column.

f. Place the insertion point in the blank paragraph below the phone number in the middle column.

g. Select Page Layout ➡ Breaks ➡ Column. A column break is inserted and the text below the break is moved to the next column.

h. Apply the Title style to the "Karen's Tutoring Service" paragraphs.

i. Place the insertion point to the left of "Karen's " in "Karen's Tutoring Service" and press Enter until "Karen's Tutoring Service" is near the middle of the column.

⑤ **FORMAT THE SECOND PAGE OF THE BROCHURE**

a. Place the insertion point in the blank paragraph below the "Karen's Tutoring Service" paragraphs.

b. Select Page Layout ➡ Breaks ➡ Column. A column break is inserted and text is moved to the next page.

c. In the first column on page 2, apply the Heading 1 style to the "Karen Can Help You Get to the TOP!" paragraphs.

d. Place the insertion point to the right of the "!" in "Get to the TOP!" and press Enter three times. The SmartArt graphic is moved down.

e. Below the SmartArt graphic, place the insertion point to the left of "Services."

f. Select Page Layout ➡ Breaks ➡ Column. A column break is inserted.

g. At the bottom on the middle column, below the table, place the insertion point to the left of "About Your Tutor."

h. Select Page Layout ➡ Breaks ➡ Column. A column break is inserted.

i. Apply the Heading 2 style to "Services" at the top of the middle column and "About Your Tutor" at the top of the last column.

j. In the last column, apply the Heading 1 style to the text "Karen can help you succeed!"

⑥ SAVE, PREVIEW, AND PRINT THE BROCHURE

a. Save the modified TUTORING.

b. Preview the brochure. The pages should look similar to:

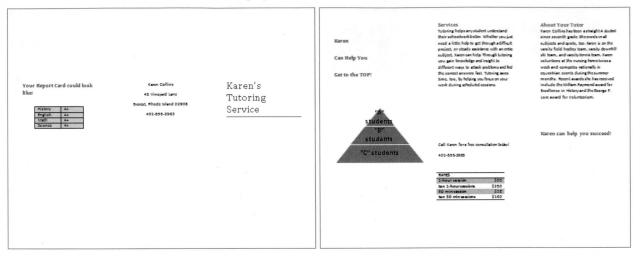

c. Add a footer to the document with your name centered.

d. Save the modified document.

e. Print a copy, then put the pages with the non-printed sides back to back. Fold in thirds, so that "Karen's Tutoring Service" is on the front and her address and phone number are on the back.

f. Close TUTORING.

Creating a Hyperlink to a Heading

Hyperlink

A hyperlink can be used to quickly scroll to a heading. For example, entries in a table of contents are hyperlinks to headings in the same document. To create a hyperlink from selected text to a heading, click Insert → Hyperlink. The Insert Hyperlink dialog box includes the Place in This Document options for inserting a hyperlink to a heading. Click a heading in the dialog box to select the destination for the hyperlink.

Once a hyperlink is created, point to the hyperlink, press the Ctrl key to change the pointer to 🖑 and click to follow the link. To remove a hyperlink, right-click the link and select Remove Hyperlink from the menu.

Text Box

Text boxes are objects that can be moved and sized like a graphic but contain text. To create a text box, click Insert → Text Box and select a style from the displayed gallery of built-in styles. The first choice in the gallery is Simple Text Box style, which creates a text box similar to:

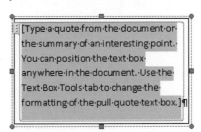

Type text to replace the placeholder text. The text can be formatted using tabs on the Ribbon just like any other text.

When a text box is selected, the Text Box Tools Format tab is displayed on the Ribbon:

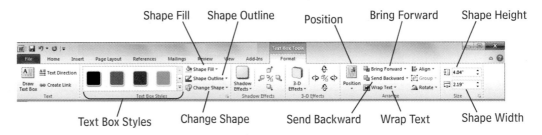

- Click Shape Fill or Shape Outline to format the fill and outline of the text box.

- Click Change Shape to change the shape of the text box.

- Change the size of the text box by dragging a handle or using Shape Height and Shape Width for precise sizing.

To position the text box on a page, move the pointer to the text box border and click to select the object:

Drag the text box border to position it on the page. Click Format → Position and select a position to quickly line the text box up with text on the page. Use options in Format → Wrap Text to adjust the wrap if necessary.

Creating a Newsletter

Companies, clubs, and organizations often produce newsletters to inform their employees or members of upcoming events and issues.

nameplate

masthead

Newsletters have several common elements. Most newsletters have a headline, byline, and body text for each article, a nameplate, a table of contents, and a masthead. The *nameplate* is the area at the top of the first page that contains the title and date of the publication. The table of contents is usually on the first page. The *masthead* is an area that includes the publisher's contact information and reprint policy. The masthead is typically placed on the second page.

Newsletters are usually formatted in two or three columns with page numbers in a header or footer. Page numbers typically are not included on the first and last page.

TIP To change the page background, select **Page Layout → Page Color.**

To create a newsletter in Word, use sections to allow for different page formats such as columns. The first page can be divided into sections with the nameplate in one section, articles in another section, and the table of contents in a text box. Additional sections can be added as needed for different page formats:

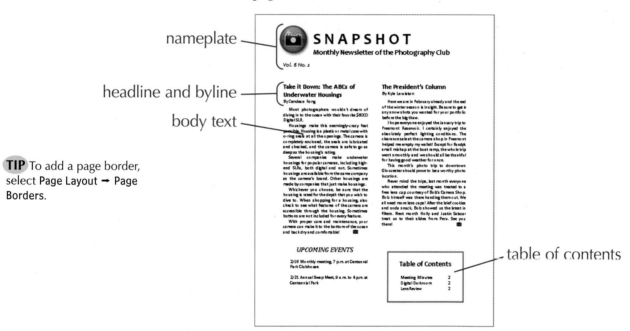

nameplate

headline and byline

body text

table of contents

TIP To add a page border, select **Page Layout → Page Borders.**

TIP PDF files are discussed in Chapter 1.

Most print shops will accept Word files and print large numbers of copies using a digital system or a printing press. PDF files are better for submitting to a print shop, because the fonts and graphics are automatically included in the file.

The printed newsletter can be bound in many ways. The most simple binding is to print the newsletter using both sides of the paper and then staple the pages together in the upper-left corner. If the newsletter is printed at a printing company, the pages may be printed on 11" x 17" paper and folded in half to create 8.5" x 11" pages, and no staple is necessary.

Traditionally, newsletters are published by distributing printed copies by mail to the recipients. An alternative method of distributing is to e-mail a file to the recipients, who can print the document as needed or just read it on the screen. When distributing in this manner, hyperlinks are helpful to the reader to quickly display other areas in the document. PDF files are better for e-mailing to recipients as well, because the document will look the same for everyone. A Word document may look different if the recipient does not have all the fonts or has different printer drivers installed.

Practice: SPACE TRANSMISSIONS

① **OPEN SPACE TRANSMISSIONS**

Open SPACE TRANSMISSIONS, which is a Word data file for this text, and display formatting marks if they are not already displayed.

② **CREATE THE TITLE AREA AND FORMAT SECTION 2 IN TWO COLUMNS**

a. Near the top of page 1, place the insertion point to the left of the "M" at the beginning of "March" in the "March Meeting" heading.

b. Click Page Layout → Breaks 📄 → Continuous. A section break is inserted. Section 1 is now the title area of the newsletter.

c. Check that the insertion point is in section 2 of the document.

d. Click Page Layout → Columns → Two. Section 2 is formatted into two columns.

e. Place the insertion point in the "March Meeting" heading, and change Page Layout → Spacing → Before to 0.

f. At the bottom of the first column, place the insertion point to the left of the "P" in the "President's Letter" heading.

g. Change Page Layout → Spacing → Before to 0.

h. With the insertion point still in the "President's Letter" heading, click Page Layout → Breaks 📄 → Column. The heading is moved to the top of the second column.

③ **FORMAT THE REMAINING PAGES IN THREE COLUMNS**

a. At the bottom of page 1, place the insertion point to the left of the "H" in the "Humans in Space" heading.

b. Click Page Layout → Breaks 📄 → Next Page. The text is moved to page 2.

c. With the insertion point still in the "Humans in Space" heading, change Page Layout → Spacing → Before to 0.

d. Click Page Layout → Columns → Three. The text is formatted in three columns.

④ **CREATE AND FORMAT A TEXT BOX**

a. At the bottom of page 1, place the insertion point after "Lopez" in the text "President M. Lopez."

b. Click Insert → Text Box → Simple Text Box. A text box is created.

c. Type the following text, with a single tab between headings and page numbers:

```
In·This·Issue¶

Humans·in·Space    →    2¶

Mission·to·Mars2¶

Recruitment·Techniques    →    2¶
```

d. Click Format → Shape Styles → Subtle Effect - Blue, Accent 1.

e. Format "In This Issue" in the Heading 1 style.

f. Format the three paragraphs below the "In This Issue" heading in the No Spacing style.

g. Format the three paragraphs below the "In This Issue" heading with a right-aligned tab stop at 2".

h. Move the pointer to the text box border and drag the text box down so that the end of the President's Message is completely displayed:

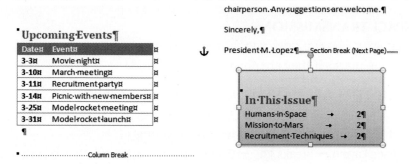

⑤ CREATE A HYPERLINK TO A HEADING

a. In the President's Message on page 1, select "recruitment techniques:"

b. Click Insert → Hyperlink. A dialog box is displayed.

1. Select Place in This Document to display those options and then click "Recruitment Techniques" in the Headings:

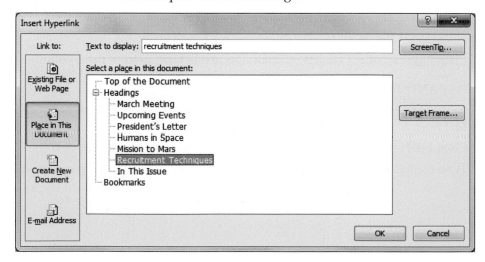

2. Select OK. The words "recruitment techniques" are now a hyperlink.

   c. Point to the hyperlink, hold down the Ctrl key until the pointer changes to 🖑 and then click. The document is scrolled to the Recruitment Techniques article on page 2, and the insertion point is placed in the heading.

⑥ SAVE THE MODIFIED SPACE TRANSMISSIONS
   a. Create a footer with your name left aligned.
   b. Save the modified SPACE TRANSMISSIONS.

⑦ PRINT AND THEN CLOSE SPACE TRANSMISSIONS

⑧ QUIT WORD

Chapter Summary

This chapter discussed formatting documents using styles, themes, columns, sections, and other features typically found in long documents. Creating tables, SmartArt graphics, brochures, and newsletters were also introduced.

A style is a named set of formats. Styles are applied using the Quick Styles gallery on the Home tab. A table of contents, or TOC, is based on heading styles applied to text and is created using the References tab.

A table consists of rows and columns of cells, and is created using the Insert tab. Text is entered in a cell and can be formatted. Using the Design and Layout tabs, rows or columns can be selected and then formatted, deleted, or added. The contents of the rows in a table can be sorted, and numbers in adjacent cells can be used in calculations.

A document is divided into sections by inserting section breaks using the Page Layout tab. Sections can have different headers and footers. Different page numbering can be applied to each section.

A document is hyphenated using the Page Layout tab, which improves the look and flow of text.

Outline view is displayed using the View tab and shows the organization of a document. In Outline view, Word uses styles to determine heading levels and body text. The Outlining tab is used to edit the outline by topic.

A bibliography is a list of sources. The entries in the list of sources are called citations. Citation is also used to describe the notation within a document that refers to a source listed in the bibliography. Using the References tab, citations can be added and a bibliography can be automatically created.

Themes are named sets of formats that change the colors, fonts, and other effects associated with styles. Text styles, table styles, footers, and TOCs are all affected by changing the theme using the Page Layout tab.

Using the Insert tab, SmartArt graphics can be created for diagrams and organization charts. SmartArt graphics can be modified in many ways using the Design and Format tabs.

A document or a section can be formatted in columns using the Page Layout tab. A document can include a hyperlink to text that has a heading style applied to it using the Insert tab.

A text box is used to place text on a page and move it like an object. Text boxes are created and formatted using the Insert and Format tabs.

Brochures and newsletters can be created in Word using many of the formatting techniques covered in this chapter, including sections, columns, and text boxes.

Vocabulary

Audience The people that read the publication.

Bibliography A list of sources.

Body The information presented in a report.

Body text The main paragraphs in a document.

Boundary The lines separating rows and columns in a table.

Brochure A single sheet of paper with information on both sides and folded two or three times to create a smaller publication.

Cell The intersection of a row and column in a table.

Citation An entry in the list of sources. Also the notation within a document that refers to a source listed in the bibliography.

Column Vertical cells in a table.

Column break Used to end a column of text. Text after the break is moved into the next column.

Elements Parts of a diagram.

Front matter Content at the beginning of a report.

Headings Titles that are often bold and in a larger and different font than the body text.

Hyphenating A process that divides a word, when necessary, at the end of a line with a hyphen (-) so part of the word wraps to the next line.

Masthead An area in a newsletter, typically placed on the second page, that includes the publisher's contact information and reprint policy.

Nameplate The area at the top of the first page of a newsletter that contains the title and date of the publication.

Outline view Displays the organization of a document.

Purpose The goal of a publication.

Quick Styles Styles included in Word to format text.

Row Horizontal cells in a table.

Section break Divides a document into sections.

SmartArt graphics Diagrams showing relationships between elements, which are used to illustrate information in documents.

Style A named set of formats.

Table of contents A list of headings and corresponding page numbers.

Text box An object that contains text but can be moved and sized like a graphic.

Theme Named set of formats that changes colors, fonts, and other effects associated with styles.

Title area A section at the top of a newsletter that contains information about the publication.

TOC *See* Table of contents.

Two-fold brochure A brochure layout that has six panels of information.

Add Bullet ⊟ Adds a bullet to a SmartArt graphic. Found on the Design tab.

Add New Placeholder Displays a dialog box used to add a placeholder for a citation if the source does not yet exist in the list of sources. Found in References → Insert Citation.

Add Shape Adds a bullet to a SmartArt graphic. Found on the Design tab.

Automatic Hyphenates a document automatically. Found in Page Layout → Hyphenation.

Bibliography Displays a gallery used to insert a bibliography. Found on the References tab.

Borders ⊞▾ Displays options used to change the cell borders. Found on the Design tab.

Breaks ⊟▾ Displays a list of breaks to insert at the insertion point. Found on the Page Layout tab.

Cell Margins Displays a dialog box used to change the distance from the cell contents to the edges of the cell. Found on the Layout tab.

Change Colors Displays a gallery of color combinations used to change the colors of a SmartArt graphic. Found on the Design tab.

Change Shape Displays other shapes for a text box. Found in the menu displayed by right-clicking a shape in a SmartArt graphic.

Clear Formatting 🔲 Changes the formatting of the paragraph to Normal style. Found on the Home tab or by clicking More Styles ▾ on the Home tab.

Close Outline View Displays the document in Print Layout view. Found on the Outlining tab.

Collapse ▬ Hides the body text under the heading. Found on the Outlining tab.

Colors 🔳▾ Displays a gallery used to change the theme color scheme. Found on the Page Layout tab.

Columns Displays options for formatting a document in columns. Found on the Page Layout tab.

Convert to Text Displays a dialog box for converting the selected table to text. Found on the Format tab.

Convert Text to Table Creates a table from selected text that is separated by tabs. Found in Insert → Table.

Delete Displays options for removing cells, columns, rows, or an entire table. Found on the Layout tab.

Delete *stylename* Delete a style completely from a document. Found in the menu displayed by right-clicking a style in the Styles window

Demote ▸ Applies the next lower level style to the paragraph containing the insertion point. Found on the Outlining tab.

Demote ▸ Moves a selected shape down a level in a SmartArt graphic. Found on the Design tab.

Demote to Body Text ⇝ Applies the Normal style to the paragraph containing the insertion point. Found on the Outlining tab.

Edit Citation Displays a dialog box used to add page numbers and make changes to a citation. Found in the menu displayed by clicking ▾ in a citation.

Effects ▣▾ Displays a gallery used to change the effects used in the theme. Found on the Page Layout tab.

Expand ⊕ Displays the body text under the heading containing the insertion point. Found on the Outlining tab.

Fonts 🄰▾ Displays a gallery used to change the fonts used in the theme. Found on the Page Layout tab.

Format Page Numbers Displays a dialog box used to change the formatting of page numbers. Found in Design → Page Number.

Formula Displays a dialog box used to add a formula in a cell that calculates numbers in adjacent cells. Found on the Layout tab.

Hyperlink Displays a dialog box used to insert a hyperlink. Found on the Insert tab.

Hyphenation ᵇᶜ▾ Displays options for hyphenating a document. Found on the Page Layout tab.

Insert Above Adds a row above the selected row in a table. Found on the Layout tab.

Insert Below Adds a row below the selected row in a table. Found on the Layout tab.

Insert Citation Displays a list of sources to choose from to add a citation at the insertion point. Found on the References tab.

Insert Left Adds a column to the left of the selected column in a table. Found on the Layout tab.

Insert Right Adds a column to the right of the selected column in a table. Found on the Layout tab.

Landscape Changes the orientation of a document to print across the widest part of the paper. Found in Page Layout → Orientation.

Link to Previous 🖼 Selected to have the same header or footer as the previous section. Found on the Design tab.

Manage Sources Displays a dialog box used to add, change, or move sources. Found on the References tab.

More Columns Displays a dialog box used to format columns in a document. Found in Page Layout → Columns.

Move Down ↓ Moves the paragraph containing the insertion point to after the preceding paragraph. Found on the Outlining tab.

Move Up ↑ Moves the paragraph containing the insertion point to before the preceding paragraph. Found on the Outlining tab.

Outline Displays a document in Outline view. Found on the View tab.

Position Displays options used to line up a selected text box with a portion of the page. Found on the Format tab.

Promote ← Applies the next higher level style to the paragraph containing the insertion point. Found on the Outlining tab.

Promote ↑ Moves a selected shape up a level in a SmartArt graphic. Found on the Design tab.

Promote to Heading 1 ⇞ Applies the Heading 1 style to the paragraph containing the insertion point. Found on the Outlining tab.

Remove from Quick Styles Gallery Removes a style from the gallery. Found in the menu displayed by right-clicking a style in the gallery.

Remove Table of Contents Deletes a table of contents. Found in References → Table of Contents.

Reset Graphic Reverses most edits made to a SmartArt graphic. Found on the Design tab.

Right to Left ⇄ Changes the arrangement of shapes in a SmartArt graphic to a mirror image. Found on the Design tab.

Save Selection as a New Quick Style Displays a dialog box used to save the selected formatting as a new style. Found in the Styles submenu displayed by right-clicking a selected paragraph.

Shading ◭ Displays options used to change the cell shading. Found on the Design tab.

Shape Effects ◯▾ Displays options for changing the look of a selected object in a SmartArt graphic. Found on the Format tab.

Shape Fill ◭ Displays options for changing the fill of a selected object in a SmartArt graphic. Found on the Format tab.

Shape Height Used to precisely size the height of a text box. Found on the Format tab.

Shape Outline ☑ Displays options for changing the outline of a selected object in a SmartArt graphic. Found on the Format tab.

Shape Width Used to precisely size the width of a text box. Found on the Format tab.

Show Levels [All Levels ▾] Changes which heading levels are displayed. Found on the Outlining tab.

SmartArt Displays a dialog box used to add a diagram or organization chart to a document. Found on the Insert tab.

Sort Displays a dialog box used to sort the contents of a table. Found on the Layout tab.

Style Set Displays a list of style sets. Found in Home → Change Styles.

Table Displays a grid used to create a table. Found on the Insert tab.

Table of Contents Displays a gallery used to insert a table of contents. Found on the References tab.

Text Box Creates an object that contains text but can be moved and sized like a graphic. Found on the Insert tab.

Text Direction Rotates the text in the cell. Found on the Layout tab.

Text Effects 𝖠▾ Displays options for changing the look of selected text in a SmartArt graphic. Found on the Format tab.

Text Fill 𝗔 Displays options for changing the fill of selected text in a SmartArt graphic. Found on the Format tab.

Text Outline ☑ Displays options for changing the outline of selected text in a SmartArt graphic. Found on the Format tab.

Themes Displays a gallery used to change the theme. Found on the Page Layout tab.

Wrap Text Used to adjust the wrap of text around an object. Found on the Format tab.

1. a) What is a style?
    b) Describe the differences between body text and headings.

2. a) What formatting does the Normal style apply to a paragraph?
    b) What formatting does the Heading 1 style apply to a paragraph?

3. How is a table with four rows and two columns created?

4. a) How is a row selected?
    b) How is a column selected?

5. a) What is a boundary?
    b) What happens when the boundary of a column is double-clicked?

6. a) How can all the numbers in a column be summed in the last cell of the column?
    b) If a number changes, how can the sum be updated?

7. a) What is a TOC?
    b) How is a table of contents created?
    c) How is a table of contents updated?

8. How can an entry in the table of contents be used to display the corresponding heading?

9. a) How is a document divided into sections?
    b) List the steps required to insert a Next Page section break at the insertion point.

10. List the steps required to have Introduction in the header on page 2 of a document, Chapter 1 in the header on page 3, and no header on the first page.

11. List the step required to have Word automatically hyphenate the open document.

12. a) What does Outline view display?
    b) How do you display the open document in Outline view?

13. a) What is a bibliography?
    b) What do citations refer to?
    c) What does a "Works Cited" list contain?

14. What does a theme affect in a document?

15. a) List the steps required to insert a SmartArt graphic at the insertion point.
    b) Describe three ways to change the look of a SmartArt graphic.

16. Find an example of a two-fold brochure and describe the purpose and audience.

17. Why would text be formatted as a hyperlink to a heading in the same document? Give an example.

18 a) Describe a document that would include text boxes.
    b) Explain two advantages of using a text box.

19 a) What is a nameplate and where is it positioned in a newsletter?
    b) Why is a newsletter created in Word divided into sections?

True/False

20. a) The body text in a document consists of the main paragraphs.
    b) A new style can be created if the built-in styles are not appropriate.
    c) Columns are horizontal.
    d) Pressing Enter in a table cell moves the insertion point to another cell.
    e) Formatting the text in a table cell in a larger font increases the row height.
    f) When a table is created, all of the column widths are equal.
    g) The formula =AVERAGE(ABOVE) calculates the average of all the numbers entered in the table cells.
    h) Each entry in a table of contents created by Word is a hyperlink to a Web site that contains more information about the topic.
    i) Word automatically updates a table of contents when changes are made to a document.
    j) A document can only have one section.
    k) A document that is divided into sections can have different headers and footers in each section.
    l) Hyphenation is a process that divides words.
    m) By default, the Metro theme is applied to a document.
    n) A SmartArt graphic with a hierarchy layout is used to create an organization chart.

Project 1

Study Time Tutoring is preparing science study sheets. Open ELEMENTS, which is a Word data file for this text, and complete the following steps:

a) Insert a table with three columns and four rows (a 3 x 4 table) in the blank paragraph below the "Alkali Metals" heading.

b) Enter the following data into the table starting in the first cell:

Element	Symbol	Atomic Number
Lithium	Li	3
Sodium	Na	11
Potassium	K	19

c) Insert a table with three columns and five rows (a 3 x 5 table) in the blank paragraph below the "Nonmetals" heading.

d) Enter the following data into the table starting in the first cell:

Element	Symbol	Atomic Number
Carbon	C	6
Nitrogen	N	7
Oxygen	O	8
Fluorine	F	9

e) Insert a table with three columns and four rows (a 3 x 4 table) in the blank paragraph below the "Noble Gases" heading.

f) Enter the following data into the table starting in the first cell:

Element	Symbol	Atomic Number
Helium	He	2
Neon	Ne	10
Argon	Ar	18

g) Bold and increase the size of the text in the first row of all the tables.

h) Decrease the width of the columns in each table appropriately.

i) Apply the Heading 1 style to the "Elements" heading and the Heading 2 style to the "Alkali Metals," "Nonmetals," and "Noble Gases" headings.

j) Add a page border.

k) Create a footer with your name right aligned.

l) Save the modified ELEMENTS and print a copy of the document in Outline view with the first and second level headings displayed.

m) Print a copy in Print Layout view.

Project 2

Study Time Tutoring is helping a student format a report. Open SATURN, which is a Word data file for this text, and complete the following steps:

a) Have Word hyphenate the document automatically.

b) On page 1, apply the Title style to "Saturn" and the No Spacing style to the "Report by Name Prof. Gemini PH104 Fall 2011" paragraphs. Replace Name with your name.

c) Apply the Heading 1 style to the "Introduction," "Around Saturn," "Missions," and "Summary" headings.

d) Apply the Heading 2 style to the "Moons," "Rings," "Pioneer 11," "Voyagers 1 and 2," and "Cassini-Huygens" headings.

e) Apply the Heading 3 style to each moon and to the "Main Rings" and "Lesser Rings" headings.

f) Use Outline view to move the topic "Moons" (including the headings and text below it) to after the "Rings" heading and text.

g) Insert a page break in the blank paragraph below "PH104 Fall 2011" on page 1.

h) At the top of page 2 insert a table of contents in the built-in **Automatic Table 2** style.

i) Place the insertion point to the left of the "I" in the "Introduction" heading and insert a **Next Page** section break.

i) In section 1, create a footer with your name followed by a space and a page number in the i, ii, iii, ... format. No footer should appear on the first page.

j) Format the page number of the footer in section 2 to be in the 1, 2, 3, … format and start at 1.

k) Scroll through the document and check the pagination, adding any page breaks as necessary to help the look of the document.

l) Update the table of contents to reflect the new page numbering.

m) Save the modified SATURN and print a copy.

Project 3

Yolanda's Catering needs a take-out menu in the form of a two-fold brochure. Your brochure should contain the following:

- An appropriate theme and color scheme
- At least one SmartArt graphic
- At least one table
- A different page color

Check the document on screen and correct any errors and misspellings. Save the document naming it Take-Out Menu and print a copy. Assemble the brochure and fold it properly.

Project 4

Create a company organization or hierarchy chart for your business venture.

a) Use a SmartArt graphic to create an organization chart that illustrates the hierarchy in the potential company.

b) Create a footer with your name.

c) Save the document naming it Hierarchy and print a copy.

Project 5

Create a brochure for your business venture. Consider the purpose and audience of the brochure in your design. Use the logo you created in Chapter 3, Project 11.

a) In Word, create a brochure. Format the brochure appropriately.

b) Check the document on screen and correct any errors and misspellings.

c) Save the document naming it Brochure and print a copy.

Project 6

Yolanda's Catering is publishing their favorite recipes. In a new document, enter and format a favorite recipe. Format the document into three continuous sections as follows:

Section 1: include the name of the recipe, your name, and a graphic
Section 2: list the ingredients for the recipe and format the section in two columns
Section 3: a numbered list of the recipe steps in one column

Save the document naming it Favorite Recipe and print a copy.

Project 7

Word includes preformatted tables called Quick Tables. The Quick Tables gallery includes several one-month calendar styles.

a) Create a new document and then click Insert → Table → Quick Tables. The gallery of Quick Tables is displayed. Click one of the Calendar styles. A table formatted as a one-month calendar is inserted.

b) Change the name and the dates in the calendar to be an accurate calendar for next month. For example, if today is October 23rd, modify the calendar to be November. Be sure to check the dates and edit them appropriately so that they are accurate.

c) Create footer with your name.

d) Save the modified Next Month and print a copy.

Project 8

Align Computers is creating technology instruction manuals for their customers. Example topics include: burning a CD, managing files, using an MP3 player, and downloading digital pictures. The instruction manual should contain the following:

- A cover page using a built-in design from the Cover Page gallery.

- An introduction page that describes the task at hand and the importance of reading the manual. Include a table of contents on this page.

- At least one page of instructions, using numbered steps and an explanation following each step. Graphics may be used to enhance the explanation. SmartArt graphics can also be used to illustrate steps or a process.

- A separate page with a conclusion that summarizes the instructions and includes any cautions or limitations. Sources can also be cited on this page, if applicable.

Apply an appropriate theme, then adjust the formatting of text, fonts, sizes, tabs and tab stops as needed. Include a footer on all but the first page with your name left aligned and a page number right aligned. Check the document on screen for errors and misspellings and make any corrections. Save the document naming it Instruction Manual and print a copy.

Project 9

Travel... With a Purpose is preparing documents to help travellers be prepared for their adventures.

a) In a new document, type a title and then below the title insert a table with two columns and eight rows (a 2 x 8 table). Apply the Title style to the title.

b) Each cell in the first column should contain a box. Use Insert → Symbol to add an empty square box of your choice. Center the boxes horizontally.

c) Each cell in the second column should describe an item or group of items needed when backpacking in another country. Add rows as needed.

d) Change the column widths appropriately. Apply an appropriate table style. If the style formats the top row as bold, change the formatting so that the top row is not bold.

e) Create a footer with your name centered.

f) Save the document naming it Backpacking List and print a copy.

An example list could look similar to:

Backpacking in July in Mexico

☐	**Passport and other identification**
☐	Money and credit cards
☐	T-shirts, long sleeve shirts, and sweaters
☐	Pants and shorts
☐	Shampoo, soap, toothbrush and paste, towel
☐	Sandals, sneakers, and boots
☐	Socks and underwear
☐	Hat, sunglasses, sunscreen and bug spray

Project 10

Create a *Travel... With a Purpose* newsletter. The newsletter should contain travel information and tips. Save the document naming it Newsletter and print a copy when complete. Be sure to check the document on screen for errors and misspellings and make any corrections. Your newsletter should contain the following:

- At least two pages, formatted in two columns per page
- At least four different stories with heading and bylines
- At least two advertisements
- At least one numbered or bulleted list
- A nameplate and a masthead
- A footer with a centered page number
- At least one table of data
- At least one text box
- At least one footnote
- At least two clip art pictures
- A 'draft' watermark

Page one of an example newsletter could look similar to:

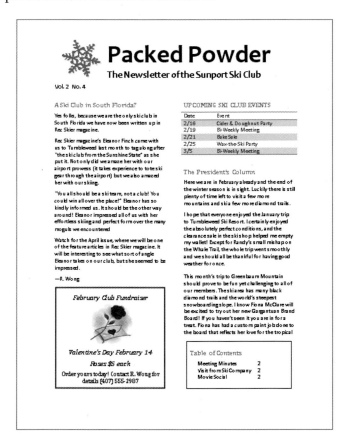

Key Concepts

Entering worksheet data
Editing cell contents
Formatting cells and applying themes
Using formulas to perform calculations
Copying and pasting between Word and Excel
Conditional formatting
Adding graphics
Protecting worksheets and workbooks
Using tools to review a worksheet
Using templates
Creating HTML files

Practice Data Files

DEPT MEMO, GADGETS LOGO, SUMMER SALES

Project Data Files

YC LOGO, TWP NEWS, TOURS, TOUR PRICES, KEYPAD, SALES ANALYSIS

Spreadsheet

Accounting activities were once tracked on large sheets of paper that spread out to form a "spreadsheet."

What is a Spreadsheet?

A *spreadsheet* is an application used to store and analyze data. There are many different uses for a spreadsheet application including payroll, inventory, data collection, personal budgets, and cost calculations. The Microsoft Excel 2010 spreadsheet application window looks similar to:

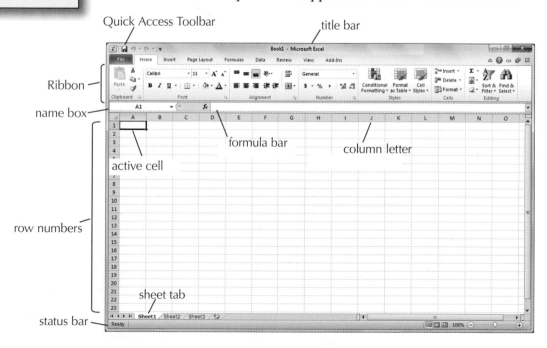

An Excel spreadsheet document is called a *worksheet*. An Excel file is called a *workbook*. A new workbook contains three worksheets, also called *sheets*. The Excel window displays information about a workbook and includes tools for working with one:

- The file name of the current workbook is displayed in the **title bar**. The name Book1 is used temporarily until the workbook is saved with a descriptive name.

- Click the **File tab** ▢ File to display commands for opening, saving, and printing a worksheet.

- Select commands and perform actions using the **Ribbon** and the **Quick Access Toolbar**.

- Click a **sheet tab** to display a sheet in the workbook.

- **Columns** are lettered from A to Z and then AA to XFD for a total of 16,384 columns. In the worksheet shown, only columns A through O are displayed.

- **Rows** are numbered from 1 to 1,048,576. In the worksheet shown, only rows 1 through 23 are displayed.

- A **cell** is the intersection of a row and column. Each cell can store a single item of data.

- A **cell reference** is the column letter and row number that identify a single cell. For example, A1 is the cell reference of the selected cell in the worksheet shown. A cell reference can be thought of as a cell's name.

- The **selected cell** is called the **active cell** and is displayed with a bold border. In the worksheet shown, cell A1 is the active cell. The column letter and row number corresponding to the active cell are orange. Type data to place it into the active cell.

- The **name box** displays the cell reference of the active cell, which is A1 in the worksheet shown.

- The active cell contents are displayed on the **formula bar**.

- View information about the current document in the **status bar**.

Cell Reference vs. Cell Contents

Each cell is identified by its cell reference, such as A3 or C2, and each cell can contain data, such as the number 5 or the label Total. This system is similar to mailboxes at the post office where each box (or cell) has a name and can store information. Be careful not to confuse the cell reference with the data it stores.

Entering Data into a Worksheet

planning a spreadsheet

Before entering data into a worksheet, it is important to develop a plan. A carefully planned worksheet presents data in a logical, organized, and easy-to-understand format. The planning process involves three steps:

1. What is the **purpose**? Determine what information the worksheet is to produce.

2. What **information** is needed? Determine the data to include.

3. How should the worksheet be **organized**? Determine which data should be in rows and which data should be in columns.

label

value, date/time

After developing a plan, enter data into a new worksheet. Worksheet *data* is either a label, value, or date/time. A *label* is text and cannot be used in calculations. A *value* is numeric and can be used in calculations. *Date/time* is either a date, such as 6/5/2011 or a time, such as 12:10 PM. A date/

TIP Click Insert → Symbol to insert symbols in a cell.

TIP To efficiently enter large amounts of numeric data, use the numeric keypad. Press the Num Lock key to turn on/off the numeric keypad.

time entry may be used in some calculations. Labels are left aligned and values and dates/times are right aligned in cells:

	A	B	C	D	E
1	Item	9/8/2011	6:30:00 AM	789	
2					

Use the keyboard to type data. As data is typed, it appears in the active cell and on the formula bar, and Cancel ✗ and Enter ✓ are activated:

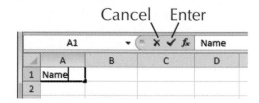

TIP To display the formula bar, click View → Formula Bar.

Click Enter ✓ to enter data in the active cell. Click Cancel ✗ to restore the original contents of the active cell. On the keyboard:

TIP Press Alt+Enter to start a new line of text within a cell.

- Press the **Enter key** to enter data and make the next cell in the column active.

- Press the **Tab key** to enter data and make the next cell in the row active. Use the Tab key to efficiently enter data across a row. Once the row is complete, press Enter, which selects the cell in the first column that contains data in the next row.

- Press an **arrow key** to enter the data and make the next cell in the direction of the arrow key active.

- Press the **Esc key** to cancel data entry and restore the original contents of the active cell.

Some data may extend beyond the width of a cell. For example, a long label is truncated when the next cell contains data:

	A	B	C	D	E
1	Current In	Quantity			
2					

Cell A1 stores Current Inventory, as shown on the formula bar, but only the characters that fit in the width of the cell are displayed. To change the column width, point to the *boundary*, the bar separating the column letters at the top of the worksheet, until the pointer changes to ✛:

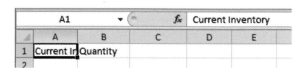

Drag the boundary to the right to increase the column width, or drag it to the left to decrease the width. The width of the entire column is changed because the width of a single cell cannot be changed:

	A	B	C
1	Current Inventory	Quantity	
2			

To change the width of a column so that it is just wide enough to display the data it contains, double-click the right boundary of the column.

Automatic Completion

Excel uses a feature called automatic completion to guess the current entry based on data in the cells above:

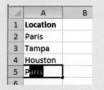

	A	B
1	Location	
2	Paris	
3	Tampa	
4	Houston	
5	Paris	
6		

Press Enter to accept the entry, or continue to type to replace the automatic entry.

Editing Cell Contents

TIP Press Ctrl+Home to select cell A1. Press the Page Up or Page Down key to select a cell one screen up or one screen down, respectively.

To change data in a cell, the cell must be active. To select a cell and make it *active*, press the arrow keys to move to the cell. The mouse may also be used to select a cell. Move the pointer onto the worksheet until the pointer changes to ✛, and then click a cell to make it the active cell.

insertion point

The contents of the active cell are displayed on the formula bar. To delete the data in the active cell, press the Delete key. To edit the data in the active cell, click the formula bar to place the insertion point. The *insertion point* is a blinking vertical line that indicates where the next character typed will be placed. Use the Backspace key to delete data one character at a time. After editing the data, click Enter ✓ or press the Enter key.

On the Quick Access Toolbar, click Undo ↺ to reverse an edit made by mistake or click Redo ↻ to repeat the last action performed. Click ▾ in Undo ↺▾ to display a list of the last actions performed. Select an option from the list to reverse that particular action.

Practice: Grades – part 1 of 5

The worksheet plan is:

1. The purpose of the worksheet is to organize student test grades. Later the worksheet will be expanded to calculate student and test averages.
2. The data needed is student names, test grades, test names, and test dates.
3. The worksheet will be organized with one student per row and one test per column. Labels will be needed to identify each student, test, and date.

① **START EXCEL**

a. Ask your instructor for the appropriate steps to start Microsoft Office Excel 2010.
b. Look at the Excel window. Note the title bar, Quick Access Toolbar, Ribbon, rows, and columns.
c. Note the bold border around the active cell. In a new workbook, the active cell is cell A1.

② **ENTER COLUMN LABELS IN ROW 1**

a. In cell A1, type Student ID, and then click Enter ✓. Cell A1 now contains the label Student ID and the active cell's contents are displayed on the formula bar.
b. Press the right-arrow key to select cell B1, and then type: Test 1
c. Press the Tab key. The label is entered and the next cell in the row is active.
d. Type: Test 2
e. Press the Tab key. The label is entered and cell D1 is the active cell.
f. Continue this procedure to place the labels Test 3 in cell D1 and Test 4 in cell E1:

E1		▾	f_x	Test 4	
	A	B	C	D	E	F
1	Student IC	Test 1	Test 2	Test 3	Test 4	
2						

③ ENTER THE TEST DATES

a. Press Enter. Cell B2 is selected because the Tab key was used to enter the data in cells B1 through D1.

b. In cell B2, type the date 9/4/2011 and press the Tab key. The date is right aligned.

c. In cell C2, type 9/14/2011 and then press the Tab key.

d. In cell D2, enter the date: 9/21/2011 and in cell E2, enter the date: 9/30/2011

④ ENTER THE STUDENT NAMES AND GRADES

Enter the following labels and values starting in cell A3 by typing the label or value and pressing the Tab key to enter the data and move to the next cell in the row. Press Enter at the end of the row. Note that the data may not be entirely displayed in column A.

10-260-001	85	73	88	95
23-781-099	92	68	75	71
15-678-023	72	63	67	72
10-433-556	57	62	75	82
22-311-444	94	91	93	84
15-778-112	70	74	60	54

⑤ WIDEN COLUMN A

a. Point to the boundary between columns A and B. The pointer changes to ✛.

b. Drag the boundary to the right approximately halfway across column B. The labels in column A should be entirely displayed. If they are not, continue to widen column A until all labels are completely displayed.

⑥ EDIT A GRADE

a. Select cell E8.

b. On the formula bar, click to the right of the number 4. The insertion point appears.

c. Press the Backspace key once to delete the number 4.

d. Type a 3 and then click Enter ✔. The grade is now 53:

	A	B	C	D	E	F
1	Student ID	Test 1	Test 2	Test 3	Test 4	
2		9/4/2011	9/14/2011	9/21/2011	9/30/2011	
3	10-260-001	85	73	88	95	
4	23-781-099	92	68	75	71	
5	15-678-023	72	63	67	72	
6	10-433-556	57	62	75	82	
7	22-311-444	94	91	93	84	
8	15-778-112	70	74	60	53	
9						

⑦ SAVE THE WORKBOOK

Save the workbook naming it: Grades

Formatting Cells

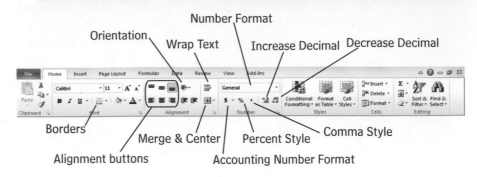

Formatting is applied to cells to make the data easier to understand. For example, data in columns is easier to read if the column headings and corresponding data have the same alignment. By default, labels are left aligned and values and dates/times are right aligned. Click Align Text Left ≡, Center ≡, or Align Text Right ≡ on the Home tab to change cell alignment:

Vertical Alignment

Click Top Align ≡, Middle Align ≡, or Bottom Align ≡ to change the vertical alignment of cell contents.

	A	B	C
1	Buyer	Date	Value
2	R. Good	3/5/2011	3500
3			

	A	B	C
1	Buyer	Date	Value
2	R. Good	3/5/2011	3500
3			

Default Alignment   *Aligned Column Headings*

Long column headings can result in an unnecessarily wide column. This can be avoided by wrapping the text:

	A	B	C	D	E	F	G
1	Last Name	First Initial	Rate	Hours	Overtime Hours	Overtime Pay	
2	Good	R.	$ 15.00	50	10	$ 225.00	
3							

Row Height

Click Format → Row Height to display a dialog box used to change row height.

or changing the orientation of the text:

	A	B	C	D	E	F	G	H
1	Last Name	First Initial	Rate	Hours	Overtime Hours	Overtime Pay		
2	Good	R.	$ 15.00	50	10	$ 225.00		
3								

To wrap text in the selected cell, click Home → Wrap Text ☰. To change the text orientation in a selected cell, click Home → Orientation ≫ and select an option such as Angle Counterclockwise.

The worksheet above contains cell borders. To add borders to a selected cell, click Home → Borders ⊞ ▾ → All Borders. Other border options are also available in Home → Borders ⊞ ▾.

In a worksheet, titles cannot be centered horizontally on the page like they can be in a word processing document. However, it is possible to merge a group of adjacent cells and center text within the merged cells.

TIP Selecting multiple cells is discussed in the next section in this chapter.

Select the cells and then click Home → Merge & Center ⊞. For example, cells A1 through D1 are merged and "Inventory" is centered within the merged cells.

	A	B	C	D	E
1		**Inventory**			
2					
3	Item	Quantity	Price	Total	
4	Handbags	100	$ 1.20	$ 120.00	
5					

To merge cells without centering the label, select the cells, and then click Home → Merge & Center ⊞ → Merge Across or Home → Merge & Center ⊞ → Merge Cells. Click Home → Merge & Center ⊞ → Unmerge Cells to restore the cells.

Cells that store numeric data should be properly formatted to reflect the type of value stored. For example, each of the cells in column B contains the value 1.5:

	A	B	C
1	Number Formats		
2			
3	General	1.5	
4	Number	1.50	
5	Currency	$1.50	
6	Accounting	$ 1.50	
7	Percentage	150.00%	
8	Fraction	1 1/2	
9	Scientific	1.50E+00	
10			

TIP A cell is automatically formatted if a $, %, or a decimal position is typed with the number.

Click Home → Numeric Format [General ▾] to display a list of numeric formats:

• General is the default format that displays numbers the way they are typed.

• Number displays a value with two decimal places. To add a thousand separator to the number, click Home → Comma Style ▸ .

• Currency displays a value with a dollar sign and two decimal places.

• Accounting is similar to Currency except the dollar sign aligns itself at the left edge of the cell. Click Home → Accounting Number Format $ to quickly apply the Accounting format.

• Short Date displays a date in a 3/29/2011 format.

• Long Date displays a date in a Thursday, March 29, 2011 format.

• Percentage displays a value as a percentage with two decimal places. Click Home → Percent Style % to quickly format a cell as percentage with 0 decimal places.

• Fraction displays a value as a fraction.

• Scientific displays a value in scientific notation with two decimal places.

• More Number Formats displays the Format Cells dialog box where Custom formats, including time formats, can be selected:

Other Currency Formats

The Accounting Number Format button contains additional currency symbols:

$ ▾

$ English (U.S.)
£ English (U.K.)
€ Euro (€ 123)
¥ Chinese (PRC)
fr. French (Switzerland)

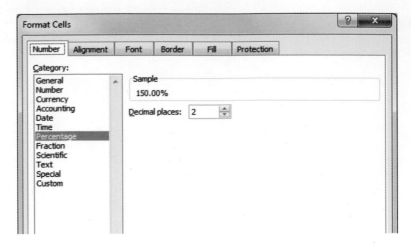

changing decimal places

To display additional decimal places, click Home → Increase Decimal. For example, a cell storing 1.5 will display 1.500 after clicking Increase Decimal twice. Click Home → Decrease Decimal to display fewer decimal places. For example, a cell storing 1.5 will display 2 after clicking Decrease Decimal once. Note that the displayed value has been rounded, but the actual value has not been changed.

#####

Formatting a cell does not change the value that is stored in the cell, only how that value is displayed. Number signs (#####) are displayed if a cell is not wide enough to display the formatted number.

Selecting Cells

Formatting multiple cells is faster when cells are selected together first. Adjacent worksheet cells can be selected together to form a range. *Adjacent cells* are cells that are next to each other. A *range* is a selection of two or more cells. Drag the pointer from one cell to another to select a range:

range

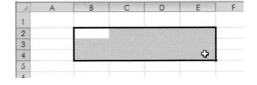

Drag from cell B2 to cell E4 to select this range

Another way to select a range is to first select the starting cell, then hold down the Shift key and click the last cell in the range. A third way to select a range is to press and hold the Shift key while pressing an arrow key to create a range in the direction of the arrow.

To select all cells in a row or column, click the row number or column letter. Click the Select All button to select the entire worksheet:

Select All button—

Applying Themes and Cell Styles

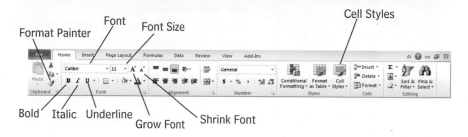

Format Painter — Font — Font Size — Cell Styles

Bold — Italic — Underline — Grow Font — Shrink Font

TIP Themes are also accessible in Word and PowerPoint. Every theme identifies one font for headings and another font for body text. In Excel, the second font is used for worksheet data.

A *theme* is a predefined set of colors, fonts, and effects used to format a worksheet. Themes are used to maintain a consistent and professional look in multiple worksheets. By default, the Office theme is applied to a new workbook.

Many companies use a specified theme for all of their documents. Typically the theme selected contains colors similar to the colors used in their company logo, sign, and so forth.

Each theme has a variety of cell styles associated with it. *Cell styles* apply several formats in one step and ensure consistent cell formatting. Click Home → Cell Styles to view the gallery of cell styles associated with the Office theme:

Page Backgrounds

Click Page Layout → Background to add a background to the entire worksheet. This feature should be used with caution because some backgrounds make it difficult to read the data.

- Titles and column headings can be formatted using the cell styles in the Titles and Headings group.

- Individual cells can be formatted using the cell styles in the Themed Cell Styles group. For example, alternate rows of similar information could be shaded, making the worksheet easier to read.

- Number formatting can be applied using the cell styles in the Number Format group.

TIP Double-click Home → Format Painter to paste the cell formats repeatedly. Click again to turn it off.

To apply a cell style, select the cells to be formatted and then click a style. To copy a cell's formatting, click Home → Format Painter ✐, and then click another cell. To remove formatting, click Home → Cell Styles → Normal or click Home → Clear ✐ → Clear Formats.

Once a cell style is applied, character formats can be modified. Using the Mini toolbar or options in the Font group on the Home tab, change the font and size using Font Calibri, Font Size 11, or Shrink Font A˅ and Grow Font A˄. Change the font style to Bold **B**, Italic *I*, and Underline U. To apply a double-underline style, click Home → Underline U ▾ → Double Underline. More than one button can be used at a time to apply multiple styles.

Changing the theme results in a different set of cell styles in the gallery. Click Page Layout → Themes to display a gallery of themes:

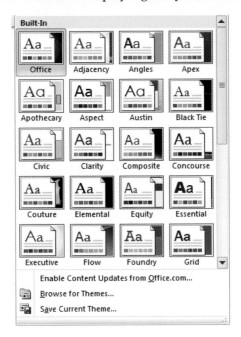

Click a theme and then click Home → Cell Styles to display the gallery of cell styles associated with that theme. For example, the cell styles associated with the Metro theme are:

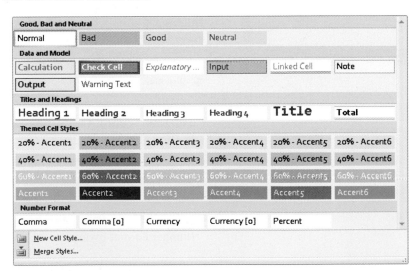

Note how the Metro cell styles differ from the Office theme cell styles shown on the previous page.

Previewing and Printing a Worksheet

Normal   Page Layout

Page Layout view

When preparing a worksheet for printing, display it in *Page Layout view*. In this view, a worksheet is displayed as pages. Page formats such as margins and headers and footers are easily modified from this view. Data can still be changed from this view as well. Click View → Page Layout to switch to Page Layout view:

Alternative Click Normal ▦ or Page Layout ▥ on the status bar to switch between views.

The Page Layout tab can then be used to adjust page formats:

Gridlines   Headings

- Click the Gridlines Print check box to include gridlines on a printout. *Gridlines* are solid lines that mark off the rows and columns, similar to what appears in the Excel window.

- Click the Headings Print check box to include row numbers and column letters in a printout.

  Click View → Normal to switch back to Normal view.

Page Break Preview

Click View → Page Break Preview or click Page Break Preview ▥ on the status bar to see where pages will break.

After formatting a worksheet in Page Layout view, select ▣ → Print to show what the printouts will look like. The worksheet cannot be modified in this view, but some formats, such as gridlines, are only visible in this view. Click Print to print a copy of the worksheet using the default print settings.

Headers and Footers

Header and Footer

Alternative If a worksheet is already in Page Layout view, click in the header or footer area to display the Design tab.

Information such as the date or the file name can be included in a header or footer to help identify printouts. Headers and footers are automatically printed at the top and bottom of each page, respectively. To add header or footer information, click Insert → Header & Footer. The worksheet is displayed in Page Layout view and the Design tab is displayed:

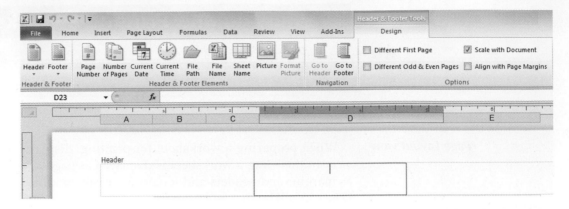

- Click Header and select an option from the displayed list to insert predefined header information.

- Click Footer and select an option from the displayed list to insert predefined footer information.

- Click one or more buttons in the Header & Footer Elements group to add additional information to the header or footer, such as the current date or the current time.

- Click Go to Header or Go to Footer to switch between the header and footer.

Practice: Grades – part 2 of 5

Excel should already be started with Grades displayed from the last practice.

① **APPLY A HEADING STYLE**

a. Drag the pointer from cell A1 to cell E1.

b. Click Home → Cell Styles → Heading 2:

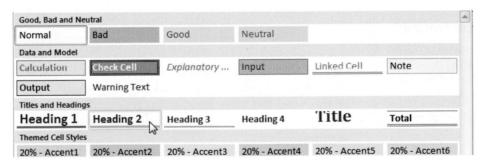

Heading 2 style is applied to the selected cells.

② **RIGHT ALIGN LABELS**

a. Select cell B1 and then hold the Shift key down and then click cell E1. Cells B1 through E1 are selected.

b. Click Home → Align Text Right ≡. The contents of the cells are right aligned:

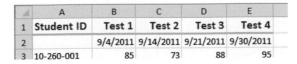

③ **FORMAT THE DATES**

   a. Select cells B2 through E2.

   b. Click Home → Number Format `Date` → More Number Formats. A dialog box is displayed. The Date options are selected.

       1. In the Type list, select a format similar to 3/14/01:

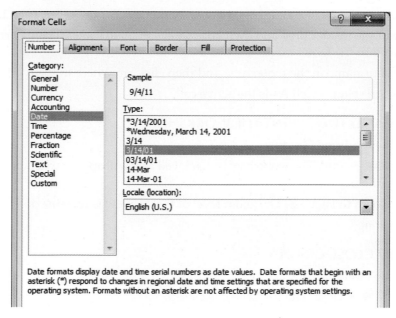

       2. Select OK. The cells are formatted:

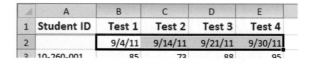

       3. Click a blank cell. The selection is removed.

④ **PREPARE THE WORKSHEET FOR PRINTING**

   a. Click View → Page Layout. The worksheet is displayed in Page Layout view. Note the rulers, page margins, and header area.

   b. Click Page Layout → Themes. A gallery of themes is displayed:

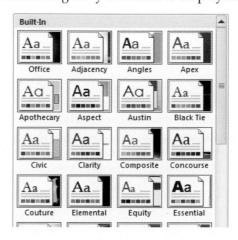

   c. Select the Equity theme. The Equity theme is applied to the worksheet. Note the color and font that is applied.

d. On the Page Layout tab, click Gridlines Print and click Headings Print. Note the column and row headings added to Page Layout view. Gridlines have also been added, but are only visible when previewing a printout.

⑤ CREATE A HEADER AND A FOOTER

a. Click Insert ➞ Header & Footer. The insertion point is placed in the header area.

b. Click Design ➞ Header and then select an option similar to Grades, Page 1.

c. Click in the header area and then click Design ➞ Go to Footer. The insertion point is placed in the footer area.

d. Type your name in the footer area and then click anywhere in the worksheet.

e. Press Ctrl+Home. Cell A1 is the active cell.

⑥ PREVIEW AND THEN PRINT THE WORKSHEET

a. Save the modified Grades.

b. Select [File] ➞ Print. The worksheet is displayed as it will appear when printed. Note the gridlines.

c. Click Zoom to Page 🔳. The zoom level of the preview is increased.

d. Select Print.

⑦ SAVE AND CLOSE GRADES

a. Save the modified Grades.

b. Select [File] ➞ Close. The worksheet is closed.

Using Formulas to Perform Calculations

formulas

One feature of a spreadsheet application is its ability to store formulas. *Formulas* are mathematical statements used to calculate values. In an Excel worksheet, a formula must begin with an equal sign (=). For example, entering the formula =25 * 3 in a cell displays the value 75.

The following arithmetic operators can be used in a formula:

Exponentiation	^	**Multiplication**	*
Division	/	**Addition**	+
Subtraction	–		

TIP Exponentiation means to raise a value to a power and is represented by the caret (^) symbol. For example, 2^3 is expressed as 2^3.

order of operations

Excel uses a specific *order of operations* to evaluate a formula. Exponentiation is performed first, multiplication and division next, and then addition and subtraction. Two operators of the same precedence are evaluated in order from left to right. For example, the formula =5 + 2 * 3 – 1 evaluates to 10 because multiplication is performed first and then the addition and subtraction from left to right. For example:

TIP When results are not as expected, check the formula bar to verify cell contents.

Formula	Resulting value
=2*2+3*2	10
=25*8/4	50
=35+12/3	39

The order in which Excel evaluates a formula can be changed using parentheses. Operations within parentheses are evaluated first. For example, the result of =(5 + 2) * 3 − 1 is 20 because 5 and 2 were added before the multiplication and subtraction were performed. For example:

Formula	Resulting value
=(3+5)*(8+7)	120
=3^2*8-4	68
=6+2^2	10

Excel automatically checks a formula for errors when it is entered into a cell. A cell with an invalid formula displays an error value and a green triangle in the upper-left corner of the cell. For example, a number cannot be divided by zero because the result is mathematically undefined. Therefore, entering =10/0 displays #DIV/0! in the cell. Select the cell with the error to display the Error Checking button ⬨. Click this button to display a description of the error and a list of options:

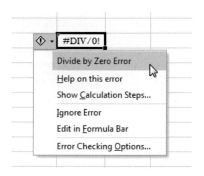

Displaying Formulas

Show Formulas

TIP The ` key is located above the Tab key on the keyboard.

To display the formulas stored in cells, press Ctrl+` (grave accent) or click Formulas ➜ Show Formulas:

	A	B	C
1	Gratuities Table		
2			
3	Amount	Tip	
4	$ 10.00	$ 1.50	
5	$ 25.00	$ 3.00	
6	$ 50.00	$ 7.50	

	A	B
1	Gratuities Table	
2		
3	Amount	Tip
4	10	=10*0.15
5	25	=20*0.15
6	50	=50*0.15
7		

Before pressing Ctrl+`*          *After pressing Ctrl+`

TIP Print the worksheet when formulas are displayed to print the formulas stored in the cells rather than the values.

When formulas are displayed column widths are adjusted automatically to view formulas entirely. Press Ctrl+` again to display values in each cell with the original column widths and formatting. Displaying formulas does not change the worksheet, only the way it is displayed.

Practice: Examples

Excel should already be started.

① CREATE A NEW WORKBOOK

a. Select [File] → New. A dialog box is displayed.

b. Select **Blank Workbook** and then select **Create**. A new workbook is displayed.

② ENTER LABELS

a. In cell A1, enter the label: Example Formulas

b. Select cell A1 and then click **Home** → **Cell Styles** → **Heading 2**.

c. Double-click the boundary between columns A and B. Column A is widened just enough to display the label.

d. Select cell A2 and enter the label: Formula

e. Select cell B2 and enter the label: Result

f. Format both labels as italic, and right align the label in cell B2:

	A	B	C
1	**Example Formulas**		
2	*Formula*	*Result*	

③ FORMAT CELLS AS TEXT

a. Select cells A3 through A8.

b. Click the **Number** group Dialog Box Launcher 🔲. A dialog box is displayed.

c. In the **Category** list, select **Text** and then select **OK**. Text format displays data exactly as entered.

④ ENTER A LABEL AND A FORMULA

a. Select cell A3.

b. Type =20/50 and then click Enter ✔. The result is a label because the cell is formatted as Text.

c. Select cell B3.

d. Type =20/50 and then click Enter ✔. The result 0.4 is displayed in the cell. Note that the formula is also displayed on the formula bar:

B3			f_x	=20/50	
	A	B	C	D	
1	**Example Formulas**				
2	*Formula*	*Result*			
3	=20/50	0.4			

⑤ ENTER FORMULAS

a. Enter the labels and formulas in the cells indicated. Note the resulting values:

In cell	enter		In cell	enter		to display
A4	=20*50		**B4**	=20*50		1000
A5	=20–50		**B5**	=20–50		–30
A6	=2+20*5+50		**B6**	=2+20*5+50		152
A7	=(2+20)*(5+50)		**B7**	=(2+20)*(5+50)		1210
A8	=20/0		**B8**	=20/0		#DIV/0!

b. Select cell B8. The Error Checking button is displayed.

c. Click the Error Checking button ◇. A menu is displayed. Note the first line of the menu indicates the type of error, "Divide by Zero Error".

d. In the menu, select Ignore Error.

⑥ CREATE A HEADER AND A FOOTER

a. Click Insert → Header & Footer. The insertion point is placed in the header area.

b. Click Design → Header → Book1.

c. Click in the header area and then click Design → Go to Footer. The insertion point is placed in the footer area.

d. Type your name in the footer area and then click anywhere in the worksheet.

e. Press Ctrl+Home and then click View → Normal.

⑦ VIEW FORMULAS

a. Save the worksheet naming it: Examples

b. Press Ctrl+` (located above the Tab key).

c. Select [File] → Print. The worksheet is displayed as it will appear when printed.

d. Select Print.

e. Press Ctrl+` to again display only the values of each cell.

⑧ SAVE AND THEN CLOSE EXAMPLES

Using Cell References in Formulas

Formulas often require values stored in other cells. To use, or refer to, a value in a cell, type its cell reference in the formula. The formula looks in the cell for the value to use in the calculation. For example, cell D2 contains a formula that references values in cells B2 and C2:

D2		▼	f_x	=B2*C2	
	A	B	C	D	
1	Item	Quantity	Price	Total	
2	Rice	180	$5.20	$936.00	

TIP The first cell reference in a formula is used to format the result.

Formulas that contain cell references are automatically recalculated when the value in a referenced cell changes. If the value in cell B2 or C2 changes, the formula automatically recalculates.

As a cell reference is typed into a formula, Excel outlines the referenced cell in a colored border. Cell references can be typed in uppercase or lowercase letters. However, Excel automatically converts a cell reference to uppercase letters.

pointing

Pointing is the best method for entering cell references into a formula because typing errors are avoided. To use this technique, type a formula up to where a cell reference should appear and then click a cell, which places its reference in the formula.

A formula cannot reference the cell it is stored in. For example, the formula in the worksheet on the previous page cannot be stored in cells B2 or C2 because this would cause an error called a *circular reference*.

circular reference

Cut, Copy, and Paste

Cut   Copy

Paste

Organizing and expanding a worksheet often requires moving and duplicating data. *Moving data* means that selected cell contents are "cut" from the worksheet and then "pasted" into other cells. *Duplicating data* means that selected cell contents are "copied" and the copy is "pasted" into other cells. Data can be moved and duplicated within the same worksheet or between two or more worksheets.

Use ✂ Cut, 🗐 Copy, and Paste on the Home tab to move and duplicate data:

1. Select the *source*, which is the cell or range to be duplicated or moved.

2. Click either Home ➞ ✂ Cut or Home ➞ 🗐 Copy. The source displays a moving dashed border.

3. Select the *destination*, which is the upper-left cell of the range where the data is to be pasted.

4. Click Home ➞ Paste. The data as well as the source formatting is pasted. Any pre-existing cell contents are replaced with the pasted data. Press the Esc key to remove the dashed border.

To copy cell contents to adjacent cells, use the Fill handle. The *Fill handle* is the solid square in the lower-right corner of a selected cell or range:

	A	B	C	D	E
1	Item	Quantity	Price	Total	
2	Rice	180	$5.20	$936.00	
3	Potatoes	45	$3.20		
4	Cereal	200	$2.00	Fill handle	
5	Bread	180	$1.80		
6	Milk	250	$4.00		
7	Bottled Water	55	$4.00		
8					

Point to the Fill handle until the pointer changes to **+**. Drag the Fill handle to copy the contents of the selected cell or range to adjacent cells:

	A	B	C	D	E
1	Item	Quantity	Price	Total	
2	Rice	180	$5.20	$936.00	
3	Potatoes	45	$3.20	$144.00	
4	Cereal	200	$2.00	$400.00	
5	Bread	180	$1.80	$324.00	
6	Milk	250	$4.00	$1,000.00	
7	Bottled Water	55	$4.00	$220.00	
8					
9					

Drag the Fill handle from cell D2 to cell D7

Alternative Right-click a cell to display a menu with the Cut, Copy, and Paste commands.

Office Clipboard

The Office Clipboard stores the last 24 cut or copied items. Click the **Clipboard** group Dialog Box Launcher 🔲 to display the Clipboard task pane. Click an item to paste it in the active cell.

Paste Options and Auto Fill Options

Depending on how data is copied from one cell to another, either Paste Options 🖫 or Auto Fill Options 🖫 will be displayed. Click the button to display a list of options for newly pasted data.

When a formula is copied, cell references automatically change relative to the new row or column. For example, if cell B10 contains the formula =B8+B9, copying this cell to cells C10 and D10 creates the formula =C8+C9 in cell C10 and =D8+D9 in cell D10. Cell references that reflect the row or column they have been copied to are called *relative cell references*.

relative cell references

Practice: Grades – part 3 of 5

Excel should already be started.

① **OPEN GRADES AND SWITCH TO NORMAL VIEW**

    a. Open Grades.

    b. Click View → Normal. The worksheet is displayed in Normal view.

② **ENTER A FORMULA**

    a. In cell F1, enter the label: Average

    b. Select cell E1 and then click Home → Format Painter 🖌 and then click cell F1. The formatting style is copied to cell F1.

    c. In cell F3, start typing a formula to average the student's grades. Type =(and then click cell B3:

AVERAGE	▾	✕ ✓ *fx*	=(B3			
	A	B	C	D	E	F	G
1	Student ID	Test 1	Test 2	Test 3	Test 4	Average	
2		9/4/11	9/14/11	9/21/11	9/30/11		
3	10-260-001	85	73	88	95	=(B3	
4	23-781-099	92	68	75	71		
5	15-678-023	72	63	67	72		

    d. Type + and then click cell C3.

    e. Enter the remainder of the formula, as shown on the formula bar, by typing and pointing:

F3	▾		*fx*	=(B3+C3+D3+E3)/4		
	A	B	C	D	E	F	G
1	Student ID	Test 1	Test 2	Test 3	Test 4	Average	
2		9/4/11	9/14/11	9/21/11	9/30/11		
3	10-260-001	85	73	88	95	85.25	
4	23-781-099	92	68	75	71		
5	15-678-023	72	63	67	72		

③ **COPY A FORMULA**

    Select cell F3 and then drag the Fill handle to cell F8. The formula is copied to the cells below with the cell references automatically changing:

	A	B	C	D	E	F	G
1	Student ID	Test 1	Test 2	Test 3	Test 4	Average	
2		9/4/11	9/14/11	9/21/11	9/30/11		
3	10-260-001	85	73	88	95	85.25	
4	23-781-099	92	68	75	71	76.5	
5	15-678-023	72	63	67	72	68.5	
6	10-433-556	57	81	75	82	73.75	
7	22-311-444	94	91	93	84	90.5	
8	15-778-112	70	74	60	53	64.25	
9							

④ CREATE ANOTHER LABEL AND FORMULA

    a. Select cell F1 and then slightly widen the column.

    b. Click Home → 🗐 Copy. The selected cell displays a moving dashed border.

    c. Select cell A9.

    d. Click Home → Paste. A copy of the label is pasted in the cell.

    e. Press the Esc key. The moving dashed border is no longer displayed.

    f. With cell A9 selected, edit the label on the formula bar to read: Test Average. Widen column A, if necessary.

    g. In cell B9, start typing a formula to average the test grades. Type =(and then click cell B3.

    h. Enter the remainder of the formula, as shown on the formula bar, by typing and pointing:

B9			f_x	=(B3+B4+B5+B6+B7+B8)/6	
	A	B	C	D	E	F
1	Student ID	Test 1	Test 2	Test 3	Test 4	Average
2		9/4/11	9/14/11	9/21/11	9/30/11	
3	10-260-001	85	73	88	95	85.25
4	23-781-099	92	68	75	71	76.5
5	15-678-023	72	63	67	72	68.5
6	10-433-556	57	62	75	82	69
7	22-311-444	94	91	93	84	90.5
8	15-778-112	70	74	60	53	64.25
9	Test Average	78.33333				
10						

⑤ COPY ANOTHER FORMULA

    Select cell B9 and then drag the Fill handle to cell E9. The formula is copied to the cells to the right with the cell references automatically changing.

⑥ FORMAT CELLS

    a. Select cells B9 through E9 and then click Number Format General ▾ → Number. The values are formatted with 2 decimal places.

    b. Click Home → Decrease Decimal .00. The averages are displayed with one decimal place.

    c. Format cells F3 through F8 as Number with one decimal place.

⑦ CHANGE A GRADE

    Change the grade in cell C6 to 81. Note how the formulas automatically recalculate the averages.

⑧ SAVE THE MODIFIED GRADES AND PRINT A COPY

Copying and Pasting Data between Word and Excel

Worksheet data can be included in a Word document. Rather than retype the worksheet data, which could introduce errors, data should be copied and pasted directly into the document from the worksheet. To copy and paste selected cells from a worksheet to a Word document, click Home → Copy, display the Word document, place the insertion point where the data is to appear, and then click Home → Paste.

Data copied from Excel is pasted as a table into a Word document:

Thank·you·to·all·team·members·for·helping·to·make·sales·this·quarter·the·best·in·12·years.·As·you·can·see·from·the·figures,·we·are·well·on·our·way·to·a·record·year!¶

TIP Refer to Chapter 1 for more information on multitasking.

Location¤	Units ·¤ Sold¢
North¤	220¤¤
South¤	525¤¤
East¤	109¤¤
West¤	323¤¤
¶	🅿(Ctrl)▾

TIP Other formatting options for pasted data include Keep Source Formatting and Keep Text Only.

Click Paste Options 🅿(Ctrl)▾ → Use Destination Styles:

Paste Options:

Use Destination Styles (S)

Information organized in a table or aligned with tabs and tab stops in a Word document can be copied to a worksheet:

1. In Word click Home → Copy.

2. Display the Excel worksheet and select the upper-left cell of the range where data is to be placed.

3. Click Home → Paste. Pasted data is automatically arranged into rows and columns similar to the way it appeared in the Word document.

Practice: DEPT MEMO

Excel should already be started with Grades displayed from the last practice.

① **OPEN DEPT MEMO**

a. Start Word.

b. Open DEPT MEMO, which is a Word data file for this text. Read the unfinished memo.

② **COPY DATA TO THE CLIPBOARD**

a. Use the taskbar to display the Grades workbook.

b. Select cells B1 through E8. All the grades are selected.

c. On the toolbar, click Home → Copy. The data is copied to the Clipboard.

③ **PASTE DATA**

a. Use the taskbar to display the DEPT MEMO document.

b. Place the insertion point in the blank paragraph below the text that reads "First quarter grades for the Business Applications class are:"

c. Click Home → Paste. The worksheet data is pasted:

First quarter grades for the Business Applications class are:

Test 1	Test 2	Test 3	Test 4
9/4/11	9/14/11	9/21/11	9/30/11
85	73	88	95
92	68	75	71
72	63	67	72
57	81	75	82
94	91	93	84
70	74	60	53

④ **COMPLETE THE MEMO**

   a. In the FROM: line, type your name.

   b. In the DATE: line, type today's date.

⑤ **SAVE THE MODIFIED DEPT MEMO AND PRINT A COPY**

⑥ **QUIT WORD**

Conditional Formatting

Conditional Formatting

Conditional formatting is formatting that is applied to a cell when a specified condition is met. Conditional formatting makes worksheet data easier to evaluate. For example, if test scores over 90 are displayed in blue and test scores below 70 are red, the worksheet becomes visually informative.

To choose formats that are applied to a cell when a condition is met, select a range of cells and then click Home → Conditional Formatting → Highlight Cells Rules, which displays a list of rules. Selecting a rule such as Greater Than displays a dialog box. Type a value or cell reference in the Format cells that are box and select a color format to be applied if the condition is true:

Select OK. More than one rule can be applied to a range of data.

Other conditional formats compare cell values within a specified range to determine formatting:

- Home → Conditional Formatting → Top/Bottom Rules includes options such as highlighting the Top 10 Items, Bottom 10%, and Below Average values. For example, the Below Average rule was applied to cells B3 through B8:

	A	B
1	Student ID	Test 1
2		9/4/11
3	10-260-001	85
4	23-781-099	92
5	15-678-023	72
6	10-433-556	57
7	22-311-444	94
8	15-778-112	70
9	Test Average	78.3
10		

TIP Color should be used sparingly to emphasize or distinguish data. Too much color can make a worksheet confusing.

- Home → Conditional Formatting → Data Bars illustrates the value of a cell relative to other cells. The bar length is scaled between the lowest and highest values in the specified range.

	A	B	C	D	E	F	G
1	Student ID	Test 1	Test 2	Test 3	Test 4	Average	
2		9/4/11	9/14/11	9/21/11	9/30/11		
3	10-260-001	85	73	88	95	85.3	
4	23-781-099	92	68	75	71	76.5	
5	15-678-023	72	63	67	72	68.5	
6	10-433-556	57	81	75	82	73.8	
7	22-311-444	94	91	93	84	90.5	
8	15-778-112	70	74	60	53	64.3	

Practice: Grades – part 4 of 5

Excel should already be started with Grades displayed from the last practice.

① **APPLY CONDITIONAL FORMATTING**

a. If a dashed border is displayed, press the Esc key.

b. Select cells B3 through E8.

c. Click Home → Conditional Formatting → Top/Bottom Rules → Below Average. Create a condition as shown:

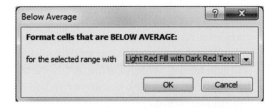

d. Select OK. Values below average are displayed with a light red fill and dark red text.

e. Select cells F3 through F8 and then click Home → Conditional Formatting → Data Bars → Light Blue Data Bar. The averages are represented by data bars:

	A	B	C	D	E	F	G
1	Student ID	Test 1	Test 2	Test 3	Test 4	Average	
2		9/4/11	9/14/11	9/21/11	9/30/11		
3	10-260-001	85	73	88	95	85.3	
4	23-781-099	92	68	75	71	76.5	
5	15-678-023	72	63	67	72	68.5	
6	10-433-556	57	81	75	82	73.8	
7	22-311-444	94	91	93	84	90.5	
8	15-778-112	70	74	60	53	64.3	
9	Test Average	78.3	75.0	76.3	76.2		
10							

② SAVE THE MODIFIED GRADES AND PRINT A COPY

③ CLOSE GRADES

Adding Graphics

Picture   Clip Art

TIP Refer to Chapter 3 for more information on the graphic editing commands on the Format tab.

A graphic, such as a business logo, can be added to a worksheet to give it a professional appearance. Click Insert → Picture to display the Insert Picture dialog box with a list of graphic files.

Clip art are files of general-purpose graphics created by an artist using illustration software. Click Insert → Clip Art 🖼 to display a task pane for finding clip art:

Clip Art	▼ ×
Search for:	
book	Go
Results should be:	
Selected media file types	▼
☑ Include Office.com content	

Copyright

Downloading graphics from the Internet may be copyright infringement unless a notice specifically states that an image is free for download.

Type a word or phrase in the Search for box and select Go to find all clip art that have the keywords in their description. To narrow a search, use the Search in list, which contains clip art collection names, and the Results should be list, which contains file formats. To place a clip art graphic into the worksheet, click the arrow to the right of the graphic and select Insert from the menu.

Once placed in a worksheet, a graphic may need to be sized. Click a graphic to select it and display handles:

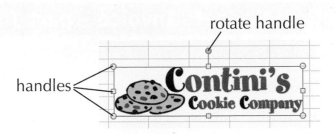

rotate handle

handles

Point to a corner handle, which changes the pointer to ⬈, and then drag to size the graphic.

To move a graphic, drag the center of a graphic (not a handle). Cut, Copy, and Paste on the Home tab can be used to create copies or move a selected graphic. Press the Delete key to delete the selected graphic. Click anywhere in the worksheet other than the graphic to remove the handles.

To adjust the color, brightness, and contrast of a selected picture, use the Format tab. Picture styles and border formatting can also be applied to graphics.

Hyperlinks in a Worksheet

When a Web site address is typed into a cell, Excel automatically turns it into a hyperlink. For example, www.lpdatafiles.com typed into a cell is automatically formatted as a hyperlink:

A reader viewing the worksheet on screen can click once to follow the link or click and hold to select the cell. Pointing to the cell changes the pointer to 👆. Clicking once displays the Web page in a browser window if there is Internet access.

Excel also recognizes an e-mail address and formats it as a e-mail hyperlink:

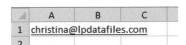

A reader viewing the worksheet on screen can click once to display a new e-mail message window.

The Insert Hyperlink dialog box contains options for inserting a hyperlink into a document. To use this dialog box, click Insert ➡ Hyperlink. Select a type of link from the Link to list and then type a label in the Text to display box. For Web page links, type a URL in the Address box. For an e-mail address link, type an address in the E-mail address box. The label is placed in the active cell, but the URL will be followed when the reader clicks the label.

To remove the hyperlink from text, right-click the link and then select Remove Hyperlink. The text remains, but is no longer a hyperlink.

Excel should already be started.

① **CREATE A NEW WORKBOOK**

② **ADD THE COMPANY LOGO**

    a. Click Insert → Picture. A dialog box is displayed.

        1. Navigate to GADGETS LOGO, which is a data file for this text.

        2. Select Insert. The logo is displayed on the worksheet.

    b. Drag the logo so that it is near the upper-left corner of the worksheet, if needed.

    c. Select the logo, if it is not already selected.

    d. On the Format tab, click the Drop Shadow Rectangle picture style:

③ **ADD A WEB SITE ADDRESS**

    a. Select cell A6, which should be just below the company logo. Size the logo by dragging a handle, if necessary, so that cell A6 is visible.

    b. In cell A6, type: www.lpdatafiles.com/gadgets.htm and press Enter. Note how the text is automatically formatted as a hyperlink:

④ **SAVE AND CLOSE THE WORKBOOK**

    a. Save the workbook naming it: Gadgets Invoice

    b. Close Gadgets Invoice.

Protecting Worksheets from Changes

There are instances when the data in a worksheet should not be changed. For example, company financial data may be sent to managers to review, but not modify. To protect the contents of the active sheet, click Review → Protect Sheet, which displays a dialog box:

Selecting a Password

Selecting a secure password requires some thought. Do not use words common to your work or name, do not use personal information such as a birth date, and use one or more numbers as opposed to just letters. Refer to Chapter 1 for more information on creating a strong password.

Specific tasks can be allowed even if a worksheet is protected. For example, click the Format cells check box to allow users to change the cell format, but not the values in the cell. Click Review → Unprotect Sheet to unprotect the sheet. If a password was typed in the Password to unprotect sheet box, the password will be needed to unprotect the sheet.

If a peer is editing a worksheet, the worksheet can still be protected while allowing specified cells to be edited. Click Review → Allow Users to Edit Ranges, which displays a dialog box. Select New to define the range that can be edited. Select OK and then select Review → Protect Sheet.

Practice: Grades – part 5 of 5

Excel should already be started.

① **OPEN GRADES**

② **PROTECT THE WORKSHEET**

    a. Click Review → Protect Sheet. A dialog box is displayed.

    b. In the Password to unprotect sheet box, type lock382 and select the check boxes as shown:

    c. Select OK. The Confirm Password dialog box is displayed:

d. In the Reenter password to proceed box, type lock382. Why would it be a good idea to write down the password in a secret location at this point?

e. Select OK.

f. Select cell A2. Try to type your name. A warning dialog box is displayed because the sheet is protected. Select OK to remove the warning dialog box.

③ **UNPROTECT THE SHEET**

a. Click Review → Unprotect Sheet. A dialog box is displayed:

b. In the Password box, type lock382 and select OK.

c. Select cell A2. Type your first and last name. You are able to enter your name because the protection has been removed from the worksheet.

④ **SAVE, PRINT, AND THEN CLOSE THE MODIFIED GRADES**

E-Mailing a Workbook

E-mail is a fast and efficient message delivery system that can include Excel workbooks attached to the message. Select [File] → Share → Send Using E-mail to display Backstage view options for sending a worksheet as an attachment. Select Send as PDF to attach a PDF copy of the workbook to an e-mail message.

Reviewing a Worksheet

Spelling   Thesaurus   New Comment   Track Changes

Excel contains several tools for proofing a worksheet. Click Review → Spelling to check the spelling of the text in the active worksheet. Select a word and then click Review → Thesaurus to display a task pane used to suggest words with similar meanings. The Review tab also contains commands to access online research and translation tools.

In many companies, a worksheet often requires data, input, or approval from several individuals or departments. This type of collaboration means working with others to create, review, and revise a workbook. Often this involves "suggested" changes that may or may not be appropriate. To facilitate this process, changes made to a worksheet can be tracked. The original creator can later decide which changes to keep and which to discard.

To track modifications, click Review → Track Changes 🖉 → Highlight Changes and then select the Track changes while editing check box. The workbook can then be e-mailed or given to a reviewer. After receiving the edited workbook, click Review → Track Changes 🖉 → Highlight Changes and then select All from the When list. Modified cells display a triangle in the upper-left corner:

<table>
<tr><td></td><td>A</td><td>B</td><td>C</td></tr>
<tr><td>1</td><td>Sales Summary</td><td></td><td></td></tr>
<tr><td>2</td><td></td><td></td><td></td></tr>
<tr><td>3</td><td>Region</td><td>Units Sold</td><td></td></tr>
<tr><td>4</td><td>North</td><td>220</td><td></td></tr>
<tr><td>5</td><td>South</td><td>525</td><td></td></tr>
<tr><td>6</td><td>East</td><td>109</td><td></td></tr>
<tr><td>7</td><td>West</td><td>323</td><td></td></tr>
</table>

The contents of cell B5 have changed

The reviewer can also add comments to help explain edits. To add a comment, click Review → New Comment.

To review changes, point to a modified cell to display information about the change. To accept or reject the change, click Review → Track Changes 🖉 → Accept/Reject Changes, which displays a dialog box. Click Accept or Reject for each change as it is displayed in a dialog box.

To stop tracking changes, click Review → Track Changes 🖉 → Highlight Changes and then clear the Track changes while editing check box.

Sharing a Workbook

Click Review → Share Workbook to allow multiple people at the same time to access and modify a workbook that is saved to a network drive.

TIP Select 📄 → Share→ Internet Fax to send a worksheet to a fax machine. You must first register with an Internet fax provider to use this tool.

TIP To better control the modifications made to the workbook, protect the workbook or sheet.

Practice: Gadgets Sales

This practice requires an e-mail client and Internet access. You are also required to work with a classmate and exchange documents through e-mail. Excel should already be started.

① **CREATE A NEW, BLANK WORKBOOK**

    a. Create a new workbook. Enter the following data and format it using the Opulent theme as shown. Cells A1 through C1 are formatted in Heading 1 style, cell A2 is formatted in Heading 4 style, and cells A4 through D4 are formatted in 60%-Accent5. Cells B5 through D8 are formatted as Currency with 0 decimal places:

	A	B	C	D
1	**Gadgets, Inc.**			
2	**2011 Sales**			
3				
4	Division	Fall	Winter	Spring
5	North	$1,467	$2,310	$1,682
6	South	$1,200	$1,196	$890
7	East	$640	$994	$1,245
8	West	$1,067	$875	$1,011

b. Click cell A1 and then click Review → Spelling. Correct any spelling mistakes.

c. Click Review → Track Changes 📝 → Highlight Changes. A dialog box is displayed.

  1. Select the Track changes while editing check box.

  2. Select OK.

d. Save the workbook naming it Gadgets Sales Name where Name is your name.

② E-MAIL A WORKSHEET FOR COLLABORATION

a. Click File → Share → Send Using E-mail → Send as Attachment. An e-mail window is displayed with the Gadgets Sales document as an attachment.

b. Type the following message, replacing Name with your name: Please add your summer sales figures. Thank you. --Name

c. In the To box, type the e-mail address of a classmate.

d. Click Send. The e-mail is sent to your classmate for collaboration.

e. Close Gadgets Sales.

③ COLLABORATE ON A WORKSHEET

a. Check your e-mail and open the e-mail from your classmate. Note that the e-mail message asks you to add summer sales figures.

b. Save the attachment to the appropriate location.

c. Open the file. The workbook is displayed in Excel. Note that [Shared] is displayed after the file name.

d. Open SUMMER SALES, which is an Excel data file for this text.

e. Select cells B4 through B8. The sales figures are selected.

f. Click Home → Copy.

g. Use the taskbar to display the Gadgets Sales workbook.

h. Select cell E4.

i. Click Home → Paste. The summer sales figures are added.

j. Select cells D4 through D8. Click Home → Format Painter 🖌.

k. Click cell E4. The summer sales figures are formatted:

	A	B	C	D	E	F
1	**Gadgets, Inc.**					
2	**2011 Sales**					
3						
4	Division	Fall	Winter	Spring	Summer	
5	North	$1,467	$2,310	$1,682	$2,030	
6	South	$1,200	$1,196	$890	$1,760	
7	East	$640	$994	$1,245	$1,380	
8	West	$1,067	$875	$1,011	$2,298	
9						

l. Save and then e-mail the modified workbook back to your classmate.

m. Close the workbook and close SUMMER SALES.

④ REVIEW CHANGES

a. Check your e-mail and open the e-mail reply from your classmate. The e-mail message includes the reviewed document as an attachment.

b. Save the attachment to the appropriate location, naming it Gadgets Sales Name Revised.xlsx where Name is your name.

c. Open the file.

d. Click Review → Track Changes 📝 → Highlight Changes. A dialog box is displayed.

  1. In the When list, select All.

  2. Select OK. The dialog box is removed and triangles are displayed in modified cells.

e. Click Review → Track Changes 📝 → Accept/Reject Changes. A dialog box is displayed.

f. Select OK. Cell E4 has a moving dashed border and another dialog box is displayed.

g. Select Accept. Cell E5 has a moving dashed border.

h. Continue to select Accept for all the modified cells.

i. Click Review → Track Changes 📝 → Highlight Changes. A dialog box is displayed.

  1. Clear the Track changes while editing check box.

  2. Select OK. Another dialog box is displayed.

  3. Select Yes.

⑤ SAVE THE MODIFIED GADGETS SALES AND PRINT A COPY

⑥ CLOSE THE WORKBOOK

Creating an HTML File

HTML is the file format for documents viewed using a browser, such as documents on the Web. A workbook in HTML format is more versatile because Excel is not needed to view it, just a Web browser.

To save a workbook in Web format, select [File] → Save As and then select a Web page type in the Save as type list. Click Change Title to give *title* the Web page a descriptive *title*, which is text displayed in the title bar of the browser window.

Saving a workbook as a Web page creates an .htm file and a folder with the same name to store any supporting files associated with the workbook, such as graphics. Saving a document as a Single File Web Page creates an .mht file that contains all supporting information.

TIP In Internet Explorer version 8, press the Alt key to display the File menu.

To view the file directly from a Web browser, open a browser, such as Internet Explorer and select File → Open.

Templates

A *template* is a master worksheet that includes the basic elements for a particular type of worksheet. Templates are used again and again whenever a worksheet of that type is needed. For example, a worksheet can be used to produce an invoice. Invoices usually contain the same data (quantity, service, unit price, and total), with only the invoice number, date, and total changing for each new invoice. Instead of adding labels and formatting cells every time, a more efficient approach would be to create a template that contains the unchanging data and then use this template each time a new invoice is needed.

To create a template, enter data in a new worksheet and apply formatting. Select File → Save As to display a dialog box. Type a file name in the File name box and select Excel Template in the Save as type list. To open a template, select File → New, which displays the New dialog box. Select My templates in the Templates list, which displays a dialog box, select the template, and then select OK.

TIP An Excel template is saved with an .xltx extension.

Alternative Select File → New to view predesigned templates from Microsoft Office Online.

Practice: Gadgets Invoice – part 2 of 2

Excel should already be started.

① **OPEN GADGETS INVOICE**

② **ENTER AND FORMAT DATA**

    a. Add labels and format using the Office theme as shown in the worksheet below. Cells C6, A8, and A12 through D12 are formatted with the cell style 20% - Accent4.

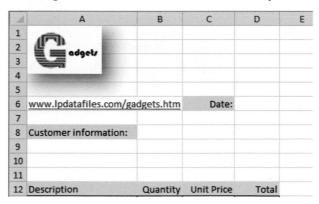

    b. Format cell D6 to display a date in a Short Date format.

    c. Format cells C13 through D17 as Currency.

    d. Select cells A13 through D17.

    e. Click Home → Borders ⊞ ▾ → All Borders.

    f. Select cells D13 through D17.

    g. Click Home → Cell Styles. Click the 20% - Accent4 color.

③ **ADD FORMULAS AND FORMAT CELLS**

    a. In cell C18, type Total Due: and then bold and right align the label.

    b. Select cell D13 and then click Home → Format Painter ✅.

c. Click cell D18. Cell D18 is now shaded with a solid border and contains currency formatting.

d. In cell D13, enter the formula =B13*C13. $0.00 is displayed.

e. Copy cell D13 to cells D14 through D17.

f. In cell D18, enter the formula =D13+D14+D15+D16+D17. $0.00 is displayed:

4 **SAVE THE TEMPLATE**

a. Select [File] → Save As. The Save As dialog box is displayed.

b. The File name box should already display Gadgets Invoice. In the Save as type list, select Excel Template:

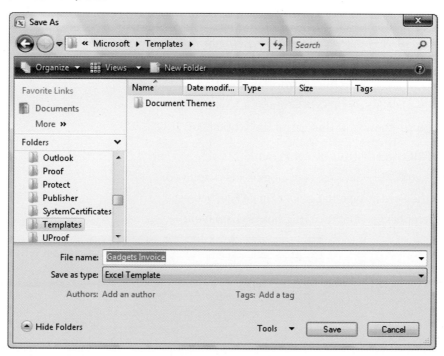

c. Select Save.

5 **CLOSE THE TEMPLATE**

⑥ CREATE A NEW WORKSHEET USING THE TEMPLATE

    a. Select ▢ File → New. A dialog box is displayed.

        1. In the Templates list, select My Templates. A dialog box is displayed.

        2. Click Gadgets Invoice and then select OK. A new workbook is displayed.

    b. Add data into the invoice so that it appears similar to the following. Note that you will not need to enter data in column D because formulas exist to calculate the data:

	A	B	C	D	E
1					
2	**G** adgets				
3					
4					
5					
6	www.lpdatafiles.com/gadgets.htm		Date:	2/2/2011	
7					
8	Customer information:				
9	Y & S Supplies				
10					
11					
12	Description	Quantity	Unit Price	Total	
13	LED Flashlight	10	$4.95	$49.50	
14	MP3 Player	7	$68.00	$476.00	
15	Smart Watch	5	$295.00	$1,475.00	
16				$0.00	
17				$0.00	
18			Total Due:	$2,000.50	

⑦ SAVE AND PRINT THE WORKBOOK

    a. Add your name in a footer. Click a blank worksheet cell.

    b. Press Ctrl+Home.

    c. Select ▢ File → Save. The Save As dialog box is displayed.

        1. In the File name box, type: YS Supplies Invoice

        2. Navigate to the appropriate location for the file to be saved.

        3. Select Save. The document is saved.

    d. Print preview and then print the worksheet.

⑧ SAVE THE WORKBOOK AS HTML

    a. Select ▢ File → Save As. A dialog box is displayed.

    b. In the Save as type list, select Single File Web Page.

    c. Click Change Title. A dialog box is displayed:

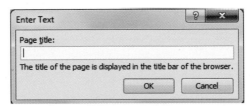

    d. Type YS Supplies Invoice in the Page title box and select OK.

    e. Select Save. If a dialog box is displayed, click Yes.

⑨ PREVIEW THE HTML DOCUMENT IN A BROWSER

    a. Start a Web browser, such as Internet Explorer.

    b. Select File → Open. A dialog box is displayed.

        1. Click Browse. A dialog box is displayed.

        2. Locate the YS Supplies Invoice.mht file, select Open, and then select OK.

    c. Expand the window, if necessary, to view the entire document. Note the title in the title bar.

    d. Close the browser window.

⑩ CLOSE YS SUPPLIES INVOICE AND QUIT EXCEL

Chapter Summary

This chapter discussed Excel, the spreadsheet application in Microsoft Office. In Excel, a spreadsheet document is called a worksheet. An Excel file is called a workbook. A new workbook contains three worksheets. Worksheets are used to present data in an organized format. Before entering data, a plan is developed.

Cells can store three types of data: labels, values, and dates/times. The width of a column is changed by dragging its right boundary.

Cells are formatted using the Home tab. Cells can be formatted to display numeric data differently, and alignments, fonts, styles, and colors can be selected for a cell. Themes and cell styles can be used to ensure consistent formatting. Conditional formatting is used to make a worksheet easier to evaluate.

A range is a selection of two or more adjacent cells, and is created by dragging from one cell to another.

Headers and footers are used to display information at the top and bottom of each worksheet page, respectively. Headers and footers are added to a worksheet using the Insert tab. A worksheet should be viewed in Page Layout view prior to printing using the View tab, which displays the worksheet as pages. A worksheet should also be previewed prior to printing.

Formulas are mathematical statements used to calculate values. Formulas must begin with an equal sign (=) and may contain cell references. Excel uses an order of operations when evaluating a formula. Excel automatically checks formulas for errors and displays an error value if the formula is invalid. Cell references can be entered into a formula using a technique called pointing. The formulas in a worksheet are displayed by pressing Ctrl+`.

Data can be cut or copied using the Home tab. Cut or copied data is placed on the Clipboard, and can be pasted in another location. Drag a cell's Fill handle to copy its contents to adjacent cells. Excel data can be copied to a Word document.

Graphics from a file or clip art are added to a sheet using the Insert tab. Graphics can be resized by dragging a handle.

A worksheet can include hyperlinks to a Web page or to an e-mail address. Pointing to a hyperlink, holding down the Ctrl key, and clicking displays the Web page or displays a new e-mail message window.

A worksheet can be protected so that the data in the worksheet is not accidentally changed. A worksheet's structure and window can also be protected.

Excel contains tools for proofing a worksheet on the Review tab. It is possible to check spelling and access a thesaurus, online research, and translation tools. Changes to a worksheet can be tracked so that the original creator can later decide which changes to keep and which to discard.

An open workbook can be e-mailed as an attachment. E-mailing attached workbooks allows for collaboration.

A template is a master workbook that includes the basic elements for a particular type of worksheet. Templates are used again and again whenever a worksheet of that type is needed.

A worksheet can be saved in HTML format, which allows the data to be viewed in a Web browser.

Vocabulary

Active cell   The cell displayed with a bold border. Also called the selected cell.

Adjacent cells   Cells that are next to each other.

Boundary   The bar separating the column letters at the top of the worksheet.

Cell   The intersection of a row and column.

Cell reference   The column letter and row number that identify a cell, such as B3.

Cell styles   Used to apply several formats in one step.

Circular reference   An error that occurs when a formula references the cell it is stored in.

Clip art   A general-purpose graphic created by an artist using illustration software.

Columns   Vertical part of the worksheet grid identified by the letters A to Z and AA to XFD.

Conditional formatting   Formatting that is applied to a cell when a specified condition is met.

Data   Information stored in a worksheet. Categorized as either label, value, or date/time.

Date   Data displayed as a calendar date.

Destination   The upper-left cell of the range where data is to be pasted.

Duplicate data   To make a copy of data and then place that copy at a different location in the worksheet or into a completely different document.

Fill handle   The solid square in the lower-right corner of a selected cell that is dragged to copy the contents of a cell to adjacent cells.

Formula   Mathematical statement used to calculate a value. A formula must always begin with an equal sign.

Formula bar   Displays the active cell's contents. Located above the cells.

Gridlines   Solid lines that mark off the rows and columns in a worksheet.

Headings   Row numbers and column letters.

HTML   The file format for documents viewed using a browser.

Insertion point   A blinking vertical line that indicates where the next character typed will be placed.

Keyword   A descriptive word used to search for clip art.

Label   Text stored in a cell that cannot be used in calculations.

Move data   Delete data from a worksheet and then place that data at a different location in the workbook or into another file.

Name box   Displays the cell reference of the active cell. Located at the top of the worksheet.

Order of operations   The precedence Excel follows to evaluate a mathematical expression.

Page Layout view   View that displays the worksheet as a printed page.

Pointing   Clicking a cell to place its reference in a formula.

Range   Selection of two or more cells.

Relative cell reference   A cell reference that reflects the row or column it has been copied to.

Row   Horizontal part of the worksheet grid identified by the numbers 1 to 1,048,576.

Selected cell   *See* Active cell.

Sheet tab   Used to display a worksheet.

Sheet   *See* Worksheet.

Source   Selected cells to be copied or moved.

Spreadsheet   An application used to store and analyze data.

Template   A master workbook that includes the basic elements for a particular type of workbook.

Time   Data displayed as a time (i.e., 12:30 PM).

Title   In an HTML document, the text that is displayed in the title bar.

Value   Numeric data that can be used in calculations.

Workbook   An Excel file.

Worksheet   Sheets in an Excel workbook.

Excel Commands

Accept/ Reject Changes Displays a dialog box prompting for which changes to review. Found in Review → Track Changes.

Accounting Number Format $ Applies the Accounting format to the active cell. Found on the Home tab.

Align Text Left ≣ Formats the active cell as left aligned. Found on the Home tab.

Align Text Right ≣ Formats the active cell as right aligned. Found on the Home tab.

Allow Users to Edit Ranges Displays a dialog box with options for editing a cell range on a protected sheet. Found on the Review tab.

Bold **B** Formats the active cell as bold. Found on the Home tab.

Borders ⊞ ▾ Used to format cell borders. Found on the Home tab.

Cancel ✖ Restores the original contents of the active cell. Found on the formula bar.

Center ≣ Formats the active cell as center aligned. Found on the Home tab.

Clip Art Displays the Clip Art task pane, which is used to place a graphic on the worksheet. Found on the Insert tab.

Comma Style ' Adds a thousands separator to a value. Found on the Home tab.

Conditional Formatting Displays a list of rules used to specify conditional formatting. Found on the Home tab.

Copy Creates a duplicate of the selected cell(s) contents for pasting. Found on the Home tab.

Cut Removes the selected cell(s) contents. Found on the Home tab.

Data Bars Displays a list of options for conditional formatting. Found in Home → Conditional Formatting.

E-mail Displays an e-mail message with the workbook as an attachment. Found in ▬File▬ → Send.

Enter ✔ Enters data in the active cell. Found on the formula bar.

Error Checking ◈ Displayed by a cell that has an error in the formula it stores.

Font Calibri ▾ Displays a list of fonts to choose from. Found on the Home tab.

Font Size 11 ▾ Displays a list of font sizes to choose from. Found on the Home tab.

Format Painter ✎ Copies cell formatting from one cell to another. Found on the Home tab.

Header & Footer Adds a header and footer to the worksheet and displays the worksheet in Page Layout view. Found on the Insert tab.

Highlight Cell Rules Displays a list of options for conditional formatting. Found in Home → Conditional Formatting.

Highlight Changes Displays a dialog box with options for tracking changes. Found in Review → Track Changes.

Hyperlink Displays a dialog box used to insert a hyperlink into the active cell. Found on the Insert tab.

Italic *I* Formats the active cell as italic. Found on the Home tab.

Merge & Center Used to merge a group of adjacent cells and center text within the merged cells. Found on the Home tab.

New Creates a new workbook. Found in Backstage view.

Number Format General ▾ Used to select number formats. Found on the Home tab.

Orientation Used to change text orientation. Found on the Home tab.

Paste Places the most recently copied or cut data into a worksheet starting at the selected cell. Found on the Home tab.

Paste Options 🗐 (Ctrl) ▾ Displayed when data is pasted on a worksheet.

Percent Style % Formats the active cell as percentage with no decimal places. Found on the Home tab.

Picture Displays a dialog box used to place a graphic on the worksheet. Found on the Insert tab.

Print Prints a copy of the worksheet. Found in Backstage view.

Print Preview Displays a worksheet as it will appear when printed. Found in ▬File▬ → Print.

Protect Sheet Displays a dialog box with options for protecting the contents of the active sheet. Found on the Review tab.

Protect Workbook Displays a dialog box with options for protecting sheets and the window. Found on the Review tab.

Remove Hyperlink Removes the blue underline from text in a cell. Found in the menu displayed by right-clicking the cell containing a link.

Redo ↻ Repeats the last action. Found on the Quick Access Toolbar.

Save As Displays a dialog box used to save a workbook as a template. Found in Backstage view.

Spelling Checks the spelling of text in the worksheet. Found on the Review tab.

Thesaurus Displays a task pane used to suggest words with similar meanings. Found on the Review tab.

Top/Bottom Rules Displays a list of options for conditional formatting. Found in Home → Conditional Formatting.

Underline U Formats the contents of the active cell as underlined. Found on the Home tab.

Undo Reverses the previous action. Found on the Quick Access Toolbar.

Unprotect Sheet Displays a dialog box with options for unprotecting the contents of the active sheet. Found on the Review tab.

Wrap Text Allows for more than one line of text within a cell. Found on the Home tab.

1. List three example uses for a spreadsheet application.

2. a) What is an Excel file called?
   b) How many worksheets does a new workbook contain?

3. a) How are individual columns identified on a worksheet?
   b) How are individual rows identified on a worksheet?
   c) What is a cell?
   d) Give an example of a cell reference.
   e) What does the name box display?
   f) What does the formula bar display?

4. What are the three steps in the worksheet planning process?

5. After selecting a cell and typing data, what happens when you:
   a) click Enter ✔?
   b) press the Enter key?
   c) press the Tab key?
   d) press the Esc key?

6. What are two ways to change the width of a column?

7. List two ways to change which cell is active.

8. If a cell contains the wrong data, how can it be corrected?

9. What is displayed when ▾ in ⌐ is clicked?

10. How many cells store each of the following types of data in part 1 of the Grades worksheet created in the Practices?
    a) labels
    b) values
    c) dates
    d) times

11. List two ways to adjust cells that contain long column headings.

12. Which numeric format has been applied to each of the following?
    a) $12.50
    b) 120,450.00
    c) 23%

    d) 1/2
    e) 1.20E+05

13. When does a cell display ####?

14. a) What is a range?
    b) List two ways to select the range B3 through C12.
    c) What button selects the entire worksheet?

15. a) What is a theme?
    b) How is the formatting removed from a cell?
    c) How can a theme be previewed?

16. a) Which view displays a worksheet as a printed page?
    b) Give one reason why a worksheet should be previewed before printing.

17. Where are headers and footers printed?

18. a) Explain what a formula is and give two examples.
    b) If 10/20 is entered into a cell, Excel considers it a label. How must the entry be changed so that 10 will be divided by 20?
    c) How can a cell be formatted so that =10/20 will appear in the cell?

19. a) Which specific order of operations does Excel use to evaluate a mathematical expression?
    b) How can the order of operations within a formula be changed?

20. What value would be calculated by Excel for each of the following formulas?
    a) =2+7*5+4
    b) =(2+7)*(5+4)
    c) =5+10/5
    d) =-(5+10)/5
    e) =2^3+4

21. a) What is displayed in a cell if an invalid formula is entered?
    b) What button is displayed when a cell with an error value is selected?
    c) Where can a description of an invalid formula error be found?

22. How can the formulas stored in the cells of a worksheet be displayed?

23. What value would be calculated by Excel for each of the following formulas if cell C15 stores a value of 6 and cell D8 a value of 3?
    a) =C15*D8
    b) =C15+5+D8
    c) =C15*5+D8
    d) =C15*(5+D8)
    e) =C15/D8

24. What is usually the best method for entering cell references in a formula? Why?

25. What is a circular reference?

26. a) Describe one way to copy the values stored in cells A1, A2, and A3 to cells T1, T2, and T3.
    b) List the steps required to move the contents of cell B4 into cell A9.
    c) What key is pressed to remove the dashed border from the source cells once the cells have been pasted?

27. a) What is a relative cell reference?
    b) What are the contents of cells D22 and E22 after copying cell C22, which stores the formula =C5 + C6, into cells D22 and E22?

28. When worksheet data is needed in a Word document, would it be best to retype the data into the document or copy and paste the data from the worksheet? Why?

29. Is it possible to copy and paste a table of data from a Word document to an Excel worksheet? If so, how will the data be organized in the worksheet?

30. Describe two conditional formats that can be applied to a range of cells.

31. a) List two ways a graphic can be added to a worksheet.
    b) Would a company logo likely be clip art? Explain.
    c) List the steps to size a clip art graphic.

32. List two ways to enter a Web site address in a cell.

33. Describe a situation where it would be important to protect worksheet data.

34. List the steps required to e-mail a workbook as an attachment.

35. Describe two proofing tools that can be used to check text on a worksheet.

36. Explain how worksheet modifications can be noted if more than one person is working on a worksheet.

37. How is e-mail important to worksheet collaboration?

38. a) Explain why a worksheet would be saved in HTML format.
    b) What software is required to view an HTML document?

39. a) What is a template?
    b) Give an example of a worksheet that would be best saved as a template.

True/False

40. Determine if each of the following are true or false. If false, explain why.
    a) A cell reference consists of a column letter only.
    b) Selected cell and active cell mean the same thing.
    c) The contents of the active cell are displayed in the name box.
    d) There are over a million rows on a worksheet.
    e) The width of just a single cell can be changed.
    f) A cell can contain only one line of text.
    g) The Accounting and Currency formats are the same.
    h) A range can consist of non-adjacent cells.
    i) The Metro theme is applied by default to a new workbook.
    j) Headers are visible in Normal view.
    k) Cell references must be typed in capital letters.
    l) The length of a Data Bar depends on the value in the cell relative to other cells.
    m) A clip art graphic can be recolored in Excel.
    n) The Underline style should be used sparingly because it could be confused with a hyperlink.
    o) Excel automatically checks the spelling of a worksheet.
    p) An open workbook can be attached to an e-mail message from Excel.

Projects

Project 1

Study Time Tutoring is designing a schedule for its students to manage their school and extra-curricular activities schedule.

a) Create a new workbook.

b) Enter the data and apply formatting using the Office theme as shown below:

	A	B	C	D	E	F
1	**Name's Weekly Schedule**					
2	TIME	Monday	Tuesday	Wednesday	Thursday	Friday
3	9:00 - 10:00					
4	10:00 - 11:00					
5	11:00 - 12:00					
6	12:00 - 1:00					
7	1:00 - 2:00					
8	2:00 - 3:00					
9	3:00 - 4:00					
10	4:00 - 5:00					
11	5:00 - 6:00					
12	6:00 - 7:00					
13	7:00 - 8:00					

c) Create an example student schedule by adding data such as school classes, athletics, extracurricular groups and clubs, studying and doing homework, and so forth.

d) Add your name in a header and the current date in a footer. Add gridlines and headings.

e) Save the workbook naming it Schedule and print a copy.

f) To have students analyze how much time they are spending on certain activities, create a new workbook. Enter the data and apply formatting as shown below:

	A	B	C	D	E	F	G
1	Activity	Mon	Tue	Wed	Thu	Fri	Total Hours
2							
3							
4							
5							

g) Using the Schedule printout as a reference, fill in all the scheduled activities in column A and the corresponding hours per day in columns B through F.

h) In column G, enter formulas that calculate the total hours spent on each activity per each work week. Format the total hours to display 2 decimal places.

i) Add your name in a header and the current date in a footer. Add gridlines and headings.

j) Save the workbook naming it Activity and print a copy.

Project 2

Yolanda's Catering uses a balance sheet to list assets (what they own), liabilities (what they owe), and stockholder's equity (total assets minus total liabilities) as of a specific date.

a) Create a new workbook.

b) Enter the data and apply formatting using the Adjacency theme as shown below. Add the YC LOGO, which is a data file for this text:

	A	B	C	D
1				
2	Yolanda's Catering			
3				
4	Balance Sheet for 2011			
5				
6	Assets:			
7		Cash	$12,000	
8		Accounts Receivable	$15,000	
9		Gym Equipment	$45,000	
10		Office Computers	$98,990	
11		Total Assets:		
12				
13	Liabilities:			
14		Accounts Payable	$75,987	
15		Short-term Debt	$1,200	
16		Total Liabilities:		
17				
18				
19		Total Stockholder's Equity:		
20				

c) Modify the logo by adding a picture style.

d) Save the workbook naming it Balance Sheet.

e) In cell C11, enter a formula that uses cell references to calculate the total assets.

f) In cell C16, enter a formula that uses cell references to calculate the total liabilities.

g) In cell C19, enter a formula that uses cell references to calculate the stockholder's equity.

h) Format cells C11, C16, and C19 in an appropriate cell style with a bottom double border.

i) Add your name in a header and the current date in a footer. Add gridlines and headings.

j) Save the modified Balance Sheet and print a copy.

k) Create an HTML document from the workbook with the title Yolanda's Catering Finances. When saving as a Web page, select Single File Web Page from the Save as type list in the Save As dialog box. This option will save the logo as well as the data in one Web page.

l) Preview the HTML file in a Web browser.

Project 3

Throughout the world, except in the United States and a few other countries, the Celsius temperature scale is used. To have travellers become familiar with the scale, complete the following steps:

a) Create a new workbook.

b) Enter the data and apply formatting using the Office theme as shown below. In cell E3 enter the formula =5/9*(B3–32) to convert the Fahrenheit temperature stored in cell B3 to degrees Celsius:

	A	B	C	D	E	F
1	Temperature Conversion					
2						
3	Fahrenheit Temp:	80		Celsius Temp:	27	

c) Save the workbook naming it Temp Conversion.

d) Format cell E3 to display 0 decimal places.

e) Apply conditional formatting to cells B3 and E3 so that negative values will be displayed in a red text color.

f) Enter the following Fahrenheit temperatures in cell B3, one at a time: 0, 32, and 80. What Celsius temperature does each of these convert to?

g) In row 5, have the worksheet convert temperatures from a Celsius temperature entered in cell B5 to a Fahrenheit temperature displayed in cell E5. Use 26 for the Celsius temperature. Include appropriate labels. The formula needed for converting from degrees Celsius to Fahrenheit is =9/5*B5+32. Display the result with 0 decimal places. Change the column widths as necessary so that all the data is displayed entirely.

h) Enter the following Celsius temperatures in cell B5, one at a time: 0, 12, and –21. What Fahrenheit temperature does each of these convert to?

i) In cell D1, add a link to a Web site, such as www.weather.com, where users could access current temperature data.

j) Add your name in a header and the current date in a footer. Add gridlines and headings.

k) Save the modified Temp Conversion and print a copy.

l) Display the formulas in the cells instead of values. Print a copy.

Project 4

Although the metric system (also called SI) is used throughout the world, the U.S. still widely depends on the English system of measurements. To help travellers with conversions, complete the following steps:

a) Create a new workbook.

b) Enter the data and apply formatting using the Median theme as shown below:

	A	B	C	D	E
1	**Metric Conversions**				
2					
3	English		Metric		
4		cubic feet		cubic meters	
5		cubic yards		cubic meters	
6		feet		meters	
7		gallons		liters	
8		inches		centimeters	
9		miles		kilometers	
10		pounds		kilograms	
11		square feet		square meters	
12		square miles		square kilometers	
13		square yards		square meters	
14		yards		meters	
15					

c) Save the workbook naming it Metric Conversions.

d) Use the information below to add the appropriate formulas that use cell references into cells C4 through C14:

     cubic meters = 0.0283*cubic feet

     cubic meters = 0.7646*cubic yards

     meters = 0.3048*feet

     liters = 3.7853*gallons

     centimeters = 2.54*inches

     kilometers = 1.6093*miles

     kilograms = 0.3732*pounds

     square meters = 0.0929*square feet

     square kilometers = 2.59*square miles

     square meters = 0.8361*square yards

     meters = 0.9144*yards

e) Check your worksheet by entering 5 in cell A4. Cell C4 should display 0.1415 because it automatically calculates the metric equivalent of 5 cubic feet.

f) Enter the following measurements into cells A4 through A14. Your worksheet should look similar to:

	A	B	C	D	E
1	Metric Conversions				
2					
3	English		Metric		
4	5	cubic feet	0.1415	cubic meters	
5	10	cubic yards	7.646	cubic meters	
6	10	feet	3.048	meters	
7	1	gallons	3.7853	liters	
8	12	inches	30.48	centimeters	
9	2	miles	3.2186	kilometers	
10	25	pounds	9.33	kilograms	
11	40	square feet	3.716	square meters	
12	12	square miles	31.08	square kilometers	
13	10	square yards	8.361	square meters	
14	5	yards	4.572	meters	
15					

g) Add your name in a header and the current date in a footer. Add gridlines and headings.

h) Save the modified Metric Conversions and print a copy.

i) Display the formulas in the cells instead of values. Print a copy.

Project 5

Estimate how much it will cost to make a recipe assuming all the ingredients need to be purchased.

a) Find a delicious recipe that requires eight or fewer ingredients.

b) Create a new workbook.

c) In cell A1, enter the title Calculating the Cost of a Recipe.

d) In cell A3, enter the name of the recipe.

e) In cell A5, enter the label Ingredient.

f) In cells B5, C5, and D5, enter the labels Store #1, Store #2, and Store #3.

g) Starting in cell A6, enter the name of each ingredient required to make the recipe.

h) Add an appropriate clip art graphic and then apply an appropriate theme and cell styles.

i) Use the Internet or newspapers to find the price of each ingredient at two different stores. Be sure the prices are for the same size container (but not necessarily the same brand name) of the ingredient.

j) Starting in cell B6, enter the corresponding ingredient prices.

k) Format the cells storing prices as currency with 2 decimal places.

l) Save the workbook naming it Recipe.

m) Add your name in a header and text Recipe in a footer. Add gridlines and headings.

n) Save the modified Recipe.

o) E-mail the worksheet to a classmate for collaboration. In the message area, add the text: Please compare prices at a third store and add the appropriate data.

p) Open the e-mail from your classmate and open the attachment. Use cell formatting to shade the best overall prices.

q) Save the modified Recipe document and print a copy.

Project 6

When determining a *budget*, it is important to come up with realistic figures. One way to determine actual expenses is to keep careful track of all money spent for a period. Keeping track of expenses for one week can work in some cases, but when there are responsibilities such as loan payments and utility bills, expenses need to be tracked for at least one month. Tracking expenses can also help determine where too much money is being spent.

a) Create a new workbook.

b) Enter data and apply formatting using the Trek theme as shown below:

	A	B	C
1	Expenses		
2			
3	Expense Description	Amount	Transaction Type
4			
5			

c) Format cells B4 through B15 as currency with 2 decimal places.

d) Save the workbook naming it Expenses.

e) Save the receipts from every purchase made over the next week and be sure to record every check in your checkbook register.

f) Update the worksheet with the saved receipts and checkbook register. Enter each transaction on a separate row in chronological order. In the Transaction Type column, enter Cash, Credit, or Check as appropriate.

g) Add your name in a header and the current date in a footer.

h) Use cell styles to shade alternate rows.

i) Add a formula that sums the expenses and a descriptive label. Format the formula and labels appropriately.

j) Save the modified Expenses.

k) Create a new Word document. Write a paragraph that analyzes your spending. Describe your source of income. Is your spending for the period too high relative to your income for the same period? Is there one type of spending that could be reduced? Spending with credit can be more expensive than spending with cash because credit incurs interest charges. Are credit expenses too high?

l) Save the Word document naming it Expenses Analyzed.

m) Below the paragraph that analyzes your spending, place a copy of the data from the Expenses worksheet.

n) Save the modified Expenses Analyzed document and print a copy.

Project 7

Worksheets can be helpful with *personal financial management*.

    a) Create a new workbook.

    b) Enter data and apply formatting as shown below:

	A	B	C	D	E
1		Transaction	Payment (Debit)	Deposit (Credit)	
2					
3	2/2/2011	Opening Deposit		$200.00	
4	2/5/2011	Cell Phone Bill	$20.00		
5	2/9/2011	Paycheck		$100.00	
6	2/10/2011	Sally's Diner	$15.35		
7	2/11/2011	Coral Square Cinema	$6.75		
8	2/17/2011	Deposit		$25.00	
9	2/18/2011	Book Palace	$15.98		
10	2/19/2011	Full Belly	$10.50		
11	2/24/2011	Coral Square Mall	$5.75		
12	2/24/2011	Coral Gas	$15.00		
13	2/27/2011	Deposit		$100.00	

    c) Save the workbook naming it Personal Finances.

    d) In cell E1, enter the label Balance. Right align and bold the label if necessary.

    e) In column E, enter formulas that use cell references to calculate the balance after each transaction. To calculate the balance, subtract the expense from the previous balance and add the income to the previous balance.

    f) In cell B14, enter the label Total: and then right align and bold it. Enter formulas that calculate the total expenses and total income for the month.

    g) Apply an appropriate theme and cell styles.

    h) Add your name in a header and the current date in a footer. Add gridlines and headings.

    i) Save the modified Personal Finances and print a copy.

    j) Display the formulas in the cells instead of values. Print a copy.

Project 8

An *income statement* lists a company's revenue (money they earn), expenses (money they pay out), and net income/loss (revenue minus expenses) for a specific time period. Align Computers wants to use a worksheet to produce an income statement.

a) Create a new workbook.

b) Enter data and apply formatting using the Metro theme as shown below:

	A	B	C	D	E
1		Align Computers			
2		Income Statement			
3		for the years 2009-2011			
4					
5		2009	2010	2011	
6	Revenue:				
7	Computer Sales	$15,500	$16,896	$17,864	
8	Service	$27,589	$26,298	$25,982	
9	Accessories	$24,980	$25,298	$25,398	
10	Total Revenues:				
11	Expenses:				
12	Advertising	$5,000	$4,500	$4,500	
13	Supplies	$2,000	$1,000	$2,750	
14	Ingredients	$13,275	$15,298	$16,490	
15	Salaries	$30,000	$30,000	$35,000	
16	Utilities	$6,570	$7,250	$8,090	
17	Total Expenses:				
18	Net Income/(Loss):				

c) Save the workbook naming it Income Statement.

d) In row 10, enter formulas that calculate the total revenue for each year.

e) In row 17, enter formulas that calculate the total expenses for each year.

f) In row 18, enter formulas that use cell references to calculate the net income or loss for each year. The net income/loss is calculated by subtracting total expenses from total revenue. Format the values as currency with 0 decimal places, if necessary.

g) Add your name in a header and the current date in a footer. Add gridlines and headings.

h) Save the modified Income Statement.

i) Display the formulas in the cells instead of values. Print a copy.

Project 9

The TWP NEWS document contains a partial newsletter. The TOURS document and the TOUR PRICES workbook contain information for the newsletter. Open TWP NEWS, TOURS, and TOUR PRICES, which are data files for this text, and complete the following steps:

a) Place a copy of all the text in the TOURS document into the TWP NEWS document in the blank paragraph at the end of the newsletter.

b) The data in cells A1 through B5 in the TOUR PRICES workbook needs to be added to the TWP NEWS newsletter. Use an appropriate theme and cell styles to appropriately format the worksheet and then place a copy of the data into the newsletter in the blank paragraph at the end of the newsletter.

c) In the TWP NEWS document, create a footer with your name.

d) Save the modified TWP NEWS and print a copy.

Project 10

A student wants to use a worksheet to create a *personal budget* for her fall semester in college.

a) Create a new workbook.

b) Enter data and apply formatting using the Office theme as shown below:

	A	B	C	D	E	F	G	H	I
1	**Personal Budget**								
2									
3		**Sep-11**		**Oct-11**		**Nov-11**		**Dec-11**	
4		**Budgeted**	**Actual**	**Budgeted**	**Actual**	**Budgeted**	**Actual**	**Budgeted**	**Actual**
5	**Income:**								
6	Loan	$7,000	$7,000	$0	$0	$0	$0	$0	$0
7	Job	$1,000	$925	$500	$465	$500	$485	$600	$725
8	Other	$5,500	$5,500	$0	$0	$0	$0	$0	$0
9	**Total:**								
10	**Expenses:**								
11	Tuition	$6,000	$5,943	$0	$0	$0	$0	$0	$0
12	Room/Board	$5,500	$5,575	$0	$0	$0	$0	$0	$0
13	Books	$700	$635	$0	$45	$0	$0	$0	$0
14	Food	$300	$315	$300	$325	$300	$320	$250	$375
15	Entertainment	$150	$0	$50	$80	$50	$0	$100	$100
16	Clothes	$50	$0	$50	$80	$50	$0	$100	$100
17	**Total:**								
18									
19									

c) Save the workbook naming it Budget.

d) In cell B9, enter a formula that calculates the total budgeted income for September. Use the cell's fill handle to copy the formula to cells C9 through I9.

e) In cell B17, enter a formula that calculates the total budgeted expenses for September. Use the cell's fill handle to copy the formula to cells C17 through I17.

f) In cell A18, enter the label: Savings: Right align the label and format it as italic. Enter formulas that use cell references to calculate the savings for each month. Savings are calculated by subtracting the total expenses from the total income.

g) Use conditional formatting to create a rule that formats the data in cells C17, E17, G17, and I17 in a light red fill if the value is a negative number. Format the columns containing the Actual data to be just wide enough to display the data.

h) Add your name in a header and the current date in a footer. Add gridlines and headings.

i) Save the modified Budget and print a copy.

j) Display the formulas in the cells instead of values. Print a copy.

Project 11

A mutual fund is a collection of stocks and/or bonds. A stock is a share of ownership in a company and a bond is a loan funded by investors. Mutual fund investors own shares that represent a portion of the mutual fund holdings. Mutual funds offer investment diversification because a single fund can consist of hundreds or even thousands of different stocks and/or bonds. Such diversification minimizes the effects of stocks performing poorly, but also dilutes the effects of stocks performing well. Important considerations for most mutual funds are:

- Mutual funds typically have a manager who buys and sells stocks and/or bonds.

- Mutual funds require fees to pay for management. These fees, called the expense ratio, reduce the return on investment.

- The majority of mutual funds do not perform as well as the market average.

Unlike most mutual funds, a stock index fund consists of only stocks from a particular index. An index is a defined subset of all stocks available on stock markets. A statement about how "the market" is doing is referring to the performance of the Dow or another index. Popular indexes include:

- **Dow Jones Industrial Average (DJIA or Dow)**   A collection of 30 blue-chip stocks. Blue-chip stocks are widely held and are considered solid, reliable, and having sustained growth. Stocks include Microsoft, Intel, Coca-Cola, McDonald's, and American Express.

- **Standard & Poor's 500 (S&P 500)**   A collection of the 500 largest company stocks. Stocks include Microsoft, Wal-Mart, and IBM.

- **Nasdaq 100**   A collection of the 100 largest company stocks listed on the Nasdaq. Stocks include Microsoft, Intel, Dell, and Yahoo!.

- **Nasdaq Composite**   A collection of all stocks listed on the Nasdaq.

- **Amex Composite**   A collection of all stocks listed on the American Stock Exchange.

- **Russell 2000**   A collection of 2,000 small-company stocks. City Bank, Zale, and Fossil are stocks in the Russell 2000.

- **Wilshire 5000**   Although the name seems to indicate a set of 5,000 stocks, the Wilshire index actually contains over 6,000 stocks. Sometimes referred to as the Total Stock Market Index because it includes the stock for nearly every U.S. corporation.

Because of its holdings, a stock index fund typically performs as well as the market average. This means stock index funds outperform most other mutual funds. Stock index funds also have very low expense ratios and are offered by many companies.

The first index fund was started in 1975 by the Vanguard Group. The Vanguard 500 Index Fund (VFINX) remains one of the most popular and outperforms the vast majority of other mutual funds. Other index funds include the Vanguard Total Stock Market Fund (VTSMX) and the Vanguard TSM VIPERS (VTI), which follow the Wilshire 5000 index.

a) Create a new workbook. Enter and format labels as shown. The current date should appear below the Price label:

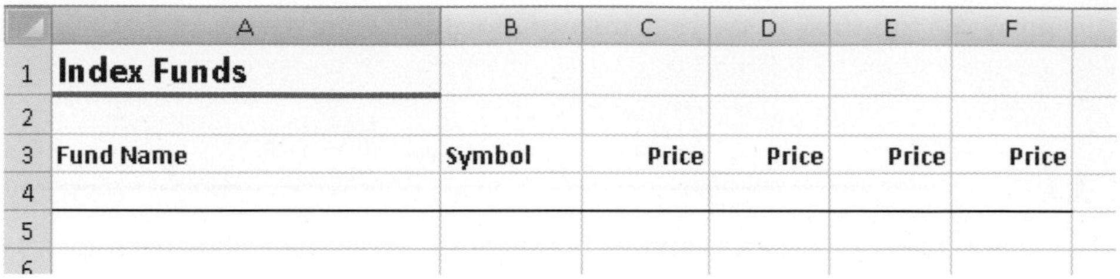

	A	B	C	D	E	F
1	**Index Funds**					
2						
3	**Fund Name**	**Symbol**	**Price**	**Price**	**Price**	**Price**
4						
5						
6						

b) Add the three Vanguard index fund names and their symbols to the worksheet.

c) Apply an appropriate theme and cell styles.

d) Save the workbook naming it Index Funds.

e) Use a Web site such as finance.yahoo.com to get a price quote for each of the funds and then enter the information into column C.

f) Format the prices as currency with 2 decimal places.

g) Research and then choose three other index funds using the Internet, newspapers, or financial magazines. Add the three selected funds, to the Index Funds workbook.

h) Update the Index Funds workbook on three different days to include new fund quotes.

Project 12

Many jobs, such as sales and marketing positions, require employees to travel outside the office using their own vehicle. For this type of travel, employees are required to keep track of their mileage on a mileage log form and then submit the form for reimbursement based on a rate per mile.

a) Create a new workbook.

b) Enter data and apply formatting using the Newsprint theme as shown below:

	A	B	C	D	E	F	G	H
1	**Travel…With A Purpose**							
2	**Monthly Mileage Log**							
3		**Employee Name:**						
4		**Submit Date:**						
5								
6	**Date**	**Description**	**From**	**To**	**Odometer**		**Mileage**	
7					**Start**	**Finish**		
8								
9								
10								
11								
12								
13								
14					**Total Mileage**			
15					**Rate**			
16					**Reimbursement**			
17								

c) In cell G8, enter a formula to calculate the mileage from the starting point to the finish point. Use the cell's fill handle to copy the formula to cells G9 through G13. In the Auto Fill Options button, select Fill Without Formatting.

d) Enter a formula to calculate the total mileage.

e) Employees are reimbursed at a rate of $0.32 per mile. Type the rate in the appropriate cell and then enter a formula to calculate the total reimbursement. Format the cells appropriately.

f) Save the worksheet as a template naming it Mileage Log and close Mileage Log.

g) Create a new workbook based on the Mileage Log template.

h) Enter your name for the Employee Name and today's date for the Submit Date.

i) Starting in cell A8, enter the data:

Date	Description	From	To	Start	Finish
4/2/2011	Microsoft Seminar	Miami	Boca Raton	33,580	33,625
4/28/2011	Sales Call	Boca Raton	Palm Beach	34,800	34,830
4/28/2011	Sales Call	Palm Beach	Boca Raton	34,830	34,860

j) Add your name in a header and the current date in a footer. Add gridlines and headings.

k) Save the worksheet naming it April Mileage Log and print a copy.

l) E-mail the worksheet to a classmate. In the message area, add the text: Attached please find my monthly mileage log.

Project 13

Many jobs require travel. When traveling for business, employees are required to fill out a travel expense form for any out-of-pocket expenses.

a) Create a new workbook.

b) Enter data and apply formatting using the Thatch theme as shown below. Cells B9 through B16 are formatted for the Accounting currency style and 0 (zero) has been typed into each cell. Accounting style displays a dash in place of 0:

	A	B	C
1	Travel...With A Purpose		
2	Expense Statement		
3			
4	Employee Name:		
5	Employee Number:		
6	Date:		
7	Travel Destination:		
8	Travel Dates:		
9	Airfare	$0.00	
10	Hotel	$0.00	
11	Food	$0.00	
12	Car rental	$0.00	
13	Gas	$0.00	
14	Entertainment	$0.00	
15	Miscellaneous	$0.00	
16	Total Expenses		
17			
18	Complete, attach all receipts, and submit to Human Resources.		
19			

c) Enter a formula to calculate the total expenses.

d) Save the worksheet as a template naming it Travel Expenses and then close Travel Expenses.

e) Create a new workbook based on the Travel Expenses template.

f) Enter your name for the Employee Name, any 4-digit number for the Employee Number, and today's date for the Date. Enter Chicago for the Travel Destination and enter 05/15/11 - 05/20/11 for the Travel Dates.

g) Use the Internet to research the cost of a five-day trip to Chicago. Include a car rental for the entire five days. Type the estimated amounts into the appropriate cells.

h) Add a header with your name. Add gridlines and headings.

i) Save the worksheet naming it Chicago Travel Expenses and print a copy.

Project 14

The numeric keypad can make the entering of large amounts of numeric data more efficient. It also allows easy access to the mathematical operators +, -, *, and /. Most keyboards require pressing the Num Lock key on the numeric keypad before numbers can be entered.

Before beginning to enter data, the right hand should be placed lightly on the keypad with slightly curved fingers. The right index finger is placed on the number 4 key, the right middle finger is placed on the number 5 key, the right ring finger is placed on the number 6 key, and the right pinky finger is placed on the + key. The right thumb is placed over the 0 key. With the fingers placed as just described, this is called the home position. Open KEYPAD, which is an Excel data file for this text, and complete the following steps:

a) Data entry into a range of cells can be made easier by selecting the range before entering the data. In a selected range, pressing Enter makes the next cell in the range active. When the last cell in a column is reached, pressing Enter makes the cell at the top of the next column in the range active. Select cells A1 through G6 and then place the right hand on the keypad in the home position as described above.

b) Enter the following numbers starting in cell A1, pressing the Enter key with the right pinky after each number. Do not look at the right hand while entering data, refer only to the picture of the keypad below. Note that the data entered will not be entered as a formula because the data does not begin with an equal sign (=).

	A	B	C	D	E	F	G
1	444	555	666	405	444	4++	55+
2	445	446	444	44+	445	5+5	445
3	455	466	400	4++	555	6+5	554
4	555	545	565	566	666	5+0	505
5	666	646	656	606	506	0+4	6+6
6	604	404	505	406	405	6++	0+0
7							

c) Repeat part (b) until the characters can be typed without referring to the keypad graphic.

d) The number 7 is typed using the index finger of the right hand, the number 8 is typed using the middle finger of the right hand, the number 9 is typed using the ring finger of the right hand and the - is typed using the pinky finger of the right hand. Select cells A8 through G13 and enter the following numbers in the same manner as part (b):

	A	B	C	D	E	F	G
7							
8	777	888	999	77-	888	999	9--
9	778	779	777	778	779	888	778
10	788	7799	898	788	799	787	878
11	888	878	989	878	878	989	9--
12	999	979	787	88-	979	7--	789
13	797	777	888	-88	797	8--	987
14							

e) Repeat part (d) until the characters can be typed without referring to the keypad graphic.

f) The number 1 is typed using the index finger of the right hand, the number 2 is typed using the middle finger of the right hand, the number 3 and the . key are typed using the ring finger of the right hand. Select cells A15 through G20 and enter the following numbers in the same manner as parts (b) and (d):

	A	B	C	D	E	F	G
14							
15	111	212	363	171	252	112	1.2
16	121	222	282	147	414	113	1.3
17	131	213	111	258	222	242	2.3
18	222	222	222	369	115	282	2.1
19	223	252	333	216	114	273	3.2
20	221	141	282	246	116	198	2.1
21							

g) Repeat part (f) until the characters can be typed without referring to the keypad graphic.

h) The / key is typed using the middle finger of the right hand, the * key is typed using the ring finger of the right hand, and the + key is typed using the pinky finger of the right hand. Select cells A22 through G27 and enter the following numbers in the same manner as parts (b), (d), and (f):

	A	B	C	D	E	F	G
21							
22	4/5	4*5	4*5	6/4	1*3	-7*3	3+3
23	5/5	5*5	5*6	5/5	5+6+9+3	-1*2	5+5
24	1*4	2-6	6+4	4*7	2+6	5+5+4	4*8
25	4*5	3+5	2+6	3+5	-4+8	1*1.5	3+2+5
26	4+5	3/3	3/3	5.6*1.3	5+3	4+6/1	4.5*4+1
27	0.5*1.3	4-5	0.6*1.08	3/6	1+1	5*8-2.5	2+9
28							

i) Repeat part (h) until the characters can be typed without referring to the keypad graphic.

j) Close the workbook without saving changes.

Project 15

Icon sets are a conditional formatting option in Excel where an icon is used to represent the value of that cell relative to the other cells in the selected range. Icon sets include:

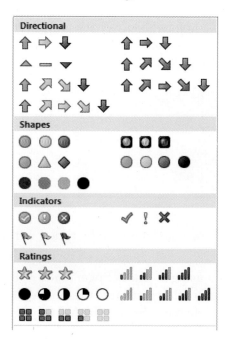

To use icon sets, select a range of data and then click Home → Conditional Formatting → Manage Rules. A dialog box is displayed. Select New Rule and then select Icon Sets in the Format Style list:

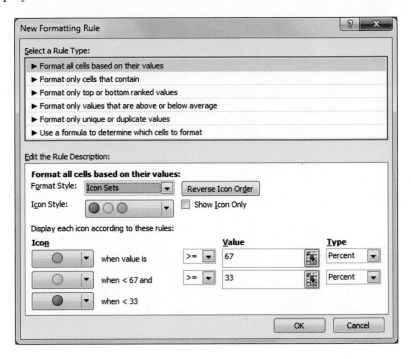

An icon style can then be selected from the Icon Style list and a rule for each icon can be specified in the appropriate Value and Type lists. Open SALES ANALYSIS, which is an Excel data file for this text, and complete the following steps:

a) In cell E1, type the heading Performance and adjust the column width appropriately.

b) In cell E2, enter a formula that calculates sales performance by subtracting the quota from the sales. Copy the formula to cells E3 through E30.

c) Select the data in column E and create a conditional formatting rule using an icon set that analyzes the performance data.

d) Add your name in a header and the current date in a footer. Add gridlines and headings.

e) Save the modified SALES ANALYSIS and print a copy.

Chapter 6
Functions and Data Organization

Key Concepts

Modifying and creating cell styles
Inserting and deleting columns and rows
Using functions
Using absolute cell references in formulas
Sorting data
Printing large worksheets
Creating amortization tables
Working with multiple sheets
Asking "What-if?" questions

Practice Data Files
PLANETS, COMMISSION SUMMARY,
PAYROLL, LOAN, CAR SALES, FUNDRAISER

Project Data Files
SCHOOL LOAN

Modifying and Creating Cell Styles

Cell Styles

An applied cell style can be modified using character formatting commands, such as Font Size `11 ▾`. However, if the cell style that needs to be modified will be used over and over again in the workbook, the cell style can be modified in the cell styles gallery. Click Home → Cell Styles to display the gallery of cell styles. Right-click a style and select Modify:

TIP Cell styles were first introduced in Chapter 5 as a means of applying several formats in one step and ensuring consistent cell formatting.

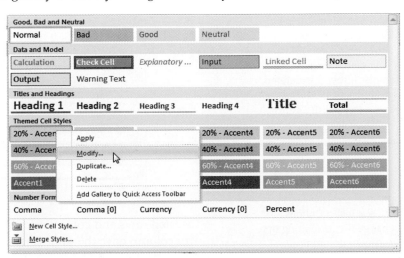

The Style dialog box is displayed:

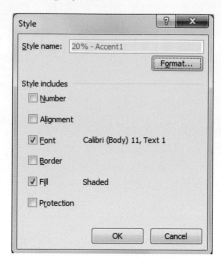

TIP A modified cell style is only accessible in the active workbook.

Select **Format** to display the Format Cells dialog box. Once changes are made, select **OK** to apply the changes to the cell style.

To create a new style, click **Home → Cell Styles → New Cell Style**. The Style dialog box is displayed. Click **Format** to specify formatting. New styles appear in the cell styles gallery under the heading **Custom**.

Inserting and Deleting Rows and Columns

Insert   Delete

Rows and columns can be inserted between data in a worksheet. To add a row or column, select a cell in the row number or column letter where the new row or column is to appear and then click **Home → Insert → Insert Sheet Rows** or **Home → Insert → Insert Sheet Columns**. For example, a new row has been inserted in the worksheet below:

TIP When cells are inserted or deleted, Excel automatically changes the relative cell references in any affected formulas. For example, if row 3 is deleted, the formula =SUM(C1:C10) changes to =SUM(C1:C9).

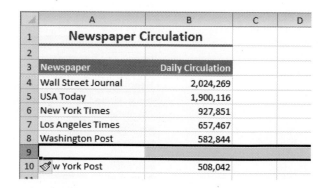

TIP Click Insert Options to change the formatting of a new row or column.

Inserted rows and columns contain no data. However, cells in the new row or column have the same formatting as the cells above or to the left of them, respectively. In the worksheet on the previous page, data added to the inserted row will automatically have the same formatting as row 8:

	A	B
1	**Newspaper Circulation**	
2		
3	Newspaper	Daily Circulation
4	Wall Street Journal	2,024,269
5	USA Today	1,900,116
6	New York Times	927,851
7	Los Angeles Times	657,467
8	Washington Post	582,844
9	Daily News	544,167
10	New York Post	508,042

TIP Click Undo ↻ on the Quick Access Toolbar to restore a deleted row or column.

To delete a row or column, select a cell and then click Home → Delete → Delete Sheet Rows or Home → Delete → Delete Sheet Columns.

Practice: PLANETS – part 1 of 2

① **OPEN PLANETS**

Open PLANETS, which is an Excel data file for this text. This worksheet lists planets and their corresponding diameter. Note that some formatting has been applied to the worksheet.

② **MODIFY A CELL STYLE**

a. Select cells A1 and B1 and then click Home → Cell Styles → Heading 1.

b. Click Home → Cell Styles.

c. Right-click Heading 1 and select Modify. The Style dialog box is displayed. Note the formats for the Heading 1 style.

    1. Select Format. The Format Cells dialog box is displayed.

    2. Select the Font tab.

    3. In the Size list, select 18:

    4. Select OK. The Style dialog box is again displayed.

d. Select OK. The modified Heading 1 style is applied to cell A1.

e. Click Home → Cell Styles. Note that the Heading 1 style modifications are reflected in the cell styles gallery.

③ **CREATE A NEW STYLE**

a. Click a blank cell and then click Home → Cell Styles → New Cell Style. A dialog box is displayed.

    1. Type Planets in the Style name box.

    2. Click Format. The Format dialog box is displayed.

3. Select the Font tab.

4. Select the Color arrow and select the Orange Accent 6, Darker 25% color:

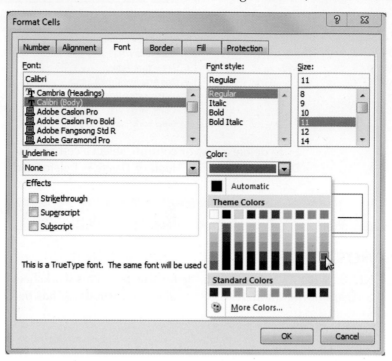

5. Select the Border tab and set the options as shown, selecting the Orange Accent 6, Darker 25% color:

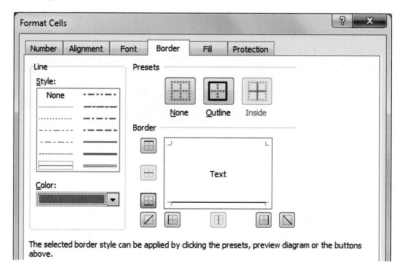

6. Select OK. The Style dialog box is again displayed.

7. Select OK. The Style dialog box is removed.

b. Select cells A3 through B9 and then click Home → Cell Styles. Note that the Planets style is listed under Custom styles.

c. Click Planets. The Planets style is applied to cells A3 through B9:

	A	B	C
1	**Planets**		
2		**Diameter (km)**	
3	Venus	12104	
4	Earth	12756	
5	Mars	6794	
6	Jupiter	142984	
7	Saturn	120536	
8	Uranus	51118	
9	Neptune	49528	
10			

④ **INSERT A ROW**

    a. Select cell A7 and then click Home → Insert → Insert Sheet Rows. A row is inserted and the data that was in row 7 and all the rows below it move down to accommodate the newly inserted row.

    b. Select cell A7 and type: Mercury

    c. Select cell B7 and type: 4878

⑤ **ADD A HEADER AND FOOTER**

    Add your name in a header and the current date in a footer.

⑥ **SAVE, PRINT, AND CLOSE THE MODIFIED PLANETS**

Using Functions to Perform Calculations

function
arguments

Excel contains built-in functions that can be included in a formula to perform common calculations. A *function* performs a calculation that results in a single value. A function requires data, called *arguments*, to perform its calculation. The arguments of a function are enclosed in parentheses after the function name and are usually cell references.

SUM

The *SUM* function adds the value of the cells in the range. For example, to add the values in cells G1, G2, and G3, use the formula:

function
=SUM(G1:G3)
arguments

TIP Function names can be typed in uppercase or lowercase letters. However, Excel automatically converts a function name to uppercase letters when entered.

A colon (:) is used to separate the first cell reference and the last cell reference in the range. Nonadjacent cells can also be used as arguments in a SUM function by separating the arguments with a comma (,). For example, to add the values stored in cells A1, B5, and E7, use the formula:

function
=SUM(A1,B5,E7)
arguments

syntax

As a function is typed, a ScreenTip illustrates the structure, or *syntax*, of the function:

⊿	A	B	C	D
1	$12.00			
2	$3.75			
3	$8.33			
4	=sum(			
5	SUM(**number1**, [number2], ...)			

Pointing is the best method for entering a cell range into a function because typing errors are avoided. After typing the opening parenthesis for the function, drag from the first cell in the range to the last:

⊿	A	B	C	D
1	$12.00			
2	$3.75			
3	$8.33			
4	=sum(A1:A3			
5	SUM(**number1**, [number2], ...)			
6				

TIP Select a range of cells to view the Average, Count, and Sum statistics in the status bar.

Press Enter to complete the formula. Excel automatically adds the closing parenthesis. The value produced from the calculation is automatically formatted with the same format as the argument cells.

Other commonly used functions include:

- The *AVERAGE* function adds the values of the cells in the range and then divides the result by the number of cells in the range. For example, =AVERAGE(E10:E15) sums the values in cells E10, E11, E12, E13, E14, and E15 and then divides the total by 6.

- The *MAX* function determines the maximum value in the range of cells. For example, =MAX(B2:B26) displays the maximum (largest) of all the values in the range B2 through B26.

- The *MIN* function determines the minimum value in the range of cells. For example, =MIN(C18:F18) displays the minimum (smallest) of all the values in the range C18 through F18.

The SUM, AVERAGE, MIN, and MAX functions ignore cells that contain text or are empty when their cell references are included as arguments.

The COUNT Fuction

The COUNT function determines the number of cells that contain values. For example, =COUNT(C1:C8) displays the number of cells in the range C1 through C8 that contain values.

Using Absolute Cell References in Formulas

As discussed in Chapter 5, relative cell references automatically change when copied. However, there are situations when a cell reference should remain the same when copied. A cell reference that does not change when copied is called an *absolute cell reference*. An absolute cell reference contains a dollar sign in front of both the column letter and row number, such as $A$1. To create an absolute cell reference, press the F4 key after entering a cell reference.

In the worksheet on the next page, shipping charges are calculated by multiplying the item's weight by a shipping cost per kg, which is stored in cell C7. The cell reference, C7, is entered into the formula as an absolute cell reference because it should not change when copied:

The formula in cell D11 contains a relative cell reference and an absolute cell reference

When the formula in cell D11 is copied to cell D12, the formula will change to =C12*$C$7.

Practice: Employee Commission

Excel should already be started.

① **CREATE A NEW WORKBOOK**

Enter the data and apply formatting using the Office theme as shown below. Format cells A1, A3, and A5 through C5 as Heading 4:

	A	B	C
1	Employee Commission		
2			
3	Rate	15%	
4			
5	Employee	Sales	Commission
6	Amanda	$12,000	
7	Pierre	$1,250	
8	Miguel	$32,560	
9	Lucia	$4,156	
10			

② **ENTER A FORMULA WITH AN ABSOLUTE CELL REFERENCE**

   a. In cell C6, type = and then click cell B6. Type * and then click cell B3. Press the F4 key. Pressing F4 places dollar signs in front of the column letter and row number. The formula bar displays =B6*$B$3

   b. Press Enter. $1,800 is displayed in cell C6. Format the cell to display 2 decimal places.

③ **COPY THE FORMULA**

   a. In cell C6, drag the Fill handle to cell C9. The formula is copied to the cells with the relative cell reference automatically changing and the absolute cell reference staying the same.

   b. Select cell C9 and then view the formula on the formula bar to see the absolute reference.

④ CALCULATE THE TOTAL COMMISSION

    a. In cell B10, enter the label Total and format it as Heading 4 cell style and then right align the label.

    b. In cell C10, type =SUM(and then drag the pointer from cell C6 to cell C9:

	A	B	C	D	E
1	Employee Commission				
2					
3	Rate	15%			
4					
5	Employee	Sales	Commission		
6	Amanda	$12,000	$1,800.00		
7	Pierre	$1,250	$187.50		
8	Miguel	$32,560	$4,884.00		
9	Lucia	$4,156	$623.40		
10		Total	=SUM(C6:C9		
11			SUM(number1, [number2], ...)		
12					

    c. Press Enter to complete the formula. Excel automatically adds a right parenthesis. The expense total is displayed in cell C10 and is automatically formatted with the same format as the argument cells.

⑤ SAVE THE WORKBOOK AND PRINT A COPY

    a. Add your name in a header and the current date in a footer. Add gridlines and headings.

    b. Save the workbook naming it Employee Commission and print a copy.

    c. Close Employee Commission.

Inserting a Function into a Formula

AutoSum   Math & Trig

Insert Function   Recently Used   Error Checking

Instead of typing the name of a function into a formula, click **Formulas** → **Insert Function**, which places an equal sign (=) in the cell and displays a dialog box for inserting functions into a formula. Select an option in the Or select a category list to limit the functions that are displayed:

Function Categories

Functions can be divided into categories. For example, the SUM function is a Math and Trigonometric function and the AVERAGE, MAX, and MIN functions are Statistical functions.

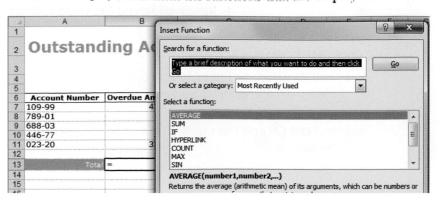

TIP Drag the title bar of the Insert Function or Function Arguments dialog box to move the dialog box and view the cells behind it.

Functions List

When an equal sign is typed in a cell, the Functions list appears on the formula bar:

SUM
SUM
AVERAGE
IF
HYPERLINK
COUNT

Click a function name from the list to display the Function Arguments dialog box for the selected function.

Select a function in the Select a function list and then OK to display the Function Arguments dialog box for the function. For example, select SUM and then OK to display the Function Arguments dialog box for the SUM function:

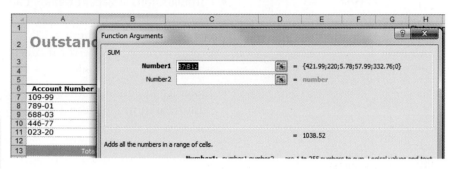

A range of cells is automatically entered in the Number1 box based on the location of the active cell. Excel assumes the range of cells is to the right or above the active cell. Type in the Number1 box or point to cells on the worksheet to change the cell range if necessary. Select OK to remove the dialog box and display the formula result in the cell.

Functions can also be inserted by clicking a button in the Function Library group on the Formulas tab. For example, click Recently Used to display a list of recently used functions. Click Math & Trig 🔢 to display a list of math and trigonometry functions, such as SUM. Click More Functions 📖 to display a menu of additional categories of functions, such as Statistical which includes the AVERAGE, MIN, and MAX functions.

Formulas ➔ AutoSum can also be used to create a formula with the SUM function. The range placed in the SUM function is the series of cells to the right or above the active cell. This range should be double-checked since Excel guesses the range. Press the Enter key to enter the formula. Click ▾ in Formulas ➔ AutoSum to display a list of other functions, such as Average, Min and Max.

Common Error Values

A cell with an invalid formula displays an error value and a green triangle in the upper-left corner of the cell. Chapter 5 discussed the #DIV/0 error. This and other common error values include:

#DIV/0 The formula is trying to divide by zero.

#REF The formula contains a reference that is not valid.

#NUM A numeric value is invalid, such as a value that is too large or too small.

#VALUE The formula is using the wrong type of argument, such as a label instead of a value.

The result of the formula is too wide to fit in the column or the result is a negative time or date value. If the result should fit in the column, check the formula for errors.

TIP Error checking rules used by Excel can be viewed by selecting 📄 File ➔ Options and then selecting Formulas in the displayed dialog box.

To correct a formula, select the cell, and then click Error Checking ◈ to display the error and a list of options.

TIP Don't assume a formula is correct. Use your estimation skills to check answers.

Some formulas may produce a result, but also display a green triangle in the cell which indicates a possible formula error. Common formula errors include:

* **Formula Omits Adjacent Cells**   The formula includes a range of values and the range does not include a value in an adjacent cell. For example, the formula =SUM(A2:25) entered in cell A26, may produce this type of error if cell A1 contains a column label that is a value, such as a date.

* **Inconsistent Formula in Region**   The formula does not match the pattern of formulas near it.

To remove the green triangle, select the cell and then click Error Checking ◈ to display the error and a list of options. If the formula does not contain an error, select Ignore Error.

The entire worksheet can also be checked for common errors by clicking Formulas → Error Checking which displays a dialog box with options for correcting common errors that are found.

Practice: COMMISSION SUMMARY

Excel should already be started.

① OPEN COMMISSION SUMMARY

Open COMMISSION SUMMARY, which is an Excel data file for this text. The worksheet summarizes commissions earned by month.

② DETERMINE THE TOTAL SALES AND COMMISSION

a. Select cell B18 and then click Formulas → Insert Function. The Insert Function dialog box is displayed:

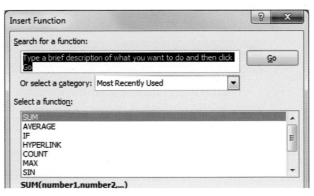

1. In the Select a function list, select SUM and then select OK. The Function Arguments dialog box is displayed:

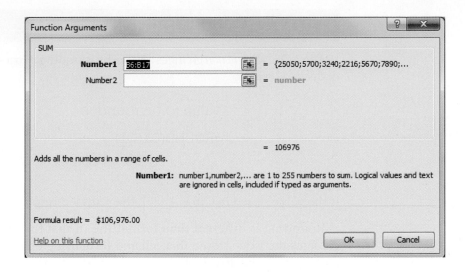

2. The range B6:B17 is automatically entered in the **Number1** box and the Formula result 106976 is displayed. Select **OK** to accept the range entered by Excel. The total sales is displayed in cell B18.

b. Copy the formula in cell B18 to cell C18. The total commission is displayed.

③ **DETERMINE THE AVERAGE MONTHLY SALES AND COMMISSION**

a. Select cell B19 and then click Formulas ➔ More Functions 📖 ➔ Statistical ➔ AVERAGE. The Function Arguments dialog box is displayed.

 1. In the **Number1** box, change the range to: B6:B17

 2. Select **OK**. The average monthly sales is displayed in cell B19.

b. Copy the formula in cell B19 to cell C19.

④ **DETERMINE THE MINIMUM MONTHLY SALES AND COMMISSION**

a. Select cell B20 and then click Formulas ➔ AutoSum ➔ Min. A formula with the MIN function is displayed in cell B20. Note that the range B6:B19 in the formula is not the correct range.

b. On the formula bar, change the range to B6:B17 and press Enter.

c. Copy the formula in cell B20 to cell C20.

⑤ **DETERMINE THE MAXIMUM MONTHLY SALES AND COMMISSION**

a. Select cell B21 and then click Formulas ➔ AutoSum ➔ Max. A formula with the MAX function is displayed in cell B21. Note that the range B6:B20 in the formula is not the correct range.

b. On the formula bar, change the range to B6:B17 and press Enter.

c. Copy the formula in cell B21 to cell C21.

d. Format cells B18 through C21 as currency with 2 decimal places.

⑥ **ADD A HEADER AND FOOTER**

Add your name in a header and the current date in a footer.

⑦ **SAVE, PRINT, AND THEN CLOSE THE MODIFIED COMMISSION SUMMARY**

The ROUND Function

The *ROUND function* changes a value by rounding it to a specific number of decimal places:

value to be rounded

=ROUND(C16,1)

decimal places

If the value stored in C16 is 42.851, the rounded result will be 42.9.

Rounding is different than formatting in that the ROUND function changes the value stored in a cell and formatting only changes the way data is displayed. Excel follows certain rules when rounding numbers. A number with a decimal portion greater than or equal to 0.5 is rounded up and a number with a decimal portion less than 0.5 is rounded down.

To round a value to the nearest whole number, a 0 is used to indicate no decimal places, as in =ROUND(AVERAGE(B3:B8), 0). A negative number as the second argument of the ROUND function rounds a value to the nearest 10s, 100s, and so forth. For example, =ROUND(72.86, –1) displays 70 and =ROUND(72.866, –2) displays 100.

> **ROUNDDOWN and ROUNDUP Functions**
>
> The ROUNDDOWN and ROUNDUP functions perform the same function as the ROUND function but always rounds a number down or up, respectively.

Sorting Data

Sort A to Z   Sort Z to A   Sort

ascending, descending

alphabetical, chronological

Arranging data in a specified order is called *sorting*. In Excel, rows can be sorted in either *ascending* (low to high) or *descending* (high to low) order based on the data in a specified column. Ascending order is also called *alphabetical* order when the data is text and *chronological* order when the data is times or dates.

To sort data, select a range and then click Data ➞ Sort A to Z ⬇. The rows will be placed in alphabetic order based on the values displayed in the first column of the range. For example, sorting the range A4:B10 displays:

	A	B	C
1	**Newspaper Circulation**		
2			
3	Newspaper	Daily Circulation	
4	Daily News	544,167	
5	Los Angeles Times	657,467	
6	New York Post	508,042	
7	New York Times	927,851	
8	USA Today	1,900,116	
9	Wall Street Journal	2,024,269	
10	Washington Post	582,844	

To sort a range in descending order, click Data ➞ Sort Z to A ⬇ .

Sort A to Z ↕ and Sort Z to A ↕ use the first column as the key sort column. The *key sort column* is the column that contains the values that a sort is based on. For example, the range A4:B10 was sorted using column B as the key sort column:

	A	B	C
1	**Newspaper Circulation**		
2			
3	Newspaper	Daily Circulation	
4	Wall Street Journal	2,024,269	
5	USA Today	1,900,116	
6	New York Times	927,851	
7	Los Angeles Times	657,467	
8	Washington Post	582,844	
9	Daily News	544,167	
10	New York Post	508,042	
11			

Find and Replace

Click Home → Find & Select → Find to display a dialog box used to search a worksheet for data, cell references, and formulas. Select Home → Find & Select → Replace to search for data and replace it with other data.

To designate a different key sort column, click Data → Sort. Select a column label from the Sort by list, select Values in the Sort On list, and select the Order, such as Largest to Smallest:

Data can also be sorted by format. Select a format option, such as Cell Color, in the Sort On list and then select an option in the Order list.

Practice: PLANETS – part 2 of 2

Excel should already be started.

① **OPEN PLANETS**

Display the worksheet in Normal view.

② **SCALE THE DIAMETER**

a. To scale the planet sizes for modeling, the diameter will be calculated to 1/1000 of its original value. In cell C2, enter the label Scale. Right align and apply the Heading 3 cell style to the label.

b. In cell C3, enter =B3/1000. The scaled value is 12.104.

③ **ROUND THE SCALED DIAMETER TO 1 DECIMAL PLACE**

a. Select cell C3.

b. On the formula bar, click between the equal sign and B3 and type: ROUND(

c. On the formula bar, click at the end of the formula and type ,1) to complete the formula: =ROUND(B3/1000,1)

d. Click the Enter button. The scaled diameter is now rounded to 1 decimal place.

e. Copy the formula in cell C3 to cells C4 through C10.

④ FORMAT SCALE

Format cells C3 through C10 as the Planets cell style.

⑤ SORT THE PLANET DATA

a. Select cells A3 through C10 to select all the planet names and their corresponding diameter and scale, which is the data to be sorted.

b. Click Data → Sort A to Z ⬇. The data is sorted in ascending order by planet name.

c. Click Data → Sort. A dialog box is displayed.

    1. In the Sort by list, select Diameter (km).

    2. In the Order list, select Largest to Smallest.

    3. Select OK. The data is sorted in descending order by diameter.

⑥ SAVE AND PRINT THE MODIFIED PLANETS

The IF Function

The *IF* function is used to make a decision based on a comparison. If the comparison is true, one value is displayed in the cell; if the comparison is false, a second value is displayed. For example, cell E7 displays "Reorder" because the stock in cell D7 is less than or equal to 10:

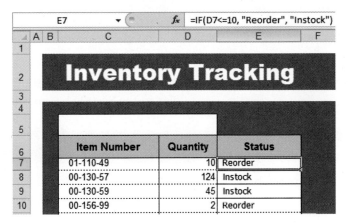

The IF function has three arguments and takes the form:

=IF(<comparison>, <value if true>, <value if false>)

For example, the formula

=IF(C4<E7, 10, 20)

displays a 10 if the value in C4 is less than the value in E7. If the value in C4 is greater than or equal to the value in E7, 20 is displayed.

The comparison argument of the IF function can contain one of the following *relational operators*, which are used to compare two values:

    =   equal to

    <   less than

    >   greater than

The COUNTIF Function

The COUNTIF function is used to calculate how many cells meet a certain condition. For example, the formula =COUNTIF(D1:D50, "Reorder") determines how many cells in the range D1 through D50 contain the label Reorder.

<table>
<tr><td><=</td><td>less than or equal to</td></tr>
<tr><td>>=</td><td>greater than or equal to</td></tr>
<tr><td><></td><td>not equal to</td></tr>
</table>

The arguments of an IF function can contain values, text, cell references, or calculations as shown in the following formulas:

=IF(N1<=25, 50, 100)

=IF(B3>=70, "Plenty", "Reorder")

=IF(B2<K25, 0, B2*15%)

=IF(C9>MIN(C2:C7), C11, C14)

=IF(D22<>F25, 0, SUM(E1:E10))

Nested Functions

A nested function is created when a function is used as one of the arguments of another function. For example, =IF(SUM(A1:A10)>10,10,0) uses a nested SUM function.

To check to see if a cell's contents are empty, two adjacent quotation marks can be used. For example, =IF(B20="", 1, 2) displays 1 if the cell contents are empty and 2 if there is data in the cell. Two adjacent quotation marks can also be used to display nothing in a cell. For example, =IF(B3>=70, "", "Reorder") displays a blank cell if the value in cell B3 is greater than or equal to 70, otherwise Reorder is displayed.

Text can also be used in the comparison part of the IF function. When compared, the alphabetical order of the text is determined. For example, the following formula displays True because apple comes before orange alphabetically:

=IF("apple"<"orange", "True", "False")

TIP Text used as an argument must be surrounded by quotation marks.

Cells that store labels can also be compared. If apple is stored in cell B3 and orange is stored in cell B5, the formula =IF(B3<B5, B3, B5) displays apple.

The IF function can be typed as part of a formula or inserted by clicking Formulas → Insert Function or clicking Formulas → Logical → IF. A dialog box is displayed where function arguments can be specified.

Printing a Large Worksheet

A worksheet that has many columns of data is often too wide to print on a single sheet of paper. When this happens, Excel prints the worksheet on consecutive sheets starting from the left-most column and proceeding to the right. The Page Layout tab can be used to help fit the worksheet on fewer sheets of paper and make each page of the printout more informative:

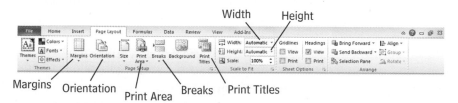

- Click Orientation → Portrait to allow more rows to be printed on a page. Portrait is the default page layout.

- Click Orientation → Landscape to print the worksheet across the widest part of the page. This allows more columns and fewer rows to fit on a page.

- Click Margins to change the margins:

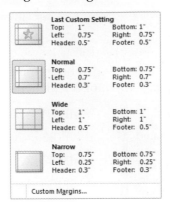

Click **Narrow** to create smaller margins, which allows more rows and columns to fit on a page. Select **Custom Margins** to display the Page Setup dialog box where custom margin settings can be set.

- Click **Breaks** → **Insert Page Break** to insert a page break before the currently selected row or column. If a single cell is selected before selecting the command, the page break is created above and to the left of that cell. A page break is indicated on the screen by a dashed line, and the effects of page breaks can be seen by previewing the worksheet.

- Select a cell in the row or column after the page break and then click **Breaks** → **Remove Page Break** to remove a page break.

- Click the **Headings Print** check box to add headings.

- Click **Print Titles** to display a dialog box where rows to repeat and columns to repeat on every printed page can be specified.

- The width and height of a worksheet can be scaled to print on a specific number of pages. Click **Width** or **Height** to select a specific number of pages for the printout.

- Click **Print Area** → **Set Print Area** to set the print area. Once the print area is set, only those cells will be included in a printout.

- Click **Print Area** → **Clear Print Area** to clear a set print area.

Practice: PAYROLL – part 1 of 3

① OPEN PAYROLL

Open PAYROLL, which is an Excel data file for this text.

② CALCULATE GROSS PAY

Gross pay is the amount earned before any deductions and is calculated by multiplying the hours worked by the employee's rate per hour.

a. In cell E7, enter the formula =C7*D7. The gross pay of $225.00 is displayed.

b. Select cell E7 and drag the Fill handle to cell E23.

③ CALCULATE SOCIAL SECURITY

Social security tax is calculated by multiplying the gross pay by the social security rate, which is stored in cell B3.

a. In cell F7, enter the formula =E7*$B$3. The social security tax of $14.63 is displayed.

b. Select cell F7 and then drag the Fill handle to cell F23.

c. Change the Social Security Rate to 6.0%. Excel automatically recalculates all the values in column F.

④ CALCULATE TAXES AND NET PAY

a. Taxes are calculated by multiplying the gross pay, which is stored in cell E7, by 15%. In cell G7, enter the formula =E7*15%. Taxes of $33.75 is displayed.

b. Net pay is the amount that the employee receives after deductions and is calculated by subtracting social security and taxes from the gross pay. In cell H7, enter the formula =E7–F7–G7. The net pay of $177.75 is displayed.

c. Select cells G7 and H7 and then drag the Fill handle to cells G23 and H23.

⑤ INSERT A COLUMN FOR THE OVERTIME HOURS

Overtime hours are hours that are worked beyond the typical work week. Often employees are paid for overtime hours at a higher hourly rate.

a. Select cell E5 and then click Home → Insert → Insert Sheet Columns. A column is inserted.

b. In cell E5, enter the label Overtime Hours. Note that the label is automatically formatted, but not entirely displayed.

c. Select the label and then click Home → Wrap Text ▤. The label "Overtime Hours" is displayed on two lines in the cell. Widen the column if necessary, until the label requires just two lines.

⑥ ENTER A FORMULA TO CALCULATE OVERTIME HOURS

An IF function is used to check to see if the Hours value stored in cell D7 is greater than 40, which is the number of hours in a work week. If the value is greater than 40, overtime hours are calculated and displayed in the cell. If not, zero is displayed. Overtime hours are calculated by subtracting the Hours, which is stored in cell D7, from 40.

a. In cell E7, enter the formula: =IF(D7>40, D7–40, 0). A ScreenTip is displayed as the formula is being typed. Since the Hours value is less than 40, 0.0 is displayed.

b. In cell E7, drag the Fill handle to cell E23.

⑦ INSERT A COLUMN FOR THE OVERTIME PAY

a. Select cell F5 and then click Home → Insert → Insert Sheet Columns. A column is inserted.

b. Click Insert Options 🖉 → Format Same As Right. Column G formatting is applied to column F.

c. In cell F5, enter the label Overtime Pay.

d. Select cell E5, click Format Painter 🖋 and then click cell F5. The wrap text format is copied to cell F5.

⑧ ENTER A FORMULA TO CALCULATE OVERTIME PAY

Overtime pay is calculated by multiplying the overtime hours by the overtime rate. The overtime rate in this case will be one and a half that of the base rate. This rate is calculated as 1.5 times the hourly rate.

a. In cell F7, enter the formula: =E7*(C7*1.5)
b. In cell F7, drag the Fill handle to cell F23.

⑨ ENTER A NEW GROSS PAY FORMULA

a. The Gross Pay formula needs to be modified to add the Overtime Pay. Modify the formula in cell G7 to =IF(D7<=40, C7*D7, C7*40+F7). Because the value in cell F7 is 0, the gross pay does not change.
b. In cell G7, drag the Fill handle to cell G23.

Check — Your worksheet should look similar to:

	A	B	C	D	E	F	G	H	I	J
1	**Payroll**									
2										
3	Soc. Sec. Rate:		6.0%							
4										
5	Last Name	First Initial	Rate/Hr	Hours	Overtime Hours	Overtime Pay	Gross Pay	Soc. Sec.	Taxes	Net Pay
6										
7	Alban	B.	$7.50	30.0	0.0	$0.00	$225.00	$13.50	$33.75	$177.75
8	Angulo	M.	$8.00	29.5	0.0	$0.00	$236.00	$14.16	$35.40	$186.44
9	Balto	Y.	$8.00	29.0	0.0	$0.00	$232.00	$13.92	$34.80	$183.28
10	Cruz	S.	$7.75	13.0	0.0	$0.00	$100.75	$6.05	$15.11	$79.59
11	Del Vecchio	E.	$9.00	43.5	3.5	$47.25	$407.25	$24.44	$61.09	$321.73
12	Eklund	E.	$9.50	31.0	0.0	$0.00	$294.50	$17.67	$44.18	$232.66
13	Esposito	S.	$11.75	43.5	3.5	$61.69	$531.69	$31.90	$79.75	$420.03
14	Hirsch	I.	$9.50	18.0	0.0	$0.00	$171.00	$10.26	$25.65	$135.09
15	Juarez	V.	$7.75	21.0	0.0	$0.00	$162.75	$9.77	$24.41	$128.57
16	Karas	A.	$8.00	15.0	0.0	$0.00	$120.00	$7.20	$18.00	$94.80
17	Keller-Sakis	G.	$8.50	20.0	0.0	$0.00	$170.00	$10.20	$25.50	$134.30
18	Lopez	R.	$9.00	17.0	0.0	$0.00	$153.00	$9.18	$22.95	$120.87
19	Parker	L.	$10.75	29.0	0.0	$0.00	$311.75	$18.71	$46.76	$246.28
20	Quinn	P.	$11.75	41.0	1.0	$17.63	$487.63	$29.26	$73.14	$385.22
21	Ramis	C.	$8.00	18.0	0.0	$0.00	$144.00	$8.64	$21.60	$113.76
22	Rappaport	L.	$7.75	18.0	0.0	$0.00	$139.50	$8.37	$20.93	$110.21
23	Rosen	R.	$9.50	10.0	0.0	$0.00	$95.00	$5.70	$14.25	$75.05

⑩ CHANGE PRINT ORIENTATION AND PRINT THE WORKSHEET

a. Click View ➔ Page Layout. The worksheet is displayed in the Page Layout view. Note that in portrait orientation the worksheet will print on two pages.
b. Click Page Layout ➔ Orientation ➔ Landscape. The worksheet will now print on one page.
c. Add your name in a header and the current date in a footer.
d. Add gridlines and headings.
e. Save the modified PAYROLL and print a copy.
f. Display PAYROLL in Normal view.

⑪ CLOSE PAYROLL

Amortization Tables and the PMT Function

installment loan

A useful application of a worksheet is an amortization table. *Amortization* is a method for computing equal periodic payments for an *installment loan*. Car loans and mortgages are often installment loans. Each installment, or payment, is the same and consists of two parts: a portion to pay interest due on the principal for that period and the remainder which reduces the principal. The *principal* is the amount of money owed and it decreases with each payment made.

principal

An *amortization table* displays the interest and principal amounts for each payment of an installment loan. For example, the monthly payment on a 30 year loan of $100,000 borrowed at 6% interest (0.5% per month) is $599.55. In the first payment, $500.00 pays the interest due (0.5% x $100,000) and $99.55 goes to reduce principal ($599.55 – $500.00). In the next payment, $499.50 pays the interest due (0.5% x ($100,000 – 99.55)) and $100.05 goes to reduce principal ($599.55 – $499.50). As payments are made, the interest due decreases because there is less principal to charge interest on. In the final payment, $2.98 pays the interest due and $596.57 pays off the principal.

The *PMT* function is used to calculate the equal periodic payment for an installment loan. The PMT function takes the form:

=PMT(<rate>, <term>, <principal>)

Alternative The PMT function can be typed as part of a formula or inserted by clicking Formulas → Insert Function → PMT or clicking Formulas → Financial → PMT.

<rate> is the interest rate per period, <term> is the total number of payments to be made, and <principal> is the amount borrowed. For example, the PMT function would be used to determine the monthly payment on a mortgage. The formula below calculates the monthly payments on a 30-year, $100,000 loan with an annual interest rate of 6%:

=PMT(6%/12, 360, –100000)

Since the payments are made monthly, the interest rate must also be computed monthly by dividing the annual interest rate of 6% by 12. The number of payments is 360, 30 years x 12 months. The principal is negative because it is the amount borrowed and it does not include a dollar sign or commas. This formula computes the monthly payment as $599.55.

Practice: LOAN

Excel should already be started.

① **OPEN LOAN**

Open LOAN, which is an Excel data file for this text. The displayed worksheet is a partially completed amortization table.

② **ENTER THE LOAN'S INFORMATION**

In order to purchase a house, a loan called a mortgage is usually obtained.

a. In cell B3, enter the yearly interest rate: 7%

b. In cell B4, enter the number of payments: 360 (30 years x 12 monthly payments)

c. In cell B5, enter the principal: $200,000

③ CALCULATE THE MONTHLY PAYMENT

In cell B7, enter the formula: =PMT(B3/12, B4, −B5)

The division by 12 is needed to convert the yearly interest rate in cell B3 to a monthly value. $1,330.60 is displayed.

④ CALCULATE TOTAL PAID AND TOTAL INTEREST

a. In cell B9, enter the formula: =B4*B7

This formula computes the total paid for the loan, $479,017.80, including principal and interest.

b. In cell B10, enter the formula: =B9−B5. The total interest paid over the 30 years, $279,017.80 is displayed:

	A	B
1	Loan Amortization Table	
2		
3	Interest rate =	7%
4	Number of payments =	360
5	Principal =	$200,000
6		
7	Monthly payment =	$1,330.60
8		
9	Total paid =	$479,017.80
10	Total interest =	$279,017.80
11		

⑤ ENTER THE FIRST PAYMENT DATA

a. In cell A13, enter: 1

b. In cell B13, enter: =B5

c. In cell C13, enter the formula: =B13*($B$3/12)

This formula calculates one month's interest on the loan. $1,166.67, which is 1% (7%/12) of the principal, is displayed. The cell reference B3 is an absolute cell reference because the interest rate will be the same for each payment.

d. In cell D13, enter the formula: =IF(C13<0.01, 0, $B$7−C13)

This formula calculates the amount of the payment which is applied to the principal, $163.94. If the value in cell C13 is less than 0.01 (less than a penny), then 0 is displayed. An IF function is used to avoid problems due to rounding.

e. In cell E13, enter the formula: =B13−D13. The new principal owed is displayed.

⑥ ENTER FORMULAS FOR THE SECOND PAYMENT

a. In cell A14, enter the formula: =A13+1

b. In cell B14, enter: −E13

c. Copy the formulas in cells C13 through E13 to cells C14 through E14:

Chapter 6 Functions and Data Organization

▲	A	B	C	D	E	F
1	Loan Amortization Table					
2						
3	Interest rate =	7%				
4	Number of payments =	360				
5	Principal =	$200,000				
6						
7	Monthly payment =	$1,330.60				
8						
9	Total paid =	$479,017.80				
10	Total interest =	$279,017.80				
11						
12		Payment	Principal	Pay to Interest	Pay to Principal	Principal Owed
13		1	$200,000.00	$1,166.67	$163.94	$199,836.06
14		2	$199,836.06	$1,165.71	$164.89	$199,671.17

(7) COMPLETE THE TABLE

Copy the formulas in cells A14 through E14 into cells A15 through E372. The principal owed is $0.00 in cell E372, which indicates the loan has been paid in full.

(8) ADD A HEADER AND FOOTER AND PRINT A PORTION OF THE WORKSHEET

a. Add a header with your name and a footer with the current date.

b. Select cells A1 through E15.

c. Click Page Layout → Orientation → Landscape.

d. Click Page Layout → Print Area → Set Print Area. Note the dashed lines around the cells indicating the print area.

e. Click anywhere to remove the selection.

f. Save the modified LOAN.

g. Select [File] → Print. Note the preview area.

h. Select Print.

i. Click Page Layout → Print Area → Clear Print Area. The print area is now set to the entire worksheet.

(9) CREATE AN AUTO LOAN MODEL

a. In cell B3, enter: 8%

b. The car loan is a 5 year loan; therefore, the number of monthly payments will be 5 x 12. In cell B4, enter: 60

c. In cell B5, enter: $22,000

d. Scroll down to row 72 which contains the last payment. The worksheet can easily model loans with less than 360 payments.

e. Save the modified LOAN and print a copy of the first three pages.

(10) ENTER YOUR OWN VALUES INTO THE LOAN WORKSHEET

a. Create different loan scenarios by changing the rate, term, and principal of the LOAN worksheet to any values you like. Change the number of payments to see how that affects the interest paid.

b. Select File → Close. Click No in the dialog box when prompted to save the file. The only change that is not saved is the experimenting with values in step 10 (a).

Using Multiple Sheets

Multiple sheets within a workbook can be used to organize, store, and link related information. For example, a workbook could contain a sheet for the 2010 Sales data, a sheet for the 2011 Sales data, and a sheet for the 2012 Forecast:

Insert Worksheet

Click a tab at the bottom of the Excel window to make a sheet active. In the workbook shown above, 2011 Sales is the active sheet. Sheets in the workbook shown have been renamed. By default, sheets are named Sheet1, Sheet2, and Sheet3. To rename a sheet, double-click the sheet tab, type a new sheet name, and then press Enter.

To insert a new sheet in front of the active sheet, select Home → Insert → Insert Sheet. To add a new sheet at the end of the existing sheets, click the Insert Worksheet tab. To delete a worksheet, right-click the sheet and select Delete from the menu. Sheet order can be changed by dragging a sheet tab to a new location within the sheet tabs.

Headers, footers, and orientation can be specified for each sheet. For example, Sheet1 can be set up to print in portrait orientation and Sheet2 in landscape orientation. The Page Layout tab is used to select options for the active sheet.

To print an entire workbook, select ▕File▏ → Print to display print options in Backstage view. Then, click Print Active Sheets in the Settings section and select Print Entire Workbook.

Copying and Moving Data Between Sheets

Data can be moved and copied between sheets. Cut ✂ , Copy 🗐, and Paste on the Home tab are used to move and duplicate data.

1. Select the *source*, which is the cell or range to be copied.

2. Click Home → Cut ✂ or Home → Copy 🗐. The source displays a moving dashed border.

3. Click the sheet tab of the worksheet that is to receive the copied data.

4. Select the *destination*, which is the upper-left cell of the range where the data is to be pasted.

5. Click Home → Paste. The data as well as the source formatting is pasted and Paste Options 🗐(Ctrl)▾ is displayed. Any pre-existing cell contents are replaced with the pasted data. Press the Esc key to remove the dashed border.

By default, pasted data is *static*, which means it does not change when the source data changes. *Linked cells* contain a reference to the original data and will automatically update if the source data changes. To link pasted data to the source data, click **Paste Options** 📋 (Ctrl) ▾ → **Paste Link**:

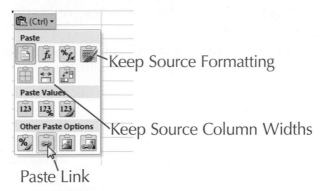

Keep Source Formatting

Keep Source Column Widths

Paste Link

Practice: CAR SALES

Excel should be already be started.

① **OPEN CAR SALES**

Open CAR SALES, which is an Excel data file for this text. This workbook contains data in three sheets: New Car Sales, Sheet2, and Used Car Sales. The Total Sales column in the New Car Sales sheet contains formulas.

② **VIEW THE DIFFERENT SHEETS IN THE WORKBOOK**

a. Click the Sheet2 tab. The second sheet in the workbook is displayed.

b. Click the Used Car Sales tab. The third sheet in the workbook is displayed.

③ **CHANGE THE ORDER OF THE SHEETS**

Drag the Used Car Sales tab to the left until a solid triangle is shown to the left of the Sheet2 tab:

The sheet order is changed.

④ **RENAME SHEET2**

a. Double-click the Sheet2 tab.

b. Type Total Sales and then press Enter.

⑤ **LINK LABELS TO THE TOTAL SALES SHEET**

a. Display the New Car Sales sheet.

b. Select cells A4 through A12.

c. Click Home → Copy 📋.

d. Display the Total Sales sheet.

e. Select cell A4.

f. Click Home → Paste. The Paste Options button 📋 (Ctrl) ▾ is displayed.

g. Click Paste Options → Paste Link. If necessary, widen the column until the names are displayed entirely.

h. Select cell A4. Note that ='New Car Sales'!A4 is displayed on the formula bar.

i. Display the New Car Sales sheet and then press the Esc key. The moving dashed line is removed.

j. In the New Car Sales sheet, copy cell E3 and then paste a copy into cell B3 in the Total Sales sheet. Link the data.

k. Use Format Painter ✔ to copy the formatting from cell E3 in New Car Sales to cell B3 in Total Sales.

l. In the Used Car Sales sheet, copy cells A4 through A14 and then paste a copy into cell A13 in the Total Sales sheet. Link the data.

Check — The Total Sales sheet should look similar to:

⑥ MODIFY LABELS

a. Display the New Car Sales sheet.

b. Select cell A12.

c. Edit the cell contents so that the name is: Bass

d. Display the Total Sales sheet. In cell A12 the cell contents have been automatically updated because the cell was linked to cell A12 in the New Car Sales sheet.

⑦ TOTAL THE SALES FOR ALL EMPLOYEES

a. Select cell B4 and then type an equal sign (=).

b. Display the New Car Sales sheet. Note that ='New Car Sales'! is displayed in the formula bar.

c. Click cell E4. The Formula bar now displays ='New Car Sales'!E4.

d. Click Enter ✔. The Total Sales sheet is displayed and cell B4 displays 157774.

e. Select cell B4 and then drag the Fill handle to cell B12.

f. Select cell B13 and then type an equal sign (=).

g. Display the Used Car Sales sheet, click cell E4, and then click Enter ✔. The Total Sales sheet is displayed and cell B13 displays 280883.

h. Select cell B13 and then drag the Fill handle to cell B23.

i. In cell A24, enter the label Total and format the label as right aligned and bold.

j. In cell B24, enter a formula to calculate the total sales for all employees.

k. Format cells B4 through B24 as Currency with 0 decimal places.

l. Bold the value in cell B24. Widen the column, if necessary, to entirely display the value.

⑧ MODIFY SALES DATA

a. In the New Car Sales sheet, select cell D4 and change the value to 143,000. The total sales in cell E4 automatically recalculates.

b. Display the Total Sales sheet. Note the total sales for Cherisma automatically updated in cell B4.

⑨ SET PRINT OPTIONS

a. Display the Total Sales sheet and then click View → Page Layout.

b. Click Page Layout → Margins → Wide. Wide margin settings are applied.

c. On the Page Layout tab, click the Gridlines and Headings Print check boxes.

d. Add a header similar to Total Sales, Page 1.

e. Click in the footer area and add a footer with your name.

f. For the New Car Sales and Used Car Sales sheets, set the margins to Wide and add a header with your name and a footer with the sheet name.

⑩ SAVE, PRINT, AND THEN CLOSE THE MODIFIED CAR SALES

a. Save the modified CAR SALES.

b. Select [File] → Print.

c. In the Settings section, select Print Entire workbook:

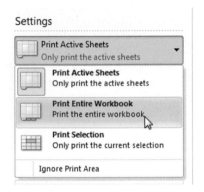

d. Select OK. All three sheets in the workbook are printed. Note that only the Total Sales sheet contains gridlines.

e. Close CAR SALES.

Asking What-If?

What-If Analysis

A worksheet is often used to answer "What-If?" questions. A *What-If question* asks how a value or set of values impacts results. For example, the following worksheet shows the profit from a fundraiser if 200 people attend. On the right, a different scenario shows the profit if 300 people attend:

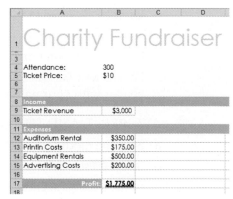

Selling an additional 100 tickets has a positive impact on the profits, with an increase of $1,000.

spreadsheet model

A worksheet that includes related data and formulas for analyzing the data is called a *spreadsheet model*. The Charity Fundraiser worksheet is a spreadsheet model. Businesses often ask "What-If" questions of their spreadsheet models in order to make predictions. This process is some-

what-if analysis

times referred to as a *what-if analysis*.

Excel contains what-if analysis tools including a scenarios feature that allows different data sets to be defined and used within the same worksheet. Scenarios can be used to forecast the outcomes in a spreadsheet model. To work with scenarios, click Data → What-if Analysis 📄 → Scenario Manager, which displays the Scenario Manager dialog box. With one scenario already added, the dialog box looks similar to:

- Multiple scenarios can be created. Select Add to display the Add Scenario dialog box. In that dialog box, type a Scenario name and type cell references that will change value in the Changing cells box.

Chapter 6 Functions and Data Organization

Select OK and then type the new cell value in the next dialog box. For the scenario shown above, the scenario name is 100 Attendance, the changing cell is B3.

- Select Show to display a scenario in the active worksheet.

- Select Summary to create a scenario summary report on a separate sheet. For example, when two scenarios have been created, the summary looks similar to:

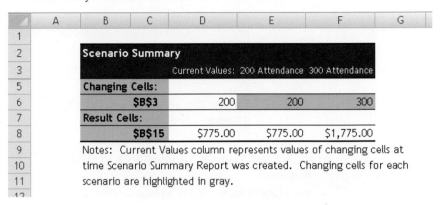

Selecting Summary displays a dialog box. In the Results cells box, enter the cell reference for the value that is affected by the changing cell. In the worksheet on the previous page, cell B17 would be the results cell.

Practice: FUNDRAISER

Excel should be already be started.

① OPEN FUNDRAISER

Open FUNDRAISER, which is an Excel data file for this text. The FUNDRAISER workbook contains the projected income and expenses involved in producing a charity event.

② ANSWER "WHAT IF" QUESTIONS

A last minute problem has required that the fundraiser be moved to a different auditorium. The organizers want to know how the profit will be affected.

a. The Auditorium Rental expense will increase from $350.00 to $500.00. Change the Auditorium Rental expense to $500.00 and note how the profit is affected.

b. The new auditorium only seats 150. Change the Attendance to 150 and note how the profit is affected.

c. The organizers have set a goal to raise a minimum profit of $425.00. Due to the increased Auditorium Rental expense and limited seating, they are forced to raise the ticket price. Change the ticket price until the minimum profit is met.

③ PRINT AND CLOSE FUNDRAISER

a. Add your name in a header and the current date in a footer.

b. Print a copy of the worksheet.

c. Close FUNDRAISER without saving changes.

④ CREATE A SCENARIO

a. Open FUNDRAISER again.

b. The organizers would like to see how changing the ticket price will affect profits. Select cell B4. This will be the cell that contains the value that will change when the scenario is selected.

c. Click Data ➔ What-if Analysis 🖳 ➔ Scenario Manager. A dialog box is displayed.

d. Select Add. Another dialog box is displayed.

   1. In the Scenario name box, type: Ten Dollars

   2. In the Changing cells box, type B4 if it is not already displayed:

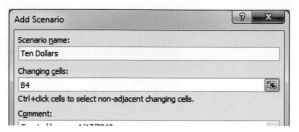

   3. Select OK. Another dialog box is displayed. The value 10 is already displayed.

   4. Select OK. The Scenario Manager dialog box is again displayed.

e. Select Add. A dialog box is displayed.

   1. In the Scenario name box, type: Twelve Dollars.

   2. In the Changing cells box, type: B4

   3. Select OK. Another dialog box is displayed.

   4. In the box, type 12:

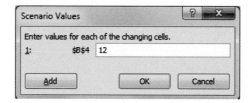

   5. Select OK. The Scenario Manager dialog box is again displayed:

f. Add a scenario for Thirteen Dollars.

g. In the Scenario Manager dialog box, select Twelve Dollars and then select Show. Cell B4 changes to $12.00 and the Profit in cell B15 recalculates to $1,175.00.

Chapter 6 Functions and Data Organization

h. In the Scenario Manager dialog box, select Thirteen Dollars and then select Show. Cell B4 changes to $13.00 and the Profit in cell B15 recalculates.

i. Select Summary. A dialog box is displayed.

1. Select the options as shown:

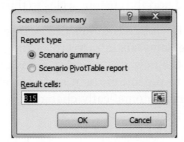

2. Select OK. A summary report of the three scenarios is displayed in a separate sheet that is automatically named Scenario Summary:

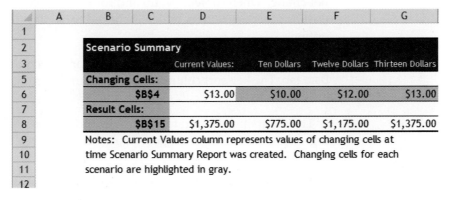

⑤ ADD YOUR NAME IN A HEADER AND THEN SAVE THE MODIFIED FUNDRAISER

⑥ PRINT THE SCENARIO SUMMARY SHEET, CLOSE FUNDRAISER, AND QUIT EXCEL

Chapter Summary

This chapter discussed how formatting with styles can ensure consistent formatting in a worksheet. It also explained how to create custom styles and add the custom styles to the cell styles gallery using the Home tab.

Rows and columns can be inserted between data in a worksheet using the Home tab. Inserted rows and columns contain no data. However, cells in the new row or column have the same formatting as the cells above or to the left of them, respectively. When cells are inserted or deleted, Excel automatically changes the relative cell references in any affected formulas.

The Formulas tab contains built-in functions used to perform common calculations. Functions include SUM, AVERAGE, MIN, MAX, and ROUND. Absolute cell references are used in formulas so that the cell reference does not change when copied. An invalid formula displays an error value and the Error Checking button, which is clicked to display the error and a list of options.

Excel data can be sorted in ascending or descending order using the Data tab. The key sort column is the column that contains the values that a sort is based on.

The IF function is used to make a decision based on a comparison. The arguments of an IF function can contain values, cell references, calculations, or text.

The Page Layout tab is used to change print settings. The print orientation and margins can be changed to help fit the worksheet on a single printed page. A worksheet can also be scaled to fit on a specified number of pages. Page breaks control how a worksheet is divided into pages. Part of a worksheet is printed by setting a print area.

Amortization is a method for computing equal periodic payments for an installment loan. An amortization table displays the interest and principal amounts for each payment of an installment loan. The PMT function is used to calculate the equal periodic payment for an installment loan.

Multiple sheets within a workbook are used to organize, store, and link related information.

The chapter also explained how worksheets can be used to answer "What-If?" questions. A What-If question asks how changing data will impact results. Excel contains what-if analysis tools on the Data tab, including a scenarios feature that allows different data sets to be defined and used within the same worksheet. Scenarios can be used to forecast the outcomes in a spreadsheet model.

Vocabulary

Absolute Cell Reference A cell reference that does not change when copied because a dollar sign has been placed in front of both the column letter and row number, such as $A$5.

Alphabetical order *See* Ascending order.

Amortization A method for computing equal periodic payments for an installment loan.

Amortization table Displays the interest and principal amounts for each payment of an installment loan.

Arguments The data required by a function.

Ascending order In order from lowest to highest. Also called alphabetical order when the data is text and chronological order when the data is times or dates.

AVERAGE Function that adds the values in a range of cells and then divides the result by the number of cells in the range.

Chronological *See* Ascending order.

Descending In order from highest to lowest.

Destination The upper-left cell of the range where data is to be pasted when copying or moving data between sheets.

Function Performs a calculation that results in a single value.

IF function Function that is used to make a decision based on a comparison.

Installment loan Loan that is repaid in a series of periodic payments.

Key sort column The column that contains the values that a sort is based on.

Linked cells Data that is connected to the source cell and will automatically update if the source cell is changed.

MAX Function that displays the largest value in a range of cells.

MIN Function that displays the smallest value in a range of cells.

PMT Function that calculates the periodic payment for an installment loan.

Principal The amount of money owed on a loan.

Relational operators Used to compare two values. Operators include =, <, >, <=, >=, <>.

ROUND function Changes a value by rounding it to a specific number of decimal places.

Sorting Arranging data in a specified order.

Source The cell or range of data to be copied when copying or moving data between sheets.

Spreadsheet model A worksheet containing data relating to a particular situation.

Static Copied data that is not connected to the source data.

SUM Function that adds the values in a range of cells.

Syntax The expected form or structure of a function.

What-if analysis The process of making decisions using a spreadsheet model.

What-if question A question that is answered using a worksheet model.

AutoSum Creates a formula with the SUM function. The AutoSum button arrow displays a list of other functions that can be used in formulas. Found on the Formulas tab.

Cell Styles Displays the cell styles gallery. Found on the Home tab.

Clear Print Area Clears a set print area. Found on the Page Layout tab.

Delete Removes a sheet from the workbook. Found in the menu displayed by right-clicking a sheet tab.

Delete Sheet Columns Deletes a column from the workbook. Found in Home → Delete.

Delete Sheet Rows Deletes a row from the workbook. Found in Home → Delete.

Error Checking ◈ Indicates a possible formula error. Displayed next to the cell containing the formula.

Error Checking Checks a worksheet for formula errors. Found on the Formulas tab.

Insert Function Displays a dialog box used to insert a function into a formula. Found on the Formulas tab.

Insert Options ✎ Displayed when a new row or column is inserted.

Insert Page Break Inserts a page break before the currently selected row or column. Found in Page Layout → Breaks.

Insert Sheet Inserts a new sheet in front of the active sheet. Found in Home → Insert.

Insert Sheet Columns Inserts a column. Found in Home → Insert.

Insert Sheet Rows Inserts a row. Found in Home → Insert.

Landscape A print orientation that prints a worksheet across the widest part of the page.

Margins Displays options for changing the margins. Found on the Page Layout tab.

Math & Trig ▣ Displays a list of math and trigonometry functions. Found on the Formulas tab.

More Functions ▣ Displays a menu of additional categories of functions, such as Statistical. Found on the Formulas tab.

New Cell Style Displays a dialog box used to create a new cell style. Found in Home → Cell Styles.

Options Displays a dialog box used to select error checking rules. Found in Backstage view.

Orientation Displays options for changing the print orientation. Found on the Page Layout tab.

Paste Options ▣ (Ctrl)▾ Displayed when contents of the Clipboard are placed in cells. Used to link cells between sheets.

Portrait The default print orientation that allows more rows to be printed on a page.

Print Titles Displays a dialog box where rows to repeat and columns to repeat on every printed page can be specified. Found on the Page Layout tab.

Remove Page Break Removes a page break. Found in Page Layout → Breaks.

Scenario Manager Displays a dialog box used to create worksheet scenarios. Found in Data → What-if Analysis.

Set Print Area Designates a specific range of cells to be printed. Found in Page Layout → Print Area.

Sort Displays a dialog box used to sort data. Found on the Data tab.

Sort A to Z ▲↓ Places selected rows of data in order from low to high. Found on the Data tab.

Sort Z to A ▼↓ Places selected rows of data in order from high to low. Found on the Data tab.

1. a) What formatting does a newly inserted row contain?
   b) What formatting does a newly inserted column contain?

2. The formula =SUM(C3:C22) is entered in cell C24 and used to sum the values in cells C3 through C22.
   a) If a row is inserted directly above row 20, what must be done in order to include the new cell in the sum?
   b) If a row is inserted directly above row 24, what must be done to include the new cell in the sum?
   c) If row 20 is deleted, what must be done to the formula so that the deleted cell is no longer in the range?

3. Using functions, write a formula to calculate:
   a) the sum of the values stored in cells B4, B5, B6, and B7.
   b) the sum of the values stored in cells B4, C4, D4, and E4.
   c) the average of the values stored in the column of cells D7 through D35.
   d) the average of the values stored in the row of cells F3 through J3.
   e) the maximum value stored in the range of cells D4 through Y5.
   f) the minimum value stored in the range of cells C1 through C9.

4. What is the difference between a relative cell reference and an absolute cell reference?

5. List two advantages of using the Insert Function dialog box to insert the name of a function in a formula instead of typing the formula.

6. Why is it important to check the range placed in the SUM function when using Formulas → AutoSum?

7. Using functions, write a formula to calculate:
   a) the sum of the values in cells C5, C6, C7, C8, and C9 rounded to 2 decimal places.
   b) the sum of the values in cells B5, C5, D5, and E5 rounded to the nearest integer.
   c) the average of the values in cells A1, A2, A3, B1, B2, and B3 rounded to 1 decimal place.

8. What will be displayed by the following formulas if cell D4 stores a value of 30 and cell E7 stores a value of –12?
   a) =IF(D4<=E7, 10, 20)
   b) =IF(E7*D4<–5, E7, D4)
   c) =IF(D4–42=E7, D4*2, E7*3)

9. Using functions, write a formula to:
   a) display 50 if the value stored in D20 equals the value in C70, or 25 if they are not equal.
   b) display the value in B40 if the sum of the range of cells C20 to C30 exceeds 1000, otherwise display a 0.

10. Write formulas using the IF function for each of the following:
    a) if B3 is less than or equal to C12 display Low; if greater than, display High.
    b) if A5 is equal to Z47 display Jonathan; if not equal to, display Judith.

11. Explain why it would be a good idea to change sheet names from Sheet1, Sheet2, and so forth in a workbook with multiple data sheets.

12. List two other "What If?" questions that can be answered using the Charity Fundraiser workbook.

True/False

13. Determine if each of the following are true or false. If false, explain why.
    a) A modified cell style is accessible to all new workbooks.
    b) When rows are inserted, Excel automatically changes the cell references in any affected formulas.
    c) The SUM function ignores cells that contain text when their cell references are included as arguments.
    d) An absolute cell reference changes when copied.
    e) A #### error value indicates the formula is trying to divide by zero.
    f) When a formula produces a result and a green triangle in the cell, this indicates a correct formula.
    g) There is no difference between formatting and rounding.
    h) Linked data will automatically update if the source cell is changed.

Project 1

Travel...With a Purpose want to use a worksheet to computerize their scuba diving log.

a) Create a new workbook.

b) In cell A1, type Dive Log and then select cells A1 through E1. Click Home → Merge & Center to join the selected cells into one larger cell and center the label. Apply the Heading 2 style to the label.

c) Enter the data and apply formatting as shown below:

	A	B	C	D	E
1			**Dive Log**		
2	*Date*	*Depth (m)*	*Duration (min)*	*Water Temp (Celsius)*	*Visibility (m)*
3					
4	5/8/2011	10	60	26	10
5	5/10/2011	18	45	25	12
6	5/11/2011	13	50	27	9
7	5/13/2011	27	15	23	10
8	5/14/2011	11	53	28	11

d) Save the workbook naming it Dive Log.

e) In cell A9, enter the label Average and then format the label as right aligned and italic. Enter formulas that use a function to average the depth and duration of all five dives.

f) Modify the average depth and duration formulas to use a function to round the results to 0 decimal places.

g) Two dives were not recorded. Insert the new data shown below into the worksheet so that the dates remain in chronological order:

Date	Depth (m)	Duration (min)	Water Temp (Celsius)	Visibility (m)
5/9/2011	15	45	28	11
5/12/2011	20	40	24	9

h) In rows 12 and 13, enter formulas that use functions to calculate:

- the maximum depth of the dives and the maximum duration of the dives
- the minimum depth of the dives and the minimum duration of the dives

Include appropriate labels and proper formatting.

i) Add your name in a header and the current date in a footer. Add gridlines and headings.

j) Save the modified Dive Log and print a copy.

k) Display the formulas in the cells instead of values. Print a copy.

Project 2

Yolanda's Catering wants to use a worksheet to keep track of expenses.

   a) Create a new workbook.

   b) Enter the data and apply formatting using the Aspect theme as shown below:

	A	B	C	D
1	**Yolanda's Catering**			
2	**Expenses per Pizza**			
3				
4	**Ingredients**	**Everything**	**Vegetarian**	**Pepperoni**
5				
6	Dough	$1.25	$1.25	$1.25
7	Cheese	$1.50	$1.50	$1.50
8	Sauce	$0.50	$0.50	$0.50
9	Pepperoni	$0.75	$0.00	$0.00
10	Sausage	$1.00	$0.00	$0.00
11	Onion	$0.15	$0.15	$0.00
12	Mushroom	$0.35	$0.35	$0.00
13	Green Pepper	$0.40	$0.40	$0.00

   c) Save the workbook naming it Pizza Palace.

   d) In cell A14, enter the label Cost of Pizza and then format the label as right aligned and italic. Enter formulas that use a function to calculate the total cost of each pizza type.

   e) Pepperoni pizza needs to be added to the worksheet between the Vegetarian and Cheese pizza columns. Enter an appropriate column heading and values for the pepperoni pizza. Copy the cost of pizza formula for the pepperoni pizza into cell D14.

   f) The menu price for each pizza needs to be added to the worksheet in row 15. When the cost of pizza is less than or equal to $4.00 the price is one and a half (1.5) times the cost, and it is two (2) times the cost when it is greater than $4.00. Enter formulas that use a function and cell references to calculate the menu price of the pizzas. Include an appropriate label and proper formatting.

   g) In cell A16, enter the label Profit and then format the label as right aligned and italic. Enter formulas that calculate the profit from each pizza type by subtracting the total cost of each type of pizza from the menu price.

   h) Change the price of Cheese from $1.50 to $2.00 for each pizza type and change the price of Dough from $1.25 to $1.50. How does this affect the profit?

   i) Add your name in a header and the current date in a footer. Add gridlines and headings.

   j) Save the modified Pizza Palace and print a copy.

   k) Display the formulas in the cells instead of values. Print a copy.

Project 3

The SCHOOL LOAN workbook contains a loan amortization table. Open SCHOOL LOAN, which is an Excel data file for this text, and answer the following What If? questions:

a) The tuition and room/board fees for one year at the state university are $10,250. The loan options are:

- 6% interest for a three year loan
- 7% interest for a five year loan
- 8% interest for a ten year loan

In cells B3, B4, and B5, enter the appropriate data for the three-year loan at 6%.

b) In cell B7, enter a formula that uses the PMT function with cell references to calculate the periodic payment for the three year loan option.

c) In cells B9 and B10, enter formulas that calculate the total amount paid and the total interest paid.

d) In cells C3, C4, and C5, enter the appropriate data for the five-year loan option and then calculate the monthly payment, total amount paid, and total interest paid.

e) In cells D3, D4, and D5, enter the appropriate data for the ten-year loan option and then calculate the monthly payment, total amount paid, and total interest paid.

f) Create at least two new styles and apply the new styles to the worksheet.

g) Add your name in a header and the current date in a footer. Add gridlines and headings.

h) Save the modified SCHOOL LOAN and print a copy.

i) Display the formulas in the cells instead of values. Print a copy.

Project 4

A loan amortization table can be used for any kind of loan, including car loans. Amortization tables can also be combined with What If? questions to help make decisions when purchasing a new car for your business.

a) Create a new workbook.

b) Enter the data and apply formatting using the Apex theme as shown below:

	A	B	C	D	E	F
1	New Car Loan Amortization Table					
2						
3		3 Year Loan	3 Year Loan	5 Year Loan	5 Year Loan	
4						
5	Interest rate =	7%	10%	7%	10%	
6	Number of payments =	36	36	60	60	
7	Principal =					
8						
9	Monthly payment =					
10						
11	Total paid =					
12	Total interest =					
13						

c) Save the workbook naming it Car Loan.

d) Using the Internet or a newspaper, find an advertisement for a new car.

e) Enter the price of the car in the ad as the principal of the car loan in row 7 of the worksheet.

f) In row 9, enter formulas that use the PMT function with cell references to calculate the periodic payment for the different loan interest rates and payment periods.

g) In row 11, enter formulas that use cell references to calculate the total amount paid (number of payments multiplied by the monthly payment).

h) In row 12, enter formulas that use cell references to calculate the total interest paid (total amount paid minus the principal).

i) Add your name in a header and the current date in a footer. Add gridlines and headings.

j) Save the modified Car Loan and print a copy.

k) Display the formulas in the cells instead of values. Print a copy.

Project 5

You are considering a cash advance to help fund your entrepreneurial adventure. This is usually an expensive method of borrowing money and is best used for only short periods of time or not at all. Banks typically loan money at rates between 5% and 15%. Cash advances are based on the credit card APR (annual percentage rate), which is typically 15% or higher.

a) Create a new workbook that stores the amount of money to borrow, the number of months to pay back the borrowed money, and the annual interest rate. Include labels and format cells appropriately.

b) To compare the cost of borrowing, include columns for annual interest rates ranging from 5% to 25% in increments of 5%.

c) Add formulas that calculate the monthly payment, total amount paid, and total interest paid for each of the different interest rates.

d) Add your name in a header and the current date in a footer.

e) Save the workbook naming it Credit and print a copy.

f) Add two new scenarios by changing the amount borrowed or the length of time and then create a scenario summary.

g) Add your name in a header and the current date in a footer to the Scenario Summary sheet.

h) Save the workbook naming it Credit and print a copy of the Scenario Summary sheet.

Project 6

An educated investment in the stock market has historically provided the highest rate of return on a long-term investment compared to other investment options, such as a savings account. Stocks give an investor a portion, or *share*, of ownership in publicly held companies. Stocks can provide income as well as a long-term investment, and are categorized as:

- **Income stocks** pay dividends that provide income. *Dividends* are money paid annually to investors and are calculated by multiplying a stock's dividend (the DIV amount on a stock table) by the number of shares owned.

- **Blue-chip stocks** are companies that are considered solid, reliable, and having sustained growth. They provide consistent, reliable growth with regular, but small dividends.

- **Growth stocks** are shares of young, entrepreneurial companies that are experiencing a fast rate of growth. Growth stocks show considerable rise in stock price over a period of several months or years. These stocks normally do not pay dividends. Although sometimes riskier than other types of stock, growth stocks offer more potential for appreciation.

- **Cyclical stocks** are shares of companies that are affected by economic trends. The price of these stocks tend to go down in a recession and up during economic booms.

- **Defensive stocks (non-cyclical)** are shares of companies that are considered recession-resistant. These companies often provide staples, which will be purchased regardless of how the economy doing. These stocks are least affected by economic cycles and typically maintain their value regardless of the economic outlook.

a) The stock market is sometimes referred to as being either a "bull market" or a "bear market." A *bull market* is when stocks are considered to be generally rising in value. In a *bear market*, stocks are considered to be generally falling in price. When building a stock portfolio, different types of stock should be added. Having a mix of income, blue-chip, and defensive stocks along with growth and cyclical stocks will diversify a portfolio and may help the overall performance of the portfolio during a bear market. *Portfolio* refers to a set of investments owned by an individual.

A company's Web site typically includes a link called "Company" or "Investor Information" that provides the information you will need. Be sure to also check the bottom navigation bar for links to investor information. Many sites can also be searched for investor information.

Create a workbook named Diversified Stock Portfolio to keep track of an investment of 100 shares from ten different companies. Include the company name and the stock symbol (called the *ticker symbol*). Be sure to create a diversified portfolio.

b) Use Word to create a memo to an investor that includes the Diversified Stock Portfolio worksheet data. Briefly explain to the investor why you feel the selected stocks create a diversified portfolio. In a separate paragraph, explain why the income, blue-chip, and defensive stocks hedge against a downturn in the portfolio value during a bear market. Save the document naming it Investor Proposal and then print a copy.

c) One investment strategy for choosing stocks is *fundamental analysis,* which uses actual company data to determine the value of a stock and its potential for growth. A company's annual report provides data about its financial situation and all traded companies are required to make it publicly available. The *annual report* includes a balance sheet, which shows assets, liabilities, and net worth for the past year. *Net worth* is also called the stockholder's equity. The figures in the balance sheet can be used to calculate:

- **Current Ratio** Also called Working Capital Ratio. Current Ratio is assets divided by liabilities. This measure determines if a company can meet financial obligations. A value between 1.2 and 2.0 is considered good. Less than 1 means assets cannot cover liabilities. A value greater than 2 means the company may not be reinvesting excess cash or has too much inventory.

- **Quick Ratio** Also called the Acid Test Ratio. Quick Ratio is assets minus inventories divided by liabilities. This measure determines if a company can meet short-term liability, such as employee salaries. A value greater than 1 is considered good.

Fundamental analysis also includes considering the P/E, which is listed for each stock in a newspaper stock table or by viewing a stock quote on the Internet:

- **P/E** Price to Earnings ratio. P/E is stock price divided by the trailing EPS. *Trailing EPS* is a company's earnings for the last four quarters divided by the number of shares outstanding. P/E can indicate the profitability of a company and is used to value a stock. The P/E is generally between 15 and 25. A lower P/E can mean a stock may be undervalued. However, a single P/E should not be used to value a stock. One way to use the P/E is to compare P/E ratios among companies in the same industry. Values for P/E ratios by industry can be found on the Internet.

Modify the Diversified Stock Portfolio workbook to include a new worksheet named Analysis. Add each of the stocks from Sheet1, grouped by industry where possible. For each stock, create formulas that calculate the Current Ratio and Quick Ratio. Use the Internet to find each company's annual report. Annual reports are usually PDF documents within an Investor link at a company Web site. Look for the Balance Sheet within the report, and then look for total current assets and total current liabilities for calculating the Current Ratio and Quick Ratio. For each stock, list its P/E, which can be found in the annual report or through a stock quote on the Internet.

d) Use Word to create a letter to an investor that includes the data from the Analysis sheet in the Diversified Stock Portfolio workbook. Explain to the investor what the ratios mean for each stock. Where possible compare the stock P/E ratios. In a separate paragraph, make recommendations to the investor about which stocks to keep and which to sell for a portfolio that represents a long-term investment. Save the document naming it Portfolio Analysis and then print a copy.

Project 7

Businesses must keep track of their assets in order to portray a realistic net worth. *Assets* are material items with considerable value, such as computers, machinery, and vehicles. Because assets lose value over time, a business must depreciate assets in order to determine net worth. For example, suppose the assets of a small advertising agency include a new computer. The computer was purchased for $4,000 (the cost). It is expected to meet the company's needs for 3 years (the total life). After 3 years, the agency expects to trade it in for $350 (the salvage value). When the agency purchased the computer, it used cash ($4,000) for the purchase. If the business subtracts the cash spent when the asset is acquired, the net worth for that year will go down by $4,000. However, the computer will be useful for three years. Therefore, the business should determine the depreciation per year for the computer and then subtract that value from the net worth to portray a realistic net worth.

The SLN() function uses the straight-line depreciation method to return the depreciation per period for an item.

a) Create a new workbook.

b) Label cells for the initial cost of an item, the salvage value of the item at the end of its useful life, and the total life of the item.

c) Save the workbook naming it Depreciation Calculator.

d) The SLN() function returns the depreciation of an asset for a single period. The SLN() function takes the form:

   SLN(*cost, salvage, life*)

   The cost is the initial cost of the asset, salvage is the salvage value of the asset at the end of its useful life, and life is the expected period of usefulness for the asset. The life determines the period of depreciation. If life is in months, then SLN() returns the depreciation per month. If life is in years, then SLN() returns depreciation per year.

   Label a cell SLN Value and then create a formula that includes the SLN() function to determine the depreciation per year for an item. In the example above, an item that costs $4,000 with a life of 3 years and worth $350 when salvaged will have a depreciation of $1,216.67 per year.

e) Add your name in a header and the current date in a footer. Add gridlines and headings.

f) Save and then print the modified Depreciation Calculator with $3,500 entered for the cost of an item, 4 years for the life of the item, and $25 for the salvage value of the item.

g) Display the formulas in the cells instead of the values. Print a copy.

Project 8

Yolanda's Catering is planning a remodeling project and is starting with an estimation of costs that will be incurred. Choose a room to remodel and then create a worksheet to keep track of remodelling costs.

a) Create a new workbook.

b) Enter the data and apply formatting using the Urban theme as shown below:

	A	B	C	D
1	Remodeling Costs Worksheet			
2				
3	Items	Cost		
4		Estimated	Actual	
5				
6				
7				
8				
9				
10	Subtotal			
11	Taxes			
12	Total			

c) Save the workbook naming it Remodeling Costs.

d) In the Items column, list all the items required to complete the remodelling project. More rows may need to be added.

e) In the Estimated column, estimate and enter the costs associated with each item.

f) In the Estimated column, enter a formula that uses a function to calculate the Subtotal.

g) In the Estimated column, enter a formula to calculate the Taxes based on the appropriate tax rate.

h) In the Estimated column, enter a formula to calculate the Total costs.

i) Use the Internet or catalogs to research the actual cost associated with each item. Enter the costs in the Actual column.

j) Enter formulas to calculate the Subtotal, Taxes, and Total of the Actual column.

k) Format columns B and C as currency with 2 decimal places.

l) Sort the items and corresponding costs in descending order by actual cost.

m) Add your name in a header and the current date in a footer. Add gridlines and headings.

n) Save the modified Remodeling Costs and print a copy.

o) Display the formulas in the cells instead of values. Print a copy.

Project 9

The accountant for *Align Computers* has decided to use a worksheet for the payroll.

a) Create a new workbook.

b) Enter the data and apply formatting using the Angles theme as shown below:

	A	B	C	D
1	**Align Computers**			
2				
3	First Name	Last Name	Salary	
4	Sang	Wong	$89,000	
5	Jill	Grossman	$37,000	
6	Jason	Jones	$36,500	
7	Christa	Smith	$64,500	
8	Tanya	White	$28,900	
9				

c) Save the workbook naming it Align Employees.

d) Employees are paid weekly. In cell D3, enter the label Weekly Pay and format it appropriately. Enter formulas that use cell references to calculate the weekly pay for each employee. Weekly pay is calculated by dividing the annual salary by 52 (the number of weeks in a year).

e) In cell B9, enter the label Average and then right align the label and format it as italic. In cells C9 and D9, enter formulas that use a function to calculate the average salary and average weekly pay for the employees. Format the average weekly pay as currency with 2 decimal places.

f) Modify the weekly pay formulas to use a function to round the weekly pay amounts in column D to 0 decimal places (do not round the average weekly pay formula). The average weekly pay also changes because the numbers have been rounded.

g) Two more employees have been hired. Insert the new data shown below into the worksheet so that the employee names remain in alphabetical order by last name:

First Name	Last Name	Salary
Dedra	Roberts	$28,000
Philip	Jorge	$52,000

Copy the weekly pay formula for the new employees into the appropriate cells.

h) Tax deductions are calculated by multiplying 15% by the weekly pay when the salary is less than $30,000, and 28% by the weekly pay when the salary is equal to or higher than $30,000. In column E, enter the label Taxes and then enter formulas that use a function and cell references to calculate the taxes. Right align the label and format the values as currency with 2 decimal places.

i) Social security deductions also need to be calculated. Insert two blank rows at the top of the worksheet. In cell A1, enter the label Soc. Sec. Rate:. In cell B1, enter the value 6%. In cell F5, enter the label Soc. Sec., right align it, and then enter formulas that use absolute and relative cell references to calculate social security of each employee by multiplying the rate by the weekly pay.

j) Net pay is computed by making the necessary deductions from the weekly pay. In column G, enter the label Net Pay, right align it, and then enter formulas that use cell references to deduct the taxes and social security from the weekly pay of each employee to get the net pay.

k) The employees receive yearly bonuses based on the position they hold. Wong, Smith, and Jorge are managers. The rest of the employees are assistants. Insert a column after the salary column, and enter the label Position. Enter the appropriate position for each person, either Manager or Assistant and center align the entire column.

l) Every year, managers receive a bonus of 20% of their weekly pay and assistants receive a bonus of 10% of their weekly pay. In column I, enter the label Bonus, right align it, and enter formulas that use a function and cell references to calculate the bonus amounts for each employee.

m) Format all the data appropriately. Change the column widths so that all the data is displayed entirely and fits on one page.

n) Add your name in a header and the current date in a footer. Add gridlines and headings.

o) Save the modified Align Employees and print a copy.

p) Display the formulas in the cells instead of values. Print a copy.

Project 10

Many automobile dealers offer the option of leasing rather than purchasing an automobile. When leased, a car is owned by the agency holding the lease and the user pays a monthly fee for the use of the car. Most leases are set for a fixed time, for example four years, and a maximum number of miles the car may be driven, usually in the range of 12,000 to 15,000 miles per year. If the car is driven in excess of this limit an additional fee per mile is charged. At the end of the lease the car must be returned to the lease holder.

The leasing price is usually determined by taking the purchase price of the car minus the estimated value of the car at the end of the lease and then adding an interest charge. The advantage of a lease is that a low or no down payment is usually required, but the disadvantage is that it is usually more expensive to lease than to own a car. Owning is almost always better if you plan to keep the car for an extended period of time, well over the four year lease time. It is important to realize that when you purchase an automobile you own it—the car is yours, and may be sold by you at any time. When you lease a car you are in effect renting it.

a) Develop a plan for a worksheet that compares the cost of leasing versus purchasing an automobile.

b) Use the Internet, newspapers, or local automobile dealer to research the cost associated with buying and with leasing a particular automobile.

c) Create a new workbook and enter the appropriate data, formulas, and formatting.

d) Save the workbook naming it Automobile Lease.

e) Use Word to create a document named Buy vs Lease that briefly describes the automobile and explains whether leasing or buying would be a better decision. Include the data from the Automobile Lease workbook to support the decision.

f) Add a footer with your name centered.

g) Save and then print the Buy vs Lease document.

c) In cell C8, enter a formula that uses cell references and an absolute cell reference to calculate the ticket printing.

Project 11

The RAND() function returns a random real number greater than or equal to 0 and less than 1. To generate a random real number between a specified range, the formula =RAND()*(high-low)+low is used. In this Project, random numbers will be used to create random table placements for workshop participants.

a) Create a new workbook.

b) Enter the data and apply formatting using the Office theme as shown below:

c) Save the workbook naming it Random Table Placement.

d) In cell B4 enter the formula =ROUND((RAND()*(10–1)+1),0) to generate a random number between 1 and 10, which will be the participant's table number.

e) Copy the formula in cell B4 to cells B5 through B9.

f) To recalculate the table numbers, press the F9 key. A new set of random numbers is generated.

g) Add your name in a header and the current date in a footer.

h) Save the modified Random Table Placement and print a copy.

Project 12

This chapter introduced functions. Use Excel Help to explore functions further.

a) Research a function not covered in this chapter. Use Word to create a document that explains the function in your own words. Print a copy.

b) Create a worksheet that uses the function in a formula.

c) Add your name in a header and the current date in a footer.

d) Save the worksheet naming it Function Exploration and print a copy.

Chapter 7
Creating Charts

Key Concepts

Creating pie, bar, and line charts
Moving, sizing, and deleting charts
Copying a chart to a Word document
Modifying and formatting charts
Exploring other chart types
Using sparklines

Practice Data Files
CONTINENTS, TEMPERATURE, TRAVEL, SALES QUOTA

Project Data Files
BREAK EVEN, BUSINESS ANALYSIS

Charts

A *chart* is a visual representation of worksheet data. A chart can enhance and simplify the understanding of numerical data in a worksheet because the relationship between data is illustrated:

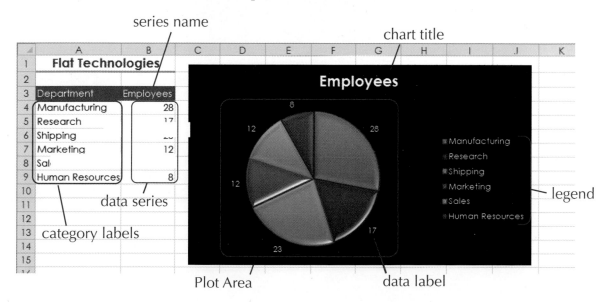

A chart is based on a range of related data. For example, cells A3 through B9 are used in the pie chart. The column with numerical data is the *data series*. The label for the data series is called the *series name*. Within a series, data is divided into *categories*. Text in cells adjacent to the data series are the *category labels*. Note that the data in cell A3 is ignored because it is to the left of the series name.

data series
series names
categories
category labels

TIP The chart symbol that represents a single data point, such as a pie slice, is called a data marker.

Chart Location

To view the data in the worksheet and its associated chart at the same time, place the chart as an object in the sheet. Place a chart that is large and complex on a separate sheet.

Charts contain different objects depending on the type of chart. In the pie chart shown:

- A **chart title** describes what is charted. Excel automatically uses the series name, if one exists.

- The **legend** corresponds to category labels.

- **Data labels** identify each value in the data series.

- The **Plot Area** is the part of the chart that displays data.

- The **Chart Area** is the entire chart and all of its elements.

A chart can be placed as an object in a worksheet as shown on the previous page or moved to a separate sheet in a workbook like the chart below:

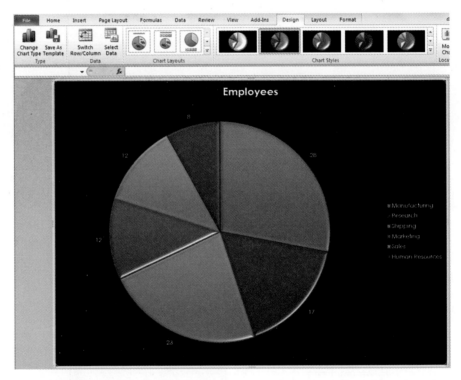

A chart is linked to the range of data it is based on. Therefore, if a value or label in the data range is changed, the chart automatically updates.

Creating Pie Charts

Pie

slice

Pie charts are best for charting data that is a percentage of a whole. A pie chart can include only one series of data. Each value from the series is represented as a *slice*. The size of a slice varies with its percentage of the series total. For example, the chart on the next page illustrates that Lawn Care accounts for 40% of the total sales. Data labels display the percentage for each slice:

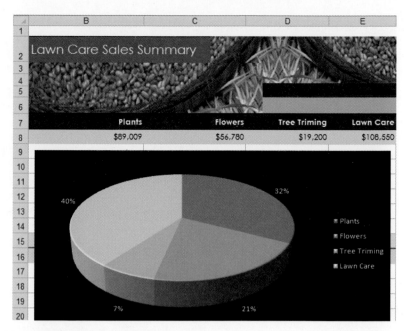

To create a pie chart, first select the data range to be charted. For the chart above, cells B7 through E8 are the data range. Next, click Insert → Pie and then click the appropriate type of pie chart from the displayed menu. The pie chart is displayed on the worksheet and the Chart Tools tabs are added to the Ribbon. Click the Layout tab to display options for data labels:

Format Selection

Data Labels

TIP To change the color of a selected pie slice, click Format → Shape Fill and select a color.

- To add data labels, click Data Labels and select an option from the displayed menu. Data labels are added to the chart with the actual data values.

- To change the labels to percentages, select the data labels and then click Format Selection. In the dialog box, select the Percentage check box and clear the Value check box.

Practice: CONTINENTS – part 1 of 2

① OPEN CONTINENTS

a. Start Excel.

b. Open CONTINENTS, which is an Excel data file for this text. The CONTINENTS workbook contains the approximate area of the seven continents of the world in square kilometers.

② CREATE A PIE CHART

a. Select cells A3 through B10:

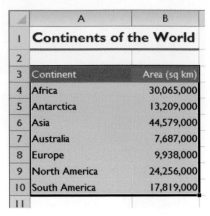

b. Click Insert → Pie. Pie chart options are displayed. Click the first 2-D Pie option:

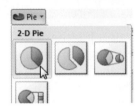

The chart is displayed on the worksheet and the data range is selected:

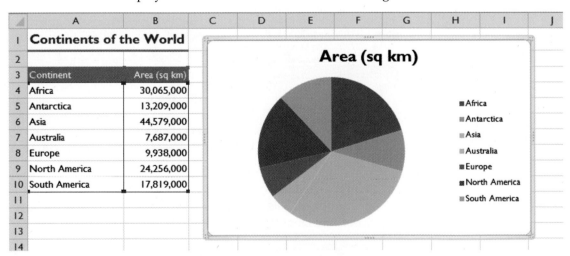

③ ADD DATA LABELS

a. Click Layout → Data Labels → Best Fit. The data value is displayed on or near the corresponding slice.

b. Click one of the data labels. All of the data labels are selected.

c. Click Layout → Format Selection. A dialog box is displayed.

    1. Select the Percentage check box and clear the Value check box:

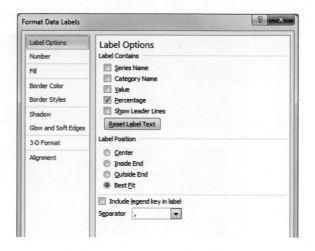

2. Select **Close**. The dialog box is removed and the data labels are displayed as percentages. Click anywhere in the worksheet to remove the selection:

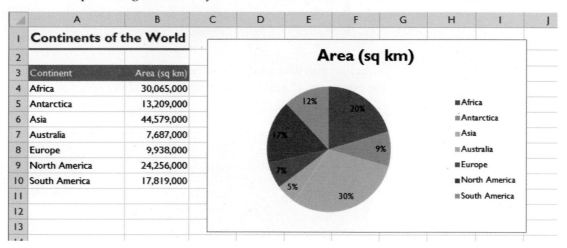

④ **CHANGE A VALUE IN THE WORKSHEET**

   a. What is the size of the Africa slice in the pie chart? Hint: pointing to a slice displays information about the slice.

   b. A mistake was made when recording the area of Africa. Type the correct value of 30,330,000 in cell B4. The chart adjusts to reflect the modified value.

⑤ **SAVE THE MODIFIED CONTINENTS**

Moving, Sizing, and Deleting Charts

Move Chart

When a chart is placed as an object on a worksheet, it may need to be moved to display data stored in cells behind the chart. To move a chart, drag a chart border:

TIP When moving a chart, avoid dragging a corner or middle handle.

Alternative Drag the Chart Area to move a chart.

A chart may also need to be sized. Point to a corner handle, which changes the pointer to ↗ and then drag to size the chart proportionately:

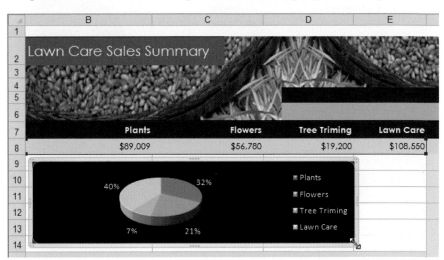

TIP To size the Plot Area, select the Plot Area and then drag a corner handle to size the area proportionately.

Click Home → Cut ✂ or press the Delete key to delete a selected chart.

To move the chart to another sheet, click Design → Move Chart, which displays a dialog box. Select New sheet, specify the sheet name, and then select OK.

Printing a Chart

A chart that is an object in a worksheet is printed when the worksheet is printed. Select [File] → Print or click View → Page Layout to determine if the chart will fit completely on a page before printing. Sizing or moving a chart may be necessary to fit it on a single sheet of paper. Changing the orientation to landscape or changing the margins may also help fit a worksheet with a chart onto a single sheet of paper. Select [File] → Print → Print to print the active worksheet with the chart.

To print only the chart on a single sheet of paper, select the chart before printing. A chart printed in this manner will not contain the worksheet header or footer. To add a header or footer to the selected chart, click Insert → Header & Footer to display the Page Setup dialog box. Select an option from the Header and Footer lists. If additional information is needed in the header and footer, select the Custom Header or Custom Footer button.

To print a chart that is in its own sheet, display the chart sheet and then select [File] → Print → Print. A header and footer can be added to a chart sheet the same way it is described in the previous paragraph.

Practice: CONTINENTS – part 2 of 2

Excel should already be started with CONTINENTS displayed from the last practice.

① SIZE AND MOVE THE CHART

    a. If the chart is not selected, click the border. The chart is selected.

    b. Move the pointer over the handle in the bottom-right corner of the chart. The pointer changes to ⤢.

    c. Drag the handle down and to the right a little. The chart is larger.

    d. Drag the chart border so that it is below the worksheet data.

② SAVE, PRINT, AND THEN CLOSE THE MODIFIED CONTINENTS

    a. Select the chart if it is not already selected.

    b. Select [File] → Print. Only the chart is displayed in the preview area.

    c. Press Esc to exit Backstage view.

    d. Click a cell in the worksheet to remove the chart border.

    e. Click View → Page Layout.

    f. Add a header with your name and a footer with the current date.

    g. Select [File] → Print → Print.

    h. Save the modified CONTINENTS workbook and close CONTINENTS.

Copying a Chart into a Word Document

Charts are often included in reports and other business documents to support and simplify the understanding of the text. To copy and paste a selected Excel chart to a Word document, in Excel click Home → Copy 📋, display the Word document, place the insertion point where the chart is to appear, and then click Home → Paste. A picture of the chart is copied from Excel and pasted into the Word document:

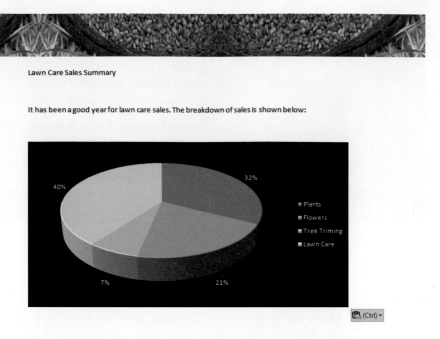

Lawn Care Sales Summary

It has been a good year for lawn care sales. The breakdown of sales is shown below:

Click Paste Options  to display a list of options for the pasted chart:

- Select Use Destination Theme & Link Data  to have the Word document chart update automatically whenever the chart changes in Excel. When a linked chart is selected in a Word document, the Design, Layout, and Format tabs are available. The Design tab is used to edit and refresh the chart data:

Edit Data   Refresh Data

  Click Design → Edit Data to start Excel and display the workbook containing the chart. Click Design → Refresh Data to update the linked chart.

- Select Picture to paste the chart as a graphic. A chart that is inserted as a graphic can be edited using the Format tab:

  A chart that is pasted as a graphic cannot be edited using Excel commands.

Creating Bar and Line Charts

Line

Column   Bar

Bar charts are useful for comparing the differences between values. A bar chart can include several series of data, with each bar representing a value. Excel can create bar charts with either vertical bars or horizontal bars. In Excel, a horizontal bar chart is called a bar chart and a vertical bar

column chart   chart is called a *column chart*:

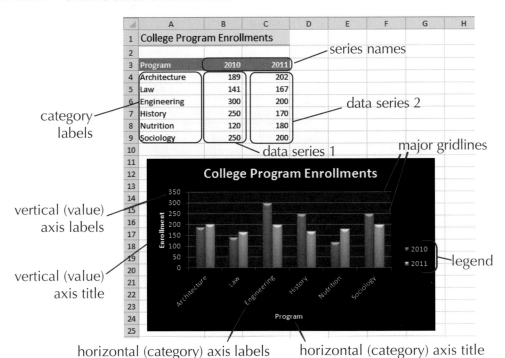

horizontal (category) axis labels   horizontal (category) axis title

Bar charts contain the following objects:

- A **chart title** describes what is charted and **axes titles** describe the data. These titles are not automatically displayed.

- The **legend** corresponds to the series names.

- The **vertical** or **value axis** contains values.

- The **horizontal** or **category axis** contains category labels.

- The **horizontal axis labels** corresponds to the category labels.

- The **vertical axis labels** are calculated by Excel based on the maximum value in the data.

- **Major gridlines** mark the major intervals on an axis.

TIP Most chart types have two axes. Pie charts do not have axes.

TIP The horizontal axis is also referred to as the x-axis. The vertical axis is also referred to as the y-axis.

To add a chart title above the chart, click Layout → Chart Title → Above Chart. Change the title text by selecting the object and then typing. To add axis titles, use Layout → Axis Titles → Primary Horizontal Axis Title and Layout → Axis Titles → Primary Vertical Axis Title, which include display options. Change the axis title by selecting the object and then typing.

Click Layout → Legend to select an option for changing the display of the legend. A legend can be removed or displayed in an alternate location.

If the data range needs to be modified on the chart, click Design → Select Data, which displays the Select Data Source dialog box. Select the appropriate object to modify and then select the data range from the worksheet. A common chart error occurs if category labels are values, rather than text. To correct this error, select Edit in the Horizontal (Category) Axis Labels in the Select Data Source dialog box and then select the horizontal axis labels on the worksheet. Next, click the axis labels entry in the Legend box and click Remove.

A *line chart* can include several series of data with each line representing a series. Each value in a series is a point on the line. Line charts are therefore useful for displaying the differences of data over time. Line charts contain similar objects to bar charts:

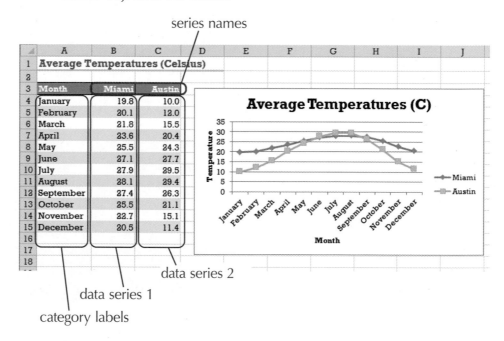

series names

data series 2

data series 1

category labels

TIP If the chart data range contains non-adjacent cells, hold down the Ctrl key while selecting the data range.

Alternative To add an adjacent range to a selected chart, drag a data range handle.

Practice: TEMPERATURE – part 1 of 2

Excel should already be started.

① **OPEN TEMPERATURE**

Open TEMPERATURE, which is an Excel data file for this text. The TEMPERATURE workbook contains the average monthly temperature of two cities.

② CREATE A LINE CHART

   a. Select cells A3 through C15:

	A	B	C
1	Average Temperatures (Celsius)		
2			
3	Month	Miami	Austin
4	January	19.8	10
5	February	20.1	12
6	March	21.8	15.5
7	April	23.6	20.4
8	May	25.5	24.3
9	June	27.1	27.7
10	July	27.9	29.5
11	August	28.1	29.4
12	September	27.4	26.3
13	October	25.5	21.1
14	November	22.7	15.1
15	December	20.5	11.4

   b. Click Insert → Line. Line chart options are displayed. Click the first 2-D Line chart in the second row:

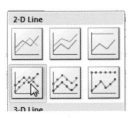

The chart is displayed on the worksheet and the data range is selected:

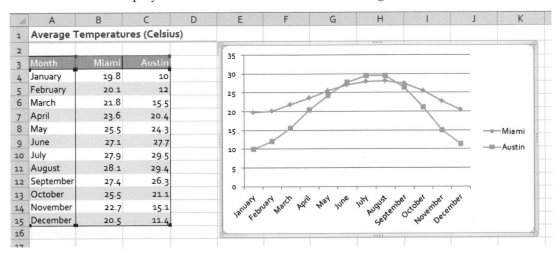

③ ADD A CHART AND AXIS TITLES

   a. Click Layout → Chart Title → Above Chart. A chart title is added above the chart.

   b. Click in the Chart Title object and replace the text with: Average Temperatures (C). Click a blank area of the chart to remove the selection.

   c. Click Layout → Axis Titles → Primary Horizontal Axis Title → Title Below Axis. An axis title is added below the horizontal axis.

   d. Click in the Axis Title object and replace the text with: Month

   e. Click Layout → Axis Titles → Primary Vertical Axis Title → Rotated Title. An axis title is added to the left of the vertical axis.

f. Click on the formula bar, type Temperature and press Enter. The axis title is changed.

g. Click Layout → Legend → None. The legend is removed.

h. Click Layout → Legend → Show Legend at Right. The legend is again displayed.

④ CHANGE THE CHART LOCATION

a. Click Design → Move Chart. A dialog box is displayed:

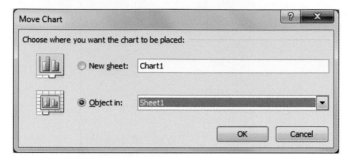

1. Click New sheet and type Avg Temp.
2. Select OK. The chart is moved to a new sheet named Avg Temp:

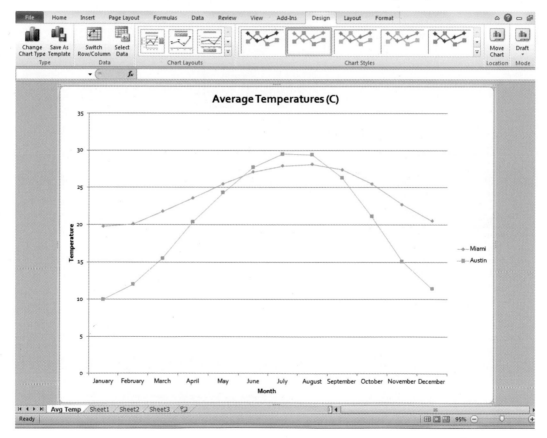

⑤ SAVE THE MODIFIED TEMPERATURE

⑥ CREATE A BAR CHART

a. Display Sheet1.

b. Select cells A5 through C6:

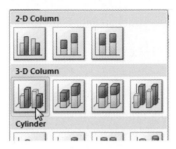

c. Click Insert → Column. Column chart options are displayed. Click the first 3-D Column option:

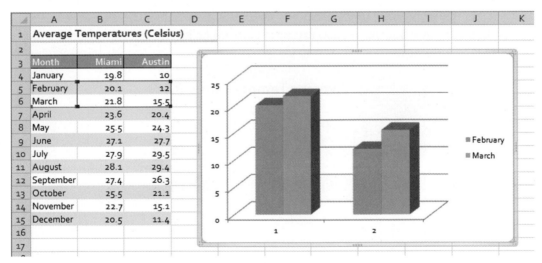

The chart is displayed on the worksheet and the data range is selected. Note that the horizontal axis labels are incorrect:

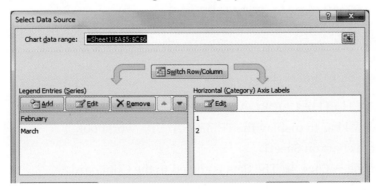

⑦ MODIFY THE DATA RANGE

a. Click Design → Select Data. A dialog box is displayed:

1. In the Horizontal (Category) Axis Labels box, click Edit. Another dialog box is displayed:

2. On the worksheet, select cells B3 and C3 and select OK in both dialog boxes. Horizontal (category) axis labels are added to the chart.

⑧ **ADD DATA LABELS**

Click Layout → Data Labels → Outside End. Data labels are displayed.

⑨ **ADD A CHART AND AXIS TITLES**

a. Click Layout → Chart Title → Above Chart. A chart title is added above the chart.

b. Change the chart title to read: Average Temperatures (C)

c. Click Layout → Axis Titles → Primary Horizontal Axis Title → Title Below Axis. An axis title is added below the horizontal axis.

d. Change the axis title to read: City

e. Click Layout → Axis Titles → Primary Vertical Axis Title → Rotated Title. An axis title is added to the left of the vertical axis.

f. Click on the formula bar, type Temperature and press Enter.

g. Select Layout → Legend → Show Legend at Bottom The legend is displayed at the bottom of the chart:

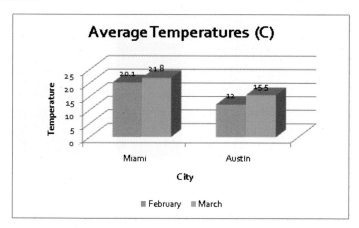

h. Move the chart below the data on Sheet1.

⑩ **SAVE THE MODIFIED TEMPERATURE**

⑪ **OPEN TRAVEL**

Start Word and open TRAVEL, which is a data file for this text. Read through the unfinished document.

⑫ **COPY DATA TO THE CLIPBOARD**

a. Use the taskbar to display the TEMPERATURE workbook.

b. Select the chart on Sheet1.

c. Click Home → Copy 🖺. The data is copied to the Clipboard.

⑬ PASTE DATA

a. Use the taskbar to display the TRAVEL document.

b. Place the insertion point in the blank paragraph after the text that reads "…average temperatures are:"

c. Click Home → Paste. The chart is pasted and Paste Options ▦ is displayed. The colors of the columns have changed to match the theme of the Word document:

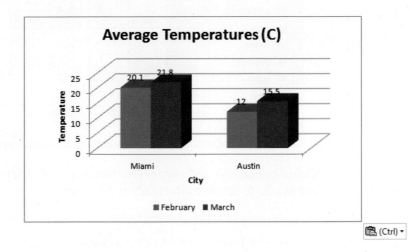

d. Click Paste Options → Picture 🖼. The chart is displayed in the same color scheme as it was displayed in Excel. The chart is no longer linked to the worksheet and the Format tab is added to the Ribbon.

e. Click Format → Corrections. Select a Brightness and Contrast option.

f. Click Format → Picture Effects → Bevel and then click a Bevel option.

⑭ CREATE A HEADER

Add a header with your name and a footer with the date.

⑮ SAVE THE MODIFIED TRAVEL DOCUMENT AND PRINT A COPY

⑯ CLOSE TRAVEL AND QUIT WORD

Chart Design

Change Chart Type

Switch Row/Column   Select Data

Chart design refers to the chart type (such as bar or line), the data for a chart, and the basic chart style and layout. To change the type of chart, click Design → Change Chart Type. A dialog box is displayed with the existing chart type selected:

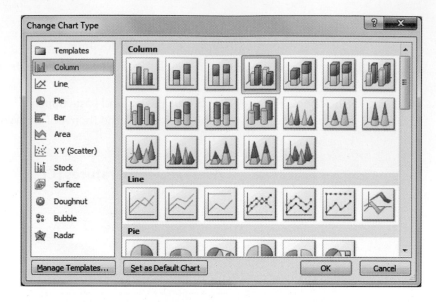

Column, bar, line, and pie are common types of charts. Other chart types are available to more effectively convey data:

- An **area chart** shows the trend of values over time.
- An **XY (scatter) chart** compares pairs of values.
- A **stock chart** displays stock prices.
- A **surface chart** shows trends in values.
- A **doughnut chart** is similar to a pie chart, but can contain more than one data series.
- A **bubble chart** compares sets of three values.
- A **radar chart** shows changes in values relative to a center point.
- **Cylinder**, **cone**, and **pyramid** charts are used to add a different chart symbol to bar and column charts.

Each chart type also has several subtypes that can be selected after selecting the chart type. For example, Area has six subtypes and XY (Scatter) has five subtypes.

To change the way data series are charted, click Design → Switch Row/Column. Data charted on the horizontal axis will move to the vertical axis and vice versa.

To add or modify data series and labels in an existing chart:

- Drag one of the handles of the outlined data to include a new series.
- Drag one of the handles of the outlined labels to include new labels.
- Select Design → Select Data to display the Select Data Source dialog box and then select Add, Edit, or Remove data and labels.

Chart layout is the placement of objects on a chart. Select a chart layout from the Chart Layouts group on the Design tab. Click More Chart Layouts ⏷ to see additional layouts.

The style of a chart can be easily modified by applying a different chart style from the **Chart Styles** group on the **Design** tab. For example, below is the same chart with two different chart styles applied:

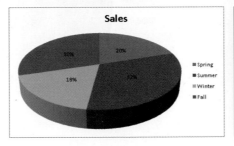 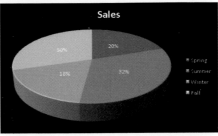

Modifying a Chart Layout

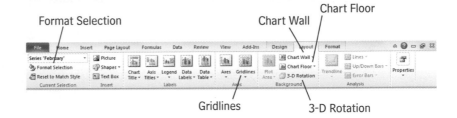

Chart layout, including the placement of titles, legends, and labels, is changed using the **Layout** tab. Other layout changes can includes axes and gridlines styles and background styles.

The **Labels** options on the **Layout** tab are used for changing the placement of titles, legends, and labels. For example, a legend can be at the top, bottom, right, or left of a chart.

Gridlines can be modified by clicking **Layout** → **Gridlines** and selecting a gridlines option. For example, below is the same chart with and without major horizontal gridlines:

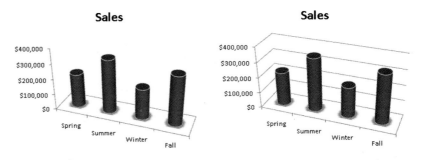

Line Chart Options

Error bars, Up/Down bars, and Trendlines can be added to line charts by clicking options on the **Layout** tab.

Certain chart types, such as 3-D column charts, allow the chart floor and chart wall to be modified. For example, the chart floor and chart wall have been filled with a selected color:

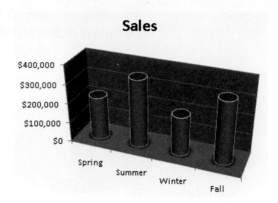

To modify the chart wall of a selected chart, click Layout → Chart Wall → More Wall Options. A dialog box is displayed with chart wall options. To modify the chart floor of a selected chart, click Layout → Chart Floor → More Floor Options. A dialog box is displayed with chart floor options.

3-D charts can also be rotated for special effects:

To rotate an axis of a 3-D chart, click Layout → 3-D Rotation. A dialog box is displayed with rotate options.

Other chart objects can be modified by clicking the chart object and then clicking Layout → Format Selection to display a Format dialog box. For example, click the vertical axis values and then click Layout → Format Selection to display the Format Axis dialog box:

TIP To change the vertical axis labels, click **Fixed** instead of **Auto** and type appropriate minimum, maximum, and unit values.

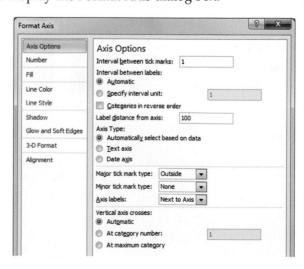

Axis scale, order of values, display units, and position of axis labels can be changed

Formatting a Chart

Shape Styles   WordArt Styles

If a chart is to be used in a report or other document, format the chart to complement the formatting used in the document or the report. Many businesses and companies have a protocol that specifies a particular theme (color scheme, fonts) and logo that should be used in all business or company documents.

Click Page Layout → Themes and select a theme from the gallery. Changing the theme will change the fonts, colors, and effects associated with both the chart and the corresponding worksheet.

Use Shape Styles on the Format tab to change the border and color of a chart. The WordArt Styles affect the look and color of the titles.

Practice: TEMPERATURE – part 2 of 2

Excel should already be started with TEMPERATURE displayed from the last practice.

① **RENAME SHEETS**

   a. Rename **Sheet1**: City Temperatures
   b. Rename **Avg Temp**: 12-Month Comparison

② **ADD DATA TO THE WORKSHEET**

   a. Select the **City Temperatures** sheet.
   b. Enter the following label and data into column D:

	A	B	C	D
1	Average Temperatures (Celsius)			
2				
3	Month	Miami	Austin	Los Angeles
4	January	19.8	10	13.4
5	February	20.1	12	13.6
6	March	21.8	15.5	14.1
7	April	23.6	20.4	15.2
8	May	25.5	24.3	16.4
9	June	27.1	27.7	17.7
10	July	27.9	29.5	19.5
11	August	28.1	29.4	20.4
12	September	27.4	26.3	20
13	October	25.5	21.1	18.5
14	November	22.7	15.1	15.7
15	December	20.5	11.4	13.5

   c. Select cells C3 through C15.

d. Click Home → Format Painter 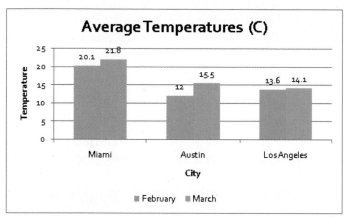.

e. Click cell D3. Formatting is applied to the data.

f. Widen column D until the label is displayed entirely.

③ ADD A DATA SERIES TO THE COLUMN CHART

a. Select the column chart. The data series and labels associated with the chart are outlined in color.

b. Drag the bottom handle in cell C6 to cell D6. The Los Angeles average temperatures for February and March and horizontal axis label are added to the chart:

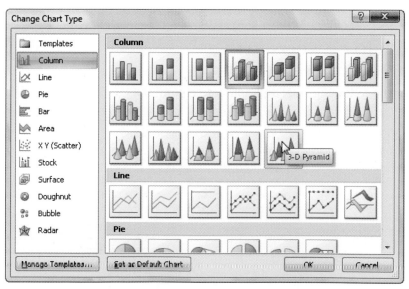

④ CHANGE THE CHART DESIGN

a. Click Design → Change Chart Type. The Change Chart Type dialog box is displayed. Click the 3-D Pyramid chart:

b. Select OK. The chart type is changed.

c. Select the chart if it is not already selected, and click Design → More Chart Styles ⬇ → Style 42. A new design is applied to the chart:

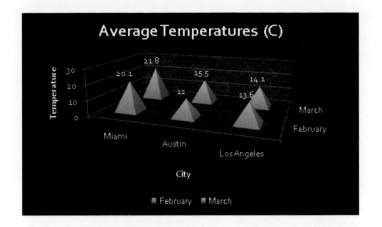

d. Select the chart if it is not already selected, and click Design → More Chart Layouts ⬇ → Layout 7. A new layout is applied to the chart. Note that this layout does not have a chart title or data labels:

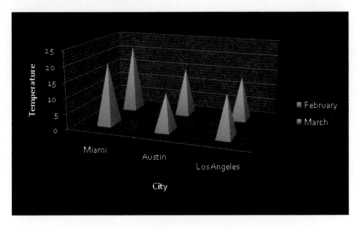

⑤ MODIFY THE CHART FLOOR AND CHART WALL LAYOUT

a. Select the chart if it is not already and then click Layout → Chart Floor → More Floor Options. A dialog box is displayed.

1. Select options as shown:

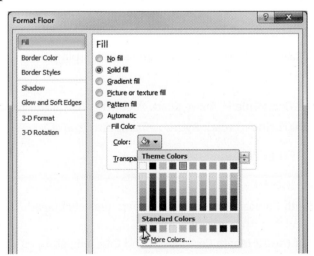

2. Click Close. The chart floor is filled in a red color.

b. Click Layout → Chart Wall → More Wall Options. A dialog box is displayed.

1. Select options as shown:

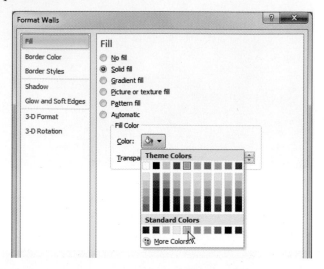

2. Click Close. The chart wall is filled in a green color.

c. Click the "Miami Austin Los Angeles" horizontal axis labels and then click Layout → Format Selection. The Format Axis dialog box is displayed.

1. Select options as shown:

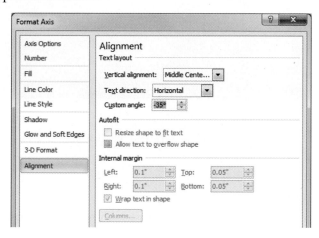

2. Click Close. The horizontal axis labels are displayed on an angle.

⑥ ADD A TITLE

a. Click Layout → Chart Title → Above Chart. A chart title is added above the chart.

b. Change the chart title to read: Average Temperatures (C)

⑦ SAVE THE MODIFIED TEMPERATURE

⑧ PRINT TWO WORKSHEETS

a. On the 12-Month Comparison and City Temperatures sheets, add a header with your name and a footer with the date.

b. Print a copy of the 12-Month Comparison and City Temperatures sheets.

⑨ CLOSE TEMPERATURE

Sparklines

Sparklines are mini-charts that can be inserted in a cell:

	A	B	C	D	E	F	G
1	**Index Funds**						
2							
3	Fund Name	Symbol	Price	Price	Price	Price	
4			9/21/2011	9/22/2011	9/23/2011	9/24/2011	
5	Vanguard 500 Index Fund	VFINX	$139.50	$137.58	$138.92	$138.68	⌄
6	Vanguard Total Stock Market Fund	VTSMX	$36.58	$36.06	$36.42	$36.33	⌄
7	Vanguard TSM VIPERS	VTI	$150.30	$148.41	$149.80	$149.35	⌄
8	Fidelity 100 Index Fund	FOHIX	$10.68	$10.54	$10.63	$10.62	⌄
9	Rydex OTC	RYOCX	$12.20	$12.55	$12.79	$13.86	⌄
10	Schwab 100 Index	SNXFX	$43.16	$43.25	$43.05	$43.88	⌄
11							

To insert sparklines, select the range of cells that the sparklines are to appear and then select the appropriate type of sparkline (☒ Line , ☷ Column , ☶ Win/Loss) from the Insert tab. After the data range is selected, the sparklines are displayed in the selected cells and the Design tab can be used to format the sparklines and display features such as high and low points.

Practice: SALES QUOTA

Excel should already be started.

1. **OPEN SALES QUOTA**

   Open SALES QUOTA, which is an Excel data file for this text.

2. **ADD SPARKLINES**

   a. Select cells E2 through E11.

   b. Select Insert → ☷ Column . A dialog box is displayed.

   c. Select cells C2 through D11 and then select OK.

   d. Select Design → Axis and then select Same for All Sparklines in the Vertical Axis Minimum Value Options category.

   e. Select a Style option.

   f. Select cell E1 and enter the label: Sales vs. Quota

   g. Widen column E and use Format Painter to copy the formatting from cell D1 to cell E1.

3. **SAVE THE MODIFIED SALES QUOTA AND QUIT EXCEL**

Chapter Summary

This chapter discussed how to create charts. A chart is a visual representation of worksheet data. By default, a chart is placed as an object in a worksheet. A chart can be moved to a separate sheet using the Design tab.

Pie charts show the percentage relationship between different parts of a whole quantity, bar charts compare different values, and line charts track data over time. In Excel a vertical bar chart is called a column chart. Various other types of charts, such as XY charts, area charts, and stock charts can be created using options on the Insert tab. Sparklines are mini charts that can be displayed in a cell.

A chart is moved by dragging the chart border and sized by dragging a corner handle. A chart should be previewed before it is printed to determine if the chart will fit completely on a page. The entire worksheet and any charts it contains can be printed by selecting the Print command. A chart can be printed by itself on a single sheet of paper by first selecting the chart.

Charts are often included in reports and other business documents to support and simplify the understanding of the text. An Excel chart can be copied to a Word document using the Home tab.

The Design tab is used to choose a data series, a chart layout, and to modify the chart style. Data in adjacent and non-adjacent data can be added to an existing chart.

The Layout tab is used to add gridlines and modify the chart floor and wall. Clicking any object in a chart and then clicking Format Selection on the Layout tab displays a dialog box where options can be selected to change the appearance of the chart.

The Page Layout tab is used to change the chart theme and the Format tab is used to change the border and color of a chart.

Vocabulary

Bar chart   Data graphed as a series of bars.

Category   The division of data within a series.

Category axis   The horizontal axis that contains category labels.

Category labels   Text displayed on the x-axis.

Chart   A visual representation of worksheet data.

Chart Area   The blank portion of a chart.

Chart title   Describes what is charted.

Column chart   Data graphed as a series of vertical bars.

Data labels   Labels that identify each value in the data series.

Data series   A set of related numerical data plotted on a chart.

Horizontal axis   *See* Category axis.

Horizontal axis label   Category labels displayed on the horizontal axis of a chart.

Legend   Corresponds to the category labels in a pie chart and series names in other chart types.

Line chart   Data graphed using a continuous line.

Pie chart   Data graphed as slices of a circular pie.

Plot Area   The part of the chart that displays data.

Series name   The label that identifies the data series.

Slice   Part of a pie chart that represents one value from the series.

Sparklines   Mini charts that can be displayed in a cell.

Static   Pasted data that will not automatically change if the source worksheet does.

Value axis   The vertical axis that contains values.

Vertical axis   *See* Value axis.

Vertical axis labels   Labels calculated by Excel based on the maximum value in the data and displayed on the vertical axis of a chart.

3-D Rotation Displays options for rotating a 3-D chart. Found on the Layout tab.

Above Chart Adds a chart title above the chart. Found in Layout → Chart Title.

Change Chart Type Displays options for changing the chart type. Found on the Design tab.

Column Displays a dialog box used to create a column chart. Found on the Insert tab.

Copy 📋 Places the selected chart on the Clipboard. Found on the Home tab.

Data Labels Adds data labels to a chart. Found on the Layout tab.

Edit Data Starts Excel and displays the workbook containing the chart. Found on the Design tab in Word.

Format Selection Displays a Format dialog box used to format a chart object. Found on the Layout tab.

Gridlines Displays options for displaying gridlines. Found on the Layout tab.

Insert Line Sparkline 📈 Line Inserts a line chart within a single cell. Found on the Insert tab.

Legend Displays options for modifying the legend. Found on the Layout tab.

Line Displays a dialog box used to create a column chart. Found on the Insert tab.

Major Gridlines Displays gridlines for major intervals on an axis. Found in Layout → Gridlines → Primary Horizontal Gridlines.

More Floor Options Displays options for modifying the chart floor. Found in Layout → Chart Floor.

More Wall Options Displays options for modifying the chart wall. Found in Layout → Chart Wall.

Move Chart Displays a dialog box used to move a chart to a new sheet. Found on the Design tab.

Page Layout Displays the worksheet in Page Layout view. Found on the View tab.

Paste Places the most recently copied chart into a document. Found on the Home tab.

Paste Options 📋 Displayed when contents of the Clipboard are placed in cells. Used to link cells between sheets.

Pie Displays options for creating a pie chart. Found on the Insert tab.

Primary Horizontal Axis Title Adds an axis title to the horizontal axis. Found in Layout → Axis Title.

Primary Vertical Axis Title Adds an axis title to the vertical axis. Found in Layout → Axis Title.

Print Prints a copy of the worksheet. Found in Backstage view.

Print Preview Displays a worksheet as it will appear when printed. Found in [File] → Print.

Refresh Data Updates linked data. Found on the Data tab. Also found on the Design tab in Word.

Select Data Displays a dialog box used to add labels to data in a chart. Found on the Design tab.

Switch Row/Column Switches data charted on the horizontal axis to the vertical axis and vice versa. Found on the Design tab.

Themes Displays a gallery of themes. Found on the Page Layout tab.

1. Explain how charts can simplify the understanding of numeric data.

2. a) How will a chart be affected if a value in a data range is changed on the worksheet?
   b) What does a legend correspond to?
   c) How many categories are in the data charted on the first page of this chapter?

3. List the two locations a chart can be placed.

4. a) How many series of data can a pie chart include?
   b) What does a pie chart use to represent values?

5. Explain how to change data labels from actual values to percentages.

6. a) What happens to the corresponding data series and labels when a chart is selected?
   b) How is a chart moved on a worksheet?
   c) List the steps required to size a chart proportionately.
   d) Why should a corner handle be used to size a chart?

7. a) List the steps required to print a chart that is stored on the same sheet as the charted data.
   b) List the steps required to print a chart that is stored on the same sheet as the charted data so that only the chart is printed.

8. Why would a chart be included in a report?

9. a) What is the difference between embedding a chart and linking a chart?
   b) Describe a situation where it would be advantageous to link a chart in a Word document to the Excel source chart.

10. In Excel, what is a vertical bar chart called?

11. What type of chart (bar, line, or pie) is best suited to display:
    a) a student's GPA over four years.
    b) the percentage each department spent of a company's total budget.
    c) the number of full-time, part-time, and temporary employees in a company.
    d) the number of books sold each day for a month at the college bookstore.

12. a) What do the axes titles describe?
    b) How are the vertical axis labels calculated?

13. List the steps required to modify a chart to include an additional adjacent series of data.

14. Describe the changes that will occur to a pie chart if the theme is changed from Office to Metro.

True/False

15. Determine if each of the following are true or false. If false, explain why.
    a) If a value in a data series changes, the corresponding chart will automatically update.
    b) Pie charts are best for showing differences of data over time.
    c) The data range for a chart always includes all of the data on the worksheet.
    d) A chart that appears as an object will print on a single sheet of paper in landscape orientation if the chart is selected before selecting [File] → Print.
    e) An Excel chart that is a linked object in a Word document can be edited in Word using the Design, Layout, and Format tabs.
    f) Bar charts are useful for comparing the differences between values.
    g) Pie charts have axes.
    h) A chart in a report should contain formatting that complements the report.
    i) Each chart type has at least one sub-type.
    j) A Surface chart shows trends in values.
    k) A Bubble chart compares sets of five values.
    l) Pie charts have a chart wall.
    m) The vertical axis on a column chart must start at the value zero.
    n) Sparklines are displayed in a single cell.

Project 1

Yolanda's Catering wants the data for the Pizza worksheet created in Chapter 6, Project 2 charted. Open Pizza Palace and complete the following steps:

a) Produce a pie chart on the active sheet that displays the ingredients and the value of their costs for the Everything pizza. Include and format the title, legend, and data labels as shown below:

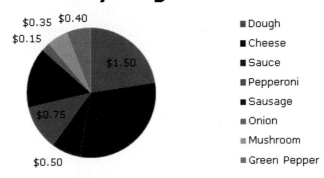

b) Be sure the chart and data fit on one page, and then save the modified Pizza and print a copy.

Project 2

The monthly payments calculated for a three year loan at two different interest rates in the Car Loan workbook created in Chapter 6, Project 4 can be compared in a column chart. Open Car Loan and complete the following steps:

a) Produce a column chart on the active sheet that displays the monthly payment for a three year loan at 7% interest and at 10% interest. Include an appropriate title, axes labels, data labels, and formatting.

b) Research the current rate for a 3 year car loan using the Internet or by contacting a local bank or financial institution. Change the 7% interest rate in cell B5 to the current rate.

c) Be sure the chart and data fit on one page, and then save the modified Car Loan and print a copy.

Project 3

A good entrepreneur uses valid statistics when doing market research. The U.S. Census Bureau carries out a census every ten years. According to the first census in 1790, there were 3,900,000 people in the United States. The census in 2000 counted 281,421,906 people in the United States. Census data also indicates how many people live in a specific city.

a) Create a new workbook.

b) Enter data and apply formatting using the Median theme similar to:

	A	B	C
1	Population Statistics		
2			
3	City	State	Population
4	New York	New York	8,008,278
5	Los Angeles	California	3,694,820
6	Houston	Texas	1,953,631
7	Philadelphia	Pennsylvania	1,517,550
8	Phoenix	Arizonia	1,321,045
9	Seattle	Washington	563,374
10	Albuquerque	New Mexico	448,607
11	Miami	Florida	362,470
12	Wichita	Kansas	344,284

c) Sort the data in descending order by population.

d) Produce a bar chart on the active sheet that compares the population of the four cities in the list with the highest population. Include an appropriate title and axes labels.

e) Add your name in a header and the current date in a footer.

f) Be sure the chart and data fit on one page, and then save the modified Population and print a copy.

Project 4

Study Time Tutoring is preparing materials to help students with their Geography studies:

a) Create a new workbook.

b) Enter data and apply formatting using the Trek theme similar to:

	A	B	C
1	Country Statistics		
2	Country	Area (sq km)	Population
3	China	9,598,086	1,313,800,000
4	United States	9,629,091	300,180,000
5	Brazil	8,514,877	187,520,000
6	Russia	17,098,242	141,800,000
7	Canada	9,970,610	32,745,000
8	Australia	7,741,220	20,700,000

c) Sort the worksheet so that the countries and their corresponding data is listed in descending order by area.

d) Produce a column chart on the active sheet that displays the area of each country. Include the title and axes labels and formatting as shown:

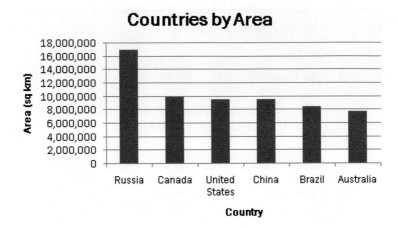

e) Manually scale the y-axis to have a minimum value of 5,000,000.

f) Save the workbook naming it Country Statistics.

g) Sort the worksheet so that the countries and their corresponding data is listed in descending order by population.

h) Produce a 3-D column chart on its own sheet that displays the population of each country:

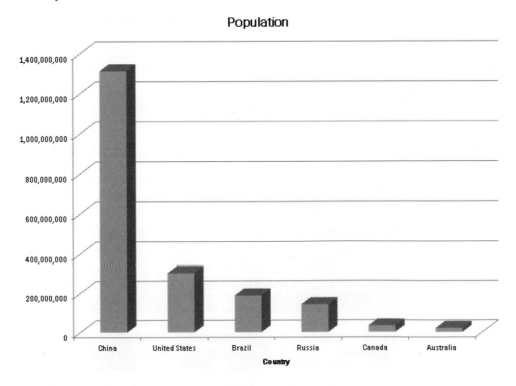

i) Rename Chart1 to Population and rename Sheet1 to Area.

j) On the Area sheet, be sure the chart and data fit on one page in landscape orientation.

k) Save the modified Country Statistics and then print a copy of the Area and Population sheets.

Project 5

Align Computer provides software training. They have four training sites located in the east, west, north, and south ends of a city. They provide Windows, Word, Access, Excel, and PowerPoint training classes.

a) Create a new workbook.

b) Enter data and apply formatting using the Office theme similar to:

	A	B	C	D	E	F	G
1		Learn Now Computer Training					
2	Course	East Site	West Site	North Site	South Site	Course Enrollment	
3	Windows	8	10	6	12		
4	Word	25	30	40	35		
5	Access	12	10	8	6		
6	Excel	20	30	35	25		
7	PowerPoint	40	42	20	12		
8	Site Enrollment						

c) Save the workbook naming it Enrollment.

d) In cell F3, enter a formula that uses a function to calculate the course enrollment. Copy the formula to the appropriate cells.

e) In cell B8, enter a formula that uses a function to calculate the site enrollment. Copy the formula to the appropriate cells.

f) Add your name in a header and the current date in a footer.

g) Produce a column chart that displays the number of students enrolled in each course at each site. Include the title, legend, and axes labels as shown below.

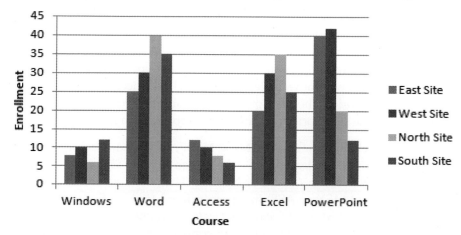

h) Move the chart to a new sheet named Enrollment.

i) Rename Sheet1 to Computer Training.

j) Add your name in a header on the Enrollment sheet.

k) Print a copy of the Enrollment and Computer Training sheets.

Project 6

In business, the break even point is when the sales revenue (money earned) equals the expenses (money paid out). A line chart can be used to determine the break even point. Open BREAK EVEN, which is an Excel data file for this text, and complete the following steps:

a) Produce a line chart on the active sheet that displays the revenues and expenses per units sold. Include the title, legend, and axes labels as shown below:

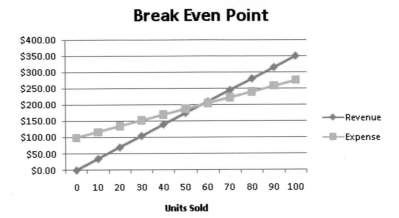

b) Add your name in a header and then save the modified BREAK EVEN.

c) Create a new Word document. Write a paragraph that defines what a break even point is. Below the definition, place a copy of the line chart from the BREAK EVEN workbook. Write another paragraph that interprets the chart data by determining where the break even point occurs and what it means.

d) Add a header with your name centered.

e) Save the Word document naming it Break Even Point and print a copy.

Project 7

A company can choose to "go public" to raise capital (money) for operations, expansion, and so on. Publicly held companies are listed on a stock exchange where a portion, or *share*, of ownership can be purchased by individuals. The price of a share of stock varies depending on supply and demand within the market. Sellers compete with other sellers for the highest price, while buyers compete with other buyers for the lowest share price. The stock price of an established company showing sustained growth is typically higher than the stock price of a younger company with no track record for profits.

There are many stock exchanges, with the AMEX, NYSE, and Nasdaq being the three largest auction markets in the world. Nearly every leading U.S. corporation as well as hundreds of non-U.S. corporations are listed on either the NYSE, the AMEX, or Nasdaq. The *New York Stock Exchange* (NYSE) and the *American Stock Exchange* (AMEX or ASE) have centralized trading floors where stocks are bought and sold. The *National Association of Securities Dealers Automatic Quotation System* (Nasdaq) is an electronic stock market with a subscriber network connecting more than 11,000 traders in more than 83 countries.

a) An educated investment in the stock market has historically provided the highest rate of return on a long-term investment compared to other investment options, such as a savings account. Choose seven companies that interest you and then use the Internet to determine the stock exchange listing for each company (NYSE, AMEX, or Nasdaq) and each company's symbol (called the ticker symbol) on the exchange. A company's Web site typically includes a link called "Company" or "Investor Information" that provides the information you need. Be sure to also check the bottom navigation bar for links to investor information. Many sites can also be searched for investor information.

Create a workbook named Stock Exchanges and in separate rows add the company name, ticker symbol, and stock exchange (NYSE, AMEX, or Nasdaq) for the seven companies you chose. Add appropriate column titles and format them as bold.

b) Stock information can be found on a stock exchange's Web site, some corporate Web sites, and in many newspapers. Newspapers print stock tables with the last price paid for a stock on the previous day, as well as other information. Stock tables have a format similar to:

	A	B	C	D	E	F	G	H	I
1	52 Week								
2	HI-LO	SYM	DIV	VOL	YLD	PE	HI-LO	CLOSE	NET CHG
3	22.55 - 30.00	MSFT	0.16	59,852,304	5	32.29	26.20 - 26.60	26.37	0.02
4									

- **52 Week Hi-Lo** is the highest and lowest prices at which the stock sold in the past year.

- **SYM** is the company stock symbol, which is the abbreviated name of the company issuing the stock. For example, MSFT is the stock symbol for Microsoft.

- **DIV** is the annual dividend paid per share to the stockholders.

- **VOL** is the volume of shares traded during the trading day.

- **YLD** is the dividend yield, which is the return on invested capital.

- **P/E** is the price to earnings ratio, which compares the price per share to the earnings per share.

- **HI-LO** is the highest and lowest price during the last trading day.

- **CLOSE** is the last price a trade was made at during the trading day.

- **NET CHG** is the difference between the closing price for the previous day and the current day in a dollar value.

Web sites contain stock data that is real-time or delayed by just minutes. When using a Web site to check stock prices, it is important to remember that the price shown is usually the price the stock is being currently traded at, not the final price for the day. Look for a previous day's close price to determine a stock's last price. The www.nyse.com, www.amex.com, and www.nasdaq.com sites each have a quote lookup on the home page for entering a ticker symbol to receive stock information.

On at least five different days, update the Stock Exchange workbook to include each stock's closing price for that day. Format the prices as currency with 2 decimal places. Add the data on each day as a column title and format it as bold.

c) Create a line chart that shows the change over time for each stock. Include an appropriate title, legend, and axes labels. Add a header with your name and print a copy.

d) If you had purchased 50 shares of each of the seven stocks, would your investment have been a wise one? *Portfolio* refers to a set of investments owned by an individual. Add a new worksheet named Portfolio to the Stock Exchange workbook and enter data that shows how the value of 50 shares of each stock changed over the investment period (the five days the worksheet was updated). Include formulas that show the dollar amount of the initial value for each stock and the dollar amount of the investment after each update. Include the total initial investment and final value.

e) On the Portfolio sheet, create a bar chart that shows the initial and final value of the 50 shares of each stock.

f) Use Word to create a letter named Portfolio Update that includes the bar chart showing investment losses and gains. Explain to the investor why you think each of the stocks either lost or gained value over the time of the investment. Print a copy.

Project 8

Stocks are tradable financial instruments that give an investor a portion, or share, of ownership in a publicly held company. There are thousands of stocks available because nearly every leading U.S. corporation as well as hundreds of non-U.S. corporations are listed on either the AMEX, the NYSE, or Nasdaq stock markets. Within the set of all stocks, subsets called *indexes* have been defined. An index is tracked to gauge the movement of the stock market as a whole. For example, the oldest index is the Dow Jones Industrial Average (DJIA or Dow), which tracks 30 blue-chip stocks. The *performance* of an index is the average of the gains or losses of the stocks in the index. A statement about how "the market" is doing is usually referring to the performance of the Dow. The Dow is one of several indexes that are used to measure the market:

- **Dow Jones Industrial Average (DJIA or Dow)**   A set of 30 blue-chip stocks. Blue-chip stocks are widely held and are considered solid, reliable, and having sustained growth. Stocks include Microsoft (MSFT), Intel (INTC), Coca-Cola (COKE), McDonald's (MCD), and American Express (AXP).

- **Standard & Poor's 500 (S&P 500)**   A set of the 500 largest company stocks. Stocks include Microsoft (MSFT), Wal-Mart (WMT), and IBM (IBM).

- **Nasdaq 100**   The set of the 100 largest company stocks listed on the Nasdaq. Stocks include Microsoft (MSFT), Intel (INTC), Dell (DELL), and Yahoo! (YHOO).

- **Nasdaq Composite**   The set of all stocks listed on the Nasdaq.

- **Amex Composite**   The set of all stocks listed on the American Stock Exchange.

- **Russell 2000**   A set of 2,000 small-company stocks. Guess (GES), Zale (ZLC), and Fossil (FOSL) are stocks in the Russell 2000.

- **Wilshire 5000**   Although the name seems to indicate a set of 5,000 stocks, the Wilshire index actually contains over 6,000 stocks and is sometimes referred to as the Total Stock Market Index.

a) The www.nyse.com and www.nasdaq.com sites each have links to index information on their home pages, as well as a quote lookup for individual stocks. Newspapers also publish stock and index performance information. Each of the indexes have corresponding Web sites, with most sites providing a list of stocks in the index.

Create a workbook named Stock Indexes that includes each of the indexes and three stocks from each index. The stock data should include the company name, ticker symbol, and index that tracks the stock. Add data for the last closing price for each of the stocks and the closing value for each of the indexes. Format the worksheet appropriately.

b) Expand the Stock Indexes workbook by adding closing stock prices and index values for at least five different days. Be sure to include dates.

c) How does individual stock performance compare to the overall performance of the index that tracks the stock? Chart the data to show this information.

d) Print a copy of the entire workbook.

Project 9

Temperatures can have an impact on business sales especially in seasonal businesses.

a) Research monthly average temperature data for your local area using the Internet or newspapers.

b) Create a new workbook.

c) Enter the researched data and apply appropriate formatting.

d) Create a line chart on the active sheet that illustrates the differences in the average monthly temperatures over a year. Include an appropriate title, legend, axes labels and formatting.

e) Add your name in a header and the current date in a footer. Add gridlines and headings.

f) Be sure the chart and data fit on one page, and then save the workbook naming it Local Temperatures and print a copy.

Project 10

The Automobile Lease workbook created in Chapter 6, Project 10 compares the cost of leasing versus purchasing an automobile. The comparison can be illustrated in a column chart. Open Automobile Lease and complete the following steps:

a) Create a column chart on the active sheet that displays the cost of leasing versus purchasing an automobile. Include an appropriate title, data labels, and formatting.

b) Open the Buy vs Lease Word document, which was created in Chapter 6, Project 10.

c) Use the chart to enhance the report by copying the column chart to the Word document and making any appropriate edits to the text.

d) Save and then print the Word document.

Project 11

Entrepreneurs often have to travel for business, which results in an expense to the business.

a) Research the driving distance (round trip) from your city or local area to six major cities.

b) Create a new workbook.

c) Enter the researched data and apply appropriate formatting. Calculate the driving expense at 30 cents a mile.

d) Decide what type of chart would best illustrate the data and create a chart on the active sheet that illustrates the distance between your city or local area and the six cities. Include an appropriate title, legend, axes labels, and formatting.

e) Add your name in a header and the current date in a footer.

f) Be sure the chart and data fit on one page in landscape orientation, and then save the workbook naming it Driving Distances and print a copy.

Project 12

An stacked area chart shows the trend of the contribution of each value over time. Open BUSINESS ANALYSIS, which is an Excel data file for this text, and complete the following steps:

a) Produce a stacked area chart on the active sheet that displays the contribution of each sales sector. Include the title, legend, and axes labels as shown:

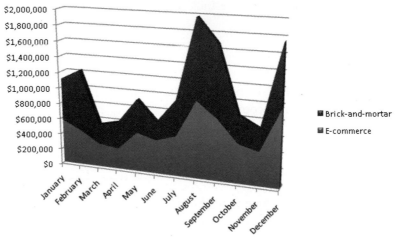

b) Add your name in a header and the current date in a footer.

c) Be sure the chart and data fit on one page in landscape orientation, and then save the modified BUSINESS ANALYSIS and print a copy.

Project 13

Excel allows many different types of charts to be created. For example, a stock chart, such as the high-low-close chart illustrates the high, low, and close price of a stock over a period of time:

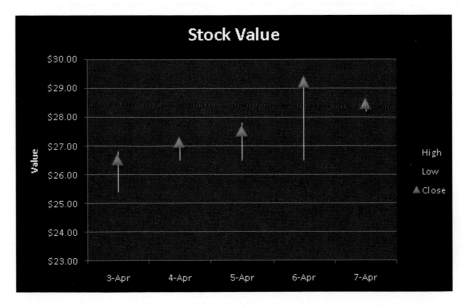

The data for the hi-low-close chart should be organized similar to:

	A	B	C	D	E
1	Stock Market Data				
2	Date	High	Low	Close	
3	3-May	$36.80	$33.02	$35.01	
4	4-May	$38.97	$35.01	$36.72	
5	5-May	$37.50	$31.60	$32.98	
6	6-May	$35.20	$31.32	$34.10	

a) Create a new workbook.

b) Use the three sheets in the workbook to enter data that can be charted using chart types other than pie, line, and bar charts. Create the corresponding chart on the active sheet. Research chart types using Excel Help before starting.

c) Add your name in a header on all three sheets.

d) Save the workbook naming it Chart Types.

e) Print a copy of the entire workbook.

Chapter 7 Creating Charts

Chapter 8
Advanced Spreadsheet Techniques

Key Concepts

Using dates and times in formulas
Creating tables
Applying data validation tools
Creating PivotTables and PivotTable Reports
Using the CHOOSE and VLOOKUP functions
Naming a cell range
Freezing cells
Creating hyperlinks to a workbook location
Embedding and linking objects
Creating macros

Practice Data Files

CORPORATE SALES, EMPLOYEE DISCOUNTS, PAYROLL MEMO

Project Data Files

FLORIDA FLIGHTS, MUSIC SALE, BUSINESS PAYROLL, FLOWER STORE, SERVICE HOURS, ADVERTISING SALES

Using Dates and Times in Formulas

Excel stores dates as sequential serial values. For example, January 1, 1900 is represented by the serial value 1 and January 1, 2011 is represented by the serial value 40544 because it is 40,544 days after January 1, 1900. To view the serial value of an existing date, format the date as General.

Because dates are stored as sequential serial values, they can be used in formulas. For example, the worksheet below determines when the next maintenance check is due by adding 180 days (approximately 6 months) to the date of the last check:

C6		fx	=B6+180	
	A	B	C	D
1	Maintenance Schedule			
2				
3		Last Check	Due Date	
4	Vehicle A	2/3/2011	8/2/2011	
5	Vehicle B	3/9/2011	9/5/2011	
6	Vehicle C	1/17/2011	7/16/2011	
7				

Time can also be used in calculations. For example, the worksheet below determines the duration it took to complete a task by subtracting the start time from the end time:

D3		fx	=C3-B3	
	A	B	C	D
1		Start Time	End Time	Duration
2	Task A	8:05 AM	10:22 AM	2:17
3	Task B	8:05 AM	6:00 PM	9:55
4				

Date and Time Functions

The =TODAY() function displays the current date.

The =NOW() function displays the current date and time. The time displayed by the NOW() function can be updated at any time by pressing the F9 key.

The result of a time calculation must be formatted as a 24-hour Time format, such as 13:30. Click Home → Number Format → More Number Formats to display a dialog box with Time format options.

Practice: Project Timeline

① CREATE A NEW WORKBOOK

a. Start Excel.

b. In a new workbook, enter the following data and format it using the Office theme as shown. Format cell A1 as Title style and merge and center the title between cells A1 through C1. Format cells B4 through C6 as Date, similar to 3/14/01. In cells A3 through C3, apply the Accent3 style and widen columns and align labels:

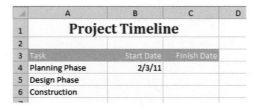

c. Save the workbook naming it: Project Timeline

② CALCULATE DATES

a. Two weeks (14 days) are required for the planning phase of the project. In cell C4, enter the formula =B4+14. What is the finish date for the planning phase?

b. The design phase will be started three days after the planning phase is finished. In cell B5, enter the formula =C4+3. What is the start date for the design phase?

c. The design phase will take 4 weeks (28 days) to complete. In cell C5, enter the formula =B5+28. What is the finish date of the design phase?

d. The construction will start one day after the design phase is finished and will take 6 months (180 days) to complete. In cells B6 and C6, enter formulas to calculate the start and finish date for the construction.

③ ADD TIME CALCULATIONS

a. Add a work schedule for the project teams. Starting in cell A8, enter the following data and formatting as shown, widening columns as necessary:

	A	B	C	D	E
1		Project Timeline			
2					
3	Task	Start Date	Finish Date		
4	Planning Phase	2/3/11	2/17/11		
5	Design Phase	2/20/11	3/20/11		
6	Construction	3/21/11	9/17/11		
7					
8	Work Schedule	Start Time	Finish Time	Hours	
9	Planning Team	9:30 AM	4:30 PM		
10	Design Team	12:30 PM	7:30 PM		
11	Construction Team	7:00 AM	5:00 PM		
12					

b. Select cells D9 through D11 and then click Home → Number Format → More Number Formats. A dialog box is displayed.

    1. Format the cells as Time, similar to 13:30, then select OK.

c. In cell D9, calculate how many hours the planning team will work in a day by entering the formula =C9–B9.

d. Copy the formula in cell D9 to cells D10 and D11. Which team works the longest hours per day?

④ SAVE, PRINT, AND THEN CLOSE THE MODIFIED PROJECT TIMELINE

a. Click View → Page Layout.

b. Add your name in a header and the current date in a footer.

c. Save the modified Project Timeline, print a copy, and then close the workbook.

Using Tables

Table

In Excel, *tables* allow a range of related data to be managed and analyzed independent of any other data in the worksheet:

TIP An Excel table is similar to a flat-file database.

To create a table, the data must be first organized into rows and columns with labels in the first row. Next, select the cells for the table and click Insert → Table. A dialog box is displayed:

Importing Table Data

Data for an Excel worksheet can be imported from an existing text file with a .txt, .cvs, or .prn extension.

Click Data → From Text, which displays a dialog box used to select a text file to import.

Select OK to create the table. Each column label in the header row includes an arrow for displaying sort commands. For example, click the Salary arrow to display:

TIP The wording of the sort commands will vary depending on whether the data is labels or values.

Select a sort command to sort the rows in the table based on the data in the selected column.

A *filter* displays only the rows that meet specific criteria. Filter commands are displayed below sort commands when a column arrow is clicked and will vary depending on the type of data a column contains:

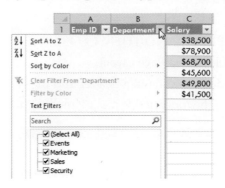

Clear check boxes to hide rows containing those entries. Select Text Filters to display a menu with additional filter commands, such as Equals or Begins With. To remove a filter, click (Select All).

Additional table options are found on the Design tab, which is displayed when a table cell is selected:

Table Name   Remove Duplicates

Resize Table   Convert to Range   Total Row   Banded Columns

- The table is named Table1 by default. To change the name, type a new name in the **Table Name** box.

- Click **Resize Table** to display a dialog box where a new table range can be typed.

- To convert the table data to a range of data, click **Convert to Range**.

- Click **Remove Duplicates** and specify columns to remove any duplicate rows in the table.

- Click **Total Row** to automatically add the label Total and the sum of any columns containing values. For example:

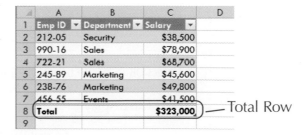

Total Row

- Click **More Table Styles** ⎘ to display additional table styles.

- Click **Banded Columns** to format even and odd columns differently. This may make the data easier to read. Similarly, click **First Column** or **Last Column** to format these columns differently.

New rows and columns can be added to a table by clicking Home → Insert → Insert Table Rows Above/Below or Home → Insert → Insert Table Columns to the Left/Right. To delete rows and columns, click Home → Delete → Delete Table Rows or Home → Delete → Delete Table Columns.

calculated column

Tables can include a *calculated column*, which allows a single formula to be entered in a cell and then the formula is automatically copied to all of the other cells in the column. For example, click cell D2, type =, point to cell C2, type * 0.1, and press Enter to enter a formula in cells D2 through D7 which calculates a 10% raise for each employee:

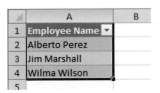

	D2	▾		f_x	=[@Salary]*0.1	
	A	B	C	D	E
1	Emp ID ▾	Department ▾	Salary ▾	Raise ▾	
2	212-05	Security	$38,500	3850	
3	990-16	Sales	$78,900	7890	
4	722-21	Sales	$68,700	6870	
5	245-89	Marketing	$45,600	4560	
6	238-76	Marketing	$49,800	4980	
7	456-55	Events	$41,500	4150	
8	Total		$323,000		
9					

TIP Pointing is the easiest method of entering a formula in a table because the formula refers to table locations as opposed to cell references

TIP Click AutoCorrect Options 🗊 to display options for a calculated column.

Formulas in a calculated column reference table locations not cells, as indicated in the formula bar above.

separating data

Table data may need to be separated into columns in order to facilitate sorting and filtering. For example, a table may have an employee's first name and last name in column A making it difficult to sort the data by last name:

	A	B
1	Employee Name ▾	
2	Alberto Perez	
3	Jim Marshall	
4	Wilma Wilson	
5		

To separate the data, select cells A2 through A4 and click Data → Text to Columns, which starts the Convert Text to Columns Wizard.

Data Validation

Data Validation

Data entry criteria can be specified for a cell or range of cells to avoid data entry errors. To create data entry criteria, select a range of cells and then click Data → Data Validation 🗊. A dialog box is displayed:

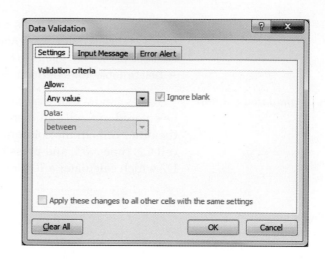

Select the type of data to allow, such as Whole numbers or Decimals, in the Allow list. A specific range of numbers can then be specified in the Data list. Cells with validation criteria will display an error message if a user enters invalid data.

creating a drop-down list

To create a drop-down list with entries that users can select from, select List in the Allow list, which displays a Source list where allowable entries can be typed.

adding a message prompt

To prompt the user with a message about the type of data to enter, select the Input Message tab and then type the message in the Input message box. The prompt is displayed when a cell is selected. For example:

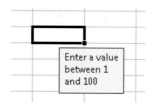

removing data validation criteria

To remove data validation criteria, select the affected cells, click Data → Data Validation 📋 → Clear All.

Practice: Art Studio Students

Excel should already be started.

① CREATE A NEW WORKBOOK

a. In a new workbook, enter the following data and format it using the Foundry theme as shown. Format cells A1 through C1 as Heading 1 style and format cells A3 through D3 as Accent1 style, formatting alignment as necessary:

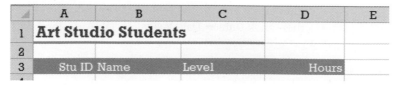

	A	B	C	D	E
1	**Art Studio Students**				
2					
3	Stu ID	Name	Level	Hours	

b. Save the workbook naming it: Art Studio Students

② SET DATA VALIDATION CRITERIA

   a. Select cells A4 through A15.

   b. The Stu ID column will contain a number for each student at the Art Studio. The numbers will be between 1 and 75. Click Data → Data Validation 📊. A dialog box is displayed. Select options as shown:

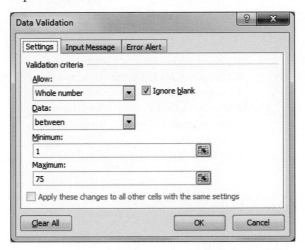

   c. Select OK. The data validation criteria is applied to cells A4 through A15.

   d. In cell A4, type 789 and then press Enter. An error message is displayed indicating the value entered is not valid. Select Cancel.

   e. Select cells C4 through C15.

   f. Click Data → Data Validation 📊. A dialog box is displayed. Select options as shown:

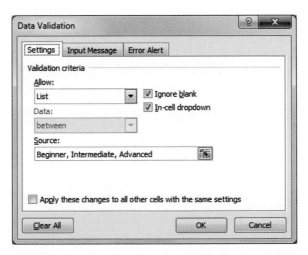

   g. Select OK. Cell C4 displays an arrow button, indicating a list is available.

③ ADD DATA TO THE WORKSHEET

Enter the following data starting in cell A4 and widen columns as necessary. The data for cells C4 through C15 can be selected from a list:

	A	B	C	D
1	**Art Studio Students**			
2				
3	Stu ID	Name	Level	Hours
4	44	Jeanette Wilson	Beginner	3
5	37	Bill Williams	Advanced	12
6	22	Kayla Russell	Intermediate	6
7	5	Bernice Rockwell	Intermediate	6
8	18	Martin Quinn	Beginner	3
9	1	Renee Marshall	Advanced	12
10	8	Madeline Manchester	Intermediate	6
11	7	Henry Jones	Advanced	9
12	12	Michelle Ianni	Beginner	3
13	52	Terry Dodds	Beginner	6
14	34	Simon Baron	Intermediate	6
15	32	Paul Andrews	Beginner	3

④ **CREATE A TABLE**

   a. Select cells A3 through D15.

   b. Click Insert → Table. A dialog box is displayed:

   c. Select OK. The table is created and the Design tab displayed.

⑤ **INSERT A COLUMN AND DISPLAY THE NAME DATA IN TWO COLUMNS**

   a. Select cell C4 and click Home → Insert → Insert Table Columns to the Left.

   b. Select cells B4 through B15 and then click Data → Text to Columns. A dialog box is displayed.

      1. Select Next. Another dialog box is displayed. Select options as shown:

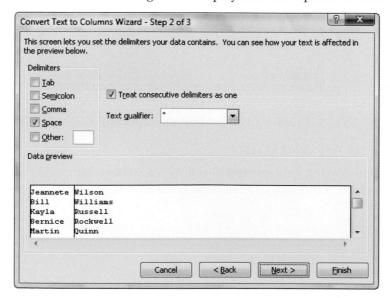

2. Select Next. Another dialog box is displayed. Note the data preview.

3. Select Finish. The name data is separated into two columns.

c. Change the label in cell B3 to: First Name

d. Change the label in cell C3 to: Last Name

e. Adjust the column widths appropriately.

⑥ CREATE A CALCULATED COLUMN

a. Select cell E4 and then click Home ➔ Insert ➔ Insert Table Column to the Right.

b. Change the label in cell F3 to: Fees

c. Each credit hour is $150. Select cell F4, type =, and then select cell E4, and then type: * 150

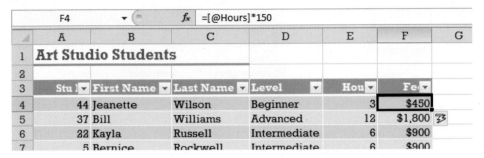

Press Enter. Fees are automatically calculated for each row.

d. Format column F as Currency with 0 decimal places.

⑦ SORT AND FILTER THE DATA

a. Click the Stu ID column arrow and then select Sort Smallest to Largest. The list is sorted in ascending order by Stu ID.

b. Click the Last Name column arrow and then select Sort Z to A. The table is resorted in descending order by Last Name.

c. Click the Level column arrow and then clear the Intermediate and Advanced check boxes, leaving the Beginner check box selected. Select OK. Just the rows where Level contains "Beginner" are displayed:

◢	A	B	C	D	E	F	G
1	**Art Studio Students**						
2							
3	Stu I ▾	First Name ▾	Last Name ▾	Level ⌐▾	Hou▾	Fe ▾	
4	44	Jeanette	Wilson	Beginner	3	$450	
8	18	Martin	Quinn	Beginner	3	$450	
12	12	Michelle	Ianni	Beginner	3	$450	
13	52	Terry	Dodds	Beginner	6	$900	
15	32	Paul	Andrews	Beginner	3	$450	
16							

d. Click the Level column arrow and then select (Select All) and then OK. All the rows are again displayed.

⑧ SAVE AND PRINT THE MODIFIED ART STUDIO STUDENTS

a. Add a header with your name.

b. Save the modified Art Studio Students and print a copy.

c. Close Art Studio Students.

PivotTables and PivotTable Reports

Pivot Table

External Data

Data for an Excel worksheet can be imported from various sources including Access, dBase, Oracle, Paradox, and text files. To connect to an external data source, click **Data → From Other Sources → From Data Connection Wizard.**

A worksheet can become very large, which makes it more difficult to analyze. For example, a corporation may track sales by major city, region, as well as comparing each city's sales to a projected sales quota:

	A	B	C	D
1	City	Region	Sales	Quota
2	Boston	East	$343,677	$400,000
3	New York	East	$677,000	$400,000
4	Miami	South East	$432,050	$500,000
5	Los Angeles	South West	$980,003	$500,000
6	Las Vegas	South West	$324,560	$200,000
7	New Orleans	South	$210,000	$200,000
8	Buffalo	North	$193,475	$200,000
9	Detroit	North	$156,233	$200,000
10	Cincinatti	Central	$120,000	$200,000

field

Rather than manually combining and organizing data to analyze it, a PivotTable and PivotTable report can be used. In a *PivotTable*, each column of a worksheet is a *field* that can be used in a report to summarize data. Like a table, data to be used in a PivotTable must be organized in rows and columns. Blank rows should be avoided. When a PivotTable is created, a PivotTable report can also be generated. A *PivotTable report* allows the worksheet data to be put into small, concise reports, simplifying data analysis.

Once the data is organized, click a cell with data, and then click Insert → PivotTable. A dialog box is displayed.

TIP Data in contiguous rows and columns are selected for a PivotTable. For example, a title with a blank row below it will not be included.

TIP To change the range for the PivotTable, select it in the sheet.

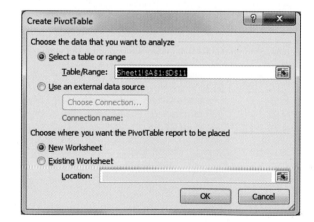

All of the data on the worksheet is automatically selected and displayed in the Table/Range box. Select New Worksheet to place the PivotTable report in a new sheet in the active workbook and then select OK. On a new worksheet, the layout area for the PivotTable report is shown and the PivotTable Field List task pane is displayed:

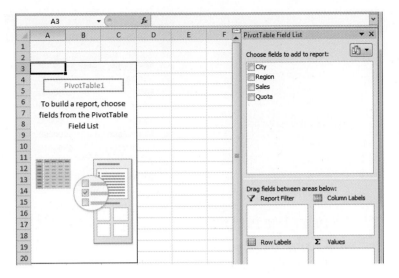

TIP Drag the title bar of the PivotTable Field List task pane to move it closer to the data, if necessary.

Select the appropriate check boxes in the Choose fields to add to report list. For example, click Region and Quota to move these fields to the layout area in a summarized format. Formatting can then be added to the report:

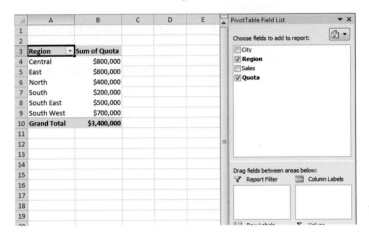

TIP If the PivotTable Field List task pane disappears, click inside the PivotTable layout area or if the PivotTable Field List task pane was closed, right-click a PivotTable cell and select Show Field List.

Data can be sorted and filtered in a PivotTable. Click a field in the PivotTable Field List to display sort and filter criteria.

Practice: CORPORATE SALES

Excel should already be started.

① OPEN CORPORATE SALES

Open CORPORATE SALES, which is an Excel data file for this text. This worksheet contains sales by city and region as well as projected sales quotas.

② CREATE A PIVOTTABLE

a. Select cell A4 and then click Insert → PivotTable. A dialog box is displayed.

b. Select OK. A sheet is added to the workbook, the layout area for the PivotTable report is shown and the PivotTable Field List task pane is displayed.

c. In the PivotTable Field List task pane, select the Region and Quota check boxes. A PivotTable report is generated. The Quota data for each region has been summed and a grand total added.

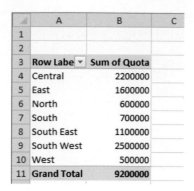

③ FORMAT THE PIVOTTABLE REPORT

a. Change the label in cell A3 to: Region

b. Right-align the column heading in cell B3.

c. Format the values in column B as Currency with 0 decimal places.

④ SORT THE PIVOTTABLE REPORT

a. If the PivotTable Field List task pane is not displayed, select a PivotTable cell.

b. In the PivotTable Field List task pane, point to Region and then click the displayed arrow:

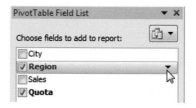

c. In the displayed menu, select More Sort Options. A dialog box is displayed.

    1. Select options as shown:

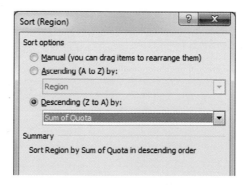

    2. Select OK. The data is sorted in descending order by Sum of Quota.

⑤ SAVE AND PRINT THE CORPORATE SALES PIVOTTABLE REPORT

a. Add your name in a header.

b. Save the modified CORPORATE SALES, print a copy of the PivotTable report, and then close the workbook.

The CHOOSE Function

The *CHOOSE function* is a lookup function that is used to return a value from a list of values. The CHOOSE function takes the form:

=CHOOSE(<choice>, <option$_1$>, <option$_2$>, ..., <option$_N$>)

<choice> is a number between 1 and 254 or a formula or reference to a cell containing a number between 1 and 254.

<option$_1$>, <option$_2$>, ... store the possible values to return.

CHOOSE returns the value in the list of arguments that corresponds to <choice>. If <choice> is 1, CHOOSE returns <option$_1$>; if <choice> is 2, then <option$_2$> is returned, and so on. For example, the worksheet below is used to determine an employee's bonus based on the performance rating score the employee received:

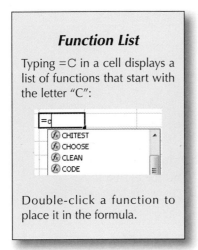

Function List

Typing =C in a cell displays a list of functions that start with the letter "C":

Double-click a function to place it in the formula.

Alternative Click Data → Insert Function to place the CHOOSE function in a formula.

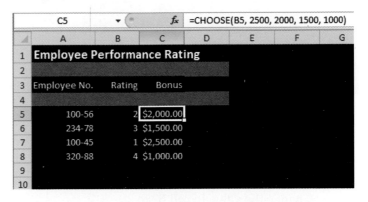

The formula bar shows that <choice> is determined by the value in cell B4. Cell C4 displays 2000 because it corresponds to <option$_2$>.

Only the integer portion of <choice> is used to determine which value to return. For example, in the worksheet above, if cell B4 stored 1.6, 2500 would be displayed because only the integer portion of the value, 1, is used. If <choice> is less than 1 or greater than N, #VALUE! is displayed, indicating a corresponding value is not available.

The options (<option$_1$>, <option$_2$>, ...) in the CHOOSE function can also include formulas, cell references, and text. For example, the formula in cell D4 uses a CHOOSE function to return text:

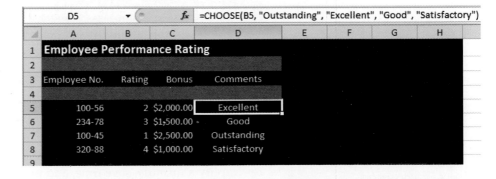

Practice: EMPLOYEE DISCOUNTS

Excel should already be started.

① **OPEN EMPLOYEE DISCOUNTS**

Open EMPLOYEE DISCOUNTS, which is an Excel data file for this text.

② **ENTER FORMULAS TO CALCULATE THE DISCOUNT**

The EMPLOYEE DISCOUNTS workbook contains a list of employees and their level ranking within the company. Each of the levels corresponds to the percentage discount an employee receives on company merchandise:

Level	Percentage
1	10%
2	15%
3	20%
4	25%

a. In cell C4, enter the formula: =CHOOSE(B4, 10%, 15%, 20%, 25%)

The CHOOSE function first looks in cell B4 to determine the value of <choice>. Because the value in cell B4 is 4, this corresponds to <option$_4$> and Excel displays 0.25, which is the decimal equivalent of 25%.

b. Copy the formula in cell C4 to cells C5 through C13.

c. Format cells C4 through C13 as Percentage with 0 decimal places.

d. Why is #VALUE! displayed in cell C7?

e. Change the value in cell B7 to 2.

f. The employee in row 6 has a ranking of 1.5 and receives a discount of 10%. Why does this employee receive the same discount as level 1 employees?

③ **SAVE, PRINT, AND CLOSE THE MODIFIED EMPLOYEE DISCOUNTS**

a. Add a header with your name and a footer with the current date.

b. Save the modified EMPLOYEE DISCOUNTS and print a copy.

c. Close EMPLOYEE DISCOUNTS.

Naming a Cell or Range

Rules for Naming

When naming a cell or range of cells, all names must begin with a letter, backslash (\), or an underscore. Single letters and names that are similar to cell references should not be used and a named range cannot include spaces.

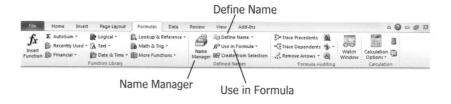

Define Name

Name Manager   Use in Formula

Complicated or repetitive formulas can use named cells or cell ranges to simplify a formula, save time, and prevent data entry errors. To name a cell or range of cells, select the cell(s), and then type a descriptive name in the name box. For example, the selected range is named Test1:

name box —

	A	B	C	D	E	F
						fx 85 (Test1)
1	Student ID	Test 1	Test 2	Test 3	Test 4	Average
2	Name	9/4/11	9/14/11	9/21/11	9/30/11	
3	10-260-001	85	73	88	95	85.3
4	23-781-099	92	68	75	71	76.5
5	15-678-023	72	63	67	72	68.5
6	10-433-556	57	81	75	82	73.8
7	22-311-444	94	91	93	84	90.5
8	15-778-112	70	74	60	53	64.3
9	Test Average	78.3	75.0	76.3	76.2	

Alternative Click Formulas → Define Name and then type a name in the displayed dialog box to create a named range.

A named range is an absolute reference. For example, using the formula =AVERAGE(Test1) in cell B9 calculates the average of the test scores in cells B3 through B8. Copying the formula to cells C9 through E9 will not change the cell references in the named cell range.

Named ranges can be selected from a list and placed in a formula by clicking the name box arrow or clicking Formulas → Use in Formula. To delete a range name, click Formulas → Name Manager, which display a dialog box. Select the named range and then select Delete. To modify a range name, a new named range must be created and then the old one deleted.

VLOOKUP Function

The *VLOOKUP function* is used to return a value from a table of values stored in the worksheet. It takes the form:

=VLOOKUP(<value>, <range>, <column>)

<value> is a number to be looked up in a table of values.

<range> is the cell range where the VLOOKUP table is stored.

Alternative Click Data → Insert Function to insert a VLOOKUP function in a formula.

VLOOKUP finds the largest number in the first column of <range> which is less than or equal to <value>, and then returns the value stored in the same row in column <column> of the VLOOKUP table. The value of <column> is usually 2 to indicate that the second column in the VLOOKUP table stores the value to be returned. The following worksheet determines the shipping cost based on the amount of the order, with orders over $1,000 receiving free shipping:

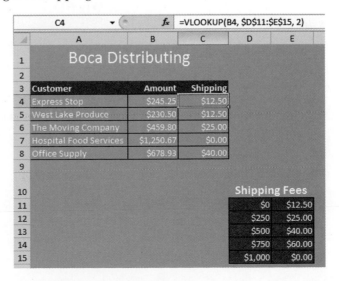

C4   fx =VLOOKUP(B4, $D$11:$E$15, 2)

Boca Distributing

	A	B	C	D	E
3	Customer	Amount	Shipping		
4	Express Stop	$245.25	$12.50		
5	West Lake Produce	$230.50	$12.50		
6	The Moving Company	$459.80	$25.00		
7	Hospital Food Services	$1,250.67	$0.00		
8	Office Supply	$678.93	$40.00		
10				Shipping Fees	
11				$0	$12.50
12				$250	$25.00
13				$500	$40.00
14				$750	$60.00
15				$1,000	$0.00

With the formula =VLOOKUP(B4, $D$11:$E$15, 2) in cell C4:

1. Excel looks in cell B4 for the lookup value, which is $245.25.

2. Excel then looks in the first column of the VLOOKUP table for the largest value which is less than or equal to $245.25, in this case $0.00 (stored in D11).

3. The corresponding value in the second column of the table, in this case $12.50, is then displayed in cell C4.

In a similar manner, the function displays $0.00 in cell C7 because cell D15 stores the largest value in the VLOOKUP table which is less than or equal to $1,250.67 (the value stored in cell B7).

The values in the first column of a VLOOKUP table must be in ascending order for VLOOKUP to work correctly. If <value> is less than the first value stored in the VLOOKUP table, #N/A! is displayed. For this reason, the first value stored in the VLOOKUP table must be less than or equal to any value that will be looked up.

In the formula containing the VLOOKUP function, absolute references are used for the VLOOKUP table range. This is necessary so that the range does not change when the formula containing the VLOOKUP function is copied.

using a named range   The range that defines the VLOOKUP table can be named to simplify the formula containing the function. For example, in the formula =VLOOKUP(B4, Shipping, 2), Shipping is the named range that defines the VLOOKUP table.

The VLOOKUP function will display text if labels are stored in the VLOOKUP table. For example, the worksheet below uses a VLOOKUP function to return a diagnosis label:

HLOOKUP Function

The HLOOKUP function is very similar to the VLOOKUP function in that both functions return a value from a table of values stored in a worksheet.

To use a VLOOKUP function, the values in the lookup table must be organized vertically in columns and to use an HLOOKUP function the values in the lookup table must be organized horizontally in rows.

Freezing Cells

Freeze Panes

TIP A worksheet must be displayed in Normal view to freeze cells.

One difficulty encountered when working with a large worksheet is that rows and columns with descriptive labels may scroll off the screen. This makes it difficult to determine which columns or rows the displayed cells are in. One way to solve this problem is to freeze selected rows and columns in place so they will not scroll when the rest of the worksheet is scrolled.

Click View → Freeze Panes → Freeze Panes to designate every row above the active cell and every column to the left of the active cell as frozen. For example, select cell B6 and then click View → Freeze Panes → Freeze Panes to freeze the cells in column A and rows 1 through 5 from scrolling:

Splitting Panes

A worksheet can be split into two panes so that the two areas can be viewed and scrolled at the same time. Select the cell one row below and a column to the right of the area to split and then click View → Split. Click View → Remove Split to remove split panes.

	A	B	C	D	E	F	G	H	I
1									
2		The Garden Store							
3									
4									
5	Product	Jan	Feb	Mar	Apr	May	Jun	Jul	Au
6	Pots and Planters	$320	$540	$2,056	$1,120	$1,980	$6,500	$7,000	$8,2
7	Stepping Stones	$125	$125	$289	$2,560	$5,026	$5,602	$3,737	$4,2
8	Lanterns	$250	$250	$389	$1,890	$2,888	$5,058	$3,500	$4,7
9	Fountains	$150	$1,200	$2,560	$8,500	$5,800	$5,860	$7,500	$5,6
10	Lawn & Patio Furniture	$800	$1,600	$2,565	$4,585	$7,857	$8,459	$19,887	$25,0
11	Rakes	$35	$240	$500	$680	$780	$2,300	$5,600	$7,8

Frozen cells are displayed with a solid border

When scrolling vertically, frozen columns remain on the screen. Frozen rows remain on the screen when scrolling horizontally.

To freeze just the top row, click View → Freeze Panes → Freeze Top Row. To freeze just the first column, click View → Freeze Panes → Freeze First Column. Click View → Freeze Panes → Unfreeze Panes to unfreeze all frozen cells.

Practice: PAYROLL – part 2 of 3

Excel should already be started.

① **OPEN PAYROLL**

Open PAYROLL, which was last modified in Chapter 6. Display the worksheet in Normal view, if it is not already.

② **FREEZE CELLS**

a. Select cell C7. Be sure that cell A1 is displayed on the screen as well.

b. Click View → Freeze Panes → Freeze Panes. The frozen cells are indicated by solid borders:

⬚	A	B	C	D	E	F	G	H	I	J
1	**Payroll**									
2										
3	Soc. Sec. Rate:	6.0%								
4										
5	Last Name	First Initial	Rate/Hr	Hours	Overtime Hours	Overtime Pay	Gross Pay	Soc. Sec.	Taxes	Net Pay
6										
7	Alban	B.	$7.50	30.0	0.0	$0.00	$225.00	$13.50	$33.75	$177.75
8	Angulo	M.	$8.00	29.5	0.0	$0.00	$236.00	$14.16	$35.40	$186.44
9	Balto	Y.	$8.00	29.0	0.0	$0.00	$232.00	$13.92	$34.80	$183.28

c. Click the right scroll arrow several times to scroll horizontally until column L is displayed beside column B. Note that columns A and B remain displayed while other columns are scrolled off the screen.

d. Click the down scroll arrow until row 45 is displayed in the window. Note that rows 1 through 6 remain on the screen.

e. Press Ctrl+Home to return to cell C7.

③ **ADD A VLOOKUP TABLE TO THE WORKSHEET**

The following tax rates will be used in calculating taxes:

Salary	Tax Rate
under $101	0%
$101 – $524	15%
$525 – $1,124	28%
$1,125 and above	31%

a. In cell J26, enter the label Tax Rate Table and bold the label.

b. Enter the following values into the indicated cells to create the VLOOKUP tax table:

In cell		enter		In cell		enter	
	J27	enter	$0	In cell	**K27**	enter	0%
	J28		$101		**K28**		15%
	J29		$525		**K29**		28%
	J30		$1,125		**K30**		31%

④ **NAME THE TABLE RANGE**

a. Select cell J27 through K30.

b. Click in the name box. Type Rate and press the Enter key:

⑤ **CALCULATE TAXES USING THE VLOOKUP FUNCTION**

In the PAYROLL worksheet, taxes are currently calculated by applying a 15% tax rate to all employees. Typically tax rates are based on gross pay, therefore the existing formula will be modified to include a VLOOKUP function to retrieve the appropriate tax rate.

a. In cell I7, replace the existing formula with: =G7*VLOOKUP(G7, Rate, 2)

The gross pay stored in cell G7 is $225.00, which is multiplied by 15% to compute the tax deduction of $33.75.

b. Copy the formula in cell I7 to cells I8 through I23.

c. Click any cell to remove the selection. The worksheet should look similar to:

	A	B	C	D	E	F	G	H	I	J	K
1	**Payroll**										
2											
3	Soc. Sec. Rate:	6.0%									
4											
5	Last Name	First Initial	Rate/Hr	Hours	Overtime Hours	Overtime Pay	Gross Pay	Soc. Sec.	Taxes	Net Pay	
6											
16	Karas	A.	$8.00	15.0	0.0	$0.00	$120.00	$7.20	$18.00	$94.80	
17	Keller-Sakis	G.	$8.50	20.0	0.0	$0.00	$170.00	$10.20	$25.50	$134.30	
18	Lopez	R.	$9.00	17.0	0.0	$0.00	$153.00	$9.18	$22.95	$120.87	
19	Parker	L.	$10.75	29.0	0.0	$0.00	$311.75	$18.71	$46.76	$246.28	
20	Quinn	P.	$11.75	41.0	1.0	$17.63	$487.63	$29.26	$73.14	$385.22	
21	Ramis	C.	$8.00	18.0	0.0	$0.00	$144.00	$8.64	$21.60	$113.76	
22	Rappaport	L.	$7.75	18.0	0.0	$0.00	$139.50	$8.37	$20.93	$110.21	
23	Rosen	R.	$9.50	10.0	0.0	$0.00	$95.00	$5.70	$0.00	$89.30	
24											
25											
26										**Tax Rate Table**	
27										$0	0%
28										$101	15%
29										$525	28%
30										$1,125	31%
31											

⑥ SAVE AND PRINT THE MODIFIED PAYROLL

Creating a Hyperlink to a Workbook Location

Hyperlink

A hyperlink can be used to quickly scroll within a workbook. To create a link from one cell to another, click Insert → Hyperlink. The Insert Hyperlink dialog box includes Place in This Document options:

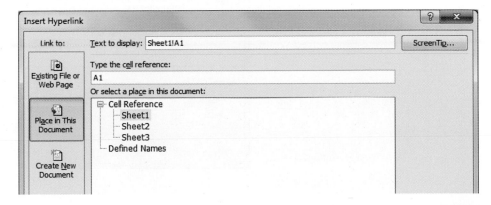

In the Text to Display box, replace the existing sheet and cell reference with a label that will be placed in the active cell. Type the hyperlink destination in the Type the cell reference box. Select ScreenTip to display a dialog box of options for creating a ScreenTip.

TIP The Hyperlink color will vary if a theme other than Office is selected.

Once a hyperlink is created, point to the hyperlink, press the Ctrl key to change the pointer to 🖑 and click to follow the link. To remove a hyperlink, right-click the link and select Remove Hyperlink from the menu.

Embedding and Linking Objects

static

When Copy 📋 and Paste are used to copy data between the Excel and Word applications, the pasted data is *static*, which means it does not change when the source data changes. Alternatively, the data can be embedded or linked using Paste Options 📋 (Ctrl)▾. For example, when Excel data is pasted in a Word document, click Paste Options 📋 (Ctrl)▾ to display:

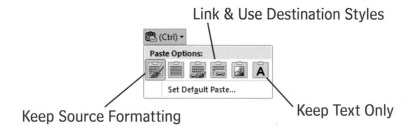

Link & Use Destination Styles

Keep Source Formatting   Keep Text Only

embedded object

- Keep Source Formatting creates an embedded object. An *embedded object* keeps the features of the application it was created in. The Excel data can then be edited in Word using Excel commands on the Design and Layout tabs.

linked object

TIP A linked object should be used if an up-to-date display of data is needed.

- Link & Use Destination Styles creates a linked object. A *linked object* automatically updates when the source data is updated. To edit a linked object in Excel, double-click the linked object.

The Paste Special dialog box can also be used to create embedded or linked objects. For example, copy Excel data, display a Word document, and then click Home → Paste → Paste Special to display the dialog box:

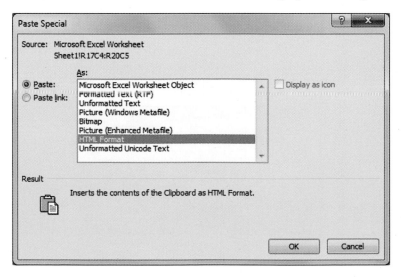

- Click **Paste** and then click the appropriate object in the **As** list to create an embedded object.

- Click **Paste link** and then click the appropriate object in the **As** list to create a linked object.

Practice: PAYROLL – part 3 of 3

Excel should already be started and PAYROLL displayed from the last practice.

① ADD A HYPERLINK TO A WORKBOOK LOCATION

a. Select cell I5.

b. Click Insert ➔ Hyperlink. The Insert Hyperlink dialog box is displayed.

   1. Select Place in This Document to display those options.

   2. In the Text to display box, verify the label is Taxes.

   3. In the Type the cell reference box, replace the existing cell reference with J26:

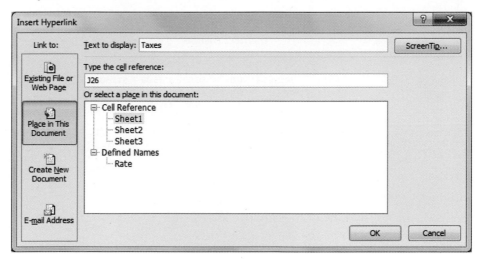

   4. Select OK. The column label is a hyperlink.

② TEST THE HYPERLINK

a. Select cell A1.

b. Click the hyperlink in cell I5. The active cell is moved to the hyperlink destination, cell J26.

③ UNFREEZE CELLS

Click View ➔ Freeze Panes ➔ Unfreeze Panes. The solid borders are removed from the worksheet.

④ COPY DATA

a. Select cells A5 through J23.

b. Click Home ➔ Copy.

⑤ CREATE A LINKED OBJECT

a. Open PAYROLL MEMO, which is a Word data file for this text. Display formatting marks if they are not already displayed.

b. Place the insertion point in the blank paragraph below the text that reads "The company payroll for the week of April 3 is summarized below:"

c. Click Paste. The Paste Options button is displayed. Click the Paste Options button and select Link & Keep Source Formatting:

d. Select OK. The worksheet data is pasted as a linked object:

Memo

To: Accounting Manager
From:
Date:
Re: Payroll Summary

The company payroll for the week of April 3 is summarized below:

Last Name	First Initial	Rate/Hr	Hours	Overtime Hours	Overtime Pay	Gross Pay	Soc. Sec.	Taxes	Net Pay
Alban	B.	$7.50	30.0	0.0	$0.00	$225.00	$13.50	$33.75	$177.75
Angulo	M.	$8.00	29.5	0.0	$0.00	$236.00	$14.16	$35.40	$186.44
Balto	Y.	$8.00	29.0	0.0	$0.00	$232.00	$13.92	$34.80	$183.28

⑥ COMPLETE THE MEMO

a. In the From: line, type your name.

b. In the Date: line, type today's date.

c. What is the hourly rate for the employee B. Alban?

⑦ UPDATE THE PAYROLL WORKSHEET

a. Use the taskbar to display the PAYROLL workbook.

b. If a dashed border is displayed, press the Esc key.

c. A data entry error was made when B. Alban's rate was entered. Modify the rate in cell C7 to $17.50. The formulas adjust to reflect the new rate.

d. Save the modified PAYROLL.

e. Use the taskbar to display the PAYROLL MEMO document. The linked object automatically reflects the changes in the source workbook. If the linked object does not change, right click the object and select Update Link.

⑧ SAVE THE MODIFIED PAYROLL MEMO, PRINT A COPY, AND QUIT WORD

⑨ CLOSE PAYROLL

Macros

Macros   Record Macro

TIP Macro names cannot contain spaces.

When creating or modifying a worksheet, a series of steps may need to be repeated. Macros can be created to perform repetitive tasks. A *macro* is a series of recorded commands and actions that perform a specific task.

The Developer tab is used to create macros. If the Developer tab is not on the Ribbon, click **File** → Options. The Excel Options dialog box is displayed. Select Customize Ribbon and then select **Developer** check box in the **Main Tabs** list.

To create a macro, click Developer → Record Macro 🔲. A dialog box is displayed:

Macro Security

Click Developer → Macro Security ⚠ to display a dialog box which can be used to change the security level for macros. For example, macro security options can be set to run macros only if they are digitally signed by a developer who is on your list of trusted sources.

Alternative To end the recording of a macro, click the Stop Recording button 🔳 on the status bar.

Type a descriptive name for the macro in the Macro name box. A macro is played or started by pressing a shortcut key. Type a letter in the Ctrl+ box to create the shortcut key for the macro. Select This Workbook in the Store macro in box to store the macro in the active workbook. Type a description of the macro in the Description box. Select OK to begin recording the macro.

Perform the sequence of steps to be recorded in the macro. Click Developer → Stop Recording to end the recording. Press the assigned shortcut key to run the macro.

To edit and delete macros, click Developer → Macros, which displays the Macro dialog box.

Practice: Company Name

You will create a macro to insert a company name and address.

① **ADD THE DEVELOPER TAB**

    a. Create a new workbook.

    b. If the Developer tab is not displayed, click **File** → Options. A dialog box is displayed.

1. Select Customize Ribbon and then select Developer check box in the Main Tabs list.

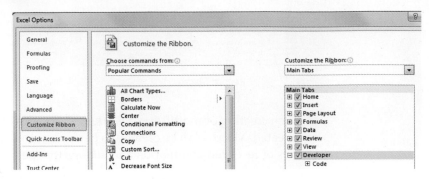

2. Select OK. The Developer tab is added to the Ribbon.

② CREATE A MACRO

The company Flat Technologies Incorporated places its name and contact information in the upper-left corner of each worksheet. Instead of having to type this information repetitively, a macro will be created.

a. Click Developer → Record Macro ⬚. The Record Macro dialog box is displayed.

1. Enter the options as shown, replacing Name with your name in the Description box:

2. Select OK.

b. In cell A1, type Flat Technologies Incorporated and format it as bold.

c. In cell A2, type 67 South West Drive Suite 501 and format it as italic.

d. In cell A3, type Delray Beach, FL 33445 and format it as italic.

e. In cell A4, type 561.555.3343 and format it as bold and italic.

f. Click Developer → Stop Recording.

③ TEST THE MACRO

a. Display Sheet2 in the workbook and select cell A1.

b. Press Ctrl+F, which is the shortcut key for the macro. The company name and address is displayed.

c. Display Sheet 3, select cell A1 and press Ctrl+F.

④ EXPERIMENT WITH MACROS

Create a macro for a task you do repetitively.

⑤ DELETE MACROS

    a. Click Developer → Macros. The Macro dialog box is displayed.

    b. Select FlatInfo in the Macro name box and then select Delete. A warning dialog box is displayed. Select Yes.

    c. Repeat steps (a) and (b) to delete the macro created in step 4.

⑥ CLOSE THE WORKBOOK AND QUIT EXCEL

    a. Close the workbook without saving changes.

    b. Quit Excel

Chapter Summary

This chapter discussed how dates and times can be used in formulas. In Excel, dates are stored as sequential serial values.

In Excel, information in a worksheet can be defined as a table using the Insert tab and then managed independently from the other data on the worksheet. Table data can be sorted, filtered, and separated. Table data can also be used to create calculated columns.

A worksheet can become very large, which makes it difficult to analyze information in the worksheet. A PivotTable and PivotTable report allows the worksheet data to be put into small, concise reports, simplifying data analysis. The Insert tab is used to create a PivotTable.

Data entry criteria can be specified for certain cells using the Data tab to avoid data entry errors. A prompt can be added to indicate to users the type of data to enter.

The CHOOSE function returns one value from a list of many. The VLOOKUP function returns values from a table that is stored in a range of cells. When given a numeric expression and the cell range where values are stored, VLOOKUP finds the largest number in the VLOOKUP table which is less than or equal to the numeric expression. It then returns the value stored in the specified column of the table. Both the CHOOSE and VLOOKUP functions can be used to display text.

The name box can be used to name a cell or range of cells. Named ranges can be used in formulas and are managed with the Formulas tab. The range that defines a VLOOKUP table can also be specified as a named range.

In a large worksheet, commands on the View tab is used to keep rows and columns containing labels from scrolling off the screen. Hyperlinks to a workbook location can help users move within a workbook. The Insert tab is used to create hyperlinks.

Paste Options and the Paste Special dialog box in Word and Excel can be used to embed and link objects. An embedded object keeps the features of the application it was created in. A linked object automatically updates when the source data is updated.

Macros can be created to help perform repetitive tasks. Macros are created using the Developer tab. A macro is run by pressing a designated shortcut key.

Calculated Column A single formula entered in a table cell and then automatically copied to all of the other table cells in the column.

CHOOSE A lookup function that returns a value from a list of many values.

Embedded object An object that keeps the features of the application it was created in.

Field A column in a worksheet.

Filter The process of displaying only the rows that meet specific criteria.

Linked object An object that automatically updates when the source data is updated.

Macro A series of recorded commands and actions that perform a specific task.

PivotTable A table of data where each column is a field that can be used to summarize data.

PivotTable report A report that allows the worksheet data to be put into small, concise reports, simplifying data analysis.

Static Pasted data that is not connected to the source file or to the source application.

Table Range of related data that can be sorted and filtered.

VLOOKUP A lookup function used to return a value from a table of values stored in the worksheet.

Excel Commands

Clear All Removes all data validation criteria. Found in Data → Data Validation.

Data Validation 📊 Displays a dialog box used to specify data entry criteria for a cell or range of cells. Found on the Data tab.

Define Name Displays a dialog box used to define a named range. Found in Formulas → Define Name.

Delete Table Columns Deletes a table column. Found in Home → Delete.

Delete Table Rows Deletes a table row. Found in Home → Delete.

Freeze First Column Designates the first column as frozen. Found in View → Freeze Panes.

Freeze Panes Designates every row above the active cell and every column to the left of the active cell as frozen. Found in View → Freeze Panes.

Freeze Top Row Designates the top row as frozen. Found in View → Freeze Panes.

Hyperlink Displays a dialog box used to insert a hyperlink into the active cell. Found on the Insert tab.

Insert Table Row Above Inserts a table row above the current row. Found in Home → Insert.

Insert Table Row Below Inserts a table row below the current row. Found in Home → Insert.

Insert Table Column To the Left Inserts a table column to the left of the current column. Found in Home → Insert.

Insert Table Column To the Right Inserts a table column to the right of the current column. Found in Home → Insert.

Macros Displays a dialog box used to edit and delete macros. Found on the Developer tab.

Name Manager Displays a dialog box used to delete a range name. Found on the Formulas tab.

Options Displays a dialog box used to add a tab to the Ribbon. Found in Backstage view.

Paste Special Displays a dialog box used to embed and link objects. Found in Home → Paste.

PivotTable Displays a dialog box used create a PivotTable. Found on the Insert tab.

Record Macro 📹 Displays a dialog box used to create a macro. Found in Developer → Record Macro.

Remove Hyperlink Removes the blue underline from text in a cell. Found in the menu displayed by right-clicking the cell containing a link.

Stop Recording Ends the recording of a macro. Found on the Developer tab.

Text to Columns Displays a dialog box used to separate data in a column. Found on the Data tab.

Table Displays a grid used create a table. Found on the Insert tab.

Unfreeze Panes Unfreezes all the frozen cells on a worksheet. Found in View → Freeze Panes.

Use in Formula Used to place a named range in a formula. Found on the Formulas tab.

Review Questions

1. a) How are dates stored in Excel?
   b) List the steps required to view the serial value of an existing date.

2. a) What is added to each column label in a table?
   b) Describe a situation where a filter could be used.
   c) Why might it be necessary to separate first and last name data into two columns?

3. Explain one way to avoid data entry errors.

4. Describe a situation where it would be useful to use a PivotTable.

5. a) Write a CHOOSE function that displays 100 if cell B20 contains a value of 1, 500 if a 2, 900 if a 3, and 1200 if a 4.
   b) Write a CHOOSE function that displays the word Excellent if cell B20 contains a value of 1, Good if a 2, Fair if a 3, and Poor if a 4.

6. a) List the steps required to name a range using the name box.
   b) Does a named range change when it is copied as part of a formula? Why or why not?

7. Describe three situations in which a VLOOKUP table could be used.

8. Gadgets, Inc. uses the following discount rates when large numbers of items are ordered:

Number of Items	Discount
100 - 149	10%
150 - 999	20%
1000 - 1999	30%
2000 and above	70%

   a) Convert this into a VLOOKUP table and make a sketch of the table.
   b) Write a formula that uses the VLOOKUP function to display the proper discount percent if cell C12 stores the number of items and cells A1 through B5 store the VLOOKUP table created in part (a).

9. What cell should be selected to freeze the cells in column A and rows 1 through 4 before selecting Freeze Panes?

10. List the steps required to insert a hyperlink in cell B7 that links to cell K38.

11. Explain the difference between linked and embedded objects.

12. a) What is a macro?
    b) List the steps required to create a macro to enter the label Date, format the label in a blue font color, and right align it.
    c) List the steps required to delete a macro.

True/False

13. Determine if each of the following are true or false. If false, explain why.
    a) The result of a time calculation must be formatted using a 24-hour Time format.
    b) More than one filter can be applied to the same table.
    c) The <choice> argument in a CHOOSE function has to be a number between 1 and 99.
    d) The name given to a cell or range of cells can contain spaces.
    e) The values in the first column of a VLOOKUP table must be in descending order to work correctly.
    f) The range that defines the VLOOKUP table can be specified as a named range.
    g) Frozen rows remain on the screen when scrolling vertically.
    h) A password is required to unfreeze cells.
    i) A hyperlink in a cell always opens a Web browser when clicked.
    j) A linked object automatically updates when the source data is updated.
    k) Macros improve productivity.

Project 1

A small commuter airline wants to use a worksheet to calculate revenue (money they collect). Open FLORIDA FLIGHTS, which is an Excel data file for this text, and complete the following steps:

a) Revenue is based on the number of tickets purchased and the type of ticket. Column B contains the type of ticket: 1 for coach, and 2 for first class. The price for tickets will be determined by the following scale:

Ticket Type	Price
1	$199
2	$425

b) Revenue is calculated by multiplying the ticket price by the number of tickets purchased. In column D, enter the label Revenue and right align it. Enter formulas that use the CHOOSE function to calculate and display the revenue earned for each route.

c) Format the revenue as currency with 0 decimal places. Change the column width as necessary so that all the data is displayed entirely.

d) Add your name in a header and the current date in a footer. Add gridlines and headings.

e) Save the modified FLORIDA FLIGHTS and print a copy.

f) Display the formulas in the cells instead of values. Print a copy.

Project 2

Study Time Tutoring wants to use a worksheet to determine how much the bookstore will pay for last semester's books.

a) Create a new workbook.

b) Enter the data and apply formatting as shown below.

	A	B	C
1	Book Title	Original Price	Condition
2	Introduction to Digital Logic Design	$75.80	1
3	A Guide to Computing Fundamentals	$125.25	1
4	College Physics	$32.50	3
5	Fiction Writing Basics	$15.45	2

c) Save the workbook naming it Used Books.

d) The bookstore buys used textbooks at a percentage of the original price based on the condition of the book:

Condition	Percentage
1	40%
2	20%
3	10%

The used price is calculated by multiplying the original price by the appropriate percentage. In column D, enter the label Used Price. Enter formulas that use the CHOOSE function to calculate and display the used price for each book.

e) Right align the label in cell D1. Format the values in column D as currency with 2 decimal places.

f) The student has decided that if the used price is over $20, it would be best to sell the book, otherwise it is best to donate the book to the library. In column E, enter the label What To Do. Enter formulas that use a function to display Sell for the books that will be sold or Donate for books that will be donated to the library.

g) Center align all the data in column E. Change the column widths as necessary so that all the data is displayed entirely.

h) Add your name in a header and the current date in a footer. Add gridlines and headings.

i) Save the modified Used Books and print a copy.

j) Display the formulas in the cells instead of values. Print a copy.

Project 3

A gym wants to use a worksheet to determine the target heart rate zone for its members.

a) Create a new workbook.

b) Enter the data and apply formatting using the Office theme as shown below.

	A	B	C
1	Gym Member	Age	Target Zone
2	Brian	25	98 to 146
3	Christine	20	100 to 150
4	Stephanie	32	95 to 142
5	Marchello	44	90 to 135

c) Save the workbook naming it Target Zone.

d) The target heart rate is based on a person's age. In cell A8, enter the label Target Heart Rate Table and bold it. Starting in cell A9, create a VLOOKUP table based on the following criteria:

Age	Target Zone
20 – 24	100 to 150
25 – 29	98 to 146
30 – 34	95 to 142
35 – 39	93 to 138
40 – 44	90 to 135
45 – 49	88 to 131
50 – 54	85 to 127

55 – 59	83 to 123
60 – 64	80 to 120
65 – 69	78 to 116
70 and older	75 to 113

e) Name the table range Zone.

f) In column C, enter the label Target Zone and format the label to match cell B1. Enter formulas that use the VLOOKUP function to display the target zone for each gym member.

g) Center align all the data in column C. Change the column width as necessary so that all the data is displayed entirely.

h) Add your name in a header and the current date in a footer. Add gridlines and headings.

i) Save the modified Target Zone and print a copy.

j) Display the formulas in the cells instead of values. Print a copy.

Project 4

The MUSIC SALE workbook contains an inventory of used musical instruments. Open MUSIC SALE, which is an Excel data file for this text, and complete the following steps:

a) The selling price is a percentage of the original price based on the condition of the instrument:

Condition	Percentage
1	60%
2	50%
3	40%
4	30%
5	20%

The selling price is calculated by multiplying the original price by the appropriate percentage. In column D, enter the label Selling Price and bold and right align it. Enter formulas that use the CHOOSE function to calculate and display the selling price for each instrument. Format the values as Currency with 2 decimal places. Change the column widths as necessary so that all the data is displayed entirely.

b) Each instrument will either be sold, donated, or thrown away based on the selling price. In cell A12, enter the label What To Do Table and format it as bold. Starting in cell A13, create a VLOOKUP table based on the following criteria:

Sale Price	What to Do?
under $100	Throw Away
$100 – $499	Donate
$500 and above	Sell

c) Name the table range Action.

d) In column E, enter the label What To Do and format the label as bold. Enter formulas that use the VLOOKUP function to display what to do with each instrument.

e) Center align all the data in column E. Change the column width as necessary so that all the data is displayed entirely.

f) Add your name in a header and the current date in a footer.

g) Save the modified MUSIC SALE and print a copy.

h) Display the formulas in the cells instead of values. Print a copy.

Project 5

The BUSINESS PAYROLL workbook will contain monthly payroll information. Open BUSINESS PAYROLL, which is an Excel data file for this text, and complete the following steps:

a) Add data validation criteria to cells C6 through C11 so that only the values 1 through 3 can be entered through a drop-down list.

b) Enter the following data starting in cell A6:

Diez, G.	$1,250.00	3
Roberts, D.	$1,250.00	1
Martin, P.	$1,650.00	1
Jorge, P.	$1,525.00	2
Romani, D.	$2,050.00	3
Berry, H.	$1,475.00	2

c) The taxes for each employee need to be calculated. Tax deductions are based on the number of dependents each employee has:

Dependents	Percentage
1	18%
2	16%
3	14%

Taxes are calculated by multiplying the monthly gross pay by the appropriate percentage. In column D, enter the label Taxes and right align the label. Enter formulas that use the CHOOSE function to calculate and display the tax for each employee. Format the data as Currency with 2 decimal places.

d) Social security is calculated by multiplying the social security rate in cell B3 by the monthly gross pay. In column E, enter the label Soc. Sec. and right align it. Enter formulas that use absolute and relative cell references to calculate the social security deductions. Format the data as Currency with 2 decimal places.

e) The net pay for each employee is calculated by making the necessary deductions from the monthly gross pay. In column F, enter the label Net Pay and right align it. Enter formulas that use cell references to deduct the taxes and social security from the gross pay of each employee to get the net pay.

f) Select cells A5 through F11 and create a table. Format the table using an appropriate table style.

g) Sort the table in ascending order by Employee.

h) Filter the table to display employees with 2 dependents.

i) Display all rows in the table.

j) Add your name in a header and the current date in a footer.

k) Save the modified BUSINESS PAYROLL and print a copy.

l) Display the formulas in the cells instead of values. Print a copy.

Project 6

The FLOWER STORE workbook will contain the items sold at a discount flower retailer. Open FLOWER STORE, which is an Excel data file for this text, and complete the following steps:

a) Add data validation criteria to cells B4 through B11 so that only decimal numbers between 20 and 99.99 can be entered.

b) Add data validation criteria to cells C4 through C11 so that only the values 1 through 4 can be entered through a drop-down list.

c) Enter the following data starting in cell A4:

Red and White Carnations	$24.00	1
Daisies and Carnations	$24.00	4
Multicolor Tulips	$26.00	2
Daisies and Yellow Roses	$27.50	2
Yellow Roses	$39.00	2
Red Roses	$39.00	1
White Roses	$39.00	3
Exotic Flowers	$46.00	4

d) The selling price of the flower arrangements are based on a percentage markup. In cell A13, enter the label Markup Table and format it as right aligned and bold. Starting in cell A14, create a VLOOKUP table based on the following criteria:

Cost	Markup
$25 and under	35%
from $26 to $45	45%
$46 and above	35%

e) Name the table range Markup.

f) In cell D3, enter the label Selling Price. Format the label to match cell C3. The selling price is calculated by multiplying the cost by the markup percentage and then adding that total to the cost. Enter formulas in column D that use the VLOOKUP function to display the selling price. Change the column widths as necessary so that all the data is displayed entirely.

g) Frequent buyers receive discounts that vary depending on the flower. Column C contains the discount codes 1 through 4. The discount on the selling price is determined by the following percentages:

Discount Code	Percentage
1	20%
2	15%
3	10%
4	5%

The discount price is calculated by multiplying the selling price by the appropriate percentage and then subtracting all of that from the selling price. In column E, enter the label Discount Price. Format the label to match cell D3. Enter formulas that use the CHOOSE function and cell references to calculate and display the discounted selling price for each item. Change the column widths as necessary so that all the data is displayed entirely.

h) Select cells A3 through E11 and create a table.

i) Add a table column to the right of column E.

j) In column F, create a calculated column with the heading Savings that subtracts the discount price from the selling price.

k) Sort the table in ascending order by Discount Price.

l) Filter the table to display arrangements with a Discount Code of 2.

m) Display all rows in the table.

n) Add your name in a header and the current date in a footer. Add gridlines and headings, and change the orientation to landscape.

o) Save the modified FLOWER STORE and print a copy.

p) Display the formulas in the cells instead of values. Print a copy.

Project 7

Most home electronic equipment is covered by a warranty. A worksheet can be used to keep track of warranty expiration dates.

a) Create a new workbook.

b) Enter the data and apply formatting using the Trek theme as shown below.

	A	B	C	D
1		Warranties		
2				
3	Item	Purchase Date	Expiration Date	
4	DVD Player	3/5/2010		
5	TV	2/1/2010		
6	Car	7/8/2009		
7	Truck	9/23/2010		
8	Computer	12/12/2010		
9				

c) The DVD player, TV, and computer have 90-day warranties. Enter a formula to calculate the warranty expiration date for this equipment.

d) The car and truck were previously owned and have 2.5 year warranties. Enter a formula to calculate the warranty expiration date of the car and truck.

e) Protect the worksheet using the password 4ghae228.

f) Add your name in a header and the current date in a footer. Add gridlines and headings.

g) Save the workbook naming it Warranties and print a copy.

Project 8

A university is holding a community service contest. The college (College of Business, College of Nursing, and so on) whose students perform the most community service hours receives ten new computers. The SERVICE HOURS workbook contains the number of community service hours completed so far.

a) In a new Word document create a one page document that promotes the contest. The document should include a short description of the contest and a paragraph about why community service is important. It should also include the deadline, which is the end of the semester. The document will be e-mailed to each college.

b) Save the document naming it Contest.

c) Add a new paragraph below the last line of text in the document and type the following text:

> To date, students have performed the following community service hours:

d) The document needs to display the number of community service hours completed for each college. Open SERVICE HOURS, which is an Excel data file for this text. Using all the data in the SERVICE HOURS workbook, insert a linked object into the Contest document below the text you just typed.

e) In the Contest document, create a header with your name centered.

f) The undergraduate students in the College of Business have just completed a total of 650 hours of community service. Edit the workbook appropriately.

g) Save the modified Contest and print a copy.

Project 9

The LOG function is used to return the logarithm of a number to a specified base. The LOG function takes the form:

    =LOG(<number>, <base>)

Number is the positive real number for which you want the logarithm. Base is the base of the logarithm. If base is omitted, it is assumed to be 10.

When quantities can vary over very large or very small ranges, it is sometimes convenient to take their logarithms in order to get a more manageable set of numbers. The measure of the loudness of sound is one example. A sound has a value of one unit if so faint that it is barely audible. All other sounds are multiples of the sound of value 1 unit. The data below lists some common sounds and their intensities:

Type of Sound	Intensity of Sound (Units)
barely audible	1
rustle of leaves	10
whisper	100
quiet conversation	1000
ordinary conversation	10 000 – 100 000
ordinary traffic	1 000 000 – 10 000 000
heavy traffic	100 000 000 – 1 000 000 000
jack hammer	10 000 000 000 – 100 000 000 000
amplified rock music	1 000 000 000 000
jet plane (20 miles away)	10 000 000 000 000 – 100 000 000 000 000

As the data conveys, stating the numerical intensity of some common sounds can be cumbersome. Logarithms are used to make the numbers more manageable. The intensity of sound is stated in decibels, which are calculated according to the formula:

$$\text{decibels(db)} = 10 \log 10 \, L$$

where L is the loudness of the sound.

a) Create a new workbook.

b) Enter the data for the types and intensities of sounds. Below the data create a decibels calculator that converts the number (sound units) typed in a cell labeled Sound to the corresponding decibels, displayed in another appropriately labeled cell.

c) Save the workbook naming it Decibels and print a copy with 10000 entered into the Sound cell.

Project 10

You have tried various advertising media to promote your new business. Open ADVERTISING SALES, which is an Excel data file for this text, and complete the following steps:

a) In cell O3, enter the label Total Sales. Change the column widths as necessary so that all the data is displayed entirely.

b) In column O, enter a formula to calculate the yearly total sales for each media. Note that an error code is displayed indicating Formula Omits Adjacent Cells. Why is it okay to ignore this error?

c) Create a PivotTable report on a separate sheet that shows the media, annual cost, and total sales. Format the PivotTable report appropriately. Were any of the advertising medias not profitable? Name the sheet appropriately.

d) Create another PivotTable report on a separate sheet that shows the category, annual cost, and total sales. Format the PivotTable appropriately. Which media was more profitable for the business? Name the sheet appropriately.

e) On each PivotTable report, add your name in a header and the current date in a footer. Add gridlines and headings.

f) Save the modified ADVERTISING SALES and print a copy of each PivotTable report.

Chapter 9
Working with a Database

What is a Database?

> **Information Age**
>
> Our present time is referred to as the "Information Age" because the computer's fast retrieval and large storage capabilities enable us to store and manipulate vast amounts of information.

A *database* is an organized collection of related data. A corporation's employee data, a store's inventory, and information about a collection are examples of data stored in a database. The computer application used for creating a database is called a *relational database management system* (RDBMS). Microsoft Access 2010 is a RDBMS.

Access is used to manage data, answer queries (questions about the data), create user-friendly forms for data entry, and generate printed reports about stored data.

Database Terminology

A database is organized into a series of tables. *Tables* contain related data, such as all of the data about a company's orders, their customers, or their employees. Within a table, *fields* store data. Access displays a table in a *datasheet*, which organizes fields into columns:

Order ID	Order Date	Customer ID	Product ID	Quantity
1	5/15/2011	WW001	S36-7	8
2	5/18/2011	MH001	L41-8	50
3	5/18/2011	PS001	V71-9	22
4	5/19/2011	WW001	S20-3	10
5	5/22/2011	MH001	S20-3	25
6	5/26/2011	WW001	M41-6	5
7	5/27/2011	PS001	S20-3	35
8	5/29/2011	AS001	V71-9	30

Each field has a name, such as Order ID or Product ID.

A *record* is a set of data for the fields in a table. The records in a datasheet are organized into rows, one record after another:

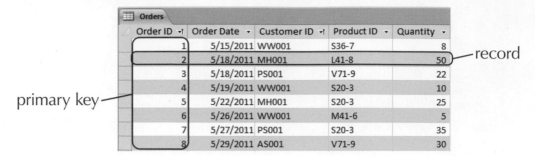

Each table contains a *primary key*, which is a unique identifier used to ensure that no two records in a table are the same.

Opening a Database

When Access 2010 is started, New options are displayed in Backstage view:

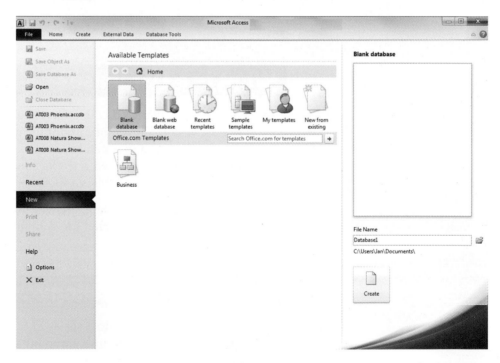

Backstage view includes Quick Commands for saving, opening, and closing a database. Along with the New tab, there are also tabs for displaying Info, Recent, Print, Share, and Help options.

An Access database is saved with an .accdb extension. To open an existing database, click Open, which displays the Open dialog box. Navigate to the appropriate location, click the database file, and then select Open. The Access interface looks similar to:

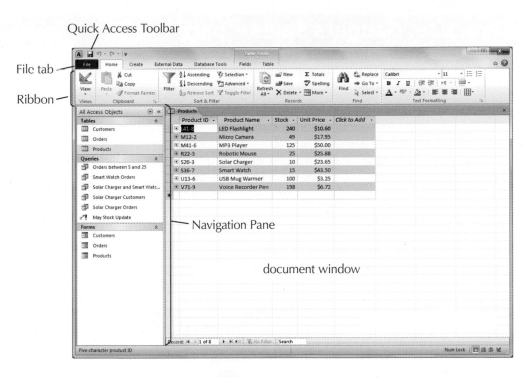

File tab

Ribbon

Navigation Pane

document window

- Click the **File tab** to display a menu of commands for opening, saving, and printing database objects.

- Select commands and perform actions using the **Ribbon** and the **Quick Access Toolbar**.

- The **Navigation pane** is used to run, open, and manage the objects of a database. Click to display the Navigation pane menu. Click « to open and close the Navigation pane.

- Open objects are displayed in a **document window**.

Flat-File Database

A spreadsheet file is sometimes referred to as a flat-file database because a worksheet organizes data into rows and columns like a database with a single table.

Note that the table in the Access window above contains four fields (Product ID, Product Name, Stock and Unit Price) and eight records.

Database Design

In a database, data is divided into tables to eliminate unnecessary data duplication, or *data redundancy*. For example, redundant data is removed when customer data (ID, name, address) is stored in one table and then other tables store just the customer ID to refer to customers.

data redundancy

database schema

Creating a new database involves determining the *database schema*, which is a description of the data and the organization of the data into tables. In a relational database, each table is related to at least one other table by a column of data. For example, the Orders and the Products tables are related by the Product ID columns:

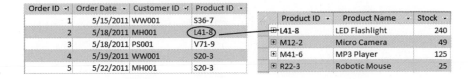

Order ID	Order Date	Customer ID	Product ID
1	5/15/2011	WW001	S36-7
2	5/18/2011	MH001	L41-8
3	5/18/2011	PS001	V71-9
4	5/19/2011	WW001	S20-3
5	5/22/2011	MH001	S20-3

Product ID	Product Name	Stock
L41-8	LED Flashlight	240
M12-2	Micro Camera	49
M41-6	MP3 Player	125
R22-3	Robotic Mouse	25

Developing a database schema is discussed further in Chapter 10.

① **START ACCESS**

Ask your instructor for the appropriate steps to start Microsoft Access 2010. Note the New options in Backstage view.

② **OPEN A DATABASE**

a. Select Open. A dialog box is displayed.

   1. Navigate to the locations where the database files are stored for this text.

   2. Select GADGET SALES.

   3. Select Open. The database contains a Customers, Orders, and Products table.

Working with Tables

The Navigation pane contains a list of the tables that have been created within the database:

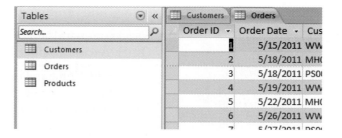

To open a table, double-click the table name. The table opens in the document window:

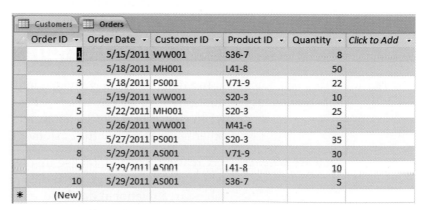

The Customers and Orders tables are open

Use the tabs to switch between open tables. Tables are closed by clicking the Close button ✕ in the top-right corner of the table.

Using Forms

A *form* is a database object used for entering records into a table and for viewing existing records. Form names are listed in the Navigation pane. If form names are not listed, click the **All Access Objects** arrow to display a drop-down menu and click **Forms**:

To open a form, double-click the form name in the Navigation pane:

TIP Select **Home → View** to switch to an alternate view of the form.

The form opens in *Form View* in the document window:

TIP Creating forms and form types are discussed in Chapter 10.

A simple form shows the data for one record

The data for a field is called an *entry*. In a form, an entry box is displayed for each field.

record controls   Record controls are displayed at the bottom of an open form and are used to display a specific record:

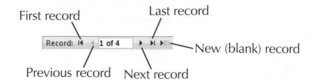

Record controls appear dimmed if they cannot be used at the current time. If a table contains no data, then its corresponding form will display an empty record.

Adding Records

Spelling

populating a database   Adding records to a database is called *populating a database*. One way to populate a database is by typing entries into a form. There are a variety of forms that can be created in Access, but data entry is usually best done with a simple form or a split form. These forms display all the fields for one record without needing to scroll, and because only one record at a time is displayed, data entry is less error-prone:

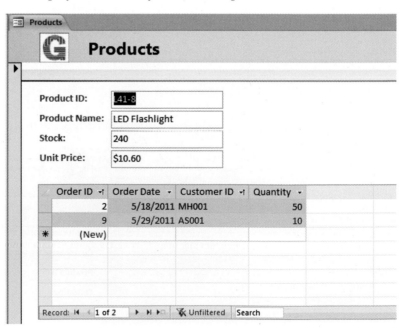

A split form shows individual records and the corresponding table

To add a new record, click New (blank) record ▸* at the bottom of a form and then type the data for the new record. Click an entry box to place the insertion point in that box. For faster data entry, keep hands on the keyboard by pressing the Enter key or the Tab key to move from entry box to entry box. Press Shift+Tab to move to the previous entry box in the form. When the insertion point is in the last entry box of the form, press Enter or the Tab key to display a new, blank record.

checking spelling   After adding records to the database, click Home → Spelling to check the spelling of all the entries. A dialog box displays words not found in the dictionary file and includes options for ignoring and correcting words.

Practice: Gadgets Sales – part 2 of 12

Access should already be started with Gadgets Sales displayed from the last practice.

① VIEWING TABLES

   a. In the Navigation pane, double-click the Customers table. The Customers table is displayed in the document window. Note the field names and records.

   b. In the Navigation pane, double-click the Orders table. The Orders table is displayed in the document window and is the active table.

   c. Click the Customers tab. The Customers table is now the active table.

   d. Click Close ×. The Customers table is removed from the document window.

   e. Close the Orders table.

② VIEWING FORMS

   a. In the Navigation pane, double-click the Customers form. The Customers form is displayed in Form View.

   b. In the Navigation pane, click «. The pane is closed, which provides more room for the form in the document window.

③ ADD A RECORD USING A FORM

   a. In the Customer ID field, type MH001 and then press the Tab key. The next field entry box is active.

   b. Continue the data entry until your form looks similar to:

Customer ID:	MH001
Customer Name:	Milla Hardware
Address:	45 Main Street
City:	Jupiter
State/Province:	FL
ZIP/Postal Code:	33481
Contact First Name:	Dale
Contact Last Name:	Milla
Contact E-mail:	dmilla@milla.lpdatafiles.com
Telephone Number:	(278) 555-1445

   c. In the record controls at the bottom of the form, click New (blank) record ▶. A new blank record is displayed. The record controls indicate that record 2 is displayed.

④ **ADD TWO MORE RECORDS**

Enter the next two records:

PS001; Pepperville Office Supplies; 14 Skyway Drive; Pepperville; NV; 89825; Marcus; Trent; mtrent@pepperville.lpdatafiles.com; (456) 555-7788

WW001; Widget World; 3900 Expressway Blvd.; Sault Ste. Marie; ON; P6A 5L3; Ann; Marchand; amarchand@ww.lpdatafiles.com; (759) 555-2554

⑤ **VIEW THE RECORDS OF THE CUSTOMERS TABLE**

a. In the record controls, click First record ⏮ to display the first record in the table.

b. Click Next record ▸ to display the next record in the table.

c. Click Last record ⏭ to display the last record in the table.

d. Close the form.

e. On the Navigation pane, click ≫ .

⑥ **ADD RECORDS TO THE PRODUCTS FORM**

a. In the Navigation pane, double-click the Products form.

b. Add the following five products records:

L41-8; LED Flashlight; 400; 10.60

M41-6; MP3 Player; 130; 50.00

S20-3; Solar Charger; 80; 23.65

S36-7; Smart Watch; 28; 43.50

V71-9; Voice Recorder Pen; 250; 6.72

c. Close the Products form.

⑦ **ADD RECORDS TO THE ORDERS FORM**

a. In the Navigation pane, double-click the Orders form.

b. The new form is displayed with (New) in the Order ID field. Press the Tab key. The Order Date entry box is selected. Note that there is a calendar icon to the right. This icon can be clicked to display a calendar for referring to dates.

c. In the Order Date entry box, type 5/15/11 and then press the Tab key. The Order ID value changes to a 1 because this is the first record entered. The date entry displays 5/15/2011 because of the formatting selected when the table was created.

d. In the Customer ID entry box, click the arrow. Note the IDs are those from Customer records entered previously. Select WW001.

e. Complete the first record so that your form looks similar to the one shown below:

Order ID	1
Order Date	5/15/2011
Customer ID	WW001
Product ID	S36-7
Quantity	8

f. Add the remaining six order records. Remember to skip the Order ID entry box when entering records:

5/18/11; MH001; L41-8; 50

5/18/11; PS001; V71-9; 22

5/19/11; WW001; S20-3; 10

5/22/11; MH001; S20-3; 25

5/26/11; WW001; M41-6; 5

5/27/11; PS001; S20-3; 35

g. Close the Orders form.

Using Datasheet View

Datasheet view displays a table in a datasheet where fields are in columns and records in rows. This view is useful for comparing records and is often used when sorting or filtering data. This view is also useful for printing data because many records can fit on a single sheet of paper.

To open a table in Datasheet view, double-click the table name in the Navigation pane:

record selector

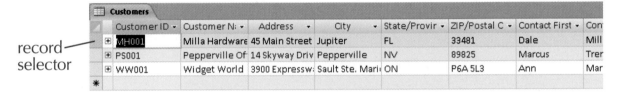

record selector

Records can be added in datasheet view. The asterisk (*) that appears to the left of the row below the last record indicates where a new record will appear. It is not a blank record and it cannot be deleted or removed. The gray box to the left of each record is a *record selector*. Click a record selector to make a record active. The first record in the table above is the active record.

boundaries

The datasheet may need some formatting in order to completely display table entries. For example, the Customers table above does not display all field entries entirely because the default datasheet column widths are too narrow. The column borders, called *boundaries*, are used to change the width of a column. Point to the right boundary until the pointer changes to ✛ and then drag the boundary to the right to increase the width of the column. Drag the boundary to the left to decrease the width. Double-click the boundary to size the column to exactly fit the data.

The order in which the fields appear in a datasheet are changed by dragging a selected field to a new location. Point to the bottom border of the field name until the pointer changes to ✣ and then drag the field to the new position. A heavy dark line indicates the field's new location.

Formatting can improve the readability of a datasheet. Use the Home tab to apply formats:

Bold Font Font Size Alternate Row Color

For example, click ⌄ in Home → Alternate Row Color and then select a color to shade every other row:

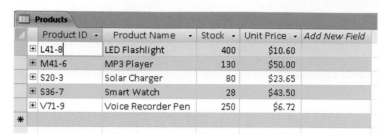

Click **Bold** to make text appear heavier. Font Calibri (Detail) ⌄ and Font Size 11 ⌄ can be used to improve readability by changing the shape of the characters and the size of the type.

Sorting Records

Advanced

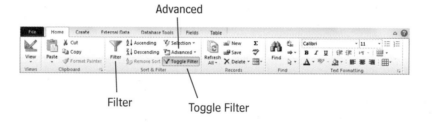

Filter   Toggle Filter

TIP Records are initially sorted in alphabetical order based on the data in the primary key field.

Placing records in a specified order is called *sorting*. In Access, records can be sorted in either ascending or descending order based on the data in a specified field. *Ascending order* places records from lowest to highest and is also called *alphabetical order* when a sort is based on a text field and *chronological order* when a sort is based on a date/time field. *Descending order* places records from highest to lowest. For example, the Products table sorted from low to high by the amount in stock looks similar to:

Alternative Click ⌄ beside a field name to display a menu with sort options.

To sort records based on the data in a field, first click that field name. Next, click Home → Ascending ᵃ↓ or Home → Descending ᶻ↓. An arrow is displayed next to the field name to indicate a sort. For example, to place the records in the Products table in ascending order by Stock, click the Stock field name and then click Home → Ascending ᵃ↓. To remove all applied sorts, click Home → Remove Sort ₂⁰.

Sorting a datasheet does not affect the order the records are displayed in a form. To change the order records are displayed in a form, click a field entry box and then click the appropriate sort button on the Home tab.

Filtering Records

Advanced

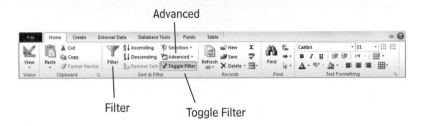

Filter   Toggle Filter

Displaying records based on specified criteria is called *filtering*. When a filter is applied, records that do not meet the specified criteria are hidden from view until the filter is removed. For example, the Orders table has been filtered to display just WW001 orders:

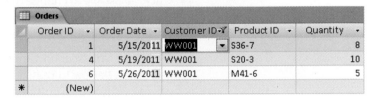

To filter records based on the data in a field, click in the field to base the filter on and then click Home → Filter to display a menu similar to:

Clear check boxes and then select OK to hide records containing those entries. Select Text Filters to create a custom filter. Text Filters commands include Does Not Equal, Begins With, and Contains.

To remove a filter, click Home → Toggle Filter. To later apply the same filter, click Home → Toggle Filter again. To remove all filters permanently, click Home → Advanced → Clear All Filters.

Previewing and Printing a Datasheet

Previewing a datasheet shows what printouts will look like. To preview the open document, select [File] → Print → Print Preview. The document appears as a printed page and the Print Preview tab is displayed:

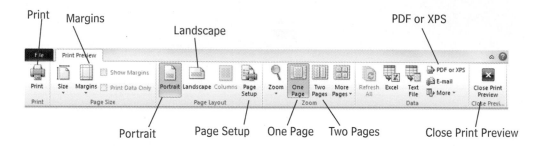

- **Portrait** is the default page layout. Portrait is a page orientation that allows more rows, but fewer columns to be printed on a page.

- Click **Landscape** to change the page orientation so that the datasheet prints across the widest part of the page. This allows more columns, but fewer rows to be printed on a page.

- Margins also affect how much data can be printed on a page. Click **Margins → Narrow** to reduce the amount of white space around the edges of the page. This will allow more rows and columns to fit on a page.

- Click **Page Setup** to display a dialog box where page orientation and margins can be specified.

- **One Page** is the default view with just one page of the document being displayed at a time. Click **Two Pages** to view two pages at once.

- Click **PDF or XPS** to export the table to a PDF or XPS document format. The **Data** group in the Print Preview tab also has commands to export the table to an e-mail, Excel file, or text file.

- Click **Print** to display a dialog box for selecting print options before printing the document.

- Click **Close Print Preview** to return to the previous view.

If a filter has been applied, only the visible records will be printed. A second way to limit the records printed is to first select the records before previewing and then use the Selected Record(s) option in the Print dialog box when printing. To select records, press and hold the Ctrl key while clicking the record selector boxes to the left of the records to print.

Practice: Gadgets Sales – part 3 of 12

Access should already be started with Gadgets Sales displayed from the last practice.

① **FORMAT THE CUSTOMERS TABLE DATASHEET**

a. In the Navigation pane, double-click the Customers table to open it. The table is displayed in Datasheet view.

b. Point to the boundary between the Customer ID and Customer Name fields. The pointer changes to ✛.

c. Double-click the boundary. The column width changes so that it is just wide enough to display the field name and field data.

d. Double-click the boundary to the right of the Customer Name field. The column expands to display the field name and data entirely.

e. Continue to double-click column boundaries until all the columns are sized to display field names and data entirely.

f. Click Home → Alternate Row Color → Light Blue 2 in the Standard Colors. **Hint**: Point to the colors to display their names.

g. Save Customers.

② PRINT THE CUSTOMERS TABLE

a. Click ▬File▬ → Print → Print Preview. A preview of the Customers table is displayed.

b. Click Print Preview → Two Pages. Two pages are displayed.

c. In the lower-left of the window, click Next Page. Note that a third page is required for the printout.

d. Click Print Preview → Landscape. Two pages are now required for the printout.

e. Click Print Preview → Print. A dialog box is displayed.

1. Select OK. The datasheet is printed.

f. Click Print Preview → Close Print Preview.

g. Close the Customers table.

③ FORMAT AND PRINT THE PRODUCTS TABLE

a. Open the Products table.

b. Double-click each field's right boundary. The columns are sized appropriately.

c. Click the Home → Alternate Row Color. Alternate rows are shaded in the Light Blue 2 selected previously.

d. Save the modified Products table.

e. Print and then close the Products table.

④ FORMAT THE ORDERS TABLE

a. Open the Orders table.

b. Size the columns appropriately.

c. Format the rows so that every other row is the Light Blue 2 color.

⑤ SORT AND THEN PRINT THE ORDERS RECORDS

a. Click any Customer ID entry box. The Customer ID field is active.

b. Click Home → Ascending ↓. The records are in alphabetical order by Customer ID.

c. Save the modified Orders table.

d. Preview the datasheet and then print a copy.

⑥ FILTER AND THEN PRINT ORDERS RECORDS

a. Click any Order Date entry box. The Order Date field is active.

b. Click Home → Filter. A menu is displayed by the Order Date field.

c. In the menu, select Date Filters → After. A dialog box is displayed.
   1. In the Order Date is on or after box, type: 5/22/2011
   2. Select OK. The filter is applied. Only three records are displayed.
d. Preview and the datasheet and then print the displayed records.
e. Click Home → Toggle Filter. The filter is removed and the hidden records are again displayed.
f. Save and the then close the Orders table.

Updating and Deleting Records

Delete

The information in a database usually requires frequent changes. These changes include modifying existing records and deleting outdated records.

Modifying a record is called *updating*. Click the record controls at the bottom of a form until the appropriate record is displayed. Next, double-click the entry to be changed and then type to replace the existing data. Click once in a field entry box to place the insertion point so that existing data can be edited. To modify a hyperlink entry, use the Tab key to select the entry and then type a new address.

To delete the active record, click Home → Delete → Delete Record. Access displays a warning dialog box before a record is deleted. Select Yes to remove the current record. Select No to retain the record.

Practice: Gadgets Sales – part 4 of 12

Access should already be started with Gadgets Sales displayed from the last practice.

① **UPDATE A PRODUCT RECORD**

a. A mistake was made when entering the stock of the LED Flashlights. Display the Products form.
b. Scroll to the LED Flashlight record with Product ID L41-8, if it is not already displayed.
c. Change the stock to 300 and then close the Products form.

Using Copy and Paste to Transfer Data

Paste   Copy

Businesses often present database information in letters, annual reports, and other documents. Rather than retype entries and records, which could introduce typing errors, data should be copied and pasted directly into the document from the database.

To select data for copying, point to the left of a table entry until the pointer changes to ⊕ and then click. Adjacent entries can be selected by dragging. To select an entire record, click the record selector. Drag from one record selector to another to select multiple records.

To copy and paste selected entries from a table to a Word document, click Home → Copy, display the Word document, place the insertion point where the data is to appear, and then click Home → Paste.

Data copied from Access is pasted as a table into a Word document:

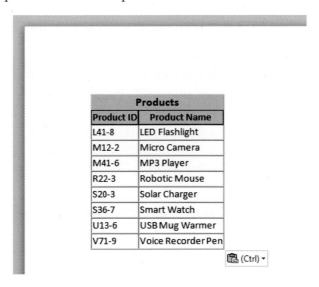

Products	
Product ID	Product Name
L41-8	LED Flashlight
M12-2	Micro Camera
M41-6	MP3 Player
R22-3	Robotic Mouse
S20-3	Solar Charger
S36-7	Smart Watch
U13-6	USB Mug Warmer
V71-9	Voice Recorder Pen

Click Paste Options 📋 (Ctrl) ▾ in the document to display a list of formatting options for the pasted data.

To copy database entries to an Excel worksheet, select entries in a table, click Home → Copy, display the worksheet, select the cell to receive the data, and then click Home → Paste. The data is pasted starting in the selected cell.

Data for a new record often comes from another document, such as a letter in an e-mail attachment. When possible, use Copy and Paste to copy data to database entry boxes to avoid typographical errors.

Access should already be started with Gadgets Sales displayed from the last practice.

① **OPEN PRODUCTION MEMO**

   a. Start Word.

   b. Open PRODUCTION MEMO, which is a Word data file for this text. Read through the unfinished memo.

② **COPY DATA TO THE CLIPBOARD**

   a. Use the Windows taskbar to display the Gadgets Sales database.

   b. Display the Products table.

   c. Select the product name and stock data:

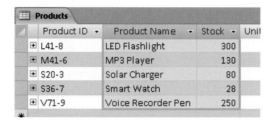

   d. Click Home → Copy. The data is copied to the Clipboard.

③ **PASTE DATA**

   a. Use the taskbar to display the PRODUCTION MEMO document.

   b. Place the insertion point in the blank paragraph below the text that reads "…will need to work overtime:"

   c. Home → Paste. The data is pasted. The memo looks similar to:

SUBJECT: Inventory update

We are into our busiest time of year, and stock is quickly dwindling. Please advise your teams of the need to increase production. Use the figures below to determine which teams will need to work overtime:

Products	
Product Name	**Stock**
LED Flashlight	300.00
MP3 Player	130.00
Solar Charger	80.00
Smart Watch	28.00
Voice Recorder Pen	250.00

 (Ctrl) ▾

④ **COMPLETE THE MEMO**

   a. In the FROM: line, type your name.

   b. In the DATE: line, type today's date.

   c. Save the modified PRODUCTION MEMO and then print a copy.

   d. Close PRODUCTION MEMO.

⑤ **ADD A NEW RETAILER RECORD**

a. Open NEW RETAILER, which is a Word data file for this text. Read through the letter.

b. Use the taskbar to display the Gadgets Sales database.

c. Close the Products table.

d. Display the Customers form.

e. Click New (blank) record ▸ to display a new record.

f. In the Customer ID entry box, type: AS001

g. Use the taskbar to display the NEW RETAILER letter.

h. Select the company name that appears at the beginning of the letter and then click Home → Copy.

i. Display the Customers form.

j. Click in the Customer Name entry box and then click Home → Paste. The company name is pasted into the Customer Name field.

k. Continue to switch between the letter and the database and copy and paste the appropriate data to complete the record. Note you will need to retype the e-mail address.

l. Close the Customers form.

m. Switch to the letter and then close NEW RETAILER and quit Word.

⑥ **ADD THREE NEW ORDER RECORDS**

a. Display the Orders form.

b. Display a new record.

c. Starting in the Order Date field, type entries for the new record:

5/29/11; AS001; V71-9; 30

5/29/11; AS001; L41-8; 10

5/29/11; AS001; S36-7; 5

d. Close the form.

Importing Data

Excel   Text File

New records can be added to a database by typing the entries or by using copy and paste to transfer data. A third way to populate a database is by importing data from an existing file. *Importing data* means that a file created in one application is converted for use by the receiving application. Excel files and text files are two file types supported by Access for importing data.

append   Imported data can be *appended*, or added, to an existing table, or used to create a completely new table. Click External Data → Excel from the Import & Link group. Select the workbook from the displayed dialog box and then use the Import Spreadsheet Wizard dialog boxes to specify the field names, primary key, and table name. Data from a text file is imported similarly. Click External Data → Text File from the Import & Link group. Select the file name from the displayed dialog box and then use the Import Text Wizard dialog boxes to specify the field names, primary key, and table name.

Practice: Gadgets Sales – part 6 of 12

Access should already be started with Gadgets Sales displayed from the last practice.

① **OPEN TINY TOYS**

     a. Start Excel.

     b. Open TINY TOYS, which is an Excel data file for this text. Note that the data is organized like the Products table in the Gadgets Sales database.

     c. Close the workbook and quit Excel.

     d. Gadget Sales is again displayed.

② **IMPORT DATA**

     a. Click External Data → Excel from the Import group. A dialog box is displayed.

         1. Select Browse and then open TINY TOYS. The File name box displays TINY TOYS.

         2. Select Append a copy of the records to the table and then select Products from the list.

         3. Select OK. The first Import Spreadsheet Wizard dialog box is displayed and the data from the worksheet is displayed.

         4. Select Next. The next wizard dialog box is displayed.

         5. Verify the column headings are being used to match the field names and select Next.

         6. The last wizard dialog box is displayed. Verify the Import to Table box displays Products.

         7. Select Finish. A final dialog box is displayed.

         8. Select Close.

     b. Open the Products table. Note the three new records.

     c. Update the three new records with the appropriate Unit Price:

         Micro Camera $17.95

         Robotic Mouse $25.88

         USB Mug Warmer $3.25

     d. Save and close the Products table.

Collecting Data with E-Mail

Create E-mail

A fourth way to populate a database is by collecting data through e-mail messages. With this approach, an e-mail message includes a data entry form for the recipient to fill out and return. Responses can be either collected for processing later or automatically processed. When responses are automatically processed, records are added to the database as the e-mails are received.

To collect data, select a table in the Navigation pane and then click External Data → Create E-mail. Use the wizard dialog boxes to specify the type of form, the fields to be added to the form, and how the data is to be processed.

Practice: Gadgets Sales – part 7 of 12

Access should already be started with Gadgets Sales displayed from the last practice. This practice requires an e-mail address, an e-mail client, and collaboration with a classmate.

① **CREATE AN E-MAIL MESSAGE FOR CUSTOMERS**

    a. In the Navigation pane, click the Customers table to select it.

    b. Click External Data → Create E-mail. A wizard dialog box is displayed:

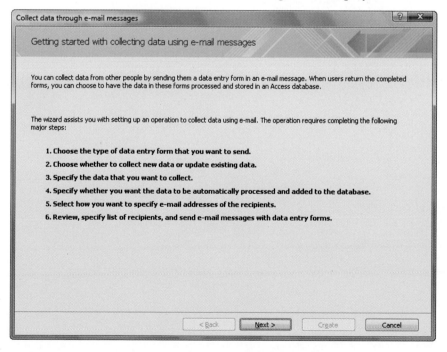

c. Read through the steps to become familiar with the steps you will be taking.

d. Select Next. The second wizard dialog box is displayed.

e. Select HTML form. This is usually the best choice because it requires only an e-mail client that supports HTML:

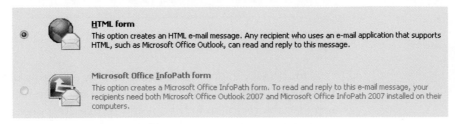

f. Select Next and then select Collect new information only:

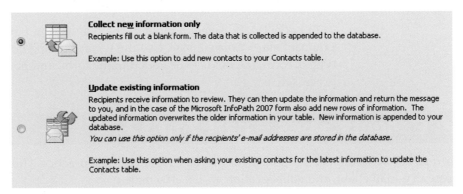

g. Select Next. Click [>>] to move all the fields to the Fields to include in e-mail message list:

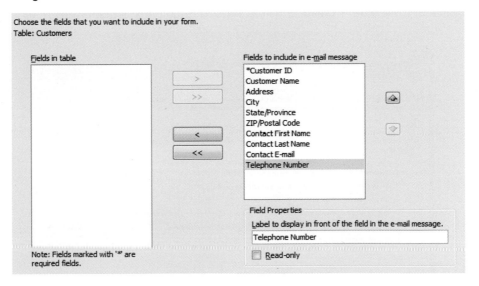

h. Select Next. Select the Automatically process replies and add data to Customers check box:

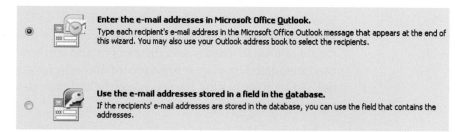

i. Select Next. Select Enter the e-mail addresses in Microsoft Office Outlook:

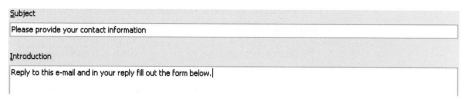

j. Select Next. The Subject and Introduction will be part of the e-mail message. Change the text to be more descriptive:

Subject
Please provide your contact information

Introduction
Reply to this e-mail and in your reply fill out the form below.

k. Select Next. Read through the information.

l. Select Create. An e-mail message is generated.

m. In the To box, type the e-mail address of a classmate.

n. Scroll through the e-mail message. The Subject and the first line of the message are what was typed in the wizard dialog box.

o. Click Send. The message is sent to the recipients for their response.

② VERIFY THE NEW ORDERS RECORD

a. Start Outlook.

b. Check your e-mail to determine if your classmate has responded. When the response arrives, there is no need to process the message in any way.

c. After the e-mail message arrives, use the taskbar to display the Gadgets Sales database.

d. Open the Customers table. A new customer record has been automatically added to the table.

e. Print the Customers table and then close Customers.

f. Close the Gadgets Sales database.

Chapter Summary

This chapter discussed Access, the Microsoft Office RDBMS application used to create a database and sort and filter data. A database is an organized collection of related data. An RDBMS contains tools to manage data, answer queries, create user-friendly forms for data entry, and generate printed reports about stored data.

A database is created based on a schema that organizes the database into tables that contain fields and records. A field stores data and has a name, type, size, and format. A record is a set of data for the fields in a table. A table must have a primary key, which is a field designated to contain unique data.

A form is a database object used for entering records into a table and for viewing existing records. In Form view, record controls at the bottom of the form are used to display specific records and add a new record. Records can be updated by displaying a record and editing an entry. Records are deleted by first making the record active and then using the Home tab to remove the record.

A table in Datasheet view displays fields in columns and records in rows. Datasheet view can be formatted for easier reading. Drag the right boundary of a column to change its width. Move a selected column to a new location by dragging it. The Home tab is used to alternate the colors in the rows, make the text bold, and change the font or font size of the text to improve readability.

There are several ways to populate a database. These include typing entries into a form, using copy and paste to transfer entries to a form, importing data from Excel worksheets or text files, and collecting data through e-mail messages. The spelling of database entries is checked using the Home tab.

Placing records in a specified order is called sorting. The Home tab is used to sort records in ascending or descending order. Displaying records based on specified criteria is called filtering. When a filter is applied, records that do not meet the specified criteria are hidden from view. Filters are useful for limiting the records to be printed.

Previewing a datasheet shows what printouts will look like. When previewed, the document appears like a printed page and the Print Preview tab is displayed. With this tab, page orientation and margins can be changed, pages can be viewed two at a time, and the Page Setup and Print dialog boxes can be displayed.

Vocabulary

Access The Microsoft Office RDBMS application.

Alphabetical order *See* Ascending order.

Append Adding data to the end of table.

Ascending order In order from lowest to highest. Also called alphabetical order when a sort is based on a text field and chronological when a sort is based on a date field.

Boundary The column borders in a table.

Chronological order *See* Ascending order.

Data redundancy Unnecessary data duplication.

Database An organized collection of related data.

Database schema A description of the data and the organization of the data into tables in a relational database.

Datasheet The data for a table organized with fields in columns and records in rows.

Datasheet view Used to display the basic structure of a table in a datasheet with fields in columns and records in rows.

Descending order In order from highest to lowest.

Entry The data for a field.

Field A column in a table. Used to store data.

Filtering Displaying records based on a specified criteria.

Form A database object used for entering records into a table and for viewing existing records.

Form view View used for entering records with a form.

Importing data Converting a file created in one application for use by the receiving application.

Landscape orientation A print setting that uses the widest part of the paper to print across.

Navigation pane Used to run, open, and manage the objects of an Access database.

Populating a database Adding records to a database.

Portrait orientation A print setting that uses the narrowest part of the paper to print across.

Primary key A field in a table that is designated to contain unique data.

RDBMS (Relational Database Management System) A software application that contains tools to manage data, answer queries, create user-friendly forms for data entry, and generate printed reports.

Record A set of data for the fields in a table.

Record controls Used for displaying a specific record in a form or for displaying a new, empty record. Located at the bottom of a form.

Record selector The gray box to the left of each record in a datasheet.

Sorting Placing records in a specified order.

Table A database object that stores related data organized into rows and columns.

Updating Modifying a record.

Access Commands

Alternate Row Color ▦▾ Shades every other row in a datasheet. Found on the Home tab.

Ascending ↓ Orders records from low to high based on the data in a specified field. Found on the Home tab.

Bold **B** Formats text as bold. Found on the Format and Home tabs.

Clear All Filters Removes all filters that have been applied to a datasheet. Found in Home → Advanced.

Close Print Preview Closes print preview. Found on the Print Preview tab.

Copy Creates a duplicate of the selected data for pasting. Found on the Home tab.

Create E-mail Starts a wizard for collecting data through e-mail messages. Found on the External Data tab.

Delete Record Deletes the active record. Found in Home → Delete.

Descending ↓ Orders records from high to low based on the data in a specified field. Found on the Home tab.

Excel Imports data from an Excel workbook file. Found on the External Data tab.

Filter Displays a menu for limiting displayed records based on specified criteria. Found on the Home tab.

First record ◄ Displays the first record in a table. Found in the record controls at the bottom of a form.

Font Calibri (Detail) ▾ Changes the font of text in a form or datasheet. Found on the Format and Home tabs.

Font Size 11 ▾ Changes the size of the text in a form or datasheet. Found on the Format and Home tabs.

Form View Displays a form in Form view where records can be added. Found in Home → View.

Landscape Changes the print orientation of a document to landscape. Found on the Print Preview tab.

Last record ► Displays the last record from a table. Found in the record controls at the bottom of a form.

Narrow Reduces the amount of white space around the edges of a document. Found in Print Preview → Margins.

New (blank) record ► Displays a new, blank record in a form. Found in the record controls at the bottom of a form.

Next record ► Displays the next record from a table. Found in the record controls at the bottom of a form.

One Page Displays one page at a time in print preview. Found on the Print Preview tab.

Page Setup Displays the Page Setup dialog box for changing print orientation and margins. Found on the Print Preview tab.

Paste Places the most recently copied data at the insertion point or in the selected cell. Found on the Home tab.

Paste Options ▦(Ctrl)▾ Displays a list of formatting options for pasted data. Found in a Word document immediately after data has been pasted.

Portrait Changes the print orientation of a document to portrait. Found on the Print Preview tab.

Previous record ◄ Displays the previous record from a table. Found in the record controls at the bottom of a form.

Print Displays the Print dialog box for printing a table or form. Found on the Print Preview tab.

Print Preview Displays a preview of a table or form. Found in File → Print.

Remove Sort ↕ Removes all sorts that have been applied to a datasheet. Found on the Home tab.

Spelling Checks the spelling of all the entries. Found on the Home tab.

Text File Imports data from a text file. Found on the External Data tab.

Toggle Filter Applies or removes a filter. Found on the Home tab.

Two Pages Displays two pages at once in print preview. Found on the Print Preview tab.

1. a) What is a database?
    b) How does an RDBMS store data?

2. What is one benefit of dividing data into tables?

3. What is a database schema?

4. a) What is a field?
    b) Explain why a field that stores more than one piece of data is considered poor design.

5. a) What is a record?
    b) Can a table contain duplicate records? Explain.
    c) What is used in a table to ensure that records are unique?

6. a) What is a form?
    b) List two kinds of forms.

7. Which view must a form be in to add records?

8. a) Where are the record controls located?
    b) What are the record controls used for?

9. How does a form make entering records less error-prone?

10 a) List one way to change a column's width in a datasheet.
    b) List the steps required to change the order of fields.
    c) List two formats and tell why they can improve the readability of a datasheet.

11. List the similarities between a datasheet and a worksheet.

12. a) What is sorting?
    b) Explain the difference between ascending and descending order.

13. a) What is filtering?
    b) Explain how a filter is different from a sort.

14. a) Why preview a datasheet before printing?
    b) How can more columns be printed on a sheet of paper?
    c) What are two ways to print only certain records?

15. a) List the steps for changing an entry in an existing record.
    b) Can an existing record be deleted? Explain.

16. Can database data be copied to a worksheet? Explain.

17. a) What does "importing data" mean?
    b) Name two file types supported by Access for importing data.

18. Explain how e-mail can be used to collect data.

19. List three ways to populate a database.

True/False

20. Determine if each of the following are true or false. If false, explain why.
    a) Each table in a database is related to another table by one field.
    b) The primary key in a database is used to prevent duplicate records in a table.
    c) A Last Name field is a good candidate for a primary key field.
    d) Adding records is called multiplying the database.
    e) Datasheet view displays one record at a time.
    f) Records can be sorted in chronological order.
    g) Filtering removes records from a database.
    h) Changing the print orientation of a datasheet may allow more columns to fit on a sheet of paper.
    i) A form is automatically updated when changes are made to the data in a corresponding table.
    j) It is not possible to copy text from a Word document and paste it as an entry in a database form.
    k) Appended data overwrites existing records in a table.
    l) E-mail cannot be used to collect data.

Project 1

Travel...With a Purpose uses a database to store information about a local museum's exhibit information.

    a) Open MUSEUM EXHIBITS, which is an Access data file for this text.

    b) Enter the following eight records in the Exhibits form:

        SE1; Minerals and Rocks; Solid Earth; 1/5/10

        SE2; Earth's Interior; Solid Earth; 3/6/11

        SE3; Atmosphere and Weather; Solid Earth; 5/3/09

        TD1; Oceans; The Deep; 5/3/11

        TD2; Icebergs; The Deep; 7/12/10

        TD3; Lakes, Rivers & Streams; The Deep; 1/1/11

        WTH1; Earthquakes and Tidal Waves; Why Things Happen; 2/7/11

        WTH2; Volcanoes; Why Things Happen; 11/23/10

    c) Enter the following 27 Attendance records:

SE1; 2010; 1,560	SE1; 2008; 1,540	SE1; 2009; 1,494
SE2; 2010; 1,298	SE2; 2008; 1,600	SE2; 2009; 1,678
SE3; 2010; 1,364	SE3; 2008; 1,467	SE3; 2009; 1,645
TD1; 2010; 1,254	TD1; 2008; 1,374	TD1; 2009; 1,575
TD2; 2010; 1,156	TD2; 2008; 1,245	TD2; 2009; 1,312
TD3; 2010; 1,324	TD3; 2008; 1,437	TD3; 2009; 1,545
WTH1; 2010; 1,256	WTH1; 2008; 1,345	WTH1; 2009; 1,512
WTH2; 2010; 1,224	WTH2; 2008; 1,435	WTH2; 2009; 1,442

    d) Format each of the table datasheets appropriately.

    e) Print preview and then print both tables using the appropriate orientation.

Project 2

Study Time Tutoring uses a database to store information on its library books.

    a) Open LIBRARY, which is an Access data file for this text and enter the following 13 Authors and Illustrators records:

        CC-54; Christopher Paul; Curtis; 1954

        EB-06; Elizabeth Barrett; Browning; 1806; 1861

        ES-08; Elizabeth George; Speare; 1908; 1994

        EW-99; E. B.; White; 1899; 1985

        GW-12; Garth; Williams; 1912; 1998

JP-40; Jack; Prelutsky; 1940

JS-20; James; Stevenson; 1920

MK-49; Maira; Kalman; 1949

MT-43; Mildred; Taylor; 1943

QB-32; Quentin; Blake; 1932

RD-16; Roald; Dahl; 1916; 1990

RM-95; Ruth; Manning-Sanders; 1895; 1988

WS-69; William; Strunk; 1869; 1946

b) Enter the following 11 Titles records:

978-0-06000-698-3; Charlotte's Web; Fiction

978-0-06051-181-4; The Mud Flat Mystery; Fiction

978-0-06076-390-9; It's Raining Pigs & Noodles; Children's Poetry

978-0-14034-893-4; Roll of Thunder, Hear My Cry; Fiction

978-0-14240-253-5; Matilda; Fiction

978-0-44022-830-1; The Sign of the Beaver; Fiction

978-0-51718-721-0; Sonnets from the Portuguese; Poetry

978-0-52526-941-0; A Book of Mermaids; Children's Stories

978-0-55349-410-5; Bud, Not Buddy; Fiction

978-0-67083-545-4; Max Makes a Million; Fiction

978-1-59420-069-4; The Elements of Style; English Language

c) Enter the following 16 Books records. Note that Copy and paste ISBNs from the Titles table to the Books form to reduce typographical errors:

978-0-06000-698-3; EW-99; *selected; blank*

978-0-06000-698-3; GW-12; *blank; selected*

978-0-06051-181-4; JS-20; *selected; blank*

978-0-06076-390-9; JP-40; *selected; blank*

978-0-06076-390-9; JS-20; *blank; selected*

978-0-14034-893-4; MT-43; *selected; blank*

978-0-14240-253-5; RD-16; *selected; blank*

978-0-14240-253-5; QB-32; *blank; selected*

978-0-44022-830-1; ES-08; *selected; blank*

978-0-51718-721-0; EB-06; *selected; blank*

978-0-52526-941-0; RM-95; *selected; blank*

978-0-55349-410-5; CC-54; *selected; blank*

978-0-67083-545-4; MK-49; *selected; blank*

978-1-59420-069-4; EW-99; *selected; blank*

978-1-59420-069-4; WS-69; *selected; blank*

978-1-59420-069-4; MK-49; *blank; selected*

d) Format each of the table datasheets appropriately.

d) Print preview and then print all three tables using the appropriate orientation.

e) Filter the Titles table for Fiction books and then print a copy of just those books.

Project 3

Yolanda' Catering uses a database to store information about its employees and payroll.

a) Open CATERING, which is an Access data file for this text.

b) Enter the following five Employees records:

EI; Edna; Incahatoe; 254 20th St.; Armine; CT; 19154-7901; (332) 555-1765

JF; Jess; Frank; 101 Red Villa Circle; Armine; CT; 19154-7901; (332) 555-2792

RD; Rita; DiPasquale; 5672 56th Ct.; Weidner; CT; 19165-3342; (332) 555-0276

TW; Thomas; Warner; 11 Roni Dr.; Weidner; CT; 19165-3342; (332) 555-2665

WF; Wimberly; Franco; 86 Luther Ct.; Weidner; CT; 19165-9088; (332) 555-1711

c) Enter the following 10 Payroll records:

1009; TW; 3/6/11; 210.24; 31.53   1032; WF; 3/13/11; 187.82; 28.17

1010; RD; 3/6/11; 175; 26.25   1044; EI; 3/20/11; 254; 38.10

1029; EI; 3/13/11; 244; 36.60   1045; JF; 3/20/11; 191.67; 28.75

1030; RD; 3/13/11; 180; 27   1046; WF; 3/20/11; 195.25; 29.28

1031; TW; 3/13/11; 225.64; 33.84   1077; JF; 3/27/11; 210.75; 31.50

d) Format each of the table datasheets appropriately.

e) Sort the Employees table in ascending order by Last Name.

f) Print preview and then print both tables using the appropriate orientation.

Project 4

Sunport Boat Storage wants to use a relational database to store information on its business.

a) Open BOAT STORAGE, which is an Access data file for this text.

b) Enter the following five Employees records:

DK86; Denita; Kilcullen; 86 Hampshire Road; Cody; WA; 12232-1207; (617) 555-1229

HW28; Hillary; Walker; 1221 Rockledge Ave.; Cody; WA; 12232-1209; (617) 555-9800

NG12; Nate; Gervin; NE 66th Plaza; Rostock; WA; 12241; (617) 555-9462

SM23; Sherman; MacGragor; 2334 12th Ave.; Cody; WA; 12232-1207; (617) 555-0993

YA12; Yvette; Archibald; 13 Cypress Creed Rd.; Rostock; WA; 12241; (617) 555-7822

c) Enter the following six Boat Owners records:

Rachell; Gundarssohn; 1671 Westchester Ave.; Poliney; WA; 12245; (232) 555-0912

Pamela; Hogart; 12 Street; Monterey; WA; 12259-4761; (232) 555-7021

Dermont; Voss; 1087 67th Terrace; Monterey; WA; 12259-4761; (232) 555-9000

Zane; McCaffrey; 689 King Blvd.; Poliney; WA; 12245-3309; (232) 555-7492

Bethany; Mulberry; 8625 West View Drive Apt. 9; Rostock; WA; 12241; (617) 555-6524

Damon; Deitrich; 4567 Sandalwood Ave.; Poliney; WA; 12245; (232) 555-2651

d) Enter the following 10 Boats records:

Donned Upon You; 10; NG12; 70; 6   SteadyAsSheGoes; 13; DK86; 60; 5

Jenny; 5; YA12; 62; 4   The Sugar Queen; 12; NG12; 45; 4

Just Desserts; 4; SM23; 50; 3   Tidal Wave; 17; SM23; 55; 2

Monkey Business; 3; HW28; 86; 2   UR Behind Me; 9; DK86; 65; 5

Shooting Star; 16; HW28; 77; 1   Viking 5; 2; SM23; 55; 1

e) Format each of the table datasheets appropriately.

f) Filter the Boats table for boats taken care of by employee SM23 and then print a copy of just those records.

g) Print preview and then print all tables using the appropriate orientation.

Project 5

A relational database can be used to allow an office manager to efficiently keep track of phone messages, visitors, and packages.

a) Open MESSAGES, which is an Access data file for this text.

b) Enter the following four Employees records:

TJ122; Trey; Jones; IT; 122; tj@lpdatafiles.com

MB234; Michelle; Brooks; Human Resources; 234; mb@lpdatafiles.com

GM319; Gretchen; Milnap; Distribution; 319; gm@lpdatafiles.com

AB235; Alfonse; Burrows; Human Resources; 235; ab@lpdatafiles.com

c) Enter the following Messages record:

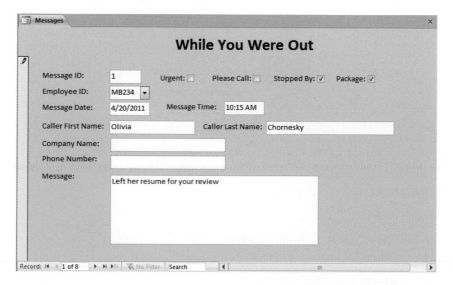

d) Enter 7 more Messages records. Note that fields that should be left empty are indicated with *blank* for their entry:

TJ122; 4/20/11; 12:39 PM; Gretchen; Milnap; *blank*; ext. 319; Bill of ladings are not printing correctly; *selected*; *selected*; *blank*; *blank*

AB235; 4/20/11; 2:20 PM; Gerald; Washburn; Office Fulfillment Services; (238) 555-9076; Cannot attend meeting; *blank*; *selected*; *blank*; *blank*

TJ122; 4/20/11; 4:12 PM; *blank*; *blank*; Downtown Delivery Services; *blank*; *blank*; *blank*; *blank*; *blank*; *selected*

GM319; 4/21/11; 8:40 AM; William; Marshall; Marshall Packaging; (376) 555-8877; *blank*; *blank*; *selected*; *blank*; *blank*

AB235; 4/21/11; 3:15 PM; *blank*; *blank*; Downtown Delivery Services; *blank*; *blank*; *blank*; *blank*; *blank*; *selected*

MB234; 4/22/11; 9:20 AM; Olivia; Chornesky; *blank*; (376) 555-2122; Would like to schedule an interview; *blank*; *selected*; *blank*; *blank*

TJ122; 4/23/11; 12:15 PM; *blank*; *blank*; Downtown Delivery Services; *blank*; *blank*; *blank*; *blank*; *blank*; *selected*

e) Display the record for GM319 in the Messages form. Select **File** → Print → Print. In the Print dialog box, click **Selected Record(s)** and then **OK** to print just the message for Ms. Milnap.

f) Format each of the table datasheets appropriately.

g) Print preview and then print both tables using the appropriate orientation.

Project 6

You want to use a relational database to store your photos and information about the photos:

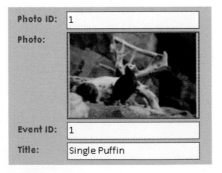

Photo ID:	1
Photo:	
Event ID:	1
Title:	Single Puffin

a) Open PHOTO COLLECTION, which is an Access data file for this text.

b) Enter the following five Photos records. Double-click the Photo entry box to add an attachment. The graphic files used for this database are data files for this text.

attach PUFFIN.JPG; 1; Single Puffin

attach BEAR1.JPG; 1; Bear in Water

attach BEAR2.JPG; 1; Bear with Fish

attach CHICKS.JPG; 2; Baby Chicks

attach LAB.JPG; 2; Dog at Farm

c) Enter the following two Events records:

    1; Alaska Trip; Alaska Sealife Center; 8/21/11; 8/30/11; Family reunion.

    2; Montana Trip; Local Farm; 9/12/11; 9/12/11; Hiking club annual trip.

d) Format each of the table datasheets appropriately.

e) Print preview and then print both tables using the appropriate orientation.

Chapter 9 Working with a Database

Chapter 10
Relational Database Techniques

Developing a Database Schema

Chapter 9 introduced database terminology and explained how to work with tables and forms. This chapter builds on those concepts by illustrating how to create and modify a simple database.

A *database schema* is a description of the data and the organization of the data into tables in a relational database. Developing a schema can be a complex project and is often handled by individuals with specialized education in database systems and database theory. However, as an introduction, below is a three-step approach for developing a schema for a simple database:

1. **Determine which information to include in the database.** This decision requires considering the purpose of the database.

2. **Divide information into related groups to create tables and then give each table a descriptive name.** Group information so that there is little or no data redundancy. However, each table must have data related to at least one other table, which will require data duplication. This is not considered data redundancy. A table with no relationship to any another table does not belong in the database.

3. **Describe the fields and determine the primary key for each table.** Determine appropriate field names, types, sizes, and formats. Designate a primary key for each table.

Creating a Database

Within a table, fields store data. A field has a name and a data type:

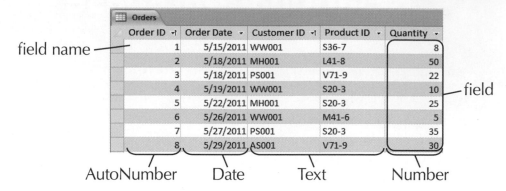

field name

field name A field has a *name* to describe the data it stores. Use the following guidelines when choosing field names:

- **Make field names unique.** Duplicate field names cannot be used to represent similar data. For example, a sales ID and a customer ID cannot be represented by two fields that are both named ID. Instead, Sales ID and Customer ID are acceptable field names.

- **Choose the shortest possible name that accurately describes the contents of the field.** In Access, field names may be up to 64 characters. When multiple words are used for a field name, begin each word with an uppercase letter.

- **Use complete words instead of numbers or abbreviations.** Some users may not understand abbreviations. For example, First Name is better than 1st Name, or F Name.

- **Avoid special characters.** For example, #1Name, ?Name, and *Name, are poor choices for field names. Some special characters are not permitted.

A well-designed database has fields that store only one piece of data for each entry. For example, a field named Full Name that stores both a first and last name is considered poor design because it limits the sorting and searching capabilities of the database. A better design includes First Name and Last Name fields to separate name data.

field type Fields are classified by the *type* of data they store:

- **AutoNumber fields** automatically store a numeric value that is one greater than that in the last record added. AutoNumber fields will automatically contain unique values.

- **Text fields** store characters (letters, symbols, words, a combination of letters and numbers) and numbers that do not require calculations, such as telephone numbers and ZIP codes.

- **Number fields** store only numeric values.

- **Date/Time fields** store dates or times.

- **Currency fields** store dollar amounts.

- **Memo fields** store several lines of text.

- **Yes/No fields** appear as a check box that is are either selected or left cleared to represent yes/no, true/false, or on/off.

- **Hyperlink fields** store links to files, e-mail addresses, and Web site addresses.

- **Attachment fields** store a file. The attached file can be opened directly from the field and edited in its native application.

- **Lookup fields** store data retrieved from a field in another table. They define a relationship between tables.

field size

Some fields types can have a specified size. The *size* of a field is the number of characters or the type of number it can store. Text fields can store up to 255 characters. The size of a number field is defined by the type of value it stores. For fields that store a number with a decimal portion, the field size *Single* is used. Fields that store only whole numbers use the *Long Integer* field size. A size cannot be defined for date/time, currency, and hyperlink fields.

field format

Numeric and date/time fields can have a specified *format* to define how the data is displayed. Text, memo, and hyperlink fields usually have no format. Numeric field formats include:

- **General Number** is the default and displays a number as typed.

- **Fixed** displays a value to a specified number of decimal places.

- **Percent** multiplies the value entered by 100 and displays it with a percent (%) sign.

- **Standard** displays the value with a thousands separator, usually a comma.

Date/time field formats include:

- **Long** (e.g., Saturday, June 24, 2011 or 10:12:30 AM)

- **Medium** (e.g., 24-June-11 or 10:12 AM)

- **Short** (e.g., 6/24/11 or 10:12)

Decimal places can be set for numeric field types. For a number field with the long integer field size, set the number of decimal places set to 0. A number greater than 0 results in the long integer data value being rounded.

The Primary Key

To ensure that no two records in a table are the same, one field in each table is designated the *primary key*:

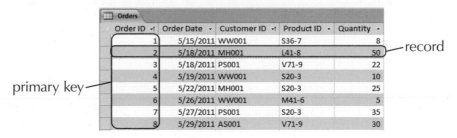

Chapter 10 Relational Database Techniques   365

The primary key column cannot contain duplicate entries. Fields such as Social Security Number, Product ID, and Serial Number make good primary keys. The primary key may also be a combination of fields designated to have a unique combination of entries.

Practice: Align Sales – part 1 of 3

You will need pencil and paper to complete a database schema for the Align Sales database. To keep track of sales, Align Computers has decided on a database with Orders, Customers, and Products tables.

① DEFINE FIELDS FOR THE ORDERS TABLE

The Orders table groups order ID (a unique number automatically generated), order date (similar to 6/24/11), customer ID (five characters), product ID (five characters), and quantity ordered information.

a. Define fields for the Orders table by writing down appropriate field names, types, sizes (keep in mind that date/time fields do not have a size), and field formats, if any (keep in mind that text fields do not have a format).

b. Determine the primary key for the Orders table, which is the field that will have a unique value for each record. Write "primary key" next to this field.

Check – Your Orders table design should look similar to:

Order ID	AutoNumber (primary key)
Order Date	Date, Short Form
Customer ID	Text, 5 characters
Product ID	Text, 5 characters
Quantity	Number, Long Integer, Fixed, 0 decimal places

② DEFINE FIELDS FOR THE CUSTOMERS TABLE

The Customers table groups customer ID (five characters), customer name, address (street address, city, state or province, ZIP or postal code), and contact information (first and last name of contact, telephone number, and e-mail address). Define the fields and primary key for the Customers table.

③ DEFINE FIELDS FOR THE PRODUCTS TABLE

The Products table groups product ID (five characters), product name, stock, and unit price information. Define the fields and primary key for the Products table.

Creating Tables and Fields

Table Design

Access displays a new table when a database is created. It is possible to complete this table by typing field names, however the field types, sizes, and formats may not be correct. To control all aspects of a table, complete it *Design view* in *Design view*. Click Home → View → Design View to switch to Design view.

To create a new table in Design view, click Create → Table Design. Create fields for the table by adding one field per row. The table window below displays four fields in Design view:

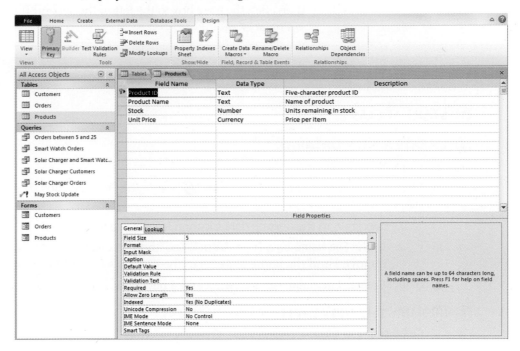

To define a field:

1. Type the field name in the first empty Field Name box.

2. Select the field type from the Data Type box. For a lookup field, select Lookup Wizard to display a series of dialog boxes for defining the data source.

3. Type a description of the field data in the Description box.

4. Type or select the field size in the Field Size box in the General tab at the bottom of the Design view window. For a text field, the size is the greatest number of characters allowed. For a number field, select either Long Integer or Single. Date/time and currency fields do not have a field size.

5. Select a field format in the Format box of the General tab. Text and memo fields do not have a format.

6. Type the number of decimal places for numeric data in the Decimal Places box of the General tab.

To complete a table, designate a primary key. First, click in the primary key field to make it the active field. Next, click Design → Primary Key:

Primary Key

The primary key field requires an entry to ensure that each record is unique. Click the Required option on the General tab, and then select Yes.

If the combination of data in two fields is required to make every record in a table unique, then designate both fields together as the primary key. Click the gray box to the left of the first field, hold down the Ctrl key, and then click the gray box to the left of the second field and then click Design → Primary Key.

Practice: Align Sales – part 2 of 3

① START ACCESS

② CREATE A NEW DATABASE

    a. Click Blank database.

    b. On the right side of the window, click 📂 beside the File Name box. A dialog box is displayed.

        1. Navigate to the appropriate location for the file to be saved.

        2. In the File Name box, type Align Sales and then select OK. The dialog box is removed and the name appears in the File Name box of the Access window.

    c. Select Create. The database is created and a new table is displayed.

③ MODIFY THE NEW TABLE IN DESIGN VIEW

    a. Click Home → View → Design View. The Save As dialog box is displayed.

        1. In the Table Name box, type: Products

        2. Select OK. The table is displayed in Design view.

    b. In the first Field Name box, type: Product ID

    c. Press the Tab key to select the Data Type box. AutoNumber is the default type for the first field. Click the arrow and change the field type to Text.

    d. Press the Tab key to move to the Description box. Type: Five-character product ID

    e. In the General tab, change the Field Size to 5, which is the maximum number of characters allowed for an entry in this field.

    f. In the next Field Name box, create a field named Product Name, of type Text, with the description Name of product, and a Field Size of 30.

    g. In the third Field Name box, create a field named Stock, of type Number, with the description Units remaining in stock, a Field Size of Long Integer, a Format of Fixed, and Decimal Places set to 0.

    h. In the fourth Field Name box, create a field named Unit Price, of type Currency, with the description Price per item, and Decimal Places set to 2.

    Check – Your table should look similar to:

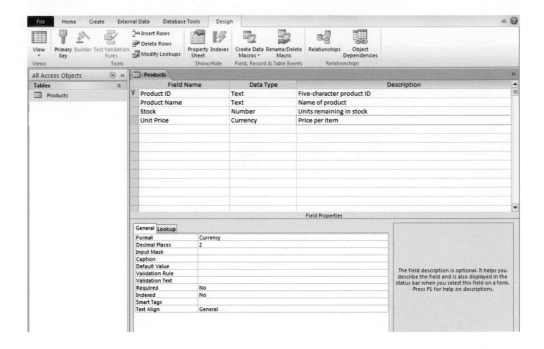

④ SELECT THE PRIMARY KEY FOR THE TABLE

   a. Click in the Product ID field.

   b. The Product ID field is the primary key for this table because each ID is unique. This field already displays 🔑 because Access automatically selects the first field as the primary key. If not, right-click the Product ID field and then select Primary Key.

   c. In the General tab, click the Required box and then select Yes from the list.

⑤ SAVE AND CLOSE THE TABLE

   a. On the Quick Access Toolbar, click Save 🖫.

   b. Close the Products table.

⑥ CREATE THE CUSTOMERS TABLE

   a. Click Create → Table Design. A new table is displayed in Design view.

   b. Create fields for the Customers table using the design below. Enter appropriate descriptions for each of the fields.

Customer ID	Text field, Field Size 5, primary key
Customer Name	Text field, Field Size 50
Address	Text field, Field Size 50
City	Text field, Field Size 25
State/Province	Text field, Field Size 2
ZIP/Postal Code	Text field, Field Size 10
Contact First Name	Text field, Field Size 20
Contact Last Name	Text field, Field Size 25
Contact E-mail	Hyperlink field
Telephone Number	Text field, Field Size 20

c. Click in the Customer ID field and then in the General tab, select Yes in the Required box. Save the table naming it Customers:

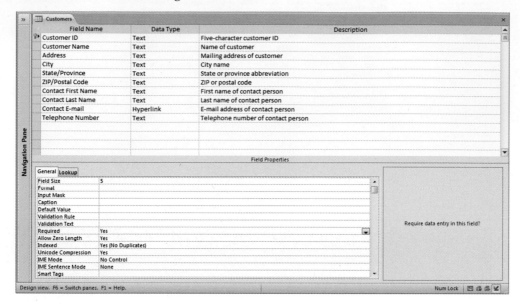

d. Close the Customers window.

⑦ **CREATE THE ORDERS TABLE**

a. Select Create → Table.

b. Create fields for the Orders table using the design below. Enter appropriate descriptions for each of the fields.

Order ID	AutoNumber field, Field Size Long Integer, primary key
Order Date	Date/Time field, Format Short Date
Customer ID	Text field, Field Size 5
Product ID	Text field, Field Size 5
Quantity	Number field, Field Size Long Integer, Format Fixed, 0 decimal places

c. Save the table naming it Orders.

Check – Your table should look similar to:

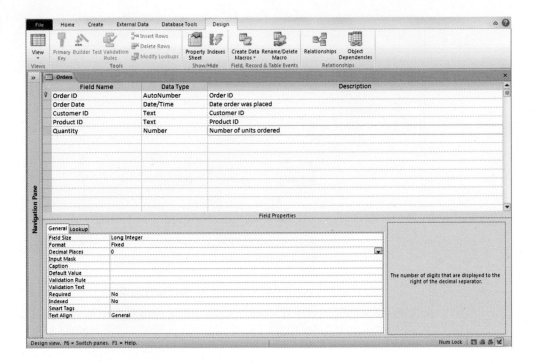

⑧ CREATE TWO LOOKUP FIELDS

The Customer ID and Product ID fields need to be lookup fields because they will store data for existing customers and products.

a. Click in the Customer ID Data Type and then click the arrow and select Lookup Wizard. A dialog box is displayed.

1. Verify the first option is selected:

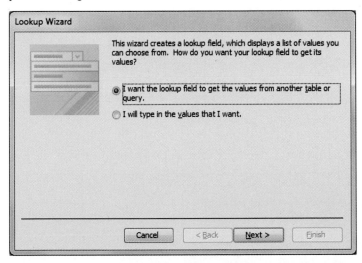

2. Select Next. The second Lookup Wizard dialog box is displayed.
3. Select Table: Customers:

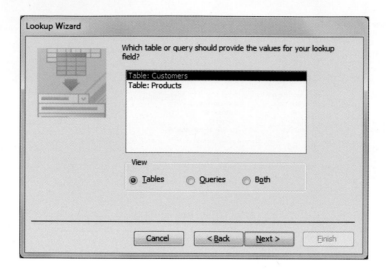

4. Select **Next**. The third Lookup Wizard dialog box is displayed.

5. With **Customer ID** selected in the **Available Fields** list, click [>] to move the field name to the **Selected Fields** list:

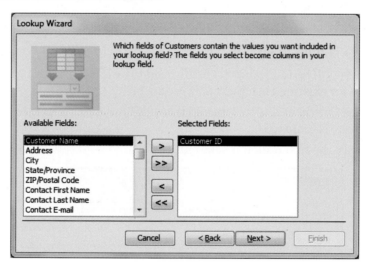

6. Select **Next**. The fourth Lookup Wizard dialog box is displayed.

7. In the first sort list, click the drop-down arrow and select **Customer ID**:

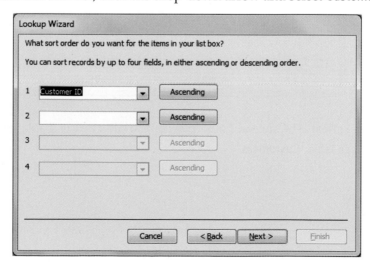

8. Select Next. The fifth Lookup Wizard dialog box is displayed:

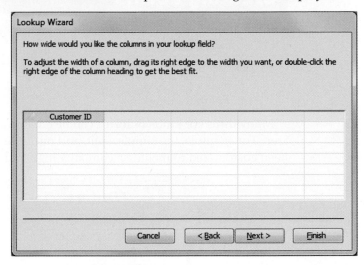

9. Select Next to accept the default size and display the last Lookup Wizard dialog box:

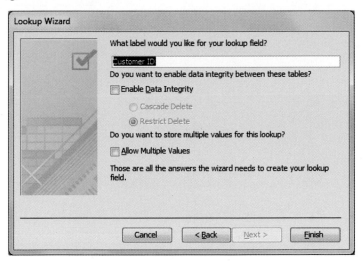

10. Select Finish to accept the default label name. A dialog box is displayed.

11. Select Yes.

b. Click in the Product ID Data Type and then click the arrow and select Lookup Wizard. Use the Lookup Wizard to create a field that looks up values in the Product ID field of the Products table. Select Yes to any warning dialog boxes.

c. Save and then close the Orders table.

⑨ USE THE NAVIGATION PANE

a. In the Navigation pane, click ▾. The Navigation pane menu is displayed.

b. Select Object Type, if not already selected.

c. From the Navigation pane menu, select All Access Objects. The Products table name is displayed under Tables.

Creating Forms

Form   More Forms

Many different kinds of forms can be created and each can be customized. For example, the simple, split, and multiple items forms below have been customized to include a company logo and formatted field names:

A simple form shows the data for one record

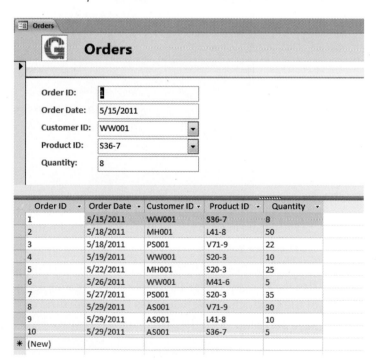

Order ID	Order Date	Customer ID	Product ID	Quantity
1	5/15/2011	WW001	S36-7	8
2	5/18/2011	MH001	L41-8	50
3	5/18/2011	PS001	V71-9	22
4	5/19/2011	WW001	S20-3	10
5	5/22/2011	MH001	S20-3	25
6	5/26/2011	WW001	M41-6	5
7	5/27/2011	PS001	S20-3	35
8	5/29/2011	AS001	V71-9	30
9	5/29/2011	AS001	L41-8	10
10	5/29/2011	AS001	S36-7	5
* (New)				

*A split form shows individual records and
the corresponding table*

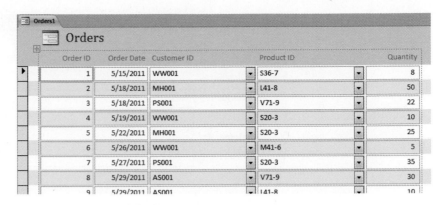

A multiple items form shows records in rows

A simple form displays a datasheet along with entry boxes when its table is related to one other table only. For example, the Products table is related to the Orders table, so its simple form will look similar to:

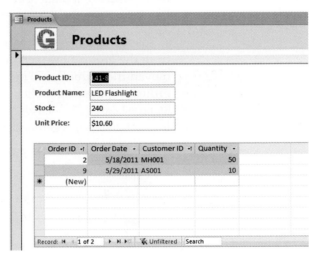

A simple form with a datasheet corresponding to each record

Note that for each product record, the related order records are shown below in a datasheet.

There can be numerous forms for a table, providing many options for entering and viewing data for a single table. To create a new form, select a table object from the Navigation pane and then click Create → Form 📇, Create → More Forms → Split Form 📰, or Create → More Forms → Multiple Items 📇. A new form based on the selected table is displayed in *Layout view* where it can be formatted. A new form with no formatting applied looks similar to:

Layout view

A new form in Layout view

Click an entry box and then drag its right border to change the size of all the entry boxes. Use the same process to size field names. Drag the right border of a datasheet to reduce or increase the extra space after the last field. Drag the datasheet ⊞ control to move the datasheet.

To individually size field names and entry boxes, they must be separated from the group. Once separated, field names and entry boxes can also be moved individually. To break apart a group, click the ⊞ control for the group and then right-click a field name or entry box and select Layout → Remove Layout. This leaves the control on the form, but removes the layout. It can then be dragged and formatted:

In Layout view, the Form Layout Tools Format and Design tabs are available:

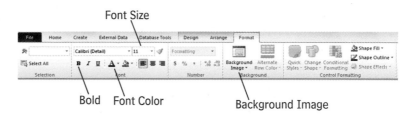

Format Layout Tools Fomat Tab

Format Layout Tools Design Tab

- Select an object and then apply character formats such as Bold **B**, Font `Calibri (Detail)`, Font Size `11`, and Font Color **A**.

- Click Background Image to add a background image to the form.

- Click Logo to add a graphic to the form.

- Click Date and Time 🖼 to add date and time objects that automatically update.

- Click Themes to display a drop-down gallery of available themes that can be applied a theme to the form.

Form view   When formatting is complete, click Design → View → Form View. *Form view* is where records are entered. Save the form to add the object to the database. To open a closed form, double-click the form name in the Navigation pane.

As a reminder of what kind of data a field stores, the status bar at the bottom of the Access window displays the description of the selected field. The field description is the text that was typed in the Description box for the field in Design view.

Practice: Align Sales – part 3 of 3

Access should already be started with Align Sales displayed from the last practice.

① **CREATE A NEW FORM**

   a. In the Navigation pane, click the Customers table to select it.

   b. Click Create → Form. A new form is displayed in Layout view. A datasheet is included because the Customers table is related to the Orders table by the Customer ID lookup field:

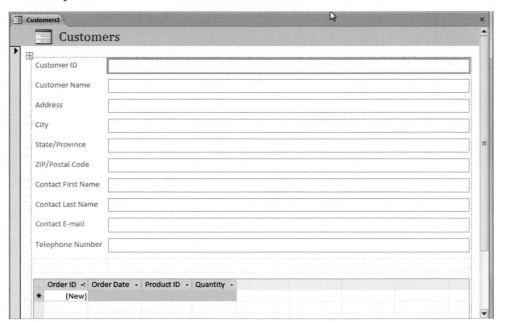

② **FORMAT THE FORM**

   a. On the Navigation pane, click « . The Pane is closed, which provides more room to format form objects.

   b. Click an entry box to select it.

   c. Drag the right border of the entry box to the left. All the entry box sizes are reduced. Size the entry boxes to handle the longest possible entry, similar to:

d. Click the first field name and then press and hold the Shift key while clicking the remaining field names. All the field names are selected.

e. Click Format → Bold **B**. The field names are bold.

f. Click the Customers title at the top the form and format it as bold.

g. Click Design → Logo. A dialog box is displayed.

    1. Navigate to ALIGN LOGO, which is a data file for this text.

    2. Select OK. The logo is added to the form. Drag a corner handle to size the logo.

h. Click Design → Themes → Austin.

Check — You form should look similar to:

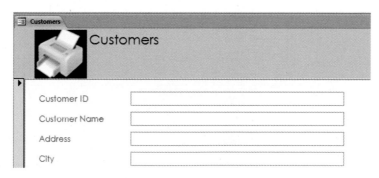

l. Save the form naming it: Customers

m. Click Home → View → Form View. The form is displayed in Form view.

n. Close the Customers form.

o. Close the Align Sales database.

Restricting Data Entry

The integrity, or reliability, of a database is as important as the database itself. Spelling errors, typos, and other mistakes in data entry will render a database untrustworthy. To help ensure accurate data, *validation rules* that check entries against specified values can be applied to a field.

A validation rule is applied to a field in Design view. For example, for a Cost field that should contain only values greater than 0, use the Validation Rule and Validation Text boxes to enter criteria and an error message:

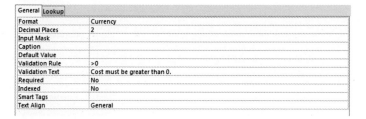

General Lookup	
Format	Currency
Decimal Places	2
Input Mask	
Caption	
Default Value	
Validation Rule	>0
Validation Text	Cost must be greater than 0.
Required	No
Indexed	No
Smart Tags	
Text Align	General

Once a validation rule is applied, field entries are restricted to values that adhere to the rule. If an entry breaks the rule, it is cleared from the entry box and the validation text is displayed in a dialog box:

Validation rules for numeric entries are often formed with one or more *relational operator*:

relational operators

<	less than
>	greater than
<=	less than or equal to
>=	greater than or equal to
<>	not equal to

If an entry does not make the validation rule true, then an error dialog box is displayed.

Validation rules can also contain logical operators. *Logical operators* form a compound expression. For example, if the cost of an item must be more than 0, but less than 10, the validation rule >0 And <10 will restrict entries to values between 0 and 10. Logical operators include:

And	requires an entry to match both criteria
Or	requires an entry to match one criteria
Not	requires an entry not match the criteria

If the possible entries for a Text field can be limited to a set of values, then a validation rule should be applied to the field. When a validation rule is applied to a Text field, only the specified values will be allowed. For example, for a Color field that should contain only green, blue, or yellow, use the validation rule "green" Or "blue" Or "yellow".

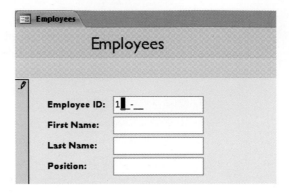

If a database is already populated, select Design → Test Validation Rules to verify that the existing data meets the validation rules.

Text and Date/Time field entries can be restricted by using an input mask. An *input mask* controls how data is entered and is useful when entries should follow a certain format. For example, an Employee ID field that requires an entry similar to 123–45, could use an input mask to show placeholder characters and a hyphen and require that five digits be entered:

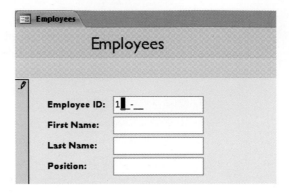

Each underscore must be replaced with a digit

Access has several existing input masks already defined. In Design view, select a field to receive a mask and then click ⊡ in the Input Mask box in the General tab to start the Input Mask Wizard:

To use an existing mask, select the mask name and then click Next. The second Wizard dialog box displays options to customize the mask.

To add a new input mask, select Edit List and then click New (blank) record ⊡. Type a name in the Description box, placeholders in the Input Mask box, a placeholder character in the Placeholder box, and an example in the Sample Data box:

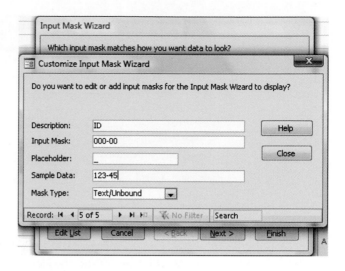

mask characters   Digits 0 and 9 are two commonly used placeholders, also called *mask characters*. A 0 means that a digit must be typed for that place. A 9 means that a digit is optional. Literal characters, such as a hyphen (-), are used along with the mask characters to force the entry to follow a certain format. During data entry, the placeholder character is displayed in the field. The underscore character (_) is a commonly used placeholder character.

Practice: MILLA HARDWARE – part 1 of 8

① OPEN A DATABASE

   a. Start Access.

   b. Open MILLA HARDWARE, an Access data file for this text. The database contains tables that represent the Milla Hardware products, departments, and employees.

② CREATE AN INPUT MASK

   a. Display the Employees table in Datasheet view. Note the variation in the way the Employee ID numbers have been entered. The ID should consist of three digits followed by a hyphen and then two more digits, in the form 123-45.

   b. Display the Employee table in Design view.

   c. Select the Employee ID field, click the Input Mask box in the General tab, and then click ⊡ in the Input Mask box. A dialog box appears.

   d. Select Edit List. A dialog box is displayed:

      1. Click New (blank) record ▶. A blank input mask record is displayed.

      2. Create an input mask as shown below. The placeholder 0 is used because each of the digits is required:

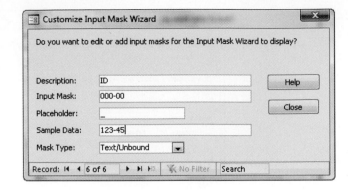

3. Select **Close**. The new input mask has been added to the list.

e. Select **ID** and then **Next**. A second Wizard dialog box is displayed.

f. Verify that the Input Mask is 000-00 and the Placeholder character is _ and then select **Finish**. Note the mask in the Input Mask box.

g. Save the modified Employees table and then display the table in Datasheet view. Note that the IDs are displayed using the input mask format.

③ **CREATE A VALIDATION RULE**

a. Display the Employees table in Design view.

b. Select the Position field and then click the **Validation Rule** box in the **General** tab.

c. Type: "Manager" Or "Associate" Or "Stocker"

d. In the **Validation Text** box, type: Enter a valid position name.

Check — Your **General** tab should look similar to:

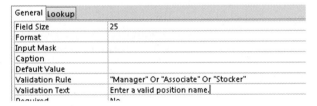

④ **TEST THE VALIDATION RULE**

a. Click **Design → Test Validation Rules**. A dialog box is displayed.

1. Select **Yes**. A second dialog box appears.

2. Select **Yes**. The modified Employees table is saved and the data is checked. A third dialog box is displayed.

3. The third dialog box should report that all data was valid for all rules. Select **OK** to remove the dialog box. (If the dialog box reported problems with the data, double-check the validation rule and then run the check again.)

⑤ **ADD AN EMPLOYEE RECORD**

a. Close the Employees table.

b. In the Navigation pane, select the Employees table.

c. Click **Create → Form**. A new form is displayed.

d. Bold the field names, select the logo and then press the Delete key to remove the logo, size the entry boxes appropriately, and then apply the Solstice predefined format.

Check — Your form should look similar to:

e. Save the form naming it Employees and then display the form in Form view.

f. Display a new record.

g. Place the insertion point in the Employee ID field.

h. Type 549 and note that the insertion point automatically moves past the hyphen.

i Type 23 for the remaining part of the Employee ID.

j. Enter Rene for the First Name field and Lamprey for the Last Name field.

k. In the Position field, type Assoc. and then press the Tab key. A dialog box displays the validation text entered in the Design view. Select OK.

l. In the Position field, enter Associate.

m. Close the Employees form.

⑥ APPLY AN EXISTING INPUT MASK

a. Display the Departments table in Design view.

b. Select the Extension field, click the Input Mask box, and then click ⊡. A dialog box is displayed.

1. Select Extension:

2. Click Next. A second Wizard dialog box is displayed.

3. Modify the Input Mask to require three digits:

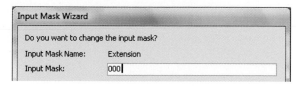

    4. Click Finish. The dialog box is removed and the mask is applied to the field.

  c. Select the Manager ID and then apply the ID input mask to the field.

  d. Save the modified Departments table and then close the table.

  e. Create a Departments form similar in format to the Employees table. You may need to close the Navigation pane to format the form.

⑦ **CREATE VALIDATION RULES FOR THE PRODUCTS TABLE**

  a. Display the Products table in Design view.

  b. For the Cost field, create the validation rule >0 and the validation text Cost must be greater than 0.

  c. For the Price field, create the validation rule >0 and the validation text Price must be greater than 0.

  d. Test the validation rules. The existing data meets all validation rules.

  e. Close the Products table.

  f. Create a Products form similar in format to the Employees table.

⑧ **ADD THREE PRODUCTS RECORDS**

  a. Display the Products form in Form view and add the following three records:

    LED Flashlight; Electrical; 10.60; 14.99

    Solar Charger; Electrical; 23.65; 44.95

    USB Mug Warmer; Housewares; 3.25; 9.95

  b. Close the Products form.

Table Relationships

Relationships

In a relational database, two tables are *related* when a field in one table corresponds to a field in another table. Every table in a relational database is related to at least one other table in the database. The related fields must have the same data type, but are not required to have the same name. To join and analyze data from multiple tables, table relationships must first be defined.

To view relationships, click **Database Tools** ➝ **Relationships**. The Relationships window opens and the **Design** tab is added to the Ribbon:

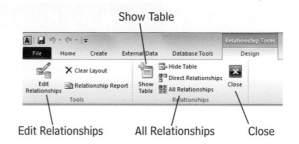

Show Table

Edit Relationships   All Relationships   Close

- Click **Show Table** to display a dialog box for adding tables to the Relationship window. If relationships have not yet been defined for a database, then the Show Tables dialog box automatically appears.

- Click **Edit Relationships** to display a dialog box for modifying a relationship between two tables.

- Click **All Relationships** ⊞ to display existing relationships.

- Click **Close** to remove the Relationships window.

To create a relationship, add tables to the Relationship window and then drag a field from one table to a related field in another table. The Edit Relationships dialog box is displayed. Verify the related fields in the dialog box and then select **Create**. Lines indicate the relationships between tables:

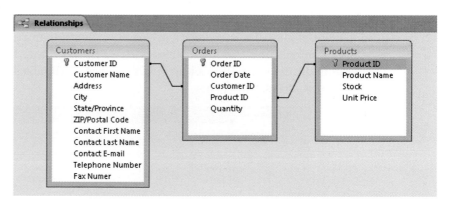

Relationships for the Gadgets Sales database

foreign key

The primary key in one table and the foreign key in another table are used to define a relationship. A *foreign key* is a field in a table that is a primary key in another table. For example, in the Gadgets Sales database, Product ID is the primary key in the Products table and a foreign key in the Orders table. Relationships formed this way are *one-to-many* which means that there is one and only one record in the primary key table that relates to zero, one, or more records in the related table. In a relational database, tables must form one-to-many relationships.

one-to-many relationship

lookup fields

A database with lookup fields will already have one or more relationships defined because Access automatically defines a relationship between the table containing the lookup field and the table containing the data used by the lookup field. The Gadgets Sales database has defined relationships, as indicated by lines connecting related fields.

deleting a relationship

To delete a relationship, click the line that connects the two tables and then press the Delete key.

Viewing Related Records

subdatasheet

Datasheet view includes *subdatasheets* of related records when relationships have been defined. A ⊞ next to records in a datasheet indicate subdatasheets are available. Click ⊞ to expand the subdatasheet for a record:

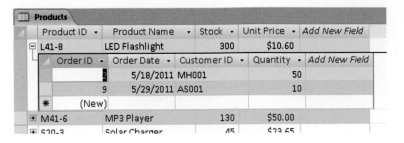

The subdatasheet shows the LED Flashlight orders because of the one-to-many relationship with the Orders table. A ⊞ changes to ⊟ when a subdatasheet is displayed. Click ⊟ to hide the subdatasheet.

Practice: MILLA HARDWARE – part 2 of 8

Access should already be started with MILLA HARDWARE displayed from the last practice.

① CREATE A RELATIONSHIP

a. Click Database Tools → Relationships. The Relationships window displays the Departments and Products tables with a line indicating the relationship formed automatically when the lookup field was created. (If tables are not displayed, click Design → All Relationships):

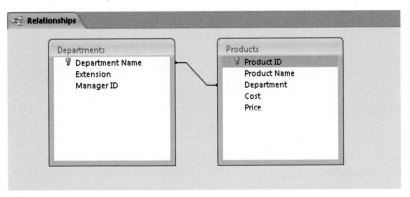

b. Click Design → Show Table. The Show Table dialog box is displayed.
   1. Click Employees and then select Add. The Employees table is added to the window.
   2. Select Close. The dialog box is removed.

c. Note the Employee ID is the primary key in the Employees table and the Manager ID is the corresponding foreign key in the Departments table. In this case, the related fields do not have the same name.

d. In the Departments table, drag the Manager ID field to the Employee ID field in the Employee table. The Edit Relationships dialog box is displayed:

e. Verify the table names and note that the Relationship Type is One-To-Many and then select Create. A line shows the relationship.

f. Save the modified MILLA HARDWARE database and then click Design → Close.

② **VIEW A SUBDATASHEET**

a. Display the Departments table. Note that each record displays a ⊞.

b. Next to the first record, click ⊞. A subdatasheet expands with items from this department.

c. Display another subdatasheet.

d. Next to each subdatasheet, click ⊓ to close the subdatasheets.

e. Close the Departments table.

③ **CLOSE MILLA HARDWARE**

The Select Query

Query Design

TIP A query is a question. Running a select query answers a question.

A *select query* is a database object that is used to retrieve, or "select," data that matches specified criteria. A select query can include any number of fields from related tables in a database. Access uses the relationships to determine how to join the data from the selected tables. The results are displayed in Datasheet view. For example, the following query selected the product name (from the Products table), the customer name (from the Customers table) and the quantities ordered (from the Orders table) from records where product name is Solar Charger:

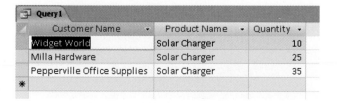

Customer Name	Product Name	Quantity
Widget World	Solar Charger	10
Milla Hardware	Solar Charger	25
Pepperville Office Supplies	Solar Charger	35

To create a select query, click **Create → Query Design**. A Query window appears and the Show Table dialog box is displayed. Select a table name from the dialog box and then select **Add** to add it to the Query window. Repeat this for every table with fields needed by the query and then select **Close** to the remove the dialog box. The tables are displayed in the Query window and the **Design** tab is added to the Ribbon.

The *design grid* is then used to specify fields and criteria:

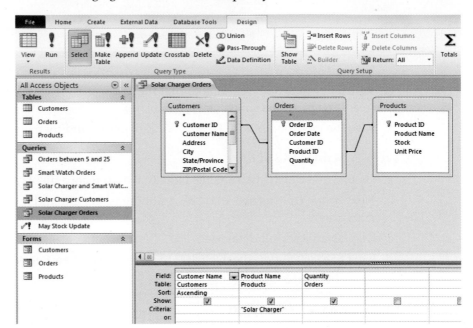

TIP To run an existing select query, double-click the query name in the Navigation pane.

TIP Access automatically encloses text criteria with quotation marks (" ") and dates with #.

After defining the select query, click **Design → Run** to display the select query datasheet.

Practice: Gadgets Sales – part 8 of 12

Access should already be started.

① **OPEN GADGETS SALES**

Open Gadgets Sales, the database created in the practices in Chapter 9.

② **ADD TABLES TO THE QUERY WINDOW**

a. Click **Create → Query Design**. A Query window appears and the Show Table dialog box is displayed:

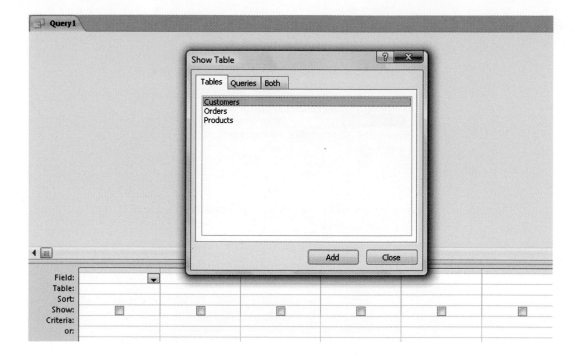

b. Click **Customers** if it is not already selected and then select **Add**. The Customers table is added to the Query window.

c. Add the **Orders** table to the Query window.

d. Add the **Products** table to the Query window.

e. Select **Close**. The Show Table dialog box is removed.

③ **ADD FIELDS TO THE DESIGN GRID**

a. Drag the Customer Name field from the Customers table to the first Field box in the design grid.

b. In the Products table, double-click the Product Name field. The Product Name field is added to the second Field box.

c. Add the Quantity field from the Orders table to the third Field box. The design grid should look similar to:

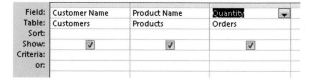

④ **SPECIFY CRITERIA AND A SORT ORDER**

a. In the Product Name **Criteria** box, type: Solar Charger

b. Click in the first **Sort** box and then click the arrow and select **Ascending**:

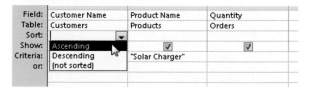

a. Click Design → Run. The database is queried and the results shown in Datasheet view. Three records are displayed:

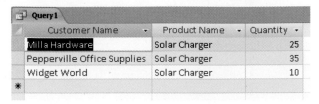

b. On the Quick Access Toolbar, click 🔲. A dialog box is displayed. In the Query Name box, type: Solar Charger Orders

c. Select OK. The query is saved and the query object appears in the Navigation pane.

d. Close the query.

Modifying a Select Query

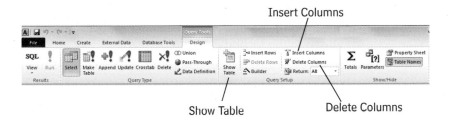

Modifications to a query can include adding or removing fields, changing a sort order, or changing the order of fields in the design grid. A select query is modified in Design view. To switch a displayed query in Datasheet view to Design view, click Home → View → Design View.

To add a field to the design grid, drag the field from the table in the Query window to the design grid. If the field should appear between two existing fields, then place the insertion point in the column where the new field should appear and then click Design → Insert Columns. A new column is added and existing columns are moved to the right. If the Query window does not contain the table with the new field, click Design → Show Table.

Delete a field from the query by deleting the appropriate column from the design grid. To do this, place the insertion point in the column to be deleted and then click Design → Delete Columns. If after removing fields a table is no longer needed, then it should be deleted from the Query window. Click the table to select it and then press the Delete key.

TIP When a new query is similar to an existing query, modify the existing query and then use the Save Object As command to give it a different name.

TIP Delete a query by selecting its name in the Navigation pane and then pressing the Delete key.

Access should already be started with Gadgets Sales displayed from the last practice.

① **DISPLAY THE SOLAR CHARGER ORDERS QUERY IN DESIGN VIEW**

    a. In the Navigation pane, double-click the Solar Charger Orders query to open it. The query is run and the datasheet displayed.

    b. Click Home → View → Design View. The query is displayed in Design view.

② **CREATE A SMART WATCH ORDERS SELECT QUERY**

    a. Change the Product Name criteria to: Smart Watch

    b. Click Design → Run. The database is queried and the results shown in Datasheet view. Two records are displayed:

    c. Select ▇File▇ → Save Object As. A dialog box is displayed. Type Smart Watch Orders as the new query name:

    d. Select OK. The new query object appears in the Navigation pane.

    e. Print the query.

    f. Close the query.

Range Queries

A select query with criteria that matches a range of values is called a *range query*. Range query criteria is specified using the relational operators <, >, <=, >=, and <>. For example, the following query selects the order date (from the Orders table) and the product name (from the Products table) where order date is after 5/16/11:

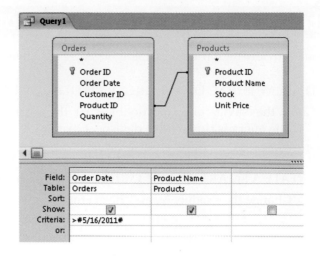

When a range query compares text, alphabetical order is used to determine which data matches the criteria. For example, to query for customers with names that come before the letter M, use the criteria <M in the Customer Name field.

Practice: Gadgets Sales – part 10 of 12

Access should already be started with Gadgets Sales displayed from the last practice.

① **CREATE AN ORDERS AFTER 5/16/11 SELECT QUERY**

    a. Click **Create → Query Design**. A Query window appears and the Show Table dialog box is displayed.

    b. Add the **Orders** and **Products** tables to the Query window and then close the dialog box.

    c. Add the Order Date field and Product Name fields to the design grid.

    d. In the Order Date **Criteria** box, type: >5/16/11

    e. In the Order Date **Sort** list, select **Ascending**:

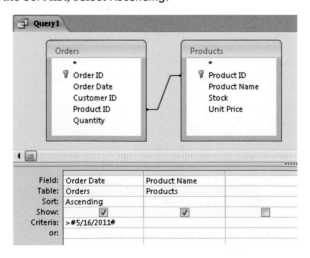

② RUN THE SELECT QUERY

a. Run the query. The database is queried and the results displayed:

b. Save the query naming it: Orders after 5/16/11

c. Check your query results:

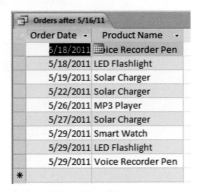

d. Close the query.

Complex Queries

A select query with multiple criteria is called a *complex query*. Complex query criteria is specified using the And and Or logical operators. For example, the following query selects the product name (from the Products table) and the order date (from the Orders table) where product name is Solar Charger And order date is after 5/16/11:

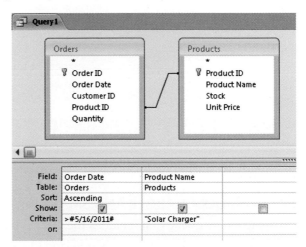

In the query above, the And operator is implied because the criteria is specified in the same row. A complex query with both criteria in the same field requires the And operator to be typed. For example, the following query selects the product name (from the Products table) and the order date (from the Orders table) where order date is after 5/16/11 And order date is before 5/30/11:

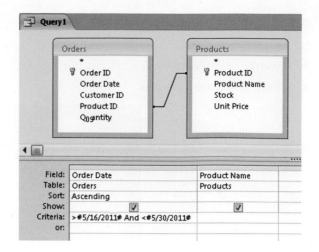

Complex queries using Or are created by using the or row of the design grid. For example, the following query selects the product name (from the Products table), the order date (from the Orders table), and the quantity (from the Orders table) where product name is Solar Charger Or product name is Smart Watch:

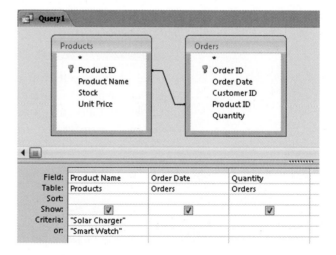

Practice: Gadgets Sales – part 11 of 12

Access should already be started with Gadgets Sales displayed from the last practice.

① **DISPLAY SOLAR CHARGER AND SMART WATCH ORDERS**
   a. Create a new query that includes the Orders table and the Products table.
   b. Add the Order Date, Product Name, and Quantity fields to the design grid.
   c. In the Order Date Sort list, select Ascending.
   d. In the Product Name Criteria box, type: Solar Charger
   e. In the Product Name or row, type: Smart Watch

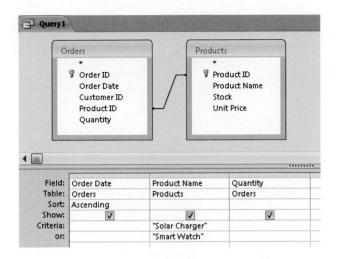

f. Run the query. Save the query naming it: Solar Charger and Smart Watch Orders.

Check your results:

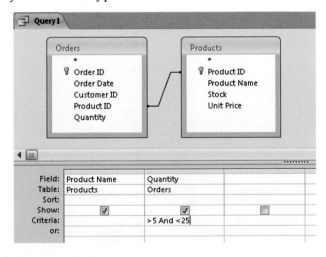

g. Close the query.

② **DISPLAY ORDERS FOR QUANTITIES BETWEEN 5 AND 25**

a. Create a new query that includes the Orders table and the Products table.

b. Add the Product Name and Quantity fields to the design grid.

c. In the Quantity **Criteria** box, type: >5 And <25

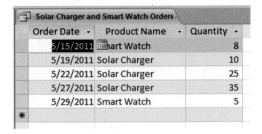

d. Run the query. The results are displayed:

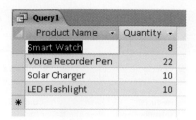

e. Save the query naming it: Orders between 5 and 25

f. Print the select query.

g. Close the query.

③ CLOSE GADGETS SALES

Using Wildcards in Query Criteria

A *wildcard* is a character that matches any one or more characters. The asterisk (*) and question mark (?) are two wildcards. The * wildcard matches any number of characters or no characters at all. For example, Brush* matches Brush, Brushless, and Brush Tray.

The ? wildcard matches any one character or no character at all. For example, Ann? matches Ann, Anne, and Anna, but not Annette.

TIP Wildcard matches are not case sensitive. For example, brush* matches Brushless.

Wildcards can be used to specify select query criteria. When wildcards are needed, use the Like operator to specify criteria. For example, the following query selects the product name (from the Products table) and the order date (from the Orders table) where product name is Like S*:

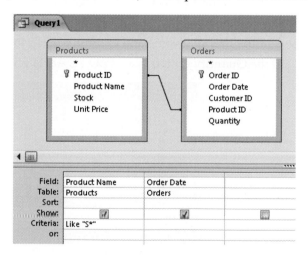

When run, the query displays:

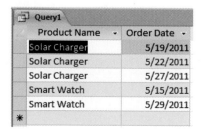

Access should already be started.

① **OPEN MILLA HARDWARE**

② **QUERY FOR BRUSH PRODUCTS**

    a. Create a select query in Design view.

    b. Add the Departments table and the Products table.

    c. From the Departments table, add the Department Name and Extension fields to the design grid.

    d. From the Products table, add the Product Name field.

    e. In the Department Name Sort list, select **Ascending**.

    f. In the Product Name **Criteria** box, type: Like *brush*

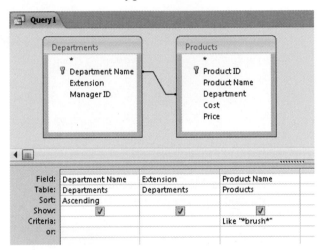

    g. Run the query. The database is queried and the results shown in a datasheet:

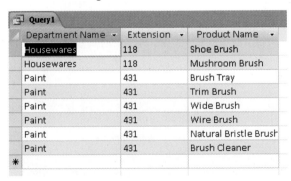

    h. Save the query naming it: Brush Items

    i. Preview and then print the select query.

    j. Close the query.

Using Fields in Query Criteria

A select query can specify another field in the criteria. For example, Milla Hardware uses their database to store prices. A select query could be used to display products with a 200% markup (a 200% markup equals three times the cost). For example, the following query selects the product (from the Products table) where price (from the Products table) is at least three times the cost (from the Products table):

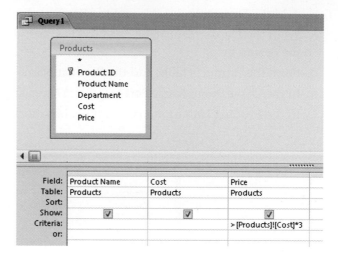

Use the format [Table Name]![Field Name] to refer to a field. If a field name is unique to the database, then the table name is not needed in the reference. However, the table must be in the Query window. When run, the 200% markup query displays:

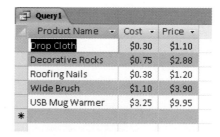

Practice: MILLA HARDWARE – part 4 of 8

Access should already be started and the MILLA HARDWARE database displayed.

① **QUERY FOR PRODUCTS WITH A MARKUP OVER 100%**

a. Create a select query in Design view.

b. Add the Products table.

c. Add the Product Name, Cost, and Price fields to the design grid.

d. In the Product Name Sort list, select Ascending.

e. In the Price Criteria box, type: >[Products]![Cost]*2

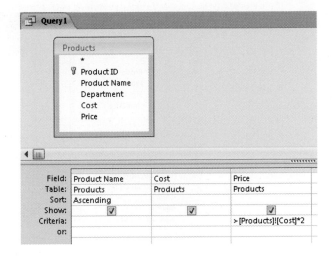

f. Run the query. The database is queried and the results displayed:

g. Save the query naming it: 100% Markup

h. Print and then close the query.

i. Close MILLA HARDWARE.

Parameter Query

A *parameter query* retrieves data that matches criteria, called a *parameter*, typed by the user when the query is run. A parameter query can include any of the fields from related tables in a database. For example, the following query selects the product name (from the Products table) and the order date (from the Orders table) where product name is what the user types when the query is run:

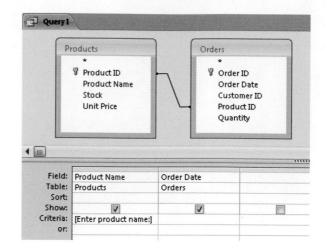

A parameter query requires a prompt enclosed by brackets in the Criteria box. Running the parameter query displays a dialog box with the prompt:

Type a value, for example, Voice Recorder Pen, and then select OK to complete the query:

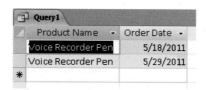

Practice: MILLA HARDWARE – part 5 of 8

Access should already be started.

① **CREATE A PARAMETER QUERY**

    a. Open MILLA HARDWARE.

    b. Create a select query in Design view.

    c. Add the Departments table and the Products table.

    d. Add the Department Name field and Product Name field to the design grid.

    e. In the Product Name Sort list, select Ascending.

    f. In the Department Name Criteria box, type: [Enter department name:]

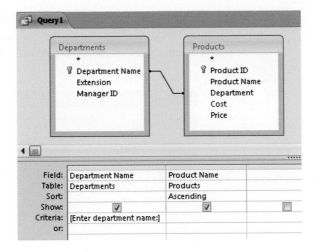

g. Run the query. A dialog box is displayed. Type: Garden

h. Select OK. The query results display the Garden department products:

i. Save the query naming it: Department Products
j. Close the query.

② **CLOSE THE MILLA HARDWARE DATABASE**

The Update Query

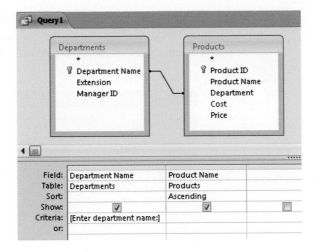

Update

An *update query* modifies, or updates, records. Criteria can be specified to limit which records are updated. If no criteria is specified, then all records containing the update field are modified. For example, the following query updates Stock (from the Products table) to Stock – Quantity (from the Orders table) where Date (from the Orders table) is in the month of May:

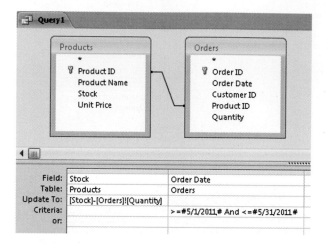

The relationship between the tables is used to match product names, and then the corresponding stock amount is decreased by the quantities ordered.

To create an update query, create a select query in Design view and then click Design → Update to add the Update To row to the design grid.

After defining the update query, run the query to update the records. A warning dialog box is displayed. Select Yes to update the records. An update query cannot be reversed after it is run.

Practice: Gadgets Sales – part 12 of 12

Access should already be started.

① OPEN THE GADGETS SALES DATABASE

    a. Open the Gadgets Sales database.

    b. Display the Products table. Note the Stock amounts shown. To make sure inventory is up to date, an update query can adjust stock amounts based on the quantities ordered.

    c. Close the Products table.

② CREATE AN UPDATE QUERY

    a. Create a select query in Design view.

    b. Add the Products and Orders tables.

    c. Click Design → Update. An Update To row is added to the design grid.

    d. Add the Stock field and the Order Date field to the design grid.

    e. In the Stock Update To row, type: [Stock]-[Quantity]

    f. In the Order Date Criteria box, type: >=5/1/2011 And <=5/31/2011

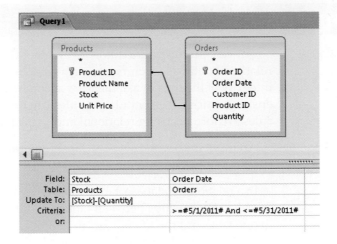

g. Run the query. A warning dialog box is displayed:

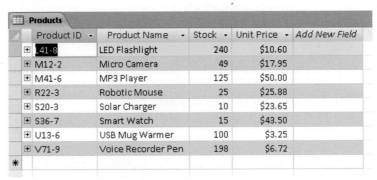

h. Select Yes. The query is executed, but the results are not automatically displayed.

i. Save the query naming it: May Stock Update

j. Close the query.

k. Display the Products table. The stock amounts have decreased:

Product ID	Product Name	Stock	Unit Price	Add New Field
L41-8	LED Flashlight	240	$10.60	
M12-2	Micro Camera	49	$17.95	
M41-6	MP3 Player	125	$50.00	
R22-3	Robotic Mouse	25	$25.88	
S20-3	Solar Charger	10	$23.65	
S36-7	Smart Watch	15	$43.50	
U13-6	USB Mug Warmer	100	$3.25	
V71-9	Voice Recorder Pen	198	$6.72	

l. Print and then close the query.

③ **CLOSE THE GADGETS SALES DATABASE**

④ **QUIT ACCESS**

This chapter explained how to create a database and also discussed relational database techniques such as data validation and queries. The integrity of the data in a database is as important as the database itself. To ensure accurate data, validation rules can be applied to fields. Validation rules are formed using relational and logical operators.

An input mask controls how data is entered and is useful when entries should follow a certain format.

In a relational database, tables must form one-to-many relationships. To do this, relationships between tables are defined using the primary key in one table and the foreign key in another table. A database with lookup fields will already have relationships defined. The **Database Tools** tab is used to define relationships. After relationships have been defined, sub-datasheets are available in a table. A subdatasheet shows corresponding records from a related table.

A select query can include any number of fields from related tables and uses relationships to determine how to join the data. The **Create** tab is used to create and run a select query. Criteria and a sort order may be specified in a select query. Select query results are displayed in Datasheet view.

A select query is modified in Design view. Tables and fields can be removed and added. The **Save As** command is used to create a query that is similar to an existing query.

A range query has criteria that matches a range of values. Relational operators are used in the criteria expression. Complex queries have multiple criteria, which are specified using logical operators. The And operator may be implied in the design grid for some complex queries. The **or** row in the design grid is used for complex queries involving Or.

Wildcards include the * and ? characters, and are specified in criteria to match any one or more characters. The Like operator is used to specify criteria with wildcards.

Select queries can include fields in their criteria by using the format [Table Name]![Field Name] to refer to a field. Parameter queries prompt the user for criteria data. Update queries change data in multiple records at once. The **Design** is needed to create an update query.

Vocabulary

Asterisk (*) A wildcard character that matches any number of characters or no character at all.

Column selector The gray box at the top of a field in the design grid of a Select Query window.

Complex query A select query with multiple criteria.

Currency field A field that stores dollar amounts.

Date/Time field A field that stores a date or time.

Design grid The part of the Query window used to specify fields and criteria.

Design view The table view that shows the field definitions for a table.

Foreign Key A field in a table that is a primary key in another table.

General number A field format that displays a number exactly as typed.

Hyperlink field A field that stores a link to a file, e-mail address, or Web site address.

Input mask Controls how data is entered and is useful when entries should follow a certain format.

Like Operator used to specify criteria that uses wildcards.

Logical operators Used to form a compound expression for a validation rule or criteria in a select query. Operators include And, Or, and Not.

Long form A date/time format that displays data in a form similar to Friday, May 5, 2009 or 10:12:30 AM.

Long Integer A field size that indicates a whole number.

Lookup field A field that stores data retrieved from a field in another table.

Medium form A date/time format that displays data in a form similar to 24-June-09 or 10:12 AM.

Mail merge The process of integrating data in an Access database with a Word document.

Mask characters The placeholders in an input mask.

Memo field A field that stores several lines of text.

Merge fields Placeholders in a Word document for data from an Access table or query.

One-to-many relationship The relationship between two tables when there is one and only one record in the primary key table that relates to zero, one, or more records in the related table.

Parameter A value used in a parameter query.

Parameter query A select query that retrieves data based on criteria typed by the user when the query is run.

Question mark (?) A wildcard character that matches any one character or no character at all.

Range query A select query with criteria that matches a range of values.

Related Two tables in a relational database with corresponding fields.

Relational operators Used to form a validation rule or specify criteria in a range query. Operators include <, >, <=, >=, and <>.

Select query A database object that retrieves data that matches specified criteria.

Subdatasheet A datasheet of related records.

Text field A field that stores characters (letters, symbols, words, a combination of letters and numbers) and numbers that do not require calculations.

Type Field classification based on the data stored.

Update query A query that modifies records based on criteria.

Validation rule Checks entries against specified values for a field.

Wildcard A character used in criteria that matches any one or more characters. Wildcard characters include * and ?.

Yes/No field A field that is either selected or not selected to represent yes/no, true/false, or on/off.

⊞   Displays a subdatasheet. Found in a table after relationships have been defined.

⊟   Hides a subdatasheet. Found in a table after relationships have been defined.

Address Block   Displays a dialog box for generating an AddressBlock merge field. Found on the Word Mailings tab.

All Relationships ▦ Displays existing relationships in the Relationships window. Found on the Design tab.

Close   Closes the Relationships window. Found on the Design tab.

Delete Columns   Deletes a column and its contents from the design grid. Found on the Design tab.

Design View   Displays a query in Design view. Found in Home → View.

Insert Columns Inserts a new column in the query design grid. Found on the Design tab.

Logo   Adds a graphic to a form. Found on the Format tab.

Multiple Items Creates a form that shows records in rows. Found in Create → More Forms.

Query Design Displays the Query window with a design grid. Found on the Create tab.

Relationships Displays the Relationships window. Found on the Database Tools tab.

Run   Executes a query. Found on the Design tab.

Save As   Displays a dialog box used for duplicating a query. Found in Backstage view.

Show Table   Displays a dialog box in the Relationships window. Found on the Design tab.

Split Form Creates a form that shows individual records and a corresponding table. Found in Create → More Forms.

Table Design   Creates a new table in Design view. Found on the Create tab

Test Validation Rules   Verifies that existing data meets validation rules. Found on the Design tab.

Update   Adds the Update To row to the design grid in the Query window. Found on the Design tab.

1. Explain how validation rules can help maintain the integrity of a database.

2. Explain the difference between a validation rule and an input mask.

3. List the relational operators and logical operators that can be used to form a validation rule.

4. Can validation rules be applied to a database that already contains data? If so, what should be done to ensure that existing data meets the validation rules?

5. a) Why is an input mask useful?
   b) What are placeholders?
   c) What are two digits commonly used for placeholders?
   d) What is the difference between placeholders and placeholder characters?

6. What types of fields are used to form a relationship between tables?

7. What is a foreign key?

8. Explain a one-to-many relationship.

9. Will the relationship between two tables need to be defined if one of the tables contains a lookup field and the other table contains the data used by the lookup field?

10. a) What is a subdatasheet?
    b) When is a subdatasheet available?
    c) How is a subdatasheet viewed?
    d) How is a displayed subdatasheet removed from view?

11. a) What is a select query?
    b) What is the design grid?

12. Compare and contrast filters (from Chapter 9) and select queries.

13. a) List the steps required to create and run a select query.
    b) How is an existing query run?

14. Consider the Gadgets Sales database. The stock manager needs to know which items have less than 50 in stock.

   a) Which fields should be used in the query?
   b) Which tables store the fields?
   c) What is the criteria expression?

15. In Design view, can a field be added between existing fields in the design grid of a select query? If so, how?

16. List the steps required to delete a column from the design grid of a select query.

17. A query similar to an existing query is needed. What is the most efficient approach to creating the new query? Explain.

18. a) What is a range query?
    b) What kind of operators are used to create the criteria for a range query.

19. How can the And operator be implied in the criteria of a complex query?

20. What is the or row of a select query design grid used for? How is this different from criteria involving And?

21. List two criteria wildcards that can be used in a select query and explain when each would be used.

22. What does the Like operator in the design grid of a select query indicate?

23. How would a reference to the Grade field in the Student table be typed as criteria?

True/False

24. Determine if each of the following are true or false. If false, explain why.
    a) Validation rules can help preserve the integrity of a database.
    b) When used in a validation rule, the And logical operator requires an entry to match one criteria or another, but not both.
    c) When used in a validation rule, the Or logical operator requires an entry to match one criteria or another or both.
    d) An input mask is used for restricting entries in numeric fields.
    e) A table does not need to be related to any other table in a relational database.
    f) A foreign key is never used to define a relationship between two tables.
    g) A one-to-many relationship means that there are many records in the key table that match many records in the related table.
    h) Tables in a relational database must form one-to-many relationships.
    i) Subdatasheets are available before relationships are defined.
    j) A select query limits the data displayed to that which meets certain criteria.
    k) The > relational operator is used to specify criteria that is greater than a particular value.
    l) In a select query, the And operator requires a record to match both criteria in order to be displayed.
    m) In a select query, the Or operator requires that a record not match any criteria in order to be displayed.
    n) The ? wildcard matches any number of characters.
    o) A parameter query displays a dialog box at run time so that criteria can be varied.
    p) An update query cannot be reversed after it is run.

Designing Queries

25. Access uses SQL (Structured Query Language) to query a database. From the Query window, click Design → View → SQL View to display the SQL associated with a select query. Because not everyone knows SQL, Access provides Design view as an easier, more visual way to create a select query.

    SQL statements have a specific format. For example, the SQL for a query for the order date of all LED flashlights looks like:
    SELECT Orders.[Order Date], Products. [Product Name]
    FROM Products INNER JOIN Orders ON Products.[Product ID] = Orders.[Product ID]
    WHERE (((Products.[Product Name])="LED Flashlight"));

    The SELECT part of the statement refers to the fields used in the query, and the FROM part refers to how the tables are joined. In this case, the records are joined when the product IDs are the same. The WHERE part of the statement refers to the criteria that the joined records must contain in order to be displayed.

    Run two existing queries for the Milla Hardware database and then switch to SQL view. For each query do the following:

    a) List the tables used in the SELECT.
    b) List the join used in the FROM.
    c) List the criteria in the WHERE.
    d) If there is an additional clause to the SELECT statement, list that clause and describe what it does.

Project 1

Travel... With a Purpose wants to use queries to analyze the data stored in its Museum Exhibits database, which was created in Chapter 9, Project 1. Open MUSEUM EXHIBITS and complete the following:

a) The Exhibits and Attendance tables are related by the Exhibit ID fields. Display the Relationships window and verify this relationship.

b) Create a select query that displays the Exhibit ID, Exhibit Name, Attendance, and Year Recorded fields of exhibits with an attendance over 1,500 in 2011. The query should sort the results in descending order by attendance. Save the select query naming it 2011 Attendance over 1,500. Print the query results.

c) Create a select query that displays the Exhibit Name, Updated, Attendance, and Year Recorded fields of exhibits with an attendance less than 1,500 in 2011 and last updated before 1/1/11. Save the select query naming it 2011 Attendance < 1,500 & Updated before 2011. Print the query results.

d) Create a select query that displays the Exhibit ID, Exhibit Name, Year Recorded, and Attendance fields. Specify criteria with the appropriate wildcard to display all the Exhibits with Exhibit IDs that begin WTH. Save the select query naming it Why Things Happen Exhibits. Print the query results.

Project 2

Study Time Tutoring wants to use queries to analyze the data stored in its Library database, which was created in Chapter 9, Project 2. Open LIBRARY and complete the following:

a) The Authors and Illustrators and Books tables are related by the ID fields. The Titles and Books tables are related by the ISBN fields. Display the Relationships window and define these relationships.

b) Create a select query that displays the Title, Subject, First Name, Last Name, Author, and Illustrator fields for all titles (no criteria needed). The query should sort the results in ascending order by title. Save the select query naming it All Titles. Print the query results.

c) Create a select query that displays the Title, ISBN, and Subject fields of fiction books. The query should sort the results in ascending order by title. Save the select query naming it Fiction Books. Print the query results.

d) Create a select query that displays the First Name, Last Name, and Illustrator fields. The criteria for a Yes/No field is specified as either True or False. Save the select query naming it Illustrators. Print the query results.

e) Create a select query that displays the Title, ISBN, First Name, Last Name, and Expanded Subjects fields. Specify the criteria with the appropriate wildcard to display all the poetry books. Save the select query naming it Poetry Books. Print the query results.

f) Create a parameter query that displays the Title, First Name, Last Name, Author, Illustrator, and ISBN fields. The query should prompt the user for the title. Save the select query naming it Search by Title. Run the query and enter Charlotte's Web.

Project 3

Yolanda's Catering wants to use queries to analyze the data stored in its CATERING database, which was created in Chapter 9, Project 3. Open CATERING and complete the following:

    a) The Employees and Payroll tables are related by the Employee ID fields. Display the Relationships window and verify this relationship.

    b) Create a select query that displays the First Name, Last Name, Check Date, Gross Pay, and Taxes fields of all payroll checks where gross pay is less than $250 and taxes are less than $30. Save the select query naming it Gross Pay < $250 & Tax < $30. Print the query results.

    c) Create a parameter query that displays the Employee ID, First Name, Last Name, Check Number, Check Date, Gross Pay, and Taxes fields. The query should prompt the user for the employee ID. Save the select query naming it Employee Payroll Lookup. Run the query and enter EI. Print the query results.

    d) Create a parameter query that displays the Employee ID, First Name, and Last Name fields. The query should prompt the user for the employee last name. Save the select query naming it Employee ID Lookup. Run the query and enter Warner. Print the query results.

Project 4

Sunport Boat Storage wants to use queries to analyze the data stored in its Boat Storage database, which was created in Chapter 9, Project 4. Open BOAT STORAGE and complete the following:

    a) Add appropriate input masks for the ZIP and Phone fields of the Employees and Boat Owners tables. To update the forms, delete the Employees and Boat Owners forms and create new ones in the same Metro predefined style.

    b) The minimum monthly fee is $45. Add data validation for the Fee field in the Boats table.

    c) Enter the following new Employee record:

        SB52; Shayla; Brooks; 912 Oak Street; Rostock; WA; 12241; (617) 555-3641

    d) Update the Boats record for the Viking 5 to store Employee ID SB52.

    e) The Boats and Boat Owners tables are related by the Owner ID fields. The Boats and Employees tables are related by the Employee ID fields. Display the Relationships window and verify these relationships.

    f) Create a select query that displays the Boat Name, Owner ID, First Name of owner, Last Name of owner, and Fee fields for those boats owned by Owner ID 2. Save the select query naming it Owner ID 2 Boats. Print the query results.

    g) Create a select query that displays the Boat Name, Fee, First Name of owner, and Last Name of owner fields of those boats with a monthly fee greater than or equal to $70. The query should sort the results in ascending order by the owner's last name. Save the select query naming it Fees >= $70. Print the query results.

    h) Create a select query that displays in ascending order by Slot Number the First Name of employee, Last Name of employee, Boat Name, and Slot Number fields of those boats stored in the first five slots. Save the select query naming it Slots 1 through 5. Print the query results.

i) Create a parameter query that displays the First Name of employee, Last Name of employee, Boat Name, and Slot Number fields. The query should prompt the user for the slotnumber. Save the select query naming it Slotnumber Lookup. Run the query and enter 16. Print the query results.

Project 5

The diamondback terrapin turtle is a threatened or an endangered species in parts of the eastern United States. In order to better track the population growth (or decline) of the diamondback terrapin turtle, researchers want to create a relational database to store their nest and hatchling data.

a) Create a relational database naming it Terrapin Research.

b) Create a Nests table for storing nest data:

Field Name	Data Type	Description	Size	Format
Nest Number 🔑	Number	Nest number of nest	Long Integer	
Nest Date	Date/Time	Date of initial observation		Short Date
Latitude	Text	Latitude using GPS	15	
Longitude	Text	Longitude using GPS	15	
Eggs	Number	Number of eggs in nest	Long Integer	
Hatch Date	Date/Time	Date of second observation		Short Date
Eggs Hatched	Number	Number of hatchlings	Long Integer	
Notes	Memo	Observations		

c) Create a Hatchlings table for storing data about the hatchlings:

Field Name	Data Type	Description	Size	Format	Decimals
Hatchling ID 🔑	AutoNumber	Hatchling ID	Long Integer		
Nest Number	Number	Hatchling nest number	Long Integer		
Date of Observation	Date/Time	Date of observation		Short Date	
CL	Number	Length of carapace (mm)	Single	Fixed	1
CW	Number	Width of carapace (mm)	Single	Fixed	1
PL	Number	Length of plastron (mm)	Single	Fixed	1
CH	Number	Height of carapace (mm)	Single	Fixed	1
Weight	Number	Weight of hatchling (g)	Single	Fixed	0

d) Create a multiple items form for the Nests table. Format the form appropriately and apply the Solstice style.

e) Enter the following ten Nests records. Since the Latitude and Longitude entries are so similar, data entry will be faster if the entries are copied and pasted from one record to another and then edited:

1; 6/11/11; 39 59 44.99 N; 74 04 30.13 W; 13; 9/4/11; 0; All desiccated

2; 6/11/11; 39 59 45.13 N; 74 04 30.57 W; 12; 9/4/11; 5; Five undeveloped

3; 6/11/11; 39 59 45.22 N; 74 04 30.68 W; 1; 9/4/11; 0; One undeveloped

4; 6/11/11; 39 59 44.57 N; 74 04 30.01 W; 6; 9/4/11; 1; One undeveloped

5; 6/11/11; 39 59 45.48 N; 74 04 30.98 W; 2; 9/4/11; 0; Two desiccated

6; 6/11/11; 39 59 45.36 N; 74 04 30.21 W; 13; 9/4/11; 10; Two unhatched

7; 6/11/11; 39 59 45.80 N; 74 04 30.79 W; 2; 9/4/11; 0; One desiccated

8; 6/11/11; 39 59 45.64 N; 74 04 30.01 W; 13; 9/4/11; 6; Six undeveloped

9; 6/11/11; 39 59 45.90 N; 74 04 30.10 W; 9; 9/4/11; 6; One desiccated

10; 6/11/11; 39 59 45.02 N; 74 04 30.80 W; 15; 9/4/09; 6; Six undeveloped, one broken

f) Create a simple form for the Hatchlings table. Format the form appropriately and apply the Solstice style.

g) Hatchling data was recorded using a spreadsheet. Import HATCHLING DATA, which is an Excel data file for this text, into the Hatchlings table.

h) Format each of the table datasheets appropriately.

i) Print preview and then print both tables using the appropriate orientation.

Project 6

A summer camp facility needs a database to coordinate counselors, cabins, activities, and campers.

a) Create a relational database naming it Summer Camp.

b) Create a Counselors table for storing counselor information:

Field Name	Data Type	Description	Size
Counselor ID 🔑	Text	ID of counselor	4
First Name	Text	First name of counselor	15
Last Name	Text	Last name of counselor	30

c) Create a Cabins table for storing data cabin assignment:

Field Name	Data Type	Description	Size
Cabin Name 🔑	Text	Name of cabin	30
Counselor ID	Text	ID of counselor assigned to cabin	4
Bunks	Number	Camper capacity of cabin	Long Integer

d) Create an Activities table storing activity information:

Field Name	Data Type	Description	Size
Activity Name 🔑	Text	Name of activity	20
Counselor ID	Text	ID of counselor running activity	4
Location	Text	Location of activity	20
Minimum Age	Number	Required camper minimum age	Long Integer

e) Modify the Activities table so that the Counselor ID field is a lookup field that looks up values in the Counselor ID field of the Counselors table.

f) Create a Campers table storing camper data:

Field Name	Data Type	Description	Size
Camper ID 🔑	Text	ID of camper	4
First Name	Text	First name of camper	20
Last Name	Text	Last name of camper	30
Age	Number	Age of camper	Long Integer
Cabin Name	Text	Cabin assignment	30

g) Modify the Campers table so that the Cabin Name field is a lookup field that looks up values in the Cabin Name field of the Cabins table.

h) Create a Schedules table for storing activity schedules:

Field Name	Data Type	Description	Size
Camper ID 🔑	Text	ID of camper	4

| Day 🔑 | Number | Activity day | Long Integer |
| Activity Name | Text | Name of activity | 20 |

The Camper ID and Day fields are a multiple-field primary key because there can only be one record for a camper on a specific day.

i) Modify the Schedules table so that the Camper ID field is a lookup field that looks up values in the Camper ID field of the Campers table.

j) The campers can choose an activity for day 1, day 2, and day 3 of their camp stay. Modify the Schedules table so that the Day field is a lookup field that uses values from a list. In the first Lookup Wizard dialog box, select the I will type in the values that I want. In the next Lookup Wizard dialog box, in the Col1 box, type the value 1, press the Tab key and type 2, and then press the Tab key again and type 3. Your dialog box should look similar to:

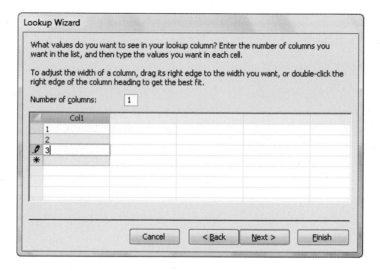

Select Next and then Finish to complete the lookup list.

k) Modify the Schedules table so that the Activity Name field is a lookup field that looks up values in the Activity Name field of the Activities table.

l) Create a simple form for each table. Format the forms appropriately and apply the Northwind style.

m) Enter the following four Counselors records:

JN01; Jessie; Neel

LW01; Leon; Washington

SP01; Sandra; Patel

TG01; Terry; Gray

n) Enter the following four Cabins records:

Alligator; SP01; 6

Egret; TG01; 8

Heron; LW01; 6

Panther; JN01; 8

o) Enter the following five Activities records:

Beading; SP01; Dining Hall; 8

Canoeing; LW01; Lake; 10

Pottery; JN01; Dining Hall; 8

Rafting; TG01; Lake; 9

Scavenger Hunt; SP01; Pavilion; 10

p) Enter the following twenty Campers records:

AD08; Anthony; Davis; 8; Heron

AB09; Ann; Bennett; 9; Panther

CH09; Carlos; Hernandez; 9; Heron

CR10; Christopher; Reed; 10; Alligator

DC10; Debi; Coleman; 10; Panther

DR11; Daniel; Ross; 11; Alligator

EW10; Evie; Wong; 10; Heron

FP11; Francisco; Perez; 11; Heron

IH10; Ivan; Hale; 10; Alligator

JB08; Jodi; Butler; 8; Egret

JC10; Jayne; Clarke; 10; Egret

JG10; Julian; Gray; 10; Alligator

JL09; James; Lewis; 9; Alligator

KN09; Karl; Neldon; 9; Alligator

LP09; Laura; Parker; 9; Egret

MC10; Marc; Cox; 10; Heron

MC11; Marguerite; Calo; 11; Egret

MR08; Martha; Ramirez; 8; Panther

MT10; Mary; Thompson; 10; Egret

SM11; Sharon; Martin; 11; Panther

q) Enter the following 60 Schedules records. Three records will be entered for each camper:

Camper	Day 1	Day 2	Day 3
AB09	Beading	Beading	Beading
AD08	Pottery	Beading	Pottery
CH09	Rafting	Rafting	Pottery
CR10	Rafting	Canoeing	Scavenger Hunt
DC10	Scavenger Hunt	Rafting	Canoeing
DR11	Canoeing	Beading	Scavenger Hunt
EC10	Scavenger Hunt	Beading	Canoeing
FP11	Canoeing	Rafting	Scavenger Hunt
IH10	Canoeing	Rafting	Scavenger Hunt
JB08	Beading	Beading	Pottery
JC10	Canoeing	Beading	Pottery
JG10	Pottery	Rafting	Canoeing
JL09	Rafting	Pottery	Scavenger Hunt
KN09	Rafting	Pottery	Rafting
LP09	Pottery	Beading	Beading
MC10	Rafting	Canoeing	Scavenger Hunt
MC11	Canoeing	Pottery	Scavenger Hunt
MR08	Pottery	Pottery	Pottery

Chapter 10 Relational Database Techniques

| MT10 | Canoeing | Beading | Pottery |
| SM11 | Canoeing | Beading | Scavenger Hunt |

r) Format each of the tables in Datasheet view appropriately.

s) Sort the Schedules table in ascending order by Day.

t) Print preview and then print all the tables using the appropriate orientation.

u) Filter the Campers table for campers staying in the Alligator cabin and print just those records.

Chapter 10 Relational Database Techniques

Chapter 11
Analyzing Data in a Database

What is a Report?

Reports present data from a database in an organized manner making the data easier to interpret and analyze. For example, in the MILLA HARDWARE report below, products have been grouped by department name and then counted:

Brush Items

Department Name	Extension	Product Name
Housewares		
	118	Mushroom Brush
	118	Shoe Brush
Brushes in Department:		2
Paint		
	431	Brush Cleaner
	431	Brush Tray
	431	Natural Bristle Brush
	431	Trim Brush
	431	Wide Brush
	431	Wire Brush
Brushes in Department:		6
Total:		8

Page 1 of 1

Once generated, reports are printed or electronically distributed.

Creating a Report

Report

record source

A report is based on a table or query. A table or query used for a report is called the report's *record source*. A report is linked to its record source so that it always reflects current data. To create a report, select a record source from the Navigation Pane and then click **Create → Report**. A new

Layout view

report based on the record source is displayed in *Layout view* where it can be formatted.

Alternative Click Create → Report Wizard to generate a report through a series of dialog boxes.

There are many sections in a report. The number of sections depends on the grouping and summaries selected for a report. A report could look similar to the Boat Fees report below:

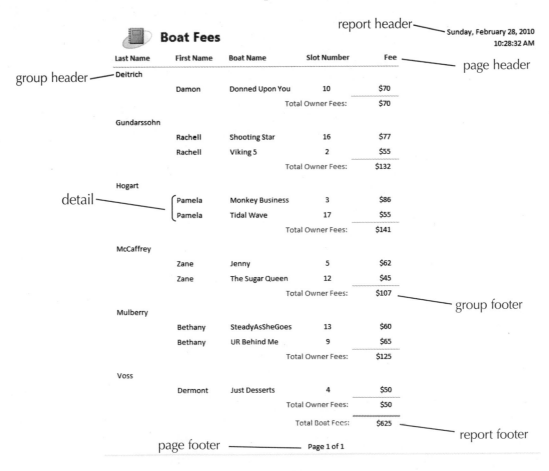

- The *report header* includes the logo, title, date, and time, and is displayed once at the top of a report.

- The *page header* is displayed at the beginning of every page and is most often includes the field names.

- The *group header* displays the group name and is included at the beginning of each group. *Grouping* organizes data based on a selected field.

- The *detail* is the main body of the report which displays the records from the record source.

- The *group footer* displays summary information for a group of records and is included at the end of each group.

- The *report footer* includes report totals and summaries and is displayed at the bottom of a report.

- The *page footer* is displayed at the end of every page and often includes page numbers.

When a report is saved, the object is added to the database and shown in the Navigation Pane. To open a closed report, double-click the report name in the Navigation Pane. To delete a report, select it in the Navigation Pane and then press the Delete key.

Modifying a Report in Layout View

In Layout view, the Design and Format tabs are used for formatting a report as well as for grouping data and sorting records:

Themes   Group & Sort   Logo

Conditional Formatting

Font group

- Select an object and then apply formats such as Bold, Center, Font, Font Size, and Font Color.

- Select a field entry and then click Conditional Formatting to display a dialog box for specifying conditional formatting rules. Conditional formatting makes report data easier to evaluate. For example, if dollar amounts less than 0 are displayed in red, the report becomes visually informative.

- Click Group & Sort to display the Group, Sort, and Total pane at the bottom of a report. The pane contains Add a group and Add a sort buttons. Click a button and select a field to group on or sort by.

- Click Logo to add a graphic to the report.

- Click Themes to apply a theme to the report.

Choosing Colors

The more contrast, or difference in lightness and darkness, of the font color and background color, the easier a report will be to read. Bright colors are difficult to view for long periods of time. Certain colors have special meaning. For example, red is associated with negative numbers.

applying conditional formats

The Conditional Formatting dialog box is used to create formatting rules:

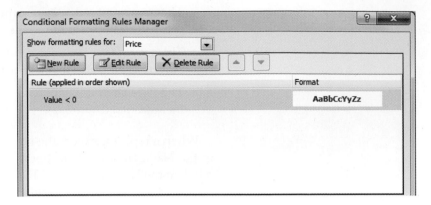

When choosing formats, consider how the report will be distributed. A black-and-white printed report cannot make use of color for making a value stand out. In this situation, use formats such as bold and italic to make data stand out.

When a group or sort has been specified, a Group on or Sort by row is displayed in the Group, Sort, and Total pane. Click a row to display options for modifying a group or sort:

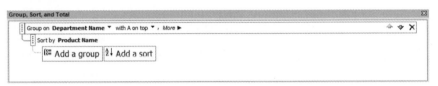

Click the Group on list to change the current grouping. In that same row, click the sort order list to specify how the groups are ordered. Options vary for text, number, and date/time data. The Sort by row contains similar options when clicked. To remove grouping or sorting options, click a row and then press the Delete key or click Delete ✕.

To change the column width of a field, click the field name, which displays a border, and then point to the right border until the pointer changes to ↔:

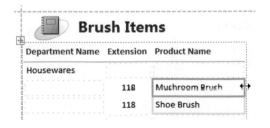

Drag to the left to narrow the column or to the right to widen the column.

To move a column of data, click the field name to select the column and then drag the column to a new location within the report.

Report view

When formatting is complete, click Design → View → Report View. *Report view* is the default view where the report is displayed but the formatting cannot be changed.

TIP Click Design → Group & Sort to display the Group, Sort, and Total pane.

TIP Dotted lines in Layout view indicate margins and page breaks.

① **OPEN MILLA HARDWARE**

a. Start Access.

b. Open MILLA HARDWARE, which was last modified in the Chapter 10.

② **CREATE A NEW REPORT**

a. In the Navigation Pane, click the Brush Items query to select it.

b. Click **Create** → **Report**. A new report is displayed in Layout view:

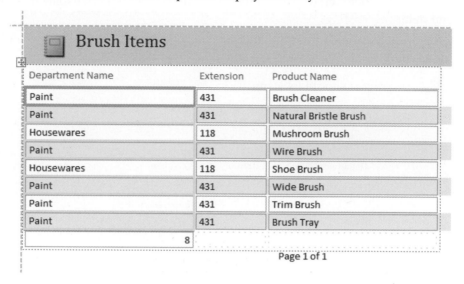

③ **GROUP DATA**

a. If the Group, Sort, and Total pane is not displayed below the report, click **Design** → **Group & Sort**. The pane is displayed with **Add a group** and **Add a sort** buttons.

b. In the Group, Sort, and Total pane, click **Add a group**. A Group on row is added to the pane and a list of field names is displayed.

c. In the list of field names, click **Department Name**. The report data is grouped by department:

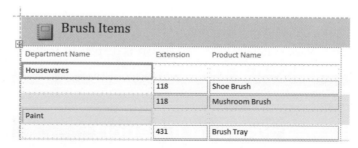

④ **SORT DATA**

a. In the Group, Sort, and Total pane, click **Add a sort**. A Sort by row is added to the pane and a list of field names is displayed.

b. In the list of field names, click **Product Name**. The report data is sorted by product name within each group.

c. Close the Group, Sort, and Total pane.

⑤ FORMAT THE REPORT

a. Click the "Brush Items" title to select it.

b. Click Format → Bold. The title is darker.

c. Bold each of the field names.

d. Click the Department Name field name. A border is displayed.

e. Point to the right border. The pointer changes to ↔.

f. Drag the right border to the left until the column is just wide enough to display the field name and entries entirely.

g. Change other field widths so that they are just wide enough to display their name and data.

h. Click an Extension entry and then click Format → Center. The entries are centered in the column.

Check — You report should look similar to:

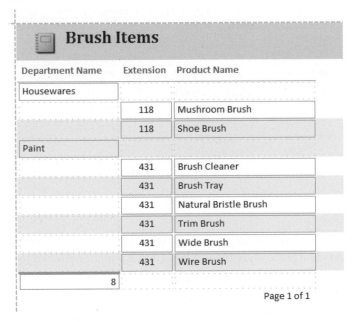

⑥ SAVE AND PRINT THE REPORT

a. Save the report naming it: Brush Items

b. Click Design → View → Report View. The report is displayed in Report view.

Printing a Report

Reports are often printed for distribution. Considerations for a printed report are readability and binding. Because the page layout of a report can affect these, select ▭ File → Print → Print Preview to see what the printout will look like. The report appears as a printed page and the Print Preview tab is displayed:

Chapter 11 Analyzing Data in a Database

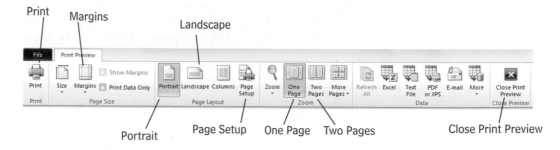

Print   Margins   Landscape

Portrait   Page Setup   One Page   Two Pages   Close Print Preview

- Portrait is the default page layout and is appropriate for most reports. Reports with many columns of data may need to be printed across the widest part of the page. In this case, click Landscape to change the page orientation. A report is more readable when related data is on the same page.

- Margins determine how much data can be printed on a page, which affects the readability of a report. Click Margins → Narrow to decrease the amount of white space around the edges of the page, which allows more columns of data per page. If a report is to be bound, margins on the binding side of the report may need to be wider. For example, a spiral binding requires holes along the binding side. Click Margins → Wide to increase the amount of white space around the edges of the page.

- Click Page Setup to display a dialog box where page orientation and margins can be specified.

- One Page is the default view with just one page of the report being displayed at a time. Click Two Pages to view two pages at once.

- Click Print to display a dialog box for selecting print options before printing the report.

- Click Close Print Preview to return to the previous view.

The preview also includes page buttons in the lower-left of the window to display the previous or next page of the document. Moving the pointer over the preview changes it to 🔍 which can be clicked to magnify the view of the document.

Summarizing Data in a Report

Totals

summary, aggregate

A *summary*, also called an *aggregate*, provides statistics on a field containing numeric data, such as an average or minimum value. A summary can also count the number of values or the number of records in a report. The Gadgets Sales report shows the total and average orders for Solar Chargers:

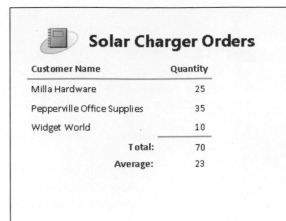

Solar Charger Orders

Customer Name	Quantity
Milla Hardware	25
Pepperville Office Supplies	35
Widget World	10
Total:	70
Average:	23

To add a summary to a report in Layout view, click a field in the report, click Design → Totals, and then click an aggregate name. Aggregates include:

- Sum computes the total for a group of values.

- Average computes the average for a group of values.

- Count Records computes the number of records in a report.

- Count Values computes the number of values in a report.

- Max determines the largest value in a group of values.

- Min determines the smallest value in a group of values.

- Standard Deviation estimates the standard deviation for a set of values.

- Variance estimates the variance in a group of values.

When report data has been grouped, a summary is added to each group footer as well as to the report footer.

Click a summary to select it. Selected summaries can be sized by dragging a border, formatted using the Format tab, and moved by dragging. To remove a selected summary, press the Delete key.

Modifying a Report in Design View

Label

Text Box

Design view   *Design view* shows the structure of a report and has different tools for modifying a report. For example, labels and text boxes can be added to a report in Design view. To display a report in Design view, click Design → View → Design View. Unlike Layout view where the actual data for a report is displayed, Design view shows only the sections of a report and the *controls* that generate the data.

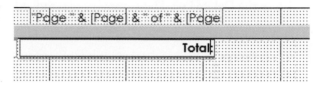

TIP In every new report, Access adds a summary that can be deleted.

Controls can be added or removed to customize the report. When adding and removing controls, the height of a section may need to be adjusted. Drag the bottom border of a section up or down to change the height.

A *label control* contains text and usually describes data nearby. For example, summaries in a report are more informative when labeled. To create a label control, click Design → Label, click in a report section, and then type the label text. The label below displays Total:

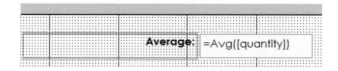

TIP Group data in Layout view before modifying a report in Design view.

A *text box control* is used for displaying data and calculations. For example, if more than one summary is needed in a report, use a text box and type a summary calculation. To create a text box control, click Design → Text Box and then click in a report section. When a text box is created, a label is also added. Modify the label to describe the data in the text box or remove it from the report:

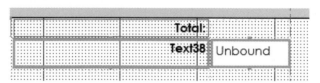

TIP "Unbound" in a new text box means that the text box is not displaying data from a field.

Summary calculations are created by typing an expression that begins with = in a text box control. A function such as Sum, Avg, or Max is then typed followed by the field name to use in the calculation. For example, the text box control has been modified to calculate an average in the report footer. Note that the field name must be enclosed in brackets:

To modify label and text box controls, click the control twice to display the insertion point. Edit the text and then click outside the control. To move an added control, click the control once to select it and then drag the large handle in the upper-left of the control. Size a control by dragging a smaller handle. Delete a selected control by pressing the Delete key.

After adding controls, switch to Layout view where formatting can be applied and the control can be more easily sized and positioned in the report.

Practice: MILLA HARDWARE – part 7 of 8

Access should already be started with MILLA HARDWARE displayed from the last practice.

① ADD A SUMMARY

    a. Open the Brush Items report if it is not already displayed.

    b. Click Home → View → Layout View. The report is displayed in Layout view.

    c. Click the Product Name field name. The selected column displays borders.

    d. Click Design → Totals → Count Records. A summary is added to the group footers and the report footer.

    e. In the Department Name column, click the summary. A border is displayed around the number 8.

    f. Press the Delete key. The summary is removed from the report.

② ADD A LABEL

    a. Click Design → View → Design View. The report is displayed in Design view. Note the section names and controls.

    b. Locate the Department Name Footer section and note the text box with the formula used to calculate the number of records in the section. Using what you know about wildcards, as discussed in Chapter 10, why do think an asterisk (*) is used in the formula?

    c. Click Design → Label.

    d. In the Department Name Footer, click to the left of the =Count(*) formula. A label with a blinking insertion point is displayed.

    e. Type Brushes in Department: and then press Enter.

    f. If necessary, drag the selected label to the left of the summary. Your footer should look similar to:

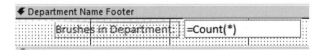

    g. In the Report Footer section, add a Total: label to the left of the summary:

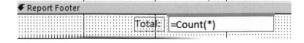

    h. Click Design → View → Layout View. The report is displayed in Layout view.

    i. Select the labels and move them, if necessary, to align with the summary data.

Check — Your report in Report view should look similar to:

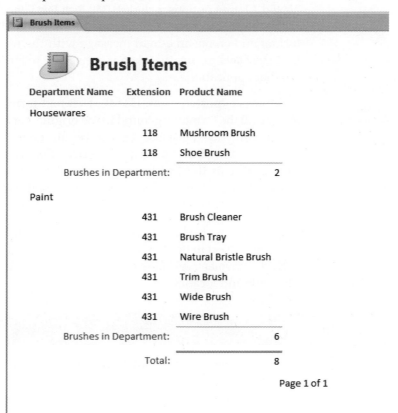

③ PRINT THE REPORT

a. Save the modified Brush Items.

b. Select **File** → Print → Print Preview. A preview of the report is displayed. Note that all the data is displayed on one page.

c. Click Print Preview → Print. A dialog box is displayed.

d. Select OK. The report is printed.

e. Close the Brush Items report.

Electronically Distributing a Report

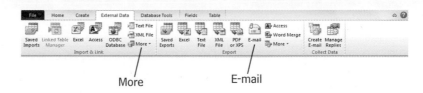

Reports are often printed on paper for distribution. However, e-mail can be a faster and more efficient means of distribution. *Posting* a report to a Web site is an efficient means of making a report available to many individuals.

To e-mail a report, click the report object in the Navigation Pane and then select External Data → E-mail. The Send Object As dialog box is displayed. Output options include HTML, Rich Text Format, Snapshot Format, and Text Files. Select an option and then OK to export the report in the selected format and create an e-mail message with the report as an attachment.

exporting data *Exporting data* means that data is converted to a file that can be used by another application.

Reports exported as an HTML, rich text format, or text file will not include all the formatting found in the original report. The PDF file format is commonly used because it preserves all the formatting in the original report. Viewing PDF files requires Adobe Reader, a free application from Adobe Systems that most users already have. To create a PDF, select the report object in the Navigation Pane and then select External Data → PDF or XPS.

Reports can also be exported to HTML format and then posted. Select the report object in the Navigation Pane and then click External Data → More → HTML Document. A dialog box is displayed for selecting the destination file name and location.

Practice: Brush Items

This practice requires browser software. Internet access is not required. Access should already be started with MILLA HARDWARE displayed from the last practice.

① **EXPORT A REPORT**

a. In the Navigation Pane, click the Brush Items report. The report is selected.

b. Click External Data → More → HTML Document from the Export group. A dialog box is displayed.

    1. Select Browse. A dialog box is displayed.

    2. Navigate to the appropriate location for the exported file to be saved and then select Save.

    3. Select the Open the destination file after the export is complete check box.

    4. Select OK. Another dialog box is displayed.

    5. Select OK. The report is displayed in a browser window. Note that some of the formatting, including lines, is no longer in the report.

c. Close the browser window. Access is again displayed.

d. Select Close to remove the dialog box.

Calculated Fields

A *calculated field* displays the result of an expression that is defined in a select query. For example, the following query includes a calculated field named Profit, which displays the difference between the Price and Cost fields for the displayed records:

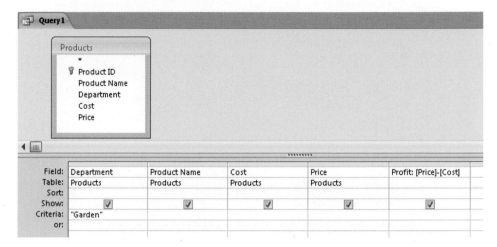

To create a calculated field, type the field name followed by a colon and an expression that uses the format [Table Name]![Field Name] to refer to a field. If a field name is unique to the database, then the table name is not needed in the reference. When run, the query displays:

Calculated fields are saved with a query, but are not stored as part of a table, and data cannot be directly entered into the field.

Numeric formats for a calculated field are specified in Design view. Right-click the calculated field name in the design grid and select Properties. The Property Sheet task pane is displayed with options including Format and Decimal Places.

Practice: MILLA HARDWARE – part 8 of 8

Access should already be started with MILLA HARDWARE displayed from the last practice.

① **CREATE TWO CALCULATED FIELDS**

    a. Create a new query that includes only the Products table.

    b. Add the Department, Product Name, Cost, and Price fields to the design grid.

    c. In the Department Sort list, select Ascending.

    d. In the next Field box, type: Profit: [Price]-[Cost]

e. In the next Field box, type: Markup: ([Price]-[Cost])/[Cost]

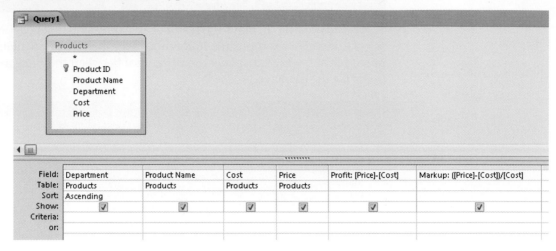

f. Right-click the Markup field and select Properties from the menu. The Property Sheet is displayed.

g. Click the Format box and then click the arrow and select Percent:

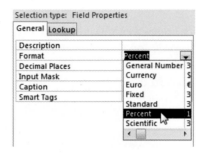

h. In the Property Sheet, type 0 for the Decimal Places.

i. Close the Property Sheet.

j. Run the query. The calculated fields are shown in a datasheet:

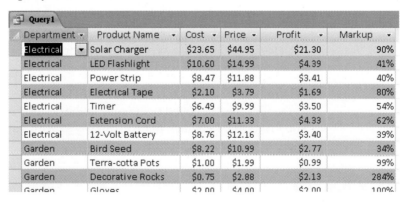

k. Save the query naming it: Profit and Markup

l. Print and then close the query.

Exporting Access Data to Excel

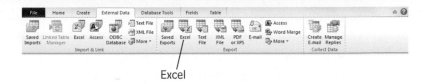

Excel

Access data can be exported as an Excel workbook so that additional calculations can be performed, "What-If?" questions asked, and charts created. To export a table or query, click the object in the Navigation Pane and then click External Data ➜ Excel in the Export group. A dialog box is displayed for selecting the name and location of the Excel file. An option for opening the new file after exporting is also available.

Practice: Garden Sale

Access should already be started with MILLA HARDWARE displayed from the previous practice.

① **EXPORT THE PRODUCTS TABLE**

    a. Open the Products table and sort the records in ascending order by Department.

    b. Save and then close the table.

    c. With the Products table still selected in the Navigation Pane, click External Data ➜ Excel in the Export group. A dialog box is displayed.

        1. Select Browse. A dialog box is displayed.

        2. Navigate to the appropriate location for the file to be saved and then type Garden Sale for the File name.

        3. Select Save. The dialog box is removed.

        4. Select the Export data with formatting and layout check box.

        5. Select OK. A dialog box is displayed.

        6. Select Close.

② **MODIFY THE SPREADSHEET TO GENERATE NEW DATA**

    a. Start Excel and then open Garden Sale, which was created in the previous step.

    b. The manager of the Garden department is planning a sale. Keep the rows in the worksheet with Garden in the Department column and delete the rest:

	A	B	C	D	E
1	**Product ID**	**Product Name**	**Department**	**Cost**	**Price**
2	26	Bird Seed	Garden	$8.22	$10.99
3	21	Terra-cotta Pots	Garden	$1.00	$1.99
4	14	Decorative Rocks	Garden	$0.75	$2.88
5	6	Gloves	Garden	$2.00	$4.00
6	17	Orchid	Garden	$8.90	$19.88
7	3	Potting Soil	Garden	$0.80	$1.50
8	24	Grass Seed	Garden	$1.90	$3.50

    c. In cell F1, type: Profit

    d. In cell F2, enter the formula: =(E2–D2)/D2

    e. Format cell F2 to display a percent with 0 decimal places. 34% is displayed. This is the profit made on the sale of seeds.

f. Copy the formula in cell F2 to cells F3 through F8.

g. In cell E10, type: Markdown Amount:

h. In cell G10, type: 10%

i. In column G, add the title Sale Price and then enter the formula =E2–(E2*$G$10) in cell G2.

j. Format cell G2 to display currency with 2 decimal places. $9.89 is displayed.

k. Copy the formula in cell G2 to cells G3 through G8.

l. In column H, add the title Sale Profit and then enter the formula =(G2–D2)/D2 in cell H2.

m. Format cell H2 to display a percent with 0 decimal places and then copy the formula to cells H3 through H8.

Check — Your worksheet should look similar to:

	A	B	C	D	E	F	G	H
1	Product ID	Product Name	Department	Cost	Price	Profit	Sale Price	Sale Profit
2	26	Bird Seed	Garden	$8.22	$10.99	34%	$9.89	20%
3	21	Terra-cotta Pots	Garden	$1.00	$1.99	99%	$1.79	79%
4	14	Decorative Rocks	Garden	$0.75	$2.88	284%	$2.59	246%
5	6	Gloves	Garden	$2.00	$4.00	100%	$3.60	80%
6	17	Orchid	Garden	$8.90	$19.88	123%	$17.89	101%
7	3	Potting Soil	Garden	$0.80	$1.50	88%	$1.35	69%
8	24	Grass Seed	Garden	$1.90	$3.50	84%	$3.15	66%
9								
10					Markdown Amount:		10%	

③ ASK WHAT IF?

a. The Garden department manager would like to see how different markdown amounts will affect profits. Click Data ➜ What-if Analysis ➜ Scenario Manager. A dialog box is displayed.

b. Select Add. Another dialog box is displayed.

 1. In the Scenario name box, type: Markdown Amount 10%

 2. In the Changing cells box, type: G10

 3. Select OK. Another dialog box is displayed. The value 0.1 is already displayed.

 4. Select OK. The Scenario Manager dialog box is again displayed.

c. Select Add and then create a scenario for named Markdown Amount 20% where cell G10 has the value 0.2.

d. Add a third scenario named Markdown Amount 30% where cell G10 has the value 0.3.

e. In the Scenario Manager dialog box, select Markdown 20% and then select Show. The worksheet changes to display the 20% markdown scenario.

f. Display the other scenarios and note the difference in the profit margins.

g. Select Summary. A dialog box is displayed.

 1. Select cells H2 through H8. The Result cells box displays the range name.

 2. Select OK. A scenario summary is displayed on a new sheet.

 3. Add your name in a header and the current date in a footer.

 4. Print just the Scenario Summary worksheet.

④ SAVE, PRINT, AND THEN CLOSE THE GARDEN SALE WORKBOOK

a. Display the Products sheet.

b. Add your name in a header and the current date in a footer.

c. Save the modified Garden Sale.

d. Print the Products sheet, close the workbook, and then quit Excel.

e. Close MILLA HARDWARE and then quit Access.

Mail Merge - Form Letters

Mail merge merges data stored in an Access database with a Word document. Mail merge is commonly used to create personalized form letters. A *form letter* is a Word document with *merge fields*, which are placeholders for data from an Access table or query. For example, a business can create a letter to their customers that is personalized by merging customer name and address data from an Access table in the company database:

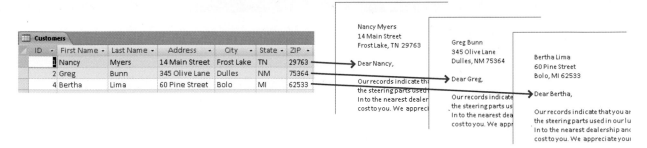

The Mailings tab on the Word Ribbon is organized for stepping through the process of creating a mail merge document:

1. Click Start Mail Merge → Letters. Other mail merge document types are also available.

2. Click Select Recipients → Use Existing List. The Select Source Dialog box is displayed. Navigate to the database containing the data to be merged. The Select Table dialog box is displayed. Select the table or select query with the fields for the merge document.

3. Click Edit Recipient List. The Mail Merge Recipients dialog box is displayed. Clear the check boxes of records that should not be included in the mail merge.

4. If the letter is to include an address block, click Address Block to automatically format and insert an address block. The Insert Address Block dialog box is displayed. Select or clear check boxes to indicate what should appear in the address block. Use the preview as a guide. Select Match Fields, if necessary, to match field names from the database to the fields in the address block.

5. Click Greeting Line to automatically format and insert a greeting. The Insert Greeting Line dialog box is displayed. Use the lists and the preview to create an appropriate greeting.

6. Type the letter, clicking Insert Merge Field to select a field name wherever data from the database should appear. The merge field is added to the letter at the insertion point.

7. Click Preview Results. Merge fields are replaced by actual data from the database. Preview Results can be used at any time during the merge process to see how a letter is developing. Click Previous Record ◀ and Next Record ▶ to see how the data from other records will appear in the letter.

8. Click Finish & Merge → Print Documents. The Merge to Printer dialog box is displayed. Use the options to select which records are printed.

Formatting can be applied to merge fields in the same way plain text is formatted.

Practice: June Sale

Access should already be started.

① **OPEN THE GADGETS SALES DATABASE**

② **CREATE A SELECT QUERY**

    a. Create a select query in Design view.

    b. Add the Customers, Orders, and Products tables.

    c. Add the Product ID, Product Name, Contact First Name, Contact Last Name, Customer Name, Address, City, State/Province, and ZIP/Postal Code fields to the design grid.

    d. In the Product Name Criteria box, type: Solar Charger

    e. Run the query. Three records are displayed.

    f. Save the query naming it: Solar Charger Customers

    g. Close the query.

③ **CREATE A NEW WORD DOCUMENT**

    a. Start Word.

    b. Create a new document, if one is not already displayed.

④ **CREATE A FORM LETTER**

    a. Click Mailings → Start Mail Merge → Letters.

    b. Click Mailings → Select Recipients → Use Existing List. The Select Data Source dialog box is displayed.

        1. Navigate to Gadgets Sales and then select Open. The Select Table dialog box is displayed.

        2. Select Solar Charger Customers query and then select OK.

    c. Click Mailings → Edit Recipient List. The Mail Merge Recipients dialog box is displayed. Note the check boxes for selecting which records will be used for the merge letter.

        1. All the records in the query will be used for the mail merge letter. Verify that all the check boxes are selected and then select OK.

d. Click Home → No Spacing. The document is formatted for single spacing.

e. Press Enter four times to move the insertion point down about 1 inch (2.54 cm).

f. Type the following address, press Enter twice, type the date, and then press Enter four times:

¶
¶
¶
¶
1·Gadgets·Blvd.¶
Middlebury,·PA·17209¶
¶
February·9,·2011¶
¶
¶
¶
¶

g. Click Mailings → Address Block. The Insert Address Block dialog box is displayed. Note the Preview does not include the contact's first and last names.

    1. Select Match Fields. The Match Fields dialog box is displayed.

        a. In the First Name list, select Contact First Name.

        b. In the Last Name list, select Contact Last Name.

        c. In the Company list, select Customer Name.

        d. In the State list, select State/Province.

        e. In the Postal Code list, select ZIP/Postal Code, if it is not already.

        f. Select OK. If a warning dialog box is displayed, select Yes.

    2. The Preview changes to include all the contact and address information:

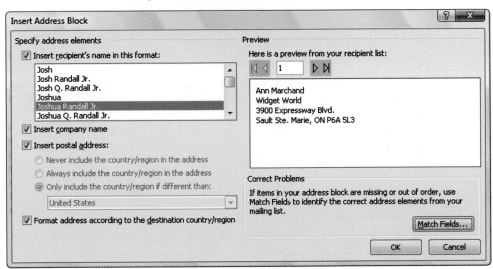

    3. Verify that your dialog box has all four check boxes selected and the appropriate recipient name style selected in the list and then select OK. An AddressBlock merge field is added to the document:

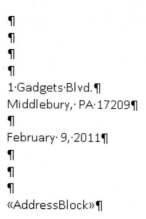

¶
¶
¶
¶
1·Gadgets·Blvd.¶
Middlebury,·PA·17209¶
¶
February·9,·2011¶
¶
¶
¶
«AddressBlock»¶

h. Press Enter twice.

i. Click Mailings → Greeting Line. The Insert Greeting Line dialog box is displayed.

    1. Select options as shown below:

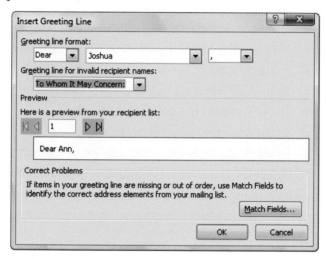

    2. Select OK. A GreetingLine merge field is added to the document.

j. Press Enter twice and then type text so that the document looks similar to:

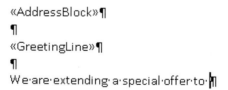

«AddressBlock»¶
¶
«GreetingLine»¶
¶
We·are·extending·a·special·offer·to·|¶

k. Click Mailings → Insert Merge Field → Product_Name. The Product_Name merge field is added to the document.

l. Type the remainder of the letter and insert merge fields as shown below, replacing Name with our name and allowing Word to wrap the text:

Chapter 11 Analyzing Data in a Database

We·are·extending·a·special·offer·to·«Product_Name»·customers.·For·the·entire·month·of·June,·the·«Product_Name»·is·being·offered·at·25%·off·the·normal·wholesale·price.·But·hurry,·offer·available·only·while·supplies·last!·Be·sure·to·specify·product·ID·«Product_ID».¶

¶
Best·regards,¶
¶
¶
¶
Name¶
Gadgets·Incorporated¶

m. Save the form letter naming it: June Sale

⑤ PREVIEW THE MERGED COPIES

a. Click Mailings → Preview Results. The merge fields are replaced by the data from the first record in the query.

b. Click Mailings → Next Record ▶. The next record in the query is merged with the letter.

c. Preview all the merge letters.

⑥ PRINT THE MAIL MERGED LETTERS AND THEN CLOSE THE DOCUMENT

a. Click Mailings → Finish & Merge → Print Documents. The Merge to Printer dialog box is displayed.

1. Select Current Record and then OK. The Print dialog box is displayed.

2. Select OK. The current mail merge document is printed.

b. Click Mailings → Preview Results. The merge fields are again displayed.

c. Select File → Print → Print to print a copy of the document with merge fields displayed.

d. Save and close June Sale.

Mail Merge - Labels

Mail merge can also be used to generate labels. A labels document is formatted for use with a specified label paper. Label paper is adhesive paper with multiple labels to a page. Word includes the dimensions for label paper provided by many different vendors including Microsoft and Avery®.

The Mailings tab is used to step through the process of creating labels:

1. Click Start Mail Merge → Labels. The Label Options dialog box is displayed. Select the appropriate label vendor and product number for the paper the labels will be printed on.

2. Click Select Recipients → Use Existing List. The Select Source Dialog box is displayed. Use the Look in list and the contents box below it to select the database containing the addresses to be merged. The Select Table dialog box is displayed. Select the table or select query with the fields for the merge document.

3. Click Edit Recipient List. The Mail Merge Recipients dialog box is displayed. Clear the check boxes of records that should not be included in the mail merge.

4. If the labels are to include an address block, click Address Block to automatically format and insert an address block. The Insert Address Block dialog box is displayed. Select or clear check boxes to indicate what should appear in the address block. Use the preview as a guide. Select Match Fields, if necessary, to match field names from the database to the fields in the address block.

5. Create the label, clicking Insert Merge Field to select a field name wherever data from the database should appear. The merge field is added to the label at the insertion point.

6. Click Update Labels. The created label is copied to all the other labels in the document.

7. Click Preview Results. Merge fields are replaced by actual data from the database. Preview Results can be used at any time during the merge process to see how the label is developing.

8. Click Finish & Merge → Print Documents. The Merge to Printer dialog box is displayed. Use the options to select which records are printed. Be sure to place the adhesive paper in the printer before printing.

Formatting can be applied to merge fields in the same way plain text is formatted. Before starting the labels, click Home → No Spacing so that paragraphs are single-spaced, which will reduce the space between lines.

Practice: June Sale Labels

Access should already be started with Gadgets Sales displayed from the last practice.

① CREATE A NEW WORD DOCUMENT

② CREATE AN ADDRESS LABEL

a. Click Mailings → Start Mail Merge → Labels. The Label Options dialog box is displayed.

1. Select the options as shown:

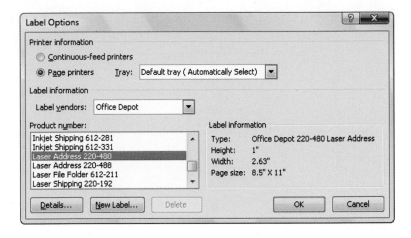

2. Select **OK**. The document is formatted for labels.

b. Click **Mailings → Select Recipients → Use Existing List**. The Select Data Source dialog box is displayed.

    1. Navigate to Gadgets Sales and then select **Open**. The Select Table dialog box is displayed.

    2. Select **Solar Charger Customers** query and then select **OK**.

c. Click **Mailings → Edit Recipient List**. A dialog box is displayed.

    1. All the records in the query will be used for the labels. Verify that all the check boxes are selected and then select **OK**.

d. Click **Home → No Spacing**. The document is formatted for single spacing.

e. Click **Mailings → Address Block**. The Insert Address Block dialog box is displayed. Note the preview does not include the customer's first and last names.

    1. Select **Match Fields**. The Match Fields dialog box is displayed.

        a. In the First Name list, select **Contact First Name**.

        b. In the Last Name list, select **Contact Last Name**.

        c. In the Company list, select **Customer Name**.

        d. In the State list, select **State/Province**.

        e. In the Postal Code list, select **ZIP/Postal Code**, if it is not already.

        f. Select **OK**. If a warning dialog box is displayed, select **Yes**.

    2. The Preview changes to include all the contact and address information:

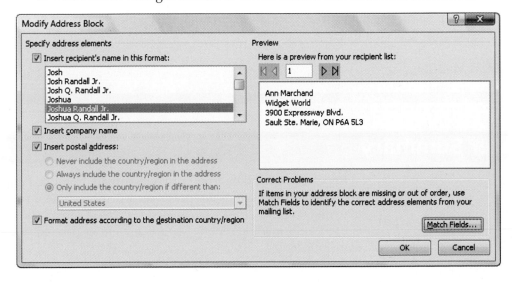

3. Verify that your dialog box has all four check boxes selected and then select OK. An AddressBlock merge field is added to the first label:

f. Click Mailings → Update Labels. The AddressBlock merge field is added to all labels:

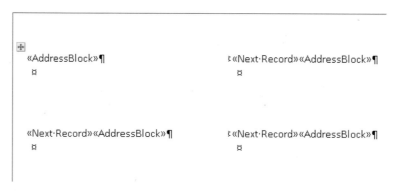

g. Save the labels document naming it: June Sale Labels

③ PREVIEW THE MERGED COPIES

Click Mailings → Preview Results. The merge fields are replaced by the data from the query.

④ PRINT THE MAIL MERGED LETTERS AND THEN CLOSE THE DOCUMENT

a. Click Mailings → Finish & Merge → Print Documents. The Merge to Printer dialog box is displayed.

1. Select All and then OK. The Print dialog box is displayed.
2. Select OK. The label document is printed onto plain paper. To create labels on adhesive paper, insert the label paper into the printer before printing.

b. Save and close June Sale Labels.

⑤ QUIT WORD

Chapter Summary

Reports present data from a database in an organized manner. Tables and queries are used as a report's record source and a report can have many sections. The Create tab is used to create a report and the Format tab is used to format the report. Reports are either printed or electronically distributed.

Considerations when printing a report are readability and binding. The print orientation and margins affect readability. Margins also affect the binding. The Print Preview tab is used to change both orientation and margins.

A summary is also called an aggregate and is used to provide statistics about the data in a report. Summaries can average, total, determine the minimum or maximum value, count records, count values, compute a standard deviation, and compute the variance. The Format tab is used to add a summary to a report.

Most report modifications can be done from Layout view. However, Design view includes the Design tab for modifying a report. With this tab, label and text box controls can be added to a report. A text box is often used to display the result of a calculation.

E-mail is an efficient means of distributing a report. When e-mailing a report, it is exported to a selected file format. Export formats include HTML, rich text format, and text.

Posting a report to a Web site makes it available to many individuals. To post a report, it must first be exported to a selected file format, similar to when e-mailing a report. In addition to the HTML and Snapshot formats, there is the PDF format. A PDF file preserves formatting, similar to the Snapshot format. PDF documents are viewed with Adobe Acrobat Reader, which is a free download. The External Data tab is used to export a report to a selected file format.

Calculated fields display the result of an expression that is defined in a select query. A calculated field is saved with a query, but not stored as a part of a table and data cannot be entered directly into the field.

An Access table or query can be exported to an Excel workbook where calculations can be performed, "What-If?" questions asked, and charts created. The External Data tab is used to export Access data.

Mail merge is used to create personalized form letters. A form letter is a Word document that includes merge fields. Mail merge is also used to create labels. Mail merge form letters and labels are created using the Mailings tab on the Word Ribbon. Before printing labels, special adhesive paper needs to be inserted into the printer.

Aggregate Also called summary. *See* Summary.

Calculated field A field that displays the result of a mathematical expression that is defined in a select query.

Controls An element in Design view that is used to generate data for a report.

Design view One of the views used for formatting a report.

Detail The report section that displays the records from the record source.

Exporting data The process of converting data to a file that can be used by another application.

Form letter A Word document with merge fields.

Group footer The report section that is displayed at the end of each group.

Group header The report section that is displayed at the beginning of each group.

Grouping Organizing report data based on a selected field.

Label control A control in Design view that is used to display text.

Layout view One of the views used for formatting a report.

Merge fields Placeholders in a Word document for data from an Access table or query.

Page footer The report section that is displayed at the end of every page.

Page header The report section that is displayed at the beginning of every page.

Report Presents data in an organized manner.

Report footer The report section that is displayed at the bottom of a report.

Report header The report section that is displayed once at the top of a report.

Record source The table or query used for a report.

Report view The default view where a report cannot be formatted.

Summary Provides statistics on a field containing numeric data. Can also count the number of records or values in a report.

Text box control A control in Design view that is used to display data or the result of a calculation.

AutoFormat Displays predefined formats for changing the color scheme and font type. Found on the Format tab.

Bold Formats text as bold. Found on the Format and Home tabs.

Center ☰ Formats text as center aligned. Found on the Format and Home tabs.

Close Print Preview Closes print preview. Found on the Print Preview tab.

Conditional Displays a dialog box for specifying a default format and a second format based on a condition.

Delete Removes a row in the Group, Sort, and Total pane.

Design View Displays a report in Design view. Found in Design → View and Home → View.

E-mail Exports a report to a selected format and then attaches it to an e-mail message. Found on the External Data tab.

Excel Exports data as an Excel workbook. Found on the External Data tab.

Font Changes the font of text. Found on the Format tab.

Font Color Changes the color of text. Found on the Format tab.

Font Size Changes the size of the text. Found on the Format tab.

Group & Sort Displays the Group, Sort, and Total pane for grouping and sorting report data. Found on the Design tab.

HTML Document Exports a report to HTML format. Found in External Data → More.

Label Adds a Label control to a report in Design view.

Landscape Changes the print orientation of a report to landscape. Found on the Print Preview tab.

Layout View Displays a report in Layout view. Found in Format → View and Home → View.

Logo Adds a graphic to a report. Found on the Design tab.

Mailings tab Generates a mail merge document such as a form letter or labels.

Narrow Reduces the amount of white space around the edges of a report. Found in Print Preview → Margins.

One Page Displays one page at a time in print preview. Found on the Print Preview tab.

Page Setup Displays the Page Setup dialog box for changing print orientation and margins. Found on the Print Preview tab.

PDF or XPS Displays a dialog box for exporting a report to a PDF format. Found on the External Data tab.

Portrait Changes the print orientation of a report to portrait. Found on the Print Preview tab.

Report Creates a report. Found on the Create tab.

Report View Displays a report in Report view where the layout cannot be changed. Found in Format → View and Home → View.

Text Box Adds a Text Box control to a report in Design view.

Totals Displays a list of aggregates. Found on the Design tab.

Two Pages Displays two pages at once in print preview. Found on the Print Preview tab.

Wide Increases the amount of white space around the edges of a report. Found in Print Preview → Margins.

1. What is a database report?

2. If a change is made to a table used in a report, is the change displayed the next time the report is viewed? Explain.

3. a) What does the report header display?
   b) Will every report contain a group header? Explain.
   c) If a record source contains 10 records, how many records will be displayed in the detail section of a report?

4. a) List three formats that could be applied to the title of a report.
   b) Give an example of conditional formatting in a report.

5. Can groups be sorted? Explain.

6. What are the considerations when printing a report?

7. What considerations should be made when determining the margins for a printed report?

8. a) What is an aggregate?
   b) List three aggregates available in Access.
   c) Where will summaries appear when report data has been grouped?

9. List the steps required to label a summary.

10. List the steps required to add a second summary to a report.

11. List three ways to distribute a report.

12. a) What are the four output file formats when e-mailing a report?
    b) What must be used to view a Snapshot file?

13. Which two file formats preserve the formatting of a report?

14. a) What is a calculated field?
    b) Can data be entered directly into a calculated field? Explain.

15. List three reasons for exporting Access data to an Excel workbook.

True/False

16. Determine if each of the following are true or false. If false, explain why.
    a) A report can use a query as its record source.
    b) A report must contain a group footer.
    c) A report header appears at the top of every page of the report.
    d) The data in a report can be sorted.
    e) The color of a report title can be changed.
    f) Margins do not affect the page layout of a report.
    g) Landscape orientation prints a report across the widest part of the part.
    h) An aggregate is also called a summary.
    i) Summaries cannot be formatted.
    j) A text box can contain a calculation.
    k) Records are displayed in Design view.
    l) The HTML file format preserves all report formatting.
    m) Reports are exported to a file type before being attached to an e-mail.
    n) A report cannot be posted to a Web site.
    o) A calculated field is added to a table.
    p) A calculated field can refer to a field in any table in the database.
    q) A query cannot be exported as an Excel workbook.
    r) Mail merge allows multiple personalized documents to be created quickly.
    s) Address labels must be individually typed even when a database of the names and addresses exist.

Project 1

Travel... With a Purpose wants to analyze the data in their relational database, which was last modified in Chapter 10, Project 1. Open MUSEUM EXHIBITS and complete the following:

a) Create a select query named Exhibit Attendance that displays the Exhibit ID, Exhibit Name, Hall, Year Recorded, and Attendance fields for all records.

b) Create a report using the Exhibit Attendance query as the record source. Group the data by Year and sort the data by Attendance. Add a summary to total the Attendance. Label the summary. Delete the summary added by Access. Format the report appropriately. Save the report naming it Exhibit Attendance by Year. Print the report.

c) Create a report using the Exhibit Attendance query as the record source. Group the data by Exhibit Name and sort the data by Year Recorded. Add a summary to total the Attendance. Label the summary. Delete the summary added by Access. Format the report appropriately. Save the report naming it Exhibit Attendance by Exhibit. Print the report.

d) Create a report using the Why Things Happen Exhibits query as the record source. Group the data by Year Recorded and sort the data by Exhibit Name. Add a summary to average the Attendance. Label the summary. Delete the summary added by Access. Format the report appropriately. Save the report naming it Why Things Happen Exhibits. Print the report.

e) Create a select query that displays the Exhibit ID, Exhibit Name, Hall, Year Recorded, and Attendance fields for all exhibits in the year 2011 and includes a calculated field named Predicted 2010 Attendance. Sunport Science Museum predicts that the attendance in 2010 will be 10% higher than the attendance in 2011. Therefore, the predicted 2010 attendance is calculated by multiplying the Attendance field by 110% (1.1). Format the calculated field as Standard with 0 decimal places. Format the query datasheet appropriately. Save the select query naming it Predicted 2010 Attendance. Print the query results.

Project 2

Study Time Tutoring wants to analyze the data in their relational database, which was last modified in Chapter 10, Project 2. Open LIBRARY and complete the following:

a) Create a report using the All Titles query as the record source. Group the data by Subject, add another group to group the data by title, and then sort the data by Last Name. Delete the summary added by Access. Format the report appropriately. Save the report naming it Titles by Subject. Print the report.

b) Create a report using the Authors and Illustrators table as the record source. Sort the data by Last Name. Add a summary to the Last Name field to count the records. Label the summary. Delete the summary added by Access. Format the report appropriately. Save the report naming it Authors and Illustrators. Print the report.

c) Create a report using the Poetry Books query as the record source. The report will be printed and handed out to the Monday Night Poetry Reading members. Delete the summary added by Access. Delete the Expanded Subject field from the report. Change the title to read Monday Night Poetry Reading List. Click Format → AutoFormat to select an appropriate predefined format. Experiment with fonts and color to make the report more interesting for the members. Save the report naming it Monday Night Poetry Reading List. Print the report.

Project 3 —————————————————————————

Yolanda's Catering wants to analyze the data in their relational database, which was last modified in Chapter 10, Project 3. Open CATERING and complete the following:

a) Create a select query named Current Employees that displays the Last Name, First Name, Address, City, State, and ZIP fields for all records.

b) Create a report using the Current Employees query as the record source. Group the data by City and sort the data by Last Name. Add a summary to the Last Name field to count the employees, if one has not already been added. Label the summary. Add the PIZZA PALACE LOGO, which is a data file for this text. Format the report appropriately. Save the report naming it Current Employees. Print the report.

c) Create a select query named Employee Payroll that displays the Employee ID, Last Name, Check Number, Check Date, Gross Pay, and Taxes fields for all records.

d) Create a report using the Employee Payroll query as the record source. Group the data by Employee ID and sort the data by Check Number. Add a summaries to total the Gross Pay and Taxes. Add the PIZZA PALACE LOGO, which is a data file for this text, to the report. Format the report appropriately. Save the report naming it Employee Payroll. Print the report.

e) Create a select query that displays the Employee ID, Check Date, Gross Pay, and Taxes fields for all employees and includes a calculated field named Net Pay. Net pay is calculated by subtracting the Taxes field from the Gross Pay field. Save the query naming it Net Pay. Print the query results.

Project 4 ———

Sunport Boat Storage wants to analyze the data in their relational database, which was last modified in Chapter 10, Project 4. Open BOAT STORAGE and complete the following:

a) Create a select query named Employee Phone Numbers that displays the First Name, Last Name, and Phone fields from the Employees table for all records.

b) Create a report using the Employee Phone Numbers query as the record source. Sort the data by Last Name. Delete the summary added by Access. Change the title to read Employee Phone List. Format the report appropriately. Save the report naming it Employee Phone List. Print the report.

c) Create a select query named Boat Fees that displays the First Name of boat owner, Last Name of boat owner, Boat Name, Slot Number, and Fee fields for all records.

d) Create a report using the Boat Fees query as the record source. Group the data by Last Name and sort the data by Boat Name. Add a summary to total the Fee field. Label the summary. Format the report appropriately. Save the report naming it Boat Fees. Print the report.

e) Create a select query that displays the Boat Name, Fee, First Name of boat owner, and Last Name of boat owner fields for all boat owners and includes a calculated field named Renewal Fee. The renewal charge is increasing by 30%. Calculate the fee by multiplying the Fee field by 130% (1.30). Save the select query naming it Renewal Fee with 30% Increase. Print a copy.

Project 5

The office manager needs to distribute an employee telephone directory. The directory can be in the form of a report from the company database, which was last modified in Chapter 9, Project 5. Open MESSAGES and complete the following:

a) Create a select query named Phone List that displays the First Name, Last Name, and Extension fields for all records.

b) Create a report using the Phone List query as the record source. Sort the data by Last Name. Delete the summary added by Access. Format the report appropriately. Save the report naming it Phone List. Print the report.

c) Create a select query named Downtown Delivery Services that displays the Message Date and Company Name fields for Downtown Delivery Services records.

d) Create a report using the Downtown Delivery Services query as the record source. Sort the data by Message Date. Format the report appropriately. Change the title to read Deliveries Made by DDS. Save the report naming it Deliveries Made by DDS. Print the report.

Project 6

A report can be used to catalog items. Open PHOTO COLLECTION, last modified in Chapter 9, Project 6, and complete the following:

Create a report using the Photos table as the record source. Add a summary to the Title field to count the number of records. Delete the summary added by Access. Format the report appropriately. Save the report naming it Photo Thumbnails. Print the report.

Chapter 12
Creating Presentations

Key Concepts

Planning and creating presentations
Editing and formatting slides
Adding and deleting slides
Viewing and printing presentations
Using themes in a presentation
Adding slide footers
Using the slide master
Adding graphics and charts
Using speaker notes
Collaborating on a presentation

Practice Data Files

BETTER BURGER, BURGER, FAT CONTENT

Project Data Files

MANAGEMENT PLAN, ALIGN LOGO

What is a Presentation?

TIP Visuals may also be on a flipchart, a white board, or handouts of printed materials.

A *presentation* is an informative speech that usually includes *visuals,* such as slides. Presentations can take other forms such as photo slide shows that run continuously and multimedia slide shows with recorded audio. A *PowerPoint presentation* consists of slides that are organized and formatted using Microsoft PowerPoint 2010

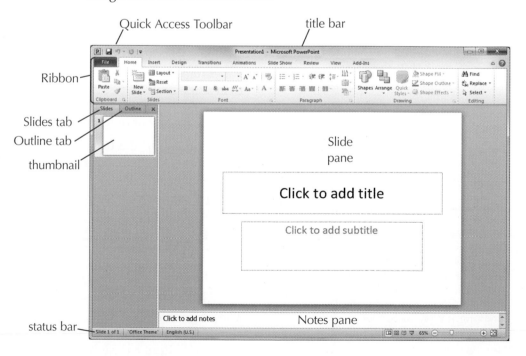

The PowerPoint window displays information about a presentation and includes tools for working with presentations:

- The file name of the current presentation is displayed in the **title bar**. The name Presentation1 is used temporarily until the presentation is saved with a descriptive name.

- Click the **File tab** to display commands for opening, saving, and printing a presentation.

- Select commands and perform actions using the **Ribbon** and the **Quick Access Toolbar**.

- The default view is **Normal view**, which divides the window into three panes. Click the **Outline tab** in the left pane to display an outline of the slide text similar to Outline view in Word. Click the **Slides tab** to display miniature versions of the slides, called **thumbnails**. Type speaker notes that correspond to the displayed slide in the **Notes pane**. Edit the current slide in the **Slide pane**. Each pane can be sized by dragging its top or right border.

- View information about the current presentation in the **status bar**.

Planning a Presentation

Before creating slides, develop a plan for the presentation. A successful presentation is carefully planned so that it clearly conveys a message. The planning process involves three steps:

1. Carefully plan the lecture or speech.

   - What is the purpose of the presentation? Determine the information to be communicated and what the effect should be on the audience, such as persuading opinions or presenting ideas.

   - Who is the audience? Identify characteristics of the audience and then determine appropriate language and speech styles. For example, young children require a different vocabulary than adults.

2. Determine the content of the slides.

   - *Content* refers to the text, graphics, and other objects on the slides. The text is created by dividing the lecture or speech into a title slide, an introduction slide, slides for each main point or topic, and a summary slide that includes contact information or any action the audience needs to take. Graphics and other objects are added to the slides to enhance the lecture or speech.

3. Determine the design and layout of the slides, and then sketch the slides using pencil and paper.

   - The *design* consists of fonts, colors, and accent graphics, and should be appropriate for the purpose and the audience. It is best to limit a design to three or less fonts, and avoid using all uppercase letters because they are more difficult to read. The text and background should be in contrasting colors. *Contrast* is the difference between the lightness and darkness of two colors. Text should preferably be a light color on a dark background or vice versa.

• What should the slides look like? Sketch the layout of each slide. The *layout* is the arrangement of text and graphics. The *title slide* usually includes the title and author and should have a different layout than the rest of the presentation.

Adding and Deleting Slides

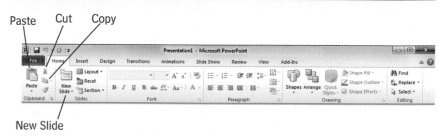

A new presentation contains one slide. To add a new slide with the same layout as the current one, click Home → New Slide. To add a new slide with a different layout, click the arrow on Home → New Slide, which displays a gallery of layouts to choose from:

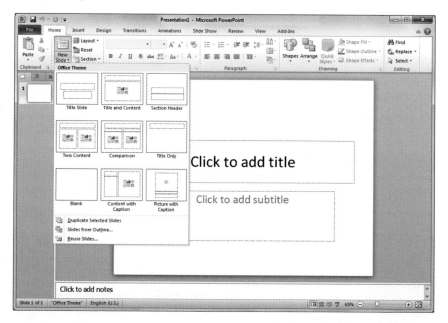

The *current slide* is the slide displayed in the Slide pane, which is indicated in the Slides tab with an orange fill around it. New slides are added after the current slide. To delete the current slide, right-click the slide in the Slides pane and select Delete Slide.

Slides can be duplicated within the same presentation. Select the slide(s) in the Outline tab or Slides tab and then click Home → New Slide → Duplicate Selected Slides. Selected slides can also be moved or copied using Home → Cut ✂ , Home → Copy 📋 , and Home → Paste.

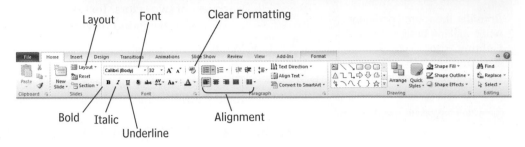

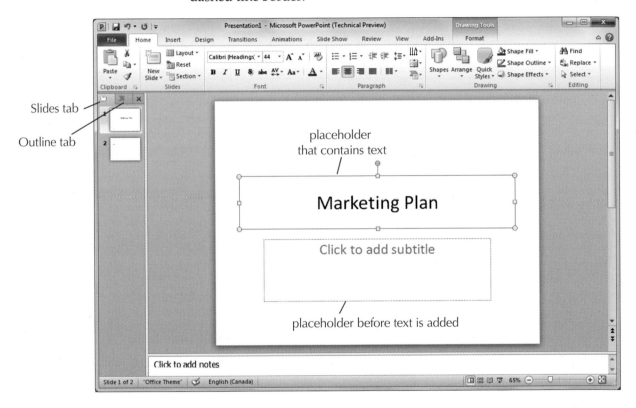

placeholders   Slides contain *placeholders* for holding text and other content such as graphics. Before content is placed, a placeholder appears as a box with a dashed-line border:

Click in a placeholder to place the insertion point and then type or edit text. The placeholder border is no longer visible after text has been added. Text can also be added or edited in the Outline tab next to the slide's icon ▣ . Selected text can be moved or copied on a slide or between slides using Home → Cut ✂ , Home → Copy ▣ , and Home → Paste.

TIP Select text by dragging the insertion point.

AutoFit   PowerPoint has a feature called *AutoFit* that automatically sizes text as it is typed so that it fits within a placeholder. AutoFit ▼ is displayed next to a placeholder when more text than can fit is typed. Click AutoFit ▼ ▾ to display a list of options that include Stop Fitting Text to This Placeholder to eliminate this feature. Sizing a placeholder larger will then display all of the text. Click a placeholder to select it and display handles, and then drag a handle to size a placeholder. Point to a placeholder border, which changes the pointer to ✥, and drag to move the placeholder.

The alignment, font, font size, and other formats can be applied to selected text in a placeholder using the Mini toolbar or Home tab. Care should be taken when formatting a presentation with different fonts. Choose no more than three different fonts for a presentation. A successful presentation is one that is easy to read. Sans serif fonts, such as Calibri and Candara, are clean-looking and a good choice for titles and headings. Serif fonts, such as Constantia, have extra lines at the ends of the letters:

No Serif (Sans Serif)   Serif

Calibri   Constantia
Candara   Cambria

A serif font is a good choice for large amounts of text. On slides, large font sizes such as 24 point are easiest to read.

To change the layout of a slide even after text has been added, click Home → Layout to display the layout gallery. Any text will be moved to the new placeholders in the new layout, if different. Multiple slides are selected by holding down the Ctrl key and clicking slides in the Slides tab or slide icons in the Outline tab. A new layout can then be applied to all the selected slides at once.

PowerPoint Views

Normal view displays the current slide in the Slide pane, and is best for editing the text and graphics on a slide. Use the vertical scroll bars or press the Page Up or Page Down key to display the next or previous slide. The left pane can be used to display slides. Click a slide in the Slides tab or click a slide icon in the Outline tab to display the slide in the Slide pane.

Slide Sorter view is useful for selecting multiple slides and changing the order of slides. Drag a slide to another position to change the order in the presentation. Slide order can also be changed in Normal view by dragging a slide icon in the Outline tab or a slide in the Slides tab.

Use the View tab to change how the presentation is displayed:

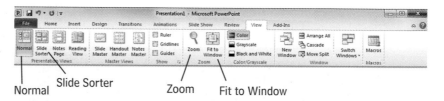

- Click Normal for the default view that divides the window into the Slides and Outline tabs, Slide pane, and Notes pane.

- Click Slide Sorter to display thumbnails of all the slides in the presentation.

- Click Zoom to display a dialog box with options for changing the magnification of the slide in Normal view.

- Click Fit to Window to display the slide as large as possible within the window.

Checking Spelling

As text is typed, spelling is automatically checked. A red wavy line appears below a misspelled word or a word not in the dictionary file. Right-click the red wavy line to display suggestions.

Alternative Hold down the Shift key and click a slide to select multiple adjacent slides.

Normal view

Alternative Click Previous Slide ⬆ or Next Slide ⬇ below the vertical scroll bar to display slides.

Slide Sorter view

Alternative To change the magnification, drag the Zoom slider or click ⊞ or ⊟ on the status bar.

Viewing a Presentation

From Beginning

Slide Show view

Slide Show view displays the presentation as it will appear to the audience. Click Slide Show → From Beginning or press F5 to start a slide show at slide 1. The slides are displayed in full-screen size and the PowerPoint window is no longer visible. Navigate through the presentation using the keyboard and mouse:

- To display the next slide, click the left mouse button or press the N key, the Page Down key, or the spacebar.

- To display the previous slide, press the P key, the Page Up key, or the Backspace key.

- To end the slide show, press the Esc key.

During a slide show, move the mouse to display a toolbar in the bottom-left corner of the screen. Buttons can be clicked to display the previous or next slide, or display a menu of options:

Alternative During a slide show, right-click the screen to display a menu of commands such as Next, Previous, Go to Slide, and End Show.

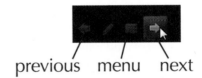

previous   menu   next

Practice: Gemstone – part 1 of 2

You will create and view a simple PowerPoint presentation. The presentation plan is:

1. The purpose of the presentation is to present basic gemstone knowledge to an audience composed of peers.

2. The content will be all text. The title slide will have a title and the author's name. An introduction slide with give an overview of the topics, and then several slides will each cover a different gemstone. A summary slide at the end of the presentation will briefly summarize the information on the gemstone slides.

3. The design should be appropriate for the purpose and the audience. The title slide will have the title in the center with the author name below it. The introduction slide will have a title at the top and two columns of bulleted list items. The rest of the slides will have a layout with a title at the top and a bulleted list below the title.

① **START POWERPOINT**

a. Ask your instructor for the appropriate steps to start Microsoft Office PowerPoint 2010.

b. Look at the PowerPoint window. Note the Slides tab, Outline tab, Slide pane, Notes pane, and status bar.

② ADD SLIDES

a. Click the arrow on Home ➝ New Slide. The layout gallery is displayed.

b. In the layout gallery, click the Two Content layout:

Two Content

A slide is added with the selected layout.

c. Click Home ➝ New Slide ➝ Title and Content. A slide is added with the Title and Content layout.

d. Click Home ➝ New Slide four times. Four more slides are added with the Title and Content layout. Check that the status bar indicates that slide 7 of 7 is displayed.

③ ENTER TEXT ON SLIDE 1

a. In the Slides tab, click slide 1 to display it.

b. In the Slide pane, click the text "Click to add title." The text disappears and the insertion point is placed.

c. Type: My Extremely Fantastic Report About Gemstones Around the World

The AutoFit feature reduces the size of the text as more text than can fit is typed.

d. Click AutoFit ⬍ and select Stop Fitting Text to This Placeholder.

e. Edit the title to read: Popular Gemstones

f. Select the text Popular Gemstones.

g. Click Home ➝ Bold. The text is formatted as bold.

h. Place the insertion point in the "Click to add subtitle" placeholder.

i. Type your name then click anywhere on the slide outside of the placeholder.

j. Click the Outline tab. Text is displayed next to the slide 1 icon.

④ ADD TEXT TO THE OTHER SLIDES

a. Click the Slides tab, then click slide 2 to display it.

b. Replace the text "Click to add title" with: Introduction

c. In the left side of the slide, click the text "Click to add text." The text disappears and the insertion point is placed.

d. Type the following text, pressing Enter at the end of each line. Note that PowerPoint adds bullets and hanging indents automatically:

- Made of minerals
- One type of mineral can form several types of gemstones
- Some are rare, others common

e. Type the following text in the placeholder on the right side of the slide, pressing enter at the end of each line:

- Found worldwide
- One type of gemstone can have several names

Check – Your slide should look similar to:

Introduction

- Made of minerals
- One type of mineral can form several types of gemstones
- Some are rare, others common
- Found worldwide
- One type of gemstone can have several names

⑤ ADD TEXT TO MORE SLIDES

a. If a placeholder is selected, click outside of the slide.

b. Press the Page Down key. Slide 3 is displayed.

c. In the title placeholder, type: Quartz

d. In the text placeholder, type the following items:

- Occurs in crystals
- Very common mineral
- Examples: amethyst, citrine

e. Click the Outline tab, then click the slide icon for slide 4. Slide 4 is displayed in the Slide pane.

f. Add the following title and text:

Beryl
- Very large crystals
- Found in Colombia, Australia, Russia
- Examples: emerald, aquamarine

g. On slide 4, select the three bulleted items.

h. Click Home → Copy 📋. The paragraphs are copied.

i. Display slide 5.

j. In the title placeholder, type: Corundum

k. Place the insertion point in the text placeholder, and click Home → Paste. The bulleted items are copied to slide 5.

l. Edit the bulleted items to read:

- Aluminum oxide material
- Found in USA, India, South Africa
- Examples: ruby, sapphire

m. Display slide 6 and add the following title and text:

Summary
- Quartz: amethyst, citrine
- Corundum: ruby, sapphire
- Beryl: emerald, aquamarine

⑥ DELETE A SLIDE

a. In the Slides pane, right-click slide 7.

b. Select Delete Slide. The slide is deleted and slide 6 of 6 is now displayed.

⑦ CHANGE THE ORDER OF SLIDES

a. Press F5. The presentation is displayed in Slide Sorter view.

b. Drag slide 5 to between slides 3 and 4. The "Corundum" slide is now slide 4.

c. Click View ➜ Normal. The presentation is again displayed in Normal view.

⑧ SAVE THE PRESENTATION

Save the presentation naming it Gemstone.

⑨ VIEW THE SLIDE SHOW

a. Click View ➜ Slide Show. PowerPoint starts the presentation by filling the screen with slide 1.

b. Press the spacebar. The next slide is displayed.

c. Press the Backspace key. The previous slide is displayed.

d. Click the left mouse button. The next slide is displayed.

e. View the entire presentation and then click the left mouse button to return to the PowerPoint window.

Themes

Themes
Colors Fonts Effects

Themes are used to maintain a consistent look throughout a presentation and in multiple documents. A *theme* is a named set of formats that changes the colors, fonts, backgrounds, and layouts of placeholders:

Office Theme

Angles Theme

Thatch Theme

Themes are accessible in Access, Word, Excel, and PowerPoint, so that documents created in all three applications can have the same theme and look like part of a professional document package.

By default, the Office theme is applied to a new presentation. To change the theme of a presentation, click a theme in the **Themes** group on the **Design** tab. To change formatting used in the applied theme, click Design ➜ Colors, Design ➜ Fonts, or Design ➜ Effects. Together these options can help implement the design and layout of a planned presentation.

TIP To change the theme of only the selected slides, right-click a theme and select **Apply to Selected Slides** in the menu. The name of the applied theme is displayed in the status bar.

Printing a Presentation

Previewing a presentation shows what printouts will look like. To preview the open presentation, select [File] → Print. Print options are displayed in Backstage view:

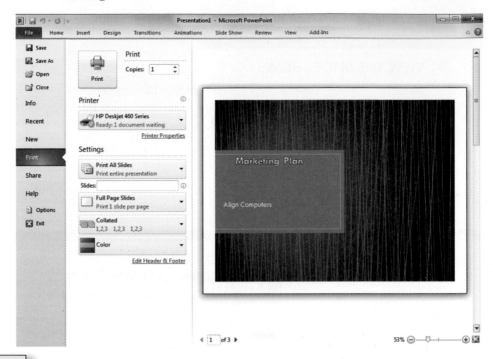

Slide 1 of the presentation is displayed in the preview area of the screen and appears as it will be printed. Use the Next Page button to view the next slide in the presentation. The Zoom slider bar in the bottom right corner of the screen is used to increase or decrease the magnification of the slide.

Print options can be changed using options in the Print, Printer, and Settings galleries. The galleries in the Settings section include options to print just the current slide, notes pages for the speaker to refer to, and to select the number of slides on a page for handouts:

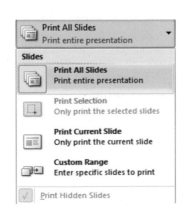

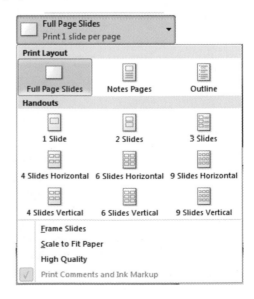

Why Print?

A presentation may be printed for a peer to edit, as notes for the speaker to use when presenting, as a handout for lecture attendees, or on transparency film for use with an overhead projector.

Design Considerations for Handouts

Consider how the audience will use the handouts. Six slides on a page may be enough to use as a reference. If the audience might need to take notes, then three slides per page with lines for notes may be more appropriate. Always include pertinent information in the header or footer, because after the presentation the attendee only has the handout.

There are also options to collate the printouts if more than one copy is being printed and to print a color presentation in grayscale or black and white:

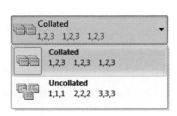

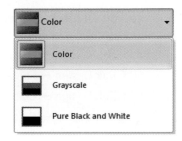

Once the print options have been selected, select Print to print the presentation.

The Edit Header & Footer link can be used to add information to the top and bottom of each printed presentation page. When the link is clicked, a dialog box is displayed. Click the Notes and Handouts tab to add header and footer information to each printed page:

- Select Date and time, and then type a date in the Fixed box or select Update automatically to insert a time stamp.

- Select Slide number to include the slide number.

- Type text in the Footer box.

- Select Don't show on title slide to hide the information on the title slide.

Practice: Gemstone – part 2 of 2

PowerPoint should already be started with Gemstone displayed from the last practice.

① CHANGE THE THEME, FONTS, AND COLOR SCHEME

   a. On the Design tab, click the Apex theme:

   The theme is applied to the entire presentation. View slides 1 and 2 and 5 to see the effects of the theme.

   b. Click Design → More Themes ⊽ → Paper:

   The theme is applied to the entire presentation. View slides 1 and 2 and 5 to see the effects of the theme.

   c. Click Design → More Themes ⊽ → Civic:

The theme is applied to the entire presentation. View slides 1 and 2 and 5 to see the effects of the theme.

d. Click Design → Fonts → Foundry. The fonts are changed in the entire presentation.

e. Click Design → Fonts → Opulent. The fonts are changed in the entire presentation.

f. Click Design → Colors → Trek. The colors are changed in the entire presentation.

g. Click Design → Colors → Office. The colors are changed in the entire presentation.

Check – Slide 1 should look similar to:

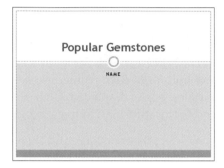

② **PREVIEW THE PRESENTATION**

a. Save the modified Gemstone.

b. Select █File█ → Print. Backstage view is displayed.

c. Click the Next Page button. The next slide is displayed.

d. Click Full Page Slides in the Settings section and select Outline from the drop-down gallery.

e. Click Outline in the Settings section and select 3 Slides from the drop-down gallery. The preview changes to show 3 slide handouts on the page.

f. Click 3 Slides in the Settings section and select 6 Slides Horizontal from the drop-down gallery. The preview changes to show 6 miniature slides on the page—this entire presentation.

③ **ADD A FOOTER TO THE PRINTOUT**

a. Click the Edit Header and Footer link under the Settings section. A dialog box is displayed.

    1. Select the Notes and Handouts tab.

    2. Set the options as shown, replacing Name with your name:

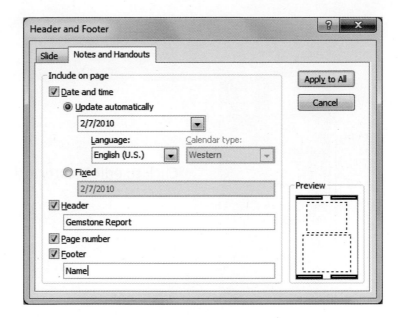

3. Select **Apply to All**. The dialog box is removed and the header and footer are added to the preview.

④ PRINT THE PRESENTATION

a. Click **Print**. The Print dialog box is displayed.

b. Select **OK**. The Gemstone presentation is printed on one page with a header and footer.

c. Click the **Home** tab to return to the presentation.

⑤ SAVE AND CLOSE THE MODIFIED GEMSTONE

The Slide Master

Slide Master

The *slide master* is the template that applies to all slides in the presentation. If there are common features in a presentation, such as a company logo on each slide, they can be added to the slide master instead of having to add them to individual slides. Click **View → Slide Master** to display the presentation in *Slide Master view*. The left pane displays thumbnails of the slide master and of all the slide master layouts. Pausing the pointer on a layout displays the layout name and indicates which slides in the presentation use that layout:

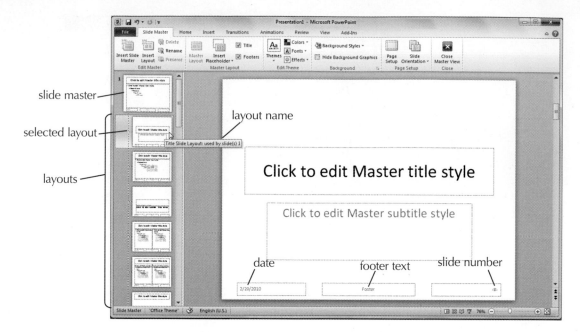

slide master

selected layout

layouts

layout name

Click the top icon in the left pane to display the slide master. On the slide master, select the text in a placeholder and then apply formatting or themes using the **Slide Master** tab, **Home** tab or **Mini toolbar**. Formatting applied to the slide master affects all the slides in the presentation. Formatting applied to a slide master layout only affects slides that use that layout.

Click **Slide Master → Close Master View** to return to Normal view.

Formatting the Background

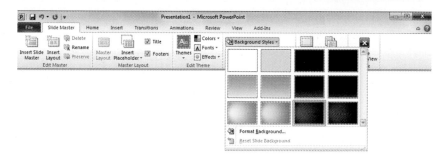

Color Considerations

The more contrast between the font color and background color, the easier it will be to read. Yellow or white text on a dark blue background has the best readability. Bright colors are difficult to view for long periods of time, and red is associated with negativity.

The background color of all the slides in a presentation can be adjusted on the slide master. Display the presentation in Slide Master view, select the slide master in the left pane, and then click **Slide Master → Background Styles**. A list of backgrounds that are available for the applied theme is displayed. To create a new background, click **Format Background**. A dialog box is displayed with options for customizing the background beyond what is included in the applied theme.

Adding Graphics to a Slide

Picture   Clip Art

Design Considerations for Graphics

Too many graphics can make a slide look busy. One main graphic on a slide is enough. If a logo or accent graphics are included, they should be relatively small.

Choose graphics carefully, because the audience is more likely to remember pictures than words. Make sure the graphics are appropriate for the topic. There may also be occasions where a graphic such as a chart can illustrate a concept better than words.

Graphics can be used to make a presentation more interesting and capture the attention of the audience. Sometimes graphics can be more informative than words and enhance a presentation. Graphics in digital format come from various sources, including scanned images, digital camera pictures, and illustration software. Click Insert → Picture to display the Insert Picture dialog box with a list of graphic files. Click Insert → Clip Art to display a task pane for finding clip art.

Graphics can be edited within PowerPoint. For example, the computer clip art is added to the slide but the background need to be modified:

TIP Use Mark Areas to Remove in the Background Removal tab to adjust the background removal.

- Click Format → Remove Background to remove the white background from the graphic:

A variety of other picture editing options, including Picture Styles, are located on the Picture Tools Format tab:

A graphic may need to be sized. Click a graphic to select it and display handles. Point to a corner handle, which changes the pointer to ⬈, and then drag to size the graphic. Drag the center of a graphic (not a handle) to move the graphic. Cut, Copy, and Paste on the Home tab can be used to create copies or move a selected graphic. Press the Delete key to delete the selected graphic. Click outside the graphic to remove the handles.

SmartArt graphics can also be added to slides. Click Insert → SmartArt to display a dialog box:

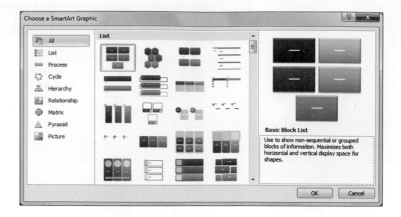

SmartArt graphics can be used to create diagrams that illustrate and simplify concepts and relationships without a lot of text. For example:

Practice: BETTER BURGER – part 1 of 2

① **OPEN BETTER BURGER**

Open BETTER BURGER, which is a PowerPoint data file for this text. The presentation has five unformatted slides with text.

② **VIEW THE SLIDE SHOW**

a. Press F5. The presentation is started with slide 1.

b. Press the spacebar. The next slide is displayed.

c. View the entire presentation and then return to the PowerPoint window.

③ **FORMAT THE SLIDE MASTER**

a. Click View ➝ Slide Master. Slide Master view is displayed.

b. In the left pane, click the top slide to select the slide master:

c. Select the text "Click to edit Master title style."

d. Click Home → Font Color 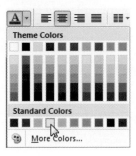 → Yellow:

The text is formatted in a yellow color.

e. With the text still selected, click Home → Font → Tahoma.

f. Select all the text in the placeholder below the title, from "Click to edit Master text styles" to "Fifth level":

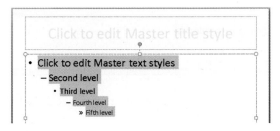

g. Format the text as Constantia.

h. Click Home → Font Color **A**. The yellow color is applied to the selected text.

i. At the bottom of the slide, in the center placeholder click Footer to select it.

j. Format the text as Constantia font in the yellow color.

k. At the bottom of the slide, in the right placeholder, format <#> as Constantia font in the yellow color.

l. At the bottom of the slide, in the left placeholder, format the date as Constantia font in the yellow color.

④ **FORMAT THE BACKGROUND**

a. Click Slide Master → Background Styles. A drop-down gallery is displayed.

b. Click Style 3:

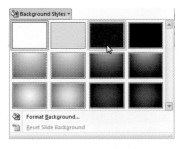

The blue background is applied to the slide master and all the layouts.

c. Click Slide Master → Close Master View. The presentation is again displayed in Normal view. Note the colors.

⑤ **ADD FOOTER INFORMATION TO THE PRESENTATION**

a. Display slide 2. Note the lack of footer information.

b. Click Insert → Header & Footer. A dialog box is displayed.

    1. Select the Slide tab, if those options are not already displayed.

    2. Set the options as shown, replacing Name with your name:

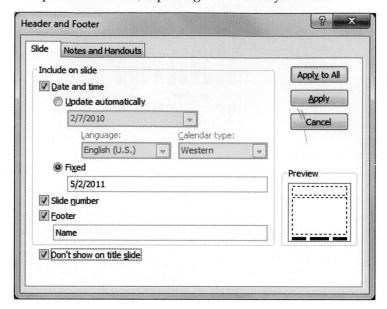

    3. Select **Apply to All**. The dialog box is removed and footer information is displayed on all but the title slide.

⑥ FORMAT TEXT ON THE TITLE SLIDE

a. Click **View → Slide Master**. Slide Master view is displayed.

b. In the left pane, click the Title Slide Layout if it is not already selected:

c. In the bottom half of the slide, select the text "Click to edit Master subtitle style."

d. Click **Home → Font Color** A . The yellow color is applied to the selected text.

e. Click **Slide Master → Close Master View**. Normal view is displayed. The subtitle on slide 1 is now yellow.

⑦ INSERT A GRAPHIC

a. Click anywhere outside the placeholders on slide 1 so that nothing is selected.

b. Click **Insert → Picture**. A dialog box is displayed.

    1. Navigate to the data files for this text.

    2. Select BURGER, which is a data file for this text.

    3. Select Insert. The graphic is displayed on the slide.

c. Point to the center of the graphic. The pointer changes to ⬩.

d. Drag the picture to be approximately centered above the title:

Creating a Chart in PowerPoint

Click Insert → Chart to place a chart on a slide. Excel is started and a worksheet is displayed. Type new data in the worksheet or open another Excel file and copy data.

⑧ SAVE THE MODIFIED BETTER BURGER

Adding a Chart to a Slide

Charts are used to illustrate numerical data, which can help the audience visualize patterns, relationships, or trends in data. Charts from an Excel workbook can be added to a slide:

1. In the workbook, select the chart to be copied.

2. Click Home → Copy 📋. The chart shows a moving dashed border.

3. In the PowerPoint presentation, display the slide in the Slide pane in Normal view.

4. Click Home → Paste. The chart is pasted on the slide, and Paste Options is displayed:

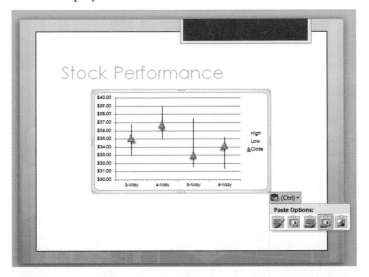

TIP Refer to Chapter 2 for more about Copy 📋 and Paste.

Click Paste Options 📋 (Ctrl) ▾ to display a list of options for the pasted chart. Options include the default Keep Source Formatting & Embed Workbook, Use Destination Theme & Embed Workbook, and Picture. Select Picture if the chart on the slide will not need to be updated when the chart changes.

When a chart is selected on a slide, options on the Design, Layout, and Format tabs can be used to modify the look of the chart.

Creating and Printing Speaker Notes

Notes Page   Notes Master

In Normal view, notes for the speaker can be typed into the Notes pane for each slide. Click the Notes pane to place the insertion point, and then type text:

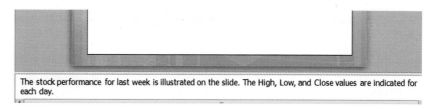

The stock performance for last week is illustrated on the slide. The High, Low, and Close values are indicated for each day.

Drag the top boundary of the pane to size it.

Notes Page view

Notes Page view

Notes Page view is used to add and format notes, add graphics to the notes, and format the layout of the Notes page. Click View → Notes Page to display one slide and the corresponding notes in Notes Page view. The notes can be printed by selecting Notes Pages in the Settings gallery in Backstage view.

TIP In addition to the notes master, click View → Handout Master to display the handout master and change the layout of handout printouts.

Similar to the slide master, the *Notes Master* is used to change the layout and look of printed speaker notes. Click View → Notes Master to display the Notes Master.

Practice: BETTER BURGER – part 2 of 2

PowerPoint should already be started with BETTER BURGER displayed from the last practice.

① **OPEN A WORKBOOK AND COPY A CHART**

    a. Start Excel and then open FAT CONTENT, which is an Excel data file for this text.

    b. Click the chart to select it.

    c. Click Home → Copy 🗐. The chart is copied to the Clipboard.

    d. Display the PowerPoint window. The BETTER BURGER presentation is displayed.

    e. Display slide 5 in Normal view.

    f. Click Home → Paste. The chart is pasted onto the slide.

    g. Click Paste Options 🗐 (Ctrl) ▾ → Picture.

    h. Size the chart if necessary and drag the chart until it is approximately centered in the lower half of the slide.

    i. Display the FAT CONTENT workbook.

    j. Close FAT CONTENT and quit Excel without saving changes.

② **CREATE SPEAKER NOTES**

    a. Display slide 2 in Normal view.

    b. Drag the top boundary of the Notes pane upwards until the Notes pane is about twice as tall as it was.

c. In the Notes pane, click the text "Click to add notes" to place the insertion point.

d. Type the following text, allowing the text to wrap:

Currently our burger has 20% more calories and 3 more grams of fat than our competition. Carbohydrates are growing in popularity as a dietary concern and our burger is loaded with carbohydrates.

e. Display slide 3 in Normal view.

f. In the Notes pane, type the following text, pressing Enter at the end of each line:

Both buns have sesame seeds.
Alternative bun costs 10% less!

g. Display slide 4 in Normal view.

h. In the Notes pane, type the following text, pressing Enter at the end of each line:

Both process cheese products are orange.
Alternative cheese has a longer shelf life.
Alternative cheese was preferred in taste tests.

③ USE NOTES PAGE VIEW TO ADD NOTES

a. Display slide 5 in Normal view.

b. Select View → Notes Page. The slide is displayed in Notes Page view. Note the slide and the notes below it.

c. Place the insertion point in the notes area and type the following text, allowing the text to wrap:

Better burger has 30% less calories, 30% less fat, and 40% less carbohydrates than our best seller.

d. Display the slide in Normal view.

④ VIEW THE SLIDE SHOW

a. Press F5. The presentation is started with slide 1.

b. View the entire presentation and then return to the PowerPoint window.

⑤ PREVIEW AND PRINT THE PRESENTATION

a. Save the modified BETTER BURGER.

b. Select ▨ File → Print. The first slide is displayed in the preview area.

c. In the Settings section, click Full Page Slides and select 6 Slides Horizontal in the Handouts section. The preview changes to show 6 miniature slides on the page—this entire presentation.

d. Select Print. The Print dialog box is displayed.

   1. Select OK. The presentation is printed on one page.

e. Select File → Print → Full Page Slides → Notes Pages. The preview changes to show one slide per page.

f. Click Next Page ▸. A notes page with a slide and speaker notes is displayed.

g. Click Print All Slides → Print Current Slide.

h. Select Print. The Print dialog box is displayed.

   1. Select OK. The presentation is printed on one page.

i. Press Esc.

⑥ SAVE AND CLOSE THE MODIFIED BETTER BURGER

E-Mailing a Presentation

E-mail is a fast and efficient message delivery system in which PowerPoint presentations can be attached to a message. Select [File] → Share → Send Using E-mail to display options for sending the presentation as an e-mail attachment in either PowerPoint, PDF, or XPS format. After selecting a format, type the e-mail address of the recipient in the To box. The file name of the presentation automatically appears as the Subject. Type text in the message box if additional information should appear in the e-mail message and then click Send to send the message.

Reviewing a Presentation

Edit Comment   Delete

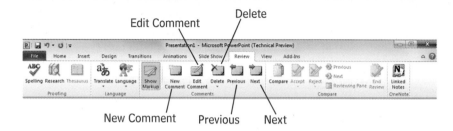

New Comment   Previous   Next

Several individuals or departments may collaborate on a presentation. To help with this process, a presentation can be e-mailed from one person to another, and each person can make edits and add comments to locations in the presentation. Comments can help explain edits.

To add a comment to the displayed slide, click Review → New Comment. Comments are indicated by icons on a slide:

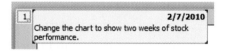

Alternative Right-click a comment to display a menu of commands such as Delete Comment.

Click a comment to view it, and double-click a comment to edit it. Press the Delete key to delete a displayed comment. Use options on the Review tab to view the Previous and Next comments, or Edit Comment or Delete a comment.

When a presentation is finished and ready to distribute to customers, employees, or other end users, be sure to delete all comments that were created in the development and reviewing process.

Practice: Butterflies

① **CREATE A NEW PRESENTATION AND ENTER TEXT**

   a. Replace the text "Click to add title" with: Report on Butterflies

   b. Replace the text "Click to add subtitle" with the text Made by followed by your name.

② **ADD A SLIDE**

   a. Click Home → New Slide → Title and Content.

   b. Replace the text "Click to add title" with: Butterfly Facts

c. Replace the text "Click to add text" with:
- Over 700 species in North America
- Most active during the day

③ **SAVE THE PRESENTATION**

Save the presentation naming it Butterflies Name replacing Name with your name.

④ **E-MAIL A PRESENTATION FOR COLLABORATION**

a. Select ▇File▇ → Share → Send Using E-mail → Send as Attachment. An e-mail window is created with the Butterflies presentation as an attachment.

b. Type the following message, replacing Name with your name: Please edit and comment on this presentation and then send it back to me. Thanks! --Name

c. In the To box, type the e-mail address of a classmate.

d. Click Send. The e-mail is sent to your classmate for review.

e. Close Butterflies.

⑤ **COLLABORATE ON A PRESENTATION**

a. Check your e-mail and open the e-mail from your classmate.

b. Save the attachment to the appropriate location.

c. Open the file.

d. View the presentation in Slide Show view.

e. Display slide 1 in Normal view.

f. Change Made to Prepared.

g. Click Review → New Comment. The insertion point is moved to the comment.

h. Type: I think Prepared sounds better.

i. Save the presentation and then select ▇File▇ → Share → Send Using E-mail → Send as Attachment. An e-mail message is displayed with the Butterflies presentation as an attachment.

j. Type the following message, replacing Name with your name:

Here are my edits. --Name

k. In the To box, type the e-mail address of a classmate.

l. Click Send. The e-mail is sent to your classmate for review.

m. Close the presentation.

⑥ **REVIEW CHANGES**

a. Check your e-mail and open the e-mail reply from your classmate. The e-mail message includes the reviewed presentation as an attachment.

b. Save the attachment to the appropriate location naming it Butterflies Name Revised.pptx where Name is your name.

c. Open the file on the hard disk.

d. Click Review → Next 🔁. The first comment is displayed.

e. Read the comment and then click Review → Delete ❌. The comment is deleted.

f. Save the modified Butterflies document.

⑦ **SAVE THE MODIFIED BUTTERFLIES AND PRINT A COPY OF SLIDE 1**

⑧ **CLOSE BUTTERFLIES AND QUIT POWERPOINT**

Chapter Summary

This chapter discussed creating presentations with Microsoft PowerPoint 2010. A successful presentation is carefully planned so that it clearly conveys a message. The purpose and audience are defined and the appearance of the slides is considered.

Slides contain placeholders for holding content. Text is typed or edited in placeholders or in the Outline tab. Alignment, font, font size and other formats can be applied to selected text using the Home tab. Content can be copied within a slide and between slides. The AutoFit feature automatically resizes text as it is typed so that it fits in a placeholder.

The Home tab is used to add new slides with various layouts of placeholders. The slide master is used to format the text, colors, backgrounds, and footer information for the entire presentation The presentation is displayed in different views using the View tab. Slides can be rearranged in Slide Sorter view. A presentation can also be displayed in Normal view, Slide Show view, and Notes Pages view. In Slide Show view, the presentation is controlled using the mouse or the keyboard.

Changing the theme changes the look of a presentation. The Design tab is used to apply a theme and to change colors and fonts used in a theme.

A presentation should be previewed before printing. Information can be added in the footer of slides or in the header or footer of printouts.

Graphics and clip art can be added to slides using the Insert tab. Notes for the speaker can be typed for each slide and then printed as notes pages. Charts from an Excel workbook can be added to a slide. When a chart is selected on a slide, options on the Format tab affect the look of the chart.

A presentation can be e-mailed as an attachment for collaboration and peer editing. Using the Review tab, comments can be added to a presentation, reviewed, edited, and deleted.

Vocabulary

AutoFit A feature that automatically resizes text as it is typed so that it fits within a placeholder.

Content The text, graphics, and other objects that appear on a slide.

Contrast Difference in lightness and darkness of two colors.

Current slide The slide displayed in the Slide pane.

Layout The arrangement of objects on a slide.

Normal view The default view which divides the window into a three panes: a left pane, Notes pane, and Slide pane.

Notes Page view Used to create and format notes and format the layout of the Notes page.

Notes pane Contains speaker notes that were typed to correspond to the current slide. Displayed in Normal view.

Notes master A master slide that changes the formatting of the notes pages.

Outline tab Displays an outline of the slide text similar to Outline view in Word.

Placeholders Container on a slide that holds text and other content such as graphics.

PowerPoint presentation A collection of slides created using Microsoft PowerPoint.

Presentation An informative speech that usually includes visuals.

Previewing a presentation Shows what printouts will look like.

Slide master A master slide that changes the formatting of all slides in the presentation.

Slide pane Displays the current slide. Displayed in Normal view.

Slide Show view Displays the current slide in full-screen size.

Slide Sorter view Displays thumbnails of all the slides in the presentation.

Slides tab Displays smaller versions of the slides.

Theme A set of layouts, formatting, and backgrounds used to quickly change the design of an entire presentation.

Thumbnail A smaller version of a slide.

Time stamp The date that is automatically updated in a footer.

Title slide The first slide in a presentation, which usually includes the title and author.

Visuals Slides, a flipchart, a white board, or handouts of printed material that are viewed while a speaker talks.

PowerPoint Commands

Apply to Selected Slides Changes the theme of the selected slides. Found in the menu displayed by right-clicking a theme.

AutoFit ⯐ Displayed next to a placeholder when more text than can fit is typed, and offers options to stop PowerPoint from automatically resizing text so that it fits in a placeholder.

Background Styles Displays backgrounds available for the applied theme. Found on the Slide Master tab.

Clip Art Displays the Clip Art task pane, used to place clip art on a slide. Found on the Insert tab.

Close Master View Returns to Normal view. Found on the Slide Master tab.

Close Print Preview Returns to Normal view. Found on the Print Preview tab.

Colors Displays a list of color schemes. Found on the Design tab.

Copy 🗎 Places a copy of the selected text or object on the Clipboard. Found on the Home tab.

Cut ✂ Moves the selected text or object to the Clipboard. Found on the Home tab.

Delete 🗙 Removes a selected comment. Found on the Review tab.

Duplicate Selected Slides Creates a new slide with the same content and layout as the selected slides. Found in Home → New Slide.

Edit Comment Displays the selected comment for editing. Found on the Review tab.

Effects Displays a list of graphical effects. Found on the Design tab.

Fit to Window Changes the magnification of the slide in Normal view to fit in the window. Found on the View tab.

Fonts Displays a list of font sets. Found on the Design tab.

Format Background Displays a dialog box used to change the background of slides. Found in Slide Master → Background Styles.

From Beginning Displays the presentation in Slide Show view, starting with slide 1. Found on the Slide Show tab.

From Current Slide Displays the presentation in Slide Show view, starting with the currently displayed slide. Found on the Slide Show tab.

Header & Footer Displays a dialog box used to add footers on slides. Found on the Insert tab.

Header and Footer Displays a dialog box used to add headers and footers to a printout. Found in Print Preview → Options.

Layout Displays a gallery of slide layouts. Found on the Home tab.

New Comment Adds a comment to the displayed slide or selected placeholder. Found on the Review tab.

New Slide Adds a new slide after the current slide. Found on the Home tab.

Next Displays the next slide in a presentation. Found in the menu displayed by right-clicking on the screen during a slide show.

Next 🗙 Displays the next comment in a presentation. Found on the Review tab.

Normal Divides the window into a three panes: a left pane, Notes pane, and Slide pane. Found on the View tab.

Notes Master Displays the Notes Master, which is used to change the look of the Notes pages. Found on the View tab.

Notes Page Displays the presentation with one slide and the corresponding notes on each page. Found on the View tab.

Options Displays a menu that contains commands for formatting the printout of a presentation. Found on the Print Preview tab.

Paste Places the contents of the Clipboard at the insertion point. Found on the Home tab.

Paste Options 📋 (Ctrl) ▾ Displays a list of options for a pasted chart. Displayed when an Excel chart is pasted onto a slide.

Picture Displays a dialog box used to place a picture on a slide. Found on the Insert tab.

Previous Displays the previous slide in a presentation. Found in the menu displayed by right-clicking on the screen during a slide show.

Previous 🔲 Displays the previous comment in a presentation. Found on the Review tab.

Print Displays a dialog box with options for printing. Found in Backstage view.

Print What Displays a list of options for printing. Found on the Print Preview tab.

Send as Attachment Sends the presentation as an attachment. Displayed after selecting 🔲 File → Share → Send Using E-mail.

Slide Master Displays Slide Master view, which includes the slide mater and its layouts. Found on the View tab.

Slide Show Displays the current slide in full-screen size. Found on the View tab.

Slide Sorter Displays thumbnails of all the slides in the presentation. Found on the View tab.

Stop Fitting Text to This Placeholder Stops PowerPoint from automatically resizing text that does not fit in a placeholder. Found in AutoFit ➕ ▾.

Zoom Displays a dialog box with options for changing the magnification of the slide in Normal view. Found on the View tab.

1. a) In Normal view, what is displayed in the Outline tab?
   b) In Normal view, what is displayed in the Slides tab?

2. a) What does the content of a slide refer to?
   b) What does the layout of a slide refer to?

3. Instead of editing text in a placeholder on a slide, where else can the text for the current slide be edited?

4. What does the AutoFit feature do?

5. a) What is displayed when the arrow below New Slide is clicked?
   b) What happens when New Slide is clicked?

6. a) Which view divides the PowerPoint window into three panes?
   b) Which view displays thumbnails of all the slides in the presentation?
   c) Which view displays the current slide in full-screen size?
   d) Which view is best for editing the text on slides?
   e) Which view is best for changing the order of slides?

7. a) How can the presentation be displayed in Slide Show view starting with slide 3?
   b) What happens when the Esc key is pressed in Slide Show view?

8. How are the fonts used in the applied theme changed?

9. List two ways to display the next page when viewing a presentation in the preview window.

10. What is printed on each page for each of the following options when printing a presentation:
    a) Outline
    b) Handouts (3 slides per page)
    c) Notes Pages

11. a) What is a time stamp?
    b) List the steps required to add the slide number and a time stamp to the footer on each slide of a presentation.

12. a) Describe a situation where the slide master would not need to be changed at all.
    b) Describe a situation where the fonts on the slide master would be changed instead of changing the fonts in the applied theme.

13. a) A company wants an elaborate, fancy script font used for all the text in a presentation. What would your recommendation be about that decision, and why?
    b) A company wants a dark blue background in a presentation and would like to know what color would be best for the text. What colors would you recommend, and why?

14. a) List the steps required to change the background of just the Two Content layout slides to a red color.
    b) Explain why a red color is a bad choice for a slide background.

15. Explain why a chart can be an effective communication tool in a presentation.

16. When you would use comments in a presentation?

True/False

17. Determine if each of the following are true or false. If false, explain why.
    a) Speaker notes are displayed when the presentation is displayed in Slide Show view.
    b) The content on a slide should include everything a speaker is going to say.
    c) The text on a slide should be formatted as small as possible.
    d) A new presentation contains three slides.
    e) Each slide layout has a separate master.
    f) The previous slide can be displayed again during a slide show.
    g) Slide Sorter view displays all the slides in the presentation in one window.
    h) The colors in a theme cannot be changed.
    i) The number of slides that are printed on a single page can be changed.
    j) A footer can be placed on individual slides and on a printout.
    k) The slide master is used to create a custom look that applies only to the first title slide in a presentation.

Project 1

Travel... With a Purpose is preparing a presentation on different maple trees in a preserve that one of their tours will be visiting:

a) Create a new presentation.

b) Modify the presentation so that it contains five slides with the following text:

> Maple Trees
> Broad-leafed Tree Series
>
> Sugar Maple
> • Sap is used for maple syrup
> • Height - 24 meters
>
> Silver Maple
> • Leaves have large teeth
> • Height - 15 meters
>
> Red Maple
> • Bright red flowers and buds
> • Height - 30 meters
>
> Tree Heights

c) Save the presentation naming it: Maple Trees

d) In a new Excel workbook, enter the tree names and their height data, and create a column chart titled Maple Trees. Save the workbook naming it: Maples

e) Place a copy of the chart on slide 5, the slide with the title "Tree Heights." Size and move the chart appropriately.

f) Apply the Median theme to the presentation.

g) Save the modified Maple Trees and print the presentation so that all the slides are printed on one page.

Project 2

Travel... With a Purpose is preparing a presentation to orient College participants to an upcoming trip.

a) Create a new presentation.

b) On slide 1, add the following text:

> Marine Biology Winter Trip: The Florida Keys
> Organized by the Biology Club and the Scuba Club

c) Add two more slides after slide 1 with the Title and Content layout.

d) Add the following text to slides 2 and 3:

> What to Expect
> • Long days in the sun and on boats
> • Some classes at night
> • Limited space for gear

What to Bring
- One duffle bag and one backpack
- Sleeping bag and mat
- Canteen and sunscreen
- Scuba gear

e) Change the background of all the slides to a dark green.

f) Change the color of the text and footers on all slides to white.

g) On slide 3, add an appropriate clip art graphic below the bulleted items. Resize and move the graphic as necessary.

h) Add your name and the slide number in the footer of all slides except slide 1.

i) Save the presentation naming it: Winter Trip Orientation

j) Print the presentation so that three slides with lines for notes are printed on each page. Include a footer with your name.

Project 3

Travel... With a Purpose is preparing a presentation on sea life for one of its tour groups.

a) Create a new presentation.

b) Modify the presentation so that it contains five slides with the following text:

Catsharks
A Brief Introduction

Characteristics
- Bottom-dwellers
- Small, up to 1 meter long

Coral Catshark
- Found in the Pacific Ocean
- White spots on dark body

Swellshark
- Found in the Pacific Ocean
- Dark brown mottled color

Striped Catshark
- Found in the Atlantic Ocean
- Dark horizontal stripes

c) Apply the Flow theme to the presentation.

d) Add the slide number and your name in the footer of all slides except slide 1.

e) Save the presentation naming it: Catsharks

f) Print the presentation so that all the slides are printed on one page. Include a footer with your name.

Project 4

Diamondback terrapins are turtles that live in brackish water along the eastern and southern coastlines of the United States. *Travel... With a Purpose* is preparing a presentation for one of its tour groups.

a) Create a new presentation.

b) Modify the presentation so that it contains four slides with the following text:

Diamondback Terrapin Turtles
An Introduction

Description
- Head, neck, and legs are spotted
- Carapace (top of shell) has rings
- Males are about 12 cm long, females can reach 22 cm long

Habitat
- Lives in brackish water
- Prefers salt marshes and tidal flats
- Hibernates in the winter, buried in mud

Other Facts
- Young terrapins are called hatchlings
- Females lay several eggs at a time, called a clutch
- Eat crabs, fish, snails, and roots
- Can live 40 years or longer

c) Apply the Concourse theme to the presentation.

d) Add the slide number and your name in the footer of each slide.

e) Save the presentation naming it: Terrapin Intro

f) Print the presentation so that all the slides are printed on one page. Include a footer with your name.

Project 5

The MANAGEMENT PLAN presentation for *Align Computers* contains 5 slides with text. Open MANAGEMENT PLAN, which is a PowerPoint data file for this text, and complete the following steps:

a) Add a new slide after slide 1 with the Title and Content layout.

b) Add the following text to the slide:

Overview
- Vision
- Employees
- Risks

c) Apply the Aspect theme to the presentation.

d) Add the slide number and the current date in the footer of all slides except slide 1.

e) Save the modified MANAGEMENT PLAN.

f) Print the presentation so that all the slides are printed on one page.

Project 6

Align Computers needs a PowerPoint presentation to go along with their sales pitch.

a) Create a new presentation.

b) On slide 1, add the following text, replacing Name with your name:

> Your Customers Want Our Computer Service
> Name, your Align Computers. Customer Service Representative

c) On slide 1, add the ALIGN LOGO graphic, which is a data file for this text. Move the picture as necessary so that it is not covering text.

d) Save the presentation naming it: Align Sales Pitch

e) Add four more slides after slide 1 with the Title and Content layout.

f) Add the following text to the slides, replacing Full Name with your full name:

> Your Customer
> • Wants Quality
> • Needs a Solution
> • Needs a Quick Turn-around
>
> Our Computers
> • Quality: we use the best materials and inspect twice
> • Variety: many different brands and models
> • Durability: tested to last
>
> Our Company
> • Orders are filled when received
> • Locations in six countries
> • Direct lines to your representative
>
> Full Name
> • fullname@gadgets.lpdatafiles.com
> • (561) 555-5000

g) Change the color of the text to a dark blue.

h) Save the modified Align Sales Pitch.

i) In a new Excel workbook, enter the following data:

> Most Important Feature
> Quality   16
> Variety   23
> Durability   11

j) Create a column chart titled Most Important Feature to 50 Customers Surveyed. Save the workbook naming it Features.

k) Place a copy of the chart on slide 2. Size and move the chart appropriately.

l) Add a date that automatically updates, the text Align Computers centered, and the slide number in the footer of all slides except slide 1. You may need to resize the text placeholder to accommodate all of the text.

m) Save the modified Align Sales Pitch.

n) Print the presentation so that the entire presentation is printed on one page.

o) Collaborate with a classmate by e-mailing the presentation to them for review, and have a classmate e-mail their Align Sales Pitch to you for review.

p) Open the e-mail from your classmate.

q) On slide 4, change the text filled when received to filled immediately.

r) Add a comment to slide 4 with the text: I changed the first bullet. I think it will sound better to the customer.

s) E-mail the reviewed presentation back to your classmate.

t) Check your e-mail and open the reviewed presentation from your classmate.

u) Read and then delete the comment on slide 4.

v) Save the modified Align Sales Pitch.

w) Print the presentation so that the entire presentation is printed on one page. Include a footer with your name.

Project 7

Align Computers needs a presentation to help train employees on proper e-mail etiquette.

a) Create a new presentation.

b) On the slide master, add the ALIGN LOGO picture, which is a data file for this text. Move the picture to the bottom-right corner of the slide. Leave a little space between the logo and the edges of the slide.

c) On slide 1, add the following text:

E-mail Etiquette
Align Computers.

d) Save the presentation naming it: Etiquette Training

e) Add two more slides after slide 1 with the Title and Content layout.

f) Add the following text to slides 2 and 3:

Message Content
• Address the client as you would in person
• Keep the message professional
• Get directly to the point

Message Formatting
• Do not type a message in all uppercase
• Use a signature block

g) Apply the Flow theme to the presentation, and change the theme colors to the Urban colors.

h) Add the following notes in the Notes pane of slide 2:

Address the client as if in person. For example, Client Z should be addressed as Ms. Z unless you would address her by her first name.
Be professional. Do not include jokes or emoticons.

i) Add the following notes in the Notes pane of slide 3:

> Using all capital letters is the equivalent of shouting.
> Use a signature block with your full name, your title, your phone number, and our company name.

j) Add a date that automatically updates and your name in the footer of all slides.

k) Save the modified Etiquette Training.

l) Print the presentation in Notes Pages layout.

Project 8

You have been hired as a *freelance writer* to create a presentation to accompany a report on the Fall Family Festival.

a) Create a new presentation.

b) On slide 1, add the following text, replacing Name with your name:

> Fall Family Festival
> Report by Name

c) On slide 1, add clip art of a leaf or leaves, above the title. Resize and move the graphic as necessary.

d) Save the presentation naming it: Festival Report

e) Add three more slides after slide 1 with the Title and Content layout.

f) Add the following text to the slides:

> Food Booths
> • Problems with trash bins
> • Not enough seating
> • Profit:
>
> Game Booths
> • Need more games for young children
> • Frisbee prizes caused problems
> • Profit:
>
> Craft Booths
> • Most popular booths
> • Not enough glue
> • Profit:

g) Change the background of all the slides to a dark green.

h) Change the color of the text and footers on all slides to a light yellow.

i) Add a date that automatically updates and the slide number to the footer of all slides.

j) Save the modified Festival Report.

k) Print the presentation so that four slides are printed on each page. Include a footer with your name.

l) Collaborate with a classmate by e-mailing the presentation to them for review, and have a classmate e-mail their Festival Report Name to you for review.

m) Open the e-mail from your classmate that you received for review and add the following dollar amounts after the Profit: text on the following slides:

Slide	Profit amount
Food Booths slide (slide 2)	$350
Game Booths slide (slide 3)	$235
Craft Booths slide (slide 4)	$440

n) Add a comment to slide 1 with the text: I added the profit amounts.

o) E-mail the reviewed presentation back to your classmate.

p) Check your e-mail and open the reviewed presentation from your classmate.

q) Read and then delete the comment.

r) In a new Excel workbook, enter the names of the booths (Food, Game, Craft) and their profit, and create a 3-D pie chart titled Profits. Include data labels that are percentages. Save the workbook naming it Festival Profits.

s) Add a slide at the end of the presentation with the title Festival Profits and place a copy of the chart on the slide. Size and move the chart appropriately.

t) Save the modified Festival Report Name.

u) Print the presentation handouts using the 6 Slides Vertical layout option.

Project 9 ☼ ───

The TRAINING document last modified in the practices of Chapter 3 has information about the Gadgets, Inc. Life-Long Learning program. The program schedule includes a session on cultural awareness and you have been asked to be a speaker.

a) Determine the purpose and audience of the presentation and write down a list of their characteristics.

b) Research one aspect of cultural awareness using the Internet and library. Write a short lecture using the information gathered during your research, keeping in mind the purpose and audience.

c) Using pencil and paper, sketch the layout and content of each slide in the presentation. Divide the content among the slides appropriately. Keep in mind the purpose and audience when designing the presentation, and include notes about which colors and fonts to use.

d) Using PowerPoint, create the presentation and save it naming it Cultural Awareness. Include appropriate clip art and slide footers, and use the colors and fonts noted in your sketches. Print the presentation so that all the slides are printed six slides to a page with your name in the footer.

e) Create speaker notes for each slide and then print all the notes pages with your name in the footer.

f) Schedule a time to give a practice presentation to your classmates. Before the scheduled practice presentation, use Word to create a rubric that can be used by your classmates for evaluating your presentation. Save the document naming it Presentation Rubric.

Some criteria are listed below, include at least one more of your own. Be sure to include a scale where appropriate:

- Were the slides appropriately designed and easy to read?
- Did the presentation appear to be well-researched and did the speaker show an understanding of the topic?
- Were the speaker's mannerisms and voice level appropriate?

If you have already created a Presentation Rubric in Project 10 or Project 11, you can use the same rubric in this Project.

g) Prepare handouts for your practice presentation. Print the handouts and a copy of the rubric for each member of your audience.

h) Give the practice presentation. After the presentation, collect the rubrics. Based on the critiques, make improvements to your presentation. In Word, write a paragraph about what you changed and why the change is an improvement. Print a copy of the document.

Project 10

The TRAINING document last modified in the practices of Chapter 3 has information about the Gadgets, Inc. Life-Long Learning program. The program schedule includes a session on assertiveness and you have been asked to be a speaker.

a) Determine the purpose and audience of the presentation and write down a list of their characteristics.

b) Research one aspect of assertiveness in the workplace using the Internet and library. Write a short lecture using the information gathered during your research, keeping in mind the purpose and audience.

c) Using pencil and paper, sketch the layout and content of each slide in the presentation. Divide the content among the slides appropriately. Keep in mind the purpose and audience when designing the presentation, and include notes about which colors and fonts to use.

d) Using PowerPoint, create the presentation and save it naming it Assertiveness. Include appropriate clip art and slide footers, and use the colors and fonts noted in your sketches. Print the presentation so that all the slides are printed six slides to a page with your name in the footer.

e) Create speaker notes for each slide and then print all the notes pages with your name in the footer.

f) Schedule a time to give a practice presentation to your classmates. Before the scheduled practice presentation, use Word to create a rubric that can be used by your classmates for evaluating your presentation. Save the Word document naming it Presentation Rubric. Some criteria are listed below, include at least one more of your own. Be sure to include a scale where appropriate:

- Were the slides appropriately designed and easy to read?
- Did the presentation appear to be well-researched and did the speaker show an understanding of the topic?
- Were the speaker's mannerisms and voice level appropriate?

If you have already created a Presentation Rubric in Project 9 or Project 11, you can use the same rubric in this Project.

g) Prepare handouts for your practice presentation. Print the handouts and a copy of the rubric for each member of your audience.

h) Give the practice presentation. After the presentation, collect the rubrics. Based on the critiques, make improvements to your presentation. In Word, write a paragraph about what you changed and why the change is an improvement. Print a copy of the document.

Project 11

The TRAINING document last modified in the practices of Chapter 3 has information about the Gadgets, Inc. Life-Long Learning program. The program schedule includes a session on organizational skills and you have been asked to be a speaker.

a) Determine the purpose and audience of the presentation and write down a list of their characteristics.

b) Research one aspect of organizational skills using the Internet and library. Write a short lecture using the information gathered during your research, keeping in mind the purpose and audience.

c) Using pencil and paper, sketch the layout and content of each slide in the presentation. Divide the content among the slides appropriately. Keep in mind the purpose and audience when designing the presentation, and include notes about which colors and fonts to use.

d) Using PowerPoint, create the presentation and save it naming it Organizational Skills. Include appropriate clip art and slide footers, and use the colors and fonts noted in your sketches. Print the presentation so that all the slides are printed six slides to a page with your name in the footer.

e) Create speaker notes for each slide and then print all the notes pages with your name in the footer.

f) Schedule a time to give a practice presentation to your classmates. Before the scheduled practice presentation, use Word to create a rubric that can be used by your classmates for evaluating your presentation. Save the Word document naming it Presentation Rubric. Some criteria are listed below, include at least one more of your own. Be sure to include a scale where appropriate:

- Were the slides appropriately designed and easy to read?
- Did the presentation appear to be well-researched and did the speaker show an understanding of the topic?
- Were the speaker's mannerisms and voice level appropriate?

If you have already created a Presentation Rubric in Project 9 or Project 10, you can use the same rubric in this Project.

g) Prepare handouts for your practice presentation. Print the handouts and a copy of the rubric for each member of your audience.

h) Give the practice presentation. After the presentation, collect the rubrics. Based on the critiques, make improvements to your presentation. In Word, write a paragraph about what you changed and why the change is an improvement. Print a copy of the document.

Project 12

Plan a presentation in which you propose a business plan for a company you wish to start. Using PowerPoint, create the presentation. Save the presentation naming it Persuade Investors. Apply an appropriate theme to the presentation. Include appropriate clip art and footer text. Add at least one chart from an Excel workbook that you create. Create speaker notes for each slide. Print the presentation using the 6 Slides Vertical handout option.

Chapter 13
Advanced PowerPoint Features

Key Concepts

Adding slide transitions and animations
Drawing annotations during a show
Creating templates and HTML files
Adding sounds and movies
Packaging a presentation
Creating hyperlinks on slides
Creating a photo album

Practice Data Files

HUMAN GEOGRAPHY QUIZ, CONTINI
LOGO, GUEST HOUSE, ROOSTER,
CHICKENS, AK BEAR, AK CARIBOU, AK
OTTER, AK SALMON, AK SHEEP

Project Data Files

MEOW, SCUBA ANEMONE, SCUBA
BUTTERFLY FISH, SCUBA CORAL, SCUBA
GRAY ANGEL, SCUBA SPONGES, BUBBLES

Adding Slide Transitions

Transitions to This Slide   Apply to All

TIP When previewing a transition, the grey background behind the slide changes to black for the duration of the transition.

A *slide transition* is the way one slide changes to the next in Slide Show view. For example, the current slide can appear to fall off the screen to reveal the next slide, or it can dissolve into the next slide. On the Transitions tab, click the Transitions to This Slide More ⊽ button to display a gallery of transitions:

Slide Timing

To have slides automatically advance, click **Transitions →** **After** and specify the time interval. To specify different timing for each slide based on the lecture of the presentation, click **Slide Show → Rehearse Timings.** When finished rehearsing the presentation, the time each slide was displayed is saved with the presentation.

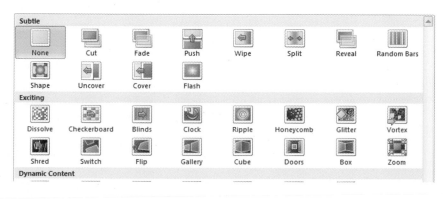

Point to a transition in the gallery to view a live preview.

Options in the Timing group affect the transition speed and what sound, if any, is played. Click Apply To All to apply the selected transition to the entire presentation. To remove transitions from a slide, apply the first option in the gallery, None.

Formatting each slide in a presentation with a different transition is perceived as choppy and disorganized, not polished and unprofessional. For a professional appearance, apply the same transition to all slides in a presentation using the slide master. Slide transitions can also be applied to multiple selected slides in Slide Sorter view.

Slide transitions are previewed by clicking the transition icon displayed next to each slide in the Slides tab or below each slide in Slide Sorter view.

Animating Objects on a Slide

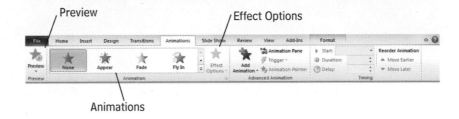

Preview   Effect Options

Animations

Animation is a visual effect in which objects appear to move. Text and objects can be animated to move onto the slide in various ways during a slide show. For example, titles can fade in and bulleted list items can slide in one by one or all together.

To animate text or an object on a slide, click the text or select the object and then click the Animation More button to display a gallery:

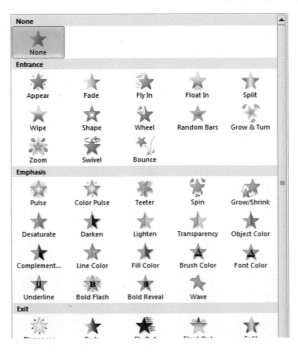

The animation styles can be applied to objects and text as they enter a slide, exit a slide, and follow a motion path.

Select Animations → Preview to view the animation. Remove an animation by selecting the text or object and then selecting None in the Animations gallery.

The direction of the animation can be adjusted by selecting Animations → Effect Options, which displays a gallery:

To make adjustments to the order of animated items, select an option in the Sequence category in the Effect Options gallery or select Animations → Animation Pane. The Animation pane is displayed. Numbers are used to identify each animated element and the order in which they are to appear on the slide:

The Animation Pane is used to reorder, time, and preview animations. To close the task pane, click Close × .

The same considerations for slide transitions apply to animations. Viewing a slide show with different animations for each item or slide is perceived as choppy and disorganized, not polished and unprofessional. For a professional appearance, apply the same animation to the same types of text or objects on all slides using the slide master.

Animations are previewed by clicking the transition icon displayed next to each slide in the Slides tab or below each slide in Slide Sorter view.

Practice: HUMAN GEOGRAPHY QUIZ – part 1 of 2

① **OPEN HUMAN GEOGRAPHY QUIZ**

    a. Start PowerPoint.

    b. Open HUMAN GEOGRAPHY QUIZ, which is a PowerPoint data file for this text.

    c. On slide 1, replace the text Name with your name.

② **ADD TRANSITIONS TO THE ENTIRE PRESENTATION**

    a. Click View → Slide Master. Slide Master view is displayed.

    b. In the left pane, click the slide master at the top.

    c. Click Transitions → More → Dissolve:

    The transition is applied and previewed.

    d. Click Transitions → More → Cube:

    The transition is applied and previewed.

    e. Click Slide Master → Close Master View. Normal view is displayed.

    f. In the Slides tab, click the transition icon next to slide 3. The slide is displayed and the transition is previewed.

③ **ADD ANIMATION TO SLIDE 1**

    a. Display slide 1 in Normal view.

    b. Place the insertion point anywhere in the words "Quiz #3…."

    c. Click Animations → More → Fly In.

    d. Click Animations → Effect Options → From Bottom Right.

④ **CUSTOMIZE THE ANIMATION FOR THE QUIZ ANSWERS**

    a. On slide 2, select the text "TRUE."

    b. Select Animations → Add Animation → Color Pulse.

    c. Change the value in the Duration box in the Timing group to 01.00.

    d. Select Animations → Preview.

⑤ **SAVE THE MODIFIED HUMAN GEOGRAPHY QUIZ**

Press F5. View the entire presentation and then return to the PowerPoint window.

Drawing Annotations in a Slide Show

annotations

Annotations are markings made on a slide that help the audience better understand the content. During a slide show, the speaker can add annotations by highlighting and drawing on slides. In Slide Show view, right-click and select Pointer Options, then select a pen type from the menu:

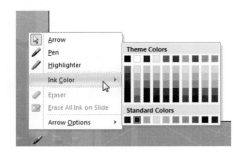

Annotation Button

During a slide show, move the mouse to display a toolbar in the bottom-left corner of the screen, then click the annotation button to display the Pointer Options submenu.

Drag to draw on the slide. Right-click and select Pointer Options → Ink Color to change the color of the ink. Annotations are removed using the Eraser or by selecting Erase All Ink on Slide. Select Arrow to return the pointer to an arrow. When the slide show is ended, a dialog box appears:

Select Keep to leave the annotations on the slides, or Discard to remove the annotations.

Practice: HUMAN GEOGRAPHY QUIZ – part 2 of 2

PowerPoint should already be started with HUMAN GEOGRAPHY QUIZ displayed from the last practice.

① VIEW THE SLIDE SHOW AND USE INK

  a. Press F5. The presentation is started with slide 1.

  b. Press the spacebar until all the text "TRUE - or - FALSE" is displayed.

  c. Anywhere on the slide, right-click and then select Pointer Options → Highlighter. The pointer changes to a small yellow rectangle.

  d. Drag the pointer across the words "cultural landscape." The text is highlighted in yellow.

  e. Drag back and forth until the words are completely highlighted.

  f. Anywhere on the slide, right-click and then select Pointer Options → Pen.

  g. Draw a circle around the word "TRUE."

h. On the same slide, experiment with other ink options and change the ink color by right-clicking and selecting Pointer Options → Ink Color.

i. Right-click and then select Pointer Options → Arrow. The pointer is an arrow again.

j. Press the spacebar until a black screen appears with the words "End of slide show, click to exit."

k. Press Esc. A dialog box is displayed.

l. Select Discard to remove the annotations and display the PowerPoint window.

② PRINT THE PRESENTATION

a. Save the modified HUMAN GEOGRAPHY QUIZ.

b. Print a copy of the presentation as Handouts with 6 horizontal slides per page.

③ SAVE AND CLOSE THE MODIFIED HUMAN GEOGRAPHY QUIZ

Creating a PowerPoint Template

A *template* is a master presentation that includes the basic formatting and elements for particular types of presentations. Templates are used again and again whenever a presentation of that type is needed. A template usually includes customized layouts, placeholders that indicate the type of information to place in them, a theme, and perhaps additional changes to the colors or fonts. For example, a company can create a template that includes their logo, corporate colors and fonts, and slide footers. The template would be used by employees to ensure a consistent design for company presentations.

TIP A PowerPoint template is saved with a .potx extension. PowerPoint templates that contain macros have a .potm extension.

To create a template, format a new presentation. Select File → Save As to display a dialog box. Select PowerPoint Template in the Save as type list and type a file name in the File name box.

To create a new presentation from a template, select File → New, then click My Templates to display a dialog box of templates. Select a template and then OK. PowerPoint creates a new, blank, untitled presentation that contains the same formatting, slides, text, and graphics as the template. This prevents accidentally saving over and changing the original template.

A variety of pre-created templates are accessible through PowerPoint. Click File → New → Sample Templates to view and select templates.

Practice: Contini, Holiday Cookies

PowerPoint should already be started.

① CREATE A NEW PRESENTATION

② FORMAT THE SLIDE MASTER

a. Click View → Slide Master. Slide Master view is displayed.

b. In the left pane, click the slide master at the top.

c. Click Slide Master ➜ Themes ➜ Solstice:

d. In the slide master, select all of the text "Click to edit Master title style."
e. On the Home tab, change the font to Cambria.
f. Drag the slide number placeholder from the bottom-right corner of the slide into the bottom of the colored bar graphic on the left side of the slide:

g. Format the slide number <#> as 16 point and bold.
h. In the left pane, click the second slide, which is the Title Slide Layout.
i. Move the "Click to edit Master title style" placeholder and the "Click to edit Master subtitle style" placeholder to the bottom half of the slide:

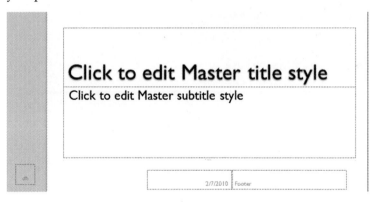

j. In the left pane, click the slide master at the top.
k. Click Insert ➜ Header & Footer. A dialog box is displayed.

    1. Select the Slide tab and set the options as shown:

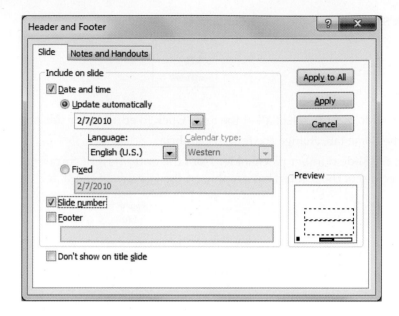

2. Select Apply to All.

③ ADD A GRAPHIC, TRANSITION, AND ANIMATION

    a. Click Insert → Picture. A dialog box is displayed.

        1. Navigate to CONTINI LOGO, which is a data file for this text, and select it.

        2. Select Insert. The graphic is placed on the slide.

    b. Drag the logo so it is to between the colored bar graphic and the date. It may cover a portion of the date's text box:

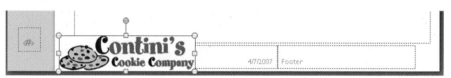

    c. Click Transitions → Dissolve:

The transition is applied and previewed.

    d. Click Slide Master → Close Master View. Normal view is displayed.

    e. On slide 1, place the insertion point anywhere in the subtitle text.

    f. Click Animations → Wipe. The animation is applied and previewed.

④ SAVE THE PRESENTATION AS A TEMPLATE

    a. Select [File] → Save As. The Save As dialog box is displayed.

        1. In the File name box, type: Contini

        2. In the Save as type list, select PowerPoint Template. Note that the Save in list has changed to display the Templates folder.

3. Select **Save**. The presentation is saved as a template.

⑤ **PRINT AND CLOSE CONTINI**

    a. Print a copy.

    b. Close Contini.

⑥ **CREATE A PRESENTATION USING THE TEMPLATE**

    a. Click ▮ File ▮ → **New**. A dialog box is displayed.

    b. Click **My Templates**. A dialog box of templates is displayed.

    c. Click Contini and then select **OK**. PowerPoint creates a new, blank, untitled presentation that contains the same formatting and graphics as the template.

⑦ **ADD CONTENT**

    a. On the slide, replace the text "Click to add title" with: Holiday Cookies

    b. Replace the text "Click to add subtitle" with the following, replacing Name with your name: Name, Director of Recipes

    c. Click **Home** → **New Slide** → **Title and Content**. A slide is added with the Title and Content layout.

    d. Click **Home** → **New Slide** again. Another slide with the same layout is added.

    e. Display slide 2 and add the following title and text:

        Last Holiday's Cookies
            • Snickerdoodles
            • Chocolate Cremes

    f. Display slide 3 and add the following title and text:

        Next Holiday's Cookies
            • Cranberry Shortbread
            • Peanut Butter Drops

⑧ **SAVE THE PRESENTATION AND VIEW THE SLIDE SHOW**

    a. Save the presentation naming it Holiday Cookies.

    b. Press F5. The presentation is started with slide 1. Notice the subtitle is not yet displayed.

    c. Press the spacebar. The subtitle wipes in.

    d. Press the spacebar again. Slide 2 dissolves in.

    e. View the entire presentation and then return to the PowerPoint window.

⑨ **CLOSE HOLIDAY COOKIES**

Adding Audio

Audio

TIP Compatible sound file formats are AIFF, AU, MIDI, MP3, MPEG, WAV, WMA.

An audio file can be added to a slide and played during a slide show. Display the slide in Normal view, and then click Insert → Audio to display a drop-down menu. Click Audio from File to display a dialog box where an audio file can be selected or click Clip Art Audio to display the Clip Art task pane with a list of sound files. PowerPoint includes a variety of sound files such as clapping and telephone sounds. Click the arrow to the right of a sound file and select Insert from the menu. A sound icon ◀ is added to the slide and Audio Tools tabs are added to the Ribbon:

Hide During Show   Loop Until Stopped

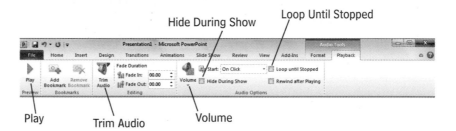

Play   Trim Audio   Volume

Alternative Click the transition icon ☆ next to a slide in the Slides tab or in Slide Sorter view to hear the sound on a slide.

- Click the Start drop-down list to play the audio start options. Select Automatically to have the audio play when the slide is displayed during a slide show or select On Click to have the audio play when the sound icon is clicked during a slide show. During a Slide Show, the audio stops playing when another slide is displayed or when the audio file ends, whichever occurs first. Select Play across slides to have the sound play across slides.

- Click Play or double-click the sound icon ◀ on the slide to play the audio.

- Click Volume to adjust the overall volume for all the sounds in the slide show.

- Select Hide During Show so that the sound icon is not displayed during the slide show.

- Click Loop Until Stopped to repeatedly play a sound until a different slide is displayed in a slide show.

- Click Trim Audio to edit the length of the audio clip.

Recording Audio

Audio can be recorded and attached to a slide by connecting a microphone to the computer and clicking Insert → Audio → Record Audio.

On a slide, a sound icon ◀ can be moved and sized like a picture. Click the icon to select it and display handles for sizing. Press the Delete key to remove a selected sound. Click outside the icon to remove the handles.

When choosing sounds, make sure the sounds are appropriate for the audience and the topic. Sounds should enhance the slides without becoming annoying. Too many sounds can have a negative effect on the audience.

Adding Video

Video clips can be added to a PowerPoint presentation using the Insert → Video command:

Video

Video can be added from a file, a Web site, or from the Clip Art task pane. To add video from the Web, select Insert → Video → Video from Website. A dialog box is displayed:

Copy the embed code from that Web site, paste it into the dialog box, and then click Insert.

To add video from a file, select Insert → Video → Video from File. Compatible video file formats include .flv, .asf, .avi, .mpg, .mpeg, .and wmv. To add clip art video, select Insert → Video → Clip Art Video. The Clip Art task pane is displayed with available video clips. Use the Search for box to find specific video clips:

The Video Tools Format tab is displayed when video is inserted:

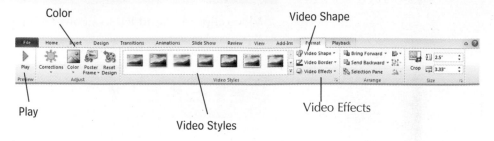

- Click Play to play the movie once.
- Click Color to modify the video color.
- Click a Video Style to apply a style to the video.
- Click a Video Shape or Video Effects change the video shape or effects.

The Video Tools Playback tab is also displayed:

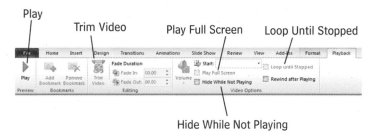

- Select Loop Until Stopped to repeatedly play a movie until a different slide is displayed in a slide show.
- Select Play Full Screen to fill the screen with the movie when it plays.
- Select Hide While Not Playing to hide the video clip when it is not playing.
- Select Trim Video to edit the length of the video clip.

Click the movie to select it and display handles for sizing. Press the Delete key to remove a selected movie. Click outside the movie to remove the handles.

When choosing movies, make sure the movies are appropriate for the audience and presentation topic. Movies should add information or enhance a topic without distracting the audience from the topic. Movies should be of good visual quality and should not be too long, so the audience does not get distracted.

Practice: GUEST HOUSE

You will need a sound card and speakers to hear the sounds in this practice. PowerPoint should already be started.

① **OPEN GUEST HOUSE**

    Open GUEST HOUSE, which is a PowerPoint data file for this text.

② **ADD A SOUND TO A SLIDE**

    a. Display slide 2.

    b. Click Insert ➙ Audio ➙ Audio from File. A dialog box is displayed.

        1. Navigate to ROOSTER, which is a sound data file for this text, and select it.

        2. Select Insert. A sound icon is added to the slide.

    c. Drag the sound icon to the end of the "Actual working farm" phrase:

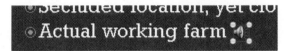

    d. Click the play button. A rooster's sound is played.

③ **ADD A MOVIE TO A SLIDE**

    a. Display slide 4.

    b. Click Insert ➙ Video ➙ Video from File. A dialog box is displayed.

        1. Navigate to CHICKENS, which is a movie data file for this text, and select it.

        2. Select Insert. The movie is added to the slide.

    c. Drag the movie to be centered below the bulleted items:

    d. Click the play button. The five-second movie plays once.

④ **SET THE MOVIE TO LOOP**

    a. Click the movie to select it if handles are not already displayed.

    b. Click Playback ➙ Loop Until Stopped. The movie will continuously loop during a slide show until it is clicked.

    c. Add appropriate animation and transition effects.

⑤ **SAVE THE MODIFIED GUEST HOUSE AND VIEW THE MULTIMEDIA SLIDE SHOW**

    a. Save the modified GUEST HOUSE.

    b. Press F5. The presentation is started with slide 1.

c. Press the spacebar until the bulleted items on slide 2 appear.
d. Click the sound icon. The rooster sound is played.
e. Press the spacebar to view slide 3 and then slide 4. Stop when the bulleted items on slide 4 appear.
f. Click the movie. The movie plays continuously, over and over.
g. Click the movie. The movie stops playing.
h. Press the spacebar to end the presentation. A black screen is displayed. Press Esc to return to the PowerPoint window.

Delivering a Presentation

There are many ways to *deliver a presentation*, which refers to the location and manner in which the audience experiences the presentation:

- A live speaker lectures or narrates while the presentation is projected onto a large screen in the same room as the audience. The presentation is typically projected using a digital projector connected to a computer.
- A live speaker in one location presents to audience members in other locations using collaborative meeting software such as Microsoft Office Live Meeting, WebEx, Adobe Acrobat Connect, or GoToMeeting. Each audience member views the presentation on a computer at their location while listening to the speaker lecture or narrate. Everyone in the meeting sees the same presentation and can communicate with each other.
- The presentation is played in a continuous loop on an unattended computer, and viewed by anyone who chooses to watch it. For example, at a kiosk or in a museum exhibit.
- The presentation is distributed on CD or published to the Web, so that the presentation can be viewed at any time.
- The presentation is printed on paper in various layouts and given to the audience to read.

Types of Projectors

LCD (liquid crystal display) projectors display colors using glass panels. DLP (digital light processing) projectors use a chip with thousands of mirrors to project light. The DLP projectors are also called digital projectors and produce better-quality, brighter images than LCD.

A PowerPoint presentation will need to be moved to the location where it will be delivered. You can package a presentation to a folder on your computer or to a CD. This process copies all of the linked and embedded files so that the presentation can be watched on most computers even if the computer does not have PowerPoint installed. As an alternative, a video can also be created using the timings, narrations, and animations in the slide show. Select File → Share to display options for sharing and packaging a presentation:

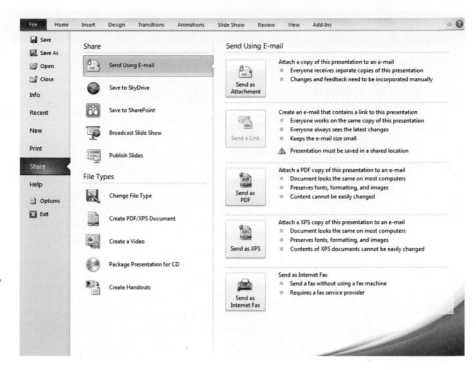

TIP Select Publish Slides to publish slides to a slide library or to a SharePoint site.

Select Package Presentation for CD → Package for CD to display a dialog box:

Rehearse Timings

Use the Rehearse Timings feature in the Slide Show tab to run a presentation automatically and display each slide for a specific number of seconds.

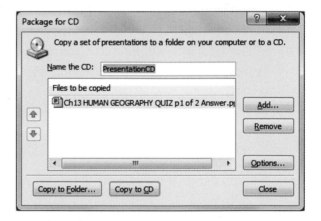

TIP Refer to Chapter 1 for information on creating a strong password.

- Type a name for the CD or the new folder in the Name the CD box.
- Select Add Files and select additional presentations and files to add to the package, such as any linked movie files.
- Select Options to display a dialog box with options for linked files, embedded fonts, and passwords that restrict opening or modifying the presentation.

Click Copy to Folder to package the presentation to a folder on a computer or network. Click Copy to CD to package the presentation to a blank, writable CD in a writable CD drive. Click Close to remove the dialog box without packaging the presentation.

Practice: Guest House Promo

PowerPoint should already be started with GUEST HOUSE open from the last practice.

① **PACKAGE THE PRESENTATION TO A FOLDER**

a. Click **File** → Share → Package Presentation for CD → Package for CD. A dialog box is displayed.

b. Select OK. A dialog box is displayed.

c. Select Options. A dialog box is displayed. Set the options as shown:

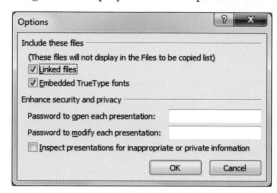

d. In the Password to modify each presentation box, type a password you can remember.

   1. Select OK. The Confirm Password dialog box is displayed.

   2. In the Reenter the password required to modify files box, type the same password and then select OK.

e. Select Copy to Folder. A dialog box is displayed.

f. In the Folder name box type: Guest House Promo

g. Select Browse to choose the location where you want the folder.

h. Select OK. A dialog box is displayed.

i. Select Yes to include linked files. A folder is created and the files are copied.

j. Select Close. The presentation, complete with viewer, fonts, and the linked movie, is in a folder and protected from modifications by a password.

② **CLOSE GUEST HOUSE AND VIEW THE PACKAGED PRESENTATION**

Hyperlinks on a Slide

Hyperlink to a Slide

To create a hyperlink from selected text to another slide, click Insert → Hyperlink. The Insert Hyperlink dialog box includes the Place in This Document options for inserting a hyperlink to another slide. Click a slide in the dialog box to select the destination for the hyperlink.

Hyperlink

When a Web site address is typed in a slide, PowerPoint automatically turns it into a hyperlink. A reader viewing the presentation on screen can click the link, which displays the Web page in a browser window if there is an Internet connection.

PowerPoint also recognizes an e-mail address and formats it as different colored, underlined characters. An e-mail address on a slide is clicked to display a new e-mail message window.

The Insert Hyperlink dialog box contains options for inserting a hyperlink into a document. To use this dialog box, click Insert → Hyperlink. Select a type of link from the Link to list and then type a label in the Text to display box. For Web page links, type a URL in the Address box. For an e-mail address link, type an address in the E-mail address box. The label is placed at the insertion point, but the URL will be followed when the reader clicks the label.

To change the hyperlink back to regular text, right-click the link and then select Remove Hyperlink from the menu. The text remains, but is no longer a hyperlink.

Creating a Photo Album

Photo Album

PowerPoint has a photo album feature that is used to create a slide show of pictures. To create a photo album presentation, click Insert → Photo Album → New Photo Album which displays a dialog box. Select File/Disk to locate and select a picture file. Add pictures one by one to the list in the dialog box. After selecting a layout in the Picture layout list, select Captions below ALL pictures to add captions to every slide. A theme can be applied in the Theme box and photos can be adjusted using buttons below the Preview. Click Create to create a new presentation with a title slide and pictures on additional slides. The presentation can be formatted like any other presentation. The photo album presentation can be packaged to a folder or CD to distribute, or published to the Web or another computer for viewing.

To edit a photo album presentation, click Insert → Photo Album → Edit Photo Album which displays a dialog box of options.

Practice: Alaska Photos

PowerPoint should already be started.

① **CREATE A PHOTO ALBUM**

  a. Select Insert → Photo Album → New Photo Album. A dialog box is displayed.

  b. Select File/Disk. A dialog box is displayed.

    1. Navigate to AK BEAR, which is a data file for this text, and select it.

    2. Select Insert. The picture is displayed in the preview and the file name is added to the Pictures in album list.

  c. Select File/Disk. A dialog box is displayed.

    1. Navigate to AK CARIBOU, which is a data file for this text, and select it.

    2. Select Insert. The picture is added.

   d. Use File/Disk to add three more pictures to the album:

        AK OTTER

        AK SALMON

        AK SHEEP

   e. In the Picture layout list, select 1 picture.

   f. Click **Create**. After a few seconds a new presentation is created with a title slide and a slide for each picture. Slide 1 is displayed in Normal view.

② **FORMAT THE PRESENTATION AND ADD A HYPERLINK**

   a. In the Slides tab, select slide 6 and press the Delete key. Slide 6 is deleted.

   b. Display slide 1, and change the text Photo Album to: Alaska Wildlife

   c. On slide 1, change the text below the title to the following, replacing Name with your name: Photography by Name

   d. Place the insertion point at the end of the your name and press Enter.

   e. Type: Alaska Tours www.lpdatafiles.com/tours.htm

   f. Type a space.

   g. Click **Design → More Themes ⌄ → Foundry**. The Foundry theme is applied.

③ **ADD CAPTIONS TO THE ENTIRE PRESENTATION**

   a. Click **Insert → Photo Album → Edit Photo Album**. A dialog box is displayed.

      1. In the Picture layout drop-down list, select 1 picture with title.

      2. Select the Captions below ALL pictures check box.

      3. Select Update.

   b. Display slide 2. The file name of the picture is the default caption.

   c. Change the text under the photo to: Grizzly Bear

   d. Display slide 3 and change the text under the photo to: Male Caribou

   e. Display slide 4 and change the text under the photo to: Sea Otter

   f. Display slide 5 and change the text under the photo to: Pacific Salmon

④ **SAVE THE PRESENTATION AND VIEW THE SLIDE SHOW, AND PRINT A COPY**

   a. Save the file naming it Alaska Photos.

   b. Press F5. The presentation is started with slide 1.

   c. This step requires a browser and Internet access. If either of these are not available, then skip this step.

      1. Click www.lpdatafiles.com/tours.htm. A browser window is opened and the Web site displayed.

      2. Close the browser window.

   d. View the entire presentation and then return to the PowerPoint window.

⑤ **SAVE, PRINT, AND CLOSE THE PRESENTATION**

   a. Save the modified Alaska Photos.

   b. Print a copy of the presentation using the 6 Slides Horizontal handouts option.

   c. Close Alaska Photos.

   d. Quit PowerPoint.

Chapter Summary

This chapter discussed features that enhance PowerPoint presentations and methods for distributing a presentation. Slide transitions and animations affect the way slides appear during a slide show and the way items move onto a slide. A professional presentation usually has one type of slide transition and animation applied to the entire presentation. Slide transitions and animations are added using the Animations tab and can be previewed in Normal view without viewing the slide show. The Custom Animation task pane includes options for formatting animations.

Annotations are notes or markings made on a slide that help the audience better understand the content. During a slide show, the speaker can add annotations by drawing and highlighting on slides. The annotations can be saved with the presentation or removed when the slide show is ended.

A PowerPoint template includes formatting and elements for presentations that need to be created over and over again. A template usually includes customized layouts, placeholders, and additional changes. Predesigned templates are also accessible through PowerPoint.

Sound files and movie files can be added to a slide using the Insert tab. Sounds and movies are played during a slide show and should be appropriate for the topic and enhance a presentation without annoying the audience.

Delivering a presentation refers to the location and manner in which the audience experiences the presentation. A PowerPoint presentation need to be packaged with the associated files to be moved to the location where it will be delivered. Presentations can be copied to a CD or to a folder on a hard disk.

When a Web site address or e-mail address is typed in a slide, PowerPoint automatically turns it into a different colored, underlined hyperlink. Blue is the default color, but may be different depending on the applied theme. Clicking the link displays the Web page in a browser window or an e-mail message window.

The photo album feature is used to quickly create a slide show of pictures. A photo album presentation can be created using the Insert tab and then packaged to a folder or CD to distribute, or published to the Web or another computer for viewing.

Vocabulary

Animated GIF A file with several graphics that display in sequence and appear animated.

Animation A visual effect that refers to the way items move.

Annotations Markings made on a slide that help the audience better understand the content.

Deliver a presentation The location and manner in which the audience experiences the presentation.

HTML The file format for documents viewed using a browser, such as documents on the Web.

Movie A digital video file from various sources, including digital cameras or illustration software.

Slide transition The way one slide changes to the next in Slide Show view.

Sound An audio file that can be added to a slide and played during a slide show.

Template A master presentation that includes the basic formatting and elements for presentations that need to be created over and over again.

Title Text in the title bar of the browser window.

PowerPoint Commands

Animate   Displays a list of animations. Found on the Animations tab.

Arrange All   Displays all open presentations at the same time. Found on the View tab.

Arrow   Changes the pointer to an arrow during a slide show. Found in the Pointer Options submenu displayed by right-clicking a slide during a slide show.

Audio from Clip Organizer   Displays the Clip Art task pane with a list of sound files. Found in Insert → Audio.

Audio from File   Displays a dialog box with a list of sound files. Found in Insert → Audio.

Custom Animation   Displays the Custom Animation task pane. Found on the Animations tab.

Edit Photo Album   Displays a dialog box used to edit a photo album presentation. Found in Insert → Photo Album.

Erase All Ink on Slide   Removes all the annotations on a slide. Found in the Pointer Options submenu displayed by right-clicking a slide during a slide show.

Eraser   Removes annotations when the pointer is dragged. Found in the Pointer Options submenu displayed by right-clicking a slide during a slide show.

Highlighter   Draws a very wide band on the slide when the pointer is dragged. Found in the Pointer Options submenu displayed by right-clicking a slide during a slide show.

Hyperlink   Displays a dialog box used to create a hyperlink. Found on the Insert tab.

Ink Color   Changes the color used to draw annotations. Found in the Pointer Options submenu displayed by right-clicking a slide during a slide show.

Loop Until Stopped   Formats a sound or movie to play continuously until the next slide is displayed during a slide show. Found on the Playbackj tab.

New Photo Album   Displays a dialog box used to create a photo album presentation. Found in Insert → Photo Album.

Package Presentation for CD   Displays a dialog box used to package an open PowerPoint presentation. Found in File → Share.

Pen   Draws a thin line on a slide during a slide show. Found in the Pointer Options submenu displayed by right-clicking a slide during a slide show.

Play Full Screen   Fills the screen with the movie when it plays during the slide show. Found on the Playback tab.

Play   Displays a list of options for playing a movie during the slide show. Found on the Playback tab.

Play   Displays a list of options for playing sound during the slide show. Found on the Playback tab.

Pointer Options   Displays a submenu of commands for making annotations. Found in the menu displayed by right-clicking a slide during a slide show.

Remove Hyperlink   Changes the selected hyperlink to regular text. Found in the menu displayed by right-clicking a hyperlink.

Save As   Displays a dialog box used to save a presentation as a template or an HTML file. Found in Backstage view.

Sound   Displays a list of options that affect the sound played during a slide transition. Found on the Transitions tab.

Video from Clip Organizer   Displays the Clip Art task pane with a list of movie files. Found in Insert →Video.

Video from File   Displays a dialog box with a list of movie files. Found in Insert → Video.

1. a) What is a slide transition?
    b) List the steps required to add a transition to all the slides in a presentation.

2. a) What is animation?
    b) List the steps required to animate the text on slide 2 with the Fade All At Once animation.
    c) What are three tasks that can be performed in the Custom Animation task pane?

3. a) Where is a transition icon displayed?
    b) What is a transition icon used for?

4. a) What are annotations?
    b) How could annotations be useful? Give an example.

5. List the steps required to draw a purple x on slide 4 with the ballpoint pen pointer option.

6. a) What is a template?
    b) How could a template be useful? Give an example.

7. a) What is audio?
    b) Where does a sound icon appear?

8. a) List the steps required to add audio from the Clip Organizer to slide 3 and have the sound play automatically during the slide show as soon as the slide is displayed.
    b) How is the volume for all the sounds in a slide show adjusted?

9. Which would be better: a different sound plays every time a new slide is displayed, or the same sound plays every time a new slide is displayed? Explain your answer.

10. What video formats are supported?

11. a) List five ways to deliver a presentation.
    b) List the steps to package an open PowerPoint presentation to a CD.

12. Why would you password protect a PowerPoint presentation that is being packaged to a CD?

13. How is a hyperlink created on a slide?

14. a) Describe the photo album feature.
    b) Describe two scenarios for using a photo album presentation. Include a description of what you would need to do to the PowerPoint file for the scenario.

True/False

15. Determine if each of the following are true or false. If false, explain why.
    a) Clicking the slide transition icon displays a slide in Slide Show view.
    b) Fade is an animation that can be applied to text.
    c) Too many different animations can distract the audience.
    d) Annotations are added in Normal view.
    e) Annotations can be saved.
    f) Ink color is always red.
    g) Templates can only be used once.
    h) By default, sound files stop when a new slide is displayed.
    i) On a slide, a movie can be sized like a graphic.
    j) An e-mail address typed on a slide requires formatting to make it a hyperlink.

Project 1

The Maple Trees presentation was created in Chapter 12, Project 1. Open Maple Trees and complete the following steps:

a) Apply an appropriate transition to all of the slides.

b) Animate the chart on slide 5.

c) Save the modified Maple Trees.

Project 2

The Winter Trip Orientation presentation was created in Chapter 12, Project 2. Open Winter Trip Orientation and complete the following steps:

a) Apply an appropriate transition to all of the slides.

b) Animate the graphic on slide 3 using an appropriate animation and effection option. Experiment with the Duration time.

c) On slide 2, add a fourth bulleted item with text and a hyperlink:

- Check the weather: www.weather.com

d) Save the modified Winter Trip Orientation.

e) Print the presentation so that three slides are printed on each page.

Project 3

The Catsharks presentation was created in Chapter 12, Project 3. Open Catsharks and complete the following steps:

a) Apply the Vortex transition to all the slides.

b) Apply the From Bottom effect option to all the slides.

c) On slide 1, add the MEOW sound, which is a data file for this text. Position the sound icon in the upper-right corner of the slide. Format the sound to automatically play once when the slide is displayed.

d) Save the presentation naming it: Catsharks

e) Print the presentation so that all the slides are printed on one page.

Project 4

There are other presentation applications in addition to Microsoft Office PowerPoint 2010. Use the Internet and library to research and compare the cost and features of three other presentation programs that are currently available.

a) Create a new presentation and modify it to include a title slide and at least one slide for each researched presentation program or one slide for each feature. Include pictures if possible.

b) Include a hyperlink to each presentation program's home page.

c) Save the presentation naming it: Presentation Software

d) Apply an appropriate theme to the presentation.

e) Apply an appropriate transition to all the slides.

f) Add a slide at the end of the presentation with notes about when each presentation program would be best suited to be used. Include notes in the Notes pane that explain your findings.

g) Save the modified Presentation Software.

h) Print the presentation so that six slides are printed on each page, with a footer that includes your name.

i) Print the last slide as Notes Pages.

Project 5

Digital projectors are commonly used in classrooms and in business to project presentations onto a screen. Common features that vary between projectors are:

Brightness The greater the brightness, the farther the projector can be from the screen. *Lumens* is the unit used to express brightness.

Keystone Correction A *keystone effect* refers to one side to the projected image being larger that the other side. Keystone effect usually happens when the projector is tilted. Some projectors have a feature that corrects the keystone effect.

Lamps The lamp is the bulb that provides light in the projector. Replacement lamps vary by cost and life (how long they last).

Display Technology Two of the most common display technologies are LCD and DLP.

Use the Internet and library to research and compare the cost and features of three digital projectors.

a) Create a new presentation and modify it to include a title slide and at least one slide for each researched projector or one slide for each projector feature. Include pictures if possible.

b) Include a hyperlink to the home page of each company that produces the projectors.

c) Save the presentation naming it: Digital Projectors

d) Apply an appropriate theme.

e) Apply an appropriate animation to the bulleted items on all the slides.

f) Save the modified Digital Projectors.

g) Print the presentation using the 6 Slides Horizontal Handouts option.

Project 6

Choose one of the ways to deliver a presentation discussed earlier in this chapter and make a list of all the technology needed to deliver a presentation using that method. For example:

> A live speaker in one location presents to audience members in other locations using collaborative meeting software such as Microsoft Office Live Meeting. Each audience member views the presentation on a computer at their location while listening to the speaker lecture or narrate. Everyone in the meeting sees the same presentation and can communicate with each other.

> The technology for this method needed would be collaborative meeting software, and computers with speakers and microphones.

Use the Internet and library to research and compare the cost and features of the technology for the delivery method you chose.

a) Use a template to create the presentation and modify it to include a title slide and at least one slide for each researched technology. Include notes for each slide that expand on the points on the slide.

b) Save the presentation naming it: Presentation Delivery

c) Apply an appropriate theme to the presentation.

d) Apply the Fly In animation to the bulleted items on all the slides and then an appropriate transition to all the slides.

e) Add a slide to the end of the presentation, with the words The End. Add a sound to the slide from the Clip Organizer called "Claps Cheers" to the last slide. Format the sound to automatically play once when the slide is displayed.

f) Save the modified Presentation Delivery.

g) Print the presentation so that the notes are included on each page, with a footer that includes your name.

h) Schedule a time to give a practice presentation to an audience of your peers. Before the scheduled practice presentation, use Word to create a rubric that can be used by your peers for evaluating your presentation. Save the document naming it Presentation Rubric. Some criteria are listed below, include at least one more of your own. Be sure to include a scale where appropriate:

- Were the slides appropriately designed and easy to read?
- Did the presentation appear to be well-researched and did the speaker show an understanding of the topic?
- Were the speaker's mannerisms and voice level appropriate?

If you have already created a Presentation Rubric in Chapter 12 Projects 9, 10, or 11, you can use the same rubric in this Project.

i) Prepare handouts for your practice presentation. Print the handouts and a copy of the rubric for each member of your audience.

j) Give the practice presentation. After the presentation, collect the rubrics. Based on your peer critique, make improvements to your presentation.

Project 7

The scuba club wants to see a slide show of photos from a recent dive trip.

a) Create a new photo album in the **1 picture** Picture layout. Use the following photos, which are data files for this text:

    SCUBA ANEMONE
    SCUBA BUTTERFLY FISH
    SCUBA CORAL
    SCUBA GRAY ANGEL
    SCUBA SPONGES

b) Save the presentation naming it Scuba Photos.

c) Change the title on slide 1 to Photos from Pompano Beach.

d) On slide 1, change the text below the title to the following, replacing Name with your name: Photography by Name

e) Add the BUBBLES sound, which is a data file for this text, to each slide that has a photo. Set the sound to not be visible during the slide show, and to play once on each slide as it is displayed.

f) Change the background of all the slides to a dark blue.

g) Apply an appropriate transition to all the slides.

h) Add a caption to all the slides, and then remove the word SCUBA from each caption.

i) Save the modified Scuba Photos.

j) Print the presentation so that all the slides are printed on one page, with a footer that includes your name.

k) Package the presentation to a folder (or a CD if possible).

Project 8

Chapter 1 in the text discussed a variety of technology-related topics. Expand your knowledge by choosing one of the following topics and researching it using books, magazines, or the Internet:

- Ergonomics
- IT Careers
- The history of computers
- Viruses
- Computer privacy issues
- Networks
- Communication etiquette
- Operating systems

a) Develop a well-designed PowerPoint presentation to document your research.

b) Include speaker notes for each slide.

c) Save the presentation naming it Technology Lecture.

Chapter 14
Desktop Publishing

Practice Data Files

SOS QUARTERLY, PEACE RIVER, BINOCULARS, SAGE'S OUTDOOR SUPPLIES

Project Data Files

MUSIC LESSONS, INSTRUMENTS, MUSIC LIST

What is Desktop Publishing?

publication

Desktop publishing is the process of combining text and graphics into one file, called a *publication*. A desktop publishing application such as Microsoft Publisher 2010 has tools and features for creating publications such as flyers, brochures, gift certificates, business cards, and posters:

- A flyer is a single sheet of paper, usually printed on one side, that communicates information about an announcement or event. Flyers are usually posted on walls but may be distributed by hand, mailed in an envelope, or placed in a strategic location for interested people to pick up.

- Booklets, cards, and brochures are created by printing on one or both sides of a paper and then folding the paper in various ways. These publications may be distributed by hand, mailed, or posted in a strategic location.

- Business cards, gift certificates, and postcards are created by printing on special paper that separates into pre-cut shapes after printing.

- Banners and posters are created by printing on large paper or gluing or taping several pages together.

The types of publications that can be created are limited only to the imagination. A folded card, for example, can be used as a greeting card or an invitation. A single-sheet publication can be a newsletter by adding pages to the publication and printing the pages back to back.

Publication Design

Publication design is the process of determining the format and layout and then creating a publication. *Format* is the finished size, materials, and binding. *Layout* is the arrangement of elements on a page. The format and layout are determined by the purpose and audience. *Purpose* is the intent of the publication, and the *audience* is who will read it.

Publication design has several steps:

1. Determine the purpose, audience, format, and layout.

2. Sketch the layout.

3. Review and revise sketches.

4. Create the publication and print a copy.

5. Review the publication and make any changes.

Creating a New Publication

TIP If Publisher is already running, select [File] → New to create a new publication.

When Publisher is started, the Getting Started window is displayed with numerous publication types to choose from:

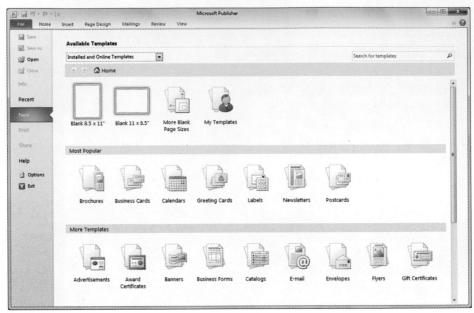

template   A *template* is a master publication that includes the basic elements for particular types of publications. Templates are used again and again whenever a document of that type is needed. Click More Blank Page Sizes to display different sizes of blank publications or click a publication type, such as Brochures to display templates:

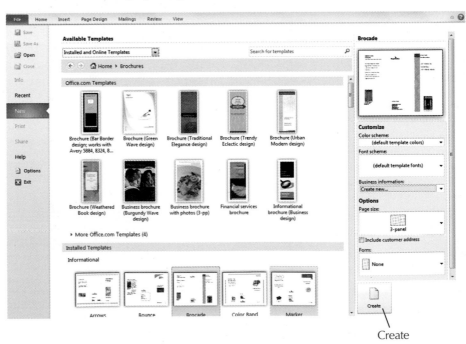

Create

TIP Selecting an Office.com Template displays a Download button instead of a Create button.

Click a template and then select a color and font scheme in the Customize options. Select Create to create the new publication:

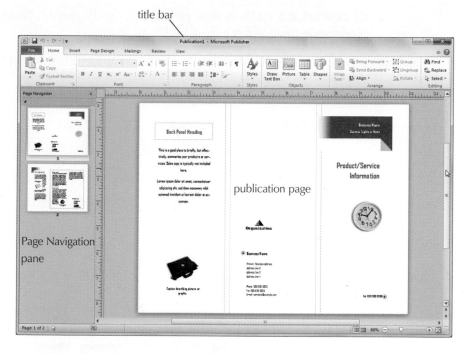

Page Navigation pane

The publication window displays information about a document and includes tools for working with documents:

- The file name of the current document is displayed in the **title bar**. The name Publication1 is used temporarily until the publication is saved with a descriptive name.

- Select commands and perform actions using the **Ribbon**. For example, the Page Design tab is used to change the color and font scheme and to add a page background:

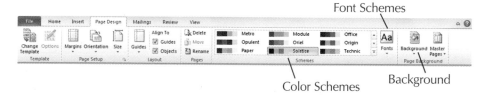

Font Schemes

Color Schemes   Background

- The **publication page** is the page as it will appear when printed.

- The **Page Navigation** pane is used to navigate the pages in a document.

- The dashed blue lines on the publication page are **margin guides**, which indicate the margins.

- The grey area around the publication is referred to as the **scratch area**. This area is used as a holding place for objects that will be used in the publication, but haven't been positioned yet.

Practice: Picnic Flyer – part 1 of 3

① CREATE A PUBLICATION

a. Ask your instructor for the appropriate steps to start Microsoft Office Publisher 2010.

b. Click Blank 8.5 x 11". A new publication is displayed. Note the Ribbon, Page Navigation pane, scratch area, and margin guides.

② SELECT A COLOR SCHEME, FONTS, AND A BACKGROUND

    a. Select Page Design → Solstice.

    b. Select Page Design → Fonts → Metro.

    c. Select the Page Design → Background → 10% tint of Accent 2 Solid Background:

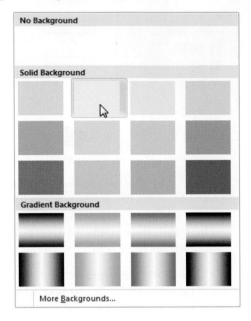

③ SAVE THE PUBLICATION NAMING IT PICNIC FLYER

    Select File → Save. A dialog box is displayed.

       1. Navigate to the appropriate location for the file to be saved.

       2. In the File name box, type: Picnic Flyer

       3. Select Save. The publication is saved with the name Picnic Flyer.

Text Boxes

Text cannot be typed directly onto a publication page, a *text box* must first be created and then text typed into the box. To create a text box, select Insert → Draw Text Box and then drag the + on the publication page. A text box is created with the insertion point in it, ready for text to be typed:

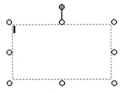

When selected, a text box has a dashed outline and handles. To resize a text box, point to a handle until the pointer changes to ⤢, and then drag. To move a text box, point to the dashed outline until the pointer changes to ✥, and then drag to move the box.

Once text is typed into a box, it can be edited and formatted using buttons on the toolbars or commands in the Format menu. Note that resizing a text box changes the wrap of the text in it.

Right-clicking a text box displays a menu:

TIP Use the green dot ◉ to rotate a selected text box.

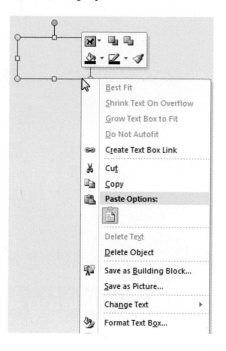

Use Cut ✄ , Copy 🗐 , and Paste to edit text and the text box. If text is selected, these commands manipulate the selected text. If no text is selected, the entire text box is cut or copied. Select Delete Object to delete the text box, or select Delete Text to remove selected text. Use Fill 🖌 to change the background color of the text box.

When a text box is selected, the Text Box Tools Format tab is used to format the text:

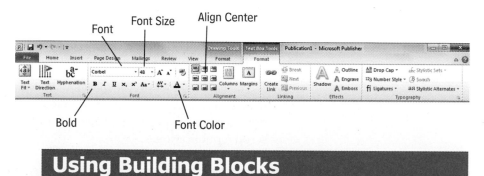

Using Building Blocks

Building Blocks

Various page parts, such as heading, sidebars, and pull quotes can be quickly added to a publication by selecting Insert → Page Parts. Other objects, such as calendars, borders, and advertisements can also be added using commands in the Building Blocks group. For example, selecting Insert → Advertisements displays:

Click an advertisement to add it to the publication.

Viewing a Publication

Whole Page

Two-Page Spread

100%

Page Width

The Zoom group in the View tab is used to magnify, or zoom into, a publication page. Select View → Whole Page to display the entire page or View → Page Width to display the page as wide as possible. The Zoom list, which is set to 71% in the Ribbon above, can be used to zoom to a specific percentage.

To zoom into a selected object, press the F9 key. Press F9 again to return to the previous magnification.

The Layout group in the View tab contains commands to view a single page or a two-page spread. In any view, use the scroll bars to display hidden parts of the page. The Page Up and Page Down keys also vertically scroll a publication.

Practice: Picnic Flyer — part 2 of 3

Publisher should already be started with Picnic Flyer displayed from the last practice.

① CHANGE VIEWS

    a. Select View → Page Width. The publication page is displayed as wide as possible.

    b. Press the Page Down key. The lower part of the publication page is displayed.

    c. Select View → Whole Page. The entire publication page is displayed.

② **ADD A BORDER**

   a. Select Insert → Borders & Accents. The Borders & Accents drop-down gallery is displayed.

   b. Select the Diamond Line border:

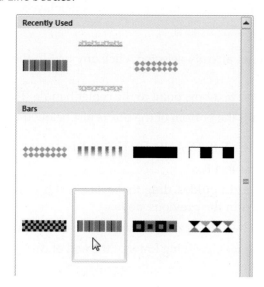

   c. Drag the border so that it creates a half-inch border across the top of the page:

③ **CREATE A TEXT BOX**

   a. Select Insert → Draw Text Box. The pointer changes to + when moved into the publication.

   b. Drag from the lower-left corner of the border to the bottom-right corner of the margin guides. A text box is created and the insertion point is in the upper-left corner of the box.

④ **ZOOM INTO THE TEXT BOX AND ENTER TEXT**

   a. Press the F9 key. The view is zoomed into the insertion point in the new text box.

   b. Type the following text, pressing Enter at the end of each line:

      The 2011
      Lasker
      Company Picnic
      Food!
      Fun!
      Swimming!

c. Select the "The 2011 Lasker Company Picnic!" text and format it as 48 point, bold, and center aligned.

d. Select the "Food! Fun! Swimming!" text and format it as 28 point, bold, and center aligned.

e. Press the F9 key. The entire publication page is displayed.

⑤ **RESIZE THE TEXT BOX**

a. If the text box is not already selected, click any text in the text box. Handles are displayed.

b. At the bottom of the text box, point to the center handle. The pointer changes to ↕.

c. Drag upwards until the bottom of the box is just below the "Swimming!" text.

⑥ **CREATE ANOTHER TEXT BOX AND ENTER TEXT**

a. Select Insert → Draw Text Box. .

b. Inside the blue margin guides, drag to create a text box that fills the space below the text box created in the previous steps.

c. Press the F9 key. The view is zoomed into the insertion point in the new text box.

d. Type the following text, pressing Enter at the end of each line:

    Saturday, July 25
    10 a.m. to 4 p.m.
    Heron Park

e. Select all of the text and format it as 18 point, italic, and aligned bottom right.

f. Press the F9 key. The entire publication page is displayed:

⑦ **SAVE THE MODIFIED PICNIC FLYER**

Adding Graphics

Graphics in the form of clip art or pictures can be placed on a publication page using the Insert tab. The publication below is a series of text frames and pictures:

To add an image, select Insert → Picture. A selected picture can then be edited and enhanced using commands on the Picture Tools Format tab:

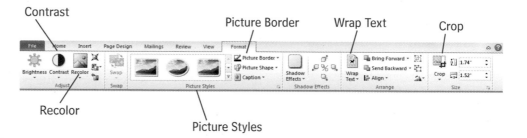

Contrast

Recolor

Picture Border

Wrap Text

Crop

Picture Styles

- Recolor changes the colors.
- Contrast adjusts the difference between the lightest and darkest areas.
- Picture Styles change the appearance of the picture.
- Picture Border adds a border.
- Wrap Text changes the way text wraps around the picture.
- Crop trims away areas of the graphic.

To add clip art to a publication, select Insert → Clip Art to display the Clip Art task pane. Type a word or phrase in the Search for box and select Go to find all the clip art that have the keyword in their description. To narrow a search, use the options in the Search in and the Results should be lists. For example, type flower in the Search for box and then select Go to display pictures similar to:

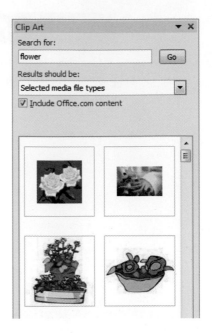

To place a clip art graphic into the document, click a graphic in the task pane or click the arrow to the right of the graphic and select Insert.

Once placed in a document, a graphic may need to be sized. Click a graphic to select it and display handles:

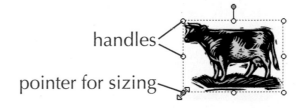

Point to a corner handle, which changes the pointer to ⟋ and then drag to size the graphic.

<span></span>

TIP Dragging a center handle causes distortion. Drag a corner handle to size a graphic without distorting it.

To move a graphic, drag the center of it (not a handle). Wherever a graphic is moved, text moves to make room. Cut ✂ , Copy 📋 , and Paste can be used to create copies or move a selected graphic. Press the Delete key to delete the selected graphic. Click anywhere in the document other than on the graphic to remove the handles.

The Master Page

The *master page* is used to create a design that applies to every page in the publication. Select View → Master Page to view the master page and display the Master Page tab:

Objects such as graphics and text boxes placed on the master page appear on all the pages in the publication. Click Close Master Page to display the publication.

Styles

Styles are a set of formatting rules that can be applied to text. They are used to format text in a consistent manner. Click Home → Styles to view the Styles gallery:

Click a style to apply it to selected text. A new style is created by selecting the New Style command at the bottom of the Styles gallery.

Typography

Drop Cap   Stylistic Sets

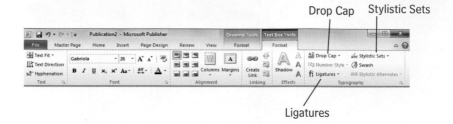

Ligatures

The Typography group in the Text Box Tools Format tab contains commands for creating stylistic text features:

- Stylistic Sets are available for some OpenType fonts, such as Gabriola. For example:

- Drop Cap creates a large capital letter at the beginning of a paragraph. Drop Cap gallery options include:

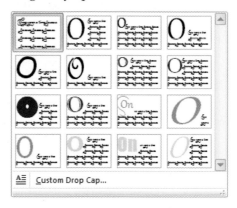

- Ligatures are combinations of two or more characters into a single character to create more readable text:

Previewing and Printing a Publication

Previewing a publication shows what printouts will look like. To preview the open publication, select File → Print. The preview area is displayed on the right side of Backstage view:

Binding

Binding describes various methods of securing together the pages or sections of a book or booklet. Binding methods include stitching, staples, wire, plastic, tape, and glue.

The Print options in Backstage view contains the categories Print, Printer, and Settings. The galleries in each category are used to modify the default print options. For example, click Composite RGB and select Composite Grayscale to print as a grayscale publication.

Practice: Picnic Flyer – part 3 of 3

Publisher should already be started with Picnic Flyer displayed from the last practice.

① **APPLY A STYLISTIC SET**

    a. Select The 2011 Lasker Company Picnic!

    b. Select Home → Font → Gabriola.

    c. Select Text Box Tools Format → Stylistic Sets and then select an option in the Individual category.

② **PLACE AN IMAGE**

    a. Select Insert → Clip Art. The Clip Art task pane is displayed.

    b. In the Search for box, type picnic and press Enter.

    c. Click one of the picnic graphics. The graphic is added to the publication.

③ **MOVE THE IMAGE**

    a. Drag the graphic so that it is in the left side of the bottom text box.

    b. Drag a corner handle to size the graphic is appropriately.

Check – Your publication page should look similar to:

④ SAVE, PRINT, AND THEN CLOSE THE MODIFIED PICNIC FLYER
   a. Save the modified Picnic Flyer.
   b. Select File → Print → Print.
   c. Select File → Close. The publication is closed.

Creating a Template

Microsoft Office includes many templates. There may also be publications for which a template needs to be created. For example, a blank office memo with the company logo and colors, or a flyer that is needed once a month.

To create a template, create a new publication, add objects and apply formatting. When the publication is saved, select Publisher Template in the Save as Type list. The file is saved to the Templates folder.

To use a template in Publisher, create a new publication and click Templates in the New from a design list. A new publication with all the objects from the template is created.

Practice: Meeting Flyer, Jan Flyer

Publisher should be already started.

① CREATE THE PUBLICATION
   a. Select File → New.
   b. Click Blank 8.5 x 11". A new publication is displayed.

② ADD TEXT BOXES
   a. Create a text box that fits from the upper-left corner of the margin guides to the bottom-right corner of the margin guides.

b. Press F9 and then type the following text, pressing Enter at the end of each line, adding blank paragraphs as needed, and replacing Name with your name:

Crabby Lake
Shell Club
Month
Meeting

Meetings are held in the Civic Center.
Everyone is welcome!
Meetings start promptly at 7 p.m.
Call Name for information: 555-1234

c. Format the "Crabby Lake Shell Club Month Meeting" text as 48 point, bold, and center aligned.

d. Format the rest of the text, from "Meetings are held…" to "…and topic" as 18 point, bold, and italic.

e. Press the F9 key. The entire publication page is displayed.

③ MODIFY THE PAGE DESIGN

a. Select Page Design → Metro.

b. Select Page Design → Fonts → Metro.

c. Select Page Design → Background → 10% tint of Accent2.

④ INSERT A PAGE PART AND ADD A BORDER

a, Place the insertion point after the last line of text.

b. Select Insert → Page Parts → Pure (Layout 2) in the Sidebars category.

c. Drag the sidebar to the bottom right corner of the page.

d. Replace the TITLE TEXT with PRESENTATION: and the body text with Speaker and Topic.

e. Select Insert → Borders & Accents. Select an appropriate border for the top and bottom of the page.

Check – Your publication page should look similar to:

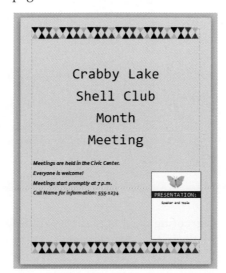

⑤ SAVE THE PUBLICATION AS A TEMPLATE
   a. Select File → Save. A dialog box is displayed.
      1. In the File name box, type: Meeting Flyer
      2. In the Save as Type list, select Publisher Template.
      3. Select Save. The publication is saved as a template named Meeting Flyer.
   b. Close Meeting Flyer.

⑥ USE THE TEMPLATE
   a. Select File → New.
   b. Click My Templates.
   c. Click Meeting Flyer and then Create. A new publication with the same objects as the template is displayed.
   d. In the sidebar, replace the words "Speaker and Topic" with: Olav Rios will present his collection of Strombidae.

⑦ SAVE, PRINT, AND THEN CLOSE THE PUBLICATION
   a. Save the publication in the appropriate folder naming it: Jan Flyer
   b. Print a copy and then close Jan Flyer.

Creating Greeting Cards

Publisher contains a variety of greeting card templates that can be downloaded:

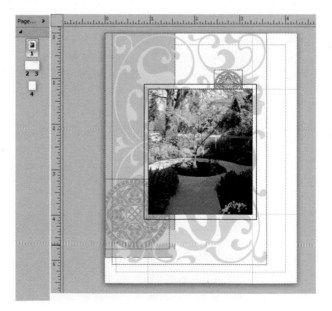

A greeting card is made by folding an 8.5" x 11" piece of paper, which results in four panels (pages) in the Page Navigation pane:

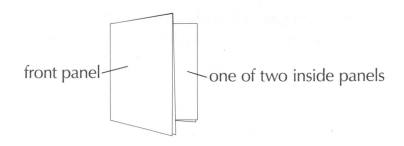

front panel — — one of two inside panels

To create a blank card, create a new publication and select More Blank Page Sizes and then select the Greeting Cards folder in the Publication Types section. Select a card size and then use the Customize section to select a color and font scheme. Select Create and then complete the card in Publisher by modifying the existing objects, or by placing text boxes and graphics in the publication and formatting as needed. Use the Page Navigation pane to move between the card pages. The four "pages" are then printed on a single sheet of paper and folded to make the card.

Using Ruler Guides

Publications have colored lines called *guides* which are used to precisely arrange objects on a page. The blue guides are *layout guides* and include margin guides and column guides. *Ruler guides* are green and can be added anywhere on a page and moved around. To create a ruler guide, move the pointer into the blue area of a ruler until the pointer changes to ⬍, and then drag off the ruler to the publication page:

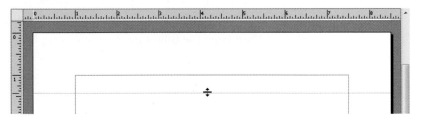

As an object is moved near a guide, it "snaps" or "jumps" exactly to the guide. This helps to precisely arrange objects on a page.

To move a ruler guide, point to the ruler guide until the pointer changes to ⬍ and then drag the guide to a new position. Delete a ruler guide by dragging it off the publication page.

Practice: Gadgets Birthday, Birthday Party

Publisher should be already started.

① **CREATE A BIRTHDAY CARD**

    a. Select File → New.

    b. Click More Blank Page Sizes to display those templates.

    c. Click the Greeting Cards folder.

    d. Click the 1/2 Letter Top Fold 8.5 x 5.5" :

    e. In the Customize options, in the Color scheme list, select Prairie.

    f. In the Customize options, in the Font scheme list, select Metro.

    g. Select **Create**. A dialog box is displayed.

    h. Select **Yes**. A new, blank publication with four panels (pages) is created.

② **ADD ELEMENTS TO PAGE 1**

    a. Select **Page Design** → **Background** → **30% tint of Accent 1**.

    b. Create a text box that fits from the left margin guide to the right margin guide.

    c. In the text box, type the following text, pressing Enter at the end of each line, and replacing Name with your name:

        Happy Birthday
        Name!

    d. Center align the text and select an appropriate font and size. For example:

③ **DISPLAY PAGE 3 AND ENTER TEXT**

    a. In the Page Navigation panel, click the Page 2 and 3 thumbnail.

    b. Create a text box on page 3 (the page on the bottom) that fits from the left margin guide to the right margin guide. You may need to scroll to view page 3.

    c. Press F9 and then type the following text, pressing Enter at the end of each line:

        Have a wonderful year!
        From all of us at Gadgets, Inc.

    d. Format all of the text using an appropriate font, size, and alignment.

    e. Click anywhere outside of the text box so that it is no longer selected.

④ **SAVE, PRINT, AND THEN CLOSE THE PUBLICATION**

    a. Save the publication in the appropriate folder naming it: Gadgets Birthday

    b. Print a copy of Gadgets Birthday.

    c. Close Gadgets Birthday.

⑤ **FOLD THE CARD**

Adding and Deleting Pages

To add a page to a publication, select **Insert** → **Page** and select from the options **Insert Blank Page** or **Insert Duplicate Page**. To insert more than one page, select **Insert Page**, which displays a dialog box:

Specify the number of new pages and whether the new pages should be added before or after the current page. Other options in the Insert Page dialog box help create objects. Select Create one text box on each page to automatically include a text box on each added page. Select Duplicate all objects on page to automatically include a copy of all the objects on a specified page on the newly added pages.

To delete a page, right-click the page in the Page Navigation pane and select Delete.

Connecting Text Boxes

Publications with multiple columns or multiple page have many text boxes. Even a simple report will have a text box on each page. Text flows from one text box to another by *connecting* the text boxes. Connecting text boxes does not mean that the boxes are physically connected or touch each other. The separate boxes are linked to each other in the publication so that as text is added or deleted to one box, it can flow into or out of the next connected box. Text in overflow ⊡ can be flowed into another text box by connecting the boxes.

To connect text boxes:

1. Create a new text box.
2. Click the Overflow button ⊡. The pointer changes to 🖟.
3. Move the pointer over the second text box until the pointer changes to 🖟, and click once to flow the text and connect the boxes.

Selecting a connected box displays Go to Previous Text Box ◀, Go to Next Text Box ▶, or both buttons. Click a button to select the previous or next connected text box.

Practice: SOS QUARTERLY – part 1 of 2

Publisher should already be started.

① OPEN SOS QUARTERLY

Open the SOS QUARTERLY publication, which is a Publisher data file for this text.

② ADD AND DELETE PAGES

    a. Select Insert ➡ Page ➡ Insert Page. A dialog box is displayed.

        1. In the Number of new pages box, type: 2

        2. Select OK. Two new pages are added to the publication after page 1, and page 2 is displayed.

    b. In the Page Navigation pane, right-click page 3 and Delete. Page 3 is deleted, and the publication now contains two pages.

③ CHANGE THE MARGINS

    a. Select Page Design ➡ Margins ➡ Custom Margins. A dialog box is displayed.

        1. Select the Margin Guides tab.

        2. In the Left, Right, Top, and Bottom boxes, type: 0.75

        3. Select OK. All the margins are changed to 0.75".

    b. In the Page Navigation pane, click the page 1 thumbnail. Page 1 is displayed. Note that the layout guides have also been changed on this page.

④ MOVE THE TEXT BOX AND THE GRAPHICS

    a. Move the "SOS Quarterly…" text box so that its upper-right corner is against the margin guides in the upper-right corner of the page.

    b. Move the graphic of outdoor supplies so that its upper-left corner is against the margin guides in the upper-left corner of the page.

    c. Move the mountain graphic so that its bottom-right corner is against the margin guides in the bottom-right corner of the page.

    Check – Your publication page should look similar to:

⑤ CREATE A TEXT BOX

    In the first column, create a text box that fits across the column, with its top is against the green ruler guide and its bottom is against the bottom margin guide.

⑥ INSERT TEXT

    a. Place the insertion point in the text box if it is not already there.

    b. Select Insert ➡ Insert File. A dialog box is displayed.

        1. Navigate to the data files for this text.

        2. Select PEACE RIVER, which is a Word data file for this text.

        3. Select OK. A The text has automatically flowed to page 2.

⑦ CONNECT TEXT BOXES

a. On page 1, in the second column, create a text box that fits across the column, with its top is against the green ruler guide and its bottom is against the bottom margin guide.

b. In the first column, select the text box, which already has text in it.

c. Select Text Box Tool Format → Break. The Link to Page 2 has been broken and the Text in Overflow indicator is displayed.

d. Click the Text in Overflow indicator and move the pointer to the text box in the second column. The pointer changes to 🐝.

e. Click once. The text is flowed into the text box in the second column. Notice Go to Previous Text Box ◄ at the top of this box.

⑧ INSERT MORE TEXT

a. In the third column, create a text box that fits across the column, with its top is against the green ruler guide and its bottom about 2" above the mountain graphic. Use the markings on the vertical ruler for measuring.

b. Place the insertion point in the text box if it is not already there.

c. Select Insert → Insert File. A dialog box is displayed.

    1. Navigate to the data files for this text.

    2. Select BINOCULARS, which is a Word data file for this text.

    3. Select OK. The BINOCULARS document is inserted into the text box. The Text In Overflow indicator ⊡ indicates that there is text that is not displayed.

d. Resize the text box so that its bottom is against the top of the mountain graphic. The Text In Overflow indicator ⊡ no longer appears because all text is displayed.

e. Change the name "Sara Andersen" to your name.

⑨ SAVE THE MODIFIED SOS QUARTERLY

Using Mail Merge in a Publication

Mail merge integrates the information stored in an Access database with a publication. To create a mail merge publication, select Mailings → Mailings Merge → Step by Step Mail Merge Wizard to display the Mail Merge task pane and then:

TIP Select Mailings → E-mail Merge to merge data into a publication that will be sent as e-mail.

1. In the task pane, select Use an existing list and then at the bottom of the task pane click Next: Create or connect to a recipient list. A dialog box is displayed.

2. Navigate to the database to use for the mail merge and then select Open. A dialog box of tables in the database is displayed.

3. Select the table that contains the merge fields and then select OK.

4. Select the recipients and then OK.

5. Add fields to the publication by clicking fields in the task pane. At the bottom of the task pane, click Next: Create merged publication.

6. Click Print preview to preview the pages. Scroll through the merged documents using Next Sheet ▸ and Previous Sheet ◂ .

7. Click Print to print the merged documents.

Database Terminology

A database is a collection of related information organized into *tables*, which contain a series of related *records*. Within the records, each piece of data is referred to as a *field*. Access is the Microsoft Office database application.

Publisher should already be started with SOS QUARTERLY displayed from the last practice.

① **ADD TEXT TO PAGE 2**

    a. On page 2, create a horizontal ruler guide at 5.5" on the vertical ruler.

    b. Create a text box that fits across all three columns, with its top is against the top margin guide, and its bottom is just above the ruler guide at 5.5".

    c. Zoom in and type the following text, pressing Enter at the end of each line and replacing Name with your name:

        Fall Clearance Sale
        September 6 and 7
        10 a.m. to 6 p.m.
        Sage's Outdoor Supplies
        Name, Manager

    d. Select all of the text and format it as 36 point, bold, italic, and center aligned.

    e. Press the F9 key. The publication page is zoomed out.

    f. Click in a blank area outside the text box. The box is no longer selected.

② **CREATE A TEXT BOX**

    a. Create a horizontal ruler guide at 8" on the vertical ruler.

    b. Below the ruler guide, create a text box that fits across the second and third columns, with its top is against the ruler guide at 8" and its bottom is against the bottom margin guide.

③ **ADD MERGE FIELDS**

    a. Select Mailings → Mailing Merge → Step by Step Mail Merge Wizard. The Mail Merge task pane is displayed.

    b. In the task pane, select Use an existing list.

    c. At the bottom of the task pane click Next: Create or connect to a recipient list. A dialog box is displayed.

        1. Navigate to the data files for this text.

        2. Select SAGE'S OUTDOOR SUPPLIES, which is an Access data file.

        3. Select Open. A dialog box of tables in the database is displayed.

        4. Select the Customers table and then select OK. A dialog box is displayed.

        5. Be sure all four records have check marks and then select OK.

    d. Place the insertion point in the text box below the ruler guide at 8" and then press the F9 key.

    e. In the task pane, in the list of fields, click First Name. The field marker is added to the text box in the publication.

    f. Insert the Last Name field, Address field, and the City, State, and ZIP fields.

    g. In the text box, format all of the merge fields as 18 point.

    h. Add spaces, type a comma, and press Enter where needed so that the merge fields look similar to:

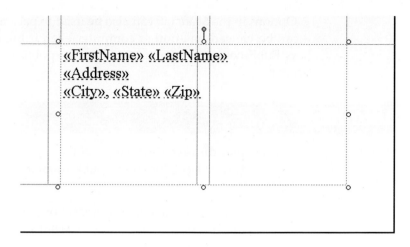

«FirstName» «LastName»
«Address»
«City», «State» «Zip»

    i. Click outside the text box.

    j. At the bottom of the task pane, click Next: Create merged publication.

    k. In the task pane, click Print preview to preview the pages that will print. The field markers are replaced with data from the Customers table in the database.

    l. On the toolbar, click Next Sheet ▸ and Previous Sheet ◂ to scroll through the four merged documents.

④ SAVE AND PRINT THE MERGED PUBLICATIONS

    a. Save the modified SOS QUARTERLY.

    b. Select Print. Four copies are printed, one for each of the customers in the database.

    c. Close the publication.

    d. Quit Publisher.

Sharing a Publication

Once a publication is finished, the Share tab in Backstage view has many options for sharing the publication. There are a variety of options for sending a publication in an e-mail including sending the attachment as a PDF file or in the message body as HTML:

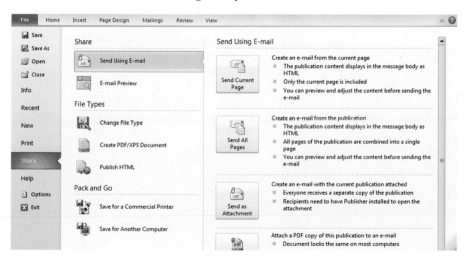

Options in the Share tab can also be used to pack a publication so that it can be viewed on another computer even if the computer does not have Publisher installed and to prepare the publication for a commercial printer.

Chapter Summary

This chapter discussed desktop publishing, which is the process of combining text and graphics into a publication using an application such as Microsoft Publisher.

To add text to a publication, draw a text box and then type and edit the text in the box. A text box can be moved, sized, cut, copied and pasted.

The magnification of the publication page can be changed using commands in the View tab. The F9 key is used to quickly zoom in and out.

The Building Blocks group in the Insert tab is used to add page parts, advertisements, and borders. Graphics can also be placed on a publication page and then moved and resized as needed.

The master page is used to create a design that applies to the every page in the publication. Objects such as graphics and text boxes placed on the master page appear on all the pages in the publication.

Although many templates are available in Publisher, a template can also be created. Templates include the basic elements for particular types of publications and can be used again and again.

Guides are used to precisely arrange objects on a page. The blue guides are layout guides and include margin guides and column guides. Margins can be changed, and page can be formatted with multiple columns. Ruler guides are green and can be added anywhere on a page and moved around.

Word documents can be inserted into an existing text box in a publication, allowing the text to be created and edited in the word processor before it is placed in Publisher.

The Text In Overflow indicator is displayed at the bottom of any text box that has more text than can be displayed. Text in overflow can be flowed into another text box by connecting the boxes.

Mail merge integrates the information stored in an Access database with a publication. The Mail Merge task pane is used to create a mail merged publication.

Options in the Share tab can be used to e-mail a publication and to prepare a publication to be viewed on another computer or for a commercial printer.

Vocabulary

Connected text boxes Text boxes that are linked to each other so text can flow into or out of the next connected box.

Desktop publishing The process of combining text and graphics into one file.

Guides Colored lines on the publication page used to precisely arrange objects.

Layout guides Blue lines on the publication page that indicate margins and columns.

Mail merge The integration of information stored in an Access database with a publication.

Master page Used to create a design that applies to the every page in the publication.

Objects Text boxes and graphics.

Overflow Text that does not fit in a text box and is therefore hidden.

Page Navigation pane Used to navigate the pages in a document. Found on the left side of the window.

Previewing a publication Shows what printouts will look like.

Publication A desktop publishing file.

Publication page The page as it will appear when printed.

Ruler guides Green lines on the publication page used to precisely arrange objects on a page

Scratch area Used as a holding place for objects that haven't been positioned yet.

Template A master publication that includes the basic elements for particular types of publications.

Text box An object that contains text.

Publisher Commands

Advertisements Quick way to add advertisements to a publication. Found on the Insert tab.

Clip Art Displays the Clip Art task pane used to insert clip art onto a publication page. Found on the Insert tab.

Copy 📋 Places a copy of the selected graphic on the Clipboard. Found on the Home tab.

Cut ✂ Moves the selected text to the Clipboard. Found on the Home tab.

Delete Deletes the currently displayed page. Found in the menu displayed by right-clicking a page in the Navigation pane.

Delete Object Deletes the selected text box. Found in the menu displayed by right-clicking a text box.

Delete Text Deletes the selected text in the text box. Found in the menu displayed by right-clicking a text box.

Draw Text Box Used to create a text box. Found on the Insert tab.

Drop Cap Displays a gallery of drop capitals. Found on the Text Box Tools Format tab.

Fill 🎨 Changes the background color of a text box. Found on the Home tab.

Go to Next Text Box ▶ Selects the next connected text box. Displayed below a selected connected text box.

Go to Previous Text Box ◀ Selects the previous connected text box. Displayed above a selected connected text box.

Insert File Displays a dialog box used to insert text from a Word document into a text box. Found in the Insert menu.

Ligatures Displays ligatures options. Found on the Text Box Tools Format tab.

Master Page Displays the master page. Found on the View tab.

Page Displays a dialog box used to add pages to a publication. Found on the Insert tab.

Page Parts Quick way to add headings, sidebars, and pull quotes to a publication. Found on the Insert tab.

Page Width Displays the page as wide as possible. Found on the View tab.

Paste Places the contents of the Clipboard at the insertion point. Found on the Home tab.

Picture Displays a dialog box used to add a picture to a publication. Found on the Insert tab.

Print Prints the publication without displaying the Print dialog box. Found in File → Print.

Share Displays e-mail and pack and go options for the publication. Found in File → Share.

Styles Displays a styles gallery. Found on the Home tab.

Step by Step Mail Merge Wizard Displays the Mail Merge task pane. Found in Mailings → Mailing Merge.

Stylistic Sets Displays a gallery of stylistic sets. Found on the Text Box Tools Format tab.

Whole Page Displays the entire page. Found on the View tab.

Two-Page Spread Displays a two-page spread. Found on the View tab.

1. What is desktop publishing?

2. a) What is a publication?
   b) List three examples of publications.
   c) What is a template?
   d) List two examples of templates that are available in Publisher.

3. What is a text box used for?

4. List two ways to zoom into a selected text box and then zoom back out again.

5. Describe two ways graphics can be edited in Publisher.

6. What kind of objects are usually placed on the master page?

7. What would you use commands in the Building Blocks group for?

8. a) Describe how a template is created and then used.
   b) Give two examples of templates that a grocery store might create.

9. a) List the steps required to create a side fold card to be used as an invitation.
   b) Describe how an 8.5" x 11" piece of paper is folded to create a greeting card.

10. a) How do you know which page in a multiple-page publication is displayed?
    b) How can you display page 3 in a publication that has 4 pages?

11. a) What are layout guides?
    b) What are ruler guides?
    c) List the steps required to create a vertical ruler guide at 3" on the horizontal ruler.
    d) Can a ruler guide be deleted? If so, how?

12. a) List the steps required to add three pages to a publication that currently has one page.
    b) How is the currently displayed page deleted from a publication?

13. List the steps required to insert text from a Word document named Badminton into a new, blank publication.

14. a) What is overflow text?
    b) List two ways to display text in overflow.

15. List the steps required to connect two text boxes, one with text in overflow and one empty text box.

16. What is mail merge?

17. What are two formats a publication can be converted to when it is sent as an e-mail attachment?

True/False

18. Determine if each of the following are true or false. If false, explain why.
    a) Text is added to a publication in a text box.
    b) Handles are used to size text boxes and graphics.
    c) Pressing the F10 key changes the publication's magnification.
    d) Graphics from a digital camera can be added to a publication.
    e) Objects on the master page appear on every document in the publication.
    f) Pages have to be added to a publication one at a time.
    g) A ruler guide is deleted by clicking the guide and pressing the Delete key.
    h) Clicking the Text In Overflow indicator creates a new text box.

Projects

Project 1

Yolanda's Catering needs a flyer that advertises Friday's lunch specials.

    a) Create a new publication based on the Blank 8.5 x 11" publication type with the Tropics color scheme and the Casual font scheme.

    b) Save the publication naming it Lunch Flyer.

    c) Use the Building Blocks group to add appropriate page parts and a border.

    d) Create a text box and type the following text, pressing Enter at the end of each line and replacing NAME with your name:

> Yolanda's Catering
>
>
> FRIDAY
> LUNCH
> SPECIALS!
>
> Burritos $4.50
> Tacos $2 each
> Taco Salad $6.95

    e) Format all of the text as bold and center aligned.

    f) Format "FRIDAY LUNCH SPECIALS!" as 48 point, and the rest of the text as 36 point.

    g) Resize and move the text box if necessary so that it fits inside the border.

    h) Save the modified Lunch Flyer and print a copy.

Project 2

Study Time Tutoring is going to offer a fingerpainting class for young children. A flyer is needed to advertise the class.

    a) Create a new publication using a Flyer template.

    b) Add the following text, replacing Name with your name:

> Name's Art School
> presents
>
> ADVANCED
> FINGERPAINTING
>
> Sunday, November 11
> 9 a.m. to 3 p.m.
> $5 per Child
>
> Call for reservations
> 555-MESS

c) Format all of the text appropriately.

d) Save the publication naming it Fingerpaint Flyer and print a copy.

Project 3

Study Time Tutoring needs a brochure for the parents when they register their children.

a) Create a new publication using a Brochure template.

b) The purpose of the brochure is to promote Study Time Tutoring's services. The audience is parents of students who may need tutoring support. Design the brochure appropriately.

c) Save the publication naming it Study Time Brochure and print a copy.

Project 4

Thank you cards are a courteous way to express appreciation for a gift, for assistance, or anything thoughtful that someone else has done for you.

a) Create a new publication using the 1/4 Letter Side Fold Card 4.25 x 5.5" publication type with the Moss color scheme and the Aspect font scheme.

b) Save the publication naming it Thank You Card Green.

c) Add an appropriate border to page 1.

d) Add a horizontal ruler guide at 2" on the vertical ruler.

e) Create a text box that fits across the margin guides, with its top against the ruler guide at 2". In the text box type: With Appreciation

f) Format the text as 14 point, italic, and center aligned.

g) On page 3, add a horizontal ruler guide at 2" on the vertical ruler.

h) Create a text box that fits across the margin guides, with its top against the ruler guide at 2". In the text box type the following text, pressing Enter at the end of each line and replacing Name with your name:

    Many Thanks
    from Name

i) Format the text as 12 point, italic, and center aligned.

j) On page 3, add a clip art graphic that represents the gift you received. Move the graphic so that its bottom-right corner is against the bottom and right margin guides. Resize the graphic if necessary so that it is completely inside the layout guides on the page.

k) Save the modified Thank You Card Green.

l) Print a copy and fold the paper to make a card.

Project 5

A printed invitation is more formal and official than a verbal invitation. A printed invitation is helpful because it provides all the information that the guest needs to attend the party.

a) Create a new publication using the Potluck 3 template in the Invitation Cards templates Theme Party section. Use the Citrus color scheme, the Casual font scheme, the Quarter-page side fold page size, and the sketch layout.

b) Save the publication naming it Pool Party.

c) Change the inside and outside margins to 0.75" and the top margin to 1.5".

d) On page 1 create a text box and type the following text, pressing enter at the end of each line:

> POOL
> PARTY!

e) Format the text as 24 point, bold, and in Dark Red.

f) Resize the text box to just fit the text, and move the text box so that its left side is against the left margin guide and its bottom is against the bottom margin guide:

g) On page 2, zoom in and fill in the following text in the text boxes, replacing all occurrences of Name with your name:

h) On page 3, format the text "You're Invited" in Accent Color 1, the same color applied in step (e).

i) Save the modified Pool Party.

j) Print a copy and fold the paper to make an invitation.

Project 6

Newsletters are easily created in Publisher because all the elements, such as text boxes and graphics, can be moved around the page.

a) Create a new publication based on the Blank 8.5 x 11" publication type, with the Concourse color scheme and the Concourse font scheme.

b) Save the publication naming it Music Monthly.

c) Change all the margins to 0.75" and format the publication with two columns.

d) Add a horizontal ruler guide at 3" on the vertical ruler.

e) Create a text box for the nameplate of the newsletter that fits across the margin guides, with its bottom against the ruler guide at 3". Type the following text, pressing Enter at the end of each line:

MUSIC MONTHLY
Distributed FREE at all Mockingbird Music Locations
Volume 10, October 2011

f) Format the text "MUSIC MONTHLY" as 48 point, bold, and center aligned. Format the rest of the text as 18 point, bold, italic, and center aligned.

g) Create a text box that fits across the first column, with its top against the ruler guide at 3" and its bottom is against the bottom margin guide. Insert the text from MUSIC LESSONS, which is a Word data file for this text. Format the headings "Are You Ready for Winter Music Lessons," "Lessons Offered," and "The Instructors" as 20 point and bold. There will be text in overflow.

h) Create a text box that fits across the second column, with its top against the ruler guide at 3" and its bottom is against the bottom margin guide. Connect it to the first text box, flowing the text into it. There should no longer be any text in overflow. Format the text in each article as 11 point.

i) Add a new page after page 1.

j) On page 2, add a horizontal ruler guide at 8" on the vertical ruler.

k) On page 2, create a text box that fits across the first column, with its top against the top margin guide and its bottom is against the ruler guide at 8". Insert the text from INSTRUMENTS, which is a Word data file for this text. There should not be any text in overflow. Format the heading "Instruments Available at Mockingbird Music" as 20 point and bold. Format the text in the article as 11 point. Format the subheadings "New and Used Instruments" and "Repair and Tuning" as 14 point and bold.

l) On page 2, create a text box that fits across the second column, with its top against the top margin guide and its bottom is against the bottom margin guide. Insert the text from MUSIC LIST, which is a Word data file for this text. There should not be any text in overflow. Format the text as 16 point and italic.

m) On page 2, add an appropriate clip art graphic. Move the graphic so that its bottom-left corner is against the bottom-left margin guides at the bottom of the first column. If necessary, resize the graphic so that it is completely inside the first column.

n) Save the modified Music Monthly and print a copy.

Project 7

Your new business needs to create an advertisement to announce the grand opening and highlight some opening day specials.

    a) Create a new publication using one of the Advertisement templates.

    b) All the appropriate text, graphics, and other objects.

    c) Save the publication as a template naming it Opening Specials.

    d) Print or e-mail a copy of the publication.

Project 8

You are having a celebration barbecue at 11:00 a.m. on June 20. The barbecue will take place at the Mango Hills Park and guests are asked to bring their own lawn chairs.

    a) Create a new publication using an appropriate Flyers templates.

    b) Save the publication naming it Barbecue.

    c) Change the information in the text boxes to appropriate information.

    d) Change the text "Contact person" to your name.

    e) Save the modified Barbecue and print a copy.

Project 9

The greeting card templates in Publisher have many attractive designs that can be customized.

    a) Create a new publication using one of the Greeting Cards templates.

    b) On page 4, change the text below "Made especially for you by" to your name.

    c) Save the publication naming it Birthday Card Design.

Project 10

Create a two-page *Align Computer* newsletter that contains hardware and software news and tips. Save the publication naming it Computer News. Use an appropriate color scheme and font scheme, format it with three columns, and include at least one clip art graphic. Print a copy.

Project 11

A calendar is a great promotional item that any recipient will look at many times over the year. Each time they view the calendar, they will see the company name and other information on the calendar. Publisher has templates for month and year calendars.

a) Create a new publication and click the Calendars publication type to view the calendar templates. Click the Mobile template and in the Customize options select the Brown color scheme and Metro font scheme. In the Options options select One year per page. Select Create to create the publication.

b) In the upper-right corner of the page, replace the text "Business Tag line or Motto." with an appropriate tag line or motto.

c) At the bottom of the page, change the text "Business Name" to the name of your business.

d) Replace the "Primary Business Address" text and all the "Your Address" lines with appropriate text:

e) Replace the phone numbers and e-mail with appropriate text:

f) Save the publication naming it Promotional Calendar and print a copy.

Chapter 15
Using OneNote

What is OneNote?

As you have been working through the text, you have probably noted that Office applications are used to store a variety of data. If you need to store and organize numerical data you would probably use Excel, but what about a passing thought, an image you might want to use in a future project, a website link you would like to go back to, the name of an author, or a podcast? All of these 'pieces' of information can be stored in OneNote 2010:

OneNote is a note-taking and information-management program where you can capture ideas and information in electronic form. OneNote has a hierarchical storage system consisting of:

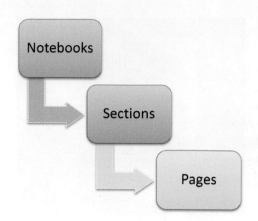

notebooks
sections
pages

Folders are called *notebooks* and each notebook consists of a series of color-coded tabs called sections. Each *section* consists of one or or more pages. The *pages* are used to enter free-form notes.

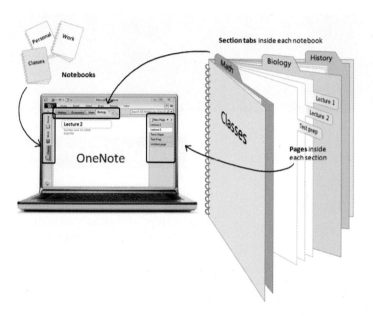

Creating a New Notebook

Notebooks can be saved on a local computer or they can be shared with others:

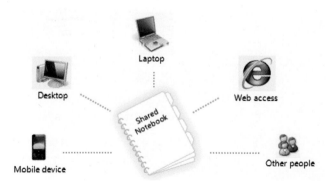

TIP Use Windows Live SkyDrive, Microsoft's file storage and sharing service, to create a Web notebook.

To create a new notebook, select File → New. New options are displayed in Backstage view:

Quick Access Toolbar

Ribbon

Create Notebook

To save a notebook on a local computer, select **My Computer** and type a name for the notebook, such as Work, in the **Name** box. Navigate to an appropriate location to save the notebook by selecting the **Browse** button and then click **Create Notebook**. A new notebook consisting of one section and one page is created:

TIP When OneNote is started, a Personal notebook is automatically created.

By default, there is a title box and below is the current date and time to indicate exactly when the note was created. The name of the notebook is listed in the **Notebooks** pane on left side of the screen.

Organizing Information with Sections

A OneNote notebook contains a collection of data from a variety of sources. To avoid an unorganized mess, each notebook should only contain related information. Within each notebook, the second level of organization is the section. *Sections* are represented by a tab at the top of the notebook and are used to breakdown the Notebook's overall topic into subtopics. For example, a college notebook could be broken into sections for each course. Navigate to a section by clicking the section tab.

There is no limit on the number of sections in a Notebook. However, there is a limit on the amount of data that can be stored in a single section. Each section corresponds to a file within the Notebook folder. Section files are saved with the .one extension.

To create a new section, click the Create a New Section tab:

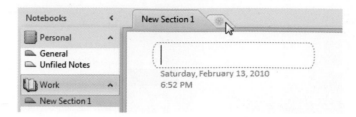

TIP To display the full title of a section, hover the mouse over the tab.

New sections are named New Section 1... by default. To rename a section, right-click the section tab and select Rename.

Section tabs can be color-coded to help organize sections with similar material. Right-click a Section tab and select Section Color to display a gallery of colors:

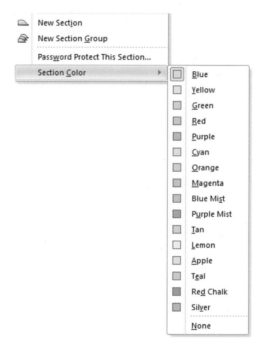

Sections can also be grouped to organize a large number of sections. Right-click a Section tab and select New Section Group. Move a section into a group by dragging the section tab and dropping it into the section group.

Practice: Work Notebook – part 1 of 3

① START ONENOTE

    a. Ask your instructor for the appropriate steps to start Microsoft OneNote 2010.

    b. Look at the OneNote window. Note the Notebooks pane, Ribbon, and Quick Access toolbar.

② CREATE A NEW NOTEBOOK

    a. Select File ➔ New. New options are displayed in Backstage view.

b. Set options as:

c. Click **Browse** and navigate to the appropriate location to save the notebook.

d. Click **Create Notebook**. A new notebook is created:

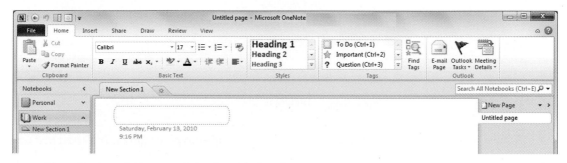

e. Type Project A Research in the title header:

Project A Research
Saturday, February 13, 2010
9:16 PM

③ **MODIFYING THE SECTION TAB**

a. Right click the **New Section 1** tab and select **Rename**.

b. Type: Project A

c. Press Enter.

d. Right-click the **Project A** tab and select **Section Color → Red**:

Working with Pages

TIP A pen-input device can be used to write notes instead of typing them.

Pages are blank slates into which data is inserted. Data can be added anywhere on the page simply by clicking on a page location to create a *note container*.

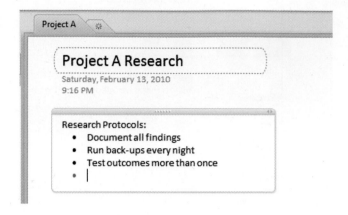

TIP Note containers can be moved by dragging the top center bar and sized by dragging the sizing handle in the top right corner of the container.

Buttons on the Home tab can be used to format text that is added to a page:

Buttons on the Insert tab are used to place data other than text on the page. For example, select Insert → Equation to add a mathematical equation to the page and display the Equation Tools Design tab:

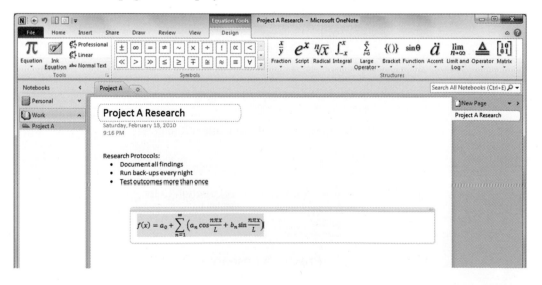

To attach a file to the page, click Insert → Attach File and then navigate to the file. An icon is used to represent the file on the page:

TIP Add rule lines to the page by selecting View → Rule Lines and selecting an option such as College Ruled or Small Grid.

Double-clicking the file icon, opens the file.

Images and screen shots are added to the page by clicking Insert → Picture and Insert → Screen Clippings. The Draw tab can be used to insert shapes and create original drawings:

If the appropriate hardware is attached to the computer, scanner print-outs, audio, and video recording can also be added to a page using buttons on the Insert tab.

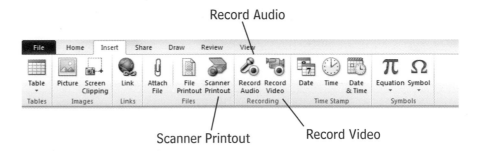

When a section is created, OneNote populates it with a blank page. To add an additional page, select the New Page drop-down arrow and select New Page. A new page tab is added:

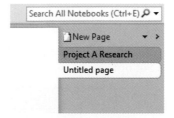

Initially the page tab is named Untitled page, until a page title is typed in the title box on the page. Navigate between pages by clicking a page tab.

Practice: Work Notebook – part 2 of 3

① **ADD DATA TO THE PAGE**

a. Click below the date and time.

b. Type the following in the note container:

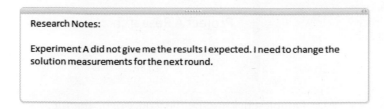

Research Notes:

Experiment A did not give me the results I expected. I need to change the solution measurements for the next round.

c. Click outside the Research Notes area and select Insert ➔ Table. Create a 3 x 3 table:

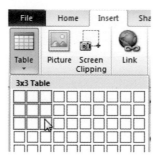

d. Add column headings to the table:

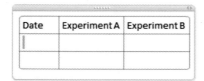

Date	Experiment A	Experiment B

② ADD A NEW PAGE

a. Select the **New Page** drop down arrow and then select **New Page**. A new page tab is added.

b. In the title box, type Research Links. The title is added to the page and the name of the Page tab changes from **Untitled page** to Research Links.

c. Click in a blank area of the page and then select Insert ➔ Link. A dialog box is displayed. Set options as:

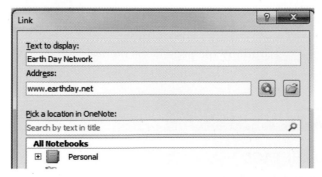

d. Select OK. The link is displayed on the page:

Earth Day Network

e. Click the link to view the page in a Web browser.
f. Close the Web browser.

③ **NAVIGATE PAGES**

Click the Project A Research tab. The Project A Research page is displayed.

Tags

OneNote contains several predefined tags that can be used flag your notes. Click Home → More ⊽ Tags to display the Tags gallery:

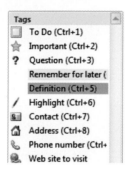

Tagging notes is an effective way of grouping similar information because notes can be searched for tagged items. Selecting Home → Find Tags displays a Tags Summary:

OneNote is ideal to organize and prioritize tasks and to-do lists. The ToDo tag is used to add a check box to the left of the paragraph:

☐ Experiment A did not give me the results I expected. I need to change the solution measurements for the next round.

The check box can be clicked when the task is completed.

Searching for Notes

One of the main advantages of using OneNote instead of a traditional paper notebook is the ability to search the information and quickly find what you are looking for. Click the Change Search Scope arrow to change the scope of the search:

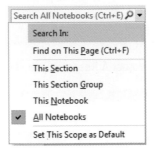

Next, type the search text. Matches are listed below the search box:

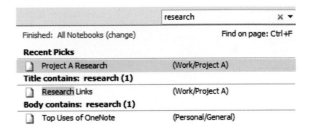

Search for the keyword 'research'

Click a match to view the information within the notebook.

Practice: Work Notebook – part 3 of 3

① **ADD TAGS**

    a. Display the Project A Research page if it is not already.

    b. Select the Research Notes container.

    c. Select Home → More ▾ Tags. The Tags gallery is displayed.

    d. Select To Do. A check box is placed to the left of the research note:

       ☐ Experiment A did not give me the results I expected. I need to change the solution measurements for the next round.

    e. Click the Research Links page tab. The Research Links page is displayed.

    f. Select the Earth Day Network container.

    g. Select Home → More ▾ Tags. The Tags gallery is displayed.

    h. Select Web site to visit. A globe icon is placed to the left of the link:

Earth Day Network

② **VIEW TAGS SUMMARY**

a. Select Home → Find Tags. A Tags Summary is displayed:

b. Click the Create Summary Page button at the bottom of the Tags Summary pane. A new page is created in the notebook that lists all of the tags:

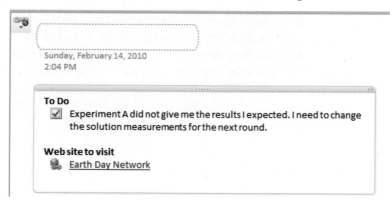

③ **SEARCH FOR INFORMATION**

a. Click the Project A Research page tab.

b. In the Search box, type: experiment

c. Click one of the matches to view the corresponding information.

d. Click outside the search box and then quit OneNote. Note that there is no need to save your work as it is saved automatically.

Working with Other Programs

OneNote works with other programs in the Office suite. For example, in Outlook, select Home → OneNote to send the contents of an e-mail message to OneNote.

In another example, PowerPoint slides can be sent to a section or page in OneNote. In PowerPoint, select File → Print and then in the Printer drop-down gallery select Send to OneNote 2010. The Select Location in OneNote dialog box is displayed:

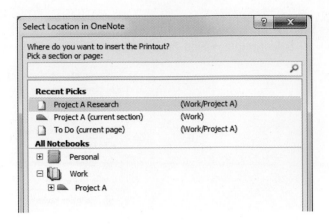

Select a location and the PowerPoint slides are then sent to that OneNote page.

In Word, select Review → Linked Notes to create notes about the Word document. After indicating where to save the notes in OneNote, OneNote docs itself on the side of the Desktop. In the docked OneNote pane, add a note. The note becomes linked to the Word document and clicking the Word icon in OneNote opens the Word document:

Chapter Summary

OneNote is a note-taking and information-management program where you can capture ideas and information in electronic form. OneNote has a hierarchical storage system consisting of notebooks, sections, and pages:

- Notebooks can be saved on a local computer or they can be shared with others on the Web or on a network drive.

- Sections are represented by a tab at the top of the notebook and are used to breakdown the Notebook's overall topic into subtopics.

- Pages are blank slates into which data is inserted. Data can be added anywhere on the page simply by clicking on a page location to create a note container.

One of the main advantages of using OneNote instead of a traditional paper notebook is the ability to search the information and quickly find what you are looking for. OneNote contains several predefined tags that can be used flag your notes. Tagging notes is an effective way of grouping similar information because notes can be searched for tagged items.

OneNote works with other programs in the Office suite. For example, In Outlook, you can send information from an e-mail message to a notebook page in OneNote.

Vocabulary

Note container   Area on a page used to create a note.

Notebooks   Folders consisting of a series of color-coded tabs called sections.

OneNote   A note-taking and information-management program where you can capture ideas and information in electronic form.

Pages   Located in notebook sections and used to enter free-form notes.

Section Areas in a notebook that consist of one or or more pages.

Tags   A method of grouping similar information.

OneNote Commands

Attach File   Attaches a file to a page. Found on the Insert tab.

Create a New Section tab   Creates a new section. Found next to the last section tab.

Equation   Inserts an equation in a note container and displays the Equation Tools Design tab. Found on the Insert tab.

Find Tags   Displays a Tags Summary. Found on the Home tab.

More ⏷ Tags   Displays the Tags gallery. Found on the Home tab.

New   Creates a new notebook. Found in the File tab.

New Page   Inserts a new page in the section. Found in the New Page drop-down menu.

Picture   Inserts a picture on a page. Found on the Insert tab.

Rename   Renames a section tab. Found by right-clicking a section tab.

Screen Clippings   Used to insert a screen shot on a page. Found on the Insert tab

Section Color Changes the color a section tab. Found by right-clicking a section tab.

1. What is OneNote used for?

2. Explain the OneNote hierarchy.

3. List three places a notebook can be stored.

4. a) Describe how a school notebook could be organized.
    b) Describe how a personal finance notebook could be organized.

5. Why is it important to rename sections (from Section 1, Section 2...) and color-code them?

6. List five types of data that can be added to a page.

7. Give an example of two predefined tags.

8. Which tag is useful for creating a to-do list?

9. What is one of the main advantages of using OneNote over a traditional paper notebook?

10. List three programs in the Office Suite that OneNote integrates with.

True/False

11 Determine if each of the following are true or false. If false, explain why.

    a) OneNote is a note-taking program.
    b) Folders are called sections.
    c) Notebooks can be saved on a local computer.
    d) Notebooks can be shared on a network drive.
    e) The title box on a page is used to name the page.
    f) Section tabs can be renamed.
    g) Page content cannot be formatted.
    h) Audio files can be saved in a notebook.
    i) Only one notebook can be searched at a time.
    j) The contents of an e-mail message can be sent from Outlook to OneNote.
    k) PowerPoint slides can be added to a notebook page from PowerPoint.

Project

Become familiar with OneNote by creating and organizing a notebook that you can use for school or to manage your personal life:

a) Create at least 4 sections and be sure to name the sections appropriately.

b) Experiment with adding content to the pages. Be sure to add images, equations, audio/video, and so forth.

c) Tag your items and try creating a to-do list.

d) Try searching for information.

e) Send the contents of an e-mail message from Outlook to OneNote.

f) Send PowerPoint slides from PowerPoint to OneNote.

g) Link a Word document to OneNote.

An Introduction to Digital Images

A digital image is any graphic that is stored in a file. Digital images are widely available and affordable. Even the least expensive digital cameras and scanners can produce quality images for use in printed matter, presentations, and on the Web. Digital images can also be purchased from companies that sell stock photography and clip art.

Bitmap Graphics

TIP The terms *image* and *graphic* are interchangeable.

Scanned and digital camera images are *bitmap graphics,* which are based on rows and columns of tiny dots that are square in shape. Each square is a *pixel* and is made up of one solid color. Many pixels of varying color create an image:

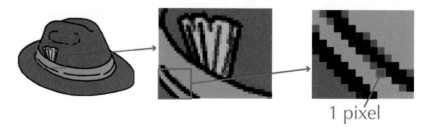

1 pixel

Vector Graphics

Another type of frequently-used graphics are *vector graphics,* which are composed of lines connected by points. Vector graphics can be resized smoothly, without developing a jagged-edge look that is common in low-resolution bitmap graphics.

The number of *dots per inch (dpi)* is called the *resolution.* The larger the number of dpi, the better the quality of the graphic. Common bitmap graphic formats are BMP, JPG, TIFF and GIF.

Digital Image File Formats

digital camera images

When a digital camera takes a photograph, a chip in the camera collects light and converts it to data. Settings in the digital camera, such as JPEG, TIFF, and RAW, determine what the camera does with the collected data. The JPEG setting processes the data into a .jpg file and the TIFF setting processes the data into a .tif file. These files can be transferred from the camera to a computer or printer. The TIF format has better quality than a JPG and is the better choice for printed matter such as newsletters, flyers, and brochures. The file size of a TIF is usually too large for use on the Web, and browsers may not be able to display a TIF, so any TIF must be converted to a JPG for use in a Web page.

The RAW setting indicates that the data for a photograph has not been processed in the camera. The photograph's data must be transferred to a computer that has software from the camera manufacturer installed. The RAW file is then manipulated using the software and can be saved in many file formats, which is one reason why many professional photographers use the RAW setting.

Manipulating, or processing, a RAW file can be thought of as developing the image just like film is developed, because it allows adjustments such as exposure and color balance to be made. RAW file names have different extensions depending on the camera, for example .mrw is a Minolta camera RAW file, .crw is a Canon camera RAW file, and .nef is a Nikon camera RAW file.

scanning images

A *scanner* is used to scan a photograph or drawing and create a digital image. Many applications have features that allow the scanner to be operated through the application. Common file formats of scanned images include TIF or TIFF, BMP, and JPG.

Maintaining Image Quality in JPG Files

Setting a digital camera to process the photograph data as JPEG is a fast, convenient way to produce image files for use in a Web page. However, every time a JPG image is saved, it is compressed again and loses data because the JPG format has lossy compression.

To retain excellent image quality, the camera should be set to process the photograph data as TIFF, and then the TIF file can be modified on a computer as needed and saved in JPG format. This way, the image will have much better quality than if it was processed as JPG and then modified and saved a few times.

When using a high-resolution digital camera such as a three or more megapixel camera, processing the photograph data as JPG is acceptable. Because the image is at such as high resolution, it can be used in printed matter or saved at the proper resolution for use in a Web page.

Smaller, not Larger

The dimensions of a bitmap graphic should never be changed to a larger size because the software extrapolates data information to fill in additional pixels, which results in poor image quality. The resolution (dpi) also cannot be increased without resulting in poor image quality.

Digital Image Resolution

Digital cameras and scanners have settings that affect the resolution of the saved images. Scanner options are usually simply expressed in *dpi* or dots per inch. In a digital camera, these settings may be called something similar to "File Size" or "Quality" and have settings such as Large, Medium, and Small, which affect the resolution of the image file processed by the camera. For example, selecting Large may result in images that are 1600 x 1200 pixels, and Small may result in images that are 640 x 480 pixels. The file size (in kilobytes) of the Large image will be larger than the file size of the Small image because it contains more data.

Megapixels and Resolution

One megapixel is roughly one million pixels. The megapixel specification for a digital camera is dependent on the number of pixels on the chip in the camera that collect light and convert it to data. For example, a camera with a chip that is 1,600 pixels wide and 1,200 pixels tall has a total of 1,920,000 pixels and is considered to be a two megapixel camera with a resolution of 1,600 x 1,200.

Modifying a Graphic

Microsoft Word, Excel, PowerPoint, and Publisher include features for modifying graphics.

When a graphic is selected in Word, Excel, PowerPoint, or Publisher the Format tab is displayed. The Format tab is used to change the look of a selected graphic:

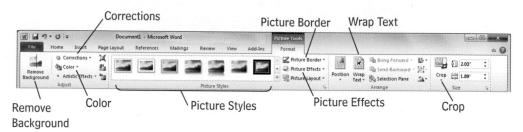

Corrections • Picture Border • Wrap Text

Remove Background • Color • Picture Styles • Picture Effects • Crop

- Remove Background remove unwanted areas of the graphic.
- Color changes the colors.
- Corrections adjusts the brightness and contrast. Also sharpens and softens.
- Artistic Effects applies artistic effects.
- Picture Border adds a border.
- Picture Effects adds effects such as bevels and shadows.
- Picture Styles apply several picture formats in one click.
- Crop trims away areas of the graphic that are not needed.
- Reset Picture removes the formatting.
- Wrap Text positions a graphic in relation to the text on a page.

Index

sorting records 340
Sort Z to A button 224
sound
  icon 496
source 234
source cell or range 172
sources 127
S&P 500 205, 290
space
  after or before a paragraph 74
  between lines of text 75
  between paragraphs 74
spaces, one after a period 36
spam 21
Spam e-mail folder 15
sparklines 279
speaker notes 468
speakerphone etiquette 107
Spelling button 182
spelling checker
  Access 337
  e-mail 16
  PowerPoint 452
  Word 38
spider 10
Split button 311
Split Form button 375
splitting panes 311
spoofing 15
spreadsheet 155. *See
  also* workbook; *See
  also* worksheet
spreadsheet model 238
stacked area chart 292
Standard Deviation command 424
Standard field format 365
Standard & Poor's 500 205, 290
Start Mail Merge button 433, 437
static 235, 314
statistics
  adding to a report 423
status bar 2, 36, 156, 450
  Section indicator 122
  Track Changes indicator 56
stock chart 272
stock exchanges 288
stockholder's equity 197
stock indexes 290
stocks 205
Stock tables 289
Stop button
  Help 24
Stop Recording button 317
storage media 6
storyboard 450
style 113
  creating 114
  deleting 114
styles 113, 523
Style Set command 114
Stylistic Sets 524
stylus pen 3

subdatasheet 386
subscript 46
SUM
  Excel 217
  Word 118
Sum command 424
summary, report 423
superscript 46
surface chart 272
Switch Row/Column button 272
Symbol button 51, 53
Symbol command 157
synonyms 52
syntax 217

T
Tab key 77
  dialog box 5
  entering data 157
table 297. *See also* datasheet
  calculations 118
  convert to range 298
  create 297
  displaying 339
  exporting 431
  formatting 339
  name 298
  printing 339
  remove duplicates 298
  sizing 298
  sort 297
  sorting 118
tab leader 78
Table button 116, 297
table data
  importing 297
  separating into more columns 299
Table Design button 367
Table Name box 298
table of contents 121
  updating 121
Table of Contents button 121
tables 331
tabloid paper size 71
Tabs dialog box 78
tab selector 77
tabs, on Ribbon 5
tab stop 77
  removing 78
tagging notes 555
Tags Summary 555
taking test 67
taskbar 2, 13
task pane
  Clip Art 521
  Clipboard 42
  Research 52
task pane, Clip Art 87, 463
telephone etiquette 107
temperature conversion 198
temperatures 291

template
  Excel 186
  local 93
  PowerPoint 492
  Publisher 514, 526
  Word 92
terrapin. *See* diamondback terrapin
text
  body 113
  columns in Word 77
  comparing 227
  finding 44
  replacing 44
  selecting 41
text box 516
  in a dialog box 5
  report 425
Text Box button
  Access 425
  Excel 139
text boxes
  connecting 531
Text Direction button 117
Text effects 46
Text Effects button 133
Text field 364
Text File button 348
text files 304, 428
Text Fill button 133
Text Filters command 341
text format 19
Text Outline button 133
Text to Columns button 299
thank you letter 64
themes
  Access 376
  Excel 163
  PowerPoint 457
  Word 128
Theme Colors button 128
Thesaurus button 52, 182
thumbnail
  PowerPoint 450
  taskbar 13
thumbnails
  photos 447
ticker symbol 289
TIF 86, 564
TIFF 563, 564
time
  Excel 295
  header or footer, Excel 166
  in calculations 295
  in formulas 295
  using in formulas 295
  Word 84
time stamp
  PowerPoint 459
timing
  slide 487
title
  Web page 95, 185